corrections today

SECOND EDITION

Corrections ToDaY

LARRY J. SIEGEL

University of Massachusetts, Lowell

CLEMENS BARTOLLAS

University of Northern Iowa

WADSWORTH
CENGAGE Learning·

Australia · Brazil · Japan · Korea · Mexico · Singapore · Spain · United Kingdom · United States

Corrections Today, Second Edition
Larry Siegel and Clemens Bartollas

Editor-in-Chief: Linda Ganster

Senior Acquisitions Editor: Carolyn Henderson Meier

Senior Developmental Editor: Shelley Murphy

Assistant Editor: Rachel McDonald

Editorial Assistant: Casey Lozier

Media Editor: Ting Jian Yap

Senior Marketing Manager: Michelle Williams

Senior Marketing Communications Manager: Heather Baxley

Senior Content Project Manager: Christy A. Frame

Senior Art Director: Maria Epes

Senior Manufacturing Planner: Judy Inouye

Rights Acquisitions Specialist: Thomas McDonough

Production Service: Linda Jupiter Productions

Photo Researcher: Kim Adams Fox

Text Researcher: Pablo D'Stair

Copy Editor: Lunaea Weatherstone

Proofreader: Mary Kanable

Indexer: Katherine Stimson

Illustrator: Scientific Illustrations

Text Designer: Lisa Delgado

Cover Designer: Riezebos Holzbaur Group

Cover Images:

Casual young man (arm and green shirt): Shutterstock/Andrei Zarubaika

Man (legs and shoes): Shutterstock/Yuri Arcurs

Empty warehouse wall (right side background): Shutterstock/donatas1205

Dirty wall with grunge floor (left side background): Shutterstock/L.Watcharapol

Ankle monitor: CORBIS/Jacques M. Chenet

Criminal: Getty Images/Joshua Ets-Hokin

Compositor: PreMediaGlobal

Library of Congress Control Number: 2012934916

ISBN-13: 978-1-133-93365-6

ISBN-10: 1-133-93365-3

Wadsworth
20 Davis Drive
Belmont, CA 94002-3098
USA

Cengage Learning is a leading provider of customized learning solutions with office locations around the globe, including Singapore, the United Kingdom, Australia, Mexico, Brazil, and Japan. Locate your local office at **www.cengage.com/global.**

Cengage Learning products are represented in Canada by Nelson Education, Ltd.

To learn more about Wadsworth, visit **www.cengage.com/wadsworth**

Purchase any of our products at your local college store or at our preferred online store **www.cengagebrain.com.**

Printed in the United States of America
1 2 3 4 5 6 7 16 15 14 13 12

This book is dedicated to my children, Eric, Andrew, Julie, and Rachel,
and to my grandchildren, Jack, Kayla, and Brooke. It is
also dedicated to Jason Macy (thanks for marrying Rachel) and
Therese J. Libby (thanks for marrying me).

—LJS

To my wife, Linda, and my children, Kristin, Mya, and Kristen, and my
grandchildren, Jake, Jordan, Rayne, Starley, Khosi, and Irie Sky.

—CB

about the authors

The author with his wife, Therese.

The author with his wife, Linda.

LARRY SIEGEL Larry Siegel was born in the Bronx in 1947. While living on Jerome Avenue and attending City College of New York in the 1960s, he was swept up in the social and political currents of the time. He became intrigued with the influence contemporary culture had on individual behavior: Did people shape society or did society shape people? He applied his interest in social forces and human behavior to the study of crime and justice. After graduating CCNY, he attended the newly opened program in criminal justice at the State University of New York at Albany, earning both his M.A. and Ph.D. degrees there. After completing his graduate work, Dr. Siegel began his teaching career at Northeastern University, where he was a faculty member for nine years. After leaving Northeastern, he held teaching positions at the University of Nebraska–Omaha and Saint Anselm College in New Hampshire. He is currently a professor at the University of Massachusetts–Lowell. Dr. Siegel has written extensively in the area of crime and justice, including books on juvenile law, delinquency, criminology, criminal justice, and criminal procedure. He is a court certified expert on police conduct and has testified in numerous legal cases. The father of four and grandfather of three, Larry Siegel and his wife, Terry, now reside in Bedford, New Hampshire, with their two dogs, Watson and Cody.

CLEMENS BARTOLLAS Clemens Bartollas is Professor of Sociology at the University of Northern Iowa. Dr. Bartollas holds a B.A. from Davis and Elkins College, a B.D. from Princeton Theological Seminary, an S.T.M. from San Francisco Theological Seminary, and a Ph.D. in sociology, with a special emphasis in criminology, from The Ohio State University. He taught at Pembroke State University from 1973 to 1975, Sangamon State University from 1975 to 1980, and at the University of Northern Iowa from 1981 to the present. He has received a number of honors at the University of Northern Iowa, including Distinguished Scholar, the Donald McKay Research Award, and the Regents' Award for Faculty Excellence. Dr. Bartollas also worked four years in a maximum-security juvenile facility in Ohio and one year in a medium-security adult prison in North Carolina. He has testified in a number of death penalty cases. Dr. Bartollas, like his coauthor, is the author of numerous articles and more than thirty books. Clemens Bartollas and his wife, Linda, live in Cedar Falls, Iowa, where their three children and five grandchildren visit on holidays and other occasions.

BRIEF CONTENTS

contents

PART I ▪ WHY DO WE PUNISH?

PART II ▪ HOW DO WE PUNISH?

PART III ■ HOW DO WE CORRECT IN THE COMMUNITY?

PART V ▪ HOW DO WE REHABILITATE?

PART VI ■ WHAT ARE SPECIAL NEEDS POPULATIONS?

PART VII ▪ WHAT IS THE FUTURE OF CORRECTIONS?

Who can forget the news on that awful day in 2007 in Cheshire, Connecticut, when two men invaded the home of the Petit family, severely beat Dr. William Petit, raped and strangled his wife, Jennifer Hawke-Petit, and then killed the couple's two daughters? Though the girls were still alive when police arrived at the scene, one of the intruders, Steven J. Hayes, hoping to destroy evidence, poured gasoline on the girls and set fire to the home; the two young girls, Hayley, 17, and Michaela, 11, died from smoke inhalation before they could be rescued.

The murderous intruders, Steven Hayes and his partner Joshua Komisarjevsky, were quickly apprehended, tried, convicted, and eventually sentenced to death. The evidence presented at trial was so gruesome that jurors were offered post-decision counseling.

Komisarjevsky and Hayes were classic career criminals. Komisarjevsky had been involved in felony offenses since age 14, breaking into houses in Cheshire and surrounding areas. Hayes had spent most of his life in and out of prison for burglary, larceny, and car theft. Both were also persistent drug abusers, using cocaine and crystal methamphetamine. The pair met at a residential drug treatment center and halfway house in Hartford. Not surprisingly, both killers had a long history of involvement with the criminal justice system. Hayes had been arrested for the first time at 16; burglarized a house at 24; was reprimanded in prison for assault at 29; arrested for drug possession at 38. He had been incarcerated in a total of 17 prisons and detention centers over a 25-year period. Komisarjevsky had started breaking into homes as a teen; in 2002, he confessed to more than a dozen burglaries, and was sentenced to nine years in prison followed by six years of supervised parole. The state's Board of Pardons and Paroles granted him early parole in 2007. He was ordered to wear an electronic ankle bracelet for 90 days; the murders occurred 6 days after it was removed.

How could these career criminals have been free to commit such a horrible crime? Shouldn't they still have been behind bars rather than free on parole? Is the system to blame? Cursed with antiquated facilities, inadequate support, insufficient and poorly trained staff, and a burgeoning population of younger, more violence-prone recidivists, the correctional system may not have the resources necessary to help inmates turn their lives around. And when the system fails, as it did in this case, politicians are quick to call for remedies that include even tougher measures, which are aimed at controlling violent offenders and protecting the public but also serve to strain an already overcrowded correctional system.

Is it possible for the correctional system to become effective? While the correctional crisis is not over, there are reasons to be optimistic. Over the past 20 years, a new generation of administrators has been appointed to positions in federal, state, local, and private corrections, bringing with them a new vision, an infusion of energy, and a spirit of professionalism. As part of the "new corrections," their emphasis has been on staff training and development, proactive leadership, support of accreditation and standards, and human treatment of offenders in community and institutional settings.

GOALS AND OBJECTIVES

Despite sharing the same sense of horror and frustration felt by many Americans over the system failure in the Petit murders, we believe in this "new corrections" so much so that we wanted to create a textbook specifically designed to help train the "new corrections professional." We have had the opportunity to channel our interests in punishment and corrections into careers as professors of criminal justice, between us spending more than 50 years teaching, working within the corrections system, and consulting with correctional personnel. We have incorporated this lifetime of knowledge and service into *Corrections Today*, which describes, probes, and analyzes the new ideology, priorities, and programs found in corrections. The text is designed to be informative and scholarly, while at the same time being practical and career oriented. We examine the field of corrections through the lens of students who are giving serious thought to careers in corrections or are now working in corrections. Our text aims to be highly readable, engaging, and authoritative, without losing sight of its goal and target audience. So while the topics covered include historical and theoretical perspectives in corrections, we strive to provide the type of context and concrete illustration that makes such material meaningful and relevant to the career-minded student.

    Corrections Today has at its core a number of unique attributes:

- **It is realistic.** We conducted a "reality check" by conducting interviews with "spokespersons" for corrections: probationers, inmates, parolees, correctional personnel, and correctional administrators. We constantly asked them: Is this the way it is? Is this a fair assessment? Do we have it right?

- **It is research oriented.** We include the most recent studies of corrections and have tried to explain findings in a user-friendly way aimed at increasing student interest—resulting in a book that is briefer but no less academically sound than more encyclopedic texts.

- **It emphasizes evidence-based research findings.** In nearly every chapter, we include studies of evidence-based research findings. For example, in Chapter 9 we explore the existing evidence on wrongful convictions in order to help students understand how often miscarriages of justice actually occur and how many people are wrongfully convicted each year. In Chapter 7, an Evidence-Based Corrections feature reviews the Prison Rape Elimination Act of 2003 (PREA), designed to make the prevention of prison rape a top priority.

- **It also emphasizes the expanding role of technology in the field.** Unique TechnoCorrections boxes spotlight the use of cutting-edge technology to supervise offenders in the community and in correctional institutions—providing an essential and compelling look at a major emphasis in corrections today.

- **It does not pull punches.** In nearly every chapter, there is an evaluation of what is taking place in the correctional system today, where the problems lie, and what can be done to correct them.

- **It focuses on how to become a corrections professional.** Our goal is to help students with career choices and explore what careers are out there in the correctional system. So not only does every chapter include interviews with practicing professionals as well as a practical Careers in Corrections box, each also features real-world Thinking Like a Corrections Professional activities and Career Destinations research tips.

- **It is hopeful.** Time after time in this text, those who work in the field remind students that corrections has been a very positive and fulfilling career for them, that they feel they have made a difference, and they invite students to join them in this exciting journey.

ORGANIZATION OF THE TEXT

This text has 15 chapters. Parts I and II of the text set out to address the key questions of why and how we punish. Part III introduces students to the increasingly important world of community corrections. Part IV addresses institutional corrections. Rehabilitation in corrections is the focus of Part V of the text. Part VI addresses special populations in corrections. Finally, Part VII looks at the future of corrections.

Chapter 1, The Correctional System, covers the goals and philosophy of punishment as well as the history of punishment from the Middle Ages through the Enlightenment through the origins of American corrections up to the twentieth century, and concludes with a discussion of the corrections system today, including the extent and consequences of prison overcrowding, the cost of corrections, and what it means to be a professional in corrections.

Chapter 2, Sentencing and the Correctional Process, focuses on *how* we punish—discussing the basic goals and philosophy of sentencing, the various types of sentencing and sentencing guidelines, three-strikes laws, and truth-in-sentencing.

Chapter 3, Community Corrections: Diversion and Probation, begins by explaining diversion and diversionary programs, considers community corrections legislation, and then focuses on probation services.

Chapter 4, Intermediate Sanctions, identifies and discusses the continuum of intermediate sanctions, including fines, forfeiture, house arrest, and electronic monitoring, and places a major emphasis on restorative justice.

Chapter 5, The Jail: Detention and Short-Term Confinement, offers comprehensive coverage of jails, from its origins through the various generations of jail supervision, as well as issues concerning jail confinement, such as overcrowding, violence, and suicide.

Chapter 6, Correctional Institutions, covers the main types of federal, state, and private prisons, including an examination of the levels of security from minimum to supermax, architectural design innovations, and prison administration.

Chapter 7, The Prison Experience: Males, focuses on the changing social structure of men's prisons, including gangs, racial tensions, contraband, violence, and sex in prison.

Chapter 8, The Prison Experience: Females, identifies the differences between men's and women's prisons when it comes to social structure, focuses on issues such as motherhood, health concerns, and sexual abuse, and discusses professionalism among workers in women's prisons.

Chapter 9, Prisoners' Rights, identifies what First, Fourth, Eighth, and Fourteenth Amendments substantive rights have been awarded to inmates and addresses the consequences of the Prisoners' Litigation Reform Act to prisoners' rights.

Chapter 10, Correctional Programs and Services, looks at the role of treatment and services in prisons today, discussing the classification for treatment, individual-level treatment programs, group programs, and inmate self-help programs.

Chapter 11, Parole and Release to the Community, examines parole practices today, how the parole board functions, the various roles of parole officers, the legal rights of parolees, and the problems faced by ex-offenders returning to the community.

Chapter 12, Special Prison Populations, reviews seven types of inmates who pose particular challenges to correctional administrators and who face challenges themselves in adjusting to prison environments—the drug-addicted inmate, the sex offender, the HIV-infected inmate, the chronic mentally ill inmate, the illegal immigrant, the terrorist, and the elderly inmate.

Chapter 13, Capital Punishment and the Death Row Inmate, examines the status of the death penalty today, its legality and role in contemporary society both nationally and internationally, and describes the positions and responsibilities of those working on death row.

Chapter 14, The Juvenile Offender, looks at the juvenile offender as he or she is processed through the juvenile justice system and then considers the transfer of juveniles to adult court and the placement of juveniles in boot camps and adult prisons.

Chapter 15, Today's Corrections Professional: Characteristics, Challenges, and Opportunities, considers how far professionalism has brought the field of corrections, the characteristics of professionalism today, and the future challenges for greater advances of professionalism.

WHAT'S NEW IN THE SECOND EDITION

We have made a number of revisions to the Second Edition. To better align with the average-length college term, we have trimmed the book to 15 chapters by reducing the coverage of history—which also gives us more room to expand discussion of today's most compelling and challenging issues: community-based corrections, net widening, the economic crisis and its impact on corrections, recidivism, and more. We have also chosen to spotlight another of today's most powerful drivers, evidence-based corrections, with a unique new boxed feature in every chapter highlighting correctional policies and practices supported by solid research. And on a more basic level, we have dramatically expanded our in-text discussion of core concepts in corrections—increasing the number of key terms by over 25 percent—and expanded our art and photo program by almost this same percentage, producing a book that is more student-centric than ever. Finally, we have made the following chapter-by-chapter changes:

Chapter 1 The chapter now opens with a vignette on Anders Behring Breivik and his killing spree in the city of Oslo, Norway. We now cover the reasons why we punish and the theories of punishment. There is new material on the history of corrections during the Middle Ages and the development of American corrections. All data and statistical tables have been revised and updated. There is a new Evidence-Based Corrections feature on the work of sociologists Stephen Bahr, Lish Harris, James Fisher, and Anita Harker Armstrong that sought to identify what differentiates successful parolees from those who fail on parole.

Chapter 2 The chapter now opens with an update on the Natalee Holloway case and discusses Joran van der Sloot, the man suspected in her disappearance who was later convicted on charges of killing another young woman in Peru. There are new sections on the actors in the sentencing process—prosecutor, judge, and probation staff, a new Careers in Corrections feature on the pretrial officer, and an Evidence-Based Corrections box addressing the role of race in sentencing.

Chapter 3 This chapter includes new information on the risk-need-responsivity (RNR) model, new sections on federal probation and improving probation effectiveness, plus new Voices Across the Profession boxes spotlighting state and federal probation officers, and an Evidence-Based Corrections feature on registering sex offenders on the Internet.

Chapter 4 There is a new Voices Across the Profession feature on Ronald P. Corbett, Jr., the commissioner of probation in Massachusetts, as well as an Evidence-Based Corrections box covering the effectiveness of drug courts and an expanded discussion of how to evaluate the effectiveness of restorative justice programs.

Chapter 5 This chapter now opens with the account of Dr. Conrad Murray, the physician who treated Michael Jackson and who was convicted of contributing to the pop star's untimely death. There is a new section on the historical origins of the jail. There is also a table that covers the recent decline in jail populations in large urban areas, as well as a new section on the emerging OmniView Total Supervision concept for prisons, which comprises the fourth generation of jail supervision.

Chapter 6 The chapter begins with material on the effect that prison closings have on the community. There is a new section on the Federal Bureau of Prisons. New exhibits cover state correctional systems and the development of privatization, and an Evidence-Based Corrections feature looks at the effectiveness of supermax prisons.

Chapter 7 Two new exhibits cover social roles in prison and prison argot. The section on combating prison gangs has been updated and expanded, and there is also a new section on racial conflict in prison and what is being done to reduce tension. The new Evidence-Based Corrections box covers the critical topic of eliminating prison rape.

Chapter 8 The chapter begins with a new opener on Kathy Boudin, a Sixties radical who turned her life around while in a women's prison. A new section covers the history and characteristics of women's prisons, and a new Voices Across the Profession discusses the career of Judy Anderson, a prison warden in South Carolina. The section on doing time in a women's prison has been completely revamped. Some of the classic studies of life in a female institution are set out in some detail, and an exhibit provides a comparison of some of their critical findings. There is a revised section on the contemporary prison experience of women in prison; it is accompanied by an exhibit that compares contemporary studies of women in prison. There is a new Evidence-Based Corrections feature on prison nursery programs.

Chapter 9 The chapter now opens with the story of Michael Morton, a man wrongfully convicted of murder who has been found innocent. There is an accompanying Evidence-Based Corrections feature on wrongful convictions. The section "Foundations of Prisoners' Rights Law" has been expanded, revised, and updated. A new exhibit sets out amendments to the Constitution that affect inmates' rights.

Chapter 10 The chapter now contains an Evidence-Based Corrections feature on the Getting Ready program in Arizona—a correctional initiative that begins preparing prisoners for reentry to society from their first day in prison. It helps inmates answer a fundamental question: how would people in the real world tackle life's problems? The section on cognitive behavioral therapy has been revised and expanded. There is a new section on drug and alcohol treatment programs, and the section on prison industry has been expanded. Finally, there is a new career box on the psychiatric social worker.

Chapter 11 The chapter has been thoroughly reorganized and tightened to enhance readability. It also includes two new sections, one on the history of parole and another that covers the legal right to parole. A new TechnoCorrections feature reviews New Jersey's Sex Offender Monitoring Pilot Project Act.

Chapter 12 This chapter contains a number of new exhibits comparing special offense/special needs inmates as well as an Evidence-Based Corrections box on therapeutic communities.

Chapter 13 There are a number of new figures and sections in the chapter, including a map of methods of executions, a substantial new section on the retentionist versus abolitionist arguments for capital punishment, and an expanded discussion of the process of death. Also included is a new Evidence-Based Corrections feature addressing the question of how racial intolerance may foster support of the death penalty.

Chapter 14 There is now an expanded section on juveniles in the adult system and an expanded section on juveniles serving life without parole. There are a number of new exhibits, including ones that cover comparisons of the juvenile and adult justice systems; the effectiveness of juvenile institutions; types of waiver to adult court; and the death penalty for juveniles. There is a new Evidence-Based Corrections box on the disproportionate minority confinement/contact (DMC) directive.

Chapter 15 This is a new chapter. The opener discusses a case involving New Jersey corrections officers fired for infractions. The American Correctional Association Code of Ethics is included, as are major new sections on professionalism addressing such topics as emerging professionalism, professionalism today, and what remains to be done. There is a career box on the internal affairs investigator and new sections on today's challenges as well as the future of corrections.

LEARNING TOOLS

In keeping with our desire to create the most student-centric text available, we have created a complete learning system. Each chapter begins with learning objectives, which are also keyed to the summary at the end of the chapter for optimum reinforcement. Key terms are boldfaced in the text where they are introduced and defined and are repeated in the running marginal glossary.

Additionally, we have included the following boxes and features to help students get the most out of the course:

VOICES ACROSS THE PROFESSION Each chapter has at least one Voices Across the Profession feature in which real-world professionals share their experiences and give students a concrete view of what it's like to work in a variety of corrections careers (see pp. xxvii–xxix for a complete list of the individuals profiled in these boxes).

CAREERS IN CORRECTIONS Throughout the book, we highlight a variety of careers in corrections, discussing the nature of the job, qualifications and required education, job outlook, earnings and benefits, and more. Careers identified are as follows:

- Director of corrections
- Pretrial officer
- Probation officer
- Substance abuse counselor
- Jail officer
- Prison warden
- Correctional officer
- Correctional counselor
- Corrections ombudsman
- Parole officer
- Forensic psychologist
- Social worker
- Internal affairs investigator

CORRECTIONAL LIFE This feature asks probationers, inmates, or parolees to discuss their life in correctional institutions: What are the problems? How do they cope? The purpose is to bring the reader as close as possible to life behind the walls: What is it really like living on death row? How do parolees/probationers make it in the community?

EVIDENCE-BASED CORRECTIONS As noted, this new box focuses on policies and practices that are supported by research, a key driver in the field today, as underscored by several of the professionals interviewed for our Voices feature when they comment that they are expected to use evidence-based practices to justify the efficacy of the programs they implement.

TECHNOCORRECTIONS These boxes spotlight the use of cutting-edge technology to supervise offenders in the community and in correctional institutions. Topics include a New Jersey pilot project concerning round-the-clock global positioning system (GPS) monitoring for the state's most dangerous registered sex offenders as well as possible future technologies, such as scanning devices that can help detect illegal contraband, and much more.

MYTH/FACT BOXES Each chapter contains two or more Myth/Fact boxes designed to separate myth from reality and thereby inform students of the incorrect notions, perceptions, and biases they bring to class as a result of what they see on television or read in fiction and on the Internet.

END-OF-CHAPTER REVIEW In addition to the end-of-chapter summary linked back to the chapter-opening learning objectives, we include the following assignment-based materials:

Critical Thinking Questions: A number of questions designed to help students think critically about the material.

"Thinking Like a Corrections Professional" Activities: Students have an opportunity to make a decision on how they think a corrections professional would handle a particular situation. Many of these features represent actual situations that have taken place, while others are possible scenarios.

Career Destinations: Suggestions for appropriate online resources to help students who are considering corrections careers.

Ancillaries

To access additional course materials, including CourseMate, please visit www.cengagebrain.com. At the CengageBrain.com home page, search for the ISBN of your title (from the back cover of your book) using the search box at the top of the page. This will take you to the product page where these resources can be found.

An extensive package of supplemental aids accompanies this edition. Many separate items have been developed to enhance the course and to assist instructors and students. Available to qualified adopters. Please consult your local sales representative for details.

INSTRUCTOR'S RESOURCE MANUAL WITH TEST BANK The manual includes learning objectives, key terms, a detailed chapter outline, a chapter summary, discussion topics, student activities, and a test bank. Each chapter's test bank contains questions in multiple-choice, true/false, fill-in-the-blank, and essay formats, with a full answer key. The test bank is coded to the learning objectives that appear in the main text, and includes the page numbers in the main text where the answers can be found. Finally, each question in the test bank has been carefully reviewed by experienced criminal justice instructors for quality, accuracy, and content coverage. Our Instructor Approved seal, which appears on the front cover, is our assurance that you are working with an assessment and grading resource of the highest caliber. The manual is available for download on the password-protected website and can also be obtained by e-mailing your local Cengage Learning representative.

POWERLECTURE WITH EXAMVIEW This one-stop digital library and presentation tool includes preassembled Microsoft® PowerPoint® lecture slides linked to the learning objectives for each chapter. Also included are an electronic copy of the Instructor's Resource Manual with Testbank, ExamView computerized testing, and more. Based on the learning objectives outlined at the beginning of each chapter, the enhanced PowerLecture lets you bring together text-specific lecture outlines and art from this text, along with new video clips, animations, and learning modules from the Web or your own materials—culminating in a powerful, personalized, media-enhanced presentation. The PowerLecture DVD includes ExamView®, a computerized test bank available for PC and Macintosh computers, with software for customizing tests of up to 250 items that can be delivered in print or online. With ExamView you can create, deliver, and customize tests and study guides (both print and online) in minutes. You can easily edit and import your own questions and graphics, change test layouts, and reorganize questions. And using ExamView's complete word-processing capabilities, you can enter an unlimited number of new questions or edit existing questions.

THE WADSWORTH CRIMINAL JUSTICE VIDEO LIBRARY So many exciting new videos—so many great ways to enrich your lectures and spark discussion of the material in this text. Your Cengage Learning representative will be happy to provide details on our video policy by adoption size. The library includes these selections and many others.

- *ABC® Videos.* ABC videos feature short, high-interest clips from current news events as well as historic raw footage going back 40 years. Perfect for discussion starters or to enrich your lectures and spark interest in the material in the text, these brief videos provide students with a new lens through which to view the past and present, one that will greatly enhance their knowledge and understanding of significant events and open up to them new dimensions in learning. Clips are drawn from such programs as *World News Tonight, Good Morning America, This Week, PrimeTime Live, 20/20*, and *Nightline*, as well as numerous ABC News specials and material from the Associated Press Television News and British Movietone News collections.

- *Cengage Learning's "Introduction to Criminal Justice Video Series"* features videos supplied by the BBC Motion Gallery. These short, high-interest clips from CBS and BBC news programs—everything from nightly news broadcasts and specials to *CBS News Special Reports, CBS Sunday Morning, 60 Minutes*, and more—are perfect classroom discussion starters. Designed to enrich your lectures and spark interest in the material in the text, these brief videos provide students with a new lens through which to view the past and present, one that will greatly enhance their knowledge and understanding of significant events and open up to them new dimensions in learning.

CRIMINAL JUSTICE MEDIA LIBRARY Cengage Learning's Criminal Justice Media Library includes nearly 300 media assets on the topics you cover in your courses. Available to stream from any Web-enabled computer, the Criminal Justice Media Library's assets include such valuable resources as: Career Profile Videos featuring interviews with criminal justice professionals from a range of roles and locations, simulations that allow students to step into various roles and practice their decision-making skills, video clips on current topics from ABC® and other sources, animations that illustrate key concepts, interactive learning modules that help students check their knowledge of important topics, and Reality Check exercises that compare expectations and preconceived notions against the real-life thoughts and experiences of criminal justice professionals. Most importantly, the Criminal Justice Media Library can be uploaded and used within many popular Learning Management Systems, and all video assets include assessment questions that can be delivered straight to the LMS' gradebook. Please contact your Cengage Learning representative for ordering and pricing information.

WEBTUTOR™ ON BLACKBOARD® AND WEBCT® Jump-start your course with customizable, rich, text-specific content within your Course Management System. Whether you want to Web-enable your class or put an entire course online, WebTutor delivers. WebTutor offers a wide array of resources, including media assets, test bank, practice quizzes linked to chapter learning objectives, and additional study aids. Visit www.cengage.com/webtutor to learn more.

LESSON PLANS The Lesson Plans bring accessible, masterful suggestions to every lesson. This supplement includes a sample syllabus, learning objectives, lecture notes, discussion topics, in-class activities, a detailed lecture outline, assignments, media tools, and "What if …" scenarios. Current events and real-life examples in the form of articles, websites, and video links are incorporated into the class discussion topics, activities, and assignments. The lecture outlines are correlated with PowerPoint slides for ease of classroom use. Lesson Plans are available on the PowerLecture resource and the instructor website.

ANNOTATED INSTRUCTOR'S EDITION This essential resource features teaching tips, discussion tips, technology tips, and video tips to help professors engage students with the course material.

COURSE360: ONLINE LEARNING TO THE NEXT DEGREE

Course360 from Cengage Learning is a complete turnkey solution that teaches course outcomes through student interaction in a highly customizable online learning environment. Course360 blends relevant content with rich media and builds upon your course design, needs, and objectives. With a wide variety of media elements including audio, video, interactives, simulations, and more, Course360 is the way today's students learn.

For the Student

STUDY GUIDE An extensive study guide has been developed for this edition. Because students learn in different ways, the guide includes a variety of pedagogical aids to help them. Each chapter is outlined and summarized, major terms and figures are defined, and self-tests are provided.

COURSEMATE Cengage Learning's Criminal Justice CourseMate brings course concepts to life with interactive learning, study, and exam preparation tools that support the printed textbook. CourseMate includes an integrated eBook, quizzes mapped to chapter learning objectives, flashcards, videos, and more, and EngagementTracker, a first-of-its-kind tool that monitors student engagement in the course. The accompanying instructor website offers access to password-protected resources such as an electronic version of the instructor's manual and PowerPoint® slides.

CAREERS IN CRIMINAL JUSTICE WEBSITE *Can be bundled with this text at no additional charge.* Featuring plenty of self-exploration and profiling activities, the interactive Careers in Criminal Justice website helps students investigate and focus on the criminal justice career choices that are right for them. Includes interest assessment, video testimonials from career professionals, résumé and interview tips, and links for reference.

CLEBOOK CLeBook allows students to access Cengage Learning textbooks in an easy-to-use online format. Highlight, take notes, bookmark, search your text, and, in some titles, link directly into multimedia: CLeBook combines the best aspects of paper books and eBooks in one package.

ACKNOWLEDGMENTS

We would like to give thanks to our terrific and supportive editor Carolyn Henderson Meier and our wonderful and fantastic developmental editor Shelley Murphy. This text would not have been possible to complete without their assistance and TLC.

The preparation of this text would not have been possible without the aid of our colleagues who helped by reviewing the manuscript.

Gerlad Bayens, Washburn University

Robert Boyer, Luzerne County Community College

Eben Bronfman, ASA Institute

Terry Campbell, Kaplan University

Eugene J. Evans, Jr., Camden County College

Ronald Fennell, Lock Haven University

Ida Flippo, Clackamas Community College

Brett E. Garland, Missouri State University

Joy Hadwiger, Rogers State University

Richard M. Hough, Sr., University of West Florida

Jessie Krienert, Illinois State University

Frank Leonard, Tallahassee Community College

Samantha Lewis, Miami Dade College

William McDonald, Monroe College

Trevor Milton, State University of New York, Old Westbury

Joe Morris, Northwestern State University of Louisiana

Angela L. Ondrus, Owens Community College

O. Elmer Polk, Kennesaw State University

Dr. Cassandra L. Renzi, Keiser University, Daytona Beach

Kristen M. Zgoba, Rutgers University

We are also grateful to the individuals who were willing to be interviewed and become our Voices Across the Profession boxes. Further, we express our appreciation to those who helped us in various ways during the preparation of the manuscript: Brannon Carter, Gloria Hadachek, Austin Howard, Allison Sorg, and James Wertz.

Many thanks to all.

Larry Siegel
Clemens Bartollas

VOICES ACROSS the PROFESSION

Chapter 1 James H. Bruton is a former warden and administrator for the Minnesota Department of Corrections. He is also the author of several books, including one on maximum-security prisons. Bruton's Voices feature provides the empowering message that we need to go to work each day believing that inmates can change and that we can have impact on their lives.

Chapter 2 Steven Clark, a district court judge in Blackhawk County, Ohio, tells what it is like to be a judge. A judge since 1984, he has been both a trial judge and a juvenile court judge.

Chapter 3 James Dare is the deputy court administrator in the Montgomery County Common Pleas Court, Dayton, Ohio. He has been a probation officer since 1984. He reminds us of the challenges of being a probation officer, including balancing power, understanding diversity, and imposing sanctions proportionate to the violation. Derek Dufresne, another Voice in the chapter, is a United States probation officer in Providence, Rhode Island. He identifies how probation is a delicate balance between law enforcement and social work.

Chapter 4 Dr. Ronald P. Corbett, Jr., is commissioner of the Massachusetts Probation Department. He talks about his basic responsibilities as commissioner of the department and the various intermediate sanctions that are being conducted at the present time. Another Voice in this chapter is Kay Pranis, a former restorative justice planner with the Minnesota Department of Corrections. She is presently a consultant and speaker for restorative justice programs across the United States. She is also an author of several books and many papers on restorative justice. Her Voices feature communicates the power and potential of restorative justice to bring healing to offenders and victims.

Chapter 5 Dr. Arnett Gaston has been a deputy commissioner and warden of two jails, and commanding officer at Rikers Island, New York, the largest jail complex in the free world, with 18,000 prisoners and 11,000 staff. His Voices feature discusses how they were able to reduce violence at Rikers Island. His statement reveals the type of proactive and professional leadership that is currently taking place in the jails of this nation. Carol Higgins O'Brien, who has worked in corrections for thirty years, is currently the assistant superintendent/warden of human services for the Middlesex Sheriff's Office at the House of Corrections (Massachusetts). She reminds us that it is often necessary to do more with less, bringing creativity and outside-the-box thinking to utilize available resources.

Chapter 6 Mark Thielen, warden of the Minnesota Correctional Facility, Faribault, is the featured Voice in this chapter. As warden of the largest prison in Minnesota, he discusses how he must maintain a safe environment for staff and inmates, but at the same time cultivate an environment that encourages inmates to change.

Chapter 7 Captain Steven Ayers has worked at the Oak Park Heights Maximum Security Prison for the past twenty-three years. As the highest ranking uniformed officer in the prison, responsible for the overall security of this supermax prison, he reports that he looks forward to coming to work every day and works "hard to do the 'right thing' even though at times it may not be viewed favorably by staff and/or offenders."

Chapter 8 Judy Anderson has been warden of the Camille Graham Camp facility in Columbia, South Carolina since 2003. In this women's prison, Anderson sees that her major challenge is to be everything to everybody, which includes public safety as well as the welfare and jobs of employees, and at the same time be responsive to the concerns of inmates.

Chapter 9 Alvin J. Bronstein was the director of the National Prison Project of the American Civil Liberties Union. In his Voices feature, he talks about the history and early accomplishments of the National Prison Project and concludes by discussing how the Prison Litigation Reform Act has had an adverse reaction on prisoners' rights.

Chapter 10 Diana Bailey is the workforce development/transition coordinator with the Maryland State Department of Corrections. She works inside the mobile units, which provide transitional information and library services for inmates in the prerelease system. In her Voices feature, she describes this exciting support system as used in Maryland to prepare men and women for release from incarceration.

Chapter 11 Jennifer Reynoldson has been a probation/parole officer supervisor for the Fifth Judicial District in Des Moines, Iowa, for the past seven years. Her discussion of the implementation and utilization of evidence-based practices into daily work with offenders is a reminder how important this is seen in corrections today. A second Voice in this chapter is James Young, who is a lead probation parole officer III and training officer for the Fifth District also in Des Moines, Iowa. He currently supervises high-risk parolees, and talks about some of the challenges of his job.

Chapter 12 Mary Leftridge Byrd has been a superintendent of both women's and men's prisons and served as assistant secretary for the division of Offender Treatment and Reentry Programs for the Washington State Department of Corrections. In 2009, she accepted a senior executive service position with the Department of Homeland Security. In her Voices feature, she begins by saying how much she loved her job as warden. She reports that one of the challenges of the job is working with the diverse types of inmates that are placed in prisons today.

Chapter 13 Kelly Culshaw is a group supervisor in the Ohio Public Defender's Death Penalty Division. She has worked there since 1997 when she graduated from The Ohio State University School of Law. In her Voices feature, she talks about the importance of her work as a public defender because of what she sees as fairness issues with the death penalty.

Chapter 14 Jean Tomlinson worked in various positions for the Texas Youth Commission before becoming superintendent of a private facility in Texas. In her Voices feature, she relates how she has a real passion for her work in juvenile corrections. She also identifies areas in which she feels juvenile corrections needs to focus and expresses concern about the quality of some private operations working with institutionalized youngsters.

Chapter 15 Ray Stantel is presently an investigator for the Georgia Department of Corrections. Stantel's Voices feature tells us that he is passionate about his work in corrections, that he loves his job as an investigator, and that he considers corrections to be an excellent career. Another Voice in this chapter is Norman C. Carlson, who served as director of the Federal Bureau of Prisons from 1970 to 1987, and is acknowledged as a corrections pioneer and important contributor to the development of professionalism, the definition of which is the subject of his Voices feature. Finally, we hear from Mark Kleiman, a professor at the UCLA School of Public Policy. In his Voices feature, he proposes alternatives to our present policy of mass incarceration.

corrections today

On July 22, 2011, Anders Behring Breivik, a right-wing extremist, began a murder spree that left 77 innocent people dead and many more wounded. His rampage began when he set off a car bomb explosion at the executive government quarter of Oslo, outside the office of Prime Minister Jens Stoltenberg, killing eight people. Then, dressed as a police officer, he preceded to a youth camp organized by the Norwegian Labour Party on the island of Utøya where he mercilessly gunned down 69 people, mostly young teens. When police finally arrived, the 32-year-old Breivik quickly surrendered.

Was this the work of a deranged person or a calculated hate crime? While at first glance Breivik's actions would appear to be the product of a serious mental defect, his violent shooting spree was carefully planned and executed. Months earlier, he had traveled to Prague in order to purchase weapons, having read on the Internet that it was easy to obtain automatic weapons in the Czech Republic. Failing to obtain weaponry abroad, Breivik worked at obtaining valid gun permits in Norway, actually taking shooting lessons at a local gun club. Just before his murderous rampage was carried out, he published on the Internet a long manifesto explaining his views and motivations.

On the other hand, some of Breivik's actions seemed to be the product of a diseased mind. He wrote a 1,500-page compendium which he published on the Web just before his murder spree. He wrote about such events as taking his mother out for a good meal, praying to

Norwegian killer Anders Behring Breivik arrives handcuffed at a hearing at a courthouse in Oslo, February 6, 2012. Breivik killed 77 people in a terror attack on July 22, 2011, and is currently awaiting trial. He was diagnosed as a paranoid schizophrenic by court-appointed psychiatrists. According to their report, Breivik acted compulsively based on a delusional thought universe. His ideas included organizing Norwegians in reservations and using them in breeding projects. In the pretrial hearing, Breivik read a prepared statement demanding to be released and treated as a hero for his "preemptive attack against traitors," including Moslems and other minorities. He said, "They are committing, or planning to commit, cultural destruction . . . of the Norwegian ethnic group and . . . of Norwegian culture. This is the same as ethnic cleansing."

God that he might be successful, seeking out methods for the purification of bomb ingredients, and getting his equipment and gear in order. He signed it: "Sincere regards, Andrew Berwick, Justiciar Knight Commander, Knights Templar Europe, Knights Templar Norway."[1] It seems he wanted to end Muslim influence in Norway by destroying the future of the liberal, pro-immigration Labour Party; he also hoped to spark a race war in Europe between Christians and Muslims. After his capture, Breivik claimed that he was acting in self-defense. He told a Norwegian judge that his bombing and shooting rampage was aimed to save Europe from a Muslim takeover and that two more cells existed in his organization.[2] He later refused to plead guilty, believing he acted out of necessity. Was he deranged? While his acts were extreme, Breivik purchased high-powered weapons, loaded them with exploding ammunition, disguised himself as a police officer, methodically stalked his prey, and surrendered to police even though he still had ammunition left in his guns. His acts seemed more calculating and shrewd than random and disorganized. His trial is expected to take place in 2012.[3]

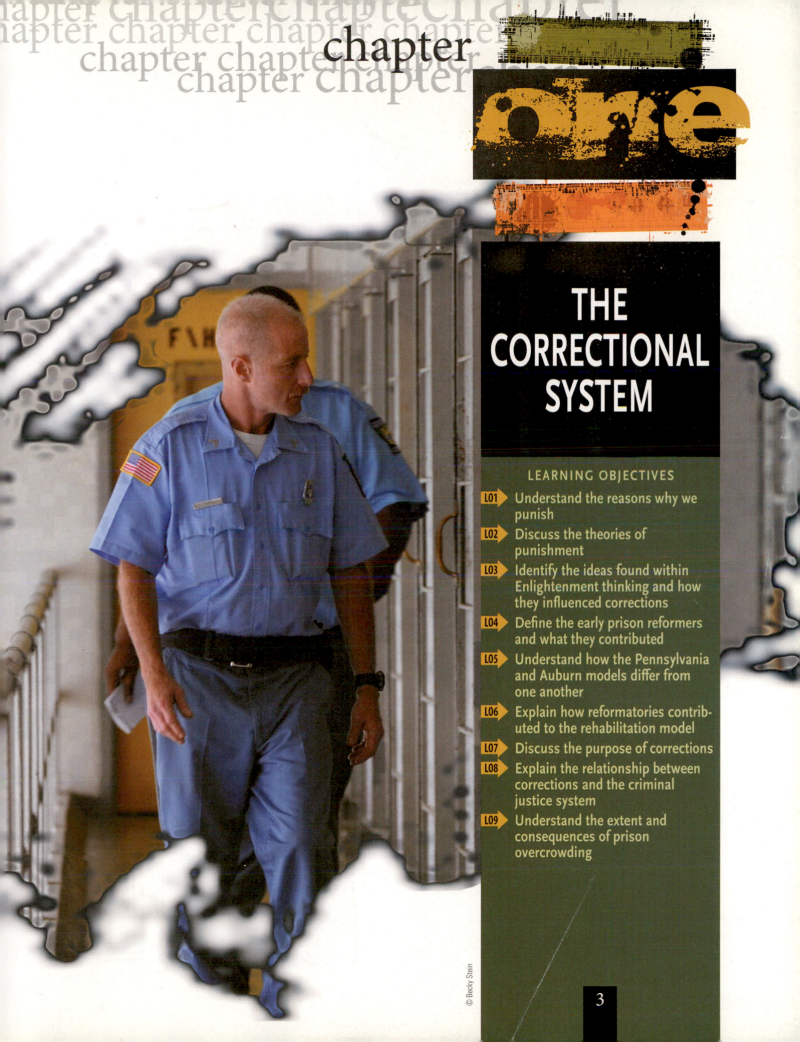

one

THE CORRECTIONAL SYSTEM

LEARNING OBJECTIVES

LO1 Understand the reasons why we punish

LO2 Discuss the theories of punishment

LO3 Identify the ideas found within Enlightenment thinking and how they influenced corrections

LO4 Define the early prison reformers and what they contributed

LO5 Understand how the Pennsylvania and Auburn models differ from one another

LO6 Explain how reformatories contributed to the rehabilitation model

LO7 Discuss the purpose of corrections

LO8 Explain the relationship between corrections and the criminal justice system

LO9 Understand the extent and consequences of prison overcrowding

© Becky Stein

It is the responsibility of federal, state, and county government, established by both law and practice, to protect us from evildoers, treat them, and reduce their potential for social harm. A key part of this mission is to prevent those convicted of both serious felonies and petty misdemeanors from repeating their criminal activities. To accomplish this goal, a correctional system has developed to confine, manage, and provide rehabilitative programs for those convicted of crime, all within a safe, secure, and humane environment. To carry out this task, the correctional system utilizes the services of trained professionals who are committed to public safety, the rehabilitation of inmates, and, after completion of their sentence, the reentry of offenders into society.

While the contemporary correctional system is functionally independent, it is also a subsystem of a broader *criminal justice system*—those agencies of social control: police, courts, and corrections—that are responsible for investigating criminal conduct, gathering evidence, identifying suspects, making arrests, bringing charges, conducting trials, deciding sentencing, and treating criminal offenders. **Corrections** also takes place in particular social contexts—environments and situations that influence people's response to events and shape their beliefs about crime and punishment. Because of its place in the social context of society, all the participants in the correctional process are important: victims, criminals, employees, professionals, and the general public that pays for the correctional system and is concerned about its effectiveness and efficiency. In the Voices Across the Profession feature, James H. Bruton discusses the role of corrections in contemporary society and identifies its most significant contributions.

In this chapter, the role of punishment is examined. Throughout history, people have struggled to determine the proper punishment for crime, hoping to find a formula that is neither too harsh nor too lenient. In nearly every age, some people cry out for draconian punishments against criminals while others urge the humane treatment of those who violate the law. The history of punishment and corrections is examined, beginning with the Middle Ages and ending with the development of the correctional system in the United States. Finally, an overview of the correctional system is presented, including critical issues of corrections, and the development of professionalism in the field of correctional service.

L01 WHY DO WE PUNISH?

The purpose of punishment—or what rulers, legislatures, and judges claimed was the purpose—has changed over time. Depending on the era and the culture, offenders were subject to extremely harsh physical punishments; they were hanged, decapitated, tortured, mutilated, incarcerated, ostracized, publicly humiliated, or otherwise restrained from the enjoyment of life and freedom. While today the cruel and public punishments of years past are usually no longer found, incarceration for life and execution are still routinely used for those committing the most serious crimes.

What are the justifications for punishment in contemporary society? What purpose is served when a fellow human being suffers punishment? After all, punishment involves applying pain, often long after the evil deed has been committed. At its core, criminal punishments result in harm to another human being—something that is in opposition to the moral values of modern society. Nonetheless, criminal punishment is considered justified because it is applied by (a) a duly authorized governmental body on (b) somebody who has violated the laws of society. Yet, how can a practice that results in the loss of personal liberty and freedom be justified in a nation such as ours? Punishment is considered justified in modern society for the following reasons:

- *Punishing law violators provides beneficial consequences.* Although it can be harsh and demeaning, punishing law violators is believed to create

CORRECTIONS The institutions and methods that society uses to correct, control, and change the behavior of convicted offenders.

© James H. Bruton

"The most important message I can give to anyone working in the field of corrections is to have an internal belief that every day you have the opportunity to make a difference in people's lives."

JAMES H. BRUTON,
CORRECTIONS PROFESSIONAL

James Bruton has worked in corrections for more than 35 years, including 14 in correctional facilities, and served as the warden at the Minnesota Correctional Facility, Oak Park Heights, from 1996 to 2001. He has been the vice chairman of the state parole board, and worked for nine years as both a juvenile and adult probation and parole officer. Bruton has also been the deputy commissioner of corrections in charge of institutions. He is the author of *The Big House: Life Inside a Supermax Security Prison* (Osceola, WI: Voyageur Press, 2004). Here is what he has to say about the field of corrections:

"The most important message I can give to anyone working in the field of corrections is to have an internal belief that every day you have the opportunity to make a difference in people's lives. In order to be successful in this difficult business, you have to have a dedicated and committed desire to look forward to going to work, keeping in mind the philosophical belief of making a difference. In conjunction with this mindset, whether you are working in a correctional facility or individually with a client, you must find a way to create an environment conducive to rehabilitation for those offenders who want to make a change in their lives. Your job, along with all of the inherent duties and responsibilities that come with it, is to provide a catalyst for the change in people's behavior to take place.

"It is important to recognize that the courts administer the punishment to the client. It is not the job of the corrections official to extend the punishment beyond the court's disposition. With respect to the administration of prisons, this conceptual philosophy is often misunderstood. The public often is confused and wants standards set both ways. For example, they may want the prison system to expand the punishment with substandard conditions and limited resources for the inmates, and then want the offender to be completely rehabilitated upon release. It quite simply cannot work like that. Keeping in mind that 95 percent of offenders sent to prison will at some point be released, we must find ways for the environment to be filled with incentive-based programming. We must find ways for each inmate to get up every day and look forward to doing something positive and productive. Good behavior will bring about rewards, and negative behavior will result in consequences. This philosophy is effective and it does work."

James Bruton is saying that the purpose in corrections is not to punish offenders—the courts have already done that. Bruton suggests that we resolve to go to work each day believing that offenders can change and that we can have an impact on their lives. Bruton is espousing the goal of reform, but, as documented throughout this chapter, the goal of repression has also been a constant theme of corrections.

Source: Interviewed in 2012.

benefits for law-abiding citizens. Both the threat and application of criminal punishment are a cost-effective means to an end: protecting the public, preventing disorder, and reducing social harm. Some might argue that while punishing people to improve society may be effective it sometimes presents a moral dilemma: would it be just and fair to execute a mentally ill criminal even if his execution helped lower crime rates? Those who believe that punishment is justified by its consequences counter that it is aimed at controlling harmful behavior. To paraphrase Mr. Spock (in *Star Trek II: The Wrath of Khan*), "The needs of the many outweigh the pain of the few." According to this view, even a morally unjust punishment—isolating and torturing terrorists in a harsh prison—is justified if it produces beneficial consequences: locating a deadly bomb they had planted. Critics might retort that it is unlikely that people willing to apply immoral and draconian punishments such as torture could be trusted to do so in a just and fair manner.

In one of the most controversial incidents in recent years, neighborhood watch volunteer George Zimmerman (left) was charged with second-degree murder in the wake of his killing an unarmed black teenager, Trayvon Martin (right) on February 26, 2012, in Sanford, Florida. While patrolling the neighborhood, Zimmerman became suspicious of Martin because he was out late at night and wearing a "hoodie." Zimmerman claimed that, during a brief confrontation between the two, he shot Martin in self-defense after he was knocked down and his head was beaten against the ground. One of the fundamental questions in the case is whether and how Zimmerman should be punished. While the fact that he took a young man's life is unquestioned, his motivation will determine his sentence. If a jury finds that he acted in self-defense, he would be freed without punishment; if they believe he acted with "depraved indifference" to another person, he would get a sentence of 25 to life in prison. Under current penal law, motive and state of mind, rather than the act itself, determine punishment.

BLAMEWORTHY The law defines that a person is criminally liable for his or her behavior.

JUST DESERTS Punishment that is commensurate with the seriousness of the offense or the harm done.

RETRIBUTION Something given or demanded as repayment for wrongdoing; "getting even" for violating the social contract on which the law is based.

■ *Punishment is deserved.* Criminal sanctions are justified because those who voluntarily break the law forfeit some of the rights claimed by citizens. They are **blameworthy:** their wrongdoing justifies treatment that under other circumstances would be considered coercive and/or a violation of civil rights, such as imprisonment or confiscation of wealth. According to the **just deserts** philosophy, punishment is justified only when it conforms to what the guilty deserve, no more and no less. Because law violations involve taking an unfair advantage over those who obey the law, the purpose of punishment is to remove or neutralize any benefit gained through illegal activity. For example, a person who does not pay his proper share of taxes gains an unfair advantage over another who meets this civic burden. The tax cheat can use his excess wealth to invest and make even more money. It would be fair not only to demand the taxes he owed originally, but to penalize him further to recover his ill-gotten gains from having use of the funds denied to the upstanding and law-abiding taxpayer.

■ *Punishment expresses public outrage.* Criminal punishment is a method of expressing public outrage over the commission of a heinous crime. Because such wrongdoing provokes anger and sorrow, the public demands that the perpetrator suffer to "pay for their sins." While a private citizen may seek *revenge* for the pain they feel, the public demands **retribution** for its collective grief by forcing those who caused it to suffer in turn. In this sense, punishment embodies and expresses the public's moral indignation aroused by crime and the anger toward its perpetrator. State-sponsored punishment justifies their anger. By taking responsibility for retribution, the state eliminates the need for personal vengeance and the social chaos that follows in its wake.

■ *Punishment teaches a lesson.* By punishing wrongdoers, the state demonstrates its disapproval of their behavior and in so doing teaches them not to repeat their misdeeds. Just as a parent punishes a misbehaving child so she won't repeat her behavior, so too does the government punish a citizen who violates its rules. The educative effect of punishment is not lost on the general population, which learns from the mistakes of others. Corrections serves as a substitute for language, and its important message is that society condemns the behavior committed.

■ *Punishment helps maintain the government, the social structure, and society.* A state cannot survive unless it maintains a set of rules that create, support, and protect its structure and process. As the government becomes more structured, these rules are formalized into laws designed to control behaviors that threaten state security and well-being. The law provides that people may be corrected or punished if they engage in socially proscribed wrongs—conduct that is condemned as wrong and threatens the social norm. The American economic system, based on capitalism and free enterprise, could not exist unless there were laws protecting private property and protecting businesspeople from fraud and embezzlement. Because criminal laws are designed to protect the social fabric, the defendant must answer not just to the individual victim, but to the whole polity through its criminal courts.

GOALS AND PHILOSOPHY OF PUNISHMENT

While criminal punishments are ideally designed to maintain the social order, there is no single vision of who should be punished, how the sanctions should be administered, and the ultimate goals that justify the application of punishment. Concepts are constantly shifting, reflecting the social, economic, and political realities of the time. Today, the objectives of criminal punishment can be grouped into seven distinct areas: general deterrence, specific deterrence, incapacitation, rehabilitation, retribution/just deserts, restoration, and equity/restitution. Each is discussed below in some detail.

General Deterrence

Deterrence is a goal of punishment designed to prevent others from committing similar crimes. The public application of punishment produces a **general deterrent effect,** designed to signal the community at large that *crime does not pay.* The logic is quite simple: By severely punishing those people convicted of crime, others who are contemplating criminality will be frightened, deterred, and discouraged from their planned actions.[4] Anyone, the argument goes, would be foolish to commit crime if they see another person languishing in prison or actually being executed for the same offense. The state's need to deter criminals, however, must be balanced against the mandate to dispense fair and equal justice to all citizens. In addition, if sentences are too lenient, they may encourage criminal conduct, but if sentences are too severe, they may also provoke anger, revenge, and disrespect for the law. A good example of this would be if the crime of rape were punished by the death penalty. Though some potential rapists might be deterred, others might be encouraged to kill their victims to avoid identification since a conviction for either murder or rape produced the same consequences.

The effectiveness of general deterrence is compromised by the ability of the criminal justice system to effectively identify, apprehend, and punish criminals. To be an effective deterrent, punishment must be certain: people must believe if they violate the law they will almost certainly be caught, convicted, and punished. But typically only 20 percent of all recorded criminal acts result in arrest, and only about 20 percent of arrestees wind up in prison, so the ability of punishment to deter crime is undermined by lack of system effectiveness and efficiency.[5] Most offenders are never arrested, and many who are arrested have their cases dropped. Still other offenders are given community-based sanctions rather than prison sentences. For some crimes, such as larceny, relatively few offenders are ever caught or punished.

If the chances of getting caught and punished are relatively small, and punishment does not deter crime per se, why then has the crime rate dropped for the past decade? Some criminal justice experts reason that the recent decline in crime rates is due to the fact that criminal penalties have been toughened for many criminal offenses. They find that once individuals are arrested, they have a greater chance of being convicted than in the past, which is referred to as *expected punishment;* this can be defined as the number of days in prison that a typical offender can expect to serve for each crime committed.[6] It stands to reason that the likelihood of being apprehended and convicted, as well as the length of

GENERAL DETERRENT EFFECT The idea that punishing one person for his or her criminal acts will discourage others from committing similar acts.

sentences, influences offenders' expected punishments. Crime rates fell significantly during the past two decades because expected punishments rose.

The percentage of convicted offenders who receive a prison sentence has been declining recently.[7] Cost cutting and budget deficits may consciously or unconsciously encourage some judges to rely more on community sentences such as probation that are significantly less expensive than jail or prison. It is possible that if this trend continues, expected punishment will decrease and, therefore, crime rates may increase.

<table>
<tr><td>**MYTH**</td><td>The fear of punishment can deter crime. The more harshly we punish crimes, the less likely people will risk committing criminal acts.</td><td>The association between crime and punishment is less than clear cut. Many criminals are not apprehended, neutralizing the effect of punishment. For some crimes, relatively few offenders are ever caught or punished. If expected punishments could increase, crime rates might go down.</td><td>**FACT**</td></tr>
</table>

Specific Deterrence

The philosophy of **specific deterrence** focuses on the fact that individual offenders should learn firsthand that crime does not pay when they experience harsh criminal penalties. What this position suggests is that the suffering caused by punishment should inhibit future criminal activities. Historically, physical punishments were designed to inflict so much pain that only the bravest or most demented criminal would risk reoffending. In our society, a stay in a violent and dangerous prison should be enough to convince people that crime does not pay. But does it work?

Although a few research efforts have found that punishment can have significant specific deterrence on future criminal behavior, these studies are balanced by research that has failed to uncover specific deterrence effects. Most prisoners (more than 80 percent) who are released from prison have had prior convictions, and the great majority (68 percent) will reoffend soon after they are released.[8] The fact that most convicted criminals reoffend weakens the argument that experiencing punishment produces a specific deterrent effect.

The effectiveness of specific deterrence may be crime specific. For example, parking offenses that have a rapidly increasing scale of punishment and a high rate of ticketing will affect parking behaviors.

Incapacitation

Another goal of punishment is to incapacitate dangerous people so they do not have the opportunity to harm others. Offenders are sentenced to prison to restrain them physically so during the time they are confined society is protected, a concept known as **incapacitation.** Sentencing for the purpose of incapacitation is embraced by both liberals and conservatives. According to liberals, prison was to be reserved for especially dangerous repeat offenders who require incapacitation to protect society while they are being treated and reformed. Conservatives may be less concerned about treatment but view incapacitation as a crime-prevention strategy that can reduce crime rates by imprisoning significant numbers of felons.

Although considerable research has been done on the effects of incapacitation in reducing crime, the results are inconclusive.[9] While it is true that the current prison population is extremely high and the crime rate has been in decline, the prison population also jumped in the decade between 1980 and 1990, while the crime rate increased substantially. It is possible that crime rates have little relationship to incarceration trends and that the reductions in crime are related to such factors as the economy, police effectiveness, and declining drug use.[10]

SPECIFIC DETERRENCE The idea that an individual offender will decide against repeating an offense after experiencing the painfulness of punishment for that offense.

INCAPACITATION Isolating offenders to protect society.

SELECTIVE INCAPACITATION

According to the policy of **selective incapacitation,** because only a small number of offenders commit a significant portion of all crimes, it is more effective to sentence repeat offenders to long prison terms while granting first-time and nonviolent offenders shorter and more lenient sentences.[11] As a result, "career offenders" are locked up for long periods, while one-time or occasional criminals are given probation or other community sentences.[12] While enticing, selective incapacitation is not without its drawbacks. It relies on predicting who will commit future crimes, something that has proven quite elusive to calculate. It also produces false positives—some people are severely punished who may never commit another crime. Is it ethical to punish people whom we believe may be dangerous in the future based on what they have done in the past?

Prison conditions are a significant concern for correctional administrators. Inmate Dennis Howie, 53, a three-strike offender, is pictured at the Mule Creek State Prison in Ione, California. The prison, which houses murderers, child molesters, thieves, and other criminals, is one of the most overcrowded in California. Some inmates have to share triple bunk beds in large public areas, including gyms, because of a shortage of prison cells. The Supreme Court has ordered California to release more than 30,000 inmates or take other steps to ease overcrowding in its prisons to prevent "needless suffering and death." California's 33 adult prisons were designed to hold about 80,000 inmates and now have about 145,000. The United States has more than 2 million people in state and local prisons. It has long had the highest incarceration rate in the world.

© Stringer/USA/X01447/Reuters/Corbis

Rehabilitation

The **rehabilitation** aspect of sentencing suggests that people who violate the law are "society's victims." They have been maltreated by their family, forced to live in poverty, or suffered some life trauma which through no fault of their own has forced them into a life of crime. They will refrain from further criminal activity if they can be successfully helped and treated rather than condemned and punished.

Rehabilitation is also based on being able to predict the future needs of the offender, not on the gravity of the current offense. For example, if a judge sentences a person convicted of a felony to a community-based program, the judge's actions reflect his or her belief that the offender can be successfully treated and presents no future threat to society.

During the twentieth century, the concept of rehabilitation dominated sentencing and corrections. People were placed behind bars until they were thought to be "cured" and then released. The parole board took control of determining when an offender was rehabilitated and thus ready to return to the community. Sentence length shifted from the control of the judge to the correctional system.

Support for rehabilitation-based sentencing practices began to erode when reformers raised questions about the ethics of the rehabilitation model. The erosion accelerated in the early 1970s when criminal justice researcher Robert Martinson and his associates failed to find any systematic evidence that indeterminate sentencing actually worked and prison programs rehabilitated inmates.[13] It was also charged at the time that parole boards were unable to determine when inmates eligible for release had been cured of their criminal propensities. The combined evidence made a mockery of the term "correctional institution." It also raised fundamental questions about the wisdom of maintaining a sentencing policy that was not only failing to achieve its primary objective but doing so in a manner that lacked fairness and consistency.

After more than 40 years, rehabilitation has made a comeback. Many private, community, and even institutional corrections are rehabilitative focused, and

SELECTIVE INCAPACITATION Identifying high-rate offenders and providing for their long-term incarceration.

REHABILITATION Changing an offender's character, attitudes, or behavior patterns so as to diminish his or her criminal propensities.

many are readopting the principles of rehabilitation. Also, a number of comprehensive reviews of research on the effectiveness of correctional treatment have found that some treatment programs do have positive outcomes in improving the attitudes of offenders and in reducing recidivism.[14] The challenge is to identify which program will work with what offenders in what setting.[15]

EVIDENCE-BASED PROGRAMS The norm for planners and correctional administrators in many jurisdictions today is to use the research on evidence-based programs to design programs that work with offenders. **Evidence-based programs** rely on careful analysis of program outcomes using scientifically approved methods, and are designed to discover which programs work with which offenders, in what types of settings, and in what frequency of treatment. One of the tenets of evidence-based practices is "targeted interventions." This principle essentially states that a jurisdiction's most expensive and intensive resources should be directed to those offenders who pose the highest risk to reoffend. Throughout this text we will focus on some of the most effective evidence-based programs. See the accompanying Evidence-Based Corrections feature.

Retribution/Just Deserts

A retributionist position is that punishment is justified if and only if it is deserved because of a past crime. Similarly, the theory of just deserts holds that it is unfair to deprive a person of liberty as a consequence of committing a criminal act for any other reason than the act they engaged in *deserves* to be punished. One should be punished because they deserve it and not to deter others or reduce future criminality. These views of sentencing are retrospective rather than prospective; those who administer punishment need not be concerned with future outcomes, only with providing appropriate punishment for a given harm.[16]

The task of just deserts is to assess the magnitude of the harm and to devise a punishment that is proportionate in severity. The assessment of the magnitude of the harm is typically defined by the type of crime (e.g., petty theft would be seen as less serious than felonious assault) and the offender's prior record. A one-time offender might be treated more leniently than a chronic criminal. Motivation might also be considered. A person who embezzles to maintain a lavish lifestyle would be judged more harshly than one who embezzles the same amount for the more noble purpose of subsidizing the company's underpaid and exploited overseas workers.[17]

Restorative Justice

The **restorative justice** goal of sentencing is designed to reintegrate the criminal offender back into the community. Restorative justice has roots in the concept of reparation, something done or paid to make amends for harm or loss. In victim-oriented reparation, the offender returns to the rightful owner either what has been taken away or its equivalent, usually in money or service. In community-oriented reparation, the offender either pays a fine or renders community service; the community thus functions as a substitute victim. By helping the victim and the community, the offender begins to understand the harm caused by their actions. Rather than being cast out of society, they are given the opportunity to be restored in good standing.[18]

Restorative justice is grounded in the concept that the government should surrender its control over responses to crime to those who are most directly affected—the victim, the offender, and the community. This expression of punishment is based on the premise that communities will be strengthened if

EVIDENCE-BASED PROGRAMS This approach is an analysis of programs with scientifically approved methods to discover what works with which offenders.

RESTORATIVE JUSTICE Making amends to the victim or to society for the harm resulting from a criminal offense.

EVIDENCE-BASED CORRECTIONS

Successful Reentry: What Differentiates Successful and Unsuccessful Parolees?

In a recent study, sociologists Stephen Bahr, Lish Harris, James Fisher, and Anita Harker Armstrong sought to identify what differentiates successful parolees from those who fail on parole. Their goal was to achieve a better understanding of the reentry process in order to enable professionals, friends, and family members to help former inmates adjust to life outside of prison and successfully complete their parole.

To achieve their research objective, they followed 51 parolees during the three years that followed their release from parole. They found that at the end of the three-year period, 55 percent (28) of the parolees had successfully completed their parole and were formally discharged, 25 percent (13) remained on parole, and 20 percent (10) were back in prison.

What differentiated the successes from the failures? One big reason for parole failure, as might be expected, is continued trouble with the law. Successes committed fewer crimes and were arrested less than failures: the mean number of arrests for those who successfully completed parole was 0.28—only 5 of the 28 successful parolees had been arrested. By contrast, those who returned to prison had been arrested at least twice within the three years after release.

Another factor that shaped parole outcome was participation in a prison-based treatment program. Those who succeeded on parole were more likely to have taken a substance abuse class while in prison, an experience that helped some parolees succeed in their attempt to stay off drugs after release and change their identity. The class may have provided the skills, motivation, and support useful in learning to remain substance free.

A number of other economic, personal, and social factors contributed to successful reentry into society. Those who worked at least 40 hours a week were more likely to have completed parole successfully. Work may be important in establishing routines that reduce opportunities and time for associations with deviant peers. Full-time work may also help parolees establish a conventional identity.

Nurturing family ties and friendship networks were also important for parole success. Conventional family and friendship networks insulated the successful parolees from the influence of friends who used drugs. Those without social supports drifted back into crime because they were less connected and more alone.

In sum, success on parole was a multifaceted construct, involving support from family and friends as well as institutional support from employees and the correctional system.

Source: Stephen J. Bahr, Lish Harris, James K. Fisher, and Anita Harker Armstrong, "Successful Reentry: What Differentiates Successful and Unsuccessful Parolees?" *International Journal of Offender Therapy and Comparative Criminology* 54 (October 2010): 667–692.

---

local citizens participate in the response to crime, and this response is tailored to the needs and preferences of victims, communities, and offenders. The discussion of restorative justice will be expanded in Chapter 4 on intermediate sanctions.

Equity/Restitution

The **equity goal of punishment** means that convicted offenders must pay back their victims for their loss, the justice system for costs related to processing their cases, and society for the disruptions caused because of their crimes. In drug trafficking, the social costs may include expenses involved with drug enforcement efforts, day treatment centers, and care for infants born to drug-addicted mothers. In predatory crimes, the costs may include services of emergency room physicians, lost workdays and productivity, and therapy for long-term psychological problems. To help meet these costs, convicted defendants might be required to pay fines, do community service, make financial restitution to victims, forfeit the property they acquired through illegal activities, and reimburse the state for costs related to the criminal process. Thus, the demands of justice require that offenders who have profited from their crimes lose privileges and rights to restore the social balance.

EQUITY GOAL OF PUNISHMENT That offenders usually gain from criminal violations makes it seem just and right that they repay society and victims for losses, expenses, and damages that result from their crimes.

The English lock up their poor in institutions known as workhouses and hold their criminals in bridewells.

Protestants of Amsterdam build a house of corrections for women.

The French create the largest and most complex web of penal institutions when Louis XIV establishes the Hospital General hospital-prison complex.

England begins transporting all felons serving sentences of three years or more to New South Wales (Australia).

| 1500s | 1558–1603 | 1593 | 1603 | 1656 | 1703 | 1718 | 1748 |

During the rule of Elizabeth I, roughly a dozen English common-law crimes are punishable by execution.

Protestants of Amsterdam build a house of corrections for men.

In Rome, Pope Clement XI builds the famous Hospice of San Michele Prison as a house of correction for younger offenders.

Montesquieu writes *The Spirit of the Laws.*

THE HISTORY OF CORRECTIONS: FROM VENGEANCE TO REFORM

To understand the present, it is necessary to examine the past of corrections. In this section, we present a brief review of the development of corrections and show its evolution since the first formal punishments were employed in early societies to development of modern corrections in Europe and the United States.

Development of Formal Corrections

As states, kingdoms, and empires superseded clan and tribal societies, the state assumed the role of punishing violators of societal norms. For the state to take over private vengeance, it was necessary to formalize the system of government, and written laws accomplished this purpose. The importance of the early codes, or written laws, is that they embodied the customs by which organized societies dealt with violators of the norms of conduct. See the Timeline for the development of corrections from ancient times to the nineteenth century.

The first formal legal code was the **Code of Hammurabi,** created by the king of Babylonia (the region which is now Iraq) in about 1780 BCE. Hammurabi's laws set out specific crimes and punishments and were based on the principle of *lex talionis* or "an eye for an eye." While people were punished commensurate for the harm they caused (a thief's hand was cut off, for example), the code also rewarded compensation in the event that the perpetrator could not be identified. Take for instance the crime of robbery. If the thief was not caught, the code called for compensation to the victim of a robbery by the authorities of the city in which the robbery occurred. By making the state directly responsible for restitution, Babylonian law reduced intergenerational feuds and blood vengeance between families, a practice that has stood the test of time.[19]

Punishment During the Middle Ages

A number of punishments were used for criminals in medieval Europe. The most widely used were flogging and branding, torture, servitude as galley slaves, the

CODE OF HAMMURABI Law code issued during the reign of Hammurabi of Babylon. The law of *lex talionis* makes its appearance in this code, one of the first comprehensive views of the law.

| 1764 | 1776 | 1777 | 1790 | 1816 | 1829 | 1857 | 1870 | 1876 | 1920s |

Above the timeline:

Transportation of criminals to the American colonies ends. (1776)

Reform in the Walnut Street Jail in Philadelphia. (1790)

Eastern State Penitentiary is ready for occupancy. (1829)

First Correctional Congress held in Cincinnati. (1870)

Howard B. Gill implements the medical model at the Norfolk Prison Colony in Virginia. (1920s)

Below the timeline:

Beccaria writes *Of Crimes and Punishment*. (1764)

Howard writes *The State of the Prisons in England and Wales*. (1777)

New prison in Auburn, New York, is ready for occupancy. (1816)

Transportation of criminals to Australia ends. (1857)

Brockway becomes the superintendent of Elmira, New York, and develops the reformatory model. (1876)

gallows or other forms of execution, and banishment and transportation. Criminals were seen as menaces to the community and as insults to God. Punishments of appalling cruelty were administered to make certain that the contrast between the riches of the few and the miseries of the many did not diminish.

Some of the first correctional institutions were developed during the medieval period and were still used in the seventeenth and eighteenth centuries. These included (a) **monastic confinement** for violations of penal law; (b) jails, which were used for the temporary detention of debtors and those who had committed minor offenses; (c) **bridewells** or poor-houses, almshouses, and hospitals intended primarily for those incapable of looking after themselves; and (d) **houses of corrections** or workhouses, where vagrants, beggars, and delinquents would be forced to work by way of discipline and punishment.[20] As a general rule, incarceration was not used as a means of correction but as a secure detention of suspected wrongdoers until they could be punished by execution, corporal punishment, or exile. Incarceration was also used to temporarily constrain the liberty of high-status persons who had fallen out of favor because they were political opponents of the ruling regime.[21] While minor offenders might receive corporal punishment such as whipping or branding, criminals who committed more serious offenses received sentences to the galleys and gallows or were transported to one of the penal colonies.

Enlightenment Thinkers and the Development of Corrections

LO3

The philosophical ideas that underlie modern corrections can be traced to three Enlightenment philosophers: Montesquieu, Beccaria, and Bentham. **Charles-Louis de Secondat, Baron de Montesquieu** (1689–1755) wrote about the need to moderate punishment. He contended that in a moderate and lenient government, "the greatest punishment of a bad action is conviction. The civil laws have therefore a softer way of correcting, and do not require so much force and severity."[22] **Cesare Bonesana Beccaria** (1738–1794) based the legitimacy of criminal sanctions on the social contract. The authority to make laws rested with the

MONASTIC CONFINEMENT Prisons established by the Church in the Middle Ages for those laity involved in offensive acts, such as incest and magic.

BRIDEWELLS Houses of corrections run by local authorities to teach habits of industry to vagrants and idlers.

HOUSES OF CORRECTIONS Workhouses where vagrants were forced to work to achieve the purposes of discipline and punishment.

CHARLES-LOUIS DE SECONDAT, BARON DE MONTESQUIEU One of the founders of the classical school of criminology, who advocated the moderation of punishment.

CESARE BONESANA BECCARIA One of the founders of the classical school of criminology, who advocated that punishment should be public, immediate, and necessary.

legislator, who should have only one view in sight: "the greatest happiness of the greatest number." Beccaria considered punishment a necessary evil and suggested that "it should be public, immediate, and necessary; the least possible in the case given; proportioned to the crime; and determined by the laws."[23] **Jeremy Bentham** (1748–1832) believed that the law should accomplish some utilitarian purpose, and the socially desirable outcome from criminal sanctions was the protection of society. He contended that punishment would deter criminal behavior if it was made appropriate to the crime. Beccaria and Bentham believed that offenders are responsible for their behavior and should be punished, but they also believed that the goal of the state should be deterrence, not revenge.

The Early Prison Reformers

Early prisons were indeed harsh environments. The worst felons were cut off from all contact with other prisoners; they had no hope of pardon to relieve their solitude or isolation. They were forced to remain alone and silent during the entire day, and breaking rules resulted in brutal punishments. This practice, which led to mental breakdowns, suicides, and self-mutilations, and the harsh and demeaning conditions of confinement in the eighteenth century inspired some leaders to call for prison reform. **John Howard** (1726–1790) was the first English prison reformer. Appointed high sheriff of Bedfordshire in 1773, Howard inspected the county prison and was shocked by the squalor in which inmates lived. He went on to inspect prisons throughout England and was particularly concerned about prisoners who were held indefinitely because they could not pay the jailer's fee—money paid to the owner or keeper of the prison for upkeep. In addition, terrible living conditions and poor hygiene produced plagues and other illnesses. Indeed, jail fever or typhus was endemic in most jails, and Howard himself died of typhus following his inspection of a jail in Russia. Before his death, Howard provided the English government with detailed proposals for improving the physical and mental health of prisoners, including where prisons should be located, the provision of clean water, proper diet, and adequate hygiene, and guidelines for hiring qualified prison personnel. He also advocated an independent inspection process to make sure reforms were being implemented.[24]

Alexander Maconochie (1786–1860) served as director of the prison colony on Norfolk Island in Australia. There, inmates were "doubly convicted," having been convicted of a crime after being transported from Britain for a previous crime. Norfolk Island was considered the end of the line for both inmates and prison administrators. Instead of continuing the previous brutal treatment of prisoners, when Maconochie took up duties as commandant of the penal settlement in 1840, he set up a system where newly arriving convicts were awarded marks to encourage effort and thrift. Sentences were served in stages, each increasing in responsibility. Cruel punishments and degrading conditions were reduced, and convicts' sense of dignity was respected. In many ways, Maconochie succeeded far better than could be anticipated, but the political unpopularity of what he was doing eventually resulted in his recall to England. Maconochie left his post certainly feeling that his experiment had not worked the way he had hoped.

Walter Crofton (1815–1897), a retired army officer, developed what became known as the "Irish mark system," an innovation that made him a celebrity in international penology circles. Crofton believed in reformation, and inmates could earn early release or "tickets-of-leave" if they demonstrated achievement and positive attitude change. The system applied to convicts serving terms of three years or more. It was separated into three stages. The first stage lasted eight or nine months, depending on the man's conduct. The second stage included four classes, and in each class, a prisoner had to earn marks for a maximum of nine per month. The third stage was spent at Lusk Commons, where convicts were

JEREMY BENTHAM One of the founders of the classical school of criminology, who believed that the law should accomplish the utilitarian purpose of the protection of society.

JOHN HOWARD English sheriff who advocated jail reform.

ALEXANDER MACONOCHIE Served as director of the prison colony in Australia and set up the "mark" system.

WALTER CROFTON Prison reformer who developed the Irish mark system, which eventually spread to the United States and influenced the development of parole.

housed in dormitories and given vocational training to fit them for employment when finally released. Aided by widespread foreign interest, Crofton's system became the standard in England. It was adopted at the Elmira Reformatory in the 1870s in the United States, and parole, as it was called in America, soon spread across the nation.[25]

The Origins of American Corrections

The American experience of corrections was shaped from a particular context, both from the culture that existed in this nation and from what had taken place in Europe. For the most part, punishments were derived from European methods, which featured harsh criminal codes and often sadistic punishments. But the idealism and social activism upon which the American colonies were founded led to the development of distinctly American legal practices, such as the penitentiary.[26]

The use of severe punishment in the United States can be traced back to the early settlers who routinely used strict correctional punishments, including mutilations, hangings, burnings, and brandings, to enforce their strict legal codes. They viewed the deviant as willful, a sinner, and a captive of the devil so they did not hesitate to resort to tough punishments, such as this 1676 public hanging. Punishments were often public and served the dual purpose of punishing the wicked and deterring those who might be planning to commit crime.

© MPI/Getty Images

THE QUAKERS AND CRIMINAL LAW After the adoption of the Declaration of Independence, the Pennsylvania legislature repealed the British laws that the colonies had enacted. A series of statutes abolished capital punishment for all crimes other than first-degree murder.[27] For the major felonies, terms of imprisonment were provided. Fines or jail terms replaced the whipping post, the pillory, and the stocks. A system of state prisons was established to accommodate felons avoiding the gallows under the terms of the new laws. It has been argued that "a more thorough transformation in the character of a penal code, by peaceful legislation, is not recorded in the world's history than that which took place in Pennsylvania during the eighteen years immediately following the Declaration of Independence."[28] Inmates began to be held in the city jails, including a new one located on Walnut Street in Philadelphia.

PENNSYLVANIA PRISON SOCIETY AND THE WALNUT STREET JAIL While the new laws were considered humane, public reaction against the display of convicts on the streets of the city and the disgraceful conditions in city jails led to the formation in 1787 of the Philadelphia Society for Alleviating the Miseries of Public Prisons (renamed the Pennsylvania Prison Society in that same year).[29] Members of the society were appalled by the overcrowded, unsanitary, and corrupt conditions of the Walnut Street Jail and appealed to the legislature for reform. In 1790, an act was passed that brought about sweeping reforms. The act authorized a penitentiary house with 16 cells to be built in the yard of the jail to carry out solitary confinement with labor for "hardened atrocious offenders," thus removing them from the general inmate population.[30]

LO5 **DEVELOPMENT OF THE PENITENTIARY** Pennsylvania's major innovation in penal reform, the **penitentiary,** had actually a long process of development.[31] The word *penitentiary* was first used in the English Penitentiary Act of 1779, which authorized the building of national penitentiaries in which convicts

PENITENTIARY A prison in which persons found guilty of a felony are isolated from normal society.

Courtesy of the Library Company of Philadelphia

FIGURE 1.1 The Layout of Eastern State Penitentiary in Philadelphia
An early print showing the "hub and spoke" model of prison design. In this model, guards could patrol the penitentiary from a central location. ∧
A floor plan of Eastern State Prison, created in 1836. The prison would see additions over the next century. <

Source: Norman Bruce Johnston, Kenneth Finkel, Jeffrey A. Cohen, and Norman Johnson, *Eastern State Penitentiary: Crucible of Good Intentions* (Philadelphia: Philadelphia Museum of Art, 1994).

would be kept in order with strict discipline and hard labor. But the buildings were never actually constructed. Not until 1818 did the legislature authorize construction of two new penitentiaries, one near Pittsburgh and the Eastern State Penitentiary in Philadelphia.[32] The American version of the penitentiary was designed to isolate people found guilty of a felony from normal society. It was believed that penitence, pastoral counseling, and reasonable discipline would correct antisocial behavior.

The **Eastern State Penitentiary** was finished in 1829 and became a model for prisons in several European countries. It had a radial design, with seven wings, each containing 76 cells, radiating from a central hub, where control personnel were stationed (see Figure 1.1). Each cell was 12 feet long, 8 feet wide, and 10 feet high, designed for single occupancy.[33] A separate exercise yard, in which the prisoner was allowed to be in the open air for an hour a day, was provided

EASTERN STATE PENITENTIARY A fortress-like prison in Philadelphia consisting of seven wings radiating from a control hub. Prisoners were kept in solitary confinement. It became a model for prisoners in several European countries.

adjacent to the cell. Cells were separated by stone partitions 18 inches thick, which effectively prevented communication from prisoner to prisoner. Solitude was the goal, and prisoners spent their days alone. Even at compulsory chapel services they could not see one another, because they were seated in chairs that looked like upended coffins. The building was a massive fortress, resembling a medieval castle, intended to deter would-be offenders.

The **Pennsylvania model** was a penal system based on the belief that most prisoners would benefit from the experience of incarceration.[34] However, within a few years, when crowding became a problem, prisoners were doubled up in cells and solitude was no longer possible. It was not long before the conditions of imprisonment at the Eastern State Penitentiary were investigated, and charges of brutality were launched and substantiated against it at hearings that took place in 1834.[35] By the end of the Civil War, the penitentiary's population had reached 1,117 prisoners.[36]

A cell at Eastern State Penitentiary, located in Philadelphia, Pennsylvania. Opened on October 25, 1829, Eastern State was the world's first penitentiary. It used solitary confinement as a form of rehabilitation. The term *penitentiary*, which comes from the word "penance," hinted at the institution's original goal: prisoners were expected to open up to God and seek salvation as a method of reform. As this contemporary photo shows, the cells were concrete and many of them contained a single glass skylight, designed to make the prisoners believe that God was always watching them. Outside the cell, there was an individual area for exercise, enclosed by high walls so prisoners couldn't communicate.

THE NEW YORK PENAL SYSTEM

In 1796, New York enacted legislation abolishing capital punishment for all offenses other than first-degree murder and treason. To accommodate felons who now would do time rather than be subjected to flogging or the gallows, Newgate Prison was built in 1797 in what is now Greenwich Village in Manhattan. A crime wave at the end of the War of 1812 led to overcrowding at Newgate Prison, and in 1816 the legislature authorized a new prison at the western New York town of Auburn. It became a model for maximum-custody prisons. When Auburn filled up in 1825, the legislature authorized the building of Sing Sing Prison at Ossining on the Hudson River. Sing Sing was built in three years by convict labor, except for three civilians—a master carpenter, a blacksmith, and a mason.[37]

Two years after the completion of the prison at Auburn, a new wing was built that became famous as the **"Auburn cellblock."**[38] Prisoners assigned to this block, first occupied Christmas Day in 1821, were not allowed to work nor were they permitted to sit or lie down during daylight hours.[39] The rationale for this austere program was to make incarceration so unpleasant that inmates would never dare reoffend.[40] Suicides, attempted murders, and various mental and physical infirmities attributed to the requirement that men be on their feet all day became so prevalent that this regimen was ended in 1825.

Auburn officials were committed to the idea that solitude is essential to prison discipline. The challenge was to maintain solitude while large numbers of prisoners were eating, working, and moving together through the prison. An ingenious deputy warden, John D. Cray, found a solution that became known as

MYTH The first large prisons to hold convicted criminals can be traced back to European dungeons of the Middle Ages.

FACT Before their creation in the United States, penal institutions were used mostly to house criminal defendants before their trial, while they arranged to pay back a debt, or while they were awaiting execution. The use of prison for reform is an American invention.

PENNSYLVANIA MODEL A penal system based on the belief that most prisoners would benefit from the experience of incarceration.

AUBURN CELLBLOCK An austere prison setting in Auburn, New York, in which inmates were made to endure great suffering.

the **Auburn silent system.** It was the successful alternative to the Pennsylvania model, and, like the Auburn cellblock, was the basis of practical penology until the mid-twentieth century. This system demanded silence from all convicts at all times. They marched in lockstep from the cellblock to the mess hall and to the factory. With right hand on the right shoulder of the person immediately ahead, face turned toward the watching guards, each convict in the platoon of silent offenders was watched for any attempt to communicate.[41] The prison was renamed the Auburn Correctional Facility in the 1970s and is still in use today.

Both the Pennsylvania and Auburn systems must be seen as an attempt to meet the urgent requirements of justice. The Pennsylvania system had the merit of adopting Bentham's goals of the reformation and deterrence of the offender. The Auburn system, in contrast, was a pragmatic effort to administer the processes of punishment as thriftily as possible. The pragmatics of the times called for measures that we would now see as unacceptably brutal but that were tolerable in an age when criminals were thought to be uniformly defective in mind and morals.

THE REHABILITATION MOVEMENT BEGINS

In 1870, a group of reformers, including wardens and politicians, unhappy with the Auburn system, convened the leading figures in penology to hear proposals for change in the management of prisons. The **First Correctional Congress,** held in Cincinnati in 1870, was carefully planned and chaired by Ohio's Governor Rutherford B. Hayes, who was later to become the 19th president. Speakers from the United States and abroad were invited to present new and progressive ideas, such as giving prisoners educational opportunities and religious instruction. Practical prison men from 22 states, Canada, and Latin American nations enthusiastically "rose above the monotony of four gray walls, men in stripes shuffling in lockstep, sullen faces staring through the bars, coarse mush and coffee made of bread crusts, armed sentries stalking the walls. They forgot it all and voted their remarkable Declaration of Principles."[42]

The Declaration of Principles passed by this correctional congress emphasized that the reformation of prisoners should be the goal of corrections. To achieve it, prisoners should be classified on the basis of a marks system, rewards should be provided for good behavior, and indeterminate sentences should be substituted for fixed sentences. The prison's aim should be to create industrious free men, rather than orderly and obedient prisoners. Prisons should be small, and separate institutions should exist for different types of offenders.[43]

THE REFORMATORY MODEL AT ELMIRA

Zebulon Brockway, warden of the Detroit House of Correction, attended the First Congressional Congress and presented a paper entitled "The Ideal Prison System for a State." In this paper, he urged that the very word "prison" be stricken from the statutes: "The true attitude of government is that of guardian; its true function to shelter, shield, help, heal."[44] In 1876, Brockway became superintendent of the Elmira Reformatory in New York, where his proposals for a model reformatory were to have free rein.

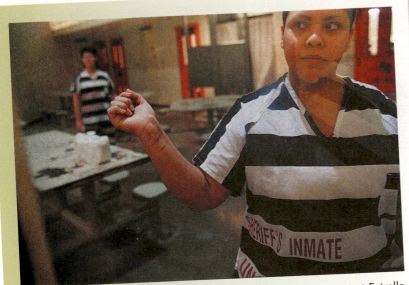

An inmate shows the cuts on her wrist from a failed suicide attempt at Estrella Jail in Phoenix, Arizona. The Estrella Jail was built in 1991, is podular/dormitory in design, and holds approximately 1,000 inmates, predominantly female. The jail has a fully staffed and equipped medical clinic, a nondenominational chapel area for religious services, and three classrooms where inmates can attend educational, drug rehabilitation, or life-skills classes. It is also home to the only female chain gang in America. Inmates stay in their tiny 8-foot by 12-foot cells 23 hours of the day during lockdown, unless they are out on assigned chain gang duty. The inmates must memorize 10 rules of conduct, addressing grooming, behavior, and attitude. Chain gang and other privileged duties can be suspended for infractions such as swearing. The chain gangs work six days a week contributing thousands of hours of free labor to the community. The tough regimen is viewed by jail administrators as a means of rehabilitating the inmates through hard work.

© Scott Houston/Corbis

Brockway felt strongly about the merits of what has been called the **reformatory model.** He advocated indeterminate sentencing as "quite indispensable to the ideal of a true prison system" and an essential part of his rehabilitative model.[45] Admission was restricted to first offenders between the ages of 16 and 30. All inmates received an indeterminate sentence—no minimum sentence but a statutory maximum. The program was aimed at changing the prisoner's character, and the superintendent would then decide when the change in the convict's character justified release. All releases were conditional, and discharge depended on conduct while under supervision in the community over a period of six months.

Elmira was the first correctional institution to pay wages to prisoners as a reward for diligence and productivity. From their wages, inmates paid for room and board, clothing and other necessities, and medical care. The economics of the system were arranged so that at the time of discharge there would be some money to the prisoner's credit. The Elmira program was emulated in 12 other states by the turn of the twentieth century and in 11 more by 1933, despite growing doubts about the success of the system.[46]

The reformatory model, as established in Elmira and other prisons, made some lasting contributions to corrections—the system of indeterminate sentencing, the payment of inmates for work, the supervision of inmates in the community, a system of behavior modification, and the development of what later came to be parole.

THE MEDICAL MODEL OF REHABILITATION
By the 1920s, the **medical model** was implemented in correctional institutions throughout the United States. Many correctional authorities looked forward to a time when the diagnosis and treatment of criminals would match the successes of modern medicine. The prison would become an analogue to the hospital. Cures would be found for most if not all forms of criminal behavior.

One of the earliest advocates of the treatment prison was **Howard B. Gill** (1889–1989), who proposed that the Norfolk Prison Colony in Virginia rehabilitate offenders by curing criminals of the "disease of crime." He carried the hospital metaphor even further. Hospitals had to diagnose before treatment could be initiated, so he devised a classification system for sorting out the "mental diseases" from which his inmates suffered. This was a "scamp" system, an acronym for five categories of convicts: situational offender, custodial (old and senile), asocial cases, medical (handicapped, deformed, tubercular), and personality (psychotics, neurotics, and those with personality difficulties). However, in the aftermath of an escape attempt by a team of inmates, a successful escape by two inmates, and increasing institutional disorders, Gill was dismissed.[47]

While attempts were being made to introduce treatment in institutions housing men, women did not fare as well. Typical women's prisons during the nineteenth century were harsh and disciplinary institutions in which the reformatory tradition was ignored and little concern was shown for the incarcerated women.[48] In the twentieth century, growing numbers of African Americans and descendants of immigrants from southern and eastern Europe filled women's institutions.[49] Chapter 8 discusses women in prison in the twentieth and twenty-first centuries.

THE PURPOSE AND FUNCTION OF THE CORRECTIONS SYSTEM TODAY

After this long history, the contemporary correctional system has emerged as an institution that serves to provide sufficient consequences to individuals convicted by the courts for violating the law so that the public will be protected, fear of crime will be reduced, and offenders are given a chance to reform. Over the centuries, these goals have taken on various meanings and emphasis. Consequently,

REFORMATORY MODEL A penal system for youthful offenders featuring indeterminate sentencing and parole, classification of prisoners, educational and vocational training, and increased privileges for positive behavior.

MEDICAL MODEL The idea that criminality is a sickness that can be cured through psychological intervention.

HOWARD B. GILL Developed the "scamp" system at the Norfolk Prison colony in Virginia.

the tactics used to achieve correctional goals have shifted from one generation to the next.

The general public's reaction to crime has a major influence on the types of punishable behavior and the punishments that are acceptable at a given time. Today, the public's reaction to crime, intensified by the fear of terrorist attacks, has encouraged a conservative, hard-line approach to corrections even though the actual crime rate has been in decline. This approach affects the number of offenders sent to correctional institutions and the duration and severity of their punishments. In this climate of fear, we should not expect a great deal of public sympathy for those who commit violent crimes.

While the correctional system may be used for punishment, it is also a venue for treatment and rehabilitation. In the midst of the sanctions given offenders because they have harmed society, there are those individuals who work with offenders to help them become productive, law-abiding citizens. It is important to examine their roles and how they do their jobs. There are, of course, sad stories of corruption, abuse, and incompetence, but there are also thrilling stories of those who pursue integrity in everything they do.

LO8 ▶ The Criminal Justice System and Corrections

Corrections today is an important cog in the contemporary criminal justice system. These agencies, located at the federal, state, and local levels of government, serve as society's instruments of social control. They are designed to regulate behaviors considered so dangerous that they cannot be tolerated within the confines of society. The justice system is therefore designed to maintain and control people considered so destructive that they must be monitored and/or confined. The agencies of justice—law enforcement, the courts, and corrections—control these outlawed behaviors by apprehending, adjudicating, and sanctioning lawbreakers. Society maintains other forms of informal social control, such as religious institutions, but these deal with moral—not legal—misbehavior. Only the criminal justice system maintains the power to control crime and punish behavior in its role as the operational arm of criminal law.

Criminal justice agencies are political entities lodged within the legislative, judicial, and executive branches of the government.

- The legislature creates law, defines its content, and establishes criminal penalties. The legislative branch of government also appropriates funds for criminal justice agencies, thereby shaping their structure and mission.

- The judiciary interprets the existing law and determines whether it meets constitutional requirements. It provides oversight on criminal justice practices and has the power to insist that they meet legal obligations. The courts have the right to overturn or ban policies that are in conflict with constitutional rights.

- The executive branch helps set justice policy and appoints key leaders within the justice system, such as the head of the prison system and judges.

Agencies of the Criminal Justice System

Because of its varied and complex mission, the contemporary criminal justice system in the United States is monumental in size. It now costs federal, state, and local governments about $228 billion per year for civil and criminal justice, up more than 300 percent since 1982.[50]

One reason the justice system is so expensive to run is because it employs more than 2.4 million people. The nation has almost 18,000 law enforcement agencies, nearly 17,000 courts, more than 8,000 prosecutorial agencies employing more than 80,000 people, about 1,200 correctional institutions such as jails and prisons, and more than 3,500 probation and parole departments.

The system is massive because it must process, treat, and care for millions of people. Although the crime rate has been in decline for most of the past decade, more than 14 million people are still being arrested each year, including more than 2 million for serious felony offenses.[51] In addition, about 1.5 million juveniles are handled by the juvenile courts. State and federal courts convict a combined total of over 1 million adults on felony charges each year.[52]

EXHIBIT 1.1 Elements of the Correctional System

Probation	Court-ordered community supervision of convicted offenders by a probation agency. Offenders on probation are required to obey specific rules of conduct while in the community.
Parole	Community supervision after a period of incarceration.
Jail	A county correctional facility that holds people pending trial, awaiting sentencing, serving a sentence that is usually less than one year, or awaiting transfer to other facilities after conviction.
Prison	A state or federal correctional facility that houses convicted criminals sentenced to a period of confinement that is typically more than one year.

More than 7 million people are under some form of correctional supervision, including 2.2 million men and women in the nation's jails and prisons and an additional 5 million adult men and women being supervised in the community while on probation or parole (see Figure 1.2 and Exhibit 1.1). Though the crime rate has declined substantially, this correctional population continues to grow, and the number of people in the correctional system has trended upward. How can this trend be explained? Though there is less crime, people are more likely to be convicted than in the past and, if sent to prison or jail, more likely to serve more of their sentence.

The Formal Criminal Justice Process

Another way of understanding criminal justice is to view it as a process that takes an offender through a series of decision points beginning with arrest and concluding with reentry into society. During this process, key decision makers resolve whether to maintain the offender in the system or to discharge the suspect without further action. This decision making is often a matter of individual discretion, based on a variety of factors and perceptions. Legal factors, including the seriousness of the charges, available evidence, and the suspect's prior record, are usually considered legitimate influences on decision making. Troubling is the fact that extralegal factors such as the suspect's race, gender, class, and age may also influence decision outcomes.

Few cases are actually processed through the entire formal justice system. Most are handled informally and with dispatch. The system of justice has been roundly criticized for its "backroom deals" and bargain justice. Although informality and deal making are in fact the rule, the concept of the formal justice process is important because it implies that every criminal defendant charged with a serious crime is entitled to a full range of rights under law. The fact that most criminal suspects are treated informally may be less important than the fact that all criminal defendants are entitled to the full range of legal rights and constitutional protections. About 30 percent of people arrested on felony charges are eventually convicted in criminal court; however, almost one-third of those convicted on felony charges are sentenced to probation and released back into the community without doing time in prison.[53] For every 1,000 crimes, about 20 people are sent to prison.

In actual practice, many suspects are released before trial because of a procedural error, evidence problems, or other reasons that result in case dismissal by the prosecutor (***nolle prosequi***). Though most cases that go to trial wind up in a conviction, others may be dismissed by the presiding judge because of a witness or a complainant's failure to appear or procedural irregularities. So the justice process can be viewed as a funnel that holds many cases at its mouth and relatively

Jail and prison inmates

Probation and parole

FIGURE 1.2 Populations of Community-Based and Institutional Corrections

Source: Lauren E. Glaze, *Correctional Population in the United States, 2010* (Washington, DC: Bureau of Justice Statistics; U.S. Department of Justice, December 2011), Table 1, p. 2.

NOLLE PROSEQUI A formal entry in the record of the court indicating that the prosecutor does not intend to proceed any further in this case.

EXHIBIT 1.2 The Criminal Justice Process

The System: Agencies of Crime Control	The Process
Police	1. Contact
	2. Investigation
	3. Arrest
	4. Custody
Prosecution and defense	5. Complaint/charging
	6. Grand jury/preliminary hearing
	7. Arraignment
	8. Bail/detention
	9. Plea negotiations
Courts	10. Adjudication
	11. Disposition
	12. Appeal/postconviction remedies
Corrections	13. Correction
	14. Release
	15. Postrelease

LO9

CORRECTIONAL LIFE
Tim: An Ex-Offender Speaks Out

"One time I was placed in jail and was still a little intoxicated. You never want to cause problems in jail in the middle of the night. I said something to one of them, and they took me in a side room. They beat me until I s—on myself. Then they took me into a tiny cell, hog-tied me, and gave me mace, probably two inches from my face. I was not giving up, and I told them that they were punks and cowards. They gave me mace a couple more times. I laid in there all night long. They knew what they were doing and didn't leave bruises or anything. In the morning, one of the shift supervisors got me out of there and cleaned me up. I thought this was extreme punishment for lipping off a bit.

Then there was the experience I had with this civilian who worked in the prison. She did not like me. One day, while I was working the chow line, she humiliated me in front of other inmates. She tried to make me look like an idiot. I simply turned to her and said, "You can't tell me s—." She went into the office and called the goon squad. I did about ten days in the "hole" as punishment, or administrative segregation. And if this wasn't enough, I was taken to a special needs, or mental health, ward. In prison, if you have a mental health disorder, you are called a "bug." You are not down there with the status of child molesters, but you don't have much higher status. This was the special section of the correctional facility where I would spend the rest of my time. The warden came and talked with me and told me that he was making an example of me."

Source: Interviewed in 2009.

few at its end. Exhibit 1.2 shows the interrelationship of the component agencies of the criminal justice system and the criminal justice process.

Corrections in the Criminal Justice System

While corrections is an element within a complex set of criminal justice organizations and processes, it is functionally independent from the other agencies, with a unique set of values, procedures, and policies. It also faces problems and issues unknown in other agencies such as the police and court system. What are some of these challenges?

SYSTEM OVERLOAD One of the major challenges affecting the ability of corrections to function as a system is overload. The past four decades can be defined as a period of **mass incarceration.** There are now 2.2 million men and women who are serving time in jails and prisons in the United States. What this means is that nearly one in every fifty people in the United States, excluding the elderly and juveniles, is in prison. The U.S. prison population has increased nearly five-fold since 1980 (see Figure 1.3). Significantly, a larger proportion of the U.S. adult population is in prison than anywhere else in the world. With 5 percent of the world's population, the United States has nearly a quarter of its prisoners. The U.S. incarceration rate of more than 724 per 100,000 is five to twelve times the rate of western European countries and Japan.[54]

Since 1995 there has been nearly a 40 percent increase in the inmate population with a 33 percent increase in male prisoners and a 51 percent increase in female prisoners.[55] A closer examination of prison overcrowding reveals that the rate varies significantly from one region to another and from one state to another. The South has the highest rate of imprisonment, followed by the West, Northeast, and Midwest.[56] The Federal Bureau of Prisons has the largest number of inmates, followed closely by California and Texas; these three jurisdictions have nearly 34 percent of the U.S. prison population. See Table 1.1 for the number of state and federal prisoners in the seven largest jurisdictions as of December 2009.

Prison crowding leads to increased inmate defiance and makes prisons (especially maximum-security and supermax prisons) more dangerous places to work. In 2011, for example, the California prison system was beset by prolonged hunger strikes by inmates who were protesting degrading conditions in isolation cells and gang-security measures that unfairly punish prisoners. In July of that year, thousands of inmates staged a three-week hunger strike at prisons across the state.[57]

The federal courts have intervened to mandate strict population ceilings for individual prisons and, in some cases, for entire state systems. Ironically, efforts to reduce prison crowding have led to the overcrowding of county jails, where convicted felons wait for vacant cells in a state prison.

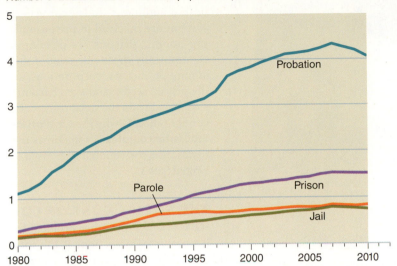

Number of adults in the correctional population (millions)

FIGURE 1.3 Adult Correctional Populations

Source: Lauren E. Glaze, *Correctional Population in the United States, 2010* (Washington, DC: Bureau of Justice Statistics; U.S. Department of Justice, December 2011), Table 1, p. 2.

TABLE 1.1 Seven Largest Jurisdictions of Prisoners Under the Jurisdiction of State or Federal Correctional Authorities

	Number of Prisoners 12/31/09	Percent Change 2008–2009
Federal Bureau of Prisons	208,118	7.5
California	171,275	−.6
Texas	171,249	−.3
Florida	96,632	3.1
New York	58,687	−4.7
Georgia	53,371	3.4

Source: Heather C. West and William J. Sabol, *Prisoners in 2009* (Washington, DC: U.S. Department of Justice, December 2010).

THE BUSINESS OF CORRECTIONS Another difference between corrections and the other agencies of justice is the shift in public perception about its role and value. While police and courts are perceived as a drain on local budgets, prisons are now viewed as a economic savior for local economies. At one time few wanted to see a prison or jail built in their community. Today, this "not in my backyard" philosophy has been replaced with welcome mats. Take for instance Canon City, Colorado, which now calls itself the "Corrections Capital of the World." In Leavenworth, Kansas—a community that recently added a private facility to its already well-known corrections stockade—a billboard reads, "How about doin' some TIME in Leavenworth?" A prison has become a quick way to fix the economic struggles of small counties. Towns that are economically strapped know that if they can induce jail and prison construction, they will receive jobs and attract other businesses such as fast food chains, department stores, and motels—all of which contribute to their tax base. As a result, they are more than willing to

MASS INCARCERATION A term given to the high rates of incarceration in the United States.

MYTH: No one wants a prison in their backyard, and most areas fight prison construction tooth and nail in order to preserve their communities.

FACT: Many rural communities see prison construction as an economic boon and fight to have state governments build institutions in their community. Prisons provide jobs and bolster the local economy. Prison construction is especially welcome during tough economic times.

There are many hidden costs of the correctional system. Here is a photo of the fortress-like San Quentin prison in San Quentin, California, taken on May 20, 2009. San Quentin, with 5,300 inmates, is located in upscale Marin County not too far from San Francisco. Rather than being tucked away in the woods, it sits on some of the most prized waterfront land in the country. Facing billion-dollar budget deficits, every few years someone proposes shutting down the prison and selling off the land at market rate. Some Californians suggest that it be torn down and sold to developers. It would be more valuable as a condo complex than as a prison.

AP Photo/Eric Risberg

offer land, cash incentives, and cut-rate deals on utilities.[58] Today, correctional systems are involved in prison-building booms. Prisons are developing economically profitable relationships among politicians, corporations, and the private sector, and even becoming a commodity on the stock market. This configuration is why the term **prison-industrial complex** is sometimes used to describe correctional systems in the United States.

THE SOCIAL COST OF CORRECTIONS
Another problem that is unique to corrections is the social costs that the policy of mass confinement has had on the American public. While law enforcement and the courts have a relatively short-term impact on people's lives, correctional confinement is a long, drawn-out process that affects both people and the communities in which they reside.

Corrections has had a significant impact on urban neighborhoods in the United States. Most immediate is the effect on the families of prisoners. There are now about 1.5 million children who have a parent in prison. For African American children, one of every fourteen has a parent behind bars on any given day. For these children, shame, stigma, and loss of financial and psychological support are profound aspects of their life experience.

The toll of corrections is often borne by minority group members. According to Marc Mauer, the effect on these communities is compounded by the fact that imprisonment has become a commonplace experience of growing up as an African American male in the United States. Government figures show that an African American male born today has a one in three chance of spending at least a year in prison at some point in his life. While children in well-off communities grow up with the expectations that they will go to college, many in low-income communities grow up with the prospect of doing time in prison.[59]

FINANCIAL COST OF CORRECTIONS
The economic problems of the past decade have impacted all the agencies of justice, including corrections (see Figure 1.4). With virtually every state in the United States facing huge deficits, most have begun cutting prison budgets and closing institutions, especially prison camps and minimum-security prisons, to help balance the budget. This process is found not only in the United States, but also in other countries such as Canada, the United Kingdom, and Australia.[60]

States have recently responded to this crisis in a variety of different ways:

- North Carolina closed seven prisons and nine others had major changes. This eliminated 516 positions for a $22.3 million annual savings.

- Washington State closed nine institutions. Three hundred employees statewide stood to lose their jobs.

- Texas eliminated one prison, three Texas Youth Commission lockups, and 2,000 private prison beds. About 1,562 prison jobs were also chopped. Probation programs saw funding cut by 20 percent, parole supervision

PRISON-INDUSTRIAL COMPLEX A term given to describe the multimillion-dollar prison-building boom in which powerful corporate interest groups, large businesses, and politicians join together to profit from the burgeoning corrections industry.

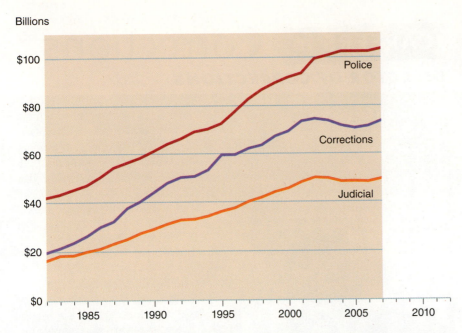

Billions

FIGURE 1.4 Direct Expenditure by Criminal Justice Function

Source: Bureau of Justice Statistics, *Employment and Statistics in the U.S., 2007* (Washington, DC: U.S. Department of Justice, 2011).

cut by almost 9 percent, and the agency construction and maintenance cut, along with 90 jobs. The victims services division was also eliminated.

■ Oregon shut down a minimum-security prison, marking the first prison closure in Oregon history. This was part of a $2.5 billion budget cut that included laying off 63 prison employees.

■ Michigan closed three prisons and five prison camps in 2009 in hopes of narrowing a $1.4 billion budget gap.[61]

PROFESSIONALISM IN CORRECTIONS   All agencies of justice have strived for **professionalism,** requiring education, training, and innovation in order to improve the effectiveness of services. The corrections system has also confronted the need for professionalism, though its mission sometimes makes this goal difficult to achieve. For those who have been in a maximum-security prison or a supermax prison, with their tall walls or razor-wire fences, tiny cells, foreboding segregation units, and ever-present dangers, concepts such as valued career or professionalism may seem totally foreign, unrealistic, and idealistic. Certainly, corrections is not an easy job. Corrections is a complex field riddled with critical issues and deeply disturbing realities, focused on human tragedy and failure. It is a field so shaped by its social context that political and economic realities at times make it seem impossible either to maintain or to change.

One corrections professional, Norman C. Carlson, who served as director of the Federal Bureau of Prisons from 1970 to 1987, was an individual who did as much as anyone to introduce professionalism into correctional service. Carlson's vision of corrections as a profession was one of the earliest themes he articulated once he became director. At that time, corrections was considered anything but a profession. In state departments of corrections, horror stories were commonplace—the inmate trusties in Arkansas who carried weapons and brutalized inmates, the backbreaking work of stoop, or field, labor in the fields of Texas, and the staff brutality that was an ever-present feature in American corrections. Even in the federal system, there were incidents of staff brutality, and Carlson wanted the bureau's staff to know what would be tolerated and what would not be tolerated.

It was not long before signs of professionalism began to appear in state correctional systems. State correctional training academies were established across

PROFESSIONALISM The conduct, aims, or qualities that characterize or make a profession or professional person.

CAREERS in Corrections

DIRECTOR OF CORRECTIONS

Preparation for the Job

Good writing and speaking skills as well as the ability to handle complex managerial decisions are mandatory. In addition to these personal attributes, the observations of others who are performing well in their respective corrections jobs are helpful. It is also wise to avoid staying in comfortable positions as individuals begin their corrections careers. In contrast, young correctional professionals should try to expand their horizons by searching out and accepting new challenges in the workplace.

Nature of the Job

The director of corrections is responsible for directing the implementation of the agency's mission and all aspects of adult corrections in that state. The director of the Federal Bureau of Prisons (BOP) is responsible for the mission of the BOP in community-based facilities, federal jails, and federal correctional institutions. His or her duties are to provide vision and leadership, direct internal/external communication, develop and direct agency budgets, manage policies and procedures, and direct the agency's human resources. This involves performing a number of tasks, including using management practices that encourage staff innovation, educating others regarding agency mission and services, presenting budgets, establishing priorities to direct and redirect resources, and promote and ensure delivery of staff training programs. The state's director has the important responsibility of establishing good relations with members of the legislature, as he or she meets with them concerning the budget and questions they may have. The BOP's director must meet with the Congress to gain approval for programs and budgets, and to answer inquiries about this federal agency.

the nation. Accreditation, spearheaded by the American Correctional Association, was developed and spread throughout community-based agencies and correctional institutions. Affirmative action policies were developed and implemented throughout corrections. The abuse of inmates began to be replaced by the belief that inmates were to be treated with dignity and respect. Some states moved more quickly than others, but this spirit of professionalism is now found throughout the nation. The characteristics and attitudes of what it means to be a corrections professional can be summarized as follows:

- To see yourself as a person of integrity and to live at integrity level. A definition of integrity is to do the right thing even when no one else is around.

- To treat offenders with dignity and respect. As one corrections professional puts it, treat inmates as you would want your father or brother to be treated in a correctional setting.[62]

- To model positive behaviors. One way this can be done is to adhere to the ethical principles set forth by the American Correctional Association.[63]

- To be a person committed to a learning model and to be open to new ways of doing things. Such a person seeks to learn throughout his or her career and is always willing to pursue all the training opportunities available.

- To believe that it is possible to make a difference. Believe that you can have an impact and are not limited by what others have done.

Qualifications and Required Education

The director of corrections is appointed by the governor. Usually, he or she has had responsible positions in correctional agencies before being appointed director. It is not unusual for the person appointed to this position to have served a period of time as associate or assistant director. The person appointed to this position today almost always has a B.A., and many have gone on to earn an M.A.

Job Outlook

There are only fifty of these jobs across the nation (one per state), and the director's job is not secure, as he or she serves at the pleasure of the governor. If the department of corrections has problems that would embarrass the governor, this could put the director's job in jeopardy. If members of the legislature have problems with the director, they too could persuade the governor that it is time for a change. Or if a new governor is elected, he or she may decide to bring in another director. For these and other reasons, directors usually stay only two or three years on the job. Yet this is a highly desired corrections position.

Earnings and Benefits

Directors are well paid. Many earn more than $100,000 a year. The California Department of Corrections and Rehabilitation pays more than $200,000 a year. In addition, the BOP's director who has completed 20 years of service is eligible to retire at age 50.

Sources: National Institute of Corrections, Longmont, CO, www.nicic.org/Library/012265 (accessed February 13, 2012); interviews with a number of directors of state corrections; and the Federal Bureau of Prisons website, www.bop.gov (accessed February 13, 2012).

- To keep your personal stuff from getting in the way. Do not let your personal problems or issues keep you from doing an effective job.[64]

- To refuse to accept unethical behavior from fellow staff members.

- To stay positive and do what is possible to create a workplace that is safe, healthy, and free of harassment in any form.[65]

Throughout this book, we highlight a number of careers in corrections. In this chapter, we examine the director of corrections, who can also be referred to as the commissioner of corrections or the secretary of corrections. One of the hopeful signs of corrections is the increase in professionalism among these top corrections officials.

Other careers in corrections covered in this book include pretrial officer, probation officer, substance abuse counselor, jail officer, warden, correctional officer, correctional counselor, corrections ombudsman, forensic psychologist, parole officer, correctional supervisor, social worker, and investigator. For each career, we discuss the preparation for the job, nature of the job, qualifications and required education, job outlook, and earnings and benefits.

In addition to these careers, it is possible to obtain employment in corrections in a number of other jobs, including accountant, office manager, secretary, business manager, building-grounds maintenance staff, dental hygienist, dentist, food service worker, registered nurse, physician, storekeeper, programmer/analyst, boiler operator, and treatment plant operator.

WHAT THE FUTURE HOLDS FOR CORRECTIONS

What does the future hold for the correctional system? One of the biggest problems—overcrowding and system overload—may be on the wane. The nation's prison population may soon be "maxing out." Budget cutbacks and belt tightening may halt the expansion of prison construction and the housing of ever more inmates in already crowded prison facilities. Although new modular construction techniques and double- and triple-bunking of prisoners make existing prisons expandable, the secure population probably cannot expand endlessly. As costs skyrocket, some states are now spending more on prisons than on higher education. The public may begin to question the wisdom of a strict incarceration policy. There may also be fewer criminals to incarcerate. The waning of the crack cocaine epidemic in large cities may hasten this decline, because street crimes will decline and fewer offenders will be eligible for the long penalties associated with the possession of crack.[66]

Another long-term trend may be the introduction of technology to monitor offenders. Rather than depend on people, personal monitors and tracking devices will be used as a cost-saving method. We will be discussing these technological innovations throughout the text.

In the final analysis, changes in corrections may depend on the faith judges and legislators place in incarceration as a crime control policy. As long as policy makers believe that incarcerating predatory criminals can bring down crime rates, the likelihood of a significant decrease in the institutional population seems remote. If there is little evidence that this costly system does lower crime rates, less costly and equally effective alternatives may be sought.

SUMMARY

LO1 Understand the reasons why we punish

The justifications for punishment are that it provides beneficial consequences, it is deserved, it expresses public outrage, it teaches a lesson, and it helps maintain the government

LO2 Discuss the theories of punishment

The objectives of criminal punishment can be grouped into seven distinct areas: general deterrence, specific deterrence, incapacitation, rehabilitation, retribution/just deserts, restoration and justice, and equity/restitution.

LO3 Identify the ideas found within Enlightenment thinking and how they influenced corrections

During the Enlightenment, Montesquieu, Beccaria, and Bentham wrote about the need to moderate punishment. The most important of these ideas were that punishment should be swift and certain as well as moderate, that the purpose of punishment was to prevent and deter the commission of crime, and that the reform of punishment meant the rejection of torture and the end of the indiscriminate application of capital punishment to hundreds of crimes.

LO4 Define the early prison reformers and what they contributed

John Howard, Alexander Maconochie, and Walter Crofton were widely hailed for the reforms they attempted to bring to corrections during the eighteenth and nineteenth centuries. Howard attacked the abuses in jails in England and on the European continent. Maconochie attempted to improve the treatment of convicts in Australia by installing the mark system on Norfolk Island, and Crofton adapted the mark system to a prison setting in Ireland.

LO5 Understand how the Pennsylvania and Auburn models differ from one another

The Pennsylvania penitentiary, with its solitary confinement and penitence model, was widely hailed both in the United States and Europe. The Auburn silent system demanded silence from convicts at all times. They marched in lockstep from the cellblock to the mess hall and to the factory.

LO6 Explain how reformatories contributed to the rehabilitation model

The reformatory model contributed to the rehabilitation model because of its system of indeterminate sentencing, the payment of inmates for work, the supervision of inmates in the community, and a system of behavior modification.

LO7 **Discuss the purpose of corrections**

The purpose of corrections is to provide sufficient consequences to individuals convicted by the courts so that the public will be protected, crime will be reduced, and offenders will learn that crime does not pay.

LO8 **Explain the relationship between corrections and the criminal justice system**

Corrections in the United States has developed as part of the larger criminal justice system, of which the police, the court system, and corrections are the three components or subsystems.

LO9 **Understand the extent and consequences of prison overcrowding**

One of the major issues in corrections today is prison overcrowding. There are currently more than 2.2 million inmates in U.S. prisons and jails. The consequences of prison overcrowding are that it leads to increased inmate defiance and makes prisons more dangerous places to work.

Key Terms

corrections, 4
blameworthy, 6
just deserts, 6
retribution, 6
general deterrent effect, 7
specific deterrence, 8
incapacitation, 8
selective incapacitation, 9
rehabilitation, 9
evidence-based programs, 10
restorative justice, 10
equity goal of punishment, 11
Code of Hammurabi, 12

monastic confinement, 13
bridewells, 13
houses of correction, 13
Charles-Louis de Secondat, Baron de Montesquieu, 13
Cesare Bonesana Beccaria, 13
Jeremy Bentham, 14
John Howard, 14
Alexander Maconochie, 14
Walter Crofton, 14
penitentiary, 15
Eastern State Penitentiary, 16
Pennsylvania model, 17

Auburn cellblock, 17
Auburn silent system, 18
First Correctional Congress, 18
Zebulon Brockway, 18
reformatory model, 19
medical model, 19
Howard B. Gill, 19
nolle prosequi, 21
mass incarceration, 23
prison-industrial complex, 24
professionalism, 25

? Critical Thinking Questions

1. Which of the reasons why we punish has the greatest influence on the public and its policy makers today?

2. Do you think retribution will continue to be as popular as it has been in recent years? Will the costs of corrections affect this desire to incarcerate so many, for so long, and in long-term institutions?

3. With the rise of professionalism in corrections, what can be done about those who continue to demonstrate a retributive spirit and express brutality toward inmates?

4. In *Voices Across the Profession,* James Bruton, who has been a correctional professional throughout his career, claims that we can make a difference. Do you agree that it is possible to make a difference in corrections?

5. What were the advantages and disadvantages of public executions of offenders? Would you favor televised public executions of offenders? If not, why not?

6. Alexander Maconochie thought that prison governors or wardens should belong to a profession. If so, how would the warden qualify as a professional? What experience and talents are needed?

7. What can corrections today learn from the correctional systems found at the Eastern State and Auburn penitentiaries? It can be argued that the reforms proposed in the First Correctional Congress, held in 1870, still have not been fully implemented in contemporary corrections? Why is that? Why did the reformatory model fall short of its hopeful goals? Is the medical model of rehabilitation an appropriate model for a prison setting?

Thinking Like a Corrections Professional

The governor has appointed you chairman of a task force to bring reform to your state's correctional efforts. She is particularly concerned that you find ways to reduce prison population, without compromising public safety. Whom will you appoint to your committee? What is your strategy for developing this plan of reform? What is your plan to disseminate the results of your report?

Career Destinations

Notes

1. Duncan Gardham, "Norway Killings: Breivik's Countdown to Mass Murder," *The Telegraph*, July 26, 2011, www.telegraph.co.uk/news/worldnews/europe/norway/8663758/Norway-killings-Breiviks-countdown-to-mass-murder.html (accessed February 13, 2012).
2. Peter O'Neil, "Norway Mass-Murder Suspect Anders Behring Breivik Denied Public Forum," Europe Bureau, *Postmedia News*, July 24, 2011.
3. Ibid.
4. For a study that concludes that crime, prison costs, and imprisonment numbers can be reduced simultaneously if policy makers shift from a reliance on severity-based policies to a more effective use of police to make the costs of crime clearer and the consequences of criminal activity faster and more certain, see Steven N. Durlauf and Daniel S. Nagin, "'Imprisonment and Crime: Can Both be Reduced," *Criminology and Public Policy* 10 (2011): 13–54.
5. Steven N. Durlauf and Daniel S. Nagin, "The Deterrent Effect of Imprisonment," in *Controlling Crime: Strategies and Tradeoffs*, ed. Philip J. Cook, Jens Ludwig, and Justin McCrary (Chicago: University of Chicago Press, 2011).
6. See Bruce A. Jacobs, "Deterrence and Deterrability," *Criminology* 48 (May 2010): 417–441.
7. Matthew R. Durose, Donald J. Farole, and Sean P. Rosenmerkel, *Felony Sentences in State Courts, 2006* (Washington, DC: Bureau of Justice Statistics, 2009).
8. David M. Kennedy, *Deterrence and Crime Prevention: Reconsidering the Prospect of Sanction* (New York: Routledge, 2009).
9. Durlauf and Nagin, "The Deterrent Effect of Imprisonment."
10. Tomislav Kovandzic and Lynne Vieraitis, "The Effect of County-Level Prison Population Growth on Crime Rates," *Criminology and Public Policy* 5 (2006): 213–244.
11. Peter Greenwood did the research that brought selective incapacitation to the attention of others. See Peter W. Greenwood, with Alan Abrahamse, *Selective Incapacitation* (Santa Monica, CA: Rand, 1982).

12. Kathleen Auerhahn, *Selective Incapacitation and Public Policy: Evaluating California's Imprisonment Crisis* (Albany, NY: SUNY Editions, 2003).
13. Robert Martinson, "What Works? Questions and Answers about Prison Reform," *Public Interest* 35 (Spring 1974): 22–54.
14. See Chapter 10 for these various studies suggesting that some treatment programs have had positive outcomes. I don't have Ch. 10 yet, so I can't confirm this.
15. For examination of the revival of rehabilitation as a penal strategy, see Gwen Robinson, "Late-Modern Rehabilitation: The Evolution of a Penal Strategy," *Punishment and Society* 10 (2008): 429–445; Tony Ward and Shadd Maruna, *Rehabilitation: Beyond the Risk Principle* (London: Routledge, 2007); Mark W. Lipsey and Francis T. Cullen, "The Effectiveness of Correctional Rehabilitation: A Review of Systematic Reviews," *Annual Review of Law and Social Science* 3 (2007): 297–320.
16. Matthew Haist, "Deterrence in a Sea of 'Just Deserts': Are Utilitarian Goals Achievable in a World of 'Limiting Retributivism'?" *Journal of Criminal Law and Criminology* 99 (2009): 789–822.
17. Ibid.
18. Mark S. Umbreit, Robert B. Coates, and Betty Vos, "Restorative Justice Dialogue: A Multi-Dimensional, Evidence-Based Practice Theory," *Contemporary Justice Review* 1 (March 2007): 25–41.
19. C. H. Johns, *The Oldest Code of Laws in the World* (Edinburgh: T & T Clark, 1905). See also Peter Watson, *Ideas: A History of Thought and Invention* (New York: Harper Perennial, 2005), pp. 93–95.
20. Norman Johnston, *Forms of Constraint: A History of Prison Architecture* (Urbana and Chicago: University of Illinois Press, 2000), p. 5. See also P. Spierenburg, *The Prison Experience: Disciplinary Institutions and Their Inmates in Early Modern Europe* (New Brunswick, 1991), p. 1–11.
21. Johnston, *Forms of Constraint*, pp. 40–41.
22. Cesare Bonesana Beccaria, *Of Crime and Punishments*, trans. Kenelm Foster and Jane Grigson (New York: Oxford University, 1964),

p. 13; originally published as *Dei Deletion Della Penne* (1764).
23. Ibid.
24. Marie Gottschalk, *The Prison and the Gallows: The Politics of Mass Incarceration in America* (London: Cambridge University Press, 2006), p. 80
25. Ibid.
26. Ibid., p. 18.
27. One reformer, Dr. Benjamin Rush, the leading physician of Philadelphia, argued vigorously but unsuccessfully against the death penalty even in case of murder.
28. Harry Elmer Barnes, *The Evolution of Penology in Pennsylvania* (Whitefish, MT: Literary Licensing, 2011), p. 73, quoting from Pennsylvania Prison Society, *A Sketch of the Principal Transactions of the Philadelphia Society for Alleviating the Miseries of Public Prisons* (Philadelphia: Merrihew and Thompson, 1859), p. 5.
29. Norman Johnston, *Prison Reform in Pennsylvania*, www.prisonsociety.org/about/history.shtml (accessed February 13, 2012).
30. Ibid.
31. Adam Jay Hirsch, *The Rise of the Penitentiary: Prisons and Punishment in Early America* (New Haven: Yale University Press, 1992), p. 32.
32. Ibid., p. 83.
33. Note that, at 96 square feet, these cells far exceeded the 60 square feet called for in the present Standards of Accreditation of the American Correctional Association.
34. Barnes, *Evolution of Penology in Pennsylvania*, pp. 159–160.
35. Norman Johnston, "The World's Most Influential Prison: Success or Failure?" *Prison Journal* 84 (December 2004).
36. For an expansive treatment of this prison, see Negley K. Teeters and John D. Shearer, *The Prison at Philadelphia: Cherry Hill* (New York: Columbia University Press, 1957).
37. Ibid.
38. W. David Lewis, *From Newgate to Dannemora: The Rise of the Penitentiary in New York, 1796–1848* (Ithaca, NY: Cornell University Press, 1965).
39. Ibid. The Auburn officials were an unsentimental lot.

40. Ibid, p. 68. Lewis is quoting from the *Journal of the State Assembly* (1822), p. 218.

41. Blake McKelvey, *American Prisons: A Study in American Society* (Montclair, NJ: Patterson Smith, 1977).

42. For a condensed version of this landmark speech, see Zebulon Brockway, *Fifty Years of Prison Service* (Ithaca, NY: Cornell University Library, 2009).

43. Ibid.

44. McKelvey, *American Prisons*.

45. Ibid.

46. Ibid.

47. Ibid.

48. Lewis, *From Newgate to Dannemora*, p. 159.

49. Mark Colvin, *Penitentiaries, Reformatories, and Chain Gangs: Social Theory and History of Punishment in Nineteenth-Century America* (New York: St. Martin's Press, 2000), p. 181.

50. Brian A. Reaves, *Census of State and Local Law Enforcement Agencies 2008* (Washington, DC: Bureau of Justice Statistics, 2011).

51. Federal Bureau of Investigation, *Crime in the United States, 2010*, www.fbi.gov/about-us/cjis/ucr/crime-in-the-u.s/2010/crime-in-the-u.s.-2010 (accessed February 21, 2012).

52. Matthew R. Durose and Patrick A. Langan, *Felony Sentences in State Courts, 2002* (Washington, DC: Bureau of Justice Statistics, 2004).

53. Ibid.

54. Gottschalk, *The Prison and the Gallows*, p. 1. See also Marie Gottschalk, "The Past, Present, and Future of Mass Incarceration in the United States," *Criminology and Public Policy* 10 (August 2011): 483–504.

55. *Prison and Jail Inmates at Midyear 2009* (Washington, DC: Bureau of Justice Statistics, 2010).

56. Ibid.

57. Robert Lopez, "State Prison Officials Vow to Crack Down on Inmate Hunger Strikes," *Los Angeles Times,* September 9, 2011, http://latimesblogs.latimes.com/lanow/2011/09/california-prison-hunger-strikes.html (accessed February 13, 2012).

58. Michael Welch, "Force and Fraud: A Radically Coherent Criticism of Corrections as Industry," *Contemporary Justice Review* 6 (2003): 234. See also Marc Mauer, "Addressing the Political Environment Shaping Mass Incarceration," *Criminology and Public Policy* 10 (August 2011): 699–705.

59. Marc Mauer, "Don't Throw Away the Key: Lessons from the 'Get Tough on Crime' Initiates," *Resist Newsletter* (March–April 2006).

60. Randall G. Shelden, "Imprisonment Binge Comes Home to Roost," www.sheldensays.com/imprisonmentbinge.htm (accessed February 13, 2012).

61. Ibid.

62. Clemens Bartollas, *Becoming a Model Warden: Striving for Excellence* (Landham, MD: American Correctional Association, 2004), p. 26.

63. The Code of Ethics for the American Correctional Association can be found online at www.aca.org/pastpresentfuture/ethics.asp (accessed February 13, 2012).

64. Bartollas, *Becoming a Model Warden*, p. 83.

65. Code of Ethics for the American Correctional Association.

66. Andrew Lang Bolub, Farrukh Hakeem, and Bruce Johnson, *Monitoring the Decline in the Crack Epidemic with Data from the Drug Use Forecasting Program, Final Report* (Washington, DC: National Institute of Justice, 1996).

In 2005, the nation was transfixed by the plight of Natalee Holloway, 18, from the Birmingham, Alabama, suburb of Mountain Brook, who disappeared on the island of Aruba while celebrating her high school graduation with about 100 classmates and several parent chaperones.

Three young men, Joran van der Sloot and brothers Deepak Kalpoe and Satish Kalpoe, were arrested, but the police could not come up with sufficient evidence to make the charges stick, and the Kalpoes and van der Sloot were released.

The three men had told the police that they took Holloway to Arashi Beach, on Aruba's northern tip, and at 2 a.m. dropped her off at her hotel, where they saw her being approached by a security guard as they drove off. This was one of several stories circulating about the case, including claims that Holloway had been sold into sexual slavery and that she had died on the beach and her body was dumped at sea.

The case remains unsolved but not forgotten. In 2010, it was suddenly back on the front page: Van der Sloot approached Natalee Holloway's family in an effort to extort money from them in exchange for information on their daughter, including the location of her body. After being paid $15,000 for information that turned out to be false, van der Sloot used the money to travel to Lima, Peru. There,

AP Photo/Karel Navarro, File

Dutch citizen Joran van der Sloot is shown being escorted by police outside a police station near the border with Chile in Tacna, Peru. Joran van der Sloot was arrested for the murder of a young Peruvian woman, Stephany Ramírez, in his Lima hotel room on May 30, 2010, after the two left a casino together. The murder occurred nearly seven years after he became the prime suspect in the unsolved disappearance of American teenager Natalie Holloway on holiday in Aruba. On January 13, 2012, a Peruvian court sentenced van der Sloot to 28 years in prison. It is possible for him to be released in 14 years with evidence of good behavior, including work and study. According to van der Sloot, he killed Ramírez in a fit of rage after she discovered information on his laptop about his involvement in the Holloway case. Should someone like van der Sloot be eligible for early release? How should someone like him be sentenced?

on May 30, 2010, the fifth anniversary of Holloway's disappearance, a local girl, Stephany Tatiana Flores Ramírez, 21, was found dead in the Hotel TAC; the room had been registered in the name of Joran van der Sloot! Witnesses put the unfortunate young woman with van der Sloot in the hotel together, and a video showed the two playing cards at the same table at a local casino. Ramírez's jewelry, ID, and credit cards were missing, as well as over $10,000 she had won earlier that evening at the casino. On January 13, 2012, Joran van der Sloot pleaded guilty to the murder of Stephany Tatiana Flores Ramírez. The judges claimed they took his confession into account, but they still gave him a sentence two years short of the 30-year maximum. Due to time already served, the judges said van der Sloot's sentence would end in June 2038. But under Peru's penal system, van der Sloot could become eligible for parole after serving half of the sentence with good behavior, including work and study. Van der Sloot could be freed sometime in his late 30s if paroled after serving half of his 28-year sentence. After sentencing, van der Sloot was transferred to Piedras Gordas maximum security prison, north of Lima.[1]

TWO

SENTENCING AND THE CORRECTIONAL PROCESS

LEARNING OBJECTIVES

LO1 Explain the role of the court team in the sentencing process

LO2 Explain what is meant by indeterminate sentencing

LO3 Understand the various forms of determinate sentencing

LO4 Describe the role of sentencing guidelines

LO5 Know what is meant by truth-in-sentencing

LO6 Identify the most serious issues in sentencing

© Bill Roth/*Anchorage Daily News*/MCT via Getty Images

How and why we punish people who break the law is a critical element of corrections. Some crimes are relatively minor and merit minor sentences. Other crimes seem beyond any punishment we can imagine. Is a 28-year sentence sufficient for someone like Joran van der Sloot who took the life of one young woman and perhaps two? Should convicted killers be considered for parole and released after serving only half their sentence? In 2012, Mississippi Governor Haley Barbour made headlines when he pardoned more than 200 convicted criminals, including 17 convicted of murder, 10 convicted of manslaughter, 8 convicted of aggravated assault, and 5 convicted of drunken-driving incidents that caused deaths.[2] The victims' families were outraged—are you? And as the TechnoCorrections feature

TECHNOCORRECTIONS — Cell Phones in Prison

AP Photo/Rich Pedroncelli, File

What can be a technological innovation to some can be an instrument of crime to another. An inmate escaped from a Kansas prison with the aid of a phone smuggled in by an accomplice. In Texas, a death row inmate charged with killing four persons, including two teenage girls, used a wireless phone from within the prison to threaten a prominent state senator and his family. These incidents serve as just two examples where individuals used cell phones to facilitate criminal acts from within a correctional institution.

Because of incidents such as these, correctional administrators have sought to place restrictions that not only limit the number of persons an inmate may call but dictate that none of the individuals called have a criminal record. As a general matter, correctional staff may monitor inmate calls when "pursuant to a policy statement" and when prisoners receive "reasonable notice that monitoring of telephone conversations might occur." Authorities may also impose restrictions on telephone use based on the security level in which an inmate is housed. While prisoners may use their cell phones for benign purposes, such as maintaining

contact with family and friends, the devices also may provide inmates with an avenue for conducting criminal activity without concerns about the restrictions imposed on landline telephone use. Prisoners have used them to, for example, intimidate and threaten witnesses; transmit photographs, including offensive pictures sent to victims; orchestrate crimes, such as gang activity; coordinate escapes; bribe prison officers; order retaliation against other inmates; text other prisoners; gain access to the Internet; and create security breaches.

Detection by Authorities

As a result of the influx of wireless phones within facilities, officials have taken aggressive measures to detect them. Authorities have implemented not only random cell inspections but perimeter searches. Some institutions have used traditional security measures to detect cell phones, such as metal detectors, X-ray technology, and routine searches of staff, visitors, and contractors. Officials also have used body orifice security scanner (BOSS) systems to detect cell phones and parts concealed in body cavities.

An innovative proactive approach to detection is the use of dogs. For instance, as part of their crackdown on cell phone possession by inmates, the Maryland Department of Public Safety and Correctional Services uses canines trained specifically to detect wireless devices, including even the

small SIM cards, which is important because prisoners often store them separately, "minimizing the loss in case a phone is seized." The use of dogs to sniff out cell phones has proved quite successful. Some agencies have begun to use electronic cell phone detection systems, which can indicate to security staff when a device is in use in a facility. Some such systems rely on wireless sensors to detect phone signals. Others may be hardwired within a facility. Although effective, use of these technologies requires startup costs.

Another approach is jamming using radio frequency (RF) technology in order to disrupt cell phone signals. While this may seem like an attractive possibility, it is illegal unless done pursuant to specific authorization by a court authority. Currently, Congress is examining the possibility of permitting the proactive use of jamming to prevent inmates' use of cell phones in correctional institutions. One bill under consideration would allow state governors or the director of the Federal Bureau of Prisons to petition the FCC to permit mobile jamming in prisons.

All these efforts have their downsides, both legal and practical. But there is little doubt that correctional authorities will continue to devise innovative methods to control inmate use of this technology within prison walls.

Source: Tod W. Burke and Stephen S. Owen, "Cell Phones as Prison Contraband," FBI Law Enforcement Bulletin, July 2010, www.fbi.gov/stats-services/publications/law-enforcement-bulletin/july-2010/cell-phones-as-prison-contraband (accessed March 19, 2012).

shows, once incarcerated many inmates use technology to continue their criminal careers. Should their punishment also include removing such personal items as cell phones and access to other electronic devices?

In this chapter, we will explore the intersection of punishment and corrections in the contemporary criminal justice system. We begin by looking at the role of court personnel in making sentencing decisions, then turn to the different type of sentences now being used in the United States. Finally, we will review the social and economic forces that impact on the sentencing process.

ACTORS IN THE SENTENCING PROCESS

While sentence type and length are typically created by some legislative body, the sentencing process rests in the hands of a number of actors, nested within the court system, who use their power and discretion to shape the administration of criminal punishments. Choosing the "correct" sentence is a complex decision. Why we punish, how we punish, and whom we punish are concepts that are constantly shifting, reflecting the social, economic, and political realities of the time. Who makes these decisions and what guides their judgments?

The Prosecutor

A member of the practicing bar, the prosecutor is typically an appointed or elected official who is responsible for bringing the state's case against the accused. He or she focuses the power of the state on those who disobey the law by charging them with a crime and eventually bringing them to trial or, conversely, releasing them after deciding that the evidence at hand does not constitute proof of a crime.

Although the prosecutor's primary duty is to enforce the criminal law, his or her fundamental obligation as an attorney is to seek justice as well as convict those who are guilty. If, for example, the prosecutor discovers facts suggesting that the accused is innocent, he or she must bring this information to the attention of the court. In recent years, prosecutors have gained greater leverage to extract guilty pleas from defendants and, as a result, reduce the number of cases that go to trial. New laws have resulted in giving prosecutors more power in the courtroom. With the advent of mandatory sentences and other harsher penalties, it is now possible for prosecutors to use the threat of more serious charges to get criminal defendants to accept pleas and cooperate in other ways.[3]

Defendants can choose to have their day in court, but they risk facing a judge and jury who may place them in prison for more years, sometimes far more years, than the plea bargain they were offered. In some courtrooms, the increased use of the plea bargain has nearly put the trial system out of business. One study of nine states found that in 1970, about one in 12 cases made it to trial; today, fewer than one in 40 felony cases are tried in court. The decline has been steeper in federal courts.[4]

The *Florida v. Shane Guthrie* case illustrates why plea bargaining has become the norm. In this case, Guthrie, 24, was arrested in 2010, accused of beating his girlfriend and threatening her with a knife. He was offered a deal by the prosecutor of two years in prison plus probation. Guthrie rejected this and a later offer of five years, because he believed he was not guilty. The prosecutor's response was severe. He filed a more serious change that would mean life imprisonment if Guthrie were convicted later in 2011 or 2012. The sentence would be mandatory.[5] As this book goes to press, this case has moved from the pretrial to trial process.

What has taken place is that there has been a transfer of power to prosecutors from judges that has undercut the formal court process with a more informal system shaped by backroom deals and agreements.[6]

In most jurisdictions it is the presiding judge who decides on criminal punishments. Here, Circuit Judge Don Lester speaks to Jarred Harrell, February 3, 2012, in the Clay County Courthouse in Green Cove Springs, Florida. Harrell, an unemployed restaurant worker, pleaded guilty in the abduction, sexual battery, and slaying of Somer Thompson, a 7-year-old Florida girl who was found in a landfill. Dozens of her family and friends packed a crowded courtroom wearing shades of purple, the little girl's favorite color, and saw Harrell admit that he raped and murdered Somer in October 2009. Judge Lester then sentenced him to six life sentences without the possibility of parole.

AP Photo/*Florida Times–Union*, Will Dickey, Pool

The Judge

The senior officer in a court of criminal law, a judge's duties are quite varied and are far more extensive than the average citizen might suspect. During trials, the judge rules on the appropriateness of conduct, settles questions of evidence and procedure, and guides the questioning of witnesses. When a jury trial occurs, the judge must instruct jury members on which evidence can be examined and which should be ignored. The judge also formally charges the jury by instructing its members on what points of law and evidence they must consider before reaching a decision of guilty or innocent. When a jury trial is waived, the judge must decide whether the defendant is guilty. Finally, and most importantly for our purposes, upon a guilty finding, the judge decides on the sentence. This duty includes choosing the type of sentence, its length, and—in the case of probation—the conditions under which it may be revoked. Even where sentences are legislatively determined, the judge can sometimes use his or her discretion to lighten the defendant's burden. Obviously, this decision has a significant effect on an offender's future.

The public's expectations of the judge's role contain several erroneous assumptions. It is often assumed that the judge is in isolation from the political and social pressures that appear to dominate other public officials; that the judge is always a neutral arbitrator; that he or she carefully follows the statutory and legal prescriptions applicable to the case and is not swayed by personal opinion; and that the judge dominates the criminal justice system, from arrest through sentencing.[7] Judges' actual behavior represents a blend of the duties they are expected to perform, the public's expectations and influence, tradition, political pressure, and the realities and pressures of their jobs.

Sentences are given by judges, who because they are only human often share the public's sentiments and reactions to crime. Those who are elected officials are aware that unpopular sentences may result in their being voted out of office. Some may have a particular value or bias that shapes their approach to punishment.[8] For example, a judge may have little regard for people who drink and be especially harsh on alcoholics who commit crime. Others may have greater sympathy for the mentally handicapped and feel compelled to grant them more lenient sentences.

In the Voices Across the Profession feature, the formal role expectations of the judge are discussed by Judge Steven C. Clarke.

Probation Staff

Before sentencing takes place in felony cases, it is common for the court's probation staff to conduct a presentence investigation. An inquiry, performed by a probation officer attached to a trial court, contains information about the defendant's background, prior criminal record, education, previous employment, and family. The defendant may be interviewed, and interviews also may be conducted with neighbors, acquaintances, and employers. Treatment staff may be asked to evaluate the defendant's mental and/or physical condition. The report may contain information that would be inadmissible as evidence at a trial but is influential and important at the sentencing stage.

This presentence investigation serves as the basis for sentencing and has a significant influence on whether the convicted defendant will be granted community release or sentenced to secure confinement. In the event that the offender is placed on probation, the investigation becomes useful as a tool to shape treatment and supervision efforts.

The pretrial officer is the focus of the Careers in Corrections feature in this chapter. The pretrial officer is related to probation services, but serves the primary purpose of recommending defendants who are eligible to be released to pretrial release.

IMPOSING THE SENTENCE

The sentence is usually imposed by the judge, but sentencing may also be exercised by a jury or may be mandated by statute, such as mandatory prison sentences for certain crimes.[9] In the majority of felony cases, excluding required mandatory prison terms, sentencing is generally based on the information available to a judge. Some jurisdictions permit victims to make impact statements that receive consideration at the sentencing hearing. Most judges also consider a presentence investigation report prepared by a probation officer in making the sentencing decision. The report is based on a social and personal history of the defendant, including the defendant's prognosis of successful integration into the community. Some judges give this report greater weight than others.

Concurrent versus Consecutive Sentences

The person who is convicted of two or more charges must receive a sentence on each charge. **Concurrent sentence** means that multiple sentences begin on the same day and are completed when the longest term has been served.

In contrast, **consecutive sentence** means that on completing the sentence for one crime, the offender begins serving time for the second of what may be multiple crimes. Concurrent sentences are usually the norm, but consecutive sentences are requested for the most serious offenders and for those who refuse to cooperate with authorities. Figure 2.1 shows the difference between consecutive and concurrent sentences.

CONCURRENT SENTENCES One or more sentences imposed at the same time and served simultaneously.

CONSECUTIVE SENTENCES One or more sentences imposed at the same time and served one after the other.

Preparation for the Job

Previous experience in probation services or in parole services is helpful, as well as volunteer experiences in working with offenders in probation.

Nature of the Job

This position performs correctional work in the areas of pretrial release, supervised release, classifications, and frequently inmate worker program coordination and work release. The pretrial officer is responsible for interviewing detainees to obtain detailed information, verifying alleged offenses committed by detainees, communicating with various agencies and officials as well as friends, family, and employers of detainees. He or she prepares a variety of related documents to include establishing and maintaining files; serves as an officer in various hearings and is required to testify in court; interacts with courts, district attorneys, victim witnesses, public defenders, private attorneys, law enforcement agencies, and the general public; and interviews newly arrested inmates for pretrial release, supervised release classification, inmate worker and work-release consideration.

Qualifications and Required Education

Applicants must have a minimum of two years of college or vocational training in criminal justice, criminology, corrections, social services, or related field, and be familiar with the operation of computers and software applications to perform word processing, database, and spreadsheet projects. The ability to communicate effectively, both orally and in writing and the knowledge of federal and state statutes applicable to law enforcement are also required. Applicants must be able to efficiently multitask, have strong organizational skills, and demonstrate proficiency in time management. This includes knowing interviewing techniques and procedure, having the ability to verify information received, and being comfortable with one-on-one contact with inmates or detainees.

Job Outlook

The job possibilities are promising. With the constant shifting of judicial districts, there are new jobs for pretrial officers. Pretrial officers are also often promoted to adult probation officers and sometimes to juvenile probation officers.

Earnings and Benefits

Salaries in most jurisdictions are $30,000 to $40,000 a year.

Source: Government Jobs, www.governmentjobs.com/view_job.cfm?JobID=365722 (accessed February 15, 2012).

The Effect of Good Time

Judges sentencing defendants to prison know and take into account the fact that the amount of time spent in confinement is reduced by the implementation of "time off for good behavior." This was first used in 1817 in New York and was quickly adopted in other jurisdictions. **Good time** is still found in prisons today but not in all jurisdictions. In some states, prisoners can accrue as much as 10 days per month of good time. Some correctional authorities also grant *earned* sentence reductions to inmates who participate in educational and vocational programs, treatment groups, or who volunteer for experimental medical testing programs. Accordingly, in some correctional systems, it has been possible to earn up to half of a sentence by accumulating both standard and earned good time.

GOOD TIME A deduction of time awarded to inmates for good behavior.

A major advantage of good time is that it permits prisoners to calculate their release date at the time they enter prison by subtracting the anticipated good time from their sentence. However, if prisoners become involved in serious disciplinary offenses or attempt to escape, they can lose their good time. Some jurisdictions even return former prisoners to prison to serve the balance of their unexpired sentence when their good time is revoked for failing to comply with conditions set down for their release, such as abusing drugs or failing to report to postrelease supervision.

Sentencing Sanctions

The forms of **sentencing sanctions** available to judges vary from jurisdiction to jurisdiction, but generally include diversionary programs, fines, probation, intermediate sanctions, confinement in jail, incarceration in a state or federal prison, and the death penalty. These sanctions will be examined in some detail in later chapters. The death penalty, a form of sanction that is available in some jurisdictions across the nation, is not only a sentence but has created a class of incarcerated people on death row: the death row inmate. Because this special population is so important to corrections, it is discussed in great detail in Chapter 13. The responsibility of the judge is to weigh the costs and benefits to the defendant and to society in arriving at the appropriate disposition. The judge also has the responsibility to escalate the punishment to fit the crime.

Former Illinois governor Rod Blagojevich arrives at his home after receiving a 14-year prison sentence for attempting to sell President Obama's former Senate seat in Chicago. Blagojevich, who reported to prison on March 15, 2012, was eligible to get two years off his sentence for good behavior. In some jurisdictions, inmates can shave a significant portion off their sentence by entering treatment programs.

AP Photo/Paul Beaty

Sentencing Models

Sentencing is the beginning of the correctional process.[10] Criminal sentencing and sanctions imposed by it represent society's most powerful means to discourage repeated unlawful behavior. Society expects sentences that are appropriate to

SENTENCING SANCTIONS The various types of sentences that can be awarded by the courts.

FIGURE 2.1 Consecutive versus Concurrent Sentences

Example: In state X
1. Rape is punishable by 10 years in prison
2. Possession of a handgun is punishable by 3 years
3. Possession of heroin is punishable by 4 years

Consecutive sentence
Rape + possession of a handgun + possession of heroin
10 + 3 + 4 = 17 years
(each sentence must be served individually)

Concurrent sentence
Rape + possession of a handgun + possession of heroin
10 years
(all sentences served simultaneously)

the seriousness of the criminal act, that incarcerate violent criminals, and that prevent innocent people from becoming victims of crime. The sentencing of convicted offenders is being transformed in a number of ways today. The discretion available to judges has decreased over the past decade, as many states have experimented with one or more types of sentencing reform—sentencing guidelines, determinate sentencing, mandatory sentences, and alternative forms of punishment. The purposes of sentencing have shifted from an emphasis on utilitarian aims, especially rehabilitation, toward a greater focus on appropriate punishment proportionate to the harm done.

Indeterminate Sentences

The **indeterminate sentence** first appeared in the late nineteenth century. Prison reformers, such as Enoch Wines and Zebulon Brockway, called for the creation of indeterminate sentences that could be tailored to fit individual needs. Offenders, it was argued, should be placed in confinement until they were rehabilitated and then they should be released on parole. As previously discussed, criminals were presumed to be sick, not bad, and could be successfully treated in prison. Rather than holding that "the punishment should fit the crime," reformers believed that "the treatment should fit the offender." This meant the establishment of a low minimum sentence that had to be served and a much longer maximum sentence that defined the outer boundary of the punishment. For example, a sentence of 1 to 15 might be given for a burglary. After a year, in this case, the average burglar would be eligible for parole (i.e., serve the remaining part of his sentence in the community) providing this person had entered treatment programs, cooperated with authorities, and otherwise proven he had been rehabilitated. On the other hand, if the inmate refused treatment, got into scrapes, or tried to escape, he could be forced to serve the entire 15-year sentence behind bars. Under this model, the amount of time to be served in prison was at the discretion of the parole board rather than the judge.

The law never allowed an indeterminate sentence to be completely indeterminate. For the minor felonies—auto theft, for example—a sentence ranging from between one and five years would be prescribed in a typical penal code. More serious felonies would carry a longer minimum sentence and sometimes would allow a maximum sentence of life imprisonment. For first-degree murder, when the convicted person was not to be executed, the sentence would always be for life.

The indeterminate sentence has been subjected to considerable criticism. Some critics complain that it creates sentencing disparity (offenders with similar crimes receive diverse sentences from one jurisdiction to another). Others charge that it takes sentencing discretion out of the hands of judges and gives it to parole boards who determine when an offender is released even if he or she has served only a small portion of the sentence behind bars. Another argument is that because it is impossible to tell what the future holds, sentencing should not be based on predictions of future outcomes but rather on what people did in the past (i.e., based on their crimes). Today the primary purpose of indeterminate sentences remains an effort to individualize each sentence in the interest of rehabilitating offenders. Yet no one can accurately determine who can be rehabilitated and who are poor candidates for treatment. Should sentencing be based on guesswork? In *Tapia v. United States* (2011), the U.S. Supreme Court found that federal law does not allow rehabilitation to be used as a factor when handing down a sentence. Tapia was given a lengthened sentence of imprisonment for the purpose of providing sufficient sentence length for her to participate in the Bureau of Prisons' Residential Drug Abuse Program (RDAP); she felt this was unfair and filed suit. The Supreme Court found in her favor and acknowledged that prison has no rehabilitative properties and that a judge cannot extend a sentence that would have typically been handed down in the interest of rehabilitation.[11]

One advantage of indeterminate sentencing is that it permits flexibility both in the type of sentences that are imposed and in the length of time that has to be served.

INDETERMINATE SENTENCE Sentence that permits early release from a correctional institution after the offender has served a required minimum portion of his or her sentence.

Jurisdictions using indeterminate sentencing often employ statutes that specify minimum and maximum terms but permit judicial discretion to fix the actual sentence given within these limits. Typically, minimum sentences are at least one year; a few state jurisdictions require a two-year minimum sentence be given to felons.

Even though rehabilitation and parole have been under heavy attack by critics who argue that criminals should be punished and not coddled, the indeterminate sentence is still the most widely used type of sentence. Today, more than 30 states retain some form of indeterminate sentencing.[12]

Determinate Sentences

Determinate sentences give the defendant a fixed term of years, the maximum set in law by the legislature, which is to be served by the offender sentenced to prison for a particular crime. For example, if the law provides for a sentence of up to 20 years for robbery, the judge might sentence a repeat offender to a 15-year term. Yet, another robber with few violations might receive a more lenient sentence of 5 years.

Determinate sentences were the ones used early in the nation's history but gave way to the indeterminate model in the 1870s when reformers began to stress treatment and rehabilitation of inmates. However, 100 years later a rising crime rate created dissatisfaction with the indeterminate sentence and the treatment model. Conservatives disliked the apparent leniency of parole and early release, which seemed to link short sentences to good grades in school and satisfactory reports from work supervisors. Liberals were critical of the charade of coerced rehabilitation performed by prisoners in order to gain parole. Both sides of the political spectrum agreed that sweeping changes in the penal code were in order. What was difficult to decide was the direction of change—toward a harder line or toward shorter but better-defined sentences. Nevertheless, in 1977, liberals and conservatives combined their usually incompatible forces to produce a federal Determinate Sentencing Law (DSL), referred to as Senate Bill (SB) 42. Under SB 42, judges were required to fix, within a very narrow range of choice, sentences at the time of the offender's conviction. The DSL allowed judges to give much harsher sentences, a provision that subsequently increased prison overcrowding.

Determinate sentencing reform has been implemented in a dozen states: Alaska, Arizona, California, Connecticut, Colorado, Illinois, Indiana, Maine, Minnesota, North Carolina, Pennsylvania, and Washington. A number of other legislatures are considering determinate sentencing acts. Moreover, parole practices and policies have undergone significant reform in Oregon, Minnesota, and the federal government, to cite several jurisdictions.

LO3 Structured Sentences

In order to regulate sentence length and curb judicial discretion, most determinate sentencing jurisdictions have developed methods to structure and control the sentencing process and make it more rational. To accomplish this task, **sentencing guidelines** have been implemented by determinate sentencing states and the federal government. Guidelines give judges a recommended sentence based on the seriousness of a crime and the background of an offender. The more serious the crime and the more extensive the offender's criminal background, the longer the prison term recommended by the guidelines. For example, guidelines might recommend a sentence of five years for robbery if the offender had no prior offense record and did not use excessive force or violence. For a second offense, the recommended sentence would increase to seven years; those who used force and had a prior record would have three years added to their sentence, and so on. By eliminating judicial discretion, guidelines are designed to reduce racial and gender disparity.[13]

The first four states to develop **presumptive sentencing** guidelines—a form of sentencing determination in which the legislature sets the penalties for criminal acts—were Minnesota (1980), Washington (1981), Pennsylvania (1982), and

DETERMINATE SENTENCE Sentencing that imposes a sentence for a definite term. Its main forms are flat-time sentences, mandatory sentences, and presumptive sentences.

SENTENCING GUIDELINES Federal and state guidelines intended to ensure fair sentencing by ending the reduction of terms in prison by grants of parole, ensuring that persons committing similar crimes serve similar terms, and ensuring that sentences reflect the severity of the criminal conduct.

PRESUMPTIVE SENTENCING Sentencing in which the legislature sets penalties for criminal acts.

Florida (1983). About twenty states and the federal government established sentencing guidelines in the final two decades of the twentieth century. Eighteen of these guidelines are still in effect. Sentencing guidelines have been particularly well received in Delaware, Minnesota, Oregon, Pennsylvania, and Washington.[14] A good many other states have rejected guidelines because they perceive them as an improper interference with the role of the judiciary or because respected judges have been vocal in their opposition. See Minnesota Sentencing Grid (Figure 2.2).

FIGURE 2.2 Minnesota Sentencing Grid

Criminal History Score

Severity Level of Conviction Offense		0	1	2	3	4	5	6 or more
Murder, 2nd-degree (intentional murder; drive-by shootings)	XI	306 261–367	326 278–391	346 295–415	366 312–439	386 329–463	406 346–480[2]	426 263–480[2]
Murder, 3rd-degree murder, 2nd-degree (unintentional murder)	X	150 128–180	165 141–198	180 153–216	195 166–234	210 179–252	225 192–270	240 204–288
Assault, 1st-degree controlled substance crime, 1st degree	IX	86 74–103	98 84–117	110 94–132	122 104–146	134 114–160	146 125–175	158 135–189
Aggravated robbery, 1st-degree controlled substance crime, 2nd degree	VIII	48 41–57	58 50–69	68 58–81	78 67–93	88 75–105	98 84–117	108 92–129
Felony DWI	VII	36	42	48	54 46–64	60 51–72	66 57–79	72 62–86
Assault, 2nd-degree felony in possession of a firearm	VI	21	27	33	39 34–46	45 39–54	51 44–61	57 49–68
Residential burglary Simple robbery	V	18	23	28	33 29–39	38 33–45	43 37–51	48 41–57
Nonresidential burglary	IV	12[1]	15	18	21	24 21–28	27 23–32	30 26–36
Theft crimes (over $2,500)	III	12[1]	13	15	17	19 17–22	21 18–25	23 20–27
Theft crimes ($2,500 or less) Check forgery ($200–$2,500)	II	12[1]	12[1]	13	15	17	19	21 18–25
Sale of simulated controlled substance	I	12[1]	12[1]	12[1]	13	15	17	19 17–22

Italicized numbers within the grid denote the range within which a judge may sentence without the sentence being deemed a departure. Offenders with nonimprisonment felony sentences are subject to jail time according to law.

☐ Presumptive commitment to state imprisonment. First-degree murder is excluded from the guidelines by law and continues to have a mandatory life sentence. See section II.E. Mandatory Sentences for policy regarding those sentences controlled by law.

☐ Presumptive stayed sentence; at the discretion of the judge, up to a year in jail and/or other nonjail sanctions can be imposed as conditions of probation. However, certain offenses in this section of the grid always carry a presumptive commitment to state prison. See sections II.C. Presumptive Sentence and II.E. Mandatory Sentences.

[1] One year and one day.

[2] M.S. § 244.09 requires the Sentencing Guidelines to provide a range of 15 percent downward and 20 percent upward from the presumptive sentence. However, because the statutory maximum sentence for these offenses is no more than 40 years, the range is capped at that number.

FEDERAL SENTENCING GUIDELINES

Federal sentencing guidelines had their beginning in October 1984, when Congress passed the Comprehensive Crime Control Act, which among other things abolished parole as of November 1987.[15] The United States Sentencing Commission was created in a companion Sentencing Reform Act of 1984.

Forty-three levels of offenses were specified, and most federal crimes were assigned to a defined level. Departures by the sentencing judges from the guidelines are discouraged. If a judge believes he or she has to depart from the guidelines, the judge is expected to justify that departure in writing and expect that it would be appealed. For example, on October 12, 2011, a 11-year prison term was handed down to Raj Rajaratnam, founder of the Galleon Group hedge fund; this was the latest example of an inside trader receiving a lighter sentence than suggested by federal guidelines. U.S. District Judge Richard Holwell said that under the federal guidelines, Rajaratnam faced a minimum of 19.5 years in prison. In opting for a substantially lighter sentence, Holwell took both Rajaratnam's charitable works and impending kidney failure into consideration.[16]

EVALUATIONS OF FEDERAL GUIDELINES

The federal sentencing guidelines have been criticized on several fronts:

- Judges complain about their complexity and difficulty of use along with the fact that they limit the exercise of judicial discretion.

- Defense counselors have little use for them because of their harshness and because they shift sentencing authority from judges to prosecutors and are based on prior record and offense elements rather than on conviction charges.

- Many federal officials also dislike the guidelines because of their dissimilarity to the prior system of sentencing and because of the disruption they brought to a system that was working well enough before the change. Some complain the guidelines were developed with insufficient attention paid to either ethical considerations of basic justice or basic concerns about their effects on prison populations.

- Some experts argue that there are biases against African Americans and Hispanics, despite the stated goal of removing discrimination from the sentencing process.[17] The most notorious of the federal guidelines is the one requiring that the possession of crack cocaine be punished far more severely than the possession of powdered cocaine. Critics rightly claim that this amounts to racial bias because African Americans are much more likely to possess crack cocaine, while whites are more likely to use powdered cocaine.[18]

- Some defense attorneys oppose the use of guidelines because they believe they result in longer prison terms and prevent judges from considering mitigating circumstances. Some jurisdictions give longer sentences if defendants had prior juvenile convictions or if they are on juvenile probation or aftercare (parole) at the time of their arrest.

LEGALITY OF SENTENCING GUIDELINES

Two recent U.S. Supreme Court cases have placed a moratorium on the use of presumptive guidelines. In *Blakely v. Washington* (2004), the Court found that Washington State's sentencing guidelines violated a defendant's Sixth Amendment rights because they permitted a judge to consider aggravating factors that would increase the sentence. The Court held that no criminal sentence in state courts can be enhanced beyond the allowable maximum guideline for an offender, unless the defendant waives the right to a jury or admits the facts in his or her guilty plea.[19]

FEDERAL SENTENCING GUIDELINES These guidelines were adopted by Congress and until the U.S. Supreme Court ruled otherwise were to be binding on federal judges.

Then, in *United States v. Booker* (2005), the Court ruled on two questions of whether the federal guidelines were unconstitutional and whether the federal guidelines violate the Sixth Amendment right to trial by jury. On the first question, the Court found that a sentence cannot be increased based on facts that were found by a judge and were not found by a jury or admitted by the defendant. On the second question, rather than striking down the federal guidelines, the Court held that the guidelines could be taken into consideration by federal judges but that they no longer had to be regarded as mandatory.[20]

These two cases did not in fact outlaw guidelines but ruled that changes must take place in how they are administered, particularly if they involve sentencing enhancement. The decisions in these cases made the future of guidelines seem questionable. However, a 2006 report by the Federal Sentencing Commission found that even though federal courts interpreted the *Booker* decision in different ways, the majority of cases continue to be sentenced within the range of existing sentencing guidelines. The guidelines may now be advisory, rather than mandatory, but they still have considerable impact on sentencing decisions.[21] Sentencing guidelines are also still being used in this advisory fashion in Minnesota as well as other states.[22]

Mandatory Minimum Sentences

A further attempt to limit judicial discretion while at the same time getting tough on crime has been the development of **mandatory minimum sentences**.[23] A mandatory minimum sentence specifies a certain required number of years of incarceration for specific crimes.[24] It can take a number of different forms:

- The legislature may prohibit defendants convicted of certain violent crimes, drug offenses, or other crimes from being placed on probation.

- The legislature may require that certain offenses, such as drug sales and/or gun possession, carry a mandatory term of imprisonment.

The purpose of mandatory minimum sentences is to provide equal treatment for all offenders who commit the same crime, regardless of sex, age, race/ethnicity, or other personal characteristics. More than 35 states have replaced various forms of discretionary sentencing with fixed-term mandatory sentences for such crimes as violent offenses, kidnapping, gun possession, arson, and sale of hard drugs.

Mandatory sentencing carries its own set of baggage. It has helped increase the size of prison populations to record levels, because many offenders who would formerly have been placed on probation are now being incarcerated. An example of this is women offenders who are minimally involved in drug crime but are punished disparately by the existing criminal justice system. These women became involved in crime because of their financial dependence on, romantic attachment to, or fear of a male drug trafficker. These "women of circumstance" find

Hope Sykes is taken away in tears after being sentenced by Judge Terry LaRue to a mandatory minimum sentence of 15 years in prison on drug charges at the Putnam County (Florida) courthouse. Sykes was 18 when she was arrested in January 2012 on a charge of trafficking after she, her cousin Ronald Cummings, 26, and Misty Croslin, 18, were recorded selling 25 hydrocodone pills in an undercover officer's car. The use of mandatory minimums for drug offenses has helped keep the prison population at record levels.

AP Photo/*Florida Times–Union*, Jon M. Fletcher

themselves imprisoned and subject to draconian sentences because the men in their lives persuaded, forced, or tricked them into carrying drugs.[25]

Three-Strikes Laws

During the 1990s, 25 states and Congress passed **three-strikes laws** for those who are repeat offenders.[26] Popularly known as "three strikes and you're out" (3×) laws or habitual offender statutes, these rules require long sentences without parole for those convicted of a third or higher-order felony. California and Washington's three-strikes laws are well known, and the Federal Crime Act of 1994 requires a mandatory life sentence for any offender convicted of three felony offenses. The legality of the three-strikes concept has been challenged in two critical cases, *Andrade* and *Ewing*, and these are set out in Exhibit 2.1.

EXHIBIT 2.1 Three-Strikes Laws

California's controversial three-strikes law sends repeat offenders to prison for 25 years to life for violent and even nonviolent crimes. The three-strikes movement continues the trend toward determinate sentencing that began in the 1980s. California's law is the harshest of the states that have recently adopted similar laws. In California, Leandro Andrade was given a 50-years-to-life sentence for shoplifting videotapes from Kmart, and Gary Ewing was given 25-years-to-life for attempting to steal three golf clubs from a country club pro shop. He slipped them down the leg of his pants, and a shop employee called the police when he noticed Ewing was limping from the shop.

Andrade and Ewing were given stiff sentences because on the third offense California's three-strikes law considers some misdemeanors, including shoplifting, as felonies. California approved the law overwhelmingly in 1994, largely because of the kidnapping-murder of 12-year-old Polly Klaas by a repeat offender out on parole.

There have been efforts to repeal these laws which have led to court action. The Ninth U.S. Circuit Court of Appeals in San Francisco threw out Andrade's sentence; the court said that it was "grossly disproportionate" to the crime of stealing $153 worth of videotapes. It was appealed to the U.S. Supreme Court, and in April 2002, the Court decided to review whether the law forces judges to mete out "cruel and unusual punishment."

On March 7, 2003, a divided Supreme Court upheld California's three-strikes law, rejecting constitutional challenges to sentences for the two men convicted of petty theft. The rulings in *Ewing v. California* and *Lockyer v. Andrade* were 5 to 4. The Court could not agree on the precise reasoning for upholding the sentence. Nevertheless, with the decisions in the two cases, the Court effectively foreclosed criminal defendants from arguing that their non-capital sentences were disproportional to the crime they had committed.

Justice Sandra Day O'Connor wrote an opinion for herself, Chief Justice William H. Rehnquist, and Justice Anthony M. Kennedy. She observed that the three-strikes law represented a new trend in criminal sentencing: "These laws respond to widespread public concerns about crime by targeting the class of offenders who pose the greatest threat to public safety: career criminals." Such laws were a "deliberate policy choice" on the part of legislatures to isolate those who "repeatedly engaged in serious or violent criminal behavior." Although California's three-strikes law, O'Connor reasoned, may have generated some controversy, "we do not sit as a superlegislature to second guess" the policy choices made by particular states. "It is enough," she concludes, "that the State of California has a reasonable basis for believing that dramatically enhanced sentences for habitual felons advances the goals of its criminal justice system in any substantial way."

Sources: *Ewing v. California*, 538 U.S. 11 (2003); Patrick Marshall, "Three-Strikes Laws," *CQ Researcher*, May 10, 2002.

THREE-STRIKES LAWS Rules for repeat offenders that require long sentences without parole for conviction of a third or higher-order felony.

TIMELINE

Chronology of Sentencing in the United States

Congress and the states adopt get-tough sentencing policies.

Congress repeals mandatory sentences for drug violations.

New York State's so-called Rockefeller laws require lengthy sentences for drug crimes.

In another key Eighth Amendment ruling, the Supreme Court in *Solem v. Helm* overturns a mandatory life-without-parole sentence for a defendant convicted of passing a $100 bad check.

| 1950–Present | 1956 | 1970 | 1972 | 1973 | 1980 | 1983 | 1984 |

Narcotic Control Act establishes minimum sentences for drug crimes.

The first clear call for sentencing guidelines comes from Federal District Court Judge Marvin Frankel in his groundbreaking book, *Criminal Sentences: Law Without Order*.

U.S. Supreme Court issues key ruling applying the Eighth Amendment's ban on cruel and unusual punishment. In *Rummel v. Estelle*, it upholds a life sentence for a man convicted of obtaining $120 under false pretenses after two prior credit card forgery convictions. Defendant is eligible for parole after 12 years.

Sentencing Reform Act of 1984 creates the U.S. Sentencing Commission. The act also reintroduces mandatory-minimum sentences for drug and firearms offenses.

LO5 Truth-in-Sentencing

From the time that indeterminate sentencing was first imposed in the 1870s until late in the twentieth century, the amount of time offenders served in prison was almost always shorter than the time they were sentenced to serve by the court. Prisoners released in 1996 served an average of 30 months in prison and jail, or 44 percent of their sentence. Many states have recently enacted **truth-in-sentencing** laws that require offenders to serve a substantial portion of their sentence and to reduce the discrepancy between the sentence imposed and the actual time served in prison.[27]

To ensure that convicted offenders serve a large portion of their sentence, the U.S. Congress authorized funding for additional state prisons and jails through the Violent Crime Control and Law Enforcement Act of 1994. In 1998, incentive grants were awarded to 27 states and the District of Columbia that met the eligibility criteria for the truth-in-sentencing program (requiring offenders to serve 85 percent of their sentence). Another 13 states have adopted a truth-in-sentencing law requiring certain offenders to serve a certain percent of their sentence.[28] Parole eligibility and good time credits are greatly restricted or eliminated under truth-in-sentencing legislation.

Truth-in-sentencing, guidelines, three-strikes laws, and other changes have revolutionized the way punishment is distributed in the United States. They have contributed to overcrowded prisons and have resulted in offenders staying longer in prison and, as a result, increased the expenditures for already fiscally challenged correctional systems. For the sentencing changes in the past 50 years, see the Timeline.

HOW PEOPLE ARE SENTENCED

The federal government conducts surveys on state and federal courts' sentencing practices.[29] A recent survey revealed that more than one million adults are convicted of felonies each year. About two-thirds (69 percent) of all felons convicted

TRUTH-IN-SENTENCING A close connection between the imposed sentence and the actual time served in prison. The time that offenders actually serve on their sentence.

The Firearm Owner's Protection Act and the Anti-Drug Abuse Act require enhanced sentences for subsequent convictions.

Washington becomes the first state to enact a three-strikes law. Within a few years, 24 other states pass similar laws.

The Supreme Court ruled in the *Lockyer v. Andrade* and *Ewing v. California* cases to uphold California's three-strikes law.

In a similar case, the Court in *United States v. Booker* held that the guidelines could be taken into consideration by federal judges, but that they no longer had to be regarded as mandatory.

In *Tapia v. United States*, the U.S. Supreme Court ruled that federal law does not allow rehabilitation to be used as a factor when handing down a sentence.

1986	1991	1993	1994	2003	2004	2005	2007	2011

In *Harmelin v. Michigan*, the U.S. Supreme Court upholds a mandatory life sentence for a first-time offense of possessing about one and a half pounds of cocaine. Justice Anthony M. Kennedy's plurality opinion notes that the Eighth Amendment prohibits sentences "grossly disproportionate" to the offense but says this sentence is justified because of the "grave harm" posed by illegal drugs.

California voters approve the country's harshest three-strikes law: 25-years-to-life for a third conviction, even for petty crimes, if the two prior convictions were for serious felonies. The Violent Crime Control and Law Enforcement Act provides funds to states that require offenders to serve 85 percent of their sentences.

The Supreme Court in *Blakely v. Washington* found that Washington State's sentencing guidelines violated a defendant's Sixth Amendment rights because they permitted a judge to consider aggravating factors that would increase the sentence.

The Supreme Court ruled in *Rita v. United States* that courts of appeals may apply presumption of reasonableness when reviewing a sentence imposed within the sentencing range, and affirmed the within-guidelines sentence imposed in the case.

in state courts are sentenced to a period of confinement—41 percent to state prisons and 28 percent to local jails. The remaining third are sentenced to straight probation, with no jail or prison sentence to serve. Felons who are sentenced to a state prison average a sentence of four and a half years but are likely to serve only half of that sentence—or just two and a quarter years before release. In addition to being sentenced to incarceration or probation, 36 percent of convicted felons also are ordered to pay a fine, pay victim restitution, receive treatment, perform community service, or comply with some other penalty. A fine is imposed on about 25 percent of convicted felons. Violent offenders who are given an incarceration sentence receive about five years, while property offenders are typically sentenced to about two years.[30]

MYTH Violent felons receive very long prison sentences.

FACT Only about 40 percent of convicted felons go to prison, the rest receiving a jail or community sentence. Even violent felons may escape a prison sentence, and those who do not, go on to state prisons and average about five years. Most are eligible for parole and other early-release programs. So their sentence is actually three years or less.

 ## Excessive Length of Sentences

Sentences given by state and federal courts have traditionally been long in the United States. The late Norval Morris, well-known student of corrections and professor of law at the University of Chicago Law School, posed throughout his career the questions: "Why should America for identical nonviolent crimes with identical nonviolent

Guevara Vilca, a 26-year-old Peruvian man charged with 454 counts of possessing child pornography, talks with his defense attorney Lee Hollander during a courtroom recess at the Collier County (Florida) courthouse on October 3, 2011. On November 4, 2011, a circuit court judge sentenced Vilca to life in prison without the possibility of parole. The severity of the justice meted out to Vilca, who had no previous criminal record, has led some criminal justice experts to question whether increasingly harsh penalties delivered in cases involving the viewing of pornography really fit the crime. Had Vilca actually molested a child he might have received a lighter sentence. Compare his sentence for possessing child pornography with the one Joran van der Sloot will serve for murder.

© Greg Kahn/*Naples Daily News*

crime rate hand out punishments in bucketfuls when Western Europe hands out punishments in spoonfuls? Why are we so excessive in our punishment?"[31] Of course, critics would retort that European crime rates have skyrocketed while those in the United States are in sharp decline.

The answer to why the United States has been so punitive in its sentencing practices is tied up in the social and political factors of our history. Yet, as much as the indeterminate sentence was faulted, it did serve to reduce the length of sentences. Inmates were usually paroled after they had served a fraction of their original sentence. However, with the rise of determinate sentences, sentencing guidelines, and mandatory sentences, inmates began serving a longer part of their original sentence. The three-strikes laws were draconian for those inmates with three felony convictions in those states that implemented this sentencing structure. This sentencing legislation still applied to a small percentage of inmates. But with the rise of truth-in-sentencing laws, supported financially by the federal government, more and more inmates were sentenced to prison and required to serve 85 percent of their sentence.[32]

It is the length of prison sentences that really distinguishes American prison policy. American prisoners stays are much longer than found in other industrial nations. For example, burglars in the United States stay an average of 16 months in prison, compared with five months in Canada and seven months in England.[33] In addition, the U.S. is the only advanced nation to incarcerate individuals from minor property crimes, such as passing bad checks. In most European countries today, sentences over a year are uncommon and human rights norms make sentences longer than 12 to 14 years unconstitutional.

Nonlegal Factors Affecting Sentencing

There are a number of **nonlegal factors in sentencing** that can legitimately influence the length of prison sentences, including:

- The severity of the offense
- The offender's prior criminal record
- Whether the offender used weapons
- Whether the offender was involved in violence
- Whether the crime was committed for money

Research does reveal a strong correlation between these legal variables and the type and length of sentence received. Beyond these legally appropriate factors, however, some critics believe that extralegal and therefore inappropriate factors influence judges when they make sentencing decisions. In other words, while it is appropriate for judges to consider a defendant's prior record in making their decision, age, race, and income cannot and should not influence the color of justice. What are some of the suspected factors?

NONLEGAL FACTORS IN SENTENCING These include contextual factors, social class, gender, age, and victim characteristics.

CONTEXTUAL FACTORS Judges in courts with smaller caseloads appear to sentence more severely than judges in larger courts. Similarly, counties that have larger jail capacities seem to send more defendants to jail.

SOCIAL CLASS Some evidence lends support to an association between social class and sentencing decisions. Lower-class offenders have typically expected to receive longer prison sentences than higher-class defendants, and they find that this frequently is true. One reason for this is that lower-class defendants often are less able to obtain quality legal representation than more affluent defendants or are unable to make bail, both factors influencing sentencing decisions.[34]

GENDER Most research reveals that women receive more favorable outcomes the further they are processed in the criminal justice system.[35] They are more likely to receive preferential treatment from a judge at sentencing than is accorded them by a police officer making the arrest or the prosecutor seeking the indictment.[36] This preferential treatment from judges seems especially to be true if women have dependent children; they are the ones who are more likely to receive leniency, no doubt because judges are reluctant to incarcerate a child's basic caregiver.[37]

AGE Judges may further be influenced by the extra-legal factor of age. The elderly may receive greater leniency, while younger defendants receive more punitive sentences.[38] Yet judges may wish to protect some younger defendants from a prison sentence fearing they will be attacked and brutalized in prison.[39]

VICTIM CHARACTERISTICS The characteristics of victims may also affect sentencing outcomes. This is especially true when it comes to victim impact statements before the sentencing judge. In victim impact statements, victims tell of their experiences and ordeals stemming from the crime, or in the case of a murder trial, surviving family members can tell of the effect that the murder has had on their lives.[40] But other studies have found that the impact of victim and witness statements is insignificant.[41]

The rising population of elderly inmates is an offshoot of the excessive criminal sentences routinely used in the nation's court system. Shown here is a "perm inmate," who is permanently housed at the maximum-security Georgia Diagnostic and Classification Prison, taking a midday stroll. The routine use of excessively long sentences accompanied by reduction in parole eligibility has produced an aging inmate population. The older inmate must be housed and treated for serious problems ranging from heart disease to liver failure. Many have long histories of drug abuse that substantially increase the risk of health problems and add to correctional costs. Would you keep people in prison past age 65?

© Becky Stein

Racial Disparities of Sentencing

There has been a long history of **racial disparity in sentencing**.[42] Yet some recent research indicates that the association is far from linear: in some instances research shows a distinct pattern of discrimination, while other efforts indicate that sentencing may be more racially neutral than previously believed.[43]

Research supportive of racial discrimination in sentencing generally shows that for some categories of criminals—those convicted of drug offenses, those who accumulate more serious prior criminal records, those who refuse to plead guilty, and those unable to secure pretrial release—minorities are singled out for harsher treatment.[44] Minority defendants receive harsher sanctions if their victims are white than if their victims are fellow minority group members. Those minorities who murder whites are more likely to receive the death penalty than those who kill other minorities. In addition, minority defendants are more likely to be prosecuted under habitual offender statutes where the likelihood increases that there will be a white victim (burglary and larceny) than if they commit violent crimes that are largely interracial.[45]

RACIAL DISPARITY IN SENTENCING An actual pattern of racial discrimination in sentencing.

Social status may influence sentencing because judges see the lower income and higher unemployment percentage of minorities and therefore view them as "social dynamite"—individuals more dangerous and more likely to be repeat offenders than white offenders.[46] Minority defendants who earn less on average than white defendants are less likely to afford bail and, as a result, are more likely to receive more severe sentences than those who have received pretrial detention. Finally, minorities are less likely than whites to be able to afford a private attorney who can put on a vigorous legal defense with the use of highly paid expert witnesses. All of these factors contribute to minorities being placed at a disadvantage during the sentencing process and contribute to sentencing disparity.

The issue of racial disparity in sentencing is explored more fully in the Evidence-Based Corrections feature.

EVIDENCE-BASED CORRECTIONS

Does Race Influence Criminal Sentencing?

It is commonly believed that race influences sentencing, and that because of racial bias African Americans routinely receive harsher sentences than whites. When Ojmarrh Mitchell and Doris MacKenzie conducted a thorough empirical review of the existing evidence on the effects of race on sentencing, they found that after taking into account a defendant's criminal history and current offense seriousness, African Americans and Latinos were generally sentenced more harshly than whites. The greatest disparity was found in crimes involving drug offenses and in decisions involving incarceration versus community sentencing. In addition, they found evidence to suggest that sentencing guidelines were associated with smaller sentencing disparities. Overall, their findings suggest that policy makers need to reevaluate sentencing practices, especially in regard to drug offenses and the decision to incarcerate.

The association between race and criminal court sentencing outcome is quite complex. While some evidence shows that racial bias in sentencing exists, other studies are not so clear cut, finding little evidence that judges are racially biased. Why does the critical issue of racial disparity in sentencing remain so murky? One reason may be that the conditions that produce sentencing disparity may actually occur before the trial takes place. This would suggest that system disparity rather than judicial bias is the true cause of any differences in sentencing outcomes. Research efforts show that because of economic disparity minorities are less likely than whites to make bail and therefore more likely to be detained in jail before trial; pretrial detention significantly increases the chance of an incarceration sentence upon conviction. When Tracy Nobiling, Cassia Spohn, and Miriam DeLone, as well as Pauline Brennan, examined race and sentencing, they found that racial status influences sentencing partially because minority group members have a lower income than whites and are more likely to be unemployed, rendering them less likely to make bail, afford high-priced private lawyers, or pay for expert witnesses. Each of these factors impacts on sentencing.

There is also evidence that racial bias in sentencing flows through the victim's status and not the criminal's. Minority defendants are sanctioned more severely if their victim is white than if their target is a fellow minority group member; minorities who kill whites are more likely to get the death penalty than those who kill other minorities. In their research, Charles Crawford, Ted Chiricos, and Gary Kleck found evidence that African American defendants are more likely to be prosecuted under habitual offender statutes if they commit crimes where there is a greater likelihood that their victim will be white (larceny and burglary) than if they commit violent crimes that are largely intraracial. In other words, judges may base sentencing decisions on the race of the victim and not the race of the defendant.

While clear-cut evidence of bias is insufficient to cast a shadow over judicial decision making, the empirical evidence clearly shows that race does play a role in sentencing outcomes, a result that is unacceptable in our democratic society.

Sources: Pauline Brennan, "Sentencing Female Misdemeanants: An Examination of the Direct and Indirect Effects of Race/Ethnicity," *Justice Quarterly* 23 (2006): 60–95; Ojmarrh Mitchell and Doris MacKenzie, "The Relationship Between Race, Ethnicity, and Sentencing Outcomes: A Meta-Analysis of Sentencing Research," report to the United States Department of Justice, 2004, www.ncjrs.gov/pdf files1/nij/grants/208129.pdf (accessed February 16, 2012); Tracy Nobiling, Cassia Spohn, and Miriam DeLone, "A Tale of Two Counties: Unemployment and Sentence Severity," *Justice Quarterly* 15 (1998): 459–486; Charles Crawford, Ted Chiricos, and Gary Kleck, "Race, Racial Threat, and Sentencing of Habitual Offenders," *Criminology* 36 (1998): 481–511.

SUMMARY

LO1 ▶ **Explain the roles of the court team in the sentencing process**

The sentencing process rests in the hands of a number of actors—the prosecutor, the judge, and the probation staff. A major change in recent years is the increased power of the prosecutors in affecting sentencing decisions.

LO2 ▶ **Explain what is meant by indeterminate sentencing**

More than 30 states still retain some form of indeterminate sentencing. This is a sentence that permits early release from a correctional institution after the offender has served a required portion of his or her sentence.

LO3 ▶ **Understand the various forms of determinate sentencing**

The variations of determinate sentencing discussed in this chapter include sentencing guidelines, mandatory minimum sentences, three-strikes laws, and truth-in-sentencing. Determinate sentencing remains popular in nearly one-third of the states.

LO4 ▶ **Describe the role of sentencing guidelines**

Beginning with the federal sentencing guidelines, about 20 states have adopted sentencing guidelines. Their purpose is to provide direction to judges when they impose sentences.

LO5 ▶ **Know what is meant by truth-in-sentencing**

Many states have enacted truth-in-sentencing laws that require a close connection between the imposed sentence and the actual time served in prison. The goal of this law is to require offenders to serve a substantial portion of their imposed sentence in prison.

LO6 ▶ **Identify the most serious issues in sentencing**

The three most serious issues in sentencing are excessive length of today's sentence; the nonlegal factors, including age and gender, that influence sentencing; and the racial disparities that are present in sentencing outcomes.

Key Terms

concurrent sentences, 37
consecutive sentences, 37
good time, 38
sentencing sanctions, 39
indeterminate sentence, 40

determinate sentence, 41
sentencing guidelines, 41
presumptive sentencing, 41
federal sentencing guidelines, 43
mandatory minimum sentence, 44

three-strikes laws, 45
truth-in-sentencing, 46
nonlegal factors in sentencing, 48
racial disparity in sentencing, 49

Critical Thinking Questions

1. Tomorrow you will appear before the judge. Are you hoping for an indeterminate or a determinate sentence? Why? Compare the two types of sentencing.

2. Of the various goals of sentencing, which one do you favor? Why? Explain the disposition suitable to your choice.

3. Do you believe the punishment should fit the crime or the needs of the offender? Explain your reasoning.

4. Do you think a just system of sentencing is possible? Why or why not?

5. Attend a criminal trial and describe the difficulties you would have in imposing a just and reasonable sentence.

Thinking Like a Corrections Professional

You are a district court judge, and a 30-year-old public school teacher is appearing before you on a bench trial. She is charged with having sex with two male students in high school, both of whom are juniors. She has pleaded guilty and is awaiting your sentence. The teacher is six months pregnant and has been divorced for a number of years.

What will be your sentence? What are the most important factors leading you to your sentence? Is it important that you make an example of her so that other similar cases will not take place in nearby school districts?

Career Destinations

Where are schools of forensic psychology located? Find them at:
www.gradschools.com/Subject/Forensic-Psychology/337.html

Read more about one particular program:
www.mspp.edu/academics/degree-programs/forensic-ma/

There are also careers in the field of sentencing. The Sentencing Project evaluates the use and effectiveness of punishment in the United States:
www.sentencingproject.org

Notes

1. CNN, "Missing Teen's Mother Leaves Aruba," August 1, 2005, www.cnn.com/2005/LAW/07/31/aruba.missing (accessed February 16, 2012); CNN, "Van der Sloot Sentenced to 28 Years for Peru Murder," January 13, 2012, www.cnn.com/2012/01/13/world/americas/peru-van-der-sloot-sentence (accessed February 16, 2012).
2. Holbrook Mohr, "Haley Barbour Pardons: Former Mississippi Gov. 'Very Comfortable' with Decision," *Huffington Post*, January 15, 2012, www.huffingtonpost.com/2012/01/13/haley-barbour-pardons-mississippi-governor_n_1205450.html (accessed February 16, 2012).
3. Richard A. Oppel, Jr., "Sentencing Shift Gives New Leverage to Prosecutors," *New York Times*, September 25, 2011.
4. Ibid.
5. Ibid.
6. Ibid.
7. John Wooldredge, "Judges' Unequal Contributions to Extralegal Disparities in Imprisonment," *Criminology* (May 2010): 539–567.
8. Ibid.
9. For an overview of sentencing in the United States, see Nicole D. Porter, *The State of Sentencing 2010* (Washington, DC: The Sentencing Project, February 2011).
10. For a current statement on the status of sentencing in the United States, see Ryan S. King, *The State of Sentencing: Developments in Policy and Practice* (Washington, DC: The Sentencing Project, 2009).
11. *Tapia v. United States*, 18 U.S.C. AS 3582(a), 2011.
12. Don Steman and Andres F. Rengifo, "Policies and Imprisonment: The Impact of Structured and Determinate Sentencing on State Incarceration Rates, 1978–2004," *Justice Quarterly* 28 (February 2011): 174–201; Michael Tonry, "Reconsidering Indeterminate and Structured Sentencing," *Sentencing and Corrections: Issues for the 21st Century* (Washington, DC: U.S. Department of Justice, 1999), p. 1.
13. Wooldredge, "Judges' Unequal Contributions to Extralegal Disparities in Imprisonment."
14. John H. Kramer and Jeffrey T. Ulmer, *Sentencing Guidelines: Lessons from Pennsylvania* (Boulder, CO: Lynne Rienner Publishers, 2008); Michael Tonry, "Sentencing Commissions and Their Guidelines," in *Crime and Justice: A Review of Research* 17 (Chicago: University of Chicago Press, 1993), p. 138.
15. For an overview of the federal sentencing guidelines, see Paul J. Hofer and Mark H. Allenbaugh, "The Reason Behind the Rules: Finding and Using the Philosophy of the Federal Sentencing Guidelines," *Criminal Law Review* (Winter 2003): 19–56; and Marc Mauer, *The Impact of Mandatory Minimum Penalties in Federal Sentencing* (Washington, DC: The Sentencing Project, 2010).
16. Andrew Longstreth, "Rajaratnam Prison Term Follows Sentencing Trends," *Reuters*, www.reuters.com/article/2011/10/13/us-galleon-rajaratnam-guidelines-idUSTRE79C7DG20111013 (accessed February 16, 2012).
17. Lisa Pasko, "Villain or Victim: Regional Variation and Ethnic Disparity in Federal Drug Offense Sentencing," *Criminal Justice Policy Review* 13 (2002): 307–328; Wooldredge, "Judges' Unequal Contributions to Extralegal Disparities in Imprisonment."
18. Michael Tonry, "Racial Policies, Racial Disparities, and the War on Crime," *Crime and Delinquency* (1994): 475–494.
19. *Blakely v. Washington*, 124 S.Ct. 2531 (2004).
20. *United States v. Booker*, No. 04-104, decided January 12, 2005.
21. United States Sentencing Commission, *Final Report on the Impact of the* United States v. Booker *on Federal Sentencing*, March 2006.
22. See Brian D. Johnson, Jeffrey T. Ulmer, and John H. Kramer, "The Social Context of Guidelines Circumvention: The Case of Federal District Courts," *Criminology* 46 (2008): 737–745.
23. For a discussion of mandatory minimum sentencing, see Natasha A. Frost, "Mandatory Minimum Sentencing," *Criminology and Public Policy* (February 2006): 1–4.
24. To further examine mandatory minimum sentences, see Jeffrey T. Ulmer, Megan C. Kurlychek, and John H. Kramer, "Prosecutorial Discretion and the Imposition of Mandatory Minimum Sentences," *Journal of Research in Crime and Delinquency* 44 (November 2007): 427–432; and Kirk J. Henderson, "Mandatory-Minimum Sentences and the Jury: Time Again to Revisit Their Relationship," *Dayton Law Review* 33 (Fall 2007): 37–57.
25. Shimica Gaskins, "'Women of Circumstance': The Effects of Mandatory Minimum Sentencing on Women Minimally Involved in Drug Crimes," *American Criminal Law Review* (Fall 2004): 1533.
26. Tomislav V. Kovandzic, John J. Sloan III, and Lynne M. Vieraitis, "'Striking Out' as Crime Reduction Policy: The Impact of 'Three Strikes' Laws on Crime Rates in U.S. Cities," *Justice Quarterly* 21 (2004): 207.
27. Paula M. Ditton, *Truth in Sentencing in State Prisons* (Washington, DC: Bureau of Justice Statistics, 1999), p. 1.
28. Ibid.
29. Matthew R. Durose and Patrick A. Langan, *Felony Sentences in State Courts* (Washington, DC: Bureau of Justice Statistics, 2007).
30. Ibid.
31. Personal correspondence with Bartollas.
32. Ditton, *Truth in Sentencing in State Prisons*, pp. 3–4.
33. Adam Liptak, "U.S. Prison Population Dwarfs That of Other Nations," *New York Times*, April 23, 2008.
34. Susan Welch, Cassia Spohn, and John Gruhl, "Convicting and Sentencing Differences Among Black, Hispanic, and White Males in Six Localities," *Justice Quarterly* 2 (1985): 67–80.
35. Fernando Rodriguez, Theodore Curry, and Gang Lee, "Gender Differences in Criminal Sentencing: Do Effects Vary Across Violent, Property, and Drug Offenses?" *Social Science Quarterly* 87 (2006): 318–339.
36. See Janet Johnston, Thomas Kennedy, and I. Gayle Shuman, "Gender Differences in the Sentencing of Felony Offenders," *Federal Probation* 87 (1987): 49–56; Cassia Spohn and Susan Welch, "The Effect of Prior Record in Sentencing Research: An Examination of the Assumption that Any Measure Is Adequate," *Justice Quarterly* 4 (1987): 286–302.
37. Barbara Koons-Witt, "The Effect of Gender on the Decision to Incarcerate Before and After the Introduction of Sentencing Guidelines," *Criminology* 40 (2002): 417–432.
38. Dean Champion, "Elderly Felons and Sentencing Severity: Interregional Variations in Leniency and Sentencing Trends," *Criminal Justice Review* 12 (1987): 7–15.
39. Darrell Steffensmeier, Jeffery Ulmer, and John Kramer, "The Interaction of Race, Gender and Age in Criminal Sentencing: The Punishment Cost of Being Young, Black, and Male," *Criminology* 36 (1998): 763–798.
40. *Payne v. Tennessee*, 111 S.Ct. 2597, 115 L.Ed.2d 720 (1991).

41. Robert Davis and Barbara Smith, "The Effects of Victim Impact Statements on Sentencing Decisions: A Text in an Urban Setting," *Justice Quarterly* 11 (1994): 453–469.

42. Michael Tonry, *Malign Neglect: Race, Crime and Punishment in America* (New York: Oxford University Press, 1995), p. 68.

43. J. D. Unnever and L. A. Hembroff, "The Prediction of Racial/Ethnic Sentencing Disparities: An Expectation States Approach," *Journal of Research in Crime and Delinquency* 25 (1987): 69–92.

44. Cassia C. Spohn, "Thirty Years of Sentencing Reform: The Quest for a Racially Neutral Sentencing Process," in *Policies, Processes, and Decisions of the Criminal Justice System*, Vol. 3, ed. J. Horney (Washington, DC: U.S. Government Printing Office, 2000), p. 428.

45. Charles Crawford, Ted Chiricos, and Gary Kleck, "Race, Racial Threat, and Sentencing of Habitual Offenders," *Criminology* 36 (1998): 481–511.

46. Tracy Nobiling, Cassia Spohn, and Miriam DeLone, "A Tale of Two Counties: Unemployment and Sentence Severity," *Justice Quarterly* 15 (1998): 459–486.

On February 24, 2005, 9-year-old Jessica Lunsford was reported missing from her home. Police checked up on known sex offenders living in the area, which included John Evander Couey, 46. He had a long list of convictions, including burglary, carrying a concealed weapon, disorderly intoxication, driving under the influence, indecent exposure, disorderly conduct, fraud, insufficient funds, and larceny. He was on unsupervised county probation at the time. A habitual drug abuser, in 1991 he had been arrested and charged with "fondling a child under the age of 16." Nineteen days after Jessica Lunsford was first reported missing, detectives returned to Couey's home, and this time found blood, but Couey had

fled and was later arrested in Georgia. While in police custody, Couey admitted that he had entered the Lunsford home at around 3 A.M. on February 24 and found Jessica asleep in her bed. He woke her, ordered her to be quiet ("Don't yell or nothing"), and told her to follow him back to his sister's house where he raped her repeatedly and kept her in a closet for three days. Couey showed investigators

This family photo shows 9-year-old Jessica Marie Lunsford of Homosassa, Florida, before she was kidnapped, raped, and killed by John Evander Couey, 46. He was on community release despite a long list of convictions, including burglary, carrying a concealed weapon, disorderly intoxication, indecent exposure, and larceny. Before he died of natural causes in 2009, he was on death row. Should dangerous offenders such as Couey be maintained in the community? Research indicates they are actually good candidates for rehabilitation.

the shallow grave where they found Jessica's body inside two tied plastic garbage bags. Her wrists were bound, but she had managed to poke two fingers through the plastic in an attempt to free herself; she had tried to escape but failed.[1] Couey had an IQ of 78, which is slightly above the level usually considered mentally disabled, but the judge rejected an argument by his lawyer that he could not be legally executed. Couey was found guilty of murder on March 7, 2007, and on August 24, 2007, was sentenced to death.[2]

On September 30, 2009, Covey, 51, died of natural causes at a Jacksonville hospital where he had been since August 12. Couey died just over a month before the Florida Supreme Court was scheduled to hear his automatic appeal.[3]

COMMUNITY CORRECTIONS: DIVERSION AND PROBATION

LEARNING OBJECTIVES

LO1 Explain what is meant by the term *community corrections act*

LO2 Compare the main types of diversion programs and identify their advantages and disadvantages

LO3 Understand the advantages of being placed on probation

LO4 Explain the risk assessment models and their current emphasis

LO5 Understand the various ways probation is administered

LO6 Understand the legal rights of probationers

LO7 Evaluate the effectiveness of probation and identify some of the promising programs in probation services

© A. Ramey/PhotoEdit Inc.

I t is hard to imagine a repeat sex offender on community release, and yet this is not uncommon. The majority of people convicted of sex offenses are placed on probation and many never set foot in jail or prison.[4] The question in the minds of many is whether sex offenders should be given a second chance. Understandably, the public and its officials have reacted to shocking sex crimes and murders by adopting tough laws and regulations that limit what sex offenders on probation can do and where they can live.[5] Sometimes things don't work out as planned: the most current research indicates that the overwhelming majority of sex offenders were not rearrested for a future sex crime, despite the fact that sex registration and notification laws have become the norm. In fact, committing other crimes such as robbery seems to be a better predictor of future sex offending than is past sex offending.[6] The Evidence-Based Corrections feature covers this topic in some depth.

EVIDENCE-BASED CORRECTIONS

Registering Sex Offenders on the Internet

In 1994, Megan Kanka, a 7-year-old New Jersey girl, was raped and murdered by Jesse Timmendequas, a sex offender who had moved into her neighborhood after being released from prison. Because Megan's family had no prior knowledge of his presence, they did not warn her to stay away from the new neighbor. Outraged because the Kankas had been left in the dark, community members successfully lobbied for the enactment of a law that requires sex offender registration and notification to the public that a sex offender is living and working in the community. Their crusade was so successful that by the mid-1990s, all 50 states and the District of Columbia had passed similar "Megan's Laws." Now many states are using the Internet to post information about sex offenders so residents can search for them by name or address.

In New Jersey, for example, sex offenders are grouped into three tiers based on their dangerousness: low (1), medium (2), and high (3). The Internet registry excludes low-risk offenders but includes the following information about moderate and high-risk sex offenders: the offender's name and address; any aliases used by the offender; any Megan's Law sex offenses committed by the offender, including a brief description and the date and location of disposition of any such offense; a general description of the offender's modus operandi, if any; the determination of whether the risk of reoffense by the offender is moderate or high; the offender's age, race, sex, date of birth, height, weight, hair, eye color, and any distinguishing scars or tattoos; a photograph of the offender and the date on which the photograph was entered into the registry; and the make, model, color, year, and license plate number of any vehicle operated by the offender. The Internet registry is continually updated with information about additional registrants added as court orders are issued authorizing Internet disclosure about those individuals.

Does It Really Work?

In 2009, Kristen Zgoba and Karen Bachar conducted an in-depth study of the effectiveness of the New Jersey registration and found that the system was expensive to maintain and did not produce effective results. Sex offense rates in New Jersey were in a steep decline before the system was installed and the rate of decline actually slowed after 1995. Their data show that the greatest rate of decline in sex offending occurred prior to the passage and implementation of Megan's Law. They also found that passage and implementation of Megan's Law did not reduce the number of rearrests for sex offenses, nor did it have any demonstrable effect on the time between when sex offenders were released from prison and the time they were rearrested for any new offense, such as a drug, theft, or sex offense.

So while using technology such as Internet registrations may seem like a panacea to some, innovations must be thoroughly tested before they can be reasonably relied upon.

Source: Kristen Zgoba and Karen Bachar, "Sex Offender Registration and Notification: Research Finds Limited Effects in New Jersey," National Institute of Justice, April 2009, www.ncjrs.gov/pdffiles1/nij/225402.pdf (accessed February 18, 2012).

© James Dare

> "Probation continues to be held to a high standard. The next generation of officers will bring new ideas, tackle new challenges, and expand the use of technology."

JAMES DARE
DEPUTY COURT ADMINISTRATOR

In 1984, I was hired as an entry-level probation officer after being turned down for the job three times. I knew I wanted to be a probation officer and my tenacity paid off. Twenty-seven years later, I'm still with the department and continue to enjoy community corrections as a professional career.

First, I want to share two paragraphs of an article titled "Hope in Community Corrections: Why Bother?" written by Carl Wicklund, executive director of the American Probation and Parole Association, in the Summer 2000 issue of *Perspectives*:

Most of us entered the field of human engineering because we wanted to make a difference and we believed we could. We entered the field filled with hope and idealism. Hope is a feeling that what we want will happen. It is a desire accompanied by expectation. It means to want and expect, and it is synonymous with optimism and desire. Hope is about dreaming and working to achieve those dreams. Hope is the most vital tool you can bring with you to the job. It is the most important gift you can give a client or a coworker. Hope is the life-blood of our dreams and the driving force behind our continued existence.

This article was written 16 years after my appointment as a probation officer; however, it summarizes an important philosophy and standard for probation officers today. Ensuring public safety is a huge responsibility besides performing the following duties: office visits, field work, jail visits, treatment visits, court appointments, conducting investigation, transports, urine collections, arrests, ensuring victims are compensated, providing meaningful interventions, ensuring compliance with court-ordered sanctions, developing case plans with clients, completing statistics, and making recommendations for or against probation. You need to be organized, flexible, and a team player.

Other challenges of being a probation officer are balancing power, understanding diversity, and imposing sanctions proportionate to the violation. Locking offenders up is easy, but providing services in the community takes work and creativity. What works for one client won't work for the next one. In probation, "one size does not fit all."

Probation officers should be encouraged to join professional organizations in order to network with other professionals, attend training, and learn about the newest technology. You may be required to be proficient with weapons, handcuffs, and other equipment, but it's your ability to assess situations and use common sense that will ensure your safety and the safety of your co-workers.

Probation continues to be held to a high standard. The next generation of officers will bring new ideas, tackle new challenges, and expand the use of technology. Probation officers will bring a new level of hope to provide the best service to the court, the client, and the community.

Source: Interviewed in 2011. James Dare is the Deputy Court Administrator, Montgomery County Common Pleas Court, Division of Criminal Justice Services, Dayton, Ohio.

Community-based programs are alternatives to institutional placements and keep offenders out of jails and federal, state, and private prisons. They are known to be more humane than overcrowded, violent, and anti-therapeutic prisons and, at the same time, can help the offender maintain family and community ties. They are more economical than costly institutionalization and are able to curtail the number of new prisons that must be built for the ever-increasing correctional population. And some evidence exists that they are more effective in reducing recidivism than short-term and long-term institutionalization.[7] These are the reasons why community placements are at an all-time high; it simply makes more sense, whenever possible, to keep offenders in the community under the supervision of trained court officers than to send offenders to prison.

The agencies of community-based corrections consist of diversion programs, probation, intermediate sanctions, reentry programs, parole, and supervision of ex-offenders. This chapter focuses on diversion and probation; the next chapter examines intermediate sanctions and restorative justice; and Chapter 11 considers parole and supervision of ex-offenders.

TIMELINE

John Augustus introduces probation in Boston.

Thirty-seven states, the District of Columbia, and the federal government pass juvenile and adult probation laws.

All states have juvenile probation laws.

National Advisory Commission on Criminal Justice Standards and Goals endorses more extensive use of probation.

U.S. Department of Justice conducts the first census of U.S. probationers.

U.S. Comptroller General's study of U.S. probation concludes it is a "system in crisis" due to inadequate funding.

1841 1878 1878–1938 1927 1954 1956 1973 1974 1975 1975 1976

Massachusetts becomes the first state to adopt probation for juveniles.

All states but Wyoming have juvenile probation laws.

All states have adult probation laws; Mississippi becomes the last state to pass authorizing legislation.

Martinson's widely publicized research purportedly proves that probation does not work.

Wisconsin implements first probation case classification system.

THE DEVELOPMENT OF COMMUNITY-BASED CORRECTIONS

Treating offenders in the community is not a new idea and is actually a tradition that can be traced back to the English common law. During the Middle Ages, judges willing to spare deserving offenders from the harsh punishments of the day used their power to grant clemency and stays of execution. This practice of **judicial reprieve** allowed judges to suspend punishment so that convicted offenders could seek a pardon or gather new evidence that they were now reformed. **Recognizance** was a practice that permitted convicted offenders to remain free if they agreed to take care of their debt obligation with the state, and **sureties** were occasionally required—individuals who made themselves responsible for the behavior of offenders who had been released.

Community-based corrections programs can also be found early in the history of the United States. The Puritans in New England attempted to punish deviants in the community, as a means to enforce their strict Puritan codes. Informal community pressures, such as gossip, ridicule, and ostracism, were found to be effective in keeping most citizens in line. Offenders might be confined in the stocks and the public cage, or for the most the serious crimes, they might be whipped, branded, banished, or hanged.

The community nature of corrections receded in importance with the rise of the American version of the penitentiary. Yet, in the middle of the nineteenth century, probation began with the volunteer services of John Augustus in Massachusetts. Born in Woburn, Massachusetts, in 1785, Augustus moved to Boston in 1829 where he started a successful boot-making business. He joined the Washington Total Abstinence Society, a group whose members abstained from alcohol themselves and were convinced that abusers of alcohol could be rehabilitated through understanding and kindness rather than punishment. As a society member, Augustus was drawn to the Boston courtroom in an effort to save people whose drinking had gotten them in trouble with the law. In 1841, he accepted his first probation client, whose offense was "yielding to his appetite for strong drink." He provided bail for this person, subject to the man appearing in court three weeks later. Beginning with this first client, he was to devote himself to the cause of probation as he became convinced that many lawbreakers only needed

JUDICIAL REPRIEVE Permitted judges to suspend judgment until offenders could seek a pardon or gather new evidence.

RECOGNIZANCE Permitted offenders to remain free if they promised to pay their debts to the state.

SURETIES Individuals who would agree to make themselves responsible for offenders who had been released from custody.

Georgia's intensive supervision probation (ISP) program claims to reduce recidivism and costs.

Rand Corporation releases study of felony probationers showing high failure rates; replications follow, showing that probation services and effectiveness vary widely across the nation.

U.S. Department of Justice funds nationwide intensive supervision demonstration and evaluation.

The 2003 state statutes reveal that possessing the power of a law enforcement/ peace officer is the only new legal proscribed function of probation officers.

1982   1983   1985   1989   1991   1993   2003   2009

Electronic monitoring of offenders begins in New Mexico, followed by a larger program in Florida.

General Accounting Office survey shows all 50 states have adopted intensive probation and other intermediate sanction programs.

Program evaluations show probation without adequate surveillance and treatment is ineffective, but well-managed and adequately funded programs reduce recidivism.

Probation population reaches 5 million.

Sources: Joan Petersilia, "Probation in the United States," in *Crime and Justice: A Review of Research* 21 (Chicago: University of Chicago Press, 1997), p. 15; and Marcus Purkiss, Misty Kifer, Craig Hemmens, and Velmer S. Burton, "Probation Officer Functions—A Statutory Analysis," *Federal Probation* 67 (June 2003): 14–20.

the interest and concern of another to be able to straighten out their lives. Augustus worked with women and children as well as with adult male offenders and in fact was willing to work with all types of offenders—drunkards, petty thieves, prostitutes, and felons—as long as he was met with a contrite heart. Over an 18-year period, Augustus bailed out and supervised approximately 2,000 probationers, helping them get jobs and establishing themselves in the community. Augustus instigated such services as investigation and screening, supervision of probationers, interviewing, and arranging for relief, employment, and education—all of which are still used today. He had a remarkably high success rate, as few of his probationers became involved in crime again. Recognizing Augustus's achievements, Massachusetts formalized probation in 1859, a year after his death, creating the nation's first paid probation officers.[8]

Following its beginnings as a voluntary movement in the late nineteenth century, probation experienced rapid growth in the first decades of the twentieth century and in the 1960s. It spread to every state and was administered by both state and local authorities and became the most common form of criminal sanction during the twentieth century. The use of volunteers had disappeared by the turn of the century, only to return in the 1950s. Probation became more treatment oriented, and early in the century, the medical treatment model was used. Later in the 1960s and 1970s, probation officers became brokers who delivered services to clients. The upgrading of standards and training was also emphasized in the 1960s and 1970s. The significant events in the development of probation in the United States are set out in the Timeline.

The Community Corrections Revolution

The social context of the 1960s was such that widespread support was given to the rehabilitative ideal, spurring the development of new forms of community-based corrections programs. Several commissions recommended the establishment of alternatives to the juvenile justice system and the development of various types of diversion programs for adults. The main rationale of diversion was to keep juvenile and adult offenders out of the justice system and avoid the stigma of criminal/juvenile delinquent labels.

The new challenge of corrections was seen as keeping offenders in the community and reintegrating them into community living. It was believed that

By teaching inmates usable skills, correctional treatment programs can help reintegrate them back into the community. Welding instructor Harry Bell (center) guides inmates Richard Johnson (left) and Tony Bailey in the weld shop at the Sheridan Correctional Center in Sheridan, Illinois, a dedicated center for the treatment of inmates with drug and alcohol abuse problems. A majority of inmates in the Illinois prison system have histories of substance abuse and/or have committed drug and alcohol-related crimes. The state opened Sheridan in January 2004 to combat a recidivism rate of 54 percent in its penal system. The recidivism rate for prisoners who have served time at Sheridan is only 7.7 percent.

© Scott Olson/Getty Images

because prisons dehumanize people and prepare inmates for lives of criminality, every effort should be made to keep offenders out of long-term institutions. The **reintegrative philosophy** of corrections—the idea that every effort should be made to return offenders to the community as law-abiding citizens—was also developed at this time. This task of corrections included building or rebuilding social ties between the offender and the community. This process of reintegrating the offender into community life included restoring family ties, obtaining education and employment, and securing for the offender a place in the normal functioning of society. This required efforts both toward the rehabilitation of offenders and toward change of the community and its institutions. As part of the expansion of community-based corrections, residential facilities were designed to house probationers having difficulties with traditional probation and high-risk parolees being released from prison.

Because it was so cost effective, probation gained the favor of judges and politicians, and the numbers of offenders on probation soared. The increasing probation population inspired state governments to reorganize and support probation initiatives, and the device they used was community corrections acts.

L01 Community Corrections Acts

A **community corrections act (CCA)** is a law passed by a state legislature in which a state grants funds to local units of government to plan, develop, and deliver correctional services and sanctions. CCAs are found in the philosophy of community-oriented corrections. One of the major purposes of community corrections acts is to encourage local sentencing options in lieu of state imprisonment.

Since the first and most developed community corrections act took place in Minnesota, about 25 states have implemented CCAs for adults (see Figure 3.1). These statutes have a number of characteristics in common:

- CCAs are legislatively authorized. Statutes provide the framework and authority for the other defining features of CCAs.

- CCAs call for decentralized program design and delivery. They provide for local control of the processes employed to serve as the basis for the development, implementation, and modification of local correctional sanctions and services.

- CCAs are authorized statewide. They mandate or authorize all localities, individually or in combination, to take advantage of the funds and authority granted.

- CCAs provide for citizen involvement and specify roles that citizens may play.

- CCAs define an intergovernmental structure. They delineate the roles to be performed and the power and authority to be exercised by involved state and local agencies or units of government.

REINTEGRATIVE PHILOSOPHY A correctional approach aimed at returning offenders to the community as soon as possible.

COMMUNITY CORRECTIONS ACT (CCA) State-based acts through which local governments that participate receive subsidies for diverting minor offenders from state prisons.

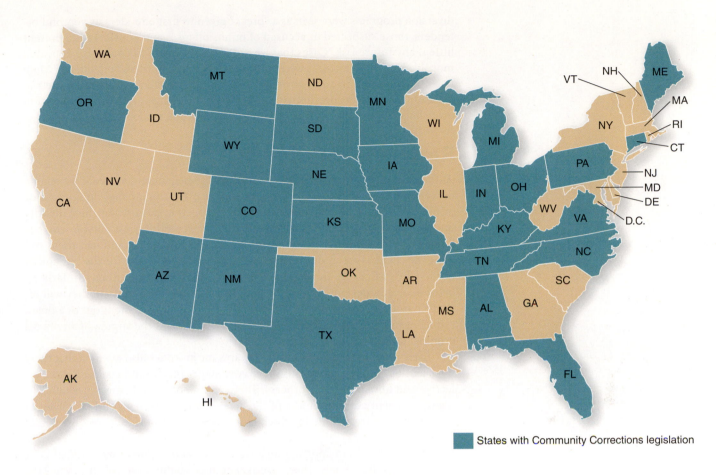

States with Community Corrections legislation

FIGURE 3.1 States with Community Corrections Legislation

Note: A number of other states have some form of community corrections policy or have initiated structured programs under an existing administrative mechanism.

Source: National Committee on Community Corrections (Washington, DC: Center for Community Corrections, n.d.).

- CCAs require local planning. They provide that local planning will serve as the basis for the development, implementation, and modification of local correctional sanctions and services.

- CCAs provide for state subsidies to support local correctional programs and services.

- CCAs process employees, assess local needs, establish local priorities, and plan local programs.

- CCAs endorse locally determined sanctions and services. They provide resources and authority for sanctions and services to be developed and delivered at the local level.[9]

Community corrections acts have spread rapidly since Minnesota's effort. Counties have found them an effective means to control offenders and to coordinate correctional efforts, and most states feel that CCAs are reducing prison populations in a promising way. In the following sections, the major forms of community corrections are laid out in some detail.

DIVERSION

The purpose of diversion in both the juvenile and adult systems is to divert offenders from further involvement with the justice system and instead enroll them in community-based treatment programs prior to a court appearance. Originally, diversion programs were seen as a "break" given to first offenders or youthful offenders, those suspected or accused of minor offenses and considered to present little if any future risk. Cases that were difficult to prove in court also appeared more likely to be diverted, as were cases with mentally disordered offenders.[10] More recently, diversion in adult corrections has been broadened to include pretrial release, pretrial diversion, diversion at the sentencing stage, and post-incarceration diversion. Yet most diversionary interventions take place prior to trial.

Rationale for Diversion

At their core, diversion programs are designed to help offenders avoid the stigma of a criminal conviction. Once offenders are officially labeled delinquent or criminal through the court process, this perspective claims that their identity undergoes an important transformation: they are no longer a person who has done a bad thing, they are now a bad person. People suspect and fear them and their life chances are undermined. Their label shadows them for the remainder of their lives. Because they are now outcasts, they may join other similarly labeled people in deviant cliques and gangs, escalating the likelihood they will repeat their illegal behaviors. To break this cycle and to keep them out of a life of crime, something must be done to help offenders avoid the stigma of an official criminal label.

Early proponents of diversion programs for juveniles also claimed that these interventions offered numerous other advantages that would lead to a more effective and humane justice process. These included the reduction of caseloads, a more efficient administration of the juvenile justice system, and provision of therapeutic environments in which children and parents could resolve family conflicts.

Other analysts, in applying diversion to the adult system, have added to or elaborated on these goals. They have also pointed to the objectives to reverse the uneven imposition of serious sanctions onto those who are already socially disadvantaged. In this sense, diversion can accomplish a variety of goals:

- Avoiding the harsh and criminogenic impacts of incarceration in prison

- Informing and providing a range of alternatives for decision makers to choose from

- Providing a "more justifying justice" for victims and communities

- Dealing with the economic, social, and personal factors associated with crime, rather than the punitively oriented alternative[11]

L02 ▶ Diversion Programs

Diversion programs can be divided into those providing **true diversion** and those seeking **minimization of system penetration**. True diversion takes place when an offender is referred to a program and the completion of this program will enable him or her to avoid criminal prosecution. For example, if an offender is referred to a deferred prosecution program and he or she is willing to participate in the program, the court will be asked to defer formal charging. In contrast, those aiming for minimization of system penetration focus on reducing the offender's interface with the justice system. In this model, the convicted drug defendant may be given a choice of either going to prison or becoming part of a therapeutic community for drug offenders.

Diversion's attractiveness has increased with the awareness of the importance of keeping minor offenders, the mentally ill, and drug offenders, whenever possible, out of the justice system.[12] Deferred prosecution, deferred judgment, and Treatment Alternatives to Street Crime (TASC) are three main types of adult pretrial diversion programs.

TRUE DIVERSION A diversion program where the offender has his or her criminal prosecution dropped upon successful completion of this program.

MINIMIZATION OF SYSTEM PENETRATION A diversion whose purpose is to minimize the offender's contact with the justice process as much as possible.

DEFERRED PROSECUTION AND DEFERRED JUDGMENT

For those who have made a mistake resulting in a criminal charge, there are programs, like deferred prosecution and deferred judgment, that make it possible for defendants to avoid criminal penalties and have an opportunity to clear their record if they stay out of further trouble with the law. The programs, though slightly different, are both designed to give offenders accused of a crime a second chance. Many are administered through special courts, including drug courts, DUI courts, or juvenile courts for youthful offenders.[13]

There are some major differences between the two: deferred judgment occurs after offenders admit to all or part of the charges against them but before the plea is entered on the record. Defendants then serve a period of informal probation, in a sense deferring judgment. In some states, such as Maryland, this is called probation before judgment (PBJ). In contrast, deferred prosecution does not require a guilty plea or the admission of facts. Offenders voluntarily serve a period of probation in lieu of court appearances and formal charges.[14]

Deferred prosecution programs have traditionally operated in one of two ways. In the first model, when an offender is arrested, he or she may be screened according to a number of pre-established criteria to determine if the problem can be handled through a formal diversion program. If so, project staff will explain the program to the accused offender, and if the offender is willing to participate in the program, the court will be asked to defer formal charging. Prosecutors are usually willing to dismiss the criminal charges for those offenders who successfully complete their diversion programs.

Under the second model, formal charges are lodged before defendants are screened for their eligibility for diversion programs. If the court and the offender agree, criminal proceedings are suspended pending the outcome of the findings and conclusions of the programs. A successful solution through the program ensures that formal charges are dropped; failure results in formal criminal charges. The length of the probation term is generally up to the prosecutor, with approval from the judge. Because this is considered a plea agreement, offenders generally will know the length of time before they agree to the program.

The Manhattan Court Employment Project, the District of Columbia's Project Crosswords, and the Flint (Michigan) Citizens Probation Authority were the pilot deferred programs. Pretrial intervention, as it is commonly termed, has included about 150 programs in 37 states. Programs have been formalized according to court rules in 2 states, and 7 states have statewide authorizing legislation.[15]

Deferred prosecution programs have focused on persons suffering from alcohol, drug, or mental health problems who can ask permission of the court to go through an intensive treatment program in lieu of being prosecuted. Successful completion of the treatment, as well as continued lawful conduct, will result in the dismissal of the charge and perhaps also avoid suspension of the person's driver's license.

Judge Andra Sparks holds gun court in Birmingham, Alabama. It used to be a given on the street: get caught with an illegal gun and you got jail. But under a new program in Birmingham—one initially derided by some police officers as a "hug a thug" rehabilitation effort—there is another option: gun court. And the results so far have been promising. Of the 240 people who have started or completed the city's gun court since it launched in February 2009, only two people participating in the program have been accused of another crime. There was a 14 percent reduction in gun seizures in the city after the program was instituted. Police have destroyed 130 weapons. The goal is to catch gun offenders early and change their mindset through a regimen of semi-monthly court visits, frequent drug testing, anger management and conflict resolution classes, fines, and community service.

DEFERRED PROSECUTION PROGRAMS Those referred to these programs benefit from having their charges dropped upon their successful completion.

TREATMENT ALTERNATIVES TO STREET CRIME (TASC) The **Treatment Alternatives to Street Crime (TASC)** program is the most widespread of the various national programs that have been designed to divert drug abusers away from the criminal justice system and into the jurisdiction of agencies offering specialized support services. TASC is centered around a screening unit, an intake unit, and a tracking unit. The screening unit attempts to identify drug users entering the criminal justice system and to offer the program to those offenders who are eligible under locally determined criteria. The intake unit diagnoses each offender referred to it and recommends the appropriate treatment program. The tracking unit constantly monitors the progress of TASC clients. Those violating the locally determined success/failure criteria are returned to the criminal justice system for appropriate action.

TASC programs are a cost-effective way of delivering treatment because of their ability to identify and link appropriate services to drug-involved individuals. By focusing on reducing the stigma associated with incarceration, drug abuse, and mental illness, TASC eases the transition to the community for clients. Supporters firmly believe that TASC's programs and the high quality of their treatment, monitoring, case management, and referrals offer a far better chance of breaking the cycles of addiction, crime, and incarceration than other programs. Yet, in the midst of extremely high risk of recidivism for drug offenders, it is not surprising that the findings on criminal recidivism for TASC programs are mixed.[16]

In sum, the outstanding feature of informal, voluntary, reconciliation-focused, community-based programs is their usefulness in keeping offenders in the community. Deferred prosecution programs appear to be a good option for most first offenders because they avoid the stigma of a criminal record and reduce the volume of persons going through the criminal justice process. The major limitations, especially of deferred prosecution and TASC programs, are that not all offenders will choose to benefit from these diversionary efforts and, more importantly, these programs may increase the numbers of those who otherwise would have been ignored by the criminal justice system in the past.

 # PROBATION

Probation is a correctional service allowing an offender to remain in the community for the duration of a sentence under supervision by an officer of the court and requiring the offender to comply with whatever conditions the court imposes. Probation is the most widely used correctional option. The basic goals of probation are to promote law-abiding behavior by the offender; to keep the adjudicated individual in the community and out of prison and, thereby, avoid the stigma of incarceration; to provide a less expensive sanction than institutionalization; and to provide a sanction that is as effective as confinement in reducing recidivism. While originally conceived as an alternative to prison, it is possible to require probationers to serve a portion of their sentence behind bars. This jail time may be served on weekends or at night, or a specified term in jail may be followed by a period of probation.

Probation generally involves suspension of the offender's sentence in return for the promise of good behavior in the community under the supervision of a probation officer. As practiced by the federal government and all 50 states, probation implies a contract between the court and the offender in which the former promises to hold or suspend a prison term while the latter promises to follow a set of rules or conditions that are mandated by the court. If the rules are violated or the probationer commits another offense, probation may be revoked, which means that the contract is terminated and the original sentence is enforced. If an offender on probation commits a second offense that is more serious than the first, this person may be indicted, tried, and sentenced on the second offense. However, probation also may be revoked if the offender has failed to meet rules and conditions of probation (called "technical violations of probation").

TREATMENT ALTERNATIVES TO STREET CRIME (TASC) A treatment program designed to divert minor drug abusers away from the criminal justice system.

PROBATION A form of punishment that permits a convicted offender to remain in the community, under the supervision of a probation officer and subject to certain conditions set by the court.

Each probationary sentence is for a fixed period of time, and it depends on the seriousness of the offense and the statutory law of the jurisdiction. Probationers must report to a probation officer as often as required. The court sets down certain conditions or rules that must be followed by the offender. Some rules are standard and are applied in every probation case. Typically, probationers cannot leave the jurisdiction and must keep their officer informed of changes in their circumstances, especially as to contacts with the police, employment, address, marital status, and income or indebtedness.

Special rules of probation vary from jurisdiction to jurisdiction and may also vary to meet the personal situation of particular offenders. The payment of fines, restitution to victims, community service assignments, random or regular urine and alcohol testing, and regular employment are common requirements. **Financial restitution** and **community service** are two conditions often placed on probationers by many courts. The use of restitution actually predates both incarceration and modern forms of community treatment; the current trend is toward a more

Community sentences are the most common form of correctional treatment. They are used in a wide variety of crimes ranging from manslaughter to disturbing the peace. Here, on September 23, 2011, eight Muslim college students from Southern California, convicted of unlawfully disrupting a speech by Israel's ambassador to the U.S., huddle with their attorneys for sentencing agreements at a court in Santa Ana, California. The defendants received three years' probation and 56 hours of community service for the conviction.

© Reuters/Alex Gallardo/Landov

purposeful and imaginative use of restitution. At times, the victim is even involved with the offender in the development of restitution agreements. (See Chapter 4 for a more extensive discussion of fines, restitution, and community service as well as involvement of the victim as part of restorative justice in the adult criminal justice process.)

Probation Populations

Today, there are more than 4 million adults on probation in the United States.[17] And though the crime rate has decreased significantly, the probation population rose continuously for more than 20 years until it went down in 2010 (see Figure 3.2). Most are concentrated in a few large states: Georgia, Texas, California, Ohio, Florida, Michigan, and Pennsylvania account for more than a third of all probationers. Probationers account for more than half the growth in the correctional population since 1990.[18]

Figure 3.3 reveals the characteristics of adult offenders on probation. White males make up about 55 percent of the adults on probation. While many people believe probation is used only with petty offenders, about 50 percent of all probationers have been convicted of a felony, including drug law violations (18 percent), property offenses (26 percent), public order offenses (18 percent), and violent offenses (19 percent).[19]

Probation supervision is made more difficult by the variety of offenders that must be supervised. The supervision of violent offenders on probation status represents a serious concern and can represent safety issues. Nearly 20 percent, or over 800,000, of all probationers have been convicted of a violent offense, such as assault, sexual assault, and domestic violence.[20] Many probationers have substance abuse problems, and while the rate of substance dependence or abuse among probationers has declined in recent years, illegal drug use among people on probation remains

FINANCIAL RESTITUTION Payment of a sum of money by an offender either to the victim or to a public fund for victims of crime.

COMMUNITY SERVICE Requires an offender to perform a certain number of work hours at a private nonprofit or government agency.

FIGURE 3.2 Annual Probation Population and Entries to Probation

Source: Lauren E. Glaze, *Probation and Parole in the United States, 2010* (Washington, DC: U.S. Department of Justice, 2011), p. 1.

Number of adults (millions)

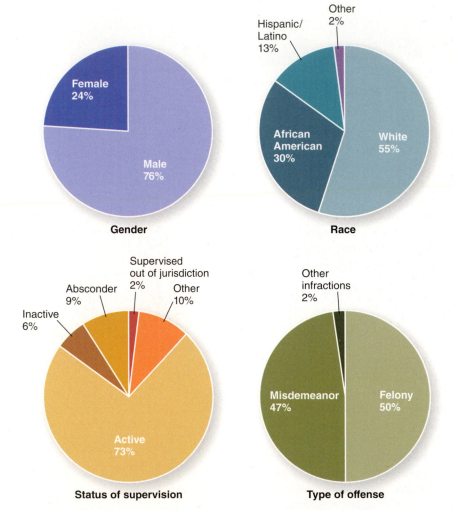

Gender

Female 24%

Male 76%

Race

Other 2%

Hispanic/Latino 13%

African American 30%

White 55%

Status of supervision

Supervised out of jurisdiction 2%

Absconder 9%

Inactive 6%

Other 10%

Active 73%

Type of offense

Other infractions 2%

Misdemeanor 47%

Felony 50%

FIGURE 3.3 Characteristics of Adults on Probation

Source: Lauren E. Glaze, *Probation and Parole in the United States, 2010* (Washington, DC: U.S. Department of Justice, 2011), p. 33.

a persistent challenge. Surveys find rates of drug abuse and dependence among probationers are two to three times higher than rates among nonprobationers. Similarly, rates of any physical illness, serious mental illness, serious psychological distress, and depression are two to three times higher among probationers than the general population. Probationers are more likely than others to have received some mental health services and are also more likely to report an unmet need for mental health services.[21] The community corrections population now serves over 700,000 individuals with an identified mental illness.[22] In view of the fact that these offenders have a difficult time adjusting to jail and prison, imprisonment is frequently an inadequate placement, especially for those mentally ill offenders deemed not dangerous or likely to create societal problems. Furthermore, about twice as many HIV-risk offenders are under community supervision as are incarcerated at a given time.[23] With high rates of injection drug use and prevalence of risky sexual behavior, it is not surprising that so many probationers are HIV positive.

Granting Probation

Probationary sentences are granted by federal and state district court judges and state superior (felony) courts. In some states, juries may also recommend probation if the case meets legally regulated criteria (for instance, it falls within a certain class of offenses as determined by statute). Yet, even in those jurisdictions that permit juries to recommend probation, judges still have the final say in the matter at their discretion. In nonjury trials, probation is granted entirely by judicial mandate. Some states have created guidelines for granting probation in an attempt to shape judicial discretion.

HOW COMMON IS THE USE OF PROBATION?

Wide variability exists in the use of probation across the nation. One study of 32 jurisdictions found that the numbers receiving probation varied from 30 percent in New York County (Manhattan) to 75 percent in Hennepin County (Minneapolis). Some of the variation is due to the sentencing laws under which these jurisdictions function. Courts in states with determinate sentencing (without a parole board) typically use probation more frequently than do courts in states with indeterminate sentencing (with a parole board). Judges may be less willing to sentence to prison when lengths of sentences are fixed.[24]

Studies also reveal that judges seem to be more willing to place felons on probation when they perceive that the probation department is able to monitor the offender closely and that the resources of the community are able to address some of the offender's underlying problems. Arizona, Minnesota, and Washington, three states that widely use probation, are well known for delivering good probation supervision and for having the resources to provide adequate treatment and services.[25]

Risk Assessment and Increased Surveillance Models

In the 1980s and 1990s, probation came under criticism as a lenient measure that allowed serious felony offenders to escape their "just deserts." Dan Richard Beto, Ronald P. Corbett, Jr., and John J. DiIulio, Jr., have addressed what they call the decline in public confidence in probation, and they recommend that probation's challenge is to get serious about the crime problem. They argue that probation can do this by becoming more aggressive about promoting public safety, which will reduce the high rates of recidivism and expand the resources given to probation services.[26]

The political backlash against rehabilitation or "being soft on crime" that occurred in the 1980s and 1990s, coupled with the decline of resources provided for probation agencies, led many large correctional and community supervision agencies to adopt new mandates involving risk management and avoidance. Their institutional focus shifted from concerns about rehabilitating or reforming probationers to minimizing the risks that these offenders posed to public order.[27] Thus, in an attempt to convince the public, as well as policy makers, that probation could be tougher on criminals, probation administrators attempted to enter into a bureaucratic-managerial stage characterized by stricter controls of probationers.[28] In shifting away from counseling and program interventions, agencies' strategies moved toward actuarial calculation and controls via offender-based data systems; drug-testing technologies, such as urinalysis, antabuse, and methadone; and classification systems.[29]

The emerging bureaucratic-managerial stage of probation began to emphasize strategies that would better ensure public protection.[30] The most widely used of these strategies have been the combination of probation and incarceration, intensive probation, and electronic monitoring and house arrest, which (excluding intensive probation) are examined in Chapter 4.

This movement in probation and parole toward a **risk management system** is what Malcolm Feeley and Jonathan Simon have called "the **new penology**." They argue that the old penology goal of normalizing individual offenders has been replaced by a new penology focused on goals aimed at regulating groups of offenders.[31] Feeley and Simon have identified three features of the new penology.

First, the language of the new penology is anchored in the discourse of system analysis and operations research. It conceives of crime as a systemic phenomenon

RISK MANAGEMENT SYSTEM A correctional system that is focused more on regulating and controlling offenders than on providing treatment or services for them.

NEW PENOLOGY A new approach in probation and other community-based corrections that focuses more on administrative control and regulation than on treatment and offering services.

and crime policy as a problem of actuarial risk management. Second, in contrast to previous efforts of transforming individuals, the new penology embraces a new objective, that of risk management and the management of the system itself.

Third, the administrative techniques are adapted from the world of insurance, financial management, and even retailing. These techniques (profiling, auditing, and screening) were introduced as ways of improving administrative knowledge of and control over penal agents and subjects. The new penology, its proponents contend, provides a useful analytic grid on which to interpret the emergent set of practices, discourses, and objectives in the criminal process.[32]

The use of these techniques has filtered into the provision of treatment services. The risk-need-responsivity (RNR) model, now being used in a number of jurisdictions, including Maine, Illinois, and Oregon, uses risk assessment tools to classify each probationer and match him or her to the right treatment program. Typically, treatment efforts are behavioral (relying on a system of rewards and punishments) and higher-risk offenders receive the most services. Cognitive behavioral and "social learning" techniques—ranging from anger management training to sessions devoted to reducing negative and antisocial attitudes—are emphasized. RNR programs rely on peers and family members to reinforce their messages. Several research efforts have found that they can cut the recidivism of high-risk offenders by as much as 20 percent.[33]

Administration of Probation

The United States has approximately 2,000 adult probation agencies. More than half are associated with a state-level agency; in about one-fourth of the states, probation is primarily a local responsibility. About 30 states combine probation and parole supervision into a single agency. A number of states have also permitted the private sector to administer probation supervision, especially for minor offenders. The federal courts also administer probation services.

LOCALLY ADMINISTERED PROBATION DEPARTMENTS In those states in which probation is a local responsibility, the state is accountable only for providing financial support, setting standards, and arranging training courses. This locally based approach accounts for about two-thirds of all probationers supervised in the United States.

One of the most persuasive arguments for local administration of probation is that citizens and agencies of the community more readily support programs that are open to their participation and are responsive to local needs and problems. Another supporting argument is that small operations are more flexible, adjust more quickly to change, and are less encumbered by bureaucratic rigidity. Yet three arguments against local administration have won the support of many policy makers: (1) A state-administered probation system can set standards of service, thereby ensuring uniformity of procedures, policies, and services. (2) A larger agency can make more effective use of funds and personnel. (3) Greater efficiency in the disposition of resources is possible when all probation officers are state employees.

STATE OR EXECUTIVE ADMINISTERED PROBATION DEPARTMENTS Assignment of probation to the executive branch on a statewide basis allows uniform standards of policy making, recruitment, training, and personnel management. Coordination with the state department of corrections and with the parole service is also facilitated. The most significant disadvantage is the development of a large probation bureaucracy with echelons of decision makers shuffling memoranda from out-basket to in-basket with little contact with the real world of the streets. Firm leadership with a grasp of sound management procedures can prevent this dismal prospect.

COMBINED PROBATION AND PAROLE DEPARTMENTS Critics of the 30 states providing both probation and parole services argue that

© Derek Dufresne

"The best thing is when your effort with an offender takes hold and contributes to their success."

DEREK DUFRESNE
U.S. PROBATION OFFICER

In the U.S. Probation Offices, we have three major components or tasks: pretrial investigation, presentence investigation, and postconviction. I am involved in the supervision unit of postconviction.

Probation is a delicate balance between law enforcement and social work. One thing I like about my job is that my caseloads are manageable. I have 80 probationers on my caseload and that allows me to intensely supervise those on release. In contrast, state probation officers may have 150 to 200 on their caseloads. Another thing I like about federal probation is that up until this year, we have had adequate resources allotted to us. This year with the budget cuts, we have had to use networking to be able to find volunteers because we cannot pay for resources.

I enjoy the fact that every day is different. One day I can do financial investigations in my office; the next day I am in the community verifying employments, community service, and education. On a daily basis, I begin the day by contacting offenders who are having problems. I complete financial reports, review monthly background checks, look at documents of offenders' progress, contact judges on progress or lack thereof, write letters to offenders, and review drug testing of those on my caseload.

In terms of supervision, we like to push education. We encourage them to get either a GED or high school diploma. We know if we can make offenders' supervision a positive experience, there is a higher chance of success. The best thing is when your effort with an offender takes hold and contributes to their success.

Source: Interviewed in 2011.

probationers, especially first-time offenders, should be kept separate from parolees, and that probation is a service to judges and should be under their control. However, it is argued that a combined system conserves scarce resources and has greater public acceptance. A combined system requires only one office, one set of directives, and one supervisory hierarchy. In both probation and parole, the same goals are sought and the same skills are required for supervision of offenders.

FEDERAL PROBATION The U.S. Probation and Pretrial Services carries out probation and pretrial services functions in the U.S. District Courts. District judges of the U.S. courts control federal probation services, but the probation division's administrative offices administer recruitment and training of personnel. In the Voices Across the Profession feature, U.S. Probation Officer Derek Dufresne talks about his job as well as how federal and state probation services differ.

PRIVATIZING PROBATION The private sector and the supervision of misdemeanant probationers were widely implemented in Florida in the 1970s. At its peak, the Salvation Army Misdemeanant Program (SAMP) in Florida employed 200 counselors in 37 counties and supervised 14,000 clients a month. Today probation agencies in 15 states use privatized probation services for low-risk offenders. Connecticut and Colorado are two states that have widely used the private sector for the supervision of low-risk probationers.

In sum, the management of probation and parole can be organized in several ways. On the whole, the executive control of probation probably utilizes more effectively the scarce resources available to probation systems. Yet decentralized services make sense in counties with a tradition of effective probation programming. In addition, statewide organization of combined probation and parole services seems to offer the best assurance of accountability and economy, given firm leadership by an administrator who knows what has to be done and how to do it. See Table 3.1.

© A. Ramey/PhotoEdit Inc.

A probation officer and police officer talk to kids being recruited into the Crips gang in California. Probation officers routinely work with police and other criminal justice organizations in crime control and treatment efforts involving community outreach. They may talk to kids about alternatives to gang membership.

Preparation for the Job

It is highly desirable, and mandatory in some offices, that an applicant for a probation officer's position has done volunteer work in some probation office

Nature of the Job

Probation officers generally work with either adults or juveniles; only in small departments are probation officers responsible for both adults and juveniles. They supervise people placed on probation by the courts and in many jurisdictions also supervise offenders released on parole. Probation officers rely upon personal interactions to supervise the offender, including asking for assistance from family members, community organizations, religious institutions, and neighbors. They will help the offender obtain substance abuse services and job training if necessary.

TABLE 3.1 Comparing the Administration of Probation Services

Responsibility	Size	Advantages
Locally administered	Two-thirds of all U.S. probationers	Citizens and agencies of the community respond to local needs and problems
State or executive	Over half the states	Allows uniform standards of policy making, recruitment, training, and personnel management
Combining probation and parole	About 30 states	Requires only one office, one set of directives, and one supervisory hierarchy
U.S. federal probation	94 U.S. district courts	Restricted to those sentenced by district courts
Privatizing	A few states	Efficient use of resources for low-risk probationers

Probation officers are also involved in the sentencing process by investigating the offender's background, writing presentence reports, and even recommending sentences. They often review these reports with the offender and the offender's family. Probation officers generally work a standard 40-hour week, which may include working evenings and/or weekends to supervise their caseload. They also may be on call at other times to assist probationers on their caseload. However, some agencies allow them to telecommute from home via computers and other equipment.

Qualifications and Required Education

Qualifications vary by state, but a bachelor's degree in social work, criminal justice, or a similar field is usually required. There may also be a training program to complete before one is eligible. A prior felony conviction may make an applicant ineligible for this position. In addition, some states require previous employment in this field. Applicants should be knowledgeable about laws and regulations pertaining to corrections. Writing and computer skills are also necessary.

Job Outlook

Jobs are more plentiful in urban areas, where a probation officer will typically work exclusively with adults or juveniles. In smaller communities, probation officers may work with both adult and juvenile offenders. Jobs for probation officers are more plentiful in those states that have more men and women on probation, such as California and Texas. Overall, growth within the criminal justice system and a large number of expected retirements of aging baby boomers suggest continued demand for new probation officers.

Earnings and Benefits

The mean annual salary is $43,510. State governments pay a median income of $39,810, and local governments pay a median income of $40,560. The lowest mean annual salary of the federal government for this position is $25,940, and the highest mean annual salary is $61,550. Wages are dependent upon government funding and the jurisdiction where one works.

Sources: "Probation Officers and Correctional Treatment Specialists," *Occupational Outlook Handbook*, 2010–2011–2012 Edition (Bureau of Labor Statistics, U.S. Department of Labor), www.bls.gov/oco/ocos265.htm (accessed March 20, 2012); "Occupational Employment and Wages, 2011: Probation Officers and Correctional Treatment Specialists" (Bureau of Labor Statistics, U.S. Department of Labor), 2011.

Basic Functions of a Probation Officer

The probation department is situated in a single court district, such as a juvenile district, superior, or municipal court. The relationship between the department and court personnel, particularly the judge, is extremely close. In a typical department, the chief probation officer (CPO) supervises hiring, sets policy, determines training needs, and may be involved with the sentencing decision with the judge. In state-controlled departments, some of the CPO's duties, such as training guidelines, are mandated at the state level. In locally controlled probation departments, the CPO has great discretion in his or her management, as long as there is judicial approval. See the Careers in Corrections feature.

The three basic functions of an adult probation officer are to manage a caseload, to supervise adult probationers, and to make presentence investigation and other reports to the courts.

CASEWORK MANAGEMENT AND OTHER ADMINISTRATIVE
DUTIES The probation officer maintains a file on each probationer for whom he or she is responsible. Within this file are the court documents that spell out the requirements of probation, chronological entries of contacts between the officer and the probationer and others whose relationship with the probationer might be significant, items of correspondence, and periodic reports made to the courts or to officials of the agency.

Commonly, probation departments divide probationers into several categories, based on their needs or on the risk they pose to the community. Some offenders are placed on minimum supervision status and are required only to mail in a report once a month or even less frequently. Offenders on medium supervision status must visit their probation officers at least once a month. Offenders on maximum or intensive supervision status must see their officers several times a month. About 90 percent of probationers in the United States are supervised on regular caseload levels, about 4 or 5 percent are placed on intensive supervision, and from 1 to 5 percent constitute specialized caseloads of individuals subject to electronic monitoring, under house arrest, or sent to boot camps.[34]

Probation officers' caseloads are so large that maintaining contact with probationers is difficult. According to one survey, caseloads ranged from around 70 cases per officer in Florida to nearly 290 in Rhode Island and 225 in Georgia. The average among those states reporting to this survey was 112 probationers per officer. For assigned probation officers who also had parolees on their caseloads, caseloads per officer ranged from around 50 in Wisconsin and West Virginia to 225 in Vermont and Ohio.[35] Probation officers with combined probation and parole caseloads averaged almost 100 clients per officer.[36]

Studies seeking to link caseload size and recidivism in probation go back 40 years. Since the late 1970s, five major studies sought to identify the impact of caseloads on recidivism, and three of the five studies found evidence supporting the contention that smaller caseloads were related to lower recidivism rates. More recently, John L. Worrall and colleagues' macro-level analysis of the relationship between probation caseloads and property crime rates in California counties found over a nine-year period that as probation loads increased, so did property crime.[37]

SUPERVISION, INVESTIGATION, AND SURVEILLANCE
The officer is required to determine as much as possible whether a client is obeying the law and complying with the terms of probation, and if not, to follow up on the violation. In some jurisdictions, probation officers are now authorized to carry handguns because the department began to require officers to spend more time visiting their clients in their neighborhoods and homes.[38]

Even though personal involvement in the supervision of offenders is no longer emphasized, officers still must establish a relationship with the probationer, establish supervision goals to comply with the conditions of probation, and decide how and when to terminate probation. The investigation and surveillance aspects of supervision call for at least periodic checks on probationers' employment, the status of their restitution payments, whether they are clean on their urine "drops," and whether they are participating in required programs.

Effective officers enjoy the respect of colleagues in the justice system and maintain good relationships within the office. Whether they are promoted or not (promotions are impossible in a one-person office and are difficult to obtain in small offices with a few officers), they are rewarded by an awareness of their reputations for fairness, genuineness, and commitment to their jobs. In short, their efforts do pay off, and they do make a difference in the lives of probationers.

Effective supervision is also critical because it protects the probation department from civil liability. The failure to supervise probationers adequately and to determine whether

CORRECTIONAL LIFE
Danny, A Probationer

"I have had one particularly helpful adult probation officer. This PO approached the job more as a service provider than as a correctional officer. I know he has gone to bat for people. He spends more time on the street than he does in his office. He takes people to job interviews; he goes to people's homes and makes sure they have enough food. He deals with offenders' mental health issues and makes sure they get their medications. He has gone to the relief office to help them get rent. He is personally involved. He treated me as a person who has intrinsic worth and potential. I drank and used drugs consistently for 38 years of my life. What helped me to stop was because there were people like Bill who had not given up on me.[39]"

they are obeying the rules of probation can result in both the officer and the department being held legally responsible for civil damages. For example, if a probationer has a history of child molestation and attacks a child while working as a school custodian, the probationer's case supervisor can be held legally responsible for failing to check on the probationer's employment activities.

PRESENTENCE INVESTIGATION REPORTS The **presentence investigation (PSI)** report is the major report required of a probation officer and is used at the time of the sentencing hearing. The main purposes of the PSI report are to help the court decide whether to grant probation, determine the conditions of probation, determine the length of the sentences, and decide on community-based or institutional placement for the defendants.

PSI reports vary somewhat in form but usually have six categories:

1. Information about the offense and a description of its exact nature
2. The defendant's prior record, including juvenile adjudications
3. Background information on the defendant's upbringing, educational background, employment, marital situation, physical and emotional health, military service, financial situation
4. A statement by the prosecution about what the appropriate disposition should be
5. A summary of the foregoing information along with sentencing alternatives available to the court
6. The probation officer's recommendation on the most appropriate sentence, based on the information in the report

In most states, a PSI report must be prepared regardless of whether the offender is eligible for probation. If he or she is sent to prison, the report will accompany the commitment document for the information of the prison authorities. The PSI may be less important in states with sentencing guidelines and not at all important for offenders sentenced using mandatory and presumptive sentencing.[40] The long form of a PSI report may take up to 20 hours to complete, but it is not uniform from one jurisdiction to another. Probations must first interview the defendant, preferably more than once, in order to verify information. Officers then review the defendant's arrest record, reports concerning the current offense, previous presentence reports, and any available psychiatric psychological reports. Occasionally they must interview the arresting officer and the defendant's employer, and they often talk with the defendant's family.

Probation officers have the authority to file a notice of violation with the court when a probationer commits a violation of the conditions of probation or is arrested again. The prosecutor may decide to prosecute the new offense, especially if the penalty exceeds revocation and he or she has a solid case. If the prosecutor decides not to prosecute, the case is placed on the court calendar, and the probationer is directed to appear in court for a preliminary hearing. If a revocation hearing is scheduled after the preliminary, the probation officer is charged before the hearing to present the judge a full violation-of-probation report documenting the charges and summarizing the probationer's degree of adjustment of probation.

LO6 What Are Probationers' Legal Rights?

The most important cases concerning probation that have been litigated by the courts have involved disclosure of PSI reports, civil rights of probationers, and the rights of probationers during probation revocation.

DISCLOSURE OF PSI REPORTS Defense attorneys prefer disclosure of the information on the PSI compiled by the probation officer because they seek the opportunity to challenge any disputable statements in the report. The question of disclosure of the PSI report to defense counsel was first raised in three cases: *Williams v. New York* (1949),[41] *Gardner v. Florida* (1977),[42] and *Booth v. Maryland*

PRESENTENCE INVESTIGATION (PSI) An investigation whose main purposes are to help the court decide whether to grant probation, to determine the conditions of probation, to determine the length of the sentence, and to decide on community-based or institutional placement for the defendant.

(1987).[43] Both in the *Gardner* and *Booth* cases, the U.S. Supreme Court decided that in death penalty cases the PSI must be available to the defense and could not contain victim impact statements that would inflame the jury.[44]

CIVIL RIGHTS The U.S. Supreme Court has ruled that probationers constitute a unique state and, as a result, are entitled to fewer constitutional protections than other citizens. In *Minnesota v. Murphy* (1984), the Court ruled that the probation officer–client relationship is not confidential, as attorney–client or physician–patient relationships are.[45] In *Griffin v. Wisconsin* (1987), the Court held that a probationer's home may be searched without a warrant on the grounds that the probation departments "have in mind the welfare of the probationer" and must "respond quickly to evidence of misconduct."[46] In *United States v. Knights* (2001), the Court upheld the legality of a warrantless search of a probationer's home for the purposes of gathering criminal evidence. The Court reasoned that the state's interest in preventing crime, along with Knights's diminished expectation of privacy, required only a *reasonable suspicion* to make the search fit within the protections found in the Fourth Amendment.[47]

REVOCATION OF PROBATION A violation of the rules or terms of probation or the commitment of a new crime can result in the **revocation of probation**, at which time the offender may be placed in an institution. Revocation because of a rule violation is referred to as a **technical violation**.

Technical violations have become a hotly debated item because of the numbers of probationers who are incarcerated in state or local facilities due to rule violations, and this, of course, has contributed to the increasing costs of corrections. For example, a Department of Justice report noted that 9 percent of all offenders who exited probation supervision were incarcerated in state or local facilities due to rule violations.[48] As the next chapter on intermediate sentencing reveals, a number of states are using intermediate sanctions as an alternative to incarceration for technical violations.[49]

Revocation is not an easy decision, but when it takes place, the officer is notified and a formal hearing is scheduled. If the charges against the probationer are upheld, the offender can be placed in a prison setting to serve the remainder of the sentence. The probationer has been given certain procedural due process at this stage of the criminal process. In four significant cases, the U.S. Supreme Court provided procedural safeguards to apply at proceedings to revoke probation (and parole):[50]

- ■ The Court ruled in *Mempa v. Rhay* (1967) that because Mempa did not have counsel at his revocation hearings, the decision of the lower courts was reversed and Mempa was to be released from prison.[51]

- ■ In *Gagnon v. Scarpelli* (1973), the Court held that both probationers and parolees have a constitutionally limited right to counsel in revocation proceedings. This means that during a probation revocation hearing, the probationer must be given counsel if he or she requires it for an effective defense.[52] On appeal in the *Gagnon* decision, the Supreme Court ruled that if a state determines a fine or restitution to be appropriate and an adequate penalty for the crime, it may not thereafter imprison a defendant solely because he or she lacks the resources to pay, because this would be a violation of a probationer's right to equal protection.[53]

- ■ In *Bearden v. Georgia* (1983), the Court ruled that a judge cannot revoke a defendant's probation for failure to pay a fine and make restitution, unless the probation is somehow responsible for the failure or the alternative forms of punishment are inadequate to meet the state's interest in punishment and deterrence. The trial court revoked probation, and the defendant was sent to prison.[54]

- ■ The Court helped clarify in the *United States v. Granderson* (1994) decision what can happen to a probationer whose community sentence is revoked. Granderson was eligible for a six-month prison sentence; instead, he was given 60 months of probation. When he tested positive for drugs,

REVOCATION OF PROBATION A violation of the rules or terms of probation or the commitment of a new crime, which may result in the offender being placed in an institution.

TECHNICAL VIOLATION A probationer violates one of the rules of probation, such as looking for a job.

his probation was revoked. Since the statute he was sentenced under required that he serve one-third of his original sentence in prison, the trial court sentenced him to 20 months. He appealed. The Court ruled that it would be unfair to force a probationer to serve more time in prison than he would have if originally incarcerated and, as a result, his proper term should have been one-third of the six months, or two months.[55]

Is Probation Effective?

The effectiveness of probation varies by the offense behavior of offenders. Recidivism rates are low among those placed on probation for a misdemeanor: data suggest that upwards of three-fourths of offenders placed on probation for a misdemeanor successfully complete their supervision.[56] In addition, adult probation is having increased success with drug offenders. Research at UCLA and elsewhere has found that drug abuse treatment is effective and that individuals coerced into treatment derive benefits similar to the benefits of those who enter voluntarily.[57] Another study followed a sample of probationers for the first eight months of their probation term and found that a significant reduction in criminal activity occurred after being placed on probation. The study did find that carrying guns or using alcohol predicted the likelihood of new criminal behavior.[58] However, in a classic study Joan Petersilia and Susan Turner found that 65 percent of those who had committed felonies and were on probation were rearrested.[59] The increased numbers of felony probationers sentenced to probation, as well as the "get tough on crime" mood in the wider society, led to the development of increased surveillance models.

Gender also appears to affect probation's effectiveness. One study found that women were more likely to be sentenced to probation for drug or property offenses, while men were sentenced to probation more for crimes of violence and for driving under the influence. Women also were less likely to be assessed court costs, fines, and probation supervision fees, largely because they were more likely to be unemployed or earned less than men. Women did perform better on probation with respect to technical violations and new arrests.[60]

IMPROVING PROBATION EFFECTIVENESS To improve probation effectiveness, several steps appear to be necessary.[61] More financial resources must be provided to implement quality programming for appropriate probation target groups. The credibility of probation with the public and the judiciary must be improved. Support is needed from a public that views the probation sanction as sufficiently punitive to make up for the harm of criminal behavior and from a judiciary that is convinced offenders will be held accountable for their behavior. More innovative programs in probation across the nation need to be implemented. In addition, probation must be made a priority research topic, such as in implementing evidence-based practice (EBP) in community programs; this will identify proven methods of reducing offender recidivism.[62] Exhibit 3.1 illustrates some of the probation practices that have proven to be successful in improving probation effectiveness.

EXHIBIT 3.1 Successful Probation Practices

■ *The use of risk and needs assessment.* Corrections research supports the use of risk and needs assessment when offenders are first placed on probation and periodically thereafter. These assessments also provide probation departments with limited resources to be able to prioritize intensive rehabilitation services.

■ *Referral to community-based programs to reduce recidivism.* Offenders are more likely to be successful while on probation provided effective treatment and assistance programs are made available. This includes drug treatment and mental health counseling, employment assistance, and anger management. In the current fiscal austerity experienced in the United States, with its high rates of unemployment, employment is particularly needed.

■ *Manageable supervision caseloads.* No national standard is available for how many probationers should be on a probation officer's caseload. Supervision generally is only effective at reducing recidivism when coupled with treatment-oriented programs.

■ *System of graduated sanctions.* One of the key strategies for effectively intervening and interrupting the cycle of reoffending is to establish a system of graduated sanctions.

■ *Program reviews and evaluations.* Implementing certain programs and practices have been found to result in better outcomes and reduced recidivism. Several states, such as Oregon, utilize assessment tools to measure programs' fidelity, a measurement of how well the program or practice is implemented. In addition to measuring programs' fidelity, it is important to collect data on probationer outcome that can indicate which programs are most effective in rehabilitating offenders.

Source: Mac Davis, *Achieving Better Outcomes for Adult Probation: Executive Summary, California* Legislative Analyst's Office, 2009, www.lao.ca.gov/2009/crim/probation/probation_052909.pdf (accessed February 18, 2012).

DEFERRED SENTENCE A sentence that delays conviction on a guilty plea until the sentenced offender has successfully served his or her probation term.

SHOCK PROBATION The offender, his or her attorney, or the sentencing judge can submit a motion to suspend the remainder of a sentence after a felon has served a period of time in prison.

BENCH, OR UNSUPERVISED, PROBATION A type of probation in which probationers are not subject to supervision.

SPLIT SENTENCE A sentence requiring an offender to spend a period of time in jail before being placed on probation in the community.

INTENSIVE PROBATION Supervision that is far stricter than standard probationary supervision.

Contemporary Probation Services

With an expanding caseload and greater responsibility to treat and care for non-traditional clients, probation departments have or are now developing a new variety of program to amplify the effectiveness of community corrections. Some of the ongoing programs include:

- Some jurisdictions allow a **deferred sentence**. This variation delays conviction on a guilty plea until the completion of a term of probation, at which time the offender withdraws the guilty plea. The court dismisses the charge, thereby clearing the offender's record of a conviction. This procedure is not the same as pretrial diversion, because a probation officer supervises the offender when the deferred sentence is imposed by a judge; in pretrial diversion the offender is diverted from the system.

- **Shock probation** calls for the shock of a few weeks in prison for a first-time offender followed by a standard term of probation.

- Some jurisdictions permit **bench, or unsupervised, probation**, especially with misdemeanants (persons convicted of a misdemeanor).

- The **split sentence**, or intermittent sentence, is also used by some jurisdictions. Offenders spend a period of time in jail before being placed on probation in the community, or they are sentenced to a number of weekends in jail while remaining in the community on probation status during the week.

- Under **intensive probation**, a probationer is supervised far more strictly than under standard services. Intensive probation is discussed more fully in Exhibit 3.2.[63]

Future of Probation Services

A number of characteristics of probation widely used in the present will likely continue. In addition, several recent innovations promise to affect probation in the future. The following is a list of some of these current trends and probable developments:

- Attention will continue to be paid to substance abusers, because of the close relationship between drugs and crime.

- Screening and classification systems will continue to guide the level of probation supervision.

- Efficiency and accountability will continue to be demanded of probation departments.

- At least 25 states now impose some form of fee on probationers to defray the cost of probation and other community programs. Massachusetts started the day fees, which are based on a probationer's wages (the typical fee is between one and three days' wages each month). Texas requires judges to impose supervision fees unless the offender is totally unable to pay, and fees make up more than half of each probation department's annual budget. It is likely this practice will increase in other states.

- Another recent innovation is the use of performance indicators that reveal whether probation is doing its job. These indicators include probationers' days free of drug use, employment rates, amount of restitution collected, and the days of community service served.

- Community partnerships will be used more frequently. These bring together community service teams to work jointly on providing treatment. Maryland's HotSpot probation initiative involves probation officers, police officers, social service professionals, and neighbors to form

EXHIBIT 3.2 Intensive Supervised Probation

Initiated in Georgia in 1982, intensive supervised probation (ISP) permits probationers to live at home but under relatively strict restrictions. ISP offenders usually are required to perform community service, work, attend school or treatment programs, meet with a probation officer or a team of two officers as often as five times a week, and submit to tests for drug and alcohol use, curfews, and employment checks. This widely used program seems especially useful with high-risk probationers. Currently, about 5 percent of those on probation or parole are assigned to ISP.

ISP programs provide several services to the justice system. Without intensive supervision, high-risk offenders would ordinarily be sent to already crowded jails or prisons. ISP lets high-risk probationers be maintained in the community, helping them maintain community ties and avoid the pains of imprisonment.

ISP programs are used in several different ways in the justice system. ISP can be a:

- Direct sentence imposed by a judge

- Post-sentencing alternative used to divert offenders from prison

- Case management tool that provides local probation staff flexibility in dealing with probationers, especially those who appear to be high risk

- Method to deal with probation violators, bringing them halfway back into the community without sending them to prison

Some jurisdictions use ISP in all of these ways. For example, New Jersey's ISP program emphasizes a law enforcement approach, but it also contains a rehabilitation component: most program participants attend peer support sessions led by probation/parole officers and receive substance abuse counseling. Moreover, senior supervisors and policy makers further encourage the rehabilitation components of the ISP program.

Evaluation of ISP Programs

Because felons sentenced to probation have high recidivism rates, ISP programs should be an effective method of controlling these more serious offenders. In a well-known study, Joan Petersilia and Susan Turner evaluated ISP programs in threecounties in California (Contra Costa, Ventura, and Los Angeles) and found that 25 percent of the ISP offenders in each site had no new incidents (technical violations or new arrests), about 40 percent had only technical violations (violations of probation conditions), and about 33 percent had new arrests during a one-year period. Evaluation of the ISP project revealed that ISP participants had more technical violations than traditional probationers simply because of the increased supervision of intensive probation. Thus, ISP may cut down on criminal offending while increasing technical violations.

There has also been criticism that ISP programs sacrifice treatment services for surveillance and control.[58] In one review, Paul Gendreau and colleagues found "that only 18 percent of ISPs surveyed in their meta-analysis offered even a modicum of treatment services, and even among those, all were of unknown quality." Gendreau and colleagues found that without the provision of treatment services, ISP programs will have marginal effects on recidivism.

It is not surprising that the failure rate in ISP caseloads is high, given that caseloads are made up of more serious offenders who might otherwise have been incarcerated and who are receiving close supervision, which can detect technical violations. Probation officers are more willing to revoke their ISP clients for fairly minor technical violations because they believe that they are a risk to the community. Evidence so far indicates that ISP appears to work better for offenders with good employment records than it does for those who are unemployed. Younger offenders who commit petty crimes are also the most likely to be failures on ISP.

Sources: "An Intensive Supervision Program that Worked: Service Delivery, Professional Orientation, and Organizational Supportiveness," *Prison Journal* 85 (2005): 445–466; Joan Petersilia and Susan Turner, "Evaluating Intensive Supervision Probation and Parole," in *Intermediate Sanctions in Overcrowded Times*, ed. Michael Tonry and Kate Hamilton (Boston: Northeastern University Press, 1995); Paul Gendreau, C. Goggin, F. Cullen, and D. A. Andrews, "The Effects of Community Sanctions and Incarceration on Recidivism," *Forum on Corrections Research* 12 (2000): 10–13; T. Huynh and H. Potter, "Effectiveness of Adult Intensive Supervision Probation," paper presented at the annual meeting of the American Society of Criminology, St. Louis, Missouri, 2011.

---

community probation teams. Using a team approach, they provide increased monitoring of offenders through drug testing, home visits, and regular meetings.[64] Whether this will expand to other states or not, this approach seems to have a great deal of utility for probation and community corrections.

- In a number of jurisdictions, probation automated management (PAM) permits low-risk probationers to report in 24 hours a day, seven days a week, using their fingerprints as biometric identifiers.[65] This is such a cost-effective measure that it is likely to spread throughout probation departments across the nation.

- Philadelphia has developed a high-tech program that may be helpful in predicting murders and intervening before they occur. In the Strategic Anti-Violence Unit (SAV-U), which was implemented in January 2007, this program gives special attention to probationers considered high risk. Using software tools and research covering thousands of past crimes, Richard Berk, professor of criminology and statistics at the University of Pennsylvania, developed a computer model for the Philadelphia probation department that identifies these high-risk probationers.[66]

- Innovative treatment approaches will continue to be developed. For example, the Good Lives Model (GLM), a framework used for sex offender treatment programs, is now being applied successfully in a case management setting. The GLM is a strengths-based approach to offender rehabilitation, premised on the idea that the capabilities and strengths of probationers must be built up, in order to reduce their risk of reoffending. According to the GLM, people offend because they are attempting to secure some kind of valued outcome in their life. As such, offending is essentially the product of a desire for something that is inherently human and normal. All too often, this desire or goal manifests itself in harmful and antisocial behavior, due to a range of deficits and weaknesses within the offender and his/her environment. Essentially, these deficits prevent offenders from securing their desired ends in prosocial and sustainable ways, thus requiring that they resort to inappropriate and damaging means—that is, offending behavior. Rather than threaten punishment, GLM focuses on developing strengths.[67]

SUMMARY

L01 **Explain what is meant by the term *community corrections act***

A community corrections act is a law passed by the state legislature in which a state grants funds to local units of government to plan, develop, and deliver correctional services and sanctions. Twenty-five states have passed community corrections acts and have made the establishment of strong community-based programs a priority.

L02 **Compare the main types of diversion programs and identify their advantages and disadvantages**

The three major types of adult diversion programs are deferred prosecution, deferred judgment, and Treatment Alternatives to Street Crime (TASC). Deferred judgment and deferred prosecution permits some minor offenders who complete a deferred program to have their formal charges dropped, and TASC is designed to divert drug abusers from the justice system and into specialized support services. The major advantage of diversion programs is avoiding justice system processing. The disadvantage is they may increase the number of those who

otherwise would have been ignored by the justice system in the past.

L03 **Understand the advantages of being placed on probation**

The major advantage of being placed on probation is that probationers are permitted to remain in the community as long as they comply with the conditions of the court under supervision of a probation officer.

L04 **Explain the risk assessment models and their current emphasis**

In the 1980s and 1990s, probation was widely criticized by those who wanted to get tough on crime. As a result, probation has gotten tougher. Probation's institutional focus shifted from concern about rehabilitating probationers to minimizing the risks that these offenders posed to public order. The risk assessment models that developed began to emphasize strategies that would better ensure public protection. The most widely used of these strategies have been the combination of probation and incarceration, intensive probation, and electronic monitoring and house arrests.

 Understand the various ways probation is administered

Probation can be administered in a variety of ways (local executive or local judicial, state executive or state judicial, or a combination), but combining probation and parole departments seems to be gaining public acceptance and is used in about 30 states. Probation can also be administered by the federal government.

 Understand the legal rights of probationers

The most important cases dealing with probationers' legal rights have involved disclosure of PSI reports, civil rights of probationers, and the rights of probationers during probation revocation.

 Evaluate the effectiveness of probation and identify some of the promising programs in probation services

Today, adult probation is the most widely used correctional option. Probation continues to demonstrate that it is as effective, if not more so, than other forms of correctional intervention. In addition to intensive probation, new approaches to probation in the present and future may include fees for probation services, performance indicators to measure probation effectiveness, and more attention to drug abusers.

Key Terms

judicial reprieve, 58
recognizance, 58
sureties, 58
reintegrative philosophy, 60
community corrections act (CCA), 60
true diversion, 62
minimization of system penetration, 62
deferred prosecution programs, 63

Treatment Alternatives to Street Crime (TASC), 64
probation, 64
financial restitution, 65
community service, 65
risk management system, 67
new penology, 67
presentence investigation (PSI), 73

revocation of probation, 74
technical violation, 74
deferred sentence, 76
shock probation, 76
bench, or unsupervised, probation, 76
split sentence, 76
intensive probation, 76

 ## Critical Thinking Questions

1. "I sentence you to 18 months of probation," the judge says. What benefits do you expect from serving out your sentence in the community?

2. Why is probation considered a second chance?

3. Probationers enjoy many of the same rights as unconvicted citizens. But a probationer's right to know on what information his or her sentence is based is a hotly debated issue. Why do many probation officers object to making PSI reports public?

4. How do you feel about placing on probation those who have committed felonies? How about placing sex offenders on probation?

5. How would one develop the attributes described as needed to be an effective probation officer?

 ## Thinking Like a Corrections Professional

You accepted a position in the Dodge County Probation Department. You lack experience and you want to be effective in your new job. Your supervisor hands you a casebook and tells you to do the best you can. She says she is swamped with reports to write and court appearances and cannot spend much time with you. What should you do first, second, and third?

During your first hours after settling into the job, six young men barge into your office. They are very belligerent. They want to know whether you are going to continue the racist actions of your predecessor, filing violations against members of their gang for wearing gang colors. What is the best way to respond to this confrontation?

Some of the other officers decide to carry a weapon, which is optional in your office. What will you do? What would be the decisive factors in your decision making?

Career Destinations

Interested in a federal probation job?
www.uscourts.gov/fedprob/

Many states maintain community corrections organizations; check one out at:
www.mass.gov/courts/admin/communitycorrections.html

Notes

1. Terry Aguayo, *New York Times*, National Desk, late edition, March 8, 2007.
2. For more recent coverage, see "The Jessica Lunsford Tragedy," *St. Petersburg Times Special Report*, March 9, 2008.
3. "Convicted Child Killer John Evander Couey Dies in Prison, Before Planned Execution," Associated Press, October 1, 2009.
4. David Ballingrud, "Probation and Sex Offenders," *St. Petersburg Times Online*, January 15, 2006.
5. David Ballingrud, "Judgment Calls," *St. Petersburg Times Online*, January 15, 2006.
6. Lisa L. Sample and Timothy M. Bray, "Are Sex Offenders Dangerous?" *Criminology and Public Policy* 3 (2003): 9–82; Franklin Zimring, Alex Piquero, Wesley Jennings, and Stephanie Hays, "The Predictive Power of Juvenile Sex Offending: Evidence from the Second Philadelphia Birth Cohort Study," June 21, 2007, Social Science Research Network, http://papers.ssrn.com/sol3/papers.cfm?abstract_id=995918 (accessed February 18, 2012).
7. See the final section of this chapter on whether probation is effective.
8. John Augustus, *First Probation Officer* (Montclair, NJ: Patterson Smith, 1972), pp. 4–5.
9. M. Kay Harris, "Key Differences Among Community Corrections Acts in the United States: An Overview," *Prison Journal* 76 (June 1996): 202.
10. Joan Nuffield, *Diversion Programs for Adults 1997–2005*, Public Safety and Emergency Preparedness Canada website, www.getprepared.gc.ca (accessed February 18, 2012).
11. Ibid.
12. K. Michael Reynolds, Sophia F. Dzigieleski, and Chris Sharp, "Serving Mentally Ill Offenders Through Community Corrections: Joining Two Disciplines," *Journal of Offender Rehabilitation* 40 (2004): 185–198.
13. "Deferred Prosecution and Deferred Judgment," www.experiencedcriminallawyers.com/articles/deferred-prosecution-deferred-judgment (accessed February 18, 2012).
14. Ibid.
15. New Jersey and Pennsylvania have had supreme court rulings authorizing intervention on a statewide basis; Arkansas, Colorado, Connecticut, Florida, Massachusetts, Tennessee, and Washington have had statewide enabling legislation.
16. M. Douglas Anglin, Douglas Longshore, and Susan Turner, "Treatment Alternatives to Street Crime," *Criminal Justice and Behavior* 26 (1999): 168–195.
17. Lauren E. Glaze and Thomas P. Bonczar, *Probation and Parole in the United States, 2009* (Washington, DC: Bureau of Justice Statistics, 2011), p. 1.
18. Ibid., p. 4.
19. Ibid., Table 5, p. 33.
20. Ibid.
21. Thomas E. Feucht and Joseph Gfroerer, "Mental and Substance Use Disorders Among Adult Men on Probation or Parole: Some Success Against a Persistent Challenge," Substance Abuse and Mental Health Services Administration, Department of Health and Human Services, 2011, http://oas.samhsa.gov/2k11/NIJ_Data_Review/MentalDisorders.htm (accessed February 18, 2012).
22. Reynolds, Dzigieleski, and Sharp, "Serving Mentally Ill Offenders Through Community Corrections," p. 185.
23. Steven Belenko, Sandra Langley, Susan Crimmings, and Michael Chaple, "HIV Risk Behaviors, Knowledge, and Prevention Education Among Offenders Under Community Supervision: A Hidden Risk Group," *AIDS Education and Prevention* 16 (2004): 367–385.
24. Joan Petersilia, "Probation in the United States," in *Crime and Justice: A Review of Research* vol. 22, ed. Michael Tonry (Chicago: University of Chicago Press, 1997).
25. Statements given by individuals who work in community-based corrections in the states of Arizona, Minnesota, and Washington.
26. Dan Richard Beto, Ronald P. Corbett, Jr., and John J. Dilulio, Jr., "Getting Serious About Probation and the Crime Problem," *Corrections Management Quarterly* 4 (Spring 2000): 1–5.
27. Michael Jacobson, *Downsizing Prisons: How to Reduce Crime and End Mass Incarceration* (New York: New York University Press, 2005), p. 151.
28. Fergus McNeil, "Developing Effectiveness: Frontline Perspectives," *Social Work Education* 20 (2001): 671–675.
29. Jacobson, *Downsizing Prisons*, p. 151.
30. Risk assessment research has begun in terms of prediction and explanation; see Daniel A. Krauss, Bruce D. Sales, Judith V. Becker, and A. J. Figueredo, "Beyond Prediction to Explanation in Risk Assessment Research," *International Journal of Law and Psychiatry* 23 (2000): 91–112.
31. Jonathan Simon and Malcolm M. Feeley, "The Forms and Limits of the New Penology," in *Punishment and Social Control*, 2nd ed., ed. Thomas G. Blomberg and Stanley Cohen (New York: Aldine De Gruyter, 2003), pp. 75–116.
32. Ibid.
33. Joan Petersilia, "Beyond the Prison Bubble," *NIJ Journal 268* (October 2011), www.nij.gov/nij/journals/268/prison-bubble.htm (accessed February 18, 2012).
34. See Richard P. Seiter and Angela D. West, "Supervision Styles in Probation and Parole: An Analysis of Activities," *Journal of Offender Rehabilitation* 38 (2003): 57–75.
35. Camille Graham Camp and George M. Camp, *The Corrections Yearbook: 2003 Adult Corrections* (Middletown, CT: Criminal Justice Institute, 2004).
36. American Correctional Association, *2004 Directory: Adult and Juvenile* (Lanham, MD: American Correctional Association, 2004), p. 75.
37. John L. Worrall, Pamela Schram, Eric Hays, and Matthew Newman, "An Analysis of the Relationship Between Probation Caseloads and Property Crime Rates in California Counties," *Journal of Criminal Justice* 32 (2004): 231–241.
38. Paul von Zielbauer, "Probation Dept. Is Now Arming Officers Supervising Criminals," *New York Times*, August 7, 2003, p. 5. Two other articles that address the risk of probation officers are Maria O'Beirne, David Denney, and Jonathan Gabe, "Fear of Violence as an Indicator of Risk in Probation Work: Its Impact on Staff Who Work with Known Violent Offenders," *British Journal of Criminology* 44 (2004): 113–126; and Hazel Kemshall, "Conflicting Knowledge on Risk: The Case of Risk Knowledge in the Probation Service," *Health, Risk, and Society* 2 (2000): 143–157.
39. Interviewed in 2009.
40. Current sentencing structures permit judges much less discretion than in the past and, as a result, the PSI is not as helpful to judges.
41. *Williams v. New York State*, 337 U.S. 241, 69 S.Ct. (1949).
42. *Gardner v. Florida*, 430 U.S. 349 (1977).
43. *Booth v. Maryland*, 482 U.S. 496 (1987).
44. *Williams v. New York State*, 337 U.S. 241, 69 S.Ct. (1949).
45. *Minnesota v. Murphy*, 465, U.S. 420, 104 S.Ct. 1136, 79 L.Ed.2d 409 (1984).
46. *Griffin v. Wisconsin*, 483 U.S. 868, 107 S.Ct. 3164, 97 L.Ed.2d 709 (1987).
47. *United States v. Knights*, 122 S.Ct. 587 (2001).

48. Alison Lawrence, *Probation and Parole Violations: State Responses* (Washington, DC: National Conference of State Legislatures, 2008), p. 1.

49. Ibid., for how a number of states are using intermediate sanctions in view of incarceration for technical violations.

50. *Morrissey v. Brewer* (1972) is an important case relating to the revocation of parole, but this will be discussed in Chapter 11.

51. *Mempa v. Rhay*, 359 U.S. 128 (1967).

52. *Gagnon v. Scarpelli*, 411 U.S. 778, 93 S.Ct. 1756, 36 L.Ed.2d 656 (1973).

53. Ibid.

54. *Bearden v. Georgia*, 33 CrL 3101 (1983).

55. *United States v. Granderson*, 114 Ct. 1259, 12 L.Ed.2d 656 (1994).

56. Petersilia, "Probation in the United States," pp. 180–181.

57. See the studies cited in Chapter 10 regarding the effectiveness of coercive treatment among drug offenders.

58. Doris Layton-MacKenzie and Spencer De Li, "The Impact of Formal and Informal Social Controls on the Criminal Activities of Probationers," *Journal of Research on Crime and Delinquency* 39 (August 2002): 243–276.

59. Petersilia, "Probation in the United States," pp. 180–181. For a more recent discussion of felony probation in California, see Kathleen Auerhahn, "Do You Know Who Your Probationers Are? Using Simulation Modeling to Estimate the Composition of California's Felony Probation Population, 1980–2000," *Justice Quarterly* 234 (March 2007): 28–47.

60. D. E. Olson, A. J. Lurigio, and M. Seng, "A Comparison of Female and Male Probationers: Characteristics and Case Outcomes," *Women and Criminal Justice* 11 (2000): 47.

61. Petersilia, "Probation in the United States," p. 185.

62. Lore Jopin, Brad Bogue, Nancy Campbell, Mark Carey, Elyse Clawson, Dot Faust, Kate Florio, Billy Wasson, and William Woodward, "Using an Integrated Model to Implement Evidence Based Practices in Corrections," paper published by the International Community Corrections Association and American Correctional Association, pp. 200–204.

63. M. A. Paparozzi and P. Gendreau, "An Intensive Supervision Program that Worked: Service Delivery, Professional Orientation, and Organizational Supportiveness," *Prison Journal* 85 (2005): 445–466.

64. Nicole Leeper Piquero, "A Recidivism Analysis of Maryland's Community Probation Program," *Journal of Criminal Justice* 31 (2003): 295–308.

65. Thomas G. Ogden, "Pagers, Digital Audio, and Kiosk: Office Assistants," *Federal Probation* 65 (2001): 35–37. See also Leanne Fiftal Alarid and Rolando V. Del Carmen, *Community-Based Corrections*, 8th ed. (Belmont, CA: Wadsworth, 2011).

66. David Ho, "Philadelphia Using Computers to Help Predict Murders," *Cox News Service*, January 5, 2007. See also Lawrence W. Sherman, "Use Probation to Prevent Murder," *Criminology and Public Policy* 6 (2007): 843.

67. The Good Lives Model, www.goodlivesmodel.com (accessed February 18, 2012).

2011 was a great year for Michael Vick.

He signed a $100 million contract to play football for the Philadelphia Eagles. However, things were not always so rosy. On July 18, 2007, a federal grand jury in Richmond indicted Vick and three other men on charges related to their alleged operation of a dogfighting ring based at a property that Vick owns in southeastern Virginia. According to the indictment, Vick decided in his rookie season of 2001 to start a dogfighting operation with two other defendants, Quanis Phillips and Tony Taylor. The indictment went on to say that this property was used as the main staging area for housing and training the pit bulls involved in the dogfighting and housing dogfights.[1] The indictment also stated that in April 2007, Purnell Peace, Phillips, and Vick "executed approximately eight dogs that did not perform well in testing sessions by various methods, including hanging, drowning, and/or slamming at least one dog's body to the ground."[2] On December 11, 2007, Vick was

sentenced up to 23 months in prison for running a dogfighting operation. Because he lied about his involvement in court, his sentence was longer than his two codefendants. On February 8, 2008, a federal judge ruled that Vick could keep all but $3.75 million of the nearly $20 million in bonus money he received from the Atlanta Falcons.[3]

On November 26, 2008, Vick pleaded guilty to a state

AP Photo/Steve Helber

Philadelphia Eagles quarterback Michael Vick is shown leaving a Newport News, Virginia, federal court after a bankruptcy hearing. Once reviled for his involvement in a dogfighting ring, Vick has emerged from the ashes (and prison) to become an NFL star. Was it necessary to put someone like Vick in prison, or would he have been a good candidate for community treatment? Was he really a threat to society?

dogfighting charge and received a three-year suspended prison sentence and a $2,500 fine on a charge of attending, sponsoring, and participating in dogfights. He also received four years of probation, and a fine that was dismissed when Vick paid his court costs and kept to his probation terms.[4] Vick was released from Leavenworth Penitentiary on May 21, 2009, and arrived home in Hampton, Virginia, that same day. He was released from home confinement in July 2009 and signed a contract to play for the Philadelphia Eagles.[5]

On December 29, 2010, President Obama called Jeffrey Lurie, the owner of the Philadelphia Eagles. Reports are that Obama praised him for taking a chance on Vick and lamented that, even after paying their debt to society, ex-cons rarely get such a second chance.[6] In 2011, until he was injured, Vick was having an MVP year. He has lectured all over the country on the horrors of dogfighting, and the terms of his probation, which he has filled without incident, will be over in 2012.[7]

chapter

Four

INTERMEDIATE SANCTIONS

LEARNING OBJECTIVES

LO1 Understand the benefits of intermediate sanctions

LO2 Identify the continuum of intermediate sanctions

LO3 Identify the sanctions that stand alone and what they contribute to intermediate sanctions

LO4 Identify the sanctions as an add-on to probation and what they contribute to intermediate sanctions

LO5 Identify the sanctions that include incarceration and what they contribute to intermediate sanctions

LO6 Understand the relationship between restorative justice and intermediate sanctions

LO7 Evaluate the effectiveness and future of intermediate sanctions

Michael Vick is one of the most promising athletes to come into the professional ranks in recent years. As quarterback for the Atlanta Falcons, beginning in the 2001 season, he had exciting moments on the football field. Then he was arrested, charged, convicted of dog-fighting and housing dogfights, and sentenced to federal prison. Should a person like Vick have been incarcerated? Does he present a danger to society? Or should his punishment serve a symbolic purpose, letting people know that no one is above the law? Forms of intermediate punishment were used on him. Following incarceration, he was placed on house arrest. Is he an example that intermediate sanctions work or are effective? Is his case similar to style guru Martha Stewart, who was convicted in a stock market scheme and sent to prison? Though no threat to society, some say she was incarcerated to set an example for others contemplating white-collar crimes. Is it fair to punish someone to send other people "a message"?

Many of those who have difficulty adjusting to probation or other sanctions pose little threat to society. It seems questionable to incarcerate them in an overcrowded and often violent prison system. It appears to make more sense, in terms of being more effective in reducing recidivism and less costly to society, to have them remain in the community in more intensive relationships than is true in traditional probation supervision. The public is concerned about the high recidivism rates of probationers and yet is unwilling to place young, inexperienced offenders in forbidding and dangerous prisons. As a consequence, local, state, and federal governments have developed a series of intermediate sanctions that enable offenders to avoid the harsh reality of prison life.

Intermediate sanctions emerged during the 1980s as a result of three trends:

- The belief that prisons were being overused for offenders who really did not need secure confinement, especially drug offenders

- Prison crowding that forced states to consider lower-cost, community-based alternatives that would impose "tough time" in the community without endangering the public

- Wide public support for "just desert" sentencing structures, sparking interest in creating community sanctions geared toward the seriousness of crime

 Rather than placing everyone on probation, the most serious offenders could receive the most severe community sanctions. The resulting intermediate sanctions provide a number of benefits:

- They are a cost-saving alternative to jails and prisons. Prisons, especially, are costly, ineffective, and damaging to inmates.

- They help reduce prison crowding and result in lower rates of recidivism.

- They can serve the needs of certain offenders who would ordinarily be sent to prison but are a low risk for recidivism and pose little danger to society.

- They can be used as a halfway-back strategy for probation and parole violators.

While these alleged advantages have been debated, what is most clear is that intermediate sanctions help fill the void between routine probation and prison. This may be a more defensible and obtainable goal than the reduction of prison crowding, cost, and offender recidivism.

Dr. Ronald P. Corbett, Jr., is commissioner of the Massachusetts Probation Department. In the Voices Across the Profession feature, he talks about his responsibilities and the various intermediate sanctions that are being conducted at the present time.

"One real satisfaction I have is in assisting probation staff to make changes in their lives so that they can be drug free, stay away from criminal behavior, and avoid disorder in their lives."

DR. RONALD P. CORBETT, JR.
COMMISSIONER OF PROBATION

The commissioner of probation is responsible for 2,000 employees over the state. We have branch offices that range from one to many probation officers. The chief is also responsible to make certain that staff conform with our practices. There is further the responsibility of hiring, firing, and evaluating the work of staff.

There are three major categories of intermediate sentencing in which we are involved:

- *Community correctional centers.* There are twenty adult centers and one juvenile center. We place high-risk cases in these centers.

- *Electronic monitoring (EM).* We are involved in two kinds—radio frequency, which is traditional and GPS, in which we have 24/7 supervision of offenders. We have a monitoring station in the middle of the state.

- *Problem-solving courts.* These are drug courts, mental health courts, and veteran courts.

Our biggest problem today is fiscal constraints. We have lost 16 percent of our management staff in the last few years. With our relatively stable offender population, this has meant fewer people chasing more cases. Another challenge is that we are working hard to implement evidence-based practices. We are trying to interface our practices with major research findings. We would like to reshape our practices into what works.

One real satisfaction I have is in assisting probation staff to make changes in their lives so that they can be drug free, stay away from criminal behavior, and avoid disorder in their lives. We want staff to have job readiness and to be successful in their jobs.

Source: Interviewed in 2011.

L02 THE CONTINUUM OF INTERMEDIATE SANCTIONS

Advocates for more effective sentencing are increasingly calling for a range of punishment options, providing graduated levels of supervision in the community. Judges are able to exercise discretion by selecting from a range of sentencing options, choosing the punishment that best fits the circumstances of the crime and the offender. Intermediate sanctions are said to allow judges to match the severity of punishment with the severity of the crime. Prisons, then, are treated as backstops, rather than backbones, of the corrections systems.[8]

Providing justice through a continuum of sanctions, ranging from being forced to pay a small fine to being placed in a community correctional facility, is now a routine element of corrections. The basic assumption behind intermediate sanctions, or alternative sanctions as they are sometimes called, is to escalate punishments to fit the crime. These sanctions are typically administered by probation departments. They involve such sanctions as intensive probation (which was examined in Chapter 3), financial restitution, community service, house arrest, and electronic monitoring. But they also involve sentences that are administered independently of probation, such as fines and forfeiture, day treatment programs, drug courts, and residential care. See Figure 4.1 for some of the range of intermediate sanctions now available.

Intermediate sanctions can be grouped from those less intrusive to offenders to those that are most intrusive. Fines are at one end of the continuum,

Fines

Sanctions that require convicted offenders to pay a specified sum of money.

Forfeiture

Sanctions that involve the government seizing property that was derived from or used in criminal action.

Restitution

Used alone or in conjunction with probation and requires completion of a payment or completion of hours of work in and for the community.

Community service orders

Court-imposed sanctions that order an offender to spend so many hours on the work project in the community.

House arrest and electronic monitoring

Offender sees probation officer three to five times a week. Probation officer also makes unscheduled visits to offender's home or workplace.

Drug courts

Sanctions designed for nonviolent offenders with substance abuse.

Day reporting centers

Clients report to a central location every day, where they file daily schedules with their supervising officer showing how each hour will be spent.

Shock probation and split sentencing

Sanctions that permit judges to grant offenders community release only after they had experienced incarceration.

Residential centers

Sanctions for selected inmates as a supplement to probation for those completing prison programs for some probation or parole violations.

Boot camps

Rigorous military-style regimen for younger offenders. Designed to accelerate punishment while instilling discipline, often with an educational component.

FIGURE 4.1 The Ladder of Intermediate Sanctions

traditional incarceration at the other. A variety of community-based corrections, such as intensive probation, community service, electronic monitoring and house arrest, and placement in residential settings, bridge the middle ground. Some of these sanctions are used in conjunction with other sanctions. Those who have been selected for intensive probation may also be assigned to house arrest and be placed on electronic monitoring. Other offenders may be sentenced to a period of confinement, such as split sentencing and shock probation. Residential confinement is a confinement that takes place prior to (halfway-in) or following imprisonment (halfway-back), and boot camps are also perceived as intermediate sanctions. See Table 4.1, which compares the various intermediate sanctions.

LO3 Intermediate sanctions are sanctions between relatively unsupervised probation on one end of the continuum and prison on the other end of the continuum. As the following discussion conveys, some of these sanctions are used more frequently than others, some are used in conjunction with other sanctions while others can be used alone, and some are used more often with juveniles than with adults.

Fines

Monetary sanctions, better known as **fines** (from the Latin term *finis*, "end," as in to end the criminal matter), can be traced to the early common-law practice of requiring that compensation be paid to the victim and the state for criminal acts. Fines are more commonly used in Europe, where they are frequently the sole punishment, even in cases involving chronic offenders who commit fairly serious offenses. Nonetheless, over $1 billion in fines are collected each year in the United States.

The purpose of fines is to equalize the financial impact of sentences on offenders. They are more frequently used in cases involving misdemeanors and lesser offenses, but they are also used in felony cases when the offender benefited financially from wrongful behavior. Fines may be used as a sole sanction or they may be combined with probation or a time in jail.

Judges sometimes claim that the reason they do not make greater use of the fine is the difficulty of collecting from offenders, who frequently are poor and who may use additional illegal acts as a means to pay their fines. Other judges contend that relying on fines may end up permitting affluent offenders to buy their way out of other punishment. While recognizing that incarcerating a person who is financially unable to pay a fine discriminates against the poor, many judges continue to incarcerate offenders for noncompliance with court orders.[9]

Prevailing evidence seems to support that judges use fines in a rational and reasonable way. Low-risk offenders are the ones most likely to receive fines

FINE A sanction that requires convicted offenders to pay a specified sum of money.

TABLE 4.1 Comparison of the Various Intermediate Sanctions

Sanctions that Stand Alone	
Fines	The court requires convicted offenders to pay a specified sum of money.
Forfeiture	The government seizes property that was derived from or used in criminal action.
Drug courts	The court assigns nonviolent offenders with substance abuse problems to these courts.
Day reporting centers	Clients report to a central location every day, where they file daily schedules with their supervising officer showing how each hour will be spent.
Sanctions as an Add-On to Probation	
Restitution	Used alone or in conjunction with probation and requires completing of a payment.
Community service orders	Court-imposed sanction that orders an offender to spend so many hours on the work project in the community.
Intensive probation	Offender sees probation officer three to five times a week. Probation officer also makes unscheduled visits to offender's home or workplace.
House arrest and electronic monitoring	Offender is confined to the house or required to wear electronic monitoring device, usually around the ankle, when he or she leaves the house.
Sanctions that Include Incarceration	
Residential centers	Used as a supplement to probation for some probation or parole violators.
Shock probation and split sentencing	Sanctions that permit judges to grant offenders community release only after they have experienced incarceration.
Work release centers	Offenders are released to these centers following incarceration as a form of gradual integration into the community.
Boot camps	Rigorous military-style regimen for younger offenders. Designed to accelerate punishment while instilling discipline, often with an education component.

instead of jail confinement: the more serious the crime, the higher the fine. Yet there has been little research finding that fines reduce recidivism rates.

DAY FINES Day fines, which are also used more frequently in Europe than in the United States, are designed to equalize the financial impact of sentences on offenders. The **day fine** addresses the concern that fines are unduly harsh on poor offenders but permit affluent offenders to buy their way out of more punitive sanctions. This concept originated in Europe, and the first day fines pilot program in the United States was designed and conducted by the Vera Institute of Justice in Staten Island, New York, between 1987 and 1989.

MYTH Fines are only used in minor cases such as traffic offenses.

FACT Fines are probably the most widely used sanction in the United States and are commonly employed in serious felony offenses. In some white-collar crimes, fines can be in the hundreds of millions of dollars.

DAY FINE A fine that represents one day of income for the defendant.

Day fines are catching on in the United States, and programs have been initiated in Arizona, Connecticut, Iowa, New York, and Oregon, among other states.[10] Judges in Phoenix use a form of day fine called FARE (Financial Assessment Related to Employability) probation. Under a FARE probation sentence, a certain number of units are assigned to a particular offense based on its seriousness—for example, 30 units for credit card forgery and 160 units for a burglary. Each unit is given a dollar value based on the offender's income. The penalty amounts range widely, from $180 for a laborer with six children who was convicted of making a false statement in an unemployment claim, to $22,000 for a restaurant owner who was convicted of money laundering.[11]

The day fine has the promise of becoming an equitable solution to the problem of setting fines for varying offenders. However, problems remain—such as discrimination against the poor, the difficulty of collecting fines, and the perception that day fines are a weak punishment. The other problem is that there is little or no evidence concerning the effectiveness of fines in terms of reducing recidivism.[12]

Forfeiture

Forfeiture involves the government seizing property that was derived from or used in criminal activity. It goes back to the Middle Ages, in which "forfeiture of estate" was a mandatory result of most felony convictions; the king could seize the property of someone convicted of a crime against the state. The modern application of forfeiture is related to the passage of the Racketeer Influenced and Corrupt Organization (RICO) Act and the Continuing Criminal Enterprise (CCE) Act, both of which permit the seizure of any property derived from illegal conspiracies or enterprises. These acts initially were designed to apply to criminal conspiracies, but they are now being applied to an extensive series of criminal acts, including white-collar crimes. In fact, more than 100 federal statutes currently use forfeiture of property as a punishment.[13] There are two forms of forfeiture—civil and criminal.[14]

CIVIL FORFEITURE The purpose of **civil forfeiture** is to confiscate property used in violation of the law and to remove the illegally gained profits from violators. Civil forfeitures are *in rem*, which means that the legal action is directly and solely against the property based on a legal finding that the property itself was used in an illegal manner. An *in rem* proceeding is not an action against a violator but against the property involved, and is a separate legal action from any criminal actions taken against the violator.

Civil forfeiture can be accomplished through administrative and/or judicial means. Administrative proceedings are conducted by the seizing agencies, while judicial proceedings are conducted in a court before a judge. The value and type of seized property and whether the forfeiture is contested determine the proceeding used.

CRIMINAL FORFEITURE Under criminal law, forfeiture takes place following conviction and requires that offenders relinquish assets related to the crime. **Criminal forfeiture** takes place as part of the criminal process, while civil forfeiture does not involve a criminal action taken against the violator. The purpose of a criminal forfeiture is to punish the violator, and it is imposed as part of that punishment following conviction. Upon completion of a criminal trial, if the defendant is found guilty, criminal forfeiture proceedings are conducted in the court before a judge. The proceedings may result in a verdict forfeiting property used in the crime or obtained with proceedings from the crime. For instance, under federal law, after arresting drug traffickers, the government can seize the boats they used to import the narcotics, the vehicles they used to carry the drugs overland, the warehouses in which the drugs were stored, and the homes they paid for with drug profits.

Since the attacks of September 11, 2001, forfeiture has been used to disrupt terrorist activities. Terrorist organizations, it can be argued, are a species of

FORFEITURE Involves the government seizing property that was derived from or used in criminal activity.

CIVIL FORFEITURE To confiscate property used in law violations and remove the illegally gained profits from violators.

CRIMINAL FORFEITURE Following conviction, offenders must relinquish assets related to the offense.

organized crime, motivated by ideological or political ends. They are usually quite clever in finding ways of money laundering, which is a process designed to give illegally obtained property the appearance of having been legally obtained. Terrorists may use the same laundering methods that organized crime groups adopt, such as shell companies and trusts. The challenge for federal officials is the seizure, detention, and forfeiture of terrorist cash.[15]

However, the use of forfeiture has met with considerable criticism. There are those who claim that the government has been overzealous in the use of forfeiture. For example, million-dollar yachts have been seized because someone aboard had a small amount of marijuana. This confiscatory practice is known as *zero tolerance*. It is also claimed that forfeiture unfairly targets a narrow range of offenders. Government employees, for instance, involved in corruption commonly forfeit their pensions, but employees of public companies are exempt from such punishments. It is further charged that the Civil Asset Forfeiture Reform Act (CAFRA) of 2000 is not responsible for significant change in the practice of civil asset forfeiture because it fails to address problems associated with assets' forfeiture and has a questionable standard of proof.[16] Finally, critics note that law enforcement is involved in a conflict of interest. Law enforcement agencies can use forfeited assets to supplement their budgets and, therefore, they may focus on cases that promise the greatest payoff rather than ones that have the highest law enforcement priority.[17]

Financial Restitution

Financial restitution (from the Latin term *restitutionem*, restoring) is payment of a sum of money by the offender either to the victim or to a public fund for victims of crime. This payment for the victim or victim's family is how financial restitution differs from fines. The amount is usually based on the crime and, in some instances, on the offender's ability to pay. Judges will sometimes order a wealthy offender's compensation be paid out of income that is derived from performing a public works or low-paid social service job, in order to avoid the situation in which a wealthy offender can easily fill a restitution order by merely writing a check.

The twin purposes of financial restitution are to compensate victims for their losses and to teach offenders financial responsibility. Offenders who do not have the resources to make their restitution payments may be confined to a correctional facility at night while they are employed elsewhere during the day to earn money for their payments.

About 30 states now operate restitution centers. Some evidence indicates that restitution may make an important contribution to the effectiveness of community sanctions. R. B. Rubeck and colleagues found from their study of financial restitution in four Pennsylvania counties that the likelihood of arrest went down as the proportion of restitution paid increased.[18]

Financial restitution offers several positive outcomes to the justice process. It can offer offenders a chance to avoid a jail or prison sentence. It can help victims regain lost property and income, and it can return something to the community without asking the community to foot the bill for an incarceration stay.

Community Service

A **community service order** is a court order that requires an offender to work a certain number of hours at a private nonprofit or government agency. Two general patterns have emerged for structuring community obligations: (1) referring

On June 29, 2011, Jimmy Tebeau sings with his Grateful Dead cover band, Schwag, at a concert at the Blue Note in Columbia, Missouri. Tebeau owns an Ozarks "campitheater" that hosts national touring acts and thousands of fans at weekend festivals. Federal prosecutors charged him with one count of maintaining a drug premises. That follows a civil lawsuit seeking forfeiture of the 350-acre property and nearly $200,000 in fines. Under forfeiture statutes, to seize the property the prosecution does not need to convict Tebeau of a crime but merely show a "preponderance of evidence" that the property was part of criminal activity. The case is still ongoing.

AP Photo/L.G. Patterson

FINANCIAL RESTITUTION The purposes of financial restitution are to compensate victims for their losses and to teach offenders financial responsibility.

COMMUNITY SERVICE ORDER A court order that requires an offender to perform a certain number of work hours at a private nonprofit or government agency.

offenders to community agencies that handle the work placement and supervise completion of the community service obligation and (2) assigning a group of offenders to provide a community service. The number of hours of community service to be completed is generally determined by the court or sometimes by program staff. Commonly assigned public service projects include cleanup work on the local streets or in city parks, volunteer service in hospitals or in nursing homes, and repair jobs in rundown housing.

At first, community service sentencing was used to permit misdemeanants, traffic defendants, minor property offenders, and other offenders who could not pay their fines to work off their obligations by working without pay for the community. Community service sentences were considered a rehabilitative alternative to jail sentences.

Today, some form of community service is used in all 50 states. Georgia, Texas, and Washington are three states that widely use community service. About one-third of Washington's convicted felons are sentenced to community service, substituting eight hours of community service for one day of incarceration. Offenders in Georgia work 1.6 million hours of community service.[19] In Texas, two-thirds of the state's corrections departments operate a specialized community service restitution unit, which is used two-thirds of the time as a supplement to probation supervision.[20]

Community service has many advocates because it can relieve jail and prison crowding by diverting certain kinds of offenders. Nevertheless, community service programs are difficult to design, implement, and manage. A program must appear punitive enough to satisfy the public that justice is being served. A sizeable staff is also needed to keep track of convicted offenders doing community service.

House Arrest

House arrest is a court-imposed sentence ordering that an offender remain confined to his or her own residence for a specific amount of time. Home confinement ranges from evening curfew to detention during all nonworking hours to continuous confinement at home. House arrest can last from several days to several years. For example, a person convicted of a drunk-driving charge might be sentenced to spend from 6 P.M. Friday to 8 A.M. Monday and every weekday after 5:30 P.M. in their home for a number of months. Current estimates reveal that more than 10,000 people are under house arrest.

The concept of house arrest, or home confinement, tends to vary from one jurisdiction to another. Some programs are administered by probation departments and others are merely judicial sentences that are monitored by surveillance officers. The Florida Community Control Program checks clients 20 or more times a month, but others only do a few curfew checks. Varying programs also produce varying degrees of offender control. Some use 24-hour confinements, while others permit offenders to attend work or school.

The most severe form of home confinement, or house arrest, requires offenders to remain in their homes, other than when they have permission to leave for employment, religious services, and medical reasons. The sanctions of house arrest can stand alone or be coupled with electronic monitoring, fines, community service, and other obligations. Monitoring techniques, a sanction widely used with home confinement, range from periodic visits or telephone calls to continuous monitoring using electronic equipment.

In the federal courts, the **home confinement program** is used with both postsentence offenders (to punish) and with pretrial defendants (to ensure their appearance in court and to protect the community). Home confinement is also used as an intermediate sanction for supervision violators and by the Bureau of Prisons for inmates in prerelease status serving the last 10 percent of their imprisonment term under the direction of probation officers. One recent study of the federal home confinement program found that house arrest can serve as an effective crime deterrent and that it lowers the recidivism rate. However, defendants with drug charges appeared to have a higher risk of flight and to pose more of a danger to the community than defendants charged with crimes against property.[21]

HOUSE ARREST A court-imposed sentence that orders an offender to remain confined in his or her residence for the duration or remainder of the sentence.

HOME CONFINEMENT PROGRAM The federal courts use this program with both postsentence offenders and with pretrial defenders.

Another study found that offenders most likely to complete the period of supervision are older, are sentenced for multiple charges, serve longer sentences, accrue fewer violations, come from less criminogenic neighborhoods, and are serving a sentence for a DIU-related offense. Significant predictors of rearrest include being sentenced for multiple charges and being younger, African American, and male.[22]

In sum, the advantages of house arrest in reducing costs and overcrowding in the correctional system clearly make further experimentation desirable. There may also be some unanticipated advantages of house arrest. For example, house arrest keeps offenders' family relations intact, and those with health problems can maintain better access to health care in the community than in prison.[23] Yet home confinement is a labor-intensive and time-consuming form of community supervision and can be dangerous. Officers provide round-the-clock coverage and respond to electronic monitoring alerts 24 hours a day. Home confinement also requires officers to make more frequent home and community visits, often in response to alerts signaling that participants may have violated program rules.[24]

ELECTRONIC MONITORING (EM) The use of electronic equipment to verify that an offender is at home or in a community correctional center during specified hours.

Electronic Monitoring (EM)

For house arrest to be effective, supervising officers must be certain that arrestees are actually at home when they are supposed to be there. Although random calls and visits are one way to check on compliance, **electronic monitoring (EM)** adds another way to determine whether offenders are complying with their home confinement orders.

Electronic monitoring can be traced back to 1964 when an electronic telemetry system based on a triangulation process using radio signals was adapted for possible criminal justice applications. During the mid-1960s, electronic monitoring systems were used in Boston to determine the location of mental patients, research volunteers, and parolees. The initial systems used multiple receivers to trace movement throughout specified areas. The number of receivers used and transmission characteristics of the environment depended on the size of the monitored area.

Electronic monitoring is usually applied in one of two ways. It can be a sanction in and of itself, or it can be used in conjunction with other sanctions—for example, offenders receive a prison or jail sanction and then are placed on electronic monitoring when they are released to the community.[25] In addition to probationers, EM can also be used with bailees and with parolees. Offenders who are electronically monitored wear devices around their wrists, ankles, or necks that send signals to a control office. There are four basic types of systems that are used: active phone line systems, passive phone line systems, remote location monitoring, and global positioning systems (GPS).

ACTIVE PHONE LINE SYSTEMS
This type of EM employs a transmitter that is attached to an offender's ankle; the receiver is inside the offender's home. The active system continually monitors offenders as the transmitter

The United States is not the only nation to employ electronic monitoring and house arrest. Here, WikiLeaks founder Julian Assange is seen with his ankle security tag at the house where he is required to stay, near Bungay, England, on June 15, 2011. Assange says his house arrest over sex allegations is hampering the work of the secret-spilling site, and his supporters accuse Britain of spying on him. The 39-year-old Australian has spent six months at a supporter's rural estate as he fights extradition to Sweden, where he is accused of the rape and sexual assault of two women. The case is still being considered in the British court system.

GLOBAL POSITIONING SYSTEM (GPS)
TECHNOLOGY This has effected EM technology by the transmitter making continuous calls to a reporting station that updates
the offender's location.

sends a signal to the central office. If offenders leave their home at an unauthorized time, this breaks the signal. A computer sends a report of the violation to a central computer, and the failure is recorded. In some cases the control officer is immediately notified by pager.

PASSIVE PHONE LINE SYSTEMS Passive systems lack a continuous signal from a transmitter to a receiver. They generally involve random phone calls generated by computers, to which offenders must respond within a certain time frame such as 30 seconds. The offender verifies his or her presence at home by placing the transmitter on the verifier box. More recent methods of confirmation permit offenders to provide voice verification or visual verification by still-picture video phone.

REMOTE LOCATION MONITORING This type of EM monitors an offender periodically or continuously throughout the day and night by means of a pager number that only the probation officer knows. The offender is instructed to call the probation officer when the pager beeps. The computer is able to determine whether or not the offender's voice matches the voice sample associated with the phone number where the call originated. Voice verification is able to determine a positive match between the voice sample and the voice on the phone.[26]

GLOBAL POSITIONING SYSTEMS EM technology has been altered dramatically by the introduction of **global positioning system (GPS) technology**. The Satellite Monitoring and Remote Tracking (SMART) program monitors offenders equipped with a GPS receiver with a microprocessor and an ankle transmitter device. The offender must remain within 100 feet of the portable receiver. The transmitter makes continuous calls to a reporting station that updates the offender's location, which is tracked by a computer.[27] The TechnoCorrections feature focuses on some of the various technology-aided services provided by EM systems.

EM TODAY More than 150,000 offenders, or approximately 20 percent of community-based supervision in the United States, are monitored at home.[28] Electronic monitoring equipment is being provided by some 20 private companies. Internationally, about 20 percent of 50,000 offenders in England and Wales who started pre- or postrelease supervision receive electronic monitoring. In Sweden, about 25 percent of all inmates are placed on electronic monitoring.[29]

Electronic monitoring advocates see many advantages to this intermediate sanction. It has relatively low cost and high security; it helps offenders avoid overcrowded and often dangerous prison environments. EM also is cost effective because offenders are monitored by computers, and an initial investment in technology can help avoid the cost of hiring more supervising officers to handle larger numbers of offenders. The public, as would be expected, supports EM, in that it provides greater security for offenders. Offenders, at least according to some surveys, prefer EM to incarceration.[30] Furthermore, EM can be used in a pretrial diversionary program, to enhance probation, or as a post-prison release sanction.[31]

However, EM does have its critics. It is claimed that this sanction is not really an alternative to incarceration but simply a new sentencing alternative that widens the net of criminal justice control. There are those who hold that offenders sentenced to EM are actually offenders who in the past would have been informally diverted from the justice system.[32] It is also held that EM has privacy issues and erodes privacy and liberty. It is further questioned whether citizens should be watched over by a computer and whether it will be employed with inappropriate offenders, such as

MYTH
Electronic monitoring of criminals is a science fiction fantasy that is based on pie in the sky technology.

FACT
EM provides a positive intermediate sanction for the justice system and is a cost-effective way of keeping offenders out of prison. There is growing evidence that it can reduce recidivism.

People usually think of electronic systems as a technological method to keep tabs on offenders in the community. However, use of the technology is expanding into a variety of applications. For example, at Bryan Adams High School in East Dallas, Texas, students who have been chronically truant are now being monitored with a global positioning system, which tracks their whereabouts 24/7 in a court-ordered attempt to keep truants in school. Across the state, in Midland, county officials started using electronic ankle monitors to track the most chronically truant students.

The use of EM to track criminal offenders who are granted community release should also expand as systems become more sophisticated. Some of the services provided by EM systems include the following:

- *Programmed contact systems* are used to contact and verify the location of offenders in their homes or elsewhere.

- *Identity verification devices* can recognize different parts of the body to ensure that the reporting person is the offender.

- *Remote alcohol detention devices* require users to blow into the device to measure blood alcohol content. Another type is Tattle Tale, which can detect alcohol or drug use by the offender. It senses these substances through the pores and perspiration.

- *Ignition interlock devices* are linked to the electrical systems of automobiles.

The driver expels deep lung air into the device, and the vehicle will not start if the driver's blood alcohol content is registered above a level deemed unsafe for driving.

- *Victim notification systems* alert the victim when the offender is approaching his or her residence. A transmitter is worn by both the offender and the victim, and a receiver is placed at both residences.

- *Field monitoring devices*, or drive-by units, are used by probation or parole officers or other authorities. They are portable devices that can be handheld or used in a vehicle with a roof-mounted antenna. When within 200 to 800 feet of an offender's ankle or wrist transmitter, the portable device can detect the transmitter's radio signals.

- *Group monitoring units* permit supervisors to monitor several offenders in the same location, in order to verify attendance of multiple offenders in a day-reporting program or to monitor offenders confined in a residential group setting.

- *GPS (global positioning system) location tracking systems* have receivers that detect satellite signals relating the exact time the signal is sent and the identity of the satellite sending the signal. This expensive technology, which

is generally used for high-risk offenders, can determine when an offender leaves an area where he or she is supposed to be (inclusion zone) or enters an area where he or she is not allowed to be (exclusion zone) as ordered by a judge. For example, Massachusetts Probation Services has implemented GPS to track sex offenders being supervised by probation who have been deemed appropriate for this type of supervision. If an offender enters an area from which they have been restricted, an alert goes off. A probation employee contacts the offender on a specialized GPS cell phone to find out why they entered the area and instruct them to leave. If the offender does not comply, the employee contacts a probation officer and an arrest warrant may be issued.

These and other EM systems should revolutionize community supervision, allowing more people to be placed in intermediate sanction programs without compromising community safety.

Sources: Sam Merten, "For Whom the Bell Tolls," *Dallas Observer*, June 26, 2008, www.dallasobserver.com/2008-06-26/news/for-whom; iSecureTrac Systems, Omaha, Nebraska, www.isecuretrac.com/Services.aspx?p=EMManagement; Massachusetts Probation Service, "The Electronic Monitoring Program Fact Sheet," www.mass.gov/courts/probation/elmofactsheet.pdf (all sites accessed February 20, 2012).

mental patients, suicidal adolescents, or even high-risk future offenders.[33] Moreover, it does provide a false sense of security, because knowing where someone is does not substitute for knowing what they are doing.

IS ELECTRONIC MONITORING EFFECTIVE? The issue of the ability of EM to reduce recidivism is an important one. The effectiveness of EM is still open for debate, but several recent studies have produced positive results.[34] For example, Kathy G. Padgett and her colleagues found that the EM program for public intoxication saved money and avoided new construction costs, without widening the net of social control. This study examined 75,661 offenders placed on home confinement in Florida and found that both radio frequency and global positioning system monitoring significantly reduced the likelihood of technical violations, reoffending, and absconding for this population of offenders. In addition, Padgett found that those placed on home confinement with EM had original charges that were significantly more serious than those placed on home confinement without EM, which challenges the net-widening charge that is sometimes made of this intermediate sanction. It appears that electronic monitoring of offenders in the community can prove to be an effective public safety alternative to prison.[35]

Drug Courts

About 80 percent of offenders in the United States were under the influence of drugs or alcohol at the time of their arrest or had a serious history of substance abuse.[36] It is not surprising therefore that intermediate sanctions have been aimed at treating the drug-involved offender.

This problem was particularly vexing when judges were left with prison as their only sentencing option for nonviolent offenders who had substance abuse problems. In 1989, at the request of presiding Judge Gerald Wetherington in Miami's Eleventh Judicial Circuit, Judge Herbert Klein proposed a strategy for dealing with the large number of drug offenders. Judge Klein's recommendation was simple: "We could help them."[37] And he proposed using **drug courts** as the means to treat drug offenders within the community.

Drug courts are designed for nonviolent offenders with substance abuse problems who require integrated sanctions and services, including (a) mandatory periodic testing for the use of controlled substances; (b) substance abuse treatment; (c) diversion, probation, or other supervised release; and (d) aftercare services such as relapse prevention, health care, education, vocational training, job placement, housing placement, and child care.

In the larger court community, Judge Klein's recommendation was initially met with an uncomfortable silence, but Judge Klein and his leadership helped drug courts become popular in Florida. Other drug courts began in Oakland, California, and the drug court movement received considerable federal support. The First National Drug Court Conference was held in Miami in December 1993. The term *drug court*, as well as the components of the drug court model, soon became common in the everyday language of criminal justice, and the ideas that underlie drug courts began to be applied in other contexts. The development of the drug courts model certainly was helped by the fact that Janet Reno, the attorney general during the Clinton administration, was one of its early proponents and supported funding for drug courts, including the 1994 Crime Act. Drug courts began to be used experimentally in Australia, Britain, and Iceland.[38] Drug courts began rapidly proliferating in the United States in the 1990s and the early years of the twenty-first century. There are more than 2,232 drug courts operating in the United States, with 204 additional drug courts in various planning stages. Drug courts are operating or being planned in 50 states, 3 U.S. territories, 62 Native American tribal courts, and 8 countries. Several states, including New York, California, Arizona, and Florida, have implemented statewide drug diversion initiatives for all nonviolent, nonrecidivist drug offenders.[39] The key elements of drug courts are set out in Exhibit 4.1 on page 97.

ARE DRUG COURTS EFFECTIVE? Adele Harrell, a drug court specialist, has argued: "The development of drug courts is a paradigm shift from court practices designed for fast and efficient delivery of penalties to court practices designed for crime prevention."[40] Still, Harrell cautions that while drug courts may be effective for some offenders, they are not a magic bullet, as many offenders involved in these courts fail.[41] There is every reason to believe that as less treatable groups participate, rates of compliance and graduation will decline and recidivism will increase.[42] Nonetheless, the success and acceptance of drug courts have prompted the creation of other specialized courts, including domestic violence courts, gun courts, and mental health courts, which employ similar principles.[43] The effectiveness of drug

DRUG COURTS Courts designed for nonviolent offenders with substance abuse problems who require integrated sanctions and services such as mandatory drug testing, substance abuse treatment, supervised release, and parole.

EVIDENCE-BASED CORRECTIONS

Are Drug Courts Effective?

Drug courts are currently being established throughout the nation and the initial evaluations have been favorable. A number of evidence-based evaluations conducted in Miami, Philadelphia, and Las Vegas reveal that drug courts can produce comparatively lower rates of recidivism. Using a nationally representative sample (including all drug courts that had been in operation for at least one year and had at least 40 program graduates), the National Institute of Justice and the Drug Court Program Office found that within one year 16 percent of drug court graduates had been arrested and charged with a serious offense (84 percent success rate), and within two years, 28 percent had been arrested and charged with a serious offense (73 percent success rate). The programs seem to work best for high-risk offenders who might normally have been sent to prison.

An analysis of the Multnomah Drug Court Program in Oregon also found the program was a success. The analysis looked at the overall impact of the drug court on the target population over time, variations over time on that impact, and external and internal conditions that influenced outcomes. A cost analysis was also conducted to assess the overall investment of taxpayer money in the court compared to its benefits. During the study period of 1991 through 2001, the entire population of offenders identified as eligible for drug court by the Multnomah County District Attorney's Office was identified and tracked through a variety of administrative data systems. Approximately 11,000 cases were identified; 6,500 participated in the drug court program during that period, and 4,600 had their case processed outside the drug court model. Data on outcomes were gathered including criminal recidivism, investment costs, outcome costs, and total costs per participant.

The researchers found that re-arrests were lower five years or more later compared to rearrests for similar drug offenders within the same county. They also found, however, that the drug courts' impact on recidivism varied by year as a result of changes in programming and judge assignments over time. Reductions in recidivism ranged from 17 to 26 percent.

Compared to traditional criminal justice system processing, treatment and other investment costs averaged $1,392 lower per drug court participant. Reduced recidivism and other long-term program outcomes resulted in public savings of $6,744 on average ($12,218 if victimization costs are included), or an estimated $79 million over 10 years.

Although general research findings are that drug courts can reduce recidivism and promote other positive outcomes such as cost savings, several factors affect a drug court program's success:

- Proper assessment and treatment
- The role assumed by the judge and the nature of offender interactions with the judge
- Other variable influences such as drug use trends, staff turnover, and resource allocation

Sources: Douglas B. Marlowe, "Evidence-Based Policies and Practices for Drug-Involved Offenders," *Prison Journal* 9 (2011): 27–47; Michael W. Finigan, Shannon M. Carey, and Anton Cox, "Impact of a Mature Drug Court over 10 Years of Operation: Recidivism and Costs," NPC Research, Inc., 2007; National Institute of Justice, "Do Drug Courts Work? Findings from Drug Court Research," http://nij.gov/nij/topics/courts/drug-courts/work.htm (accessed February 20, 2012).

courts is set out more fully in the Evidence-Based Corrections feature.

See Careers in Corrections for information about substance abuse counselors, key participants in drug courts. They are also needed in therapeutic communities, detoxification units, short-term residential programs, and outpatient treatment—such as antabuse, drug education classes, relapse prevention, and methadone or naltrexone maintenance.

MYTH Drug courts are a fad that looks good on paper but does not work in practice.

FACT Drug courts represent a major improvement in how drug offenders are treated by the criminal justice system. Though program and recidivism rates remain high for graduates from these programs, drug courts are a far more effective and more rehabilitative way of handling drug offenders than costly and often dangerous prison settings.

Day Reporting Centers

Day reporting is another form of intermediate sanction. The offender is assigned to a facility where he or she must report on a regular basis or at a specific time every day to participate in activities such as counseling, social skills training, and employment training. The goals of

SUBSTANCE ABUSE COUNSELOR

Preparation for the Job

The applicant needs an undergraduate education in psychology and substance abuse courses. A certificate in addiction or substance abuse would also be helpful.

Nature of the Job

Counselors help people with personal, family, educational, mental health, and career decisions and problems. Their specific duties are dependent upon the individual they serve and where they work. Substance abuse counselors will counsel persons who are addicted to drugs or alcohol, helping them to identify behaviors and problems related to the addiction, and then assisting them in changing the behavior. They may create and conduct programs to prevent addiction. They may work in a variety of settings, such as residential treatment facilities, prisons, or private offices.

Qualifications and Required Education

Forty-eight states and the District of Columbia have some form of counselor license that governs their practice of counseling, which typically requires a master's degree. Candidates may need a master's degree in social work or a related field from an accredited school to meet this requirement. Within the graduate program, one will also have to complete a period of supervised clinical internship experience. Counselors will also have to participate in workshops and personal studies to maintain their certificates and licensures. Candidates may also need 2 years or 3,000 hours of supervised clinical experience beyond the master's degree, passage of a state exam, adherence to ethical codes and standards, and annual continuing education courses. One should check with the state and the place one wishes to work to find out all the requirements.

Job Outlook

Overall, employment of counselors is expected to be excellent. Drug courts, residential confinement, therapeutic communities, detoxification units, short-term treatment programs, and institutional positions are expected to continue to increase. Demand is expected to be strong because drug offenders are increasingly being sent to treatment programs rather than jail. Job openings will also occur as counselors retire or leave the profession.

Earnings and Benefits

The mean annual salary for this position is $34,800. Government employers generally pay the highest wages, followed by hospitals and social service agencies. Residential care facilities often pay the lowest wages. The lowest mean annual salary for this position is $25,310, and the highest mean annual salary is $44,920.

Sources: "Counselors," *Occupational Outlook Handbook*, 2010–2011 Edition (Bureau of Labor Statistics, U.S. Department of Labor), www.bls.gov/oco/ocos067.htm (accessed February 20, 2012); "Alcohol and Drug Abuse Counselors," from *Ferguson's Careers in Focus: Social Work*, 2nd ed. (New York: Facts on File, 2006).

DAY REPORTING CENTER (DRC) A facility where an offender, usually on probation, must report every day to participate in counseling, social skills training, and other rehabilitative activities.

the **day reporting center (DRC)** are to provide a punishment in a cost-effective way, to ensure community safety, and to rehabilitate the offender through intensive programming. The number of contacts per week is normally greater than offenders would receive through normal community supervision, and the programs provide or refer offenders to services that are not available to offenders outside the DRC or are not available in as focused or intensive a manner.[44]

Day reporting centers can trace their origins to the British experience with probation day centers in the 1970s and the 1980s. The purpose of these probation centers was to divert offenders whose problems seemed to be linked to personal inadequacies. Several communities in the United States created day treatment programs to deliver therapeutic services to at-risk youth and deinstitutionalized mental patients. Over a 10-year period, beginning in the mid-1980s, the number of day reporting centers grew from a handful clustered in a few states to 114 programs in 22 states.[45]

Little evidence supports that DRCs contribute to lower rates of recidivism. A North Carolina study compared the outcome of probationers sentenced to day reporting centers along with intensive supervision to those sentenced to intensive probation alone, and it found that the addition of the day reporting center component did not reduce the rearrest rates.[46] A Cook County, Illinois, study did find that the day reporting center clients who remained in the program for at least 70 days had not been rearrested compared to one-quarter of the control group (those in the program less than 10 days). Also, two-thirds of the DRC clients remaining in the program for at least 70 days had not been reincarcerated compared with less than one-half of the control group.[47] On balance, day reporting centers remain a promising intervention, although they may require another intermediate sanction, such as intensive probation, to increase the rates of those who finish the program.

Shock Probation and Split Sentencing

Shock probation and split sentencing are intermediate sanctions that permit judges to grant offenders community release only after they have experienced incarceration. In recent years, shock probation has been largely replaced by shock incarceration, or boot camps, which will be discussed later in this chapter. The major difference between shock probation and shock incarceration programs relates to the required participation in drills and physical training in boot camp prison settings that are components of the recent shock incarceration programs.

Shock probation had its beginnings in Ohio in 1965 and has been used in Kentucky, North Carolina, Texas, Indiana, Idaho, and Maine. Ordinarily, a felon is sent to prison (usually at least for 30 days but less than 60 days) in states that have shock probation, and his or her attorney can submit a motion to suspend the remainder of the sentence and to release him or her on probation. Until the court acts on the petition, the institutionalized inmate remains uncertain about how much more time he or she will spend in prison. This sanction is based on the premise that if offenders are given a taste of incarceration, this will be sufficient to shock them into law-abiding behavior, and they will be reluctant to violate probation or commit another crime.[48]

Split sentencing is also a standard feature in many states with intensive supervision programs. The split sentence had its beginning in the federal system and requires the probationer to serve a period of confinement. Intermittent confinement means weekend, night, or vacation confinement in jail during the time a person is on probation. More than 10 percent of probationers are now given split sentences. Split sentencing, like shock probation, is based on the premise that a short jail stay or an intermittent jail stay will shock the person into law-abiding behavior.

Both shock probation and split sentencing have received praise as ways to limit prison time, maintain family ties, reintegrate the offender into the community, reduce the costs of corrections, and reduce prison populations. It is argued that even a short jail or prison sentence will make offenders more receptive to the conditions of probation because it is a warning of what awaits them if probation is violated. However, there are those who argue that shock probation and split sentencing interfere with the purpose of probation, which is to provide offenders with a nonstigmatizing, community-based treatment. These critics argue that even a short-term institutional confinement subjects a person to the stigmatizing and destructive effects of confinement.

Residential Community Corrections Centers

The role of reentry to the community was traditionally supplied by the nonsecure **halfway house**. Its purpose was to be a point of reentry for paroled or soon-to-be paroled prison inmates. Inmates would spend the last few months of their confinement in these facilities, as they were given an opportunity to learn such skills as interviewing and acquiring suitable jobs, obtaining a place to live, and managing a checking account.

Halfway houses continue to serve as prerelease centers for inmates soon to be paroled, but they also serve as intermediate sanctions. The main types of halfway houses for probationers are called probation centers, restitution centers, county work-release centers, and therapeutic communities. These programs usually are reserved for probationers who are having problems adjusting to community supervision.

Residential community corrections centers have further served as residential pretrial release centers for offenders who require immediate need of social services before their trial and as halfway-back alternatives for probation and parole violators who get a last chance before being sentenced to a correctional institution. These programs are sometimes used as a base from which offenders can be placed in drug and alcohol treatment programs, job training, and outpatient psychiatric facilities.

There are more than 2,000 state-operated community-based facilities in use today. In addition, up to 2,500 private, nonprofit programs operate in the United States. About half are used as halfway-back facilities for ex-offenders who have been released from prison, and the other half are true intermediate sanctions, including about 400 federally sponsored programs. Community-based residential treatment programs for drug users have also been increasingly developed.[49]

HALFWAY HOUSE These can vary from probation centers, restitution centers, county work-release centers, and therapeutic communities.

RESIDENTIAL COMMUNITY CORRECTIONS CENTERS Residential centers for offenders that frequently offer a last chance before an offender is sent to prison or a last chance for parole violators.

Some counties have established work-release facilities to provide more intensive services for offenders who need more than probation but less than prison. Finally, some therapeutic communities, particularly those in Minnesota, are reserved for offenders who have committed serious crimes. They are characterized by almost total reliance on in-house resources and confrontation groups (encounter groups and intensive attack therapies).

There has been a significant increase in the number and types of services purchased from private vendors operating group homes, halfway houses, and work-release programs. In addition to residential services for probationers and parolees, they sometimes offer programs to assist drug abusers, ex-offenders, and victims. Private agencies profit from being smaller operations and thus escaping some of the bureaucratic red tape that affects state residential programs. These programs depend on a variety of funding sources, including federal, state, local, and private foundations. Among these, Talbert House is well known for the high-quality services they offer to offenders.

An ex-prisoner speaks in a group therapy session at a halfway house in Los Angeles. It is common for community programs to use guided group interaction, a technique that has been shown to have great promise in dealing with both juvenile and adult offenders. Successful guided group interaction programs allow community members to learn to assume responsibility for their own and each others' successes and failures. Participants learn to solve problems by speaking honestly and frankly in small groups for which they have responsibility, but which are also monitored and guided by staff who are often ex-offenders, and use these experiences to help them make a positive return to society.

Founded in 1965 in Cincinnati, Ohio, by a group of citizens who wanted to develop a better way of returning individuals to the community, Talbert House has expanded its services through the years. It now operates multiple service sites throughout Cincinnati for clients struggling with criminal victimization, chemical dependency, personal crisis, mental illness, and criminal justice issues. The services include prevention services, adolescent treatment, outpatient services for adult substance abuse, residential treatment for drug abuse, mental health services, a community corrections center, and residential programs for women offenders. Funding is typically a problem for private programs, but Talbert House receives support from agencies such as the Hamilton County Community Mental Health Board, Hamilton County Alcohol and Drug Addiction Services Board, Ohio Department of Rehabilitation and Corrections, Hamilton County Commissioners and Courts, United Way–Community Chest, and the city of Cincinnati–Neighborhood Services Division.

Delancey Street is another of the leading residential organizations for former substance abusers, ex-convicts, homeless, and others who have hit bottom. Beginning in 1971 in San Francisco, it now also has centers in Los Angeles, New Mexico, North Carolina, and New York. The minimum stay is two years, but the average resident remains for nearly four years—drug, alcohol, and crime-free.

It has been difficult to obtain reliable evaluation data on residential facilities due to their varying programs, target populations, and treatment alternatives and goals. Some critics question their overall effectiveness, but the fact is that these programs appear to work for some types of offenders, and the approaches of some centers seem more effective than other settings. What may contribute to greater effectiveness with these programs is that instead of being used as a last resort before sentencing to incarceration in a jail or prison, residential community center placements might work more effectively with first-time offenders who have little experience with the criminal justice process; who are not users or addicted to drugs, especially crack cocaine; and who have a history of employment.[50]

BOOT CAMP A military-style facility used as an alternative to prison in order to deal with prison crowding and public demands for severe treatment.

RESTORATIVE JUSTICE Focuses on the welfare of victims in the aftermath of crime.

Boot Camps

Boot camps began in adult corrections but in recent years have been more frequently used in juvenile corrections. When boot camps are used in adult corrections, they are usually first-time offenders in their late teens or early twenties who undergo rigorous physical and behavioral training for three to six months. Boot camps are designed to give offenders a sense of responsibility and accomplishments while improving self-discipline.[51] In a survey of boot camp programs, it was found that the typical pattern was the use of strict discipline, physical training, drill and ceremony, military bearing and courtesy, physical labor, and summary punishment for minor violations of rules. Boot camps originated in Georgia and Oklahoma in 1983 and are now offered by more than 30 states.

Critics are quick to say that boot camps present a number of disturbing issues:

■ Journalistic accounts of boot camp celebrate a popular image of a dehumanizing experience marked by hard, often meaningless, physical labor. The inmate is portrayed as deficient and requiring something akin to being clubbed over the head to become "a man." This imagery is particularly troubling when it is remembered that the inmates are disproportionately minorities and underclass members.

■ Why would a facility developed to prepare people to go into war be considered to have much potential in deterring or rehabilitating offenders?

■ How do the aggressive treatment of residents and the insistence on unquestioning obedience to authority foster prosocial behavior?[52]

James O. Finckenauer sees boot camps as another failed panacea and, as a result of the growing pessimism about them, he notes that one-third have been closed.[53] Nor have the studies of recidivism rates of boot camp graduates been encouraging—the rearrest rates of boot camp graduates are similar to those of prison inmates. Some corrections experts argue that the boot camp experience does not have a lasting impact because boot camps do not do enough to meet the needs of offenders.

MYTH

Boot camps work wonders because their military atmosphere and training help whip undisciplined offenders into shape and give them a sense of achievement and responsibility.

FACT

There is growing disenchantment with boot camps. They don't seem to work and recidivism is quite high.

While the future of boot camps is in doubt, there has been some interest in developing aftercare services for boot camp graduates to reduce the recidivism rates.[54] For example, a boot camp in New York combines a military regimen with substance abuse counseling, community services, and high school equivalency classes. Upon release, the men and women in this program are required to participate in an intensive six-month aftercare program that provides them with a job and helps them stay employed. It is hoped that such aftercare services will improve their chances of success.

L06 ▶ RESTORATIVE JUSTICE

Restorative justice has recently been coupled with intermediate sanctions. Humanistic in its treatment of offenders, **restorative justice** has as its focus the welfare of victims in the aftermath of crime. In bringing criminal and victim together to heal the wounds of violation, the campaign for restorative justice advocates alternatives to incarceration, such as intensive community supervision. The most popular of the restorative strategies are victim–offender conferencing and community restitution. In many states, representatives of the victims' rights movement have been instrumental in setting up programs in which victims/survivors confront their violators. Every state has a crime victim compensation commission or some agency with a similar name to perform this function.[55]

Kay Pranis served as the restorative justice planner for the Minnesota Department of Corrections from 1994 to 2003 and is now a nationally respected consultant for restorative justice. A champion of peacemaking circles, her work focuses on promoting the use of restorative justice principles in the criminal justice system and in communities. She is the author of many published papers and *The Little Book of Circle Processes: A New/Old Approach to Peacemaking* (Good Books, 2005). In Voices Across the Profession, she tells why she feels sanctions in the community have the possibility of healing and restoration.

There are more than 1,000 restorative justice programs operating throughout North America and Europe, according to the international survey done by the Center for Restorative Justice and Peacemaking.[56] Included in this number are many programs operating inside U.S. prisons. On the international stage, the

VOICES ACROSS the PROFESSION

© Kay Pranis

"When I came to this work, I did not think that my work was about crime. It was more about community and to see crime as an opportunity to bring people together."

KAY PRANIS
RESTORATIVE JUSTICE PLANNER

I am continually humbled by human capacities for openness, heart-centered connecting, humility, compassion, understanding, and love. I find that restorative justice in general and peacemaking circles in particular help us connect with our deepest and best selves and bring these dimensions of ourselves to some of the hardest challenges we face.

When I came to this work, I did not think that my work was about crime. It was more about community and to see crime as an opportunity to bring people together. We know that crime is negative energy because crime is harm, but the restorative approach gave us opportunities to transform that negative energy into positive energy. The peacemaking circles were the most obvious example of transforming negative community-level energy around crime into positive community-building energy and of moving toward a more healthy community. It is not just when people break a law that we have to pay attention, to require them to make amends, and to correct their behavior. Lots and lots of hurt happens that is not crime. We need a way to understand the hurt that we cause to another, to be able to acknowledge and to apologize, and take some steps to make it right.

I am incredibly hopeful about this movement, and I do see it as a movement. It is not in isolation; there are movements happening in many fields that are along the same path and are congruent with restorative justice. I know that programs come and go, but the people who are involved in restorative justice make a shift in how they look at their work. And the people I see who make that shift do not go back. They take that way of thinking about how we relate with one another and how we respond to harm into whatever work they do.

Sometimes drawing out these often unexpressed human capacities leads to healings and transformations that seem miraculous to our normal ways of thinking. But mostly they provide the strength and persistence to do the hard, demanding, daily work of building and rebuilding human lives and communities.

To me, restorative justice is like ground water. You can't always see it, but it is always moving. And it will always find its way through because this work appeals to who we want to be in our best self. When you create space for people to be in touch with who they want to be in their best selves and you give them permission to bring that forward, that is a place where people want to stay.

Source: Interviewed in 2010.

thrust for a restorative vision has been embraced through the role of the United Nations, which has created formal standards of guidelines for countries to use in restorative justice programming.[57] They encourage the use of restorative justice programming by member states at all stages of the criminal justice process.

Over the past 20 years, restorative justice has emerged as a different way for communities to respond to the harm caused by crime. Several definitions of restorative justice can be found, but at the heart of most of these definitions is the conviction that those most directly involved in a crime (individual victims, offenders, families of victims and offenders, and victimized communities) are those who should be central in responding to the harm caused by crime. The focus is more on repairing the harm that was done to victims by holding offenders directly accountable for their behavior than on the law that was broken.[58]

Restorative justice processes pay attention not only to the harm inflicted on the victims of a crime, but also to the ways the crime has harmed the offender and the community. The focus then is on victim healing, offender reintegration, and community restoration. This emphasis on victim healing has persuaded some to consider restorative justice to be a victim-centered approach. Yet the emphasis on providing offenders an opportunity to make amends and to increase their awareness of the consequences of their actions has persuaded others to regard restorative justice as offender-focused. It is the third emphasis, community restoration, that puts victim healing and offender reparation into perspective.

With its roots in the rituals of indigenous populations and traditional religious practices, restorative justice represents a growing international movement with a relatively clear set of values, principles, and guidelines for practice. Its purpose is to restore the torn fabric of community and wholeness to all those affected by crime, to repair the harm that was done to the victim and the community, and to make the offender accountable to all.[59]

Restorative Justice Programs

While stressing accountability for offenses committed, restorative strategies operate with the goal of repairing injuries to victims and to communities in which crimes have taken place. Ross London, a former judge, prosecutor, and public defender, proposes that restoration and particularly the restoration of trust, be viewed as the overarching goal of all criminal justice policies and practices. It is his opinion that punishment—far from contradicting the goal of restoration—is both essential to the victim and the community, and a necessary component for offenders' reintegration.[60]

Community conferencing and circle sentencing are vital parts of restorative justice programming. Whether these conferences occur before, during, or after adjudication, they promote education and transformation within a context of respect and healing. These models are neither mutually exclusive nor complete in and of themselves. They can be combined or adapted depending on the special situation at hand.[61] Some of the most important initiatives are described in the sections that follow.

COMMUNITY CONFERENCING AND CIRCLE SENTENCING

Community conferences make it possible for victims, offenders, and community members to meet one another to resolve issues raised by the offender's trespass.[62] A particularly promising form of community conferences is called circle sentencing. Historically, sentencing circles have their roots in United States native and Canadian aboriginal cultures. These circles were adopted by the criminal justice system in the 1980s as First Nations peoples of the Yukon and local criminal justice officials endeavored to build more constructive ties between the criminal justice system and the grassroots community. In 1991, Judge Barry Stuart of the Yukon Territorial Court introduced circle sentencing in order to empower the community to participate in the justice process.

One of the most promising developments in sentencing circles is the Hollow Water First Nations Community Holistic Healing Circle, which simultaneously addresses harm created by the offender, healing the victim, and restoring community goodwill. Circles have been developed most extensively in the western provinces of Canada. They have also experienced a resurgence in modern times among American Indian tribes, for example, in the Navajo courts. Today circles increasingly may be found in most mainstream criminal justice settings. In Minnesota, circles are used in many kinds of ways for a variety of crimes and in different types of settings.[63] A Hawaii minimum-security prison has a pilot reentry restorative circles program that began in 2005.[64]

Participants in healing or sentencing circles typically speak out while passing around a "talking piece" (such as a feather or stone). Separate healing circles are initially held for the victim and offender. After the healing circles meet, a sentencing circle (with feedback from family, community, and the justice system) determines a course of action. Other circles then follow up to monitor compliance, which may involve restitution or community service.[65]

FAMILY GROUP CONFERENCES Growing out of both aboriginal and feminist approaches, family group conferences (FGCs) use a group decision-making model in order to try to stop family violence. The FGC made its mainstream criminal justice debut in New Zealand in 1989. It has been tested in Newfoundland and Labrador, as well as in communities in New Zealand, Austria, England and Wales, Canada, and the United States.[66] FGCs are used in many countries as a preferred sentencing and restorative justice forum for youthful offenders. Despite differences among jurisdictions, one common theme is overriding: family group conferences are more likely than traditional forms of dispute resolution to give effective voice to those who are traditionally disadvantaged.[67]

REPARATION AND RESTITUTION Often referred to as the "Vermont model" of reparative probation, this form of restorative justice can be implemented more quickly within existing structures and processes of the criminal justice system.[68] It involves a reparation programs track designed for offenders who commit nonviolent offenses and who are considered at low risk for reoffense. The reparative programs track mandates that the offender make reparations to both the victims(s) and the community. A reparative probation program, moreover, directly engages the community in sentencing and monitoring offenders, and depends heavily on small-scale community-based committees to deal with minor crimes. Reparative agreements are made between perpetrators and these community representatives, while citizen volunteers furnish social support in order to facilitate victim and community reparation.

RESTITUTION PROGRAMS Restitution is actually the most popular model of restorative justice. It enables in-kind or actual return of what has been lost to the victim. Restitution is best viewed within the larger context of "making amends." This includes the provision that the offender offers a sincere apology and promises to change the behavior that caused the initial injury. Ideally, restitution also encourages a move toward "balancing the scales" with a true spirit of generosity and forgiveness on both sides.[69] Victims identify and then seek redress for their losses, whether identified as material (damage to property), personal (bodily or psychological harm), or communal (injury to the quality of life of an entire community).

In many cases, offenders can offer individuals, families, or communities compensation for losses. Using a community justice focus, Ventura County, California, juvenile justice officials have implemented a successful program that emphasizes restitution as the key element of the reparative process. To compensate for material losses, youthful offenders in the South Oxnard Challenge Project offer various innovative types of financial or in-kind restitution to victims. The latter have included needed projects for victims, whether individuals or neighborhoods, such as painting a victim's garage, cleaning up graffiti, or working in an office reception area.[70]

VICTIM–OFFENDER CONFERENCING Introduced formally into the criminal justice arena in the 1980s, victim–offender conferencing encourages one-on-one victim–offender reconciliation facilitated through a mediator. Key issues include the utilization of co-mediators; the nature and duration of follow-up victim–offender meetings; the use of victim–offender mediation for more serious and violent offenses; and the implementation of victim–offender mediation in multicultural and prison settings. A growing body of empirical research worldwide reveals that successful victim-offender programs have been implemented in British Columbia and Ontario, Canada; Valparaiso, Indiana; Minneapolis, Minnesota; Quincy, Massachusetts; and Batavia, New York, as well as in Kettering, England, and Glasgow, Scotland.[71] While the verdict is still out, initial outcomes research does indicate considerable satisfaction among both victims and offenders, although the question of recidivism looms. It remains to be seen how such programs can begin to be viewed with utmost seriousness by attorneys and judges as a viable alternative to traditional retributive justice procedures.

In evaluating the effectiveness of restorative justice practices using meta-analysis techniques, Jeff Latimer, Craig Dowden, and Danielle Muise compared restorative justice programs to traditional approaches to criminal behavior. They found that restorative justice programs were significantly more effective in terms of offender and victim satisfaction, restitution compliance, and recidivism. However, the authors noted that these findings must be tempered by an important self-selection bias inherent in restorative justice programs.[72]

L07 # FUTURE OF INTERMEDIATE SANCTIONS

Agreement is widespread that graduated sanctions hold the promise for increasing compliance to the conditions of the courts and for providing cost-effective crime control measures, usually without widening the net of the criminal justice system. In addition, they reduce the overreliance on incarceration, with its rising corrections costs. Moreover, the experiences of drug courts have revealed that this approach reduces rates of substance abuse.[73] A number of benefits have been attributed to graduated sanctions:

- *Certainty* because infractions of the behavioral contract are quickly discovered and sanctioned

- *Celerity* because the response to violations is swift

- *Proportionality* because the structured sanctions menu is designed to ensure that the level of punishment is commensurate with the severity of the criminal behavior

- *Progressiveness* because the structured sanctions menu is designed to result in increasingly stringent responses to continued violations[74]

In the midst of the wide praise that intermediate sanctions is receiving today, there has been criticism. Some experts are concerned that intermediate sanctions are expanding the net of the criminal justice system. Instead of reducing the number of those sentenced to prison, it is argued that intermediate sanctions are resulting in an expansion of the overall system. One study of sentencing recommendations of probation officers found that this varied by probation officers, but in two-thirds of the cases the intermediate sanction did serve a net widening (or net repairing) function.[75] Others contend that the most serious problems with intermediate sanctions are the 40 to 50 percent rates of revocation and subsequent incarceration, and the assignment of less serious offenders than program developers anticipated to these programs.[76]

The "net widening" criticism is particularly disturbing and must be addressed by the courts and policy makers. Enough research on the reduction of recidivism has been done on intermediate sanctions indicating what is needed to improve the quality of these programs. The needs and safety of victims are a further consideration. The future efficacy of intermediate sanctions certainly depends on these criticisms being taken seriously.

SUMMARY

Understand the benefits of intermediate sanctions

Intermediate sanctions are a cost-saving alternative to jails and prisons; they help reduce prison crowding; they help serve the needs of offenders who are a low risk of recidivism and pose little danger to society; they can be used as a halfway-back strategy for probation and parole violators; and they help fill the void between routine probation and prison.

LO2 ▶ **Identify the continuum of intermediate sanctions**

The types of intermediate sanctions include intensive supervision of probation, restitution and fines, community service orders, day reporting centers, house arrest, electronic monitoring, halfway houses, drug courts, and boot camps. They can be divided into sanctions without incarceration (fines, forfeiture, and drug courts); sanctions as part of being placed on probation (community service orders, restitution, and intensive probation); and sanctions that include incarceration (shock probation and split sentencing).

LO3 ▶ **Identify the sanctions that stand alone and what they contribute to intermediate sanctions**

The sanctions that stand alone are fines, forfeiture, drug courts, and day reporting centers. They are widely used, especially drug courts and day reporting centers. They are not as restrictive as some of the other sanctions, but they provide opportunities to make changes and to become more law abiding.

LO4 ▶ **Identify the sanctions as an add-on to probation and what they contribute to intermediate sanctions**

These sanctions include restitution, community service orders, intensive probation, house arrest and electronic monitoring, and residential centers. These sanctions are added to probation because it is felt that these offenders need more restrictions. The hope is that offenders will become responsive and will not need to be sent or returned to prison.

LO5 ▶ **Identify the sanctions that include incarceration and what they contribute to intermediate sanctions**

These sanctions include shock probation and split sentencing, work release centers, and boot camps. All three of them involve incarceration: shock probation requires a prison sentence before being released on parole; work release centers' placements usually follow a term of incarceration; and boot camps are a placement for youthful offenders that is another attempt to find a means of diverting offenders before it is necessary to sentence them to a prison terms.

LO6 ▶ **Understand the relationship between restorative justice and intermediate sanctions**

The focus of restorative justice is to bring criminal and victim together to heal the wounds of violation and to advocate alternative methods of incarceration.

LO7 ▶ **Evaluate the effectiveness and future of intermediate sanctions**

The reviews of sanctions are mixed, but there seems to be general agreement that they are preferable to returning offenders to prison for technical violations of probation and that some offenders, especially drug offenders, appear to profit from these programs. The future appears to be promising for the increased use of intermediate sanctions.

Key Terms

fine, 86
day fine, 87
forfeiture, 88
civil forfeiture, 88
criminal forfeiture, 88
financial restitution, 89
community service order, 89

house arrest, 90
home confinement program, 90
electronic monitoring (EM), 91
global positioning system (GPS)
   technology, 92
drug courts, 94
day reporting center (DRC), 96

halfway house, 98
residential community corrections
   centers, 98
boot camp, 100
restorative justice, 100

Critical Thinking Questions

1. Why are intermediate sanctions one form of punishment about which individuals with competing views can reach some agreement?

2. Of the various types of intermediate punishments, which one makes the most sense to you? How would you recommend expanding it?

3. Of the various types of intermediate punishments, which makes the least sense to you? What do you feel is needed to make it more acceptable?

Thinking Like a Corrections Professional

You are a drug court judge and a drug user is appearing before you for the fourth time. This offender has more potential than you have seen in a long time. She has finished three years of college, earning high grades, but simply does not seem to successfully complete drug rehabilitative programs. What will be your approach with this offender? What sanction will you give her?

Career Destinations

Want a job in a day reporting center? Read more about one at: **www.cookcountysheriff.org/departments/departments_dcsi_dayreporting.html**

Are you interested in becoming a substance abuse counselor? You will find all the information you need for a career as a substance abuse counselor, including training, education requirements, qualifications needed for licensure and certification, and more at the website of the Substance Abuse Counselor Headquarters:

www.substanceabusecounselorhq.com

There are numerous opportunities for employment in restorative justice programs:
www.bcrjp.org

www.restorativejustice.org/job-openings-in-restorative-justice/

Notes

1. Mark Manke, "Falcons' Vick Indicted in Dogfighting Case," *Washington Post*, July 18, 2007.
2. Ibid.
3. "Federal Judge Rules Vick Can Keep More than $16 Million in Bonus Money," ESPN.com, February 5, 2008.
4. Orlando Ledbetter, "Vick Enters Guilty Plea, Gets Suspended Sentence," *Atlanta Journal Constitution*, November 28, 2008.
5. Bob Kent, "Mornhinweg Says Vick Will Play," PhiladelphiaEagles.com, September 24, 2009.
6. Anthony L. Hall, "Rehabilitation (and Vindication?) of Michael Vick," *The IPINIONS Journal*, December 29, 2010.
7. Ibid.
8. Patricia M. Harris, Rebecca D. Petersen, and Samantha Rapoza, "Between Probation and Revocation: A Study of Intermediate Sanctions Decision-Making," *Journal of Criminal Justice* 29 (2001): 308.
9. *Tate v. Short*, 401 U.S. 395, 91 S.Ct. 668, 28 L.Ed.2d 130 (1971).
10. Pennsylvania Department of Corrections, "Day Fines, 2003."
11. William M. DiMascio, *Seeking Justice: Crime and Punishment in America* (New York: Edna McConnell Clark Foundation, 1995), p. 36.

12. Doris Layton MacKenzie, "Evidence-Based Corrections: Identifying What Works," *Crime and Delinquency 46* (2000): 457–472.
13. U.S. Treasury Department, "About Forfeiture."
14. John L. Worrall, "The Civil Asset Forfeiture Reform Act of 2000: A Sheep in Wolf's Clothing," *Policing* (2004): 220–240.
15. R. E. Bell, "The Confiscation, Forfeiture, and Disruption of Terrorist Finances," *Journal of Money Laundering Control* 7 (2003): 105–125.
16. John L Worrall, "Addicted to the Drug War: The Role of Asset Forfeiture as a Budgetary Necessity in Contemporary Law Enforcement," *Journal of Criminal Justice* 29 (2001): 171–187.
17. Ibid.
18. R. B. Rubeck, J. N. Schaffer, and M. A. Logue, "The Imposition and the Effects of Restitution in Four Pennsylvania Counties: Effects of Size of County and Specialized Collection Units," *Crime and Delinquency* 50 (2004): 168–188.
19. *2001 Annual Report* (Atlanta: Georgia Department of Corrections, 2002).
20. Gail A. Caputo, "Community Service in Texas: Results of a Probation Survey," *Corrections Compendium 39* (March/April 2005): 8–9.
21. Darren Gowen, "Overview of the Federal Home Confinement Program 1988–1996," *Federal Probation* 64 (December 2000): 11–18.

22. Robert Stanz and Richard Tewksbury, "Predictors of Success and Recidivism in a Home Incarceration Program," *Prison Journal* 80 (2000): 326–344.
23. Brian Payne and Randy Gainey, "The Influence of Demographic Factors on the Experience of House Arrest," *Federal Probation* 66 (2002): 64–70.
24. Gowen, "Overview of the Federal Home Confinement Program."
25. Brian K. Payne and Randy R. Gainey, "The Electronic Monitoring of Offenders Released from Jail or Prison: Safety, Control, and Comparisons to the Incarceration Experience," *Prison Journal* 84 (December 2004): 413–435.
26. D. Gowen, "Remote Location Monitoring—A Supervision Strategy to Enhance Risk Control," *Federal Probation* 65 (2001): 38–41.
27. Ibid.
28. Jennifer Lee, "Some States Track Parolees by Satellite," *New York Times*, January 31, 2002, p. A3.
29. Ralph Gable and Robert Gable, "Electronic Monitoring: Positive Intervention Strategies," *Federal Probation* 69 (2005): 21–25.
30. Payne and Gainey, "The Electronic Monitoring of Offenders Released from Jail or Prison: Safety, Control, and Comparisons to the Incarceration Experience."

31. Ibid., p. 415.

32. Ibid., p. 414; and J. Bonta, S. Wallace-Capretta, and J. Rooney, "Can Electronic Monitoring Make a Difference?" *Crime and Delinquency* 46 (2000): 61–75.

33. J. Robert Lilly, "Issues Beyond Empirical EM Reports," *Criminology and Public Policy* (February 2006): 93–101.

34. George Mair, "Electronic Monitoring: Effectiveness and Public Policy," *Criminology and Public Policy* (February 2006): 57–60.

35. Kathy G. Padgett, William D. Bales, and Thomas G. Blomberg, "Under Surveillance: An Empirical Test of the Effectiveness and Consequences of Electronic Monitoring," *Criminology and Public Policy* (February 2006): 61–91.

36. National Center on Addiction and Substance Abuse, *Behind Bars II: Substance Abuse and America's Prison Population* (New York: National Center, 2010).

37. John S. Goldkamp, "The Impact of Drug Courts," *Criminology and Public Policy* (March 2003): 198.

38. Candace McCoy, "The Politics of Problem-Solving: An Overview of the Origins and Development of Therapeutic Courts," *American Criminal Law Review* (Fall 2003): 1513–1534.

39. "In the Spotlight," *Drug Courts: Facts and Figures* (Washington, DC: National Criminal Justice Reference Service, 2011); Douglas B. Marlowe, David S. Festinger, Patricia A. Lee, Maria M. Schepise, Julie E. R. Hazzard, Jeffrey C. Merrill, Francis D. Mulvaney, and A. Thomas McLellan, "Are Judicial Status Hearings a Key Component of Drug Courts? During-Treatment Data from a Randomized Trial," *Criminal Justice and Behavior* 30 (April 2003): 142.

40. Adele Harrell, "Judging Drug Courts: Balancing the Evidence," *Criminology and Public Policy* (March 2003): 207–212.

41. Ibid.

42. Richard S. Gebelein, "The Rebirth of Rehabilitation: Promise and Perils of Drug Courts," National Institute of Justice, www.ncjrs.gov/pdffiles1/nij/181412.pdf (accessed February 20, 2012).

43. For evidence of effectiveness of drug courts, see "GAO Highlights," *Adult Drug Courts: Studies Show Courts Reduce Recidivism but DOJ Could Enhance Future Performance Measure Revision Efforts* (Washington, DC: United States Government Accountability Office, December 2011).

44. Amy Craddock, "Estimating Criminal Justice System Costs and Cost-Savings Benefits of Day Reporting Centers," *Journal of Offender Rehabilitation* 39 (2004): 70–71.

45. James R. Brunet, "Day Reporting Centers in North Carolina: Implementation Lessons for Policymakers," *Justice System Journal* 23 (2002): 135–156.

46. Roy Sudipto, "Adult Offenders in a Day Reporting Center: A Preliminary Study," *Federal Probation* 66 (June 2002): 44–51; Roy Sudipto, "Factors Related to Success and Recidivism in a Day Reporting Center," *Criminal Justice Studies* (2004): 3–17. For a study with similar findings, see Liz Marie Marciniak, "Addition of Day Reporting to Intensive Supervision Probation: A Comparison of Recidivism Rates," *Federal Probation* 64 (June 2000): 34–39.

47. Christine Martin, Arthur J. Lurigio, and David E. Olson, "An Examination of Rearrests and Reincarcerations Among Discharged Day Reporting Center Clients," *Federal Probation* 67 (June 2003): 24–31.

48. The Ohio Department of Rehabilitation and Corrections evaluated shock probation for over two decades.

49. Michelle A. Lang and Steven Belenko, "Predicting Retention in a Residential Drug Treatment Alternative to Prison Program," *Journal of Substance Abuse Treatment* 19 (2000): 145–160; Eric J. Workowski, "Criminal Violence and Drug Use: An Exploratory Study Among Substance Abusers in Residential Treatment," in *Treating Substance Abusers in Correctional Contexts: New Understandings, New Modalities*, ed. Nathaniel J. Pallone (New York: Routledge, 2003), pp. 109–121.

50. Hung-En Sung and Steven Belenko, "Failure After Success: Correlates of Recidivism Among Individuals Who Successfully Completed Coerced Drug Treatment," *Journal of Offender Rehabilitation* 42 (2005): 75–97.

51. Faithe E. Lutze and Corney A. Bell, "Boot Camp Prisons as Masculine Organizations: Rethinking Recidivism and Program Design," *Rehabilitative Issues: Problems and Prospects in Boot Camp* (2005): 133–152.

52. Merry Morash and Lisa Rucker, "A Critical Look at the Idea of Boot Camp as a Correctional Reform," *Crime and Delinquency* 36 (April 1990): 206.

53. James O. Finckenauer, "Ruminating About Boot Camps: Panaceas, Paradoxes, and Ideology," *Rehabilitative Issues: Problems and Prospects in Boot Camp* (2005): 199–207.

54. Ojmarrh Mitchell, Doris L. MacKenzie, and Deanna M. Perez, "A Randomized Evaluation of the Maryland Correctional Boot Camp for Adults: Effects on Offender Antisocial Attitudes and Cognitions," *Rehabilitative Issues: Problems and Prospects in Boot Camp* (2005): 71–80; Brent B. Benda, Nancy J. Harm, and Nancy J. Toombs, "Survival Analysis of Recidivism of Male and Female Boot Camp Graduates Using Life-Course Theory," *Rehabilitative Issues: Problems and Prospects in Boot Camp* (2005): 88–96.

55. See Ross London, *Crime, Punishment, and Restorative Justice: From the Margins to the Mainstream* (Boulder, CO: Lynne Rienner, 2011), and John P. J. Dussich and Jill Schellenberg, eds., *The Promise of Restorative Justice: New Approaches for Criminal Justice and Beyond* (Boulder, CO: Lynne Rienner, 2011).

56. Mark Umbreit, *National Survey of Victim–Offender Mediation Programs in the United States* (St. Paul, MN: Center for Restorative Justice and Peacemaking, 2000). For a more updated international review, see Prison Fellowship International, www.pfi.org (accessed March 21, 2012).

57. D. Van Ness, "UN Expert Meeting Recommends Declaration of Basic Principles on Restorative Justice," www.restorativejustice.org/articlesdb/articles/519 (accessed February 20, 2012).

58. Mark S. Umbreit, Betty Vos, Robert B. Coates, and Katherine A. Brown, *Facing Violence: The Path of Restorative Justice and Dialogue* (Monsey, NY: Criminal Justice Press, 2003), p. 7. Also see articles at Prison Fellowship International, www.pfi.org (accessed March 21, 2012).

59. Katherine Stuart van Wormer and Clemens Bartollas, *Women and the Criminal Justice System*, 3rd ed. (Upper Saddle River, NJ: Prentice Hall, 2011), pp. 165–186.

60. London, *Crime, Punishment, and Restorative Justice*.

61. Van Wormer and Bartollas, *Women and the Criminal Justice System*, p. 181.

62. Mark Umbreit, Sheryl Wilson, and Annie Roberts, "Restorative Justice for Victims, Offenders and Community," Center for Restorative Justice and Peacemaking, University of Minnesota, School of Social Work, January 2006.

63. G. Bazemore and M. Umbreit, *A Comparison of Four Restorative Conferencing Models*, U.S. Department of Justice, Office of Juvenile Justice and Delinquency Prevention (Washington, DC: U.S. Department of Justice, National Institute of Corrections, 2001).

64. Lorenn Walker, Ted Sakai, and Kat Brady, "Restorative Circles—A Reentry Process for Hawaii Inmates," *Federal Probation* 70 (2006): 33–37, and 86.

65. Ibid. See also P. McCold, *Overview of Mediation, Conferencing, and Circles*, paper presented to the 10th United Nations Congress on Crime Prevention and Treatment of Offenders, International Institute for Restorative Practices, Vienna, April 10–17, 2000.

66. J. Hudson, B. Galaway, A. Morris, and G. Maxwell, "Introduction," in J. Hudson et al., *Family Group Conferences: Perspectives on Policy and Practice* (Monsey, NY: Criminal Justice Press, 1996), pp. 1–16.

67. Van Wormer and Bartollas, *Women and the Criminal Justice System*, p. 181.

68. D. Karp and L. Walther, "Community Reparative Boards in Vermont: Theory and Practice," in *Restorative Community Justice: Repairing Harm and Transforming Communities*, ed. G. Bazemore and M. Schiff (Cincinnati: Anderson, 2001), pp. 199–217.

69. D. Van Ness and K. H. Strong, *Restoring Justice*, 2nd ed. (Cincinnati: Anderson, 2002).

70. Karp and Walther, "Community Reparative Boards in Vermont: Theory and Practice."

71. Umbreit, Vos, Coates, and Brown, *Facing Violence: The Path of Restorative Justice and Dialogue*.

72. Jeff Latimer, Craig Dowden, and Danielle Muise, "The Effectiveness of Restorative Justice Practices: A Meta-Analysis," *Prison Journal* (June 2005): 127–144.

73. Faye S. Taxman and Adam Geib, "Graduated Sanctions: Stepping into Accountable Systems and Offenders," *Prison Journal* 79 (1999): 182–204.

74. Ibid.

75. Robert J. Homant and Mark A. DeMercurio, "Intermediate Sanctions in Probation Officers' Sentencing Recommendations: Consistency, Net Widening, and Net Repairing," *Prison Journal* 89 (December 2009): 426–439.

76. Michael Tonry and Mary Lynch, "Intermediate Sanctions" in *Crime and Justice: A Review of Research*, ed. Michael Tonry (Chicago: University of Chicago Press, 1999), pp. 99–144.

Dr. Conrad Murray was found guilty of manslaughter in the 2009 death of his patient, Michael Jackson, and sentenced to four years in county jail. Judge Michael E. Pastor ordered that Murray serve the time in Los Angeles County Jail because of the recent sentencing realignment requiring that involuntary manslaughter cases not be served in state prison. After a six-week trial that described in considerable detail Michael Jackson's final hours, many questions remain about Murray's use of an operating-room anesthetic as Jackson battled chronic insomnia.[1]

Prosecutors wanted Murray sentenced to four years, the maximum term. Defense attorneys wanted probation for the cardiologist, arguing that he would lose his ability to practice medicine "and likely face a lifetime of ostracism"—punishment enough, they claimed. But even though four years behind bars may sound harsh, in reality Murray's sentence would likely be cut in half because of jail overcrowding.[2]

Murray admitted to detectives that he had been giving Jackson nightly doses of a restricted medication called propofol to help him sleep. Propofol is supposed to be used in hospital settings and had never received approval for sleep treatments. Murray acknowledged giving it to Jackson and then leaving the room on the day he died.[3]

Murray declined to testify during his trial but did participate in a documentary in which he said that he did not consider himself guilty of any crime and blamed Jackson for entrapping him into

© Pool/Reuters/Landov

Dr. Conrad Murray shown being handcuffed (top) and led away into custody of the Los Angeles Sheriff's Department after the jury returned with a guilty verdict in his involuntary manslaughter trial in Los Angeles, California, November 7, 2011. Murray, Michael Jackson's personal doctor, was found guilty of involuntary manslaughter in the singer's death following a six-week trial that captivated Jackson fans around the world.

administering the propofol doses. His attorneys contended that Jackson gave himself the fatal dose when Murray left his bedside. Murray was deep in debt when he agreed to serve as Jackson's personal physician for a fee of $150,000 a month; ironically, the singer died before Murray had received any money.[4]

Prosecutors wrote in a filing before the sentencing: "The defendant has displayed a complete lack of remorse for causing Michael Jackson's death." They added: "Even worse than failing to accept even the slightest level of responsibility, [Murray] has placed blame on everyone else, including the one person no longer here to defend himself, Michael Jackson."[5]

While sitting inside his 5-foot by 8-foot jail cell, instead of repenting for his crime, Murray began filing an appeal on his own. Because he cannot afford an attorney, the public is forced to pay for the transcripts of the trial, including any other costs to prepare his case.[6]

chapter

Five

THE JAIL: DETENTION AND SHORT-TERM CONFINEMENT

LEARNING OBJECTIVES

LO1 Describe the purpose of the jail

LO2 Explain the bail process, pretrial release, and preventive detention

LO3 Identify the makeup of the jail population

LO4 Discuss jail administration and structure

LO5 Compare the new-generation jail with more traditional jails

LO6 Describe jail-based treatment programs

LO7 Explain the legal and administrative issues of jail confinement

LO8 Discuss the future trends of the jail

© Becky Stein

109

JAIL A facility that is authorized to hold pretrial detainees and sentenced misdemeanants for periods longer than 48 hours.

The local or county level correctional center is a pivotal institution that touches the lives of more people than does any other penal institution. The jail has a long reputation of being a problem, but, fortunately, the culture of the jail is changing in a positive way. The Voices Across the Profession feature includes an interview with Dr. Arnett Gaston, who reflects on the new culture of the jail—one built on up-to-date facilities, able jail administrators, professionalism, and training of jail staff.

Each year millions of people enter local institutions, stay there for short periods of time, and then are replaced by more people who commit petty crimes and misdemeanors. Jails typically are used to detain people before trial who cannot make or afford bail. In addition to being intake centers for the entire criminal justice system, local correctional centers also serve as a place of first

Voices ACROSS the PROFESSION

© Arnett Gaston

" We wound up reducing 78 percent of the violence through our facilities on and off the island. "

ARNETT GASTON
FORMER COMMANDING OFFICER, RIKERS ISLAND

Arnett Gaston worked in corrections for 38 years. He began as a uniformed officer in the old Tombs Prison in New York City, and has worked throughout the department. He served as a deputy commissioner and as a warden in two jails, one holding a population of 2,500 inmates and another facility having a population of 2,000 inmates. He then became chief of management planning. Gaston ended up his career as commanding officer at Rikers Island, where he had 10 facilities under his command. Rikers Island is considered the largest jail

complex in the free world, with 18,000 prisoners and 11,000 staff.

"I was part of the restructuring of the Rikers Island jail complex. I was very much involved with what ultimately became known as the reformation of the policies and practices that led to the reduction of violence. First of all, we decided that the approach we were taking was out of date. We were reacting to violence in many instances with violence, and that really did not work. We determined to take a more preemptive and analytical approach where we would analyze the problem, try to look at certain strategies, develop operational plans and put them into operations, and evaluate their success or failure.

"We started analyzing how the events occurred, who were the victims, and who were the perpetrators or predators. We classified them into various categories. In essence, we developed a violence mapping strategy. Once we began to recognize that there were certain times of the day when certain instances began to happen in certain locations, we developed operational plans to correct that. We kept doing that everywhere we found the problem. As we were able to combat the violence, we put systems in place to minimize recurrence. We did this initially in one pilot facility and eventually extended it to all the island facilities. We wound up reducing 78 percent of the violence through our facilities on and off the island.

"We thought a lot of our violence was gang activity, because we have a lot of gangs in our jails, but we found that it was more individual action based on smaller groups of inmates. Yet because part of the problem with violence was associated with gang activity, this led us to set up a gang task force to investigate the activities of the gangs. We were able to diminish much of the gang violence, but equally important, we were able to get a lot of valuable information on gangs—how they operated and what they did. From this, we developed a digitalized imaging system, where we could have a complete picture file on every person in the gang—their markings, their tattoos, and their status in the gang. We were able to share this with the NYPD [New York Police Department], and they were so impressed that they adopted their own digitalized imaging system."

Arnett Gaston reminds us that competent jail administration is what is needed to improve the quality of what takes place in the jail, that a preemptive or proactive model can do much to reduce violence and other problems of the jail, and that many contemporary administrators are operating jails in a much more professional and humane fashion that serves to diminish the ghastly reputations for violence and the sordid conditions of jails in the past.

Sources: Interviewed in 2011. See also Bert Useem and Anne M. Piehl, "Prison Buildup and Disorder," *Punishment and Society* 8 (2006): 87–115.

or last resort for individuals who belong in public health, welfare, and social service agencies.

L01
There are three different types of local correctional institutions:

- Jails have the authority to detain individuals for periods of 48 hours or longer; they also hold convicted inmates sentenced to short terms (generally a year or less) for petty offenses. Jails are usually administered by the county sheriff but are sometimes managed on a regional basis or, in a few cases, by the state or federal government.

- Lockups, sometimes called temporary holding facilities or police lockups, are generally found in city police stations or precinct houses, and they hold persons for periods of less than 48 hours.

- Workhouses and houses of corrections—operated by cities and counties and sometimes known as county prisons—hold convicted inmates sentenced to short terms. In New Hampshire and Massachusetts, a house of corrections holds convicted misdemeanants and a county jail holds pre-trial detainees.

How correctional institutions arose, how they are structured today, and what services they provide are discussed in the following sections.

ORIGINS OF THE JAIL

The local correctional center had its origin in medieval England. Although initially conceived as a place for detaining suspected offenders until they could be tried, jails gradually came to serve the dual purposes of detention and punishment. The English jail became an expression of the dominant authority of the county, which maintained control over the jails because the state had not developed its own institutions. The concept of the English jail was brought to Britain's colonies in North America soon after the settlers arrived from the Old World. The jail was used to detain individuals awaiting trial and those awaiting punishment. The stocks and pillory, and sometimes the whipping post, were usually located nearby. Instead of cells, the early colonial jails consisted of small rooms that housed up to 30 prisoners. An example of these early colonial facilities is the jail (gaol) at Williamsburg, Virginia, built in 1703–1704 (see Figure 5.1). Prisoners in each county were placed under the jurisdiction of the sheriff, who fed and lodged them. The fee system was also used in the colonies. Virginia established the first colonial jail, but it was the Pennsylvania jails that became the model for other states. At the beginning

FIGURE 5.1 Jail (Gaol) at Williamsburg, Virginia, Built 1703–1704

Source: Marcus Whiffen, *The Public Buildings of Williamsburg* (Williamsburg, VA: Colonial Williamsburg Foundation, 1958). Courtesy of the Colonial Williamsburg Foundation.

When inmates enter a correctional institution, they are subject to an initial classification procedure. They may take a battery of psychological tests and provide personal and background information. These inmates are going through a health check, which is a routine part of the classification system.

© Becky Stein

of the nineteenth century, children, debtors, slaves, the mentally ill, and the physically ill were housed in jails, but as the century progressed, children and the mentally ill were more often sent to other institutions. Jails began to house both pretrial and posttrial prisoners; some jails also held felons as well as misdemeanants.

INITIAL BOOKING AND CLASSIFICATION

Jails usually have a central area for **booking**, admitting, and releasing inmates. Deputy sheriffs or police officers bring arrested offenders to the jail, where they are identified and fingerprinted, and their property is inventoried and stored. If they are there for a misdemeanant offense, they may be quickly released on bond. These offenders sit in an unsecured part of the jail booking area until someone comes to post their bond. But if arrested for a felony, they will have to wait until an initial appearance before a magistrate to see if they are granted bail. They are placed in a general holding area within the jail, where they are housed with other offenders.

Those not released on bond or personal recognizance are first placed in a secure housing unit until they can be interviewed and some preliminary information is collected regarding their crime and past criminal history. The purpose of this classification process is to identify the dangerousness and risk of the offenders and to determine whether they should be separated from other offenders. Furthermore, such major problems as a need for detoxification or potential for suicide are identified and considered in their assignment of housing. Once they are classified, they are moved to the most suitable housing area.

 ## BAIL, PRETRIAL, RELEASE, AND PREVENTIVE DETENTION

Half of the detainees in jail are misdemeanants who could not make bail. The defendants who receive bail or pretrial release will be given an opportunity to post bail and be released from jail. Those who are unable to post bond or receive pretrial diversion must remain in jail until their trial. The average delay between arrest and trial is more than six months.[7]

The following section discusses what bail bonds and **pretrial release** are and how they are administered.

BOOKING The process of admitting an arrestee or sentenced misdemeanant to jail.

PRETRIAL RELEASE Release from jail or a pretrial detention center pending adjudication of the case.

BAIL BOND The means, financial or property, used to release a defendant from jail.

BAIL BONDSMAN Bonding agents lend money for a fee to people who cannot make bail. They normally charge a percentage of the bail amount.

Bail

Bail is generally considered at a hearing conducted shortly after a defendant has been taken into custody. At this hearing, the judge considers such issues as whether the defendant is a flight risk or is dangerous before setting bail. Some jurisdictions have developed bail schedules to make certain that the amounts are uniform based on criminal history and on crime. **Bail bonds** are generally cash deposits but may also consist of property or other valuables. Indigent defendants who are unable to make bail may turn to a **bail bondsman**.

Pretrial Release

For those defendants unable to make cash bail, pretrial alternatives to jail include **release on own recognizance (ROR)**, unsecured bail, percentage bail, third-party custody, signature bail, and supervised release.

- Defendants who are released on their own recognizance (ROR) must appear at trial when scheduled. An ROR staff member interviews arrestees and then verifies data about each defendant. A defendant who scores the required number of verified points, as determined by established criteria, is recommended for ROR (see Figure 5.2 for the pretrial release criteria used in the judicial districts of Iowa).

- **Unsecured bail** allows release without a deposit or bail arranged through a bondsman. It differs from ROR in that the defendant is obligated to pay an established fee upon default. But because the full bond amount is rarely collected, this program is basically the same as ROR.

- In **percentage bail**, the defendant deposits a portion of the bail amount, usually 10 percent, with the court clerk.

- **Third-party custody** occurs when the court assigns custody of the defendant to an individual or agency that promises to ensure his or her later appearance in court.

- A **signature bond** is usually given for minor offenses, such as minor traffic offenses, and is based on the defendant's written promise to appear in court.

- **Supervised release** programs require more frequent contact with a pretrial officer, phone calls, and office interviews. Although the purpose of supervision is to enforce the conditions imposed, the defendants also receive assistance with housing, finances, health problems, employment, and alcohol- or drug-related problems. Percentage bond, cash bail, or unsecured bail may be part of supervised release; in high-risk cases, intensive supervision may be used, requiring several contacts a week with a pretrial release officer.

BAIL REFORM Until the early 1960s, money bonds were relied upon as the basic form of pretrial release. However, a great deal of research found that the bail system was not applied in a fair and equal manner. For example, one study examining the racial and ethnic differences in the processing of felony defendants in large urban courts found that Hispanic defendants received less pretrial release than did African American and white defendants. Hispanic defendants experienced a triple burden at the pretrial release stage. As a group, they:

- Were most likely to be required to pay bail to gain release

- Received the highest bail amounts

- Were least able to pay bail

These racial/ethnic differences were most pronounced in drug cases and are consistent with the perspective that suggests Hispanics are a newly immigrated group especially prone to harsher treatment in the criminal justice process.[8] Clearly reforms were needed.

The bail reform movement is most closely linked with the **Manhattan Bail Project**, a program pioneered by the Vera Institute of Justice in New York. The early success of the ROR program resulted in bail reform that culminated with the enactment of the federal **Bail Reform Act of 1966**. The intent of this legislation was to ensure that release would be granted in all noncapital cases in which sufficient reason existed that the defendant would return to court. During the 1970s and early 1980s, public pressure over increases in crime hampered the

RELEASE ON OWN RECOGNIZANCE (ROR) The release without bail of defendants who appear to have stable ties in the community and are a good risk to appear for trial.

UNSECURED BAIL Allows defendants' release without a deposit or bail arranged through a bondsman.

PERCENTAGE BAIL Defendants deposit about 10 percent of the bail amount with the court clerk.

THIRD-PARTY CUSTODY Takes place when the court assigns custody of the defendant to an individual or agency that promises to ensure his or her appearance in court.

SIGNATURE BOND Generally given for minor offenses and based on the defendant's written promise to appear in court.

SUPERVISED RELEASE Requires more frequent contact with pretrial officers, phone calls, and officer interviews.

MANHATTAN BAIL PROJECT A Vera Institute of Justice program that provided ROR release for eligible defendants, which influenced later bail reform movements.

BAIL REFORM ACT OF 1966 Federal legislation that further spurred the bail reform movement by urging pretrial release for all noncapital cases unless the defendant appeared unlikely to return to court.

Interview by _____

Date _____

Interview	Verified	**Residence**
3	3	Present residence 1 year or more or owns dwelling
2	2	Present residence 6 months or more or present and prior 1 year
1	1	Present residence 3 months or more or present and prior 6 months
0	0	Present residence 3 months or less

		Family Ties
3	3	Lives with family (spouse or dependents)
2	2	Lives with relatives or lives w/non-family individual 1 year or more
1	1	Lives with non-family individual
1	1	Lives alone and has sufficient support and/or family contact in the area
0	0	Lives alone

		Time in Area
2	2	Five years or more, continuous, recent

		Employment/Support
4	4	Present local job 1 year or more
3	3	Present local job 6 months or present and prior 1 year
2	2	Social Services or Social Security income or full-time student for 6 months
1	1	Unemployment Compensations, family support
1	1	New student status, new job, part-time job
0	0	Unemployed, not sufficient support

		Alcohol/Drug Abuse
−1	−1	Present involvement
−2	−2	Present involvement and history of abuse

		Criminal Record
2	2	No convictions
1	1	One simple/serious misdemeanor conviction within last 5 years
0	0	One felony/aggravated misdemeanor or 2 simple/serious within last 5 years
−1	−1	Two or more felony convictions or 3 or more simple/serious convictions
−1	−1	Six months or more jail term or 3 or more jail sentences
−2	−2	Served prison term

		Current Offense Charge
−3	−3	Forcible felony/mandatory sentences
−2	−2	Present on probation or parole
−1	−1	Other criminal charges pending of aggravated misdemeanor or felony nature

		Miscellaneous (more than one may apply)
−2	−2	Previous Pre-Trial/Probation/Parole violations
−2	−2	Failure to appear or contempt of court charges
−3	−3	Flight to avoid prosecution or AWOL

		Health/Psychiatric (indicate if applicable)

Comments: _____

_____

_____

FIGURE 5.2 Pretrial Services Release Criteria in Iowa

Source: First Judicial District, State of Iowa.

BAIL REFORM ACT OF 1984 This federal act formalized preventive detention provisions for those considered dangerous or unlikely to return to court.

pretrial release movement and, as a result, the more recent federal legislation, the **Bail Reform Act of 1984**, required that no defendant be kept in pretrial detention simply because they could not afford financial bail. Yet it established the presumption for ROR in all cases in which a defendant can be bailed and formalized restrictive preventive detention provisions, which are explained in the next section.

Preventive Detention

Those defendants who are charged with serious crimes or are thought likely to escape are generally held in jail until trial. Public concern about crimes committed by those who have been granted pretrial release has given rise to the preventive detention movement. The objective of **preventive detention** is to retain in jail defendants who are deemed dangerous or likely to commit crimes while awaiting trial. This concern for public safety became so strong that by the mid-1980s well over half of the states had enacted preventive detention laws. Despite efforts of reform, millions of people either do not make bail or are denied bail and find themselves in jail awaiting trial while others who have committed misdemeanors are given a jail sentence.

PREVENTIVE DETENTION Retaining in jail defendants who are deemed dangerous or likely to commit crimes while awaiting trial.

Contemporary Jails

From their early beginnings, the contemporary jail has continued to be a social institution. It is generally located in the community, under the authority of a sheriff who must be politically elected, and dependent on local funding. Most jails are small. Today there about 1,500 jails with 1 to 49 beds, 1,300 jails with 50 to 249 beds, 500 jails with 250 to 999 beds, and fewer than 200 jails with more than 1,000 beds.[9]

The jail has developed into a complex correctional institution serving various kinds of inmate populations (see Exhibit 5.1).

MYTH All people, even dangerous felons, are entitled to pretrial release on bail.

FACT Preventive detention statutes have been created that deny bail to dangerous defendants who are charged with serious crimes or are thought likely to escape. These defendants are generally held in jail until trial.

Jail Populations

L03

Nearly 750,000 inmates are held in jails today, though there are more unconvicted inmates in jail than convicted (see Figure 5.3). The number of those in jail actually decreased a bit in 2010. Nonetheless, during the past decade the number of jail inmates rose from 220 to 250 per 100,000 U.S. residents.[10] (See Figure 5.4.) Considering reform efforts and the declining crime rate, why did jail populations increase in this period? There are a number of reasons for this phenomenon. As prisons become more overcrowded, correctional officials use local jails to house inmates for whom there is no room in state prisons. Jail populations also respond to the efforts being made to reduce or control particular crime problems, including substance abuse, spousal abuse, and driving while intoxicated (DWI). Some jurisdictions have passed legislation requiring that people arrested on suspicion of domestic violence be held in confinement for a number of hours to "cool off" before becoming eligible for bail. Other jurisdictions have attempted

EXHIBIT 5.1 Prison and Jail Inmate Populations

- Pretrial detainees, who cannot afford or were denied bail and who are held until their trial or disposition of their case
- Convicted offenders, who are housed in jail for periods of less than one year
- Convicted offenders awaiting sentences; these offenders may be federal, state, or local prisoners
- Misdemeanants, drunks, and the mentally ill
- Mandatory arrests for drunken driving, known across the nation as DWI, DUI (driving under the influence), and OMVI (operating motor vehicle while intoxicated)
- Inmates being held on retainer warrants from other states
- Probation, parole, and bail-bond violators and absconders
- Temporarily detained juveniles pending transfer to juvenile authorities
- Witnesses who are in protective custody or who are being held as witnesses prior to trial
- State and federal inmate prison overflow
- Military police detainees
- Those held for contempt of court
- Inmates about to be released after completing their prison sentence

Source: Todd D. Minton, *Jail Inmates at Midyear 2010—Statistical Tables* (Washington, DC: U.S. Department of Justice, 2011).

FIGURE 5.3 Jail Population: Convicted and Unconvicted

Source: Todd D. Minton, *Jail Inmates at Midyear 2010 – Statistical Tables* (Washington, DC: U.S. Department of Justice, 2011), p. 7.

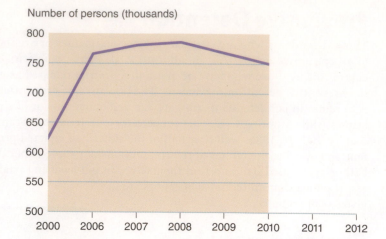

FIGURE 5.4 Persons Held in Jail

Source: Bureau of Justice Statistics, *Jail Statistics* (Washington, DC: U.S. Department of Justice, 2011).

TABLE 5.1 Large Jails and Decline of Jail Populations	
Los Angeles County, California	3,007 inmates
Maricopa County, Arizona	1,196 inmates
Orange County, California	1,143 inmates
Philadelphia, Pennsylvania	1,111 inmates
Fresno County, California	1,105 inmates
Harris County, Texas	1,096 inmates

Source: Todd D. Minton, *Jail Inmates at Midyear 2010—Statistical Tables* (Washington, DC: U.S. Department of Justice, 2011), p. 2.

to deter drunk driving by passing mandatory jail sentences for people convicted of DWI; such legislation can quickly result in overcrowded jails. The recent decline in the actual number of jail inmates may signal an end to growth in the inmate population. Perhaps the decade-long downturn in the crime rate has begun to impact the number of people in jail. Six jail jurisdictions account for nearly half of the decline in jail population (see Table 5.1).

AGE The number of juveniles held in jail peaked at about 10,000 in 1999 and then began a decade-long decline; today there are about 7,200 kids being held in adult jails.[11] The number of juveniles held in jails has declined primarily because of the Juvenile Justice and Delinquency Prevention Act (JJDPA), which grants federal money to cities and states that agree not to confine juveniles in jail. In contrast, the population of elderly jail inmates has more than doubled in size during the past decade.[12] Elderly inmates bring with them their own set of problems, such as the economic challenge of providing health care at a time when state and local budgets are being squeezed.[13]

GENDER As Figure 5.5 shows, male inmates far outnumber females; almost nine out of every 10 jail inmates are adult males. There are also racial disparities in the female jail populations: African American and Hispanic females are more likely to receive jail sentences than are white female inmates.[14]

Female jail inmates face many challenges. The majority of them have children who are dependent on them, and housing is frequently an issue when they are released from jail confinement. Most come from significantly disadvantaged backgrounds. Many have suffered abuse and severe economic disadvantage. One study of 100 female inmates found extremely high rates of lifetime trauma exposure (98 percent), current mental disorders (36 percent), and drug/alcohol problems (74 percent).[15]

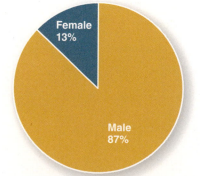

FIGURE 5.5 Percent of Jail Population by Gender

Source: Todd D. Minton, *Jail Inmates at Midyear 2010—Statistical Tables* (Washington, DC: U.S. Department of Justice, 2011), p. 7.

RACE AND ETHNICITY Blacks are almost three times more likely than Hispanics and five times more likely than whites to be in jail (see Figure 5.6 for the number of jail inmates). Euro-Americans and African Americans each make up about 40 percent of the jail population, Hispanics 15 percent, and other races (Asians, American Indians, Alaska Natives, Native Hawaiians, and other Pacific Islanders) the remainder. While African Americans and whites make up the great bulk of the jail population, American Indians are held in local jails at the highest rate of any racial group. Many Indian nations (Indian tribes have the sovereignty of a nation) are creating and running jails, regardless of the cost, because they have determined that they can provide custodial services near home communities.

SOCIAL CLASS Despite bail reform efforts, the poor are still the group least likely to make bail, the ones most likely to commit petty offenses, to have mental health issues, to be considered flight risks, and to be unable to afford restitution. It is not surprising, then, that they remain overrepresented in jail populations. Criminologist John Irwin contends that, more than anything else, jails are "dumping grounds for the poor" and catchalls for uneducated, unemployed, homeless, and impoverished offenders. He refers to these disorderly and disorganized persons as "rabble" and contends that the jail was invented and continues to be operated in order to manage society's rabble.[16] One study found that Irwin's "rabble" theory may be overstated, but the fact still remains that the jail is a social institution in which the poor are overrepresented.[17]

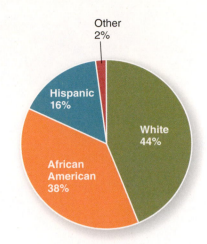

FIGURE 5.6 Jail Population by Race and Ethnicity

Source: Todd D. Minton, *Jail Inmates at Midyear 2010— Statistical Tables* (Washington, DC: U.S. Department of Justice, 2011), p. 7.

Adjustment to Jail

The jail climate is critical to the adjustment of inmates and the quality of work experience for staff. If staff and inmates are getting along, inmates are following the regulations and procedures, and rule violations and violence are at a minimum, the jail climate is much different than in a negative environment in which the jail is ripe for a disturbance, riot, or hostage situation.[18] In some jails, especially large urban ones, pretrial confinement is disruptive and traumatic, especially for a person who has not been to jail before. In this culture, the strong prey on the weak, and an adequate adjustment to jail requires that inmates have the ability to protect themselves. Self-protection becomes particularly challenging if an inmate is not connected to a gang.

Most detained prisoners live in an uncertain world. The uncertainties of jail include questions about the length of confinement, chances of obtaining pretrial release, and the results of the court process. Jail inmates also must deal with inactivity and boredom. The collective impact of the jail environment can lead to tension, anxiety, alienation, and guilt. If not handled in constructive ways, the stress of jail confinement can escalate to crisis proportions, resulting in psychological breakdowns. The rural jails have a much less frightening inmate culture than do urban jails, and other forms of adjustment become more important.

Overcrowded and understaffed jails are the scene of violence, suicide, and inmate drug abuse. Yet it is difficult to increase funding for jails at a time when many Americans are feeling economically pinched at home. Here are jail cells in Rikers Island, New York.

© Michael Yamashita/Corbis

JAIL ADMINISTRATION AND STRUCTURE

The most important features defining how jails function consist of the type of jail administration, the variation in size of other characteristics, the supervision of inmates, and the commitment to programs. County sheriffs usually have operational responsibility for the jails. In some jails, the programs that are offered are quite impressive; in other jails, especially small ones, programs may be few or nearly nonexistent.

CHAPTER 5 | THE JAIL: DETENTION AND SHORT-TERM CONFINEMENT **117**

Local and State Administration and Politics

In more than 3,000 counties in the United States, the sheriff runs the jail. A major problem with this means of jail administration is that sheriffs are politically accountable to county voters, so jails are one of the most political institutions in adult corrections. Sheriffs have received a lot of criticism for their jail administration. Some of the criticism may be deserved, but they also are criticized for things over which they have little control—for example, there may be totally inadequate jail facilities, but the sheriff is unable to get enough money to repair or build a new facility.

However, there are increasing numbers of sheriffs who are attempting to run their jails in a professional way. They have been willing to implement the minimum standards for local jails and detention facilities developed by the National Sheriffs Association. As illustrated by the career of Arnett Gaston earlier in this chapter, they use good management techniques, develop effective staff training, and do everything in their power to make the jail into a humane institution for short-term detainees. They also attempt to anticipate or prevent problems before they take place.

JAIL ADMINISTRATIVE ALTERNATIVES There are three alternatives to local control of jails:

- *State-run jails.* Four states (Connecticut, Delaware, Rhode Island, and Vermont) currently have full operational responsibility for jails. Except for five locally operated jails, Alaska, too, has a state-operated jail system. Although state-run jails offer greater operational efficiency than locally operated jails, political opposition by the counties is one important reason why more states are not likely to select this approach.

- *Cooperative (regional) arrangements.* A widely used alternative to local or state control is regional or multi-county arrangements. Kentucky, Virginia, West Virginia, North Dakota, South Dakota, Nebraska, and Kansas were the first states to adopt regional jails. This arrangement typically takes place when a jurisdiction with an adequate jail is willing to contract with neighboring cities and counties to house prisoners on a per diem basis or when a group of local governments decides that no existing facility is adequate and then decides to build a new regional jail or "detention center." Furthermore, local governments may decide to specialize and house different populations, such as juveniles, females, pretrial detainees, or convicted felons awaiting transportation to state prisons. Transportation problems, multi-jurisdiction funding problems, and turf disputes limit or prohibit the even wider use of cooperative arrangements among local governments.

- *State-subsidized programs.* State subsidies provide a third way to reach beyond locally operated jails, with their politics and financial constraints. Almost 60 percent of the states provide technical assistance to local governments having jail problems, and about 50 percent provide training for jail personnel. In addition,

CORRECTIONAL LIFE
Chris: You're in Jail

"I was in the largest jail lockup in the United States, the Los Angeles County Jail. This jail is a cement monolith that houses in excess of 1,000 men on any given day. Over 50 percent of the 150,000-plus inmates in California's 33 prisons originated from Los Angeles County. This jail is affectionately known throughout the state as the "concrete jungle." It houses the most dangerous lockups in the state, if not the country. L.A. County is a training ground for young L.A. gang members. It's where they earn their "bones"—that is, it is where they stab rival gang members and show their "homies" that they are "down" and willing to die for the clique, the gang. For the unaffiliated, inmates that are not in gangs, L.A. County is a treacherous maze. Civility is taken as a weakness. Like prison, the use of violence is the only way to gain respect. You either learn to fight and defend your person, or become a victim who is mentally and physically abused. There is no middle ground. The culture is primitive. Rehabilitation or redemption doesn't figure into the equation. Life in the concrete jungle is all about survival."

Source: Statement prepared by an inmate who was released from the Los Angeles County Jail.

some subsidy programs assist jails in complying with state standards and in making capital improvements ordered by courts.

In addition to state and local control, there has been some effort to turn jails over to private management.

FOUR GENERATIONS OF JAIL SUPERVISION

FIGURE 5.7 First-Generation Jail: Intermittent Surveillance

Source: National Institute of Corrections, *Direct Supervision, Jail Informative Packet* (Washington, DC: U.S. Department of Justice, 1993).

The four generations of jail supervision are the linear/intermittent surveillance of inmates, the indirect or podular/remote surveillance of inmates, the direct or podular/direct supervision of inmates, and the new OmniView Total Supervision (OVTS).

First-Generation Jails

First-generation jails are designed to provide linear/intermittent surveillance of inmates, which involves staff's providing supervision of inmates from time to time, as they tour the linear cellblocks (see Figure 5.7). A typical first-generation jail has inmates living in dormitories or multiple-occupancy cells. In this model, staff/inmate interaction usually takes place through bars. The layout is similar to that of a hospital in which long rows of rooms open onto a corridor. Electronic surveillance has been used to compensate for the weakness of the linear design. But officers monitoring banks of video screens find it difficult to maintain effective watchfulness because of preoccupation with other activities, having to view too many cameras, and fatigue. Management in first-generation jails assumes that they hold violent inmates who express their rage by victimizing each other, assaulting staff members, destroying property, and attempting to escape. Nonetheless, because officers can usually see into only one or two cells at a time, these facilities experience high rates of inmate sexual assaults, fights, suicides, accidents, and unexpected medical emergencies.[19]

Second-Generation Jails

Second-generation jails are designed to provide indirect or podular/remote surveillance. Because the officers' station is inside a secure room and separated from the inmates' living area, supervision is indirect. Observation is enabled through protective windows in front of a console/desk. Microphones and speakers inside the living unit permit officers to hear and communicate with inmates (see Figure 5.8). This approach gives rise to several problems:

- Although the staff can observe activity in day rooms, they are unable to respond quickly to problems.

- If a problem occurs in a pod, the officer has to call "out front" for assistance.

- The flow of information between officers and inmates is drastically reduced.

- On-duty staff often overlook minor infractions because they believe it is not worth the trouble to call for assistance.

- Staff lacks knowledge of individual inmates and thus has to make guesses about levels of stress when trouble seems to be brewing in the pod.[20]

This form of jail construction, as with first-generation jails, has the basic problem that inmates and staff are separated.

FIRST-GENERATION JAIL Focuses on staff providing linear/intermittent surveillance of inmates, which they do by patrolling the corridors and observing inmates in their cells.

SECOND-GENERATION JAIL Staff use remote supervision as they remain in a secure control booth surrounded by inmate pods or living areas.

FIGURE 5.8 Second-Generation Jail: Remote Surveillance

Source: National Institute of Corrections, *Direct Supervision, Jail Informative Packet* (Washington, DC: U.S. Department of Justice, 1993).

L05 → # New-Generation Jail

The **new-generation jail**, or direct-supervision model, originated at three metropolitan correctional centers (MCCs) operated by the Federal Bureau of Prisons in the early 1970s, and is based on the direct or podular/direct supervision of inmates, a method that uses the physical plant to manage the jail population. Increasingly popular, there are nearly 500 new-generation jails currently being employed around the United States (see Figure 5.9).[21]

Richard Werner identified five components that structure the new-generation model:

1. To create a new understanding of the role of the officer in the institution
2. To take officers out of control rooms and place them in living areas where they could interact directly with inmates
3. To implement decentralized, small living units (functional unit management)
4. To promote the use of noninstitutional environments
5. To define this new system and to identify its management principles[22]

Direct-supervision (DS) jails place the correctional officers' station within the inmates' living area, or pod, which means the officer can see and speak to inmates. During the day, inmates stay in the open area (day room). Generally, they are not permitted to go into their cells except with permission. If they do so, they must quickly return. The officer controls door locks to cells from the control panel. He or she also carries a small radio worn on the front of the shirt that permits immediate communication with other jail staff if the need arises. In addition, the day room is covered by a video camera monitored in the central control room.

Direct supervision offers many advantages: effective control and supervision of inmates; improved communication between staff and inmates; safety of staff and inmates; manageable and cost-effective operations; improved classification and

NEW-GENERATION JAIL A facility with a podular architectural design that emphasizes the interaction of inmates and staff.

FIGURE 5.9 Direct-Supervision Jail

Source: National Institute of Corrections, *Direct Supervision, Jail Informative Packet* (Washington, DC: U.S. Department of Justice, 1993).

orientation of inmates, especially programming for specialized offender groups; staff ownership of operations; and the ability to shut a pod down when populations are low.

However, there are also some disadvantages with this model, including the difficulty of selling the jail to a public that tends to see the layout as a means of "coddling" prisoners, the amount of training needed to make the transition to the new style of supervision, and the fact that the overcrowding issue makes this design hard to implement.[23] Christine Tartaro's examination of a national survey of new-generation jails found that many of these jails fail to include important components of the ideal direct-supervision jails, such as normalized living environments, in their facilities.[24]

Yet national surveys further show that direct-supervision jails are an effective means of inmate management and have been accepted as best practice by agencies at the federal, state, and local levels and by accrediting organizations. DS facilities are consistently perceived by staff and inmates to have safe environments and experience fewer violent or security-related incidents than traditional jails.[25]

Fourth-Generation Jail

The OmniView Total Supervision (OVTS) jail and prison is a concept that is being utilized in several locations. The OVTS incarceration facility encompasses a centrally placed, high-strength mirrored glass control center with a panoramic view that provides 100 percent surveillance of the entire inmate access facility. The complete interior of the cell units, recreation area, stairwells, entryway, and multipurpose rooms are totally visible.[26]

This new correctional facility design complies with the Prison Rape Elimination Act (PREA) in that it establishes a zero-tolerance standard for the incidence of prison rape in U.S. prisons. The design of the OVTS cell can be utilized in single, double, or multiple occupancy cells without any loss of total supervision, which promises to provide increased security as well as increased operational cost savings for all classification needs (see Figure 5.10).

FIGURE 5.10 OmniView Total Supervision

Source: Comparison of Incarceration Supervision Types: Final Analysis, www.radialomniview.com/pdf/scan0002.pdf (accessed March 22, 2012).

JAIL PROGRAMS

The lack of programs has long been a criticism of jails. It is difficult for small jails to develop a variety of programs because they lack space, staff, and fiscal resources. They are frequently dependent on volunteers. Large jails have more programs, but overcrowding makes it difficult to offer adequate programming for each inmate. Nevertheless, more programming exists now than was present a generation ago. Carol Higgins O'Brien, the assistant deputy warden in charge of human services, talks about programs in the Middlesex House of Corrections in Massachusetts in the Voices Across the Professions feature.

Larger jails in the United States now generally provide GED and adult basic education programs, drug and alcohol treatment programs, counseling, work release, and jail industries, including inmate work programs and inmate vocational programs. Jails also are required to provide religious services, some exercise equipment, and access to a law library for long-term convicted inmates. Jails are constitutionally mandated to make available adequate health care delivery systems. Some jails have exemplary health care delivery systems; others offer nearly no health care. Some of the crucial health care issues confronting individuals in the jail setting are the following:

- Communicable diseases such as tuberculosis, HIV disease, sexually transmitted disease, hepatitis, and measles

- Chronic diseases such as hypertension, cardiovascular disease, diabetes, renal/liver disease, and lung diseases

- Chemical/substance abuse

- Prenatal care

- Smoking

- Mental health, including caring for the homeless and the mentally incompetent, and preventing suicide

One of the most encouraging aspects of jail programming is the increasing number of programs that are offered to some qualifying jail inmates, ranging from weekend programs, electronic monitoring, day reporting, community service, other pretrial supervision, work programs, and treatment programs. Another important jail program is the interventions conducted in several jails across the nation. These programs attempt to give prisoners greater authority in the operation of their living units while at the same time using staff to teach them to control unwise behavior, instill constructive conduct, and improve communication skills. Evaluations of TC programs have revealed that they can reduce recidivism and drug use, especially when coupled with community-based aftercare.[27] (See Chapter 10 for more information on therapeutic community interventions within correctional environments.)

A model program operated in the Boulder, Colorado, County Jail has an impressive array of programs offered for inmates:

- A work release dormitory is connected to but separate from the main jail.

- A public health detox facility provides 24-hour inpatient detox services for up to 20 clients, plus a transitional residential program, daily treatment support groups, and sobriety monitoring services for clients who are sober.

- The jail has all the programs that larger jails usually provide, including adult basic education programs, drug and alcohol treatment programs, and inmate vocational programs.

A number of other programs are offered, partly because of an extensively developed volunteer program where volunteers work directly with inmates at

© Carol Higgins O'Brien

" I really love what I do. . . . I see fulfillment and the feelings of success when an inmate is ready to be released and is more equipped than he was when he came here to stay out of trouble. "

CAROL HIGGINS O'BRIEN
ASSISTANT SUPERINTENDENT/
WARDEN OF HUMAN SERVICES

I have been working in corrections for about 30 years. Currently I work at the Middlesex Sheriff's Office at the House of Correction. I have been with this department since July 2011 when I came from another sheriff's department after 11 years. In Massachusetts, we have county corrections where pretrial detainees are held in jails. Sentenced inmates can receive up to two and a half years, usually for misdemeanors but sometimes felonies.

We currently house approximately 800 inmates. This number can vary and a few years ago there were 1,200 inmates here. The main building was built in the 1920s and has three old-style tiers; the new facility is four years old and has a podular design with the direct supervision concept. The podular units are where most of the programs take place. We also have a community work building for minimum security, a work release house, and an electronic monitoring program where inmates live in the community, at home, or in a program and wear an electronic monitoring bracelet and attend a day reporting center.

As assistant superintendent/warden of human services, my responsibilities include treatment, classification, program assessment, educational and vocational programs, religious programming, and substance abuse programs. We have several programs we are proud of. Here are a few examples:

- Digital imaging print shop that teaches inmates the newest version of printing and graphic arts design, providing viable employment opportunities upon release

- Culinary arts program that teaches this industry and provides a certificate from a local technical high school and community college credits

- A custodial training program is about to begin, which will lead to custodial certification

One of the problems we face here is that inmates stay a short amount of time, which means that the time for programming and preparation for reentry is limited. As I tell inmates, they often lack the tools necessary for successful reentry; we try to give them those tools, and fill their toolbox during their stay to help facilitate greater success upon the return to the communities they came from. There is also the major problem with budget constraints. We need to do more with less. The question we face is: how creative can you be and think outside of the box, so we can utilize the resources we have? A further problem is helping staff deal with the stressful environment of a correctional facility. This is not a normal work environment and our staff needs to be able to manage the stress. We are also trying to predict future human behavior and we all know that is not an exact science.

I really love what I do. My movement through my career has always kept my job fresh. It is also very refreshing when your staff like their jobs and like what they do. I see fulfillment and the feelings of success when an inmate is ready to be released and is more equipped than he was when he came here to stay out of trouble; his toolbox is full. For example, I ran into an offender I had worked with in a state prison a few years ago. He wanted to thank me for helping him. He said he was clean and sober, was happily married, and had his own business.

Source: Interviewed in 2012.

the jail. Volunteers provide such services as literacy tutoring; Prison Dharma Network, which focuses on meditation and Buddhist spiritual teachings; the "Productive Day" program, which has a goal of eight hours of productive activity—including education, work, or treatment—for every inmate, every day; teaching crocheting and knitting, so that female offenders can create lap robes to be distributed to nursing facilities, particularly those housing low-income residents; and the Boulder County Jail Garden, where master gardeners mentor inmate workers to take care of vegetable and flower gardens.[28]

JAIL OFFICERS

The job of the more than 200,000 correctional officers in jails (sometimes designated as jail officers, corrections deputies, or sheriff's deputies) has changed in recent years.[29] Both the emergence of the new-generation jail as well as the changes resulting from the movement toward professionalism in the jail have been major factors contributing to this change.

Changing Roles

In the past, when a male applicant was interviewed for an entry-level position in the jail, he might be asked whether he could fight or liked to fight. It was widely accepted that the way to establish and maintain control over the jail population was through brute force. As a result, those who worked in the jail were expected to be physically able to handle inmates. There was little or no training given to recruits. It was also widely accepted that police deputies would spend a few years working in the jail and would be transferred to the streets when they had proven their mettle within the jail. In addition, those deputies who had disciplinary problems on patrol would be reassigned to the jail.[30]

Today, officers who work in the jail, especially more progressive ones, are seen as professionals. Women compose one-third of all jail employees, but minority employees are underrepresented in terms of their proportion among inmates. Officers are well trained in correctional academies and know how to negotiate and mediate conflicts with inmates. They are equipped to write reports, because of the realization that the vast preponderance of litigation for the sheriff comes from problems that emerge in the jail. These officers are not the rejects of law enforcement who could not make it on the streets, but individuals who have the capacity for promising careers in jail administration. The greater parity in pay and benefits has also resulted in improved morale and job longevity.[31]

Yet the role of the officer in a jail context does have its challenges. The population of the jail constantly changes, and the officer is interacting with persons from a wide variety of ethnic and social backgrounds. Working with everyone from career criminals to those who were arrested for the first time, the officer needs to be able to respond in a professional manner to as many known situations as can reasonably be expected to occur. The officer must understand that any violation of constitutional rights of an inmate may have the highest potential for personal or agency liability. In addition, occupational stress can be a problem.

The vast majority of research has been conducted on correctional officers and the prison work environment, but there is beginning to be an interest in examining the role of officers in jails. In one study examining stress among jail correctional officers in a northeastern state, the results indicated that perceived danger, role problems, job satisfaction, and organizational strengths were significant predictors of both occupational and general stress. Gender and salary predicted occupational stress, while training and correctional experience predicted general stress.[32] Another study, based on interviews with officers at a large southeastern jail, found that male and female

A jail officer takes a palm print in Santa Ana, California. Jail officers are viewed today as well-trained professionals, equipped to negotiate and mediate conflicts with inmates, write reports, and interact with prisoners from a wide range of ethnic and social backgrounds.

CAREERS in Corrections

JAIL OFFICER

Preparation for the Job

Jail officers need to be stable and mature individuals who can handle job responsibilities and the stress of working in a jail context.

Nature of the Job

Jail officers have the responsibility of overseeing individuals who have been arrested or are awaiting trial or who have been convicted of a crime and are sentenced to serve time in a jail. They maintain security and inmate accountability to prevent assaults, disturbances, and escapes. Sheriff's departments typically place newly appointed deputies in the jail for a period of time until they are transferred to law enforcement responsibilities on the streets. Some sheriff's departments will employ jail officers in permanent positions in the jail; they may be known as detention officers. In jail facilities with direct-supervision cellblocks, officers work unarmed. They are equipped with communication devices so they can summon help if necessary.

Qualifications and Required Education

Most jails require correctional officers to be at least 18 to 21 years of age and a U.S. citizen; have a high school education or its equivalent; demonstrate job stability, usually by accumulating two years of work experience; and have no felony convictions. The possibility of promotion may be enhanced by obtaining a postsecondary education. Federal, state, and some local departments of corrections provide training for correctional officers based on guidelines established by the American Correctional Association and the American Jail Association.

Job Outlook

Job opportunities for correctional officers who work in the jail are expected to be excellent. The need to replace correctional officers who transfer to other occupations, retire, or leave the labor force, along with rising employment demand, will generate thousands of job possibilities each year.

Earnings and Benefits

Today, the mean annual earnings of jailers is in the mid-$40,000s. The mean annual earnings of first-line supervisors/managers of correctional officers is in the high $40,000 range. In addition to typical benefits, correctional officers usually are provided with a uniform or a clothing allowance to purchase their own uniforms. Their retirement coverage entitles correctional officers to retire at age 50 after 20 years of service or at any age with 25 years of service.

Source: U.S. Bureau of Labor Statistics, *Occupational Outlook Handbook*, 2010–11 Edition, www.bls.gov/oco/ (accessed February 24, 2012).

officers react to conflict situations in a similar manner, although it seems that the inmate's sex is a salient factor in officers' decisions on how to resolve conflict.[33] The job of the officer in the jail is featured in the Careers in Corrections feature.

 ## ISSUES OF JAIL CONFINEMENT

The most serious issues facing the jail involve crowding, mental health placements, violence, and suicides. Like other correctional institutions in the United States, jails have not escaped the skyrocketing influx of prisoners. Mental hospitals have traditionally provided for the mentally ill, but as shrinking budgets have caused many state hospitals to close their doors, the mentally ill now circulate between mental health clinics, homelessness, and jail. Violence, especially in large facilities with linear supervision, continues to be a way of life in the jail.[34] Overcrowding and idleness among heterogeneous populations provide an ideal setting for the strong to take advantage of the weak. Suicides have always been a problem within the jail context.

Jail Crowding

Jail crowding has grown progressively worse in the past two decades. Jail populations have nearly tripled since 1985.[35] Ten states, led by Louisiana, Texas, and Mississippi, exceeded the national incarceration rate. Some jails have reached the point where crowding makes it impossible to accept more prisoners. Other jails, under court order, must find ways to reduce the number of prisoners.

A contributing factor to jail crowding is that in some states many thousands of state and federal prisoners are being held in local jails. What makes jail crowding such a serious problem is that jails have even fewer alternatives for dealing with overcrowded facilities than do federal and state institutions. The Federal Bureau of Prisons and states can transfer inmates from one facility to another. Parole boards in some overcrowded states release prisoners early. Such options are not usually available to jail administrators, who are dependent on bail reform acts, speedy trials, and the benevolence of judges to alleviate overcrowded jail conditions.

Overcrowding is particularly acute in large urban jails, which hold more than 50 percent of the U.S. jail population. The Tombs in New York City, the Cook County Jail in Chicago, the Los Angeles County Jail, the old District of Columbia jail, and the jails in Atlanta, Dallas, and Houston have continually suffered from scandalously overcrowded conditions.

One of the problems resulting from overcrowding is inmate idleness. A long-accepted adage is that busy inmates create fewer problems than idle inmates. A few jails run work farms, and the city workhouses usually have labor gangs. But in existent jail programs, makeshift work and maintenance tasks usually are not adequate. The endless empty hours in day rooms, accompanied by the usual restricted movement within the jail, result in restless prisoners. In first- and second-generation jails, idleness is one of the factors contributing to high rates of physical and sexual assaults among inmates.[36]

Mental Health Placements

The steadily increasing number of mentally ill inmates is one of the most serious issues facing jail administration. Federal statistics reveal that the number of mentally ill inmates in U.S. jails and prisons has quadrupled in recent years. More than half of all prison and jail inmates report mental health problems, including symptoms of major depression as well as manic and psychotic disorders.[37]

- Jail inmates who had a mental health problem (24 percent) were three times as likely as jail inmates without (8 percent) to report being physically or sexually abused in the past.

- Twenty-one percent of jail inmates reported having a history of a mental health problem.

- Twenty-four percent of jail inmates reported at least one symptom of psychotic disorder.

- Fourteen percent of jail inmates reported that they had used prescribed medication for a mental problem in the year before arrest or since admission.[38]

Mentally ill offenders are often arrested because community-based treatment programs do not exist, are filled to capacity, or are inconveniently located. The downsizing or elimination of community-based mental health treatment has resulted in increasing numbers of the diagnosed mentally ill being sent to jail. Officials affirm that persons with severe mental illness are commonly jailed for such minor breaches of the law as vagrancy, trespassing, alcohol-related charges, disorderly conduct, or failing to pay for a meal.

Mentally ill prisoners pose a special problem for the jail. The most common mental health services in jails are intake screening and evaluation, crisis intervention and suicide prevention, and the prescription of psychotropic medications.[39] However, officers' lack of training and insufficient intervention for mentally ill prisoners make these prisoners high risk for jail confinement. Ideally, the mentally ill prisoner would be transferred to a psychiatric facility, but these facilities are often reluctant to accept troublesome prisoners with criminal histories.

One does not have to be around a jail very long to discover the inability of mentally ill individuals to adjust to this environment. They may slump in a corner of their cell in a fetal position; they may be severely withdrawn and appear to be out of touch with what is happening to them. They may spend a good part of the day moaning or groaning in a loud voice. They may have conversations with imaginary partners or protectors. Or they may make ongoing attempts to injure themselves or commit suicide.

The Substance Abuse and Mental Health Services Administration (SAMHSA), particularly its Center for Mental Health Services (CMHS), makes federal funding available for programs designed to divert those with mental illness from jail to support services in mental health treatment programs. During the past decade, SAMHSA funded 20 proposals to implement prebooking and postbooking jail diversion programs.[40]

Violence

Violence in the jail setting consists of collective violence or riots, physical assaults (inmate/inmate, inmate/staff, and staff/inmate), and inmate suicides. Unlike long-term correctional facilities, or prisons, whose history has been checkered with riots and mass disturbances, jails have infrequently had problems with mass disturbances (such as hunger strikes of inmates or destruction of property) and almost never have inmates been organized enough to become involved in a riot and take over a cellblock.

Inmate/inmate physical assaults, including rapes, are the most frequent types of violence. The good news is that physical and sexual assaults take place less frequently in newer jails, with direct supervision of inmates. The bad news is that assaults continue to be a problem in older jails, especially large urban jails. In these jails, women and first-offending males are the most likely victims. Proactive jail administrators have contributed to the reduction of physical assaults (see Arnett Gaston in Voices Across the Profession).

Staff/inmate physical assaults have not appeared to increase with the implementation of direct supervision. And when they do occur in the jail setting, it is usually involved with a jail officer becoming injured in the process of controlling disruptive inmates. Staff/inmate assaults also appear to have decreased, even though blatant examples surface from time to time. For example, on April 13, 2007, 11 federal jail officers, including a captain and three lieutenants, were charged in the Federal District Court in Brooklyn, New York, with beating two inmates. Five were convicted for the first beating and four in the second beating.[41]

Jail Suicides

The problem of jail suicide continues to plague jail administrators. The attempt to determine the intent behind an often intoxicated or despondent inmate's verbal and physical actions can appear to be an exercise in futility.[42] Sufficient evidence is available to conclude that suicide attempt rates and successful suicide rates are much higher in jails and prisons than in the larger community. Christine Tartaro and Rick Ruddell's national study of suicide found that the prevalence of suicide is two to five times greater in smaller jails than in larger jails. Their study also revealed that special-needs inmates and long-term inmates had higher levels of suicide attempts.[43] A study of suicide victims in jails and prisons in the Netherlands revealed that bullying and suicide risk are related and that a distinction should be made between mild and serious features of bullying and their influence on suicide.[44]

While still a serious problem, jail suicides have declined steadily for the past two decades. Nonetheless, the jail suicide rate is over three times the rate in state prisons, with violent offenders the ones most likely to take their own life.[45] Reasons for the relatively high rate may include that those entering jail are cut off from drugs and alcohol which they may have used for self-medication on the outside, that they realize they may be facing a long prison sentence, and that for the first time they are cut off from the support of family and friends.

Most jails have suicide prevention programs—less than 3 percent of jails fail to have such a program.[46] If inmates are considered a high risk for suicide, they may be monitored with **suicide watch programs**, in which inmates are placed in specially equipped cells that do not contain anything (belts, sheets, blankets) that can be used for a suicide attempt and in which there is frequent supervision (generally every 30 minutes or so). Cameras are sometimes placed in the cell to maintain ongoing supervision. These methods seem to be working, as the rates of jail suicides have been in decline. Still, suicides remain a problem for jail staff, especially in terms of inmates new to the jail setting.

The TechnoCorrections feature shows how jail administrators are attempting to use technology to monitor the whereabouts of inmates, with the goal of reducing violence by increasing control over inmate movements.

 TRENDS SHAPING THE JAIL

In recent years, a number of promising proposals for jail reform have been recommended and implemented. The direct supervision of inmates that is found in the new-generation jail is becoming increasingly common across the nation. Indeed, nearly half or more of the recently constructed jails provide direct supervision.

The Commission on Accreditation of Corrections of the American Correctional Association (ACA), the National Sheriff's Association, and the federal government are proposing minimum standards for the construction and operation of jails. Thirty-two states have established standards for jails, and in 25 states these standards are mandatory. In 2004, the ACA published the *Performance-Based Standards for Adult Local Detention Facilities: Fourth Edition*, which promised to provide a "new generation" of jail standards.

In addition, seven states in recent years have enacted legislation that transfers control of local jails to state government, and many more states have established procedures for state inspection of local jails. Furthermore, regional jails, serving multiple cities or counties, have become a large part of the landscape of American jails. Privatization of the jail, whether in providing particular services or in taking over the operation of the jail, is becoming increasingly widespread on the correctional landscape.

SUICIDE WATCH PROGRAMS Inmates are placed in special cells and are supervised more frequently, usually every 30 minutes or less.

Keeping track of inmates within a jail can be challenging, especially as they move about the facility. Monitoring inmate movements requires correctional officers to accurately identify individual prisoners by sight as they pass through security posts and to be in frequent telephone and radio communication between officers at two or more security posts. They must check paper passes authorizing inmates' movements and create records to note when prisoners leave one area and enter another. Despite the best precautions and well-thought-out practices, mistakes can be made, officers' attention can be diverted, and tardy inmates not noticed or searched for promptly. This process can be critical since assaults and even murders have been committed by inmates as they moved from one part of a prison or jail to another.

Biometrics—using physiological or behavioral characteristics such as iris, retinal, and facial recognition; hand and finger geometry; fingerprint and voice identification; and dynamic signature—is now being used to keep track of jail inmates. Biometrics systems are usually deployed using a three-step process. First, a camera, scanner, or other sensor takes an image or picture. Second, that image is made into a pattern called a biometric signature. For example, with fingerprints the signature comprises minute points along a finger's ridges, splits, and end lines. Voice recognition involves patterns of cadence, pitch, and tone. Hand and finger geometry measures physical characteristics such as length and thickness. Third, the biometric signature is converted into a template using a mathematical algorithm. Templates contain biometric and other data in the form of numbers that are either embedded on a plastic card or stored in a database. Some systems use a card that can be inserted in or held near a scanner that feeds the information on the card into a computer. The computer compares the biometric signature captured by the scanner with those already in its files to find the correct match.

The Biometric Inmate Tracking System (BITS) has been tested in the U.S. Navy's prison in Charleston, South Carolina. All biometric methods—iris, facial, retinal, finger and hand geometry, voice, and fingerprint—were tested, and the fingerprint recognition method, now used in conjunction with hand geometry, was judged to work best. It provided the most accurate and reliable matches at about one-third the cost of iris, facial, and retinal methods. The fingerprint method also moved prisoners through the gates faster than the others. That's a prime consideration when, for example, correctional specialists are moving 50 or more prisoners at once from housing or work areas to the galley at mealtime. Fingerprint readers are also easier to use and more durable than other readers.

Evaluation of the system indicates that it can be a very effective way of monitoring inmates, freeing jail officers from handling paper passes and allowing them to spend more time actually watching inmates in their area. While final evaluations have not been completed, project staff are optimistic that with further testing and analysis, biometrics technology can be used successfully in U.S. prisons and jails to identify and track inmates.

Radio Frequency Identification (RFID) Technology

Corrections officials are also beginning to use radio frequency identification (RFID) technology to monitor and track jail inmates. RFID uses small transponders called tags to track movements. RFID tags can be attached to or incorporated into a variety of objects, such as wristbands. Each tag has an integrated circuit and a tiny antenna to handle radio signals and can be used with a network of sensors—called RFID readers—to track movements. For example, a few correctional institutions have used the systems to provide information on prisoners' movements and to alert staff if there is an unusual concentration of people in a certain area. Movement information can be stored in computers and could prove useful in investigations to determine who was present in a certain part of a building at a particular time. Although RFID technology is mature and has been used to track inventory in warehouses, its use in correctional facilities is relatively new and untested but still holds great promise.

Sources: Philip Bulman, "Using Technology to Make Prisons and Jails Safer," *NIJ Journal* 262 (2009), www.nij.gov/journals/262/corrections-technology.htm (accessed February 24, 2012); Christopher Miles and Jeffrey Cohn, "Tracking Prisoners in Jail with Biometrics: An Experiment in a Navy Brig," *NIJ Journal* 253 (2006), www.ojp.usdoj.gov/nij/journals/253/tracking.html (accessed February 24, 2012).

The quality of life in jail, particularly for non-urban jails, has experienced improvement. In some jails, programming has been expanded to include drug treatment, jail industries, boot camps, and self-help programs. Jail inmates have increasingly been released from jail for day reporting and treatment, community service, work release, and weekend release. One of these programs is the subject of the Evidence-Based Corrections feature. Finally, more extensive in-service training, as well as college-educated officers, is being used to improve jail operations.

Iowa's Jail-Based Assessment and Treatment Project

The Jail-Based Assessment and Treatment Project is being tested in three Iowa counties (Polk, Scott, and Woodbury) and focuses on caring for jail inmates suffering from substance abuse and criminal thinking. Clients are admitted to the project and begin their treatment while in jail. Clients take part in substance abuse and criminal thinking treatment, individual and group therapy sessions, support groups, educational classes, and discharge plan development. The program continues in the community with an outpatient component followed by aftercare. The same case manager who works with participants in jail follows them in the community during their outpatient and aftercare phases.

The district attorney, public defender, and probation/parole officer refer potential project participants to the jail assessment team. The in-jail portion of the project lasts from 45 days to 4 months, during which participants concentrate on their criminal thinking and substance abuse treatment simultaneously. Each participant has a case manager and a treatment counselor. Case managers and treatment counselors begin developing a discharge plan in jail once the participant enters the program.

Program participants are released to community outpatient treatment for six to nine months for them to continue their criminal thinking and substance abuse treatment in individual and group therapy sessions. Following outpatient treatment, participants enter the aftercare stage. Aftercare consists of a peer support group once a week. A team that usually includes a case manager, counselor, and probation officer works with program participants in the community for up to one year after release and assists them with educational and employment services and staying engaged in their treatment. Participants have the same case manager in the community that they had in jail.

Each county contracts with a private treatment agency to provide assessments and treatment in jail and in the community. Project stakeholders include public health staff, judges, probation officers, county sheriffs, risk assessment officers, public defenders, district attorneys, treatment staff, and staff from the local mental health centers. These stakeholders keep close contact with one another to maintain communication, voice concerns, and discuss various problems such as waiting lists and referrals.

Does It Work?

The Iowa Consortium for Substance Abuse Research and Evaluation, located at the University of Iowa, conducts ongoing evaluations of the Jail-Based Assessment and Treatment Project to determine the effectiveness of treatment services. The study measures outcomes along three variables—abstinence, rearrest, and employment—with follow-up interviews six and twelve months after admission to the project. (In Woodbury and Scott Counties, the typical participant will have been out of jail for about four months when the six-month interview is conducted. The typical Polk County participant will have been out of jail for about two months.) Six months after admission to the project, 77 percent of clients had abstained from drug use, 93 percent had not been rearrested, and more than half (52 percent) were employed full time, compared with 31 percent who were employed just before entering the program. Twelve months after admission, 69 percent had abstained from drug use, 84 percent had avoided arrest, and 56 percent were employed full time. At the 12-month mark, 81 percent of those who were successfully discharged from the project were abstinent from drugs, 92 percent had not been rearrested, and 68 percent were working full time. These data are evidence of the program's effectiveness.

Source: Adapted from Amy L. Solomon, Jenny W. L. Osborne, Stefan F. LoBuglio, Jeff Mellow, and Debbie A. Mukamal, "Life After Lockup, Improving Re-entry from Jail to the Community," Urban Institute, Washington, DC, 2008, www.ojp.usdoj.gov/BJA/pdf/LifeAfterLockup.pdf (accessed February 24, 2012).

SUMMARY

 Describe the purpose of the jail

The basic purpose of the jail is to hold pretrial detainees who cannot afford bail or were denied bail and convicted offenders who are housed in jail for periods of less than one year. In addition, the jail holds such populations as mandatory arrests for drunken driving, inmates being held in retainer warrants from other states, witnesses are in protective custody, and those held for contempt of court.

 Explain the bail process, pretrial release, and preventive detention

Defendants, of course, wish to receive bail, which means they are released from jail until their trial takes place. If they cannot raise the money for bail or are ineligible for pretrial release, it is necessary for them to stay in jail until their trial. Preventive detention is a recent movement with an objective to retain in jail defendants who are deemed dangerous or likely to commit crimes while awaiting trial.

LO3 ▶ Identify the makeup of the jail population

The makeup of the jail continues to be largely poor, adult, male, and minority inmates, but the numbers of female inmates have increased in recent years.

LO4 ▶ Discuss jail administration and structure

Jails are highly political institutions, with the sheriff, an elected official, responsible for jail operations. There are three alternatives to local control of jails: state-run jails, cooperative (regional) arrangements, and state-subsidized programs.

LO5 ▶ Compare the new-generation jail with more traditional jails

In recent years, a new-generation jail has increasingly replaced the traditional linear-design jail.

New-generation jails still must often deal with problems of overcrowding, but direct supervision of inmates, increased programming, and improved staff morale make this jail a more desirable placement for inmates.

LO6 ▶ Describe jail-based treatment programs

Large jails typically provide a variety of programs, including GED and adult basic education programs, drug and alcohol treatment programs, counseling, work release, and jail industries.

LO7 ▶ Explain the legal and administrative issues of jail confinement

Jail crowding, mental health services, and the possibility of violence are three of the most serious issues facing the jail.

LO8 ▶ Discuss the future trends of the jail

Voluntary and state-required jail standards, as well as regional or multi-county arrangements of jails, are other hopeful signs that the jails of the twenty-first century will be an improvement over those of the nineteenth and twentieth centuries.

Key Terms

jail, 110
booking, 112
pretrial release, 112
bail bond, 112
bail bondsman, 112
release on own recognizance (ROR), 113

unsecured bail, 113
percentage bail, 113
third-party custody, 113
signature bond, 113
supervised release, 113
Manhattan Bail Project, 113
Bail Reform Act of 1966, 113

Bail Reform Act of 1984, 114
preventive detention, 115
first-generation jail, 119
second-generation jail, 119
new-generation jail, 120
suicide watch programs, 128

 ## Critical Thinking Questions

1. Jails have been regarded as totally inadequate institutions. Why was that description frequently accurate in the past? Why is it less likely to be true today?

2. Is there such a thing as a good jail? Imagine yourself inside a good one and describe it.

3. What is pretrial diversion? Who is most likely to receive it?

4. Direct-supervision jails seem so much better than linear-design jails. What problems do you see in direct-supervision jails? How much do you believe the new-generation jail is likely to improve the overall quality of jails in the United States?

5. What programs do you believe a large urban jail needs to offer?

 ## Thinking Like a Corrections Professional

You are the undersheriff (in charge) at the Y County Jail. The rated capacity is 350, but the population for the last six months has exceeded 500. No relief is in sight. The budget is tight, and the food is meager and unappetizing. A handsome 18-year-old inmate asks for an interview with you. He tells you that the older men in the tank to which he is assigned attempted to sexually assault him after lights-out. He wants protection. He is serving a year and a day for auto theft and has nearly all of it left to serve. How would you handle this situation?

Sexual exploitation is not your only problem. The traffic in cocaine and marijuana in Y County is heavy and poorly controlled by the police. A lot of stuff is coming into the jail. A study by the district attorney's investigative staff finds that officers are bringing much of it for sale to inmate gang leaders. The investigators recommend that all officers be routinely frisked when they arrive at work. You know that many officers will protest that this is unfair to the law-abiding majority of the staff. Will you adopt the district attorney's recommendation anyway? If so, how will you deal with the protest by correctional officers that is sure to follow? What measures would you employ to eliminate traffic in drugs inside the jail?

Career Destinations

Interested in a job as a jail officer? Read this job description from Northern Neck Regional Jail in Virginia:
www.nnrj.state.va.us/employment/Jail_Officer_Full.htm

Here are the salary ranges for various jail employees at that same jail:

www.nnrj.state.va.us/about/salary%20range.pdf

Go to the American Jail Association site to learn more about careers, training, and so on:
www.aja.org

Notes

1. Tim Kenneally, "Dr. Conrad Murray Sentenced to 4 years for Michael Jackson's Death," *The Wrap*, November 29, 2011, www.thewrap.com/music/article/dr-conrad-murray-sentenced-michael-jackson-death-33129 (accessed February 23, 2012).
2. "Dr. Conrad Murray to Be Sentenced for Involuntary Manslaughter of Michael Jackson," Associated Press, November 29, 2011, www.foxnews.com/entertainment/2011/11/29/dr-conrad-murray-to-be-sentenced-for-involuntary-manslaughter-michael-jackson/ (accessed February 23, 2012).
3. Ibid.
4. Ibid.
5. Ibid.
6. Mari Fagel, "Conrad Murray's Delusional Appeal: What It Means," *Huffington Post*, December 5, 2011, www.huffingtonpost.com/mari-fagel/conrad-murrays-delusional_b_1129102.html (accessed February 23, 2012).
7. Todd D. Minton, *Jail Inmates at Midyear 2010—Statistical Tables* (Washington, DC: U.S. Department of Justice, 2011).
8. Stephen Demuth, "Racial and Ethnic Differences in Pretrial Release Decisions and Outcomes: A Comparison of Hispanic, Black, and White Felony Arrestees," *Criminology* 41 (August 2003): 873–907.
9. *National Jail and Adult Detention Directory 2012* (College Park, MD: American Correctional Association, 2012).
10. Bureau of Justice Statistics, *Jail Statistics* (Washington, DC: U.S. Department of Justice, 2011).
11. Ibid.
12. Ibid.
13. Human Rights Watch, *Old Behind Bars: The Aging Prison Population in the United States* (New York: Human Rights Watch, 2012). See also Robynn Kuhlmann and Rick Ruddell, "Elderly Jail Inmates: Problems, Prevalence and Public Health," *California Journal of Health Promotion* 3 (2005): 49–60.
14. Ibid.; and Pauline K. Brennan, "Sentencing Female Misdemeanants: A Examination

15. Bonnie Green, Jeanne Miranda, Anahita Darowalla, and Juned Siddique, "Trauma Exposure, Mental Health Functioning, and Program Needs of Women in Jail," *Crime and Delinquency* 51 (2005): 133–151.
16. John Irwin, *The Jail: Managing the Underclass in American Society* (Berkeley: University of California Press, 1985), pp. 26–38.
17. John A. Backstrand, Don C. Gibbons, and Joseph P. Jones, "What Is in Jail? An Examination of the Rabble Hypothesis," *Crime and Delinquency* 38 (1992): 219–229.
18. Gary F. Cornelius, *The American Jail: Cornerstone of Modern Corrections* (Upper Saddle River, NJ: Prentice Hall, 2008), p. 97.
19. For the three generations of jails, see William "Ray" Nelson, "New Generation Jails," http://prop1.org/legal/prisons/97jails.htm (accessed February 23, 2012); Allen R. Beck, "Deciding on a New Jail Design," www.justiceconcepts.com/design.htm (accessed February 23, 2012).
20. Beck, "Deciding on a New Jail Design."
21. Stephen I. Saunders, III, *Direct Supervision Jails: A New Management Model for the 21st Century*, www.fdle.state.fl.us/Content/getdoc/08dd615a-20f2-4367-9dd4-c6b23a45278d/Saunders.aspx (accessed March 22, 2012).
22. R. Werner, "The Invention of Direct Supervision," *Corrections Compendium* 30 (2005): 4–7, 32–34.
23. Nelson, "New Generation Jails."
24. Christine Tartaro, "Watered Down: Partial Implementation of the New Generation Jail Philosophy," *Prison Journal* 86 (2006): 284–300.
25. Richard Werner, "Effectiveness of the Direct Supervision System of Correctional Design and Management: A Review of the Literature," *Criminal Justice and Behavior* 33 (June 2006): 403.
26. Comparison of Incarceration Supervision Types: Final Analysis, www.radialomniview.com/pdf/scan0002.pdf.

of the Direct and Indirect Effects of Race/Ethnicity," *Justice Quarterly* 23 (March 2006): 60–95.

27. R. S. Silverman, J. A. Bouffard, and F. S. Taxman, "Inside the Black Box: Short- versus Long-Term On-Site Observations of Community-Based Therapeutic Communities for Drug Offenders," paper presented at the annual meeting of the American Society of Criminology, San Francisco, November 2000.
28. Website for Boulder County, Colorado, www.bouldercounty.org (accessed February 23, 2012).
29 *Sourcebook of Criminal Justice Statistics 2002* (Washington, DC: Bureau of Justice Statistics, 2004).
30. Comments made by F. E. Knowles, February 2007.
31. Ibid.
32. Tammy L. Castle and Jamie S. Martin, "Occupational Hazard: Predictors of Stress Among Jail Correctional Officers," *American Journal of Criminal Justice* 31 (2006): 65–82.
33. Nancy L. Hogan, Eric G. Lambert, John R. Hepburn, Velmer S. Burton, Jr., and Francis T. Cullen, "Is There a Difference? Definitions of and Response to Conflict Situations," *Women and Criminal Justice* 15 (2004): 143–150.
34. Leslie Lunney, "Nowhere Else to Go: Mentally Ill and in Jail," *Jail Suicidal Mental Health Update* (Washington, DC: National Center on Institutions and Alternatives and the National Institute of Corrections, 2000), p. 13.
35. Bureau of Justice Statistics, *Prison and Jail Inmates at Midyear 2006* (Washington, DC: Bureau of Justice Statistics, 2007), p. 1.
36. See Christine Tartaro, "The Impact of Density on Jail Violence," *Journal of Criminal Justice* 30 (2002): 499–510.
37. Human Rights Watch, *U.S. Number of Mentally Ill in Prisons Quadrupled*, September 5, 2006. See also Doris J. James and Lauren E. Glaze, *Mental Health Problems of Prison and Jail Inmates* (Washington, DC: U.S. Department of Justice; Bureau of Justice Statistics, 2006).
38. James and Glaze, Mental Health Problems of Prison and Jail Inmates, pp. 1–2.

39. Diane S. Young, "Non-psychiatric Services Provided in a Mental Health Unit in a County Jail," *Journal of Offender Rehabilitation* 35 (2002): 65.

40. Substance Abuse and Mental Health Services Administration, www.samhsa.gov (accessed February 23, 2012).

41. Matt Clarke, "MCC Brooklyn Sex Scandal and 11 Staff Indicted for Beating Prisoners," *Prison Legal News*, March 19, 2008.

42. For the research on the previous studies on jail suicide, see Melinda M. Winter, "County Jail Suicides in a Midwestern State: Moving Beyond the Use of Profiles," *Prison Journal* 83 (June 2003): 132–133.

43. Christine Tartaro and Rick Ruddell, "Trouble in Mayberry: A National Analysis of Suicides and Attempts in Small Jails," *American Journal of Criminal Justice* 31 (2006): 81–104.

44. Eric Blaauw, Frans Willem Winkel, and Ad J. F. M. Kerkhof, "Bullying and Suicidal Behavior in Jails," *Criminal Justice and Behavior* 28 (June 2001): 279–299.

45. Christopher J. Mumola, *Suicide and Homicide in State Prisons and Local Jails* (Bureau of Justice Statistics: U.S. Government Printing Office, 2005), p. 1.

46. James L. Stephan, *Census of Jails, 1999* (Washington, DC: U.S. Department of Justice, August 2001), p. 41.

In a 2011 report, "On the Chopping Block: State Prison Closings," the Sentencing Project, a prestigious nonprofit think tank, reported that after 40 years of record prison expansion, state lawmakers are now actually closing prisons. In 2011, at least 13 states either closed prisons or considered doing so. Michigan has led the nation in closing 21 facilities, including prison camps, as a result of parole and sentencing reforms. Overall, the state has reduced capacity by over 12,000 beds for a cost savings of $339 million. New Jersey and Kansas are other states that have also closed prisons in recent years; Maryland further reduced prison capacity when it closed the Maryland House of Corrections in 2007 and transferred 850 prisoners to other prisons.[1]

This is good news and reflects the first decline in state prison populations since 1977. What is not good news is how prison closings are affecting the economies of the local communities. When a local community hears that a prison closing is being considered, it attempts to inform local and state lawmakers and local community leaders. For example, when Camp Gabriels, a minimum-security prison in New York State, was being considered for closing, the local community organized to keep the institution open since it employed more than 180 people and contributed about $40 million to the regional economy. At a rally, veteran corrections officer Peter Martin

AP Photo/Charles Rex Arbogast

In 2008, residents of Pontiac, Illinois, packed the local high school auditorium, the foyer, and gymnasium for a public meeting of the Commission on Government Forecasting and Accountability concerning the Pontiac Correctional Center. The corrections department was threatening to close down the local prison, a source of local jobs and revenue. The protests worked: on March 12, 2009, Governor Pat Quinn cancelled plans to close Pontiac.

predicted that Camp Gabriels would continue to be around, providing good jobs and ready to house a new crop of prisoners. Martin declared, "We will have Camp Gabriels when we get done fighting. All our employees—we won't let you down. We will be there next year."[2] Martin's predictions were in vain: Camp Gabriels closed in 2009.

Sometimes local communities and their lobbies are able to prevail in preventing a prison closing. When the state of Illinois announced the closing of the Pontiac Correctional Center, central Illinois lawmakers, elected officials, and community action groups went into action to keep the prison open. On March 12, 2009, the state issued a reversal, saying that "Keeping Pontiac Correctional Center open will ensure nearly 600 people in the region keep their jobs, prevent hundreds of families from being uprooted, and allow Pontiac to maintain one of its largest sources of revenue."[3]

chapter

SIX

CORRECTIONAL INSTITUTIONS

LEARNING OBJECTIVES

LO1 Identify the extent to which prisons mirror the larger society

LO2 Describe the age, gender, and racial makeup of those sent to prison

LO3 Discuss the federal jurisdiction over prisons

LO4 Explain whether state jurisdictions are similar from one state to another

LO5 Know how many prisoners are housed in private facilities and whether there is common agreement on the effectiveness of these facilities

LO6 Understand the security types of correctional institutions

LO7 Describe what prisons look like

LO8 Define the basic responsibilities of a correctional administrator

LO9 Explain the proactive management style

© Becky Stein

135

While many people don't want a prison "in my backyard," the local residents certainly didn't feel that way about Camp Gabriels and the Pontiac Correctional Center. Contemporary prisons are seen as offering many functions. First, they get dangerous people off the streets and give them "just deserts" for their crimes. With this approach, prison success is measured by such factors as physical security, length of incapacitation, a lower crime rate, and inmates who fear criminal sanctions. The purpose of prison is to punish criminals. Second, prisons are supposed to reform criminals and keep them from recidivating after they reenter society. Third, prisons provide good jobs for local communities. In depressed rural areas, as the opening vignette reports, prisons can provide the economic life blood of a community. Finally, work in a prison can serve as an important career in corrections. In Voices Across the Profession, Mark Thielen, who is warden of the largest prison in Minnesota, talks about how he feels good about the positive effects that education, especially offender graduation ceremonies, is having on inmates.

One of the tragedies of our time is that correctional institutions—whatever form they may take—do not seem to correct, and many former prisoners recidivate soon after reentering society. Although no completely accurate statement of the recidivism rate is available and various studies differ somewhat, it is estimated that more than half of all inmates will be back in prison within six years of their release. That means that each year about 240,000 former prisoners return to prison because they failed on parole.[4]

Prisons maintained by the Federal Bureau of Prisons and every state government are very expensive to our society. The most recent government figures reveal that prisons cost taxpayers about $40 billion each year, up from about $12 billion in 1986. This amounts to an annual cost of about $125 per year for every American citizen.[5]

voices ACROSS the PROFESSION

© Mark Thielen

> "Today, our efforts to preserve a positive environment are increasingly challenged by budget cuts and yearly reductions. One must be creative and take advantage of the common practice of doing more with less."

MARK THIELEN
WARDEN

As the warden of the Minnesota Correctional Facility–Faribault, the largest prison in Minnesota, I am first responsible for enhancing public safety by providing the securities, sanctions, and controls necessary to contain and manage offenders in my custody. I must maintain a safe environment for staff and offenders, but just as crucial is my commitment to cultivate an environment and provide the means that allows and encourages men to change.

Today, our efforts to preserve a positive environment are increasingly challenged by budget cuts and yearly reductions. One must be creative and take advantage of the common practice of doing more with less. Our budget cuts routinely expand the comfort zone of our teachers and behavioral health staff and, not surprisingly, it strengthens their resolve. I know this because I participate in our offender graduation ceremonies—this is the best part of my job. Diplomas are awarded for GED, vocational training, tutors, and limited post-secondary. I see the pride and note those offenders who have taken personal inventory. I see the difference in conversation. I've seen it in interactions. More importantly, education reduces the risk to reoffend—that's a fact, a fact that I mention quite often, because I'm a teacher too.

Source: Interviewed in 2011.

Today the just desert/incapacitation philosophy of sentencing is dominant, a policy that seems effective since the crime rate has declined as the number of people in prison has risen. The connection between a declining crime rate and rising prison population is not lost on politicians who support policies favoring long-term institutions and putting people behind bars in order to energize their political campaigns.[6] Advocates of the *no frills*, or **penal harm**, movement argue that if prison is a punishing experience, criminals will be deterred from crime, and current prisoners will be encouraged to go straight. Besides, why should individuals who have engaged in antisocial activities receive benefits behind bars that are sometimes unavailable to the honest and law-abiding, such as higher education courses?

The provision of quality care and treatment remains a goal of modern corrections. It is considered a responsibility of a free and democratic society to provide quality care to inmates in institutional settings. Prison reformers, ever since the founding of the Pennsylvania Prison Society in 1787, have believed that an important aspect of quality care is to maintain constant vigilance over those placed in long-term institutions, especially those from disadvantaged backgrounds. There is common agreement among many that quality institutional care of inmates includes providing vocational and educational programs for those who desire them; treating inmates with dignity and respect; avoiding verbal or physical abuse of inmates; and being open to new ways of improving inmate care, perhaps much different from the past. Is this how the treatment of prisoners is viewed in the United States today? Does the general public believe that prison inmates are treated with dignity and respect?

The purpose of this chapter, as well as the institutional chapters that follow, will be to evaluate, describe, and analyze the state of the prison in contemporary society. What do they do, and how are they doing it? What are they supposed to be? This chapter focuses on describing prisons—what the jurisdictions over them are, what the main types are, what they look like, and how they are governed.

PENAL HARM A current movement that believes the purpose of corrections is to punish offenders as severely as possible.

TO WHAT EXTENT DO PRISONS MIRROR THE LARGER SOCIETY?

An important consideration in corrections is the relationship between the prison and the wider society. James Jacobs's classic analysis of the Stateville Penitentiary in Illinois concludes that the social organization and moral values of the larger society, as well as major society changes, are found in the micro-society within prison walls.[7] Donald Clemmer's classic study of the prison community at Menard Correctional Center in Illinois also notes the existence of numerous parallels between the prison and the free world. Clemmer writes, "In a sense the prison culture reflects the American culture, for it is a culture within it."[8]

There are those who argue that rather than the prison being a microcosm of the larger society, it is a distorted image of that society. In its analysis of the 1971 Attica Prison rebellion, the New York State Special Commission on Attica stated, "While it is a microcosm reflecting the forces and emotions of the larger society, the prison actually magnifies and intensifies these forces, because it is so enclosed."[9]

An examination of the relationship between the prison and society reveals that poverty, racial and gender discrimination, violent crime, and mental illness are found in more exaggerated forms within the prison. The vast majority of prisoners come from pockets of poverty. They have grown up in disorganized communities, have been victims of racial and sexual discrimination, have varying degrees of emotional disturbance, and have victimized others. As these individuals come into the prison, they must deal with the deprivations of confinement in an environment full of racial unrest and division. Predators in the outside world may become victims in this enclosed world. For those who have emotional problems, the world of the prison is even more chaotic.

It is challenging for inmates, regardless of their background, to find they are in an environment that is failing to prepare them for their readjustment to the wider society once they are released. The setting of the prison so frequently makes survival the prime concern of prisoners, rather than gaining skills or a positive attitude. So, within the distorted setting of the prison, inmates so often leave less able to make it in the wider society than when they were admitted to prison, sometimes many years before.

The next section will examine the state of the prison population and how it breaks down in terms of age, gender, race/ethnicity, and criminal offenses.

INMATE POPULATIONS

Federal and state correctional authorities today have jurisdiction over 1,600,000 prisoners. The federal system now holds more than 12 percent of these prisoners, while the remainder are in state institutions. This population has grown steadily despite a declining crime rate.[10] What are the characteristics of this inmate group?

 ## Age

White male prisoners tend to be older than African American and Hispanic inmates; 18 percent are aged 45 to 54 and over 11 percent are aged 40 to 44. Women aged 35 to 39 make up the largest percentage of sentenced female prisoners overall (nearly 20 percent). This is true for white, African Americans, and Hispanic female prisoners.[11]

Gender

As Figure 6.1 shows, males now make up about 93 percent of sentenced prisoners and females make up about 7 percent.

FIGURE 6.1 Inmates Under the Jurisdiction of Federal and State Correctional Systems

Source: Heather C. West and William J. Sabol, *Prisoners in 2009* (Washington, DC: Bureau of Justice Statistics Bulletin, December 2010), p. 1.

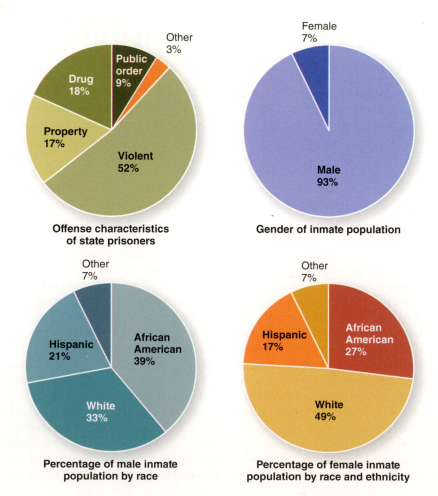

Race

Today, African American males make up about 39 percent of the inmate population, white men 33 percent, and Hispanic men 21 percent. Nearly half of the sentenced females are white; African American women make up nearly 27 percent of all sentenced female inmates and Hispanic women about 17 percent. The rate of incarceration has increased for white women and declined for African American women.

Offense Characteristics

Violent offenders make up more than 52 percent of all sentenced inmates in state prisons. Drug offenses represent the most serious charge for about 18 percent of state prisoners, and property offenses follow with 17 percent. Offense distributions differ between male and female state prisoners. More than half of males are sentenced for violent offenses, compared to 35 percent of females. Drug, weapons, and immigration offenders make up more than three-quarters of the sentenced federal prison population.

There are racial and ethnic differences in the prison population: African American and Hispanic inmates are more likely to be sentenced for violence and drug offenses than whites, who are more likely to be sentenced for property offenses.[12]

Federal and state correctional facilities hold more than 1,600,000 prisoners. This population has grown steadily despite a declining crime rate. The vast majority of prisoners come from pockets of poverty, have been victims of racial and sexual discrimination, have varying degrees of emotional disturbance, and have victimized others. These young men are inmates of Baldwin Inmate Boot Camp in Hardwick, Georgia.

© Robin Nelson/PhotoEdit Inc.

JURISDICTION OVER PRISON SYSTEMS IN THE UNITED STATES

The Federal Bureau of Prisons, state departments of corrections, and prisons funded and administered by private corporations have jurisdiction over prisons in the United States.

L03 Federal Bureau of Prisons

The Federal Bureau of Prisons was established in 1930 to ensure the administration of the 11 federal prisons in operation at that time; today, the Bureau of Prisons oversees 112 correctional institutions, 6 regional offices, a central office in Washington, D.C., 2 staff training centers, and 28 community corrections offices. The BOP is responsible for the custody and care of more than 208,000 federal offenders, of whom 85 percent are confined in bureau-operated correctional institutions or detention centers. The remaining offenders are confined through agreements with state and local governments or through contracts with privately operated community correctional centers, detention centers, and juvenile facilities.[13] Figure 6.2 shows the regions of the correctional institutions under the jurisdiction of the Bureau of Prisons.

The Bureau of Prisons has identified itself as a professional organization since Norman C. Carlson was director of corrections (1970–1987). Both management

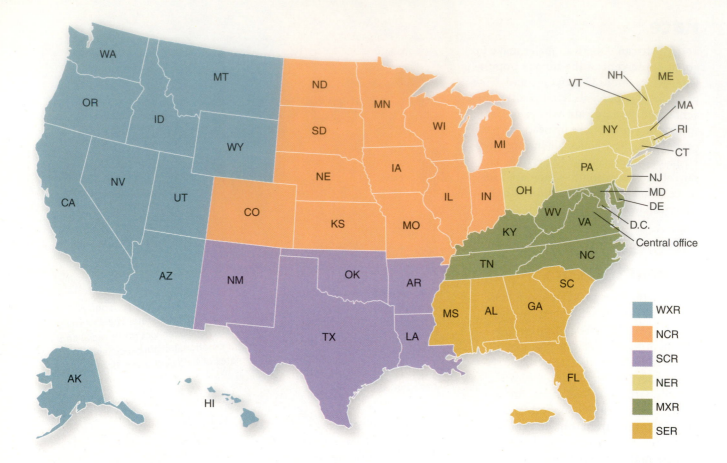

FIGURE 6.2 Bureau of Prisons Correctional Facilities

Note: Go to www.bop.gov, select a region of the map to view facilities in that area, then access information specific to an institution or office.

Source: Federal Bureau of Prisons, www.bop.gov (accessed February 25, 2012).

and nonmanagement staff typically view themselves as professionals who work as a team. Correctional officers also tend to view themselves as professionals who have the possibility of upward career mobility in the agency.[14] The majority of staff at all levels, from the director's office down, feel that the BOP offers excellent career opportunities, and that it provides up-to-date skilled management and staff training for people who want to make a difference.

The federal training centers do an able job of creating an *esprit de corps* among institutional personnel. Rotating top administrative staff every two or three years also seems to help maintain a high level of professionalism that reduces stagnation and burnout.[15]

The Bureau of Prisons offers a variety of inmate programs.[16] Nearly 50,000 inmates have completed residential drug treatment programs since 1990. In one study, individuals released to the community for at least six months after they completed the federal drug residence program were 73 percent less likely to be arrested for a new offense and 44 percent less likely to test positive for drug use, when compared to inmates who did not complete the program. The BOP has had thousands of inmates complete a general equivalency diploma (GED), and many others have completed vocational training and other educational programs. In addition, the BOP has developed a number of new life skills programs in recent years.[17]

Federal Prison Industries (FPI), or **UNICOR**, would like to think of itself as the gold standard for inmate vocational programs. FPI employs more than 20,000 inmates, about 25 percent of the sentenced and medically eligible federal inmate

UNICOR The trade name used by Federal Prison Industries.

population. FPI has up-to-date equipment, develops a strong work ethic, and pays considerably more than state prisoners receive from prison industry.[18] Yet, there is considerable question about the BOP's exploiting inmates in UNICOR by the wages they pay, which are a very small portion of the profits it makes.

The Bureau of Prisons further deserves praise because it has been willing to receive the most hard-to-control inmates from state prisons, thereby making the inmate population more manageable in state facilities. This has sometimes created problems of inmate control in federal facilities, but with the construction of high-security supermax areas in many state facilities across the nation, states may become more willing to place these difficult inmates in their own high-security housing units.

The BOP may be the standard-setter of correctional facilities, but it has had its problems. These include a disastrous fire at FCI Danbury, Connecticut, in which several inmates lost their lives; 21 inmate murders at the Atlanta Federal Penitentiary; an incident at the Marion (Illinois) Federal Penitentiary that claimed the lives of two staff members (two more were stabbed in one day); a riot at the Atlanta Penitentiary, in which inmates nearly burned the entire facility to the ground; and a federal facility in California at which some 40 staff were arrested and charged with corruption. There are other instances of staff brutality as well as staff corruption.[19] Prison crowding is at least as serious a problem in BOP facilities as it is in state institutions.[20] Federal penitentiaries also have serious problems generated by sexual exploitation, inmate defiance, and drug trafficking. In addition, inmates must endure boredom, regimentation, personal indignities, the deprivations of imprisonment, and the difficulty of daily survival.[21] The ideals of professionalism are often not realized on a daily basis, and some staff fall far short of what it means to be a professional.[22]

LO4 State Departments of Corrections

There are 50 separate state departments of corrections as well as one for the District of Columbia. The systems are difficult to compare and evaluate because of differences in ideology, structure, and programs. The quality of previous correctional leaders, the resources available, and the volume of inmates have largely shaped what takes place in corrections within a state.

Some states have few correctional institutions (New Hampshire, 6; Utah, 5; and Wyoming, 4). Other states have many (Texas, 107; North Carolina, 88; and Florida, 85). Within each state is considerable variation in the quality of institutions. There may be a maximum-security prison that resembles an old castle and a new minimum-security facility with an innovative and campus-style design. If one were to visit these facilities, it would be difficult to believe both are managed within the same jurisdiction.

IMPROVING STATE SERVICES Though the problems are immense, state correctional institutions are better than they were in the past. State departments of corrections have become concerned about improving institutional standards. By the late 1970s, state correctional administrators began to apply for institutional accreditation through the Commission on Accreditation of the American Correctional Association. Now nearly all of the 50 states have participated in the accreditation process, and 500 correctional institutions have been accredited or are in the process of accreditation.[23]

Most state departments of corrections have begun to emphasize preservice and in-service training, requiring that newly hired correctional officers must receive some type of training before they begin work in the institution. This training may take place at the state corrections academy, at the institution, or at some other location. Top institutional administrators are increasingly receiving in-service training.

State corrections departments are also now more receptive to institutional research and evaluation. In addition, directors/commissioners of state systems and wardens/superintendents of state prisons are now more open and honest about institutional problems.[24] Despite these advancements, state departments of corrections are frequently overcrowded and filled with too much violence. They often have underdeveloped programming, insufficient prison industries for inmates, and lack of resources for anything other than prison construction. Exhibit 6.1 discusses how state correctional systems are now dealing with the crisis they face on a daily basis.

Private Prisons

Private prisons are much different from federal or state prisons, which are under governmental jurisdiction. The private sector's involvement in corrections is not new. Private industry used prison labor in several ways during the early nineteenth century. The contract labor system used prison labor to manufacture goods for private companies, which furnished tools and materials and supervised the work of inmates. In the piece-price system, contractors furnished raw materials and paid prisoners for the completed goods on a per piece basis. The convict lease system provided prisoners "on loan" to work in farming, construction, mining, and on plantations, under the complete control of the lessee.[25] It should be noted that this is not what private companies do today.

The private sector now provides prisoners' work programs and medical, education, and psychological services; financing for prison or jail construction; and management and operation of prisons or jails. Two companies operate over half of the contracts of private correctional facilities: the Corrections Corporation of America and the GEO Group Inc. (formerly Wackenhut Corrections). The Corrections Corporation of America (CCA) operates facilities with 75,000 inmates in 61 correctional institutions. The GEO Group operates slightly fewer facilities and houses fewer inmates. Other companies, such as Management and Training Corporation, LCS Correctional Services, and Emerald Corrections, also hold multiple prison contracts throughout the United States.[26] Privately operated facilities are generally located in the southern and western regions of the United States and include both federal and state offenders.[27] (See Figure 6.3 and Exhibit 6.2.)

© Becky Stein

COST-EFFECTIVENESS Evaluation studies on the cost-effectiveness of private versus public institutions have been inconclusive.[28] Private prisons do seem cheaper to build, but the question pertains to the quality of private services. Mason's 2012 report, *Too Good to Be True*, concludes: "The available evidence does not point to any substantial benefits to privatizing prisons."[29]

LOWER RATES OF RECIDIVISM While some research has found that private providers have lower rates of recidivism, other studies found no difference in the rate of recidivism between public and private facilities.[30] A recent study used data from a large cohort of Oklahoma inmates and found that private prison inmates had a greater risk of recidivism.[31] Some evidence does exist that inmates released from private prisons who do reoffend may commit less serious offenses than those released from public institutions.[32] Yet private, state, and federal facilities tend to house different populations.

Inmates in a state facility in Georgia are shown walking to an afternoon activity. Though problems persist, state correctional institutions are much better than they were in the past. Great strides have been made to improve professionalism and the quality of correctional life. Nevertheless, the quality of corrections varies from state to state and among correctional administrators and officers within states.

INSTITUTIONAL OPERATIONS How do institutional operations compare between public and private prisons? When Harvey Lappin and colleagues compared the performance of private prisons and several Bureau of Prisons facilities of equivalent design and security level, they found:

- Staff surveys from the GEO Group (formerly Wackenhut) prisons revealed lower than expected scores on institutional operations.

- Staff had higher institutional commitment in the private prison.

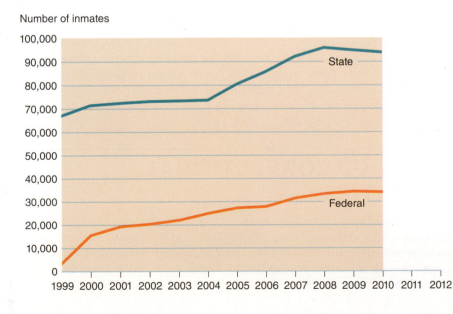

Number of inmates

FIGURE 6.3 Private Prison Populations

Source: From Cody Mason, *Too Good to Be True: Private Prisons in America*, p. 6. Copyright © 2012 by The Sentencing Project. Reproduction of this document in full or in part, and in print or electronic format, only by permission of The Sentencing Project.

- The private facility had higher staff turnover than the comparison BOP prisons.

- An inmate survey revealed that inmates perceived worse sanitation and food services at the private facility, while security and gang-activity levels were about the same as the BOP prisons.

- The private prison had higher rates of most kinds of inmate misconduct, including a higher than expected level of drug use at the private facility in comparison to the BOP prisons.[33]

Questions exist on whether private providers skimp on services and programs in order to reduce costs. Some private services providers have been sued because their services were inadequate, causing harm to inmates.[34] It is further reported that private prisons have higher rates of escapes, greater levels of institutional violence, more shoddy construction, and more poorly trained and inexperienced staff than federal and state facilities.[35] Mason's 2012 evaluation questioned the quality of services in private operations.[36]

LEGAL ISSUES The increased involvement of private enterprise in corrections raises a number of important financial, legal, and moral questions that have not been adequately addressed. One of the major legal issues is whether private correctional officers have less immunity from lawsuits than state employees. In **Richardson v. McKnight**, the Supreme Court held that correctional officers employed by a private firm are not entitled to a qualified immunity from suit by prisoners charging a section 1983 violation.[37] The case of **Correctional Services Corp. v. Malesko** defines the protections and rights of prisoners in private corporations' facilities. The U.S. Supreme Court ruled that although Malesko could sue an employee of the private correctional corporation for violating his constitutional rights (he was forced to walk up stairs when he had a heart condition), he could not sue the correctional corporation itself.[38] The *Malesko* decision shields the private prison corporation from suits brought under the federal civil rights statute. Interestingly, the state is still liable, even if the private corporation is not.[39] See Exhibit 6.3 for an evaluation of private prison operations.[40]

RICHARDSON V. MCKNIGHT   **LO6**
Supreme Court held that correctional officers employed by a private firm are not entitled to a qualified immunity from suit by prisoners, charging a section 1983 violation.

CORRECTIONAL SERVICES CORP. V. MALESKO Defines the protections and rights of inmates in private corporations' facilities.

TYPES OF CORRECTIONAL FACILITIES

Correctional institutions have been traditionally designed as minimum-, medium-, and maximum-security facilities. Maximum-security prisons have been further divided into reformatories, state penitentiaries, correctional centers, and state prisons. In the 1990s, supermax prisons were built around the nation.

Security is the byword of all prisons, especially maximum-security and supermax facilities. Correctional workers are made aware that each inmate is a potential escape risk and, therefore, the utmost security must be maintained. More secure prisons are designed to eliminate hidden corners where people can congregate, and passages are constructed so that they can be easily blocked off to quell disturbances.

Minimum-Security Prisons

Minimum-security prisons, in contrast to other types of prisons, have far more relaxed perimeter security, sometimes without fences or any other form of external security. Inmates usually have less than a year before release when they are moved to minimum security. The inmates live in less-secure dormitories, which are regularly patrolled by correctional officers. As in medium-security facilities, they have communal showers, sinks, and toilets. The inmates work, go to school, and have vocational classes. They get more freedom, so they are permitted to work outside jobs such as road crews and exterior maintenance. These facilities have generous visitation policies with contact visitation, sometimes even short home furloughs, and a safer environment for both staff and inmates.

Medium-Security Prisons

Inmates who are placed in **medium-security prisons** may sleep in dormitories on bunk beds, with lockers to store their possessions, or they may be double-bunked (two inmates per cell). They are often out of their cells most of the day. Inmates are usually allowed to work, take courses and get a GED, have visits, and use the yard.

Medium-security prisons typically have single or double fencing, guarded towers or closed-circuit television monitoring, sally-port entrances, and zonal security systems to control inmate movement within the institutions. In medium-security prisons, the emphasis is on controlled access to programs. Prisoners assigned to medium custody can be locked down in emergencies, but it is expected that they will participate in industrial and educational activities. The rationale behind medium-security facilities is that a good deal of freedom and movement and the availability of programs are allowed within a technologically secured perimeter.

EXHIBIT 6.3 Comparison of Private and Federal/State Facilities

Proponents of private operators contend that they run prisons more effectively and at less cost than public agencies. They claim they can do this because privatization:

- Increases the capacity of prisons because private corporations can build prisons more quickly

- Responds with greater flexibility to correctional needs by cutting red tape

- Attracts employees who are younger and more enthusiastic than public employees

- Brings fresh ideas into the correctional system

In contrast, critics of private prisons argue that private prisons cannot be compared to federal or state prisons because they:

- May build their facilities more quickly but too often the quality of the facilities leaves much to be desired

- Have no lower and probably higher rates of recidivism

- Have higher rates of inmate misconduct

- Provide inferior services to inmates compared to federal and state facilities

- Offer inadequate compensation to staff, who at times barely make more than minimum wage

- Pose ethical and moral issues that are yet to be resolved

MINIMUM-SECURITY PRISON A prison with relaxed perimeter security, sometimes without fences or any other means of external security.

MEDIUM-SECURITY PRISON A prison with single or double fencing, guarded towers or closed-circuit television monitoring, sally-port entrances, and zonal security systems to control inmate movement within the institution.

MYTH
Privately run institutions are much more effective than those run by the government. Cutting state bureaucracy is both effective and efficient.

FACT
There is little conclusive evidence that private institutions are any better than state-run facilities. Private institutions have their own set of problems.

Maximum-Security Prisons

Most **maximum-security prisons** are large physical plants. Some of the older maximum-security facilities are surrounded by stone walls with guard towers at strategic places. These walls may be 25 or more feet high. But new maximum-security facilities tend to be surrounded by several fences because of the expense of stone walls.

Maximum-security prisons are sometimes divided into close security and maximum security. In close security, inmates usually have one- or two-person cells that are observed from a remote control station. Each cell has its own toilet and sink. Inmates may leave their cells for work assignments or programs and may otherwise be allowed in a common room in the cellblock or an exercise yard. The fences are usually double fences with watchtowers housing armed guards, sometimes with a third, lethal-current electric fence in the middle.[41]

Maximum-security prisons also usually have two types of **segregation**: isolation and administrative segregation. Isolation is punishment; the prisoner is sent for a specific number of days to a solitary cell without contact with other inmates. Administrative segregation is just what the term implies: the prisoner is removed from the main population because his or her behavior is considered dangerous to others. The removal may be for a specific and/or indefinite period of time, the latter being subject to case review.

In maximum-security prisons, all inmates usually have individual cells with sliding doors controlled from a secure remote control station. Inmates are often allowed out of their cells one out of twenty-four hours. When out of their cells, inmates remain in the cellblock or an exterior cage. Movement out of the cellblock or "pod" is tightly restricted, using restraints and escorts by correctional officers.[42] The assumption that underlies maximum-security prisons is that the physical characteristics of the prison will be such that complete control of prisoners can be applied at any time.

There are many notorious maximum-security prisons, and no less among them is the famed Sing Sing Correctional Facility in Ossining, New York, which stands on a scenic bluff overlooking the Hudson River, about 30 miles north of New York City. The phrase going "up the river" was coined with Sing Sing in mind. It was also the place of some famous executions, including Ruth Snyder, a woman convicted of killing her husband for insurance money. Her execution in Sing Sing's electric chair on January 12, 1928, was photographed and became a national sensation; she was the first woman to be electrocuted since 1899. Altogether, 614 men and women have been executed at Sing Sing.

AP Photo/Mary Altaffer

Supermax Prisons

The **supermax prison**, based on isolation of prisoners, a system that can be traced to the old Pennsylvania model, is known by many names—security housing units, administrative segregation, intensive management unit, and extended control unit.[43] Forty-four states have embraced the idea of 23-hour lockdown for problem prisoners: some states have constructed stand-alone high-tech supermax prisons; others have added high-security units to existing facilities.[44] More than 20,000 male and female inmates are now housed in 57 supermax facilities.[45] They house such well-known gang chiefs as Jeff Fort and Larry Hoover and terrorists as Richard Reid, Terry Nichols, and Zacarias Moussaoui.

Take for instance the 484-bed federal facility (ADX) in Florence, Colorado. This prison has the most sophisticated security measures in the United States, including 168 video cameras and 1,400 electronically controlled gates. Inside the cells, all furniture is immovable; the bed, the desk, and TV stand are

MAXIMUM-SECURITY PRISON A prison in which complete control of any and all prisoners can be applied at any time.

SEGREGATION A punishment unit in which inmates are separated from other inmates and are fed in their cells. Unlike the past, inmates must be adequately fed and permitted some time out of their cells to exercise.

SUPERMAX PRISON Most secure of all prison systems, in which there is typically a 23-hour lockdown.

made of cement. All potential weapons, including toilet seats, toilet handles, and soap dishes, have been removed. The cement walls are 5,000-pound quality, and steel bars are placed so they crisscross every eight inches inside the institution. Cells are angled so that prisoners can see neither each other nor the outside scenery. This cuts down on communications and denies inmates a sense of location, to prevent escapes. The newer prisons have totally automated the traditional jobs of correction officers such as opening cell doors and surveillance.[46]

In some supermax prisons, there are security housing units (SHUs), pronounced "shoes," for inmates who are deemed to be a special danger to the security of the prison. Within these units, two categories of inmates are housed. The first category is administrative detention (AD), which is used to house inmates who are acknowledged as posing a threat to the general population, though inmates may also be placed in this unit for their own protection. The second category is disciplinary segregation (DS), which is reserved for those inmates who have been found guilty of a serious prison rule violation. Supermax facilities have both supporters and detractors; see Exhibit 6.4.

SUPERMAX VIOLENCE

In the late 1980s and 1990s, the security housing units (SHUs) of the Concoran State Prison and the Pelican Bay Prison brought the California Department of Corrections considerable adverse publicity because of the levels of violence found in these facilities. At Corcoran's SHU, staff violence reached unbelievable levels. Under an "integrated yard policy," rival groups and known enemies were routinely brought together to fight in the small group exercise yards. For nine years, inmates were used as pawns by staff in these set-up fights. Correctional officers promoted their champions and even wagered on the fights for entertainment. An estimated 8,000 of these "gladiator fights" took place between 1988 and 1997.[47]

Officers in Corcoran used guns to control the yards, and more than 2,000 shooting incidents took place. Hundreds were wounded and five were killed. An independent analysis of the five lethal shootings revealed that none was justified by the department of corrections' own criteria; yet, the "shooting review board" routinely justified every shot ever fired in the SHU yards. In a

---

EXHIBIT 6.4 The Pros and Cons of Supermax Prisons

Pros

- Supermax prisons are needed to control inmates whose behavior is so disruptive that they are unmanageable when left in the general inmate population.

- Some inmates are simply too dangerous for the average prison setting. Gang leaders, disruptive inmates from other institutions, and inmates who incite riots are those most likely to be placed in supermax facilities or units.

- Administrators uniformly agree that supermax prisons improve system-wide prison safety, order, and control, as well as contribute to many positive unintended effects.

Cons

- Supermax prisons inflict excessive levels of pain and harm.

- Because they have difficulty controlling their disruptive behavior, mentally ill prisoners are disproportionately represented in these prisons.

- Inmate-on-inmate violence is not reduced through the use of punitive confinement.

- Inmates released directly from supermax prisons are especially dangerous to society because of the harsh conditions of confinement.

- Because a high percentage of the inmates are African Americans, placement in supermax prisons may be racially motivated.

Sources: Daniel P. Mears and Jennifer L. Castro, "Wardens' Views on the Wisdom of Supermax Prisons," *Crime and Delinquency* 52 (July 2006): 421–422; Roy D. King, "The Rise and Rise of Supermax: An American Solution in Search of a Problem?" *Punishment and Society* 2 (1999): 163–186; Lorna A. Rhodes, *Total Confinement Madness and Reason in the Maximum Security Prison* (Berkeley: University of California Press, 2004); and Hans Toch, "The Contemporary Relevance of Early Experiments with Supermax Reform," *Prison Journal* 83 (2003): 221–228.

wrongful-death lawsuit brought on behalf of one inmate gunned down in the yards, former California Corrections Director Dan McCarthy testified that "The rate of violence in the Corcoran SHU in its first year of operation was absolutely the highest rate I have ever seen in any institution anywhere in the country."[48]

Pelican Bay Prison, located in Crescent City, California, was opened in 1989 to move the state's worst offenders out of antiquated facilities such as San Quentin and Folsom. Pelican Bay has two areas: the maximum-security prison and the more notorious supermaximum-security housing unit. The 1,200 inmates in the SHU live 24 hours a day in an X-shaped, windowless bunker. Everything is gray concrete: the walls, the beds, and immovable stools. It is impossible to move more than eight feet in any direction within the cells. There is a skylight two stories up, but on an overcast day, it is dark and so are the cells.[49]

According to testimony given in the legal case **Madrid v. Gomez** (1995), excessive and unnecessary force and abuse were common in the special housing unit at Pelican Bay. Examples of the violence at Pelican Bay found in *Madrid v. Gomez* included:

- Inmates were left naked in outdoor holding cages during inclement weather.

- Beatings occurred even after inmates had been restrained.

- Verbal harassment and racial taunting were commonplace.

- Inmates were shot for fistfights both on the outdoor recreation yards and inside the cellblocks.

- One mentally ill inmate suffered second- and third-degree burns over a third of his body when he was given a bath in scalding water in the prison infirmary a week after he had bitten an officer.

The judge agreed with the prisoners in this class-action suit and ruled in their favor in 1995, stating, "Dry words on paper cannot adequately capture the senseless suffering and sometimes wretched misery that defendants' [prison staff and administration] unconstitutional practices leave in their wake."[50]

The effectiveness of the supermax prison is discussed further in the Evidence-Based Corrections feature.

WHAT PRISONS LOOK LIKE

L07

The four most widely used architectural designs in American prisons are the radial design, the telephone-pole design, the courtyard design, and the campus style (see Figure 6.4). The 1980s and 1990s were years of constant prison construction, and facilities built in those decades—mostly medium- and minimum-security prisons—have influenced the description of a typical

MADRID V. GOMEZ The judge in this case found that staff at the Pelican Bay Prison in California had used excessive and unnecessary force on inmates.

Radial design   Telephone-pole design   Courtyard style   Campus style

FIGURE 6.4 Prison Designs Used in the United States

EVIDENCE-BASED CORRECTIONS

Supermax Prisons

While the supermax prison may reassure some correctional experts who applaud a facility designed to house the nation's most dangerous offenders, the question remains: does it work any better than a traditional maximum-security facility?

Some of the most significant evaluations of supermax prisons have been conducted by justice scholar Daniel Mears and his associates. Mears finds that most correctional administrators agree on the definition of the core meaning of a supermax prison: a stand-alone unit or part of another facility designated for violent or disruptive inmates. It typically involves up to 23-hour-per-day, single-cell confinement for an indefinite period of time. Inmates in supermax housing have minimal contact with staff and other inmates. In addition, Mears finds that wardens generally believe that supermax prisons serve to achieve at least four critical goals—increasing safety, order, and control throughout prison systems and incapacitating violent or disruptive inmates. However,

Mears finds a great deal of difference over the stated or perceived goals of supermax prisons. There is less agreement about whether they improve inmate behavior throughout prison systems; decrease riots, the influence of gangs, or escapes; successfully punish, reduce the recidivism of, or rehabilitate violent or disruptive inmates; or deter crime in society.

There were also some surprising positive effects. Supermax prisons increase privacy, reduce danger, and even provide creature comforts (such as TV sets) that are unavailable in general-population prisons. Staff report less stress and fear because they have to contend with fewer disruptive inmates. There can also be positive effects in other correctional institutions such as improving living conditions and outcomes for general population inmates by removing the most dangerous offenders from their midst.

On the other hand, Mears and his associates uncovered some negative effects associated with the use of the supermax prison. Staff may have too much control over inmates—a condition that damages staff–inmate re-

lationships. Long hours of isolation may be associated with mental illness and psychological disturbances. Supermax inmates seem to have a more difficult time readjusting upon release. A stay in a supermax prison inhibits reintegration into other prisons, communities, and families. Mears and Jennifer Castro surveyed wardens and found that even though they seem to favor supermax prisons, they also expressed concern that the general public considers supermax institutions inhumane, that they drain limited funds from state budgets, and that they produce increases in litigation and court interventions, as well as increased recidivism and reentry failure among released inmates. In sum, it remains unclear whether the benefits of these prison facilities outweigh their costs.

Sources: Daniel Mears, "An Assessment of Supermax Prisons Using an Evaluation Research Framework," *Prison Journal* 88 (2008): 43–68; Daniel Mears and Jennifer Castro, "Wardens' Views on the Wisdom of Supermax Prisons," *Crime and Delinquency* 52 (2006): 398–431; Daniel Mears and Jamie Watson, "Towards a Fair and Balanced Assessment of Supermax Prisons," *Justice Quarterly* 23 (2006): 232–267; Daniel P. Mears, *Evaluating the Effectiveness of Supermax Prisons* (Washington, DC: Urban Institute, 2006), www.urban.org/uploadedPDF/411326_supermax_prisons.pdf (accessed February 26, 2012).

American prison. What this means is that the maximum-security prisons depicted in 1930s movies—the prototype of prisons in the past—are no longer the dominant type of institution for adults. During the late twentieth century, technological innovations, usually to promote security, further altered the appearance of prisons.

Architectural Design for Today's Prisons

The structural design of early prisons was created to produce a specific outcome: moral reformation. The isolated cells were intended to facilitate contemplation, work, and penitence. Since Jeremy Bentham's circular Panopticon in the nineteenth century, institutional security or control, rather than reformation, has been the basic function of prison architecture.

In prisons with a **radial design**, the corridors extend like spokes from a control center at the hub. Eastern State Penitentiary in Philadelphia was the first prison to utilize the radial design. The federal penitentiary at Leavenworth

RADIAL DESIGN In this wheel-shaped configuration, corridors radiate like spokes from a control center at the hub.

(Kansas) and state penitentiaries at Rahway and Trenton (New Jersey) are other prisons with radial designs.[51]

The **telephone-pole design**, which has long central corridors, is more common for prisons built during the twentieth century. This design, the most widely used for maximum-security prisons in the United States, was used for the federal penitentiary in Marion (Illinois), and state correctional institutions at Graterford (Pennsylvania), Somers (Connecticut), and Jackson (Georgia). The telephone-pole design makes it possible to house prisoners by classification levels. A major disadvantage of this layout is that militant convicts can barricade a corridor. In the event of a riot or a hostage-taking situation, inmates can take control of a cell house and make it difficult for guards to recapture control of that cell house.

The **courtyard style design**, likely to be found in newer prisons, has housing units. The Washington Corrections Center for Women at Purdy (Gig Harbor) became a showplace among women's prisons and is built around multilevel and beautifully landscaped courtyards. The attractive buildings provided security without fences until a number of escapes in the mid-1970s resulted in the construction of eight-foot fences. Small housing units with pleasant living rooms reflect the expectation that the women will behave like human beings and also imply that they will be treated as such. The education, recreation, and training areas are ample and roomy. Away from the courtyard are attractive apartments, each containing a living room, kitchen, dining space, two bedrooms, and a bath. Women who are close to release or are on work or educational release occupy these apartments.[52]

The **campus style design**, used for minimum-security and a few medium-security prisons, utilizes an open design that allows some freedom of movement. Small housing units are scattered among the educational, vocational, recreational, and dining units of the prison. Women's prisons frequently use the campus design. The campus design is likely to be found in showplace institutions that have more generous visiting policies than do typical institutions, allow more furloughs, offer better services and programs, and permit the placement of inmates who provide a safer environment for both staff and inmates.

Changing Form of the Prison

More than half of U.S. prisons today are less than 20 years old. A major advantage of new prison construction across the nation is that these facilities permit the tearing down or closing of many of the old, dungeon-like prisons.

Some of the newly constructed prisons across the nation do not look like prisons. The Minnesota Correctional (Facility) in Oak Park Heights is one of the more technologically advanced and secure prisons in the nation. This three-story facility has some walls below ground level, and living space that faces out to a sunken central courtyard. The subterranean design saves energy, and the prison has a heat-reclaiming unit. Within this innovative facility, the freedom of movement becomes more restricted and closely monitored as inmates approach the institution's security perimeters. This restriction makes it possible to minimize guard-tower surveillance and thereby reduces costs. A sophisticated computer monitors the opening and closing of doors and other routine events. Other security elements at Oak Park Heights include a closed-circuit television monitoring system and an electronic alarm network on the roof of the facility and on the perimeter's double security fence.[53] The use of technology to maintain security in closed prison institutions is the subject of the TechnoCorrections feature.

TELEPHONE-POLE DESIGN This prison has a long central corridor serving as the means for prisoners to go from one part of the prison to another. Extending out from the corridor are cross-arms containing housing, school, shops, and recreation areas.

COURTYARD STYLE DESIGN A prison design in which corridors surround a courtyard. Housing, educational, vocational, recreational, prison industry, and dining areas face the courtyard.

CAMPUS STYLE DESIGN Open prison design that allows some freedom of movement; the units of the prison are housed in a complex of buildings surrounded by a fence.

Only a few years ago, using technology to maintain prison security was unknown. Now prison technology offers innovations that provide substantial savings in staffing costs and operations. A few of the more intriguing technological developments include:

- *Ground-penetrating radar.* Ground-penetrating radar (GPR) is able to locate tunnels inmates use to escape. GPR works almost like an old-fashioned Geiger counter, but rather than detecting metal, the system detects changes in ground composition, including voids such as those created by a tunnel.

- *Heartbeat monitoring.* Now it is possible to prevent escapes by monitoring inmates' heartbeats! The Advanced Vehicle Interrogation and Notification system (AVIAN) works by identifying the shock wave generated by the beating heart, which couples to any surface the body touches. The system takes in all the frequencies of movement, such as the expansion and contraction of an engine or rain hitting the roof, and determines if there is a pattern similar to a human heartbeat.

- *Nonlethal electrified fences.* Nonlethal electrified containment fences stop inmates without causing severe harm or death. If an inmate tries to climb or cut through the perimeter fence, he or she will receive a nonlethal jolt of electricity, which causes temporary immobilization. At the same time, the system initiates an alarm to staff that an attempt has occurred and identifies its location.

- *Backscatter imaging system for concealed weapons.* This system utilizes a backscatter imager to detect weapons and contraband. The primary advantage of this device over current walk-through portals is that it can detect nonmetallic as well as metallic weapons. It uses low-power X-rays equal to about five minutes of exposure to the sun at sea level. Although these X-rays penetrate clothing, they do not penetrate the body.

- *Body-scanning screening system.* This is a stationary screening system to detect nonmetallic weapons and contraband in the lower body cavities. It uses simplified magnetic resonance imaging (MRI) as a noninvasive alternative to X-ray and physical body cavity searches. The stationary screening system makes use of first-generation medical MRI.

- *Transmitter wristbands.* These wristbands broadcast a unique serial number by radio frequency every two seconds so that antennas throughout the prison can pick up the signals and pass the data via a local area network to a central monitoring station PC. The wristbands can sound an alert when an inmate gets close to the perimeter fence or when a prisoner does not return from a furlough on time. They can even tag gang members and notify guards when rivals get into contact with each other.

- *Personal health status monitor.* The personal health status monitor uses acoustics to track the heartbeat and respiration of a person in a cell. More advanced health status monitors are now being developed that can monitor five or more vital signs at once and, based on the combination findings, can produce an assessment of the inmate's state of health. This more advanced version of the personal health status monitor may take another decade to develop, but the current version may already help save lives that would otherwise be lost to suicide.

- *Personal alarm location system.* It is now possible for prison employees to carry a tiny transmitter linking them with a computer in a central control room. In an emergency, they can hit an alarm button and transmit to a computer that automatically records whose distress button has been pushed. A map of the facility appears onscreen, showing the exact location of the staff member in need of assistance.

- *Under-vehicle surveillance system.* An under-vehicle surveillance system utilizes a drive-over camera that records a video image of the license plate and the underside of any vehicle entering or leaving the secure perimeter of the prison. This system allows prison staff to check each vehicle for possible escape attempts and keeps a digital recording of every vehicle that enters or exits the prison.

- *Biometric recognition.* The facial recognition biometric system utilizes facial recognition by matching more than 200 individual points on the human face with a digitally stored image. The system is used to control access in buildings and rooms inside buildings; it will become more and more common in the near future.

These methods are in use today and are merely the forerunners of a technological revolution that is changing the administration of prisons while at the same time improving security.

Sources: Jeff Goodale, Dave Menzel, and Glen Hodgson, "High-Tech Prisons: Latest Technologies Drive Cost Savings and Staff Efficiencies," *Corrections Today* 67 (July 2005): 78; John Ward, "Jump-Starting Projects to Automate Correctional Processes," *Corrections Today* 66 (2006): 82–83; John Ward, "Security and Technology: The Human Side," *Corrections Today* 66 (2004): 8; Frank Lu and Laurence Wolfe, "Technology that Works: An Overview of the Supervision and Management Automated Record Tracking (SMART) Application," *Corrections Today* 66 (2004): 78–81; Gary Burdett and Mike Rutford, "Technology Improves Security and Reduces Staff in Two Illinois Prisons," *Corrections Today* 65 (2003): 109–110; and Tony Fabelo, "Technocorrections: The Promises, the Uncertain Threat," *Sentencing and Corrections: Issues for the 21st Century* (Washington, DC: National Institute of Corrections).

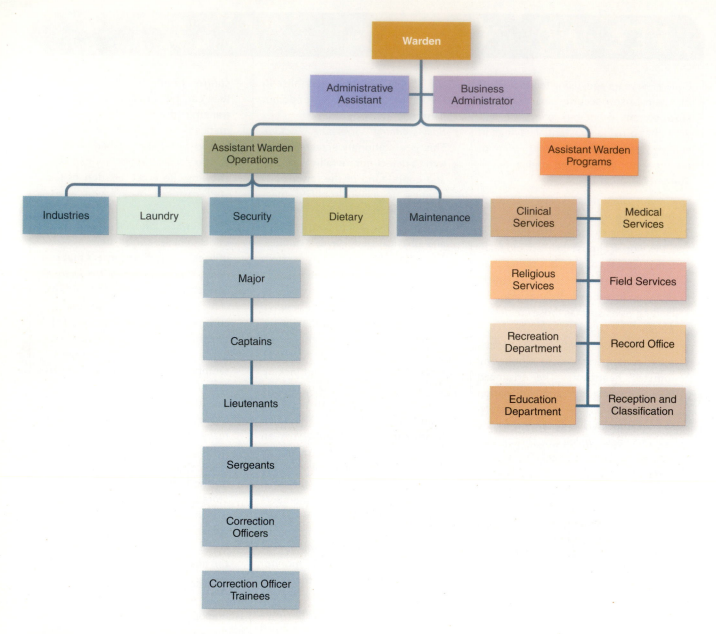

FIGURE 6.5 Institutional Table of Organization

Source: Illinois's Menard Correctional Center.

 CORRECTIONAL ADMINISTRATION: HOW ARE PRISONS RUN?

The warden or superintendent is ultimately responsible for everything that takes place within the prison. The warden delegates the responsibility for custodial services and for program services to assistant or associate wardens (see Figure 6.5). In large correctional institutions, an associate warden for management services and an associate warden for industrial and agricultural services are charged with the responsibility for those areas. The associate wardens, in turn, rely on middle managers and line staff to operate the various departments within their sphere of responsibility. Institutional administrators encompass establishment of policy, planning, civil suits, institutional monitoring, staff development, and fiscal management.[54]

Establishment of Policy

Wardens determine policy for their particular institutions, although major policy changes must be cleared with the central office. One of the challenges of determining policy stems from the number of groups that must be satisfied: the legislature, the director of corrections, the various levels of institutional staff, the public, and the inmates.

Planning

The warden is expected to develop goals and methods for their achievement. Some top administrators look to modern management principles to be helpful tools in the goal-setting process. If no long-range plan exists, most wardens know they will become involved in crisis-centered management and will have to face the same problems day after day. Staff burnout and inappropriate reactions to organizational problems are the consequences of crisis-centered management.

Dealing with Civil Suits

Civil lawsuits by inmates constitute another area in which planning is needed. Administrators who are sued by prisoners must spend much of their time responding to charges, preparing affidavits, and testifying in court. This time-consuming process is not only frustrating and draining on administrative resources but also intimidating. Administrators may end up paying exorbitant attorneys' fees or sustaining extensive damages. Court decisions that impose new procedures, standards, and personnel requirements on a correctional system can also be expensive, time-consuming, and full of problems for administrators.

Institutional Monitoring

The effective institutional administrator must have adequate information about what is taking place within the facility and must provide for special inmate needs. To keep informed, wardens must find ways to maintain good communication with prisoners. Prisoners with special needs, such as mentally restricted and emotional disturbed prisoners, sex offenders, or AIDS inmates, pose management problems for administrators and will be the subject of Chapter 12.

Staff Development

The warden is expected to develop training programs for new staff and to make changes in job assignments when necessary. The warden's style of leadership affects the way subordinates do their jobs. Most institutional administrators continue to believe that staff morale and job involvement are enhanced when all levels of personnel participate in decision making, but the degree of personnel involvement is a decision that the top manager must make.

Fiscal Management

"A good warden," as correctional administrators are fond of saying, "always has a handle on the budget." Fiscal management should be a year-round process. There should be periodic (perhaps monthly) staff meetings to keep abreast of developments and the status of the budget. The warden should maintain his or her own file on changes that will be needed and others that will be recommended for the next year's budget.

CAREERS in Corrections

PRISON WARDEN

STEPHEN UPTON
WARDEN

© Becky Stein

Stephen Upton is the warden of Georgia State Prison in Reidsville, known for housing the state's toughest criminals. A long-term corrections official, Upton also served as warden at Calhoun State Prison and Hays State Prison before his latest appointment.

Preparation for the Job

In addition to a college education, prison wardens need exposure to all levels of prison operations. As a person is promoted to increasing levels of responsibility, it is also important to observe and learn from other corrections staff.

Nature of the Job

The prison warden is in charge of operating federal, state, or private prisons, hiring staff, managing the budget, and maintaining a secure institution. The warden exercises direct supervisory authority over immediate subordinates so that applicable plans are administered. The effective warden provides opportunities for inmates to improve themselves and to earn reasonable compensation by their participation in constructive programs and assignments. The warden organizes, plans, and implements a full range of structured institution systems of inmate accountability and discipline consistent with established law, policies, and regulations.

L09 ➤ ## Proactive Wardens

An increasing number of wardens across the nation have become committed to a proactive approach. The **proactive warden** is committed to anticipating and preventing problems before they take place. The proactive warden puts a greater emphasis on programming for inmates and staff development. He or she also emphasizes the importance of direct communication and rapport between the warden and staff, the warden and inmates, and the staff and inmates.[55]

The proactive warden typically sees the context of the prison as a dynamic community with the capacity to change in a positive direction. Proactive

PROACTIVE WARDEN An approach to prison management that is focused on anticipating problems before they occur.

The superintendent of a correctional facility has the same job description, although the size of the institution may be smaller and it may be a women's facility or a minimum-security prison. The job of warden or superintendent is a 24/7 position. Wardens often find themselves in crisis-centered management on a regular basis, unless they have done a good job with training subordinate staff whom they trust and have a proactive plan to anticipate and prevent problems. For those wardens who are continually involved in crisis-centered management, it does not take them long to feel overwhelmed by their jobs.

Qualifications and Required Education

The large majority of wardens across the nation have completed some college, and a good many possess advanced degrees. The warden, as do other correctional staff, generally begins service as a correctional officer or a correctional counselor and with effective performance is promoted through various positions, including associate warden of operations and programs. Those who aspire to become a warden in the Federal Bureau of Prisons must be willing to undergo several transfers in the process. Sometimes, wardens from one state are given positions as wardens in another state.

Job Outlook

With the continued construction of new facilities, as well as the promotion, retirement, and resignation of present institutional administrators, the job outlook is very good for competent individuals to be eventually appointed the chief operating officer of a prison.

Earnings and Benefits

Salaries of prison wardens vary from one state to the other, but wardens tend to be paid very well and the job usually comes with a number of perks. For example, in California, a prison warden's compensation package of $123,264 includes $103,416 base salary, $14,400 retirement contribution, and $5,448 health benefits. The Bureau of Prisons salaries for wardens are generally $100,000 or more. In Florida, prison wardens are paid salaries between $80,000 and $91,000, and in Louisiana, prison wardens are paid from $53,000 to $113,940 a year; a $80,000 salary seems to be the average compensation of many state systems. Moreover, the job of the warden frequently includes a house to live in and a vehicle.

Sources: This description of the prison warden is collected from interviewing several prison wardens in recent years. See also a description of the warden's position from the Louisiana Department of Civil Service, the State of Minnesota, the California Department of Corrections, and the Federal Bureau of Prisons.

wardens generally have the ability to think and conceptualize well, the character development to know the right moral positions to take, the creativity to be a problem solver with sometimes very complex issues, the willingness to look upon the prison as a learning community, and the willingness to take a proprietary interest in the institution.[56] Frank Wood, former warden of two prisons in Minnesota and Commissioner of the Minnesota Department of Corrections, identified several ways in which proactive wardens are different from other wardens (see Exhibit 6.5).

The Careers in Corrections subject for this chapter is the prison warden, a key figure in achieving humane correctional care for inmates and a safe environment for both staff and inmates.

EXHIBIT 6.5 The Proactive Warden

- *Proactive* wardens believe they can make a difference. They believe that prisons can be run in such a way that inmates and staff have hope and confidence in and respect for each other.

- Proactive wardens believe in treating inmates with dignity and respect. Treating inmates with dignity and respect has to do with how the staff interact with inmates on a daily basis.

- Proactive wardens have a hands-on approach. They spend a good deal of time walking the cellblocks, visiting inmates in their cells, touring the yard, and talking with staff at their assignments. With this management-by-walking-around philosophy, proactive wardens believe they will obtain information necessary to avoid or defuse pending problems.

- Proactive wardens realize the importance of a supportive team. A major concern of these wardens is to build a team of supportive staff.

- Proactive wardens are receptive to technological innovations. They are quick to use the technological advantages that recently have become available to corrections.

- Proactive wardens model the behaviors that they want to elicit from inmates and staff. They believe that a necessary component of a human-relations approach is their willingness to demonstrate to others what involvement in and understanding of others entails.

- Proactive wardens have a plan and the commitment to execute this plan for reform of the existing institution. They have clarity in their goals and principles. Having developed their principles over the years, they are continually working on how these principles could be more effectively attained or realized in a prison context.

Source: Derived from Clemens Bartollas, *Becoming a Model Warden* (Lanham, MD: American Correctional Association, 2004), pp. 69–71, 74–76.

SUMMARY

L01 **Identify the extent to which prisons mirror the larger society**

There are numerous parallels between the prison and the free world and in many respects the prison is a microcosm of the wider society. It can be argued that the prison is a distorted image of the larger society, with the problems of the larger society found in an exaggerated form in the prison.

L02 **Describe the age, gender, and racial makeup of those sent to prison**

The prison population is made up of males (93 percent) who tend to be young and minority. Violent offenders make up a little more than 50 percent of all sentenced inmates in state prisons.

L03 **Discuss the federal jurisdiction over prisons**

The Federal Bureau of Prisons is the largest prison system, as it oversees 106 correctional institutions, 6 regional offices, a central office in Washington, D.C., 2 staff training centers, and 28 community corrections offices. The Bureau of Prisons has had its problems, but it has long been advocated as the standard-setter of American corrections. Its advantages over state prison systems include better-trained staff, higher salaries, and more adequately funded programs and operations.

L04 **Explain whether state jurisdictions are similar from one state to another**

Correctional systems of the 50 states and the District of Columbia are difficult to compare and evaluate because of differences in ideology, structure, and programs. Yet there has been marked improvement in state correctional systems in recent years.

L05 **Know how many prisoners are housed in private facilities and whether there is common agreement on the effectiveness of these facilities**

Private prisons are gaining in number and popularity, and now have more than 100,000 inmates. There is disagreement about the quality and effectiveness of private prisons.

LO6 ▶ **Understand the security types of correctional institutions**

The security levels of prisons vary from minimum-security to supermax correctional facilities. Security is the byword of all prisons, especially maximum-security and supermax facilities. Today, prison cells are still very small, prison keepers are required to keep prisoners docile if they want to keep their jobs, and solitary confinement is a way of life in the most secure prisons across the nation.

LO7 ▶ **Describe what prisons look like**

The four most widely used architectural designs in American prisons are the radial design, the telephone-pole design, the courtyard design, and the campus design.

LO8 ▶ **Define the basic responsibilities of a correctional administrator**

Correctional administrators are responsible for the establishment of policy, planning, dealing with civil suits, institutional monitoring, staff development, and fiscal management.

LO9 ▶ **Explain the proactive management style**

A proactive warden is committed to anticipating and preventing problems before they take place in the prison. This management style believes in treating inmates with dignity and respect, puts an emphasis on programming for inmates and staff development for staff, and holds to the importance of direct communication between the warden and staff and the warden and inmates. An increasing number of wardens see themselves as proactive in their approach.

Key Terms

penal harm, 137
UNICOR, 140
Richardson v. McKnight, 144
Correctional Services Corp. v. Malesko, 144
minimum-security prison, 145

medium-security prison, 145
maximum-security prison, 146
segregation, 146
supermax prison, 146
Madrid v. Gomez, 148

radial design, 149
telephone-pole design, 150
courtyard style design, 150
campus style design, 150
proactive warden, 154

? Critical Thinking Questions

1. Are all prisons like the "Big House" depicted in movies of the 1930s? Explain your answer using examples from your reading.

2. You wake up one morning and find yourself in prison. Based on your reading of this chapter, describe the sort of prison you hope it will be.

3. Why did the popularity of supermax prisons increase during the 1990s?

4. If you have not visited a prison, make arrangements to do so. Compare what you see with what you have read.

5. What are the advantages of a proactive approach to prison administration?

Thinking Like a Corrections Professional

You have just been hired as a consultant to the state prison system because of your expertise on private prison management. The governor requests your opinion about a proposal received from the well-known and respected Penal Corporation of America, which is offering to privatize a medium-security prison and guarantees substantial savings to the state. The governor asks for your advice and wants to know the pros and cons of privatization and whether she should go along with the plan. You tell her that this is a complex problem and you will submit a memorandum within a few days. Outline the contents of your memorandum.

Career Destinations

If you are interested in a career in prison management at the federal level, you might want to explore resources on the home page for the U.S. Federal Bureau of Prisons:
www.bop.gov

Before you start your career, you may want to familiarize yourself with the layout of a typical prison. Take a virtual tour through Florida's state prisons:
www.dc.state.fl.us/oth/vtour/

Notes

1. The Sentencing Project, "On the Chopping Block: State Prison Closings," 2011 report, Washington, DC, p. 1.
2. Brian Mann, "Prison Closings Trouble Upstate New York," *All Things Considered*, NPR, March 7, 2008.
3. Office of the Governor, Illinois Government News Network, March 12, 2008.
4. Heather C. West and William J. Sabol, *Prisoners in 2009* (Washington, DC: Bureau of Justice Statistics Bulletin, December 2010), http://bjs.ojp.usdoj.gov/content/pub/pdf/p09.pdf (accessed February 26, 2012).
5. Kristen Hughes, *Justice Expenditure and Employment in the United States, 2003* (Washington, DC: Bureau of Justice Statistics, 2006).
6. Thomas Stucky, Karen Heimer, and Joseph Lang, "Partisan Politics, Electoral Competition, and Imprisonment: An Analysis of States Over Time," *Criminology* 43 (2005): 211–247.
7. James B. Jacobs, *Stateville: The Penitentiary in Modern Society* (Chicago: University of Chicago Press, 1977).
8. Donald Clemmer, *The Prison Community* (New York: Holt, Rinehart & Winston, 1966), p. 298.
9. *Attica: The Official Report of the New York State Special Commission on Attica* (New York: Praeger, 1972), p. 82.
10. West and Sabol, *Prisoners in 2009*, p. 1.
11. Ibid., pp. 6–7.
12. Ibid., pp. 8–9.
13. Federal Bureau of Prisons website, www.bop.gov (accessed February 26, 2012).
14. See Bartollas's biography of Norman C. Carlson, *A Model of Correctional Leadership: The Career of Norman A. Carlson* (Alexandria, VA: American Correctional Association, 2010).
15. Ibid.
16. For a description of the BOP programs, see Mary Bosworth, *The U.S. Federal Prison System* (Thousand Oaks, CA: Sage Publishers, 2002).
17. BOP website.
18. Ibid.
19. Bartollas, *A Model of Correctional Leadership: The Career of Norman A. Carlson.*
20. In interviews, three former directors of the Bureau of Prisons—Norm Carlson, Michael Quinlin, and Kathleen Hawk Sawyer—all made this point.
21. For a vivid picture of life within a federal penitentiary, see Pete Earley, *The Hot House: Life Inside Leavenworth Prison* (New York: Bantam Books, 1992).
22. Michael G. Santos has written several books describing his incarceration in federal facilities. For example, see Michael G. Santos, *About Prison* (Belmont, CA: Wadsworth, 2004).
23. Information provided by the American Correctional Association, 2012.
24. Impressions gained from administrators of state departments of corrections and the Federal Bureau of Prisons.
25. Mark Colvin, *Penitentiaries, Reformatories, and Chain Gangs: Social Theory and the History of Punishment in Nineteenth-Century America* (New York: St. Martin's Press, 2000), pp. 243–246.
26. Cody Mason, *Too Good to Be True: Private Prisons in America* (Washington, DC: The Sentencing Project, January 2012), p. 2.
27. Corrections Corporation of America, www.cca.com, and the GEO Group, Inc., www.thegeogroupinc.com (sites accessed February 26, 2012).
28. J. Maahs and T. Pratt, "Are Private Prisons More Cost-Effective than Public Prisons? A Meta-Analysis of Evaluation Research Studies," *Crime and Delinquency* 45 (1999): 358–371.
29. Mason, *Too Good to be True*, p. 17.
30. Gerald G. Gaes, Scott D. Camp, and William G. Saylor, "The Performance of Privately Operated Prisons: A Review of Research," www.bop.gov/news/research_projects/published_reports/pub_vs_priv/oreprpriv_cm2.pdf (accessed February 26, 2012); William Bales et al., "Recidivism: An Analysis of Public and Private State Prison Releases in Florida," 2003, www.dc.state.fl.us/pub/recidivismfsu/RecidivismStudy2003.pdf (accessed February 26, 2012); William Bales, Laura Bedard, Susan Quinn, David Ensley, and Glen Holley, "Recidivism of Public and Private State Prison Inmates in Florida," *Criminology and Public Policy* 4 (2005): 57–82; and Lonn Lanza-Kaduce, Karen Parker, and Charles Thomas, "A Comparative Recidivism Analysis of Releases from Private and Public Prisons," *Crime and Delinquency* 45 (1999): 28–47.
31. Andrew L. Spivak and Susan F. Sharp, "Inmate Recidivism as a Measure of Private Prison Performance," *Crime and Delinquency* 54 (2008): 282–508.
32. Charles Thomas, "Recidivism of Public and Private State Prison Inmates in Florida: Issues and Unanswered Questions," *Criminology and Public Policy* 4 (2005): 89–100; Travis Pratt and Jeff Maahs, "Are Private Prisons More Cost-Effective than Public Prisons? A Meta-Analysis of Evaluation Research Studies," *Crime and Delinquency* 45 (1999): 358–371.
33. H. G. Lappin, T. R. Kane, W. G. Saylor, and S. D. Camp, *Evaluation of the Taft Demonstration Project: Performance of a Private-Sector Prison and the BOP* (Washington, DC: U.S. Department of Justice, Federal Bureau of Prisons, 2005).
34. Danica Coto, "Medical Care Company Names in Numerous Jail Lawsuits," *Charlotte Observer*, August 30, 2004.
35. Sasha Abramsky, "Incarceration, Inc.," *The Nation*, July 19 and 26, 2004; Gaes, Camp, and Saylor, "The Performance of Privately Operated Prisons"; and "Lawmakers Press for Private Prison Closure," *Corrections Digest* 36 (March 2005): 1–2.
36. Mason, *Too Good to Be True*, p. 17.
37. *Richardson v. McKnight*, 521 U.S. 399 (1997).
38. *Correctional Services Corporation v. Malesko*, 534 U.S.61, 122 S.Ct. 515 (2001).
39. Ahmed A. White, "Rule of Law and the Limits of Sovereignty: The Private Prison in Jurisprudential Perspective," *American Criminal Law Review* 38 (2001): 111–147.
40. Charles W. Thomas is a strong advocate of private facilities. See Thomas, "Recidivism of Public and Private State Prison Inmates in Florida: Issues and Unanswered Questions."
41. "Prison Security Levels," *Fire on the Line* prison guard blog, June 7, 2006.
42. Ibid.
43. Maureen L. O'Keefe, "Administrative Segregation from Within: A Corrections Perspective," *Prison Journal* 88 (2008): 123.
44. Daniel P. Mears, "Evaluating the Effectiveness of Supermax Prisons," Urban Institute, May 10, 2006; and Mears, "A Critical Look at Supermax Prisons," *Corrections Compendium* 30 (2005): 6–7.
45. Mears, "Evaluating the Effectiveness of Supermax Prisons."
46. Jeffrey Ian Ross, "Supermax Prisons," *Social Science and Public Policy* 44 (2007): 60–64; Corey Weinstein, "Even Dogs Confined to Cages for Long Periods of Time Go Berserk," in *Building Violence: How America's Rush to Incarcerate Creates More Violence*, ed. John P. May and Khalid R. Pitts (Thousand Oaks, CA: Sage Publications, 2000), p. 121.

47. Kate King, Benjamin Steiner, and Stephanie Ritchie Breach, "Violence in the Supermax: A Self-Fulfilling Prophecy," *Prison Journal* 88 (March 2008): 144–168.
48. Ibid.
49. Laura Sullivan, "Life in Solitary Confinement: At Pelican Bay Prison, a Life in Solitary," *NPR*, March 7, 2008.
50. *Madrid v. Gomez*, 889 F.Supp. 1146 (N.D.Cal. 1995).
51. William G. Nagel, *An American Archipelago: The United States Bureau of Prisons* (Hackensack, NJ: National Council on Crime and Delinquency, 1974), p. 1.
52. William G. Nagel, *The New Red Barn: A Critical Look at the Modern American Prison* (New York: Walker, 1973), p. 36.
53. Minnesota Department of Corrections, "A New High Security Facility for Minnesota" (St. Paul, MN: Department of Corrections, n.d.), p. 2.
54. Richard Gramley, a former Illinois warden, defined the basic responsibilities of the correctional administrator and helped shape this discussion.
55. Clemens Bartollas, *Becoming a Model Warden* (Lanham, MD: American Correctional Association, 2004), pp. 71–72.
56. Ibid., p. 72.

Ralph J. Phillips, better known as Bucky, has become a folk hero to inmates and a sought-out media interviewee. His fame is related to his notorious 2006 crime spree, which involved breaking out of jail, killing a state trooper, eluding capture for five months while hundreds of troopers tried to track him down through the backwoods of western New York, and shooting two more troopers before he was captured. For his efforts, Bucky Phillips was sentenced to life in prison in New York's Clinton County Correctional Facility. In prison, Bucky now expresses sorrow for the dead trooper, yet seems to relish his days on the run. "I enjoyed those few months more than I've enjoyed any other time in my life," he says. He is especially proud of his maneuvers to remain free: how he led two troopers on a twisted route deep into the woods and watched as a helicopter came to help find them; how he disguised himself several times as a trooper with a uniform he had obtained from an acquaintance, even chatting with another trooper who never recognized him; and how he moved around mostly at night and spent long stretches in the woods, eating rabbits and fish and sleeping on the ground. He assaulted a bounty hunter who

AP Photo/Don Heupel

Ralph J. Phillips, better known as Bucky, is shown being escorted by New York State law enforcement officers. Bucky's notoriety is related to his 2006 crime spree, which involved breaking out of jail, killing a state trooper, eluding capture for five months while hundreds of troopers tried to track him down through the backwoods of western New York, and shooting two more troopers before he was captured.

kept his picture hanging from his rearview mirror.[1]

Using what he calls "cat and mouse" tactics, Bucky would purposely allow himself to be seen and then would flee as far as Ohio, Kentucky, and West Virginia in stolen cars, only to return back to his home ground. At times, he monitored trooper activity with a police scanner. He became aware that he had become something of a cult figure when he saw strangers walking on a road with shirts bearing the name "Bucky." He also learned that there were signs and shirts reading "Run, Bucky, Run" and "Where's Bucky?" Another sign of his growing fame: a restaurant called Grandma's Kitchen created and began serving customers the "Bucky Burger."[2]

Phillips is presently serving a sentence of life without parole at the Clinton County Correctional Facility, a maximum-security prison in Dannemora, New York, near the Canadian border. On October 19, 2011, he was charged with violating prison regulations after a search of his cell turned up prohibited items. He appeared to have escape tools, but the details of what the correctional officers found in the cell were not released.[3]

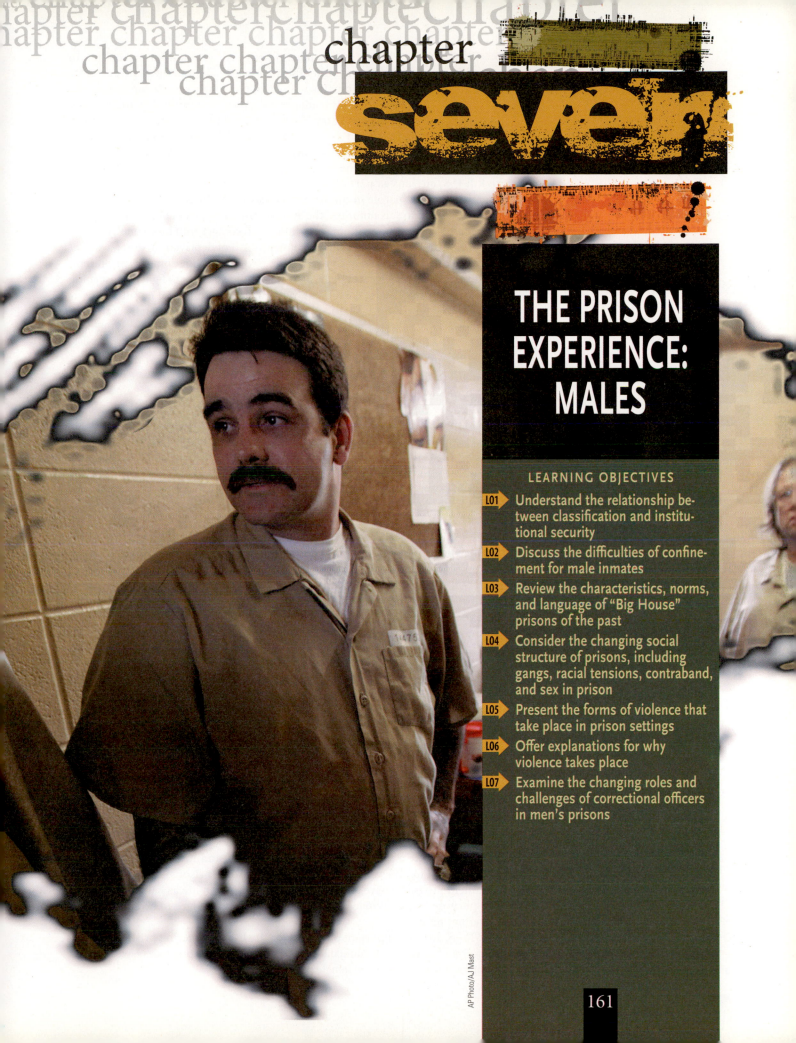

THE PRISON EXPERIENCE: MALES

LEARNING OBJECTIVES

LO1 Understand the relationship between classification and institutional security

LO2 Discuss the difficulties of confinement for male inmates

LO3 Review the characteristics, norms, and language of "Big House" prisons of the past

LO4 Consider the changing social structure of prisons, including gangs, racial tensions, contraband, and sex in prison

LO5 Present the forms of violence that take place in prison settings

LO6 Offer explanations for why violence takes place

LO7 Examine the changing roles and challenges of correctional officers in men's prisons

AP Photo/A.J. Mast

Bucky Phillips is not alone. It has been common for our culture to create folk heroes out of serious criminals, and there are currently a number of inmates who have notorious reputations—Charles Manson, the cult leader of the Manson family; legendary gang leaders such as Larry Hoover, chief of the Gangster Disciples; and terrorists such as the Unabomber (Theodore Kaczynski), shoe bomber Richard Reid, Oklahoma City terror bomb conspirator Terry Nichols, and Zacarias Moussaoui, the French citizen who was convicted of conspiring to kill U.S. citizens as part of the 9/11 attacks and who is now serving a life sentence without parole in the supermax prison in Florence, Colorado.

In contrast to this notoriety, the average inmate lives a life bereft of glamour and fame. Usually far from home with little or no contact with loved ones, inmates feel alienated. They must learn to adapt to a world of deprivation, doing without comforts and pleasures they enjoyed in the free world. Boredom is ever present. The experienced convict eventually learns to do time but has to fight against going "stir crazy." Furthermore, the total impact of incarceration—one negative experience stacked on the next—hardens a person. Male inmates, especially, learn that the best way to avoid being hurt is to repress their emotions. As one ex-offender puts it, "It took me a long time after I got out before I could feel anything. I was so used to making sure that nobody messed with me that I didn't trust nobody. I couldn't let anyone close to me. I didn't know what it felt like to love somebody. Man, I was dead."[4]

Because survival is uncertain in large dangerous institutions, men are likely to arm themselves for self-protection. In most state and federal prisons, the male prisoner also must deal with inmate gangs. As a gang member in a Midwestern prison noted, "In here you can't fly alone; you've got to join an organization if you want to survive."[5] Moreover, racial conflict is acute. Racial tension sometimes erupts in sexual victimization, in stabbings and killings, and in mass disturbances. Considerable evidence exists that incarceration has a negative impact on individuals. For example, criminologist Michael Massoglia has written widely on the relationship between incarceration and negative health in subsequent years following release.[6]

In Voices Across the Professions, Captain Steven Ayers talks about his job in a supermax prison in Minnesota.

We divide our discussion of prison life into two chapters. This chapter focuses on the male inmate and how he serves his time in prison. The next chapter examines the female inmate and how she copes with confinement.

ENTERING PRISON

Prisons in the United States are looked upon as **total institutions**. This means that inmates are segregated from the outside world, are kept under constant scrutiny and surveillance, and are forced to obey strict official rules to avoid facing formal sanctions. With their personal possessions taken from them, they must conform to institutional dress and personal appearance norms. Many human functions are strictly curtailed or limited. Some institutions employ a **no-frills policy** that was passed as an amendment to the 1994 crime bill. What this no-frills policy means is stripping prisons of weight rooms, no cable TV (even if they have a TV that works), no computers, no air conditioning (dormitories are like a blast furnace in the summer), and mediocre food (beans, potatoes, and noodles are repeatedly served in some prisons). Educational and treatment programs have also been cut, making prison life as harsh as possible. The purpose is to convince offenders that prison is no place to be and they had better not return.

There are two important processes for the inmate entering prison: the classification process and the difficulties of adjustment. These processes have much in common for both male and female prisoners.

TOTAL INSTITUTION Term coined by Irving Goffman to describe an institution that has total control over all aspects of those confined there.

NO-FRILLS POLICY Inmates will receive the bare minimum of food, services and programs, and medical care required by law.

© Steven Ayers

> "This is what drives and motivates me—that we can make a difference in offenders' lives."

STEVEN AYERS
PRISON CAPTAIN

I am working on my 26th year in corrections, of which 23 years have been at Oak Park Heights Maximum Security Prison. I started in corrections right after completing college as a correctional officer and have since held positions as a case manager, special investigator/polygraph examiner, and assistant to the warden. In 2001, I was promoted as the highest ranking uniformed officer—captain. As the captain, I am responsible for the overall security of the prison. I have had opportunities to move to higher level positions, but I made the career decision that I wanted to continue to be directly involved in operational security. This is where the "real" prison work occurs.

A typical day in the life of a captain:

- We read the incident reports/captain's report from the previous twenty-four hours.

- We prepare for the warden's executive morning meeting, held Monday through Friday.

- In the warden's executive meeting, we review all reports and develop a plan of action for the day. We update the warden on any projects/initiatives we are working on.

- We represent the interests of the correctional officers to the executive level staff.

- We are always trying to prevent major incidents such as offender physical altercations, assaults on staff, contraband in the facility, and suicides. If they occur, we work to ensure they are handled appropriately and minimize the negative impacts.

- We are responsible for developing emergency plans, officer post orders, and security policies and routinely conduct drill on our plans. We conduct weekly inspections of the entire facility.

- We respond to real and imagined concerns of offenders, and assist staff with work issues they are experiencing.

- We search, search, and search to try to keep the "neighborhood" safe.

- The security division job consists of 99 percent routine/normal operations with 1 percent responding to emergency incidents that take place. We work with staff to avoid complacency in carrying out their duties.

- Every three years we have a security audit, and I ensure that we are in compliance with the security standards and policies.

We do have our difficulties and challenges. An emerging challenge right now is the offenders' abuse of over-the-counter and prescription medications. Offenders go to great lengths to try to get high on drugs, and without access to illegal drugs, they have resorted to abusing these types of drugs. Another issue is that security threat groups used to be clearly defined along racial lines. Now the groups are made up of a mix of races and there is in-fighting with the younger and older members within the groups. This has made it much more challenging to track and monitor groups in our facility. Management of offenders suffering from mental illness in prison taxes staffing resources. Our goal is to help them so they can serve their sentences in the general population, but it can be very difficult for them to make it successfully in that environment.

In terms of job satisfaction, I really look forward to coming to work every day. I work hard on trying to do the "right thing" even though at times it may not be viewed favorably by staff and/or offenders. One needs to work on staying positive in a potentially negative work and living environment. I relieve any stress the job creates by staying physically fit. The job is filled with so much variety and there is always something refreshing and new. This is what drives and motivates me—that we can make a difference in offenders' lives. It is very fulfilling when an offender informs me that I have made a positive difference in his life, big or small. This business is not for everyone, as you need to be able to separate what the offender had done to get to prison and treat them humanely at all times. Ninety-five percent of the offenders will someday be released back into society so we need to work on creating an environment that is positive to hopefully allow them to be better people, not worse.

Source: Interviewed in 2011.

PRISON CLASSIFICATION
A method of assessing inmate risks and needs that balances the security concerns of the institution with treatment needs of the individual.

EXTERNAL CLASSIFICATION SYSTEM
Determines the level of security and control needed for the incoming prison population.

INTERNAL CLASSIFICATION SYSTEM
Determines the cell or housing unit where inmates will be housed as well as facility programs to which they are assigned.

Classification

Inmates quickly learn what the term *total institution* really means. Their first experience usually occurs in a classification or reception center, where they are given a battery of psychological and intelligence tests and are evaluated on the basis of their background, offense history, personality, and treatment needs. Specialists attempt to develop a profile that includes criminal and social history, education, job skills and work history, substance abuse, and health. Based on this information, the offender is assigned to the most appropriate custody classification and prison. Violent offenders, high-profile gang members, and hard-core and repeat offenders will usually go to the maximum-security unit. Offenders with learning disabilities may be assigned to an institution that specializes in educational services, mentally disordered offenders will be held in a facility that can provide psychiatric care, and so on. Some states have instituted rigorous classification instruments designed to maximize the effectiveness of placements, thereby cutting down on the cost of incarceration.[7] However, some inmates may find that because of overcrowding they cannot be placed in an institution that meets their needs. Instead, they may find themselves in an overcrowded institution, housing more experienced and/or more dangerous inmates, that lacks the proper treatment they need to aid in their rehabilitation.

Prison classification is a method of assessing inmate risks that balances the security needs of the institution with treatment needs of the individual. Because inmates are a heterogeneous group, possessing a variety of behavioral problems, treatment needs, and psychological conditions, it is important to evaluate them so they can be placed in the proper institution and obtain the appropriate treatment and care. Effective classification can reduce prison infractions and create a safer environment for both inmates and staff.

EXTERNAL VERSUS INTERNAL CLASSIFICATION There are both external and internal classification decisions to be made (see Figure 7.1). James Austin's nationwide review of prison classification systems highlights the difference between external and internal classification. He states that while external classification places an inmate at a custody level that will determine where he or she will be housed, internal classification determines the cell or housing unit, as well as the facility programs (e.g., education, vocational, counseling, and work assignments) to which the prisoner will be assigned.[8]

External classification systems are now being used in all federal and state prison systems in the United States. Each offender is assessed using an objective risk classification system (using data such as the sentence length, the seriousness of the committed offense, and the offender's criminal history) and is assigned to a minimum, medium, maximum, or supermax prison facility.[9]

Internal classification systems focus on those decisions that are made for the incoming prison population. This review may include assessment of:

- Dangerousness as well as other types of assessments (physical health, mental health, gang affiliation, and flight/escape risk)

- Prison rule infractions, grievances, institutional punishments or sanctions, and reclassification decisions[10]

EVALUATION OF CLASSIFICATION The National Institute of Corrections worked with eight states over a seven-year period to develop, pilot-test, implement, and evaluate internal prison classification systems. Seven models were tested. Colorado, Connecticut, and Florida developed computerized, objective, behavior-based models for housing and program assignments. Oregon developed an objective model that was based on behavioral and compatibility indicators for its female population, although preliminary results suggest that the system works equally well for male inmates. New Jersey developed a behavior-based model for identifying the aggression levels of its maximum-custody inmates. Washington

Admission to prison

Initial external classification
- Custody assessment
- Program needs assessment
- Facility designation

Transfer to facility

Initial internal classification
- Housing assignment
- Program assignment
- Work assignment

Transfer to designated housing area

Reclassification
- External classification
  - Custody
- Internal classification
  - Program
  - Housing
  - Work
  - Facility
  - Community programs

FIGURE 7.1 Prison Classification Process

Source: J. Austin and P. Hardyman, *Objective Prison Classification: A Guide for Correctional Agencies* (Washington, DC: U.S. National Institute of Corrections, 2004).

State analyzed the utility of the Adult Internal Management System (AIMS) for case management of minimum-custody inmates with long sentences. South Dakota and Missouri further developed a personality-based system, the Adult Internal Classification System (AICS), modeled after AIMS. The diversity of the models developed suggests that there is no "best model," nor should there be one. The instruments and process must be tailored and validated to the specific populations for which they will be used. However, a set of standards applicable to all internal classification systems was identified.[11]

Despite its problems, classification has a number of advantages:

- An effective classification system can reduce institutional tension by placing inmates in the prison in which they can function more effectively.

- An effective classification system can better ensure a safe environment for both staff and inmates.

- An effective classification system can avoid placing inmates in more secure and expensive housing than they really need.

- Institutions with inmate gang problems may require that gang members or leaders of rival gangs be separated from each other and a classification system is therefore indispensable.

- Inmates with special needs, including HIV inmates, the elderly, inmates with mental health problems, and sex offenders, require that they be placed in the most appropriate institutional settings.

Difficulties of Adjustment

After they arrive at the correctional institution that will perhaps house them for many years, inmates go through a variety of attitude and behavior changes as their sentence unfolds. When they arrive at prison, they are stripped, searched, showered, and assigned living quarters. Their treatment may seem harsh and inhuman, so it is not surprising that many of the men will become depressed when considering the long duration of the sentence and the loneliness and dangers of prison life. They soon realize they must learn the ins and outs of survival: which persons can be befriended, and which are best avoided?[12] To avoid victimization, inmates must learn to adopt a defensive lifestyle.[13] They must discover areas of safety and danger. Studies suggest that with limited resources and extensive personal limitations prior to their confinement, most inmates find that the challenges of incarceration further deplete their meager resources, which increases the difficulties of adjusting to prison life.[14]

TRADITIONAL MALE INMATE CULTURE: THE BIG HOUSE ERA

The so-called **Big House**—large maximum-security prisons that emphasized security and control—dominated American corrections from the 1930s through the 1950s. This type of prison emerged and spread, with considerable help from Hollywood, which portrayed this prison to the general society. States built large fortress-like institutions—Sing Sing, San Quentin, Alcatraz, and Stateville—that became stark representations of the prison experience. The Big House was a walled facility with large cellblocks that often contained three or more tiers of one- or two-man cells. Big House prison populations showed considerable homogeneity. Most of the inmates were white, were property offenders, and had spent several stints in prison during the course of their criminal careers.[15] "Convicts," as they were known then, developed a unified culture and kept their distance from the "hacks" or guards.

BIG HOUSE A type of large fortress-like prison that dominated corrections in the early part of the twentieth century.

EXHIBIT 7.1 Social Roles in the Big House Prison

- Rats and center men, who hoped to relieve their pains by betrayal of fellow prisoners

- Gorillas and merchants, who relieved deprivations by preying on their fellow prisoners, taking their possessions by force or the threat of force

- Wolves, punks, and fags, who engaged in homosexual acts either voluntarily or under coercion to relieve the deprivation of heterosexuality

- Real men, who endured the rigors of confinement with dignity, as opposed to ball busters, who openly defied authority

- Toughs, who were overtly violent, who would fight with anyone, strong or weak, and who "won't take anything from anybody"

- Hipsters, who talked tough but were really "all wind and gumdrops"

Source: Gresham Sykes, *The Society of Captives: A Study of a Maximum Security Prison* (Princeton, NJ: Princeton University Press, 1958), pp. 64–108.

In the Big House, old "cons" informed new prisoners that the guards were in control and the inmates had to make the best of it or face severe consequences. To make their time easier, convicts developed their own social roles, informal codes of behaviors, and language. In an influential study, sociologist **Gresham Sykes** delineated a typology of inmate social roles (see Exhibit 7.1).

Sykes found that inmate social roles, other than "real men," provided ways to reduce the rigors of their own prison life at the expense of fellow prisoners. Convicts fulfilling the social role of the "real men" were loyal and generous and tried to minimize friction among the other inmates. They tried to maintain social cohesion under trying circumstances and set an example that produced inmate solidarity.[16]

Inmate Social Code

During the Big House era, an informal **inmate code** of behavior developed and dominated the inmate culture. It was based on the following tenets:

- Don't interfere with inmate interests.

- Never rat on a con.

- Do your own time.

- Don't exploit fellow inmates.

- Be tough; be a man; never back down from a fight.

- Don't trust the "hacks" (guards) or the things they stand for.[17]

The inmate code was functional not only to prisoners but to prison administrators.[18] The code promoted order. It encouraged each prisoner to serve his sentence rather than create problems. Prisoners understood that disorder within the walls would mean that informal arrangements between prisoner leaders and staff would be set aside and prisoners would lose privileges it had taken them years to attain. The code also protected the self-respect of inmates because they knew they were maintaining order not for the staff but for themselves. "Hacks" were the enemy, and a convict who was worthy of his role within the prison made his animosity toward the enemy very clear.

Nevertheless, inmates and guards in the Big House knew that they depended on each other. Inmates maintained order and performed many of the tasks of running the institution. In turn, guards permitted inmates to violate certain rules and to gain privileges that were contrary to policy. What took place was an exchange. Staff and inmates accommodated each others' needs while maintaining a hostile stance toward each other.

Prisonization

Among the most influential research on the Big House culture was the research by **Donald Clemmer** in his seminal study of Menard Prison in southern Illinois. Clemmer claimed that the solidarity of the inmate world prevented

GRESHAM SYKES Developed a typology of prison social roles and inmate culture.

INMATE CODE An unwritten but powerful code regulating inmates' behavior; inmates codes are functional to both inmates and prison administrators because they tend to promote order within the walls.

DONALD CLEMMER Known for his research at Menard Correctional Center; coined the term *prisonization*, which defines how inmates learn to adapt to prison while taking on the prison culture.

prisoners from being rehabilitated. He coined the term **prisonization**, defining it as the "taking on in greater or lesser degree of the folkways, customs, and general culture of the penitentiary."[19] "Prisonization," he added, "is a process of assimilation, in which prisoners adopt a subordinate status, learn prison argot (language), take on the habits of other prisoners, engage in various forms of deviant behavior such as homosexual behavior and gambling, develop antagonistic attitudes toward guards, and become acquainted with inmate dogmas and mores."[20] Clemmer felt that when prisoners adapted to prison life they began surrendering their individuality and became dependent upon the system.

Clemmer's emphasis was on the unique situation of the prison as a community composed of unwilling members under the coercive control of state employees. The prison was viewed as a closed system, despite the fact that staff and the prisoners themselves were bringing in the outside culture and its values. Clemmer thought that all convicts were prisonized to some extent and possibly as many as 20 percent were completely prisonized. And he was convinced that upon release the highly prisonized offenders were likely to return to crime. Just as immigrants coming to the United States would be "Americanized" to a greater or lesser degree, so would a convict entering prison be more or less prisonized.[21]

Clemmer's research was highly regarded by penal experts, and numerous attempts were made to validate his findings. In one notable study conducted in the Washington State Reformatory, Stanton Wheeler found strong support for Clemmer's concept of prisonization. But Wheeler found that the degree of prisonization varied according to the phase of an inmate's institutional stay: an inmate was most strongly influenced by the norms of the inmate subculture during the middle stage of his or her prison stay (with more than six months remaining).[22]

Donald Clemmer's research highlighted the influence of **prison culture** on the psychological well-being of inmates. What intrigued prison experts was how that culture developed in the first place. Did it arise spontaneously within prison walls or did it reflect the inmate's previous life on the outside? The two explanations for prison culture that have received the most attention are the deprivation model and the importation model. According to the **deprivation model**, developed by Gresham Sykes, inmate behavior is a product of the prison environment. The model describes the prisoner's attempt to adapt to the deprivations imposed by incarceration.[23] According to the **importation model**, the prison culture is imported from the outside world.[24] Consequently, inmate culture is affected as much by the values of newcomers and events on the outside as it is by traditional inmate values. Two newer

In maximum-security prisons, inmates are well supervised and security is very tight. Inmates convicted of dangerous crimes such as murder are closely watched. Here, Grade B death row inmates exercise in 8-foot by 10-foot exercise cages and must enter and leave the grounds in handcuffs. Some, like the man in the black hat, are only allowed to exercise by themselves.

© Penni Gladstone/*San Francisco Chronicle*/Corbis

PRISONIZATION The process by which inmates learn and internalize the customs and culture of prison.

PRISON CULTURE The values, norms, and attitudes that inmates form in terms of institutional survival.

DEPRIVATION MODEL A model that views the losses experienced by an inmate during incarceration as one of the costs of imprisonment.

IMPORTATION MODEL A model that suggests that the influences prisoners bring into the prison affect their process of imprisonment.

EXHIBIT 7.2 Argot Language Used by Inmates

- Back-me-ups—friends you can count on in a fight
- Beef—a charge for the commission of a crime
- Bogus—anything false, counterfeit
- Bracelets—handcuffs or shackles
- Buy the farm—inmate who has committed suicide
- Cellie—cellmate
- Ding—mentally ill inmate
- Do a hitch—serve a prison term
- Easy time—one who is able to serve a sentence relatively trouble-free
- Fish—new inmate
- House—cell
- Jacket—label
- Kite—communication between prisoners and staff
- Pruno—prison-distilled wine made from fruit and other ingredients
- Rat—prisoner who provides information to the administration about other inmates
- Shank—prisoner-made knife or other sharp weapon
- Snitch—same as rat
- Standup guy—strong inmate who will not sell out to staff
- Yard—exercise area for inmates

Sources: Some of these are found in Lorna A. Rhodes, *Total Confinement: Madness and Reason in the Maximum Security Prison* (Berkeley: University of California Press, 2004), and others are common knowledge of the authors.

SITUATIONAL MODEL A model that suggests that prison culture is influenced by situations rather than remaining constant and can vary over time and place.

ADMINISTRATIVE-CONTROL MODEL A model that contends that the management style of the prison has influence over what takes place in inmate culture.

ARGOT A form of slang inmates use in prison settings to express how they feel.

PRISON GANG A group of inmates who are bound together by mutual interests, have identifiable leadership, and act in concert to achieve a specific purpose that generally includes the conduct of illegal activity.

SECURITY THREAT GROUPS (STGs) The name that law enforcement and corrections officials give to groups that exhibit ganglike activity.

models that have received some attention are the **situational model** and the **administrative-control model**.

Prison Language or Argot

Referring to thousands of conversations and interviews, as well as to inmate essays and biographies, Clemmer was able to identify a unique language, or **argot**, that prisoners use. The specific demands on language by a subgroup are frequently expressed through slang. Argot, which was originally defined as the jargon or language of thieves but also applied to other groups, is a particular form of slang. It can be argued that a prisoner lives, functions, and thinks within the framework defined by the argot and, therefore, the argot centers on the functions that it serves for the inmate.[25]

With the demise of inmate solidarity and the inmate code in prisons across the United States, the commonly recognized or used argot language has decreased. There still remain a number of terms that appear widely used from one prison to another; see Exhibit 7.2.

CONTEMPORARY MALE PRISON CULTURE

As the Big House era came to an end in the final decades of the twentieth century, prison culture underwent a dramatic change, taking on new forms in its structure, language, and mores. The influence of the inmate social code waned and with it the control over the inmate population by the right guys and real men. In its place has been an invasion of prison gangs and resulting racial conflicts, as well as changes in sexual expression.

L04 Prison Gang Structures

Prison gangs exist in 40 states and in the Federal Bureau of Prisons. In some states, especially California, Illinois, and Texas, prison gangs are the dominant force in inmate life. In nearly all of the other states that have prison gangs, they pose security problems and cause increased levels of violence. Prison gangs have recently been called **security threat groups (STGs)**.

ORIGINS AND DEVELOPMENT OF PRISON GANGS In the late 1960s and 1970s, gang members began to experience increasing numbers being sent to prison. It was not long before prison gangs appeared in other states, including New York, Pennsylvania, Ohio, Arizona, Michigan, and Iowa. By the 1990s, prison gangs were found in all of the larger prison systems and many of the small ones.

In California, the Mexican Mafia (chiefly from East Los Angeles) vies for power with Nuestra Familia (consisting of rural Chicanos). African Americans in California are organized into the Black Guerrilla Family, the Black Muslims, the Black Panthers, and other groups; the Neo-Nazis and the Aryan Brotherhood are white gangs that have organized to provide protection against abuse and intimidation.

In the Illinois prison system, the Gangster Disciples, the Black Gangster Disciple Nation, the Conservative Vice Lords, and the Latin Kings vie for control. James Jacobs claims that the most important factor contributing to violence at Stateville was the presence of these four Chicago street gangs.[26] All of these "super gangs" originated in the slums of Chicago, and many of the leading figures were gang leaders when in free society. Jacobs found that formal agreements among the gang leaders assured incarcerated members that members of other gangs would not molest them. Inmates unaffiliated with a gang—around 50 percent of those at Stateville—were fair game for thievery, intimidation, blackmail, assault, and sexual pressure.[27]

Prison gangs in Texas are also increasing their control over prison life. Formed in 1975 by a group of prisoners who had served time in the California prison system, the Texas Syndicate is the oldest and the second largest inmate gang in the Texas prison system. A Texas offshoot of the Mexican Mafia, Mexikanemi (or Soldiers of Aztlan), was formed in 1984 and is the largest inmate gang in Texas. The Aryan Brotherhood of Texas and the Texas Mafia are two other powerful inmate gangs. Figure 7.2 shows the tattoo insignia of these four gangs. Both the Texas Syndicate and Mexikanemi are organized along paramilitary lines. Regardless of rank, both inmate gangs require their members to abide by a strict code of conduct known as the "constitution."[28]

The Federal Bureau of Prisons (BOP) identifies the Aryan Brotherhood, Mexican Mafia, Texas Syndicate, and Black Guerrilla Family as particularly troublesome for prison officials. In addition, the BOP has identified as security threat groups (STG) other gangs such as the Arizona Aryan Brotherhood, Black Gangster Disciples, Hells Angels, and Jamaican Posse.[29]

FIGURE 7.2 Gang Tattoos in Texas Prisons

Source: From Ben M. Crouch and James W. Marquart, *An Appeal to Justice: Litigated Reform of Texas Prisons* (p. 210). Copyright © 1989 by University of Texas Press. Reprinted by permission.

ECONOMIC VICTIMIZATION Prison gangs usually specialize in economic victimization. They typically force all independent operators out of business and either divide among themselves the spoils of drugs and other inmate contraband or fight to the death to determine who will establish a monopoly within the prison.[30] A survey of security threat groups in prisons found that they dominated the inmate rackets, including the illegal sex trade, illicit food business, loan sharking scams, gambling scams, "extortion" rackets, and drug trafficking.[31]

GANGS AND VIOLENCE High levels of violence may occur when gangs are in conflict with each other. Interracial conflict disrupts institutional life when large gangs organized along racial and ethnic lines make it a deliberate policy to attack other racial and ethnic gangs. Another problem is that imprisoned gang leaders usually have tight control over what takes place within the prison where they are confined. Imprisoned gang leaders have incited prison disturbances, the taking of hostages, and inmates' refusal to work or come out of their cells.[32]

Gangs have gained control in some prisons because officials are afraid that violence will be commonplace unless gang demands are met and leaders appeased. As one prison official in Illinois put it, "We felt that we had to stay on their good side or they would take the lid off the prison."[33] According to Larry Hoover, the legendary leader of the Gangster Disciples, gangs can incite a riot any time they want. In fact, according to Hoover, the gangs had agreed, especially the Vice Lords and the Gangster Disciples, that they would maintain peace within the prison, including cutting down on prison rapes, if the administration would meet their demands.[34]

The prison gang problem is serious and getting bigger. Prison gangs spread from one state to another in several ways. Inmate gang members may be transferred to a federal or another state correctional institution, where they spread their gang's ideas. Gang members who move from one state to another and are then imprisoned for criminal activities may organize a gang in prison. Also, the leaders of some street gangs send gang members to other states specifically to establish a gang organization, and those organizers end up sentenced to prisons in that state.

COMBATING GANGS It was clear by the early 1990s that prison officials had to take away the gangs' authority over prison life. Every attempt was made to suppress the expression of gang activity within the prison. Any demonstration of gang membership or activity was a disciplinary offense and could even lead to an institutional transfer to a more secure facility, including federal facilities. Suspected gang members were closely followed by staff and even segregated from other members.[35] Prison officials developed intelligence networks to discover what was taking place with gangs and who was involved.

Prison officials have also stepped up security measures and control mechanisms to control gangs and violence. The TechnoCorrections feature discusses one commonly used method of inmate control.

Some corrections departments are making a diligent effort to prosecute gang members for crimes they have committed in the prison. Others have enforced the rule against "unauthorized activity or assembly," in which known gang members are unable to associate with each other. And a few simply lock up identified gang members and leave them in segregation while they are incarcerated. Pelican Bay State Prison in California actually mandates that identified gang members go through de-classification programs and renounce their gang ties.[36]

Changing Racial Patterns

By the 1990s, prisons were more racially polarized than ever before. Racial tension and hostility became so intense that different racial and ethnic groups avoided each other as much as possible. They sat on different sides of the dining room and when assembling to watch movies or television. Even a slight disagreement among races—for example, over changing a television channel—could quickly spark violence. If an inmate was stabbed and the stabbing did not appear to have racial overtones, there might not be any further problems. But if a person from

Prison gangs are a routine feature in correctional facilities and their control presents a significant problem for officials. One approach has been to house leaders in supermax prisons where they have little contact with fellow members. Here, on August 17, 2011, inmate Timothy Kelly, a former member of the Aryan Brotherhood prison gang, talks with reporters about the secure housing unit at the Pelican Bay State Prison near Crescent City, California. State prison officials allowed the media to tour the unit, where inmates are isolated for 22.5 hours a day in windowless, soundproofed cells, to counter allegations of mistreatment made during an inmate hunger strike. Kelly, who committed a double homicide and is serving a life sentence without the possibility for parole, has renounced his gang membership and says the secure housing unit is needed to make it more difficult for gangs to communicate.

AP Photo/Rich Pedroncelli

The use of nonlethal weapons to control inmate populations has become commonplace. Many of these weapons are manufactured by TASER International, Inc., the leading manufacturer of electronic control devices (ECDs). Generally speaking, a taser is an electroshock weapon that uses electrical current to disrupt voluntary control of muscles, producing what is called *neuromuscular incapacitation*.

Recently TASER announced its Shockwave area denial system, which can be used in correctional settings. The Shockwave system is a mobile, remote force-multiplier that uses neuromuscular incapacitation technology to deny access to strategically important areas in a prison. The device consists of a six-shot ECD that covers a 20-degree arc with 25-foot cartridges in units that can be stacked side by side or vertically, or can be daisy-chained together. The Shockwave device is used to defuse violent crowd situations by deploying multiple taser cartridges across a wide area arc. It can be triggered from a remote location, thereby reducing danger to prison security forces.

What Are the Risks?

Critics complain that taser devices cause extreme pain and even death. The American Civil Liberties Union alleges that, since 1999, at least 148 people have died in the United States and Canada after being shocked with tasers. However, a recent government-sponsored study finds that ECDs may be safer than believed. The researchers found that although exposure to ECDs is not risk free, there is no conclusive medical evidence within the state of current research that indicates a high risk of serious injury or death from the direct effects of ECD exposure; using ECD devices is safe in the vast majority of cases.

While the potential for moderate or severe injury related to ECD exposure is low, darts may cause puncture wounds or burns. Puncture wounds to an eye by a barbed dart could lead to a loss of vision in the affected eye. There is currently no medical evidence that ECDs pose a significant risk for induced cardiac dysrhythmia when deployed reasonably. Nor is there medical evidence to suggest that exposure to an ECD produces sufficient metabolic or physiologic effects to produce abnormal cardiac rhythms in normal, healthy adults. These findings suggest that the use of taser weapon technology will remain a standard security measure behind prison walls.

Sources: National Institute of Justice, "Study of Deaths Following Electro Muscular Disruption: Interim Report," June 2008, www.ncjrs.gov/pdf-files1/nij/222981.pdf (accessed February 29, 2012); TASER Shockwave Area Denial System, www.taser.com/products/law-enforcement/taser-shockwave-ecd (accessed February 29, 2012); American Civil Liberties Union, "Unregulated Use of Taser Stun Guns Threatens Lives, ACLU of Northern California Study Finds," October 6, 2005, www.aclu.org/racial-justice_prisoners-rights_drug-law-reform_immigrants-rights/unregulated-use-taser-stun-guns-th (accessed February 29, 2012). For more recent information on taser usage, see also aclu-or.org/content/aclu-use-tasers (accessed March 23, 2012).

one racial or ethnic group stabbed an inmate from a different group, retaliation usually followed.

Today, much attention is paid to the racial integration of inmates. The most significant issue is whether it is practical to adopt a policy of enforced integration.[37] Chad Trulson and James Marquart used 10 years of inmate-on-inmate assault data in Texas and compared the rates of violence between prisoners who were racially integrated and those who were racially segregated. Trulson and Marquart found that violence among integrated inmates was lower than the level of violence found among segregated inmates.[38] They argue that successful racial integration was achieved in Texas because prison officials removed disruptive inmates from the general prison population and matched compatible inmates. They conclude that housing inmates randomly is the only realistic and legally defensible strategy of prison desegregation.[39]

Conflict among gangs is the norm, regardless of ethnic or racial makeup. It is not unusual for a Hispanic gang to battle an African American gang for dominance among the prison population. Or Hispanic gangs may war among themselves for prison dominance. Intraracial gang conflict is as common as interracial.[40]

MYTH Prisons are high-security institutions where control is tight and inmates are closely monitored.

FACT Many prisons are controlled by inmate gangs rather than the correctional staff. Within prison walls, gangs run such activities as the illegal sex trade, the illicit food business, loan sharking scams, gambling, extortion, and drug trafficking.

Prison Contraband

Contraband can be defined as any unauthorized substance or material possessed by inmates, such as weapons, drugs, alcoholic beverages, prohibited appliances, and clothing. Gambling, institutional privileges, special food and canteen services, and prostitution can also be acquired through the contraband market. Contraband can also be items that would assist in an escape, such as ropes or ladders, or wire cutters that could cut a security fence. The definition of contraband has varied over time. Though cigarette smoking was commonplace in years past, tobacco products are considered contraband in some prisons today.

Inmates, of course, desire contraband. Drugs and alcohol substitutes can ease the pains of confinement. They may be used as a means to protect oneself against other inmates or even to attack staff. Contraband can help start a riot or aid in escapes. In order to control contraband, staff must spend a considerable amount of time searching inmates' cells and lockers. Staff are aware that the more contraband that can be retrieved from a prison, the safer the prison will be for both inmates and staff and the less chance that serious problems will erupt.

HOW CAN CONTRABAND GET INTO A PRISON? There are a number of ways that contraband comes into the prison:

- Contraband can be brought in by visitors. The extensiveness of this problem has resulted in more careful screening of visitors.

- Contraband may be introduced into the prison by corrupt prison staff, who can turn a lucrative profit by selling it to inmates. Some prisons have found it necessary to occasionally search staff when they come to work, over the strong objection of correctional employee unions.

- Contraband can be made by prisoners. They may make a knife, for example, out of a bedspring. Inmates have always demonstrated amazing ingenuity in what they use to make contraband.

- Inmates may be able to steal contraband from other areas of the prison, such as food or knives from the kitchen or tools from vocational shops. Inmates can also steal metal from the metal shop and use this to fashion deadly weapons.

Sex in Prison

Sex among inmates in men's prisons usually occurs in three different contexts:

- Consensual sex involving affection and/or sexual release

- Coercive sexual behavior that combines force and domination

- Sex for hire, the purchase of sexual release at various levels of domination

While sex among inmates was not unknown in the Big House era, it has undergone significant change in the contemporary correctional setting. Today, the violence and brutality of inmates toward other inmates is expressed in **sexual victimization** as well as in stabbings or slayings. Many new arrivals in prison, especially white males who have committed minor crimes, are "on trial" and may become victimized if they fail to show their toughness and resiliency. The juvenile inmate especially has a difficult time, as these inmates tend to be very vulnerable. If first-time inmates, including juveniles, have the willingness and capacity to fight, they will usually pass the trial. If not, then prison time will indeed be "hard time."[41]

HOW COMMON IS SEXUAL ASSAULT? In 2003, President George W. Bush signed the **Prison Rape Elimination Act (PREA)** to "provide for the analysis of the incidence and effects of prison rape in federal, state, and local institutions and to provide information, resources, recommendations, and funding to protect

CONTRABAND Unauthorized materials possessed by prisoners.

SEXUAL VICTIMIZATION Forcing an inmate to submit sexually to one or more inmates.

PRISON RAPE ELIMINATION ACT (PREA) This act established "zero tolerance" for rape in custodial settings, required data collection on the incidence of rape in each state, and established a National Prison Rape Elimination Commission.

individuals from prison rape."[42] A data collection instrument was developed in order to sample 10 percent of all facilities in the United States to measure the extent of jail and prison sexual victimization.[43] The act established three programs in the Department of Justice:

1. A program dedicated to collecting national prison rape statistics and data, and to conducting research
2. A program dedicated to the dissemination of information and procedures for combating prison rape
3. A program to assist in funding state programs[44]

The most recent federal data indicate:

■ An estimated 60,500 inmates (or 4.5 percent of all state and federal inmates) experienced one or more incidents of sexual victimization involving other inmates or staff.

■ Nationwide, about 2 percent of inmates reported an incident involving another inmate and 3 percent reported an incident involving staff.

■ Among the 146 prison facilities in the survey, 6 had no reports of sexual victimization from the sampled inmates; 10 had an overall victimization rate of at least 9 percent.

■ Among the 10 facilities with the highest overall prevalence rates, 3 had prevalence rates of staff sexual misconduct that exceeded 10 percent.[45]

Ironically, as Table 7.1 shows, there is more sexual abuse committed by prison staff members than by other inmates.

Other research efforts indicate that sexual assaults are far more widespread than was found by the government survey. Some indicate that at least 20 percent of all inmates are raped during their prison stay.[46] Christopher Hensley and colleagues found that 18 percent of inmates reported inmate-on-inmate sexual threats and that 8.5 percent reported that they had been sexually assaulted.[47] In another study, Hensley found that 14 percent of the inmates had been sexually targeted by other inmates.[48]

Not all research finds such high levels of violent sex. When Mark Fleisher examined sexual violence in men's high-security and women's medium- and high-security prisons, he found that sexual violence was uncommon. Most sex was consensual, rather than forced, and was used to win favors or privileges.[49]

Regardless of whether sexual assaults are seen as epidemic or as relatively infrequent, few would deny that sexual victimization has many unfortunate effects. It curbs victims' freedom to act; indeed, many victims feel that their only viable alternative is to check into

TABLE 7.1 Sexual Victimization in State and Federal Prisons

National Estimate

Type	Number	Percent
Total	60,500	4.5
Inmate-on-inmate	27,500	2.1
Nonconsensual sexual acts	16,800	1.3
Abusive sexual contacts only	10,600	0.8
Staff sexual misconduct	38,600	2.9
Unwilling activity	22,600	1.7
Excluding touching	16,900	1.3
Touching only	5,700	0.4
Willing activity	22,700	1.7
Excluding touching	20,600	1.5
Touching only	2,100	0.2

Note: Detail may not sum to total because inmates may report more than one type of victimization. They may also report victimization by both other inmates and staff.

Source: Allen J. Beck and Paige M. Harrison, *Victim Victimization in State and Federal Prisons Reported by Inmates, 2007* (Washington, DC: Bureau of Justice Statistics, 2007).

MYTH Prisons are highly dangerous places, and most inmates are sexually assaulted.

FACT Prison rape is actually less pervasive than previously believed, and most male inmates are spared sexual assaults.

protective custody. Sexual victimization also leads to feelings of helplessness and depression, the threat of AIDS, damaged self-esteem, possible self-destructive acts such as self-mutilation or suicide, lowered social status, psychosomatic illnesses, increased difficulty in adjusting to life after release, and possibly even increased risk of recidivism.

ELIMINATING SEXUAL ASSAULT Anyone who has worked in an adult prison knows how difficult it is to eliminate or even dramatically reduce sexual assaults. Double-celling and dormitories make it impossible to protect vulnerable inmates. The inmate culture, with its discouragement of those who give testimony against predators, is another obstacle to a safe facility. In addition, the physical size of correctional facilities, the overcrowded conditions, and the number of areas of indefensible space are greater restrictions to keeping vulnerable inmates safe.

Using video cameras in those areas in which inmates are more vulnerable may reduce sexual assaults. It is also important for inmates to understand that they will be prosecuted if convicted of sexual assault and that all charges of sexual assaults against them will be fully investigated. But probably the most important way to protect inmates is a vigorous and valid classification process in which more vulnerable inmates are isolated from those who may take advantage of them. The Evidence-Based Corrections feature discusses research on sexual violence in prison and how correctional administrators are using the knowledge to improve conditions.

EXPRESSIONS OF PRISON VIOLENCE

Prison violence is usually interpreted to mean a prison riot or mass disturbances, but it also means violence of inmates toward each other, toward staff, and staff's violence toward inmates. Prison violence also includes self-inflicted violence, when inmates attempt to hurt themselves or may even have successful suicide incidents.

Riots and Other Major Disturbances

Inmate disturbances can be nonviolent or violent. Nonviolent disturbances include hunger strikes, sit-down strikes, work stoppages, voluntary lock-downs (staying in one's cell even when the cellblock is open), excessive numbers of inmates reporting on sick call, and the filing of grievances by nearly everyone in a cellblock or even in the entire institution. Violent inmate disturbances include crowding around a correctional officer and intimidating him or her so that a disciplinary ticket is not written, assaulting officers, sabotaging the electrical, plumbing, or heating systems, burning or destroying institutional property, and **prison riots**—attempts to take control, with or without hostages, of a cellblock, a yard, or an entire prison.

The most well-known prison riots took place at the Attica Correctional Center in Attica, New York, in 1971 and at the New Mexico State Prison in Santa Fe in 1980. During recent decades, riots have taken place in numerous correctional facilities across the United States. A few examples include:

■ *William G. McConnell Unit in Beeville, Texas (1999).* The disturbance started when an inmate pried his way out of his cell and made it through three security doors. He stabbed a correctional officer and released 83 inmates from their cells. They were subdued by a tactical team an hour later.[50]

■ *New Castle, Pennsylvania (2007).* About 500 inmates were involved in this riot in which two staff members and seven inmates suffered minor injuries at a facility that is operated by a private company.[51]

PROTECTIVE CUSTODY A form of segregation, not for punishment but intended to isolate potential victims from predators.

PRISON VIOLENCE Can vary from riots to staff assaults, inmate assaults, staff assaults of inmates, or self-inflicted violence.

INMATE DISTURBANCE A disturbance, either violent or nonviolent, that brings disruption or even closes down the prison.

PRISON RIOT Collective response of inmates that is violent, in which they strike out against what they consider unfair prison conditions.

EVIDENCE-BASED CORRECTIONS

Eliminating Prison Rape

The Prison Rape Elimination Act of 2003 (PREA) established a "zero-tolerance standard" for prison rape and mandated that the U.S. Department of Justice (DOJ) "make the prevention of prison rape a top priority in each prison system." One of the goals of PREA was to increase the data and information on the incidence of prison rape to help improve management and administration in regard to sexual violence in correctional facilities. The law also created an independent National Prison Rape Elimination Commission, which was charged with studying the impact of sexual assault in correction and detention facilities and developing national standards to address the problem. Now there is more information available and correctional administrators have a more complete picture of sexual violence in prisons, providing them with the information and assistance they need to address this complex problem.

One research effort to assess prison violence was conducted by James Austin and his associates, which looked at sexual violence in the Texas prison system, the third largest prison system in the nation. The researchers chose this system because it had the highest rate of alleged incidents (550 alleged incidents, for a rate of 3.95 per 1,000 prisoners); on the other hand, it also has one of the lowest substantiation rates (less than 3 percent). In studying the number and nature of sexual assault allegations in this system from 2002 to 2005, they assembled "lessons learned" to help reduce sexual assaults across all correctional systems.

Among their findings in *Sexual Violence in the Texas Prison System*:

- White inmates are attacked more than any other race. Nearly 60 percent of the 43 "sustained" incidents—those proven to be true by an investigation—involved a white victim.

- Victims are generally younger than their assailants. The average age of victims in "sustained" cases was three years younger than the assailants.

- Mentally ill or intellectually impaired inmates are more likely to be victimized. Although only 12 percent of the allegations involved a mentally ill or intellectually impaired prisoner, this percentage is 8 times the proportion of mentally ill inmates in the general prisoner population (1.6 percent).

- Cellblocks with solid cell fronts may contribute to sexual assault. Solid cell fronts, while permitting privacy for the inmates and reducing noise within the unit, also provide the degree of privacy that permits sexual assaults to occur. Unlike older prison designs, in which the cell fronts consist of bars, solid doors limit visual observation by staff and, to some degree, soundproof the cells to the point that staff have difficulty hearing what is going on in individual cells.

The researchers made several recommendations, including that officials provide more structured opportunities to report sexual assault and that prisoners who have been implicated in such incidents be closely monitored. The researchers also recommended that a better system of categorizing victims and assailants be considered, and provided a characteristics checklist for correctional officials to use to help identify potential victims and assailants.

Another study, by Mark Fleisher and Jessie Krienert, looked at the sociocultural causes of prison sexual violence in men's and women's high-security prisons across the United States. Using a large cross-section of inmates (408 males and 156 females in 30 prisons across 10 states), they identified major attitudes and beliefs that inmates have about prison sexual assault, including:

- Inmate culture has a complex system of norms on sexual conduct. An act of sexual violence that occurs in one context may be interpreted differently in another context. Interpretation depends on the pre-assault behavior of the victim and the assailant, as well as other inmates' perceptions of the causes of the sexual violence.

- Inmates "self-police" against unwanted sexual predators and maintain protective relationships to facilitate safety from physical and sexual abuse.

- Inmate sexual culture allows inmates to disagree on the meaning of sexual violence in similar contexts. Some inmates may interpret sexual violence as rape, whereas other inmates may interpret a similar act as other than rape. The response of a victim toward an aggressor after the act of sexual violence plays a key role in an inmate's interpretation of sexual violence.

- Inmates judge prison rape as detrimental to the social order within the prison community—prison rapists are unwelcome.

As a result of this evidence, many states have created new policies and procedures to change the correctional culture, thereby affecting the attitudes of staff and inmates. Some now mandate training for all staff on inappropriate sexual conduct and sexual violence and offer inmate education on reporting mechanisms and services for victims. However, problems still remain such as inmate unwillingness to report victimization, staff fear of false allegations, lack of staff training, and delayed reporting of incidents. Despite these issues, with the implementation of PREA and the active engagement of correctional officials, a multifaceted effort to understand the extent of prison sexual violence and to identify solutions for reducing it is well under way.

Sources: Pat Kaufman, "Prison Rape: Research Explores Prevalence, Prevention," *NIJ Journal* 259 (2008), www.nij.gov/nij/journals/259/prison-rape.htm (accessed March 1, 2012); James Austin, Tony Fabelo, Angela Gunter, and Ken McGinnis, *Sexual Violence in the Texas Prison System*, National Institute of Justice, September 2006, www.ncjrs.gov/pdffiles1/nij/grants/215774.pdf (accessed March 1, 2012); Mark Fleisher and Jessie Krienert, *The Culture of Prison Sexual Violence*, National Institute of Justice, 2006, www.ncjrs.gov/pdffiles1/nij/grants/216515.pdf (accessed March 1, 2012).

- *Three Rivers, Texas, Federal Prison (2008).* This disturbance left one prisoner dead and 22 others injured. Criminal intelligence sources said they believe the riot might have been between Mexican American inmates who consider themselves Chicanos and inmates who have closer ties to Mexico.[52]

- *Oklahoma State Reformatory at Granite, Oklahoma (2008).* Two inmates died and 15 more were injured during rioting in an exercise yard. This disturbance between black and Native American inmates was sparked by one inmate spitting on another.[53]

HOW RIOTS OCCUR Riots may be spontaneous or planned to achieve some goal. Planning a riot usually requires a degree of inmate solidarity. When prison riots break out today, they tend to be more like the New Mexico riot rather than the inmate revolt at Attica. At Attica, inmates had a high degree of organization, solidarity, and political consciousness. The New Mexico riot was notable for inmates' fragmentation, lack of effective leadership, and disorganization. Indeed, the 1980 New Mexico riot showed the extent to which relations between prisoners had fragmented during the 1970s. Political apathy and fighting among inmates had replaced the politicization and solidarity of earlier years.[54]

Inmate Assaults on Staff

Inmates commit more than 16,000 annual assaults against staff. This is a little more than one-third of the number of assaults against other inmates. About one-sixth of the inmate-on-staff assaults require medical attention. About 70 percent of inmate assaults on staff are referred for prosecution.[55]

In one study, S. C. Light carried out a content analysis of official records dealing with nearly 700 prisoner-staff assaults in New York State.[56] He focused on the themes, or the immediate context, of the assaults and discovered that six themes accounted for over four-fifths of the cases. In decreasing order of frequency, these themes were:

- *Officer's command.* Assault followed an explicit command to an inmate.

- *Protest.* Assault occurred because the victim considered himself/herself victimized by unjust or inconsistent treatment by a staff member.

- *Search.* Assault occurred during search of an inmate's body or cell.

- *Inmates fighting.* Assault resulted from an officer intervening in a fight between inmates.

- *Movement.* Assault took place during the movement of inmates from one part of the prison to another.

- *Contraband.* Assault followed a staff member suspecting an inmate of possessing contraband items.[57]

Correctional officers are particularly concerned about being physically and sexually violated by inmates during hostage takings during a riot. One study examined 33 hostage takings and forced confinements spanning 11 years in Canadian institutions and found that of the 20 hostage takings, 7 had involved sexual assaults of staff. In this study, sexual assaults were always against women and 36.6 percent of the women were sexually assaulted.[58] Hostage taking can also result in violence toward male correctional officers, as took place during the violent conclusion of the Attica siege in September 1971, in which 11 officers and staff died,[59] and the standoff in Lucasville, Ohio, in April 1993, in which three officers died.[60]

Inmates versus Inmates

Inmate-on-inmate violence comes as no surprise. The prison environment combines a number of factors that contribute to inmates' assaults on each other. These factors include inadequate supervision by staff members, architectural designs that promote rather than inhibit victimization, the easy availability of deadly weapons, the housing of violence-prone inmates in close proximity to relatively defenseless victims, a high level of tension produced by close quarters and cross-cutting conflicts among both individuals and groups of inmates, and feedback systems through which inmates feel the need to take revenge for real or imagined slights for past victimizations.[61]

Understandably, inmates make every effort to protect themselves. Weaponry has replaced fists as the primary means of self-protection in men's institutions. A variety of objects can be weapons: chisels, screwdrivers, sharpened shanks of spoons, broomsticks, baseball bats, clubs, chunks of concrete, stiff wire, heavy-gauge metal, metal from beds, boiler plate metal, and zip guns. Smuggled weapons also appear. Correction officers collect barrelfuls of knives and other weapons during shakedowns in some institutions.

Staff Assaults on Inmates

While riots and prisoner-on-prisoner assaults tend to make headlines, severe beating of inmates by prison staff have occurred throughout much of U.S. corrections history.[62] All kinds of punitive and sadistic practices have taken place. As you may recall, federal surveys have found that a majority of sexual assaults reported by inmates involve correctional staff members. James Marquart's examination of the maximum-security Eastham Unit in Texas in the 1980s found widespread staff brutality toward inmates. In explaining this abuse, Marquart concluded that physical coercion was deeply embedded in the guard subculture.[63]

Today, there is less evidence of staff's inappropriate use of force on inmates. Prisoners' rights organizations continue to accuse staff of retaliating against rioting inmates after regaining control of cellblocks. Most of the criticism of staff brutality against prisoners has come from those who have examined high-security units or supermax prisons. Fay Dowker and Glenn Good documented a number of instances of staff brutality in high-security units or prisons. For example, in Missouri's Potosi Correctional Center, prison officials apply the "double-litter restraint" to difficult prisoners. The prisoner's hands are cuffed behind him, his ankles are cuffed, and he is forced to lie facedown on a cot. A second cot is then tightly strapped upside down over the inmate and the ends are strapped shut, which totally encloses and immobilizes him.[64] In addition, as previously discussed, correctional officers in California's Corcoran and Pelican Bay Prisons have received attention for their use of force against inmates.

Self-Inflicted Violence: Prison Suicide

State prison suicide rates have dipped sharply from 34 per 100,000 in 1980 to 14 per 100,000 inmates in 2002. Nearly 350 state prisoners commit suicide each year, which constitutes about 7 percent of all state prisoner deaths. The average annual suicide rate of state prisoners is about a third of that of local jail inmates.[65]

White inmates in state prisons are 35 percent more likely than Hispanic inmates and 58 percent more likely than African American inmates to commit suicide. Thus, African Americans are about a third as likely as whites to commit suicide in state prisons and less than half as likely as Hispanic prisoners.[66] Prison suicide is most common among young married white males, and juveniles have high rates of suicide. Suicide generally occurs early in confinement, and hanging is the usual method. Some prison homicides are in fact suicides, because inmates let themselves be murdered by violent inmates. Inmates have been known to charge the fence, knowing that guards will shoot them down. Furthermore, prisoners on death row who have lost their will to live may call off their appeals, letting the state carry out the suicidal act.[67]

There is no single explanation for either collective or individual violence, but many theories are proposed for why it takes place.

Individual Violence

- *History of prior violence.* Before inmates were incarcerated, many were violence-prone individuals who used force to get their own way.

- *Psychological factors.* Many inmates suffer from personality disorders. It is not surprising that people with extreme psychological distress may resort to violence to dominate others or that inmates with personality disorders are violently abused by others.

- *Prison conditions.* The prison experience itself causes people to become violent.

- *Lack of dispute-resolution mechanisms.* Many prisons lack effective mechanisms that enable inmate grievances against either prison officials or other inmates to be handled fairly and equitably.

- *Basic survival.* Inmates resort to violence in order to survive. The lack of physical security, inadequate mechanisms for resolving complaints, and the code of silence promote individual violence by inmates who might otherwise be controlled.

Collective Violence

- *Inmate-balance theory.* Inmate-balance theory is based on the belief that collective disorders occur when prison officials go too far in asserting their authority.

- *Administrative-control theory.* According to this theory, collective violence is caused by prison mismanagement, lack of strong security, and inadequate control by prison officials. Poor management may inhibit conflict management and set the stage for violence.

- *Overcrowding.* As the prison population continues to climb, unmatched by expanded capacity, prison violence may increase.

Sources: Grant Harris, Tracey Skilling, and Marnie Rice, "The Construct of Psychopathy," in *Crime and Justice: An Annual Edition*, ed. Michael Tonry (Chicago: University of Chicago Press, 2001), pp. 197–265; Arjen Boin and William A. R. Rattrey, "Understanding Prison Riots," *Punishment and Society* 6 (2004): 47–65; Bert Useem and Michael Reisig, "Collective Action in Prisons: Protests, Disturbances, and Riots," *Criminology* 37 (1999): 735–760.

Studies of prison suicides have found a number of explanations (see Exhibit 7.3):

- The prison experience itself, marked by deprivation, overcrowding, and violence, increases the likelihood of prison suicide.[68]

- Prisoners typically experience less social control than the general population and lower levels of integration with other people and groups. These loners are more likely to feel alienated and depressed, hence they have higher rates of suicide.[69]

- Most inmates bring psychological and emotional problems to prison when they arrive and these preconditions are related to suicide. One study of the mental health records of all 76 suicides that occurred between 1993 and 2001 in the New York Department of Correctional Services found that 95 percent had a substance abuse history, 70 percent displayed agitation or anxiety prior to the suicide, and 49 percent had a behavioral change.[70]

GUARDING THE PRISON

Historically, the paramilitary model has been used for security in most institutions. Custodial staffs wear uniforms and badges; are assigned titles such as sergeant, lieutenant, captain, and major; use designations such as company, mess hall, drill, inspection, and gig list; and maintain a sharp division between lower- and higher-ranking officers. The procedures and organizational structures that control inmates are also militaristic in form. For many years, prisoners marched to the dining hall and to their various assignments. They removed their hats in the presence of a captain and stood at attention when the warden approached.

Although the prison has been stripped of some of its regimentation, the paramilitary model is alive and flourishing. Associate wardens of custody or operations are ultimately responsible for knowing the whereabouts of all inmates at all times. Correctional officers' captains, few in number, are usually assigned to full-time administrative responsibilities or to shift command. Lieutenants are known as troubleshooters. They roam the institution dealing with volatile incidents. The lieutenant's job is to be right there with fellow officers. The lieutenants take troublesome inmates out of their cells and walk them to segregation. Sergeants, like army sergeants, manage particular units, such as cell houses or the hospital, and supervise several other officers.

The Changing Role of Correctional Officer

Higher salaries, improved standards, greater training, and unionization are signs that the role of correctional officer is undergoing change. Correctional officers are beginning to make a living wage in most states (see the Careers in Corrections box). Over half of the states now require a high school diploma or a GED certificate as their minimum employment requirement. Many states have academy training programs for preservice and in-service officers, which appear to be effective in ensuring that officers bring basic skills to their jobs. The Federal Bureau of Prisons requires three years of college for correctional officers.

Correctional officers in the majority of states are now unionized. The growth of unions among correctional officers has encouraged them to seek greater rights, more recognition, and higher pay. The unions that represent correctional officers include AFSCME (American Federation of State, County, and Municipal Employees), the Service Employees International Union (SEIU), the International Brotherhood of Teamsters, and state employee associations. Officers in Connecticut, New Jersey, New York, and Ohio have gone on strike to protest low wages or poor working conditions. When correctional officers walk out, other personnel, the state police, and sometimes even the National Guard are forced to run the institution until the strike is settled.

Conflicting Goals and Expectations

The greatest problem faced by correctional officers is the duality of their role: maintainers of order and security and advocates of treatment and rehabilitation. Added to this basic dilemma is the changing inmate role. In earlier times, correctional officers could count on inmate leaders to help them maintain order, but now they are faced with a racially charged atmosphere in which violence is a way of life. Correctional work in some institutions can be filled with danger, tension, boredom, and little evidence that efforts to help inmates lead to success. Correctional officers experience alienation and isolation from inmates, the administration, and each other. It is not surprising that correctional officers perceive significant levels of stress related to such job factors as lack of safety, inadequate career opportunities, and work overload.[71] However, those who have high levels of job satisfaction, good relations with their coworkers, and high levels of social support seem to be better able to deal with the stress of the correctional setting.[72]

MYTH Prison guards are ruthless people who enjoy their position of power over inmates, fight rehabilitation efforts, and have a "lock psychosis" developed from years of counting, numbering, and checking on inmates.

FACT Correctional officers are public servants who are seeking the security and financial rewards of a civil service position. Most are in favor of rehabilitation efforts and do not hold any particular animosity toward inmates.

Women Officers in Men's Prisons

It is not unusual to find women working as correctional officers in men's prisons. Some critics have questioned the wisdom of such assignments; they believe that women are not fit for the job because they are not strong enough, are too easily corrupted by inmates, or are poor backups for officers in trouble. Women have been criticized as being a disruptive influence because inmates compete for their attention or refuse to follow their orders. Critics also say that the presence of women violates inmates' privacy, especially when women are working shower areas or conducting strip searches. However, in a number of cases, the courts have generally tried to protect both women's right to employment and inmates' privacy as much as possible.[73]

CAREERS in Corrections

CORRECTIONAL OFFICER

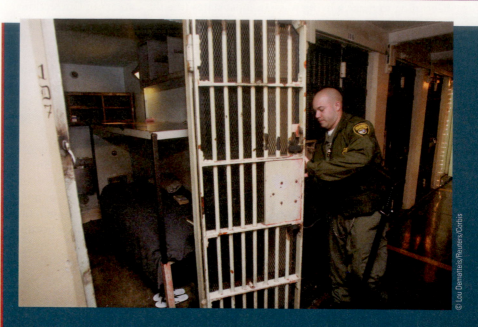

© Lou Dematteis/Reuters/Corbis

California State Correctional Officer A. Lopez closes the door to the type of cell that awaits the most serious criminal offenders in maximum-security prisons. Scott Peterson, who gained national notoriety for killing his wife Laci, is actually housed in this cell in San Quentin State Prison.

Preparation for the Job

Maturity, good communication skills, the desire to help people, and the ability to work in a stressful environment are good job preparations for correctional officers.

Nature of the Job

Correctional officers carry out their duties in several different areas:

- *Housing unit officers.* These officers are responsible for the security of the housing units. They open and close steel-barred doors, allowing entrance and exit; take inmate counts several times a day; distribute medicine, mail, and laundry; oversee maintained activities; answer the telephone, and supervise the showers of the inmates. The correctional officer must also see that inmates are fed, either in the cell house or in the central dining facility, to which they must be escorted. The inmates' daily showers must be supervised. If violations of rules occur, the cell house guard must write disciplinary tickets.

- *Work detail supervisors.* These officers monitor inmates' behavior while they are working in the kitchen, laundry, or trash pick-up inside the prison or are on outside details such as farming operations.

Those supporting the employment of female officers in men's prisons argue that departments of corrections can achieve privacy by means of administrative policies preventing women from doing strip searches. The installation of modest half-screens, fogged windows that permit figures to be seen, or privacy doors on toilet stalls offers solutions to privacy issues. Security does not have to be sacrificed, and these modifications can be made to the physical environment at little cost.

- *Industrial shop and school officers.* The responsibility of these officers is to monitor inmate activities at the various prison industry locations and in academic or vocational classes.

- *Yard officers.* These officers maintain order and ensure security while inmates participate in or watch recreation activities that take place within the prison.

- *Perimeter security officers.* In the traditional prison, perimeter officers are stationed in towers positioned along the high wall surrounding the prison. In more recently built prisons, perimeter officers typically walk and drive patrols outside the razor wire.

Officers primarily enforce regulations through communication skills and moral authority and attempt to avoid conflict at all costs. Most officers attend to their duties unarmed, but a few officers hold positions in lookout towers with the use of high-powered rifles. In addition to the custodial duties demanded of them in more secure facilities, correctional officers in federal institutions and some minimum-security state facilities are also responsible for providing rehabilitative services.

Qualifications and Required Education

Most correctional officer positions require only a high school education or its equivalent. The candidate must be at least 18 or (in some cases) 21 years of age, be a U.S. citizen, and have no felony convictions. In the Federal Bureau of Prisons and many state facilities, the salaries offered for new officers are sufficient enough to attract a large applicant pool. As a result, most of those selected have college educations or at least degrees from two-year institutions. A potential correctional officer must further be in excellent health and meet formal standards of physical fitness, eyesight, and hearing. Drug testing and background checks of applicants are usually done.

Job Outlook

With the continued construction of federal, state, and private prisons, there are jobs available for those who are interested in becoming a correctional officer. With so many existing prisons in small towns and in sometimes isolated areas, applicants may need to be willing to relocate for these positions.

Earnings and Benefits

Correctional officers in the state of California start at $70,000 or more because of the influence the powerful California's Correctional Peace Officers Association has had on salaries. In contrast, correctional officers in some private prisons start at the minimum wage or not much higher. The Federal Bureau of Prisons and most state correctional systems have starting salaries for correctional officers between $30,000 and $44,000. The possibility of overtime pay can raise this salary level another $10,000 or more per year.

Sources: "Career Profiles," *Princeton Review*; Bureau of Labor Statistics, United States Department of Labor, "Correctional Officers," *Occupational Outlook Handbook,* 2010–2011 Edition, www.bls.gov/oco/ocos156.htm (accessed March 1, 2012); and interviews with corrections officials.

Officers' Response to Problems on the Job

Like the prison culture, problem-solving skills are passed down from one generation of correctional worker to another. Old-timers tell new correctional officers about acceptable behavior on the job. Experienced officers know that all officers will be punished severely for violations of security. A mistake that leads to an escape may cost them several weeks "in the streets" (suspension) or may even result in termination. Any erosion of security makes it more likely that inmates will initiate a disturbance and that the disturbance will mushroom into a full-scale riot. Moreover, experienced officers know that inmates cannot be given too much leeway or they will end up controlling the institution and abusing their keepers. These officers try to teach newly certified correctional staff how to strike a balance between rigidly enforcing all the rules and allowing the inmates to gain control. Finally, experienced officers know that the best hope for security is fair treatment of inmates. Simply put, an inmate who is treated fairly and with respect is much less likely to become a security problem than a prisoner who feels humiliated and abused by staff.

Nevertheless, there are always a few officers who become involved in corrupt and illegal behavior that jeopardizes security and violates the law. They may agree to bring contraband into the institution because they have been set up by inmates. Some officers carry contraband for profit. Inmates who are trafficking drugs into the institution or have a drug appetite themselves seem to be able to raise large amounts of cash. According to offenders who have spent time in federal and state institutions, inmates walk and talk with each new officer and soon figure out who can be corrupted. An example is an officer in a Midwestern state who was caught in a strip search with two large bags of marijuana taped across his chest. Investigators found that he had been bringing drugs into the prison for some time and had been able to buy a Cadillac and expensive clothes with his additional tax-free income.[74]

Job Enrichment: A Challenge for Administrators

There is no question that most correctional officers want to help inmates, provide them with human services, and help them to rise as much as possible above the limitations of their institutional setting. These officers relate to inmates as human beings and see themselves as being consistent, fair, and flexible.[75] The challenge is to motivate all line staff to rise to this level of professionalism.

SUMMARY

LO1 **Understand the relationship between classification and institutional security**

Classification of inmates is an important consideration for institutional security. Classification involves both external classification, in which an inmate is sent to a particular custody level institution, and internal classification, in which the prisoner is assigned to a housing area and programs.

LO2 **Discuss the difficulties of confinement for male inmates**

The difficulties of confinement for male inmates, especially in maximum-security placements, include protecting oneself against the dangers of prison society and dealing with the loneliness and boredom of daily life.

LO3 **Review the characteristics, norms, and language of "Big House" prisons of the past**

The traditional male inmate culture, or the Big House era, had social roles, an inmate code, and

prison language or argot. All this led to a solidarity of inmate culture.

LO4 **Consider the changing social structure of prisons, including gangs, racial tensions, contraband, and sex in prisons**

The contemporary prison is a violent and unpredictable environment in which to do time. Prison gangs are found in most state correctional systems and the Federal Bureau of Prisons. Racial conflict within the walls is a relatively new feature of prison structure. Sexual assaults may be less prevalent than in the past, but many new inmates, especially those who have not done time before, will be tested.

LO5 **Present the forms of violence that take place in prison settings**

Inmate assaults on staff occur frequently in today's prisons, but the number of assaults on staff is about a third of the number of assaults against other inmates. Staff assaults on inmates still take place, though much less frequently than in the past. Prison suicide rates have dipped sharply in recent years; today suicides constitute about 7 percent of all state prisoners' deaths. The forms of violence that take place in prison settings include collective violence or riots, inmate assaults on inmates, inmate assaults on staff, staff assaults on inmates, and prison suicides. Most large prisons, especially maximum-security ones, experience a riot at one time or another.

 Offer explanations for why violence takes place

There are many theories as to why prison violence takes place, ranging from individual violence to collective violence. Individual explanations of prison violence include history of prior violence, psychological factors, prison conditions, lack of dispute-resolution mechanisms, and basic survival. Collective violence explanations include inmate-balance theory, administrative-control theory, and overcrowding.

 Examine the changing roles and challenges of correctional officers in men's prisons

Higher salaries, improved standards, greater training, and unionization are signs that the role of correctional officer is undergoing change. The greatest problem faced by correctional officers is the duality of their role in maintaining order and security and advocating treatment. In addition, correctional officers today are experiencing greater alienation and isolation from inmates. Furthermore, the correctional officer's role has shifted in recent years, as part of the growing professionalization of the prison. There are increasing numbers of officers who wish to treat inmates fairly, with consistency, and humanely.

Key Terms

total institution, 162
no-frills policy, 162
prison classification, 164
external classification system, 164
internal classification system, 164
Big House, 165
Gresham Sykes, 166
inmate code, 166
Donald Clemmer, 166

prisonization, 167
prison culture, 167
deprivation model, 167
importation model, 167
situational model, 168
administrative-control
    model, 168
argot, 168
prison gang, 168

security threat groups (STGs), 168
contraband, 172
sexual victimization, 172
Prison Rape Elimination
    Act (PREA), 172
protective custody, 174
prison violence, 174
inmate disturbance, 174
prison riot, 174

 # Critical Thinking Questions

1. You are the warden of a correctional facility that has extremely high rates of violence among racial and ethnic groups. What will your strategy be for diffusing the racial and ethnic tension?

2. Is it more difficult for an inmate to do time today than during the Big House era?

3. What causes prison riots and inmate violence? What can a prison administrator do to reduce violence?

4. Is it possible to communicate and to develop a relationship with prison gang members? What would be the purpose of such a relationship?

5. Why do you think there is so much contraband in prison? What can be done to restrict its availability?

 # Thinking Like a Corrections Professional

As the warden of an adult prison, you hear from inmates who work in the kitchen that correctional officers are taking food home that was intended for inmates. What would you do to investigate these charges? Would you dismiss these accusations because you believe that your officers would not become involved in such inappropriate behavior? Would you hand this investigation over to your associate warden for operations and trust that he or she will handle the investigation in an appropriate way? Would you hand this investigation over to a security staff member, such as a captain, but stay involved yourself?

If it was discovered from the investigation that two correctional officers were regularly taking meat and other food intended for inmates, how would you handle this situation? Would it be sufficient grounds for termination?

Career Destinations

There are many careers in secure corrections. A number of states maintain websites that either advertise positions or discuss qualifications. Here is one example:
www.doc.state.al.us

This site has job postings, links, and information:
www.corrections.com/networks/careers

Notes

1. "Phillips Case: Ex-Fugitive 'Bucky' Phillips Pleads Guilty to Shooting Trooper," *Niagara Gazette*, November 29, 2006.
2. Ibid.
3. Associated Press, "Inmate Who Killed Trooper Is Said to Have Escape Tools," October 19, 2011, www.nytimes.com/2011/10/20/nyregion/ralph-phillips-who-killed-trooper-is-accused-of-harboring-escape-tools-in-dannemora-prison.html (accessed February 27, 2012).
4. Interviewed in 1995.
5. Interviewed in 1999.
6. See Michael Massoglia, Martin Y. Iguchi, James Bell, Rajeev N. Ramchard, and Terry Fain, "How Criminal System Racial Disparities May Translate into Health Disparities," *Journal of Health Care for the Poor and Underserved* 16 (2005), pp. 48–56.
7. Richard Berk, Heather Ladd, Heidi Graziano, and Jong-Ho Baek, "A Randomized Experiment Testing Inmate Classification Systems," *Criminology and Public Policy* 2 (2003): 215–242.
8. J. Austin, *Findings in Prison Classification and Risk Assessments* (Washington, DC: U.S. National Institute of Corrections, 2003), p. 2.
9. James M. Byrne and April Pattavina, "Institutional Corrections and Soft Technology," in *The New Technology of Crime, Law and Social Control*, ed. James M. Byrne and Donald J. Rebovich (Monsey, NY: Criminal Justice Press, 2007), p. 247.
10. Ibid., pp. 264–265.
11. Patricia L. Hardyman, James Austin, Jack Alexander, Kelly Dedel Johnson, and Owan C. Tulloch, *Internal Prison Classification Systems: Case Studied in Their Development and Implementation* (Washington, DC: National Institute of Corrections, 2002), p. 22.
12. Christopher Hensley, Mary Koscheski, and Richard Tewksbury, "Examining the Characteristics of Male Sexual Assault Targets in a Southern Maximum-Security Prison," *Journal of Interpersonal Violence* 20 (2005): 667–679.
13. John Wooldredge, "Inmate Lifestyles and Opportunities for Victimization," *Journal of Research in Crime and Delinquency* 35 (1998): 480–502.
14. Andy Hochstetler, Daniel S. Murphy, and Ronald L. Simons, "Damaged Goods: Exploring Predictors of Distress in Prison Inmates," *Crime and Delinquency* 50 (2004): 436.
15. The early twentieth-century prison writings describe this prison environment.
16. Ibid.
17. Adapted from Gresham M. Sykes and Sheldon L. Messinger, "The Inmate Social System," in *Theoretical Studies in the Social Organization of the Prison*, ed. Richard A. Cloward (New York: Social Science Research Council, 1960), pp. 6–8.
18. Gresham Sykes, *The Society of Captives: A Study of a Maximum Security Prison* (Princeton, NJ: Princeton University Press, 1958), pp. 64–108.
19. Donald Clemmer, *The Prison Community* (New York: Holt Rinehart & Winston, 1958), p. 209.
20. Ibid., pp. 299–300.
21. Ibid.
22. Stanton Wheeler, "Socialization in Correctional Institutions," *American Sociological Review* 26 (October 1961): 697–712.
23. Sykes, *The Society of Captives*.
24. Ibid., pp. 142–155.
25. B. Useem and M. Reisig, "Collective Action in Prisons: Protests, Disturbances, and Riots," *Criminology* 37 (1999): 735–760, at 735.
26. James B. Jacobs, *Stateville: The Penitentiary in Mass Society* (Chicago: University of Chicago Press, 1977), p. 146.
27. Ibid.
28. Ben M. Crouch and James W. Marquart, *An Appeal to Justice: Litigated Reform of Texas Prisons* (Austin: University of Texas Press, 1989).
29. D. Orlando-Morningstar, *Prison Gangs* (Washington, DC: Federal Judicial Center, 1997).
30. Ibid., and Lee Bowker, *Prison Victimization* (New York: Elsevier, 1980).
31. George W. Knox, "The Problem of Gangs and Security Threat Groups (STGs) in American Prisons Today: A Special NGCRC Report," *Journal of Gang Research* 12 (Fall 2004): 1–76.
32. Personal interview, 2009.
33. Personal interview, 2009.
34. Personal interview, 2009.
35. Mark S. Davis and Daniel J. Flannery, "The Institutional Treatment of Gang Members," *Corrections Management Quarterly* 5 (2001): 37–46.
36. John Hancock, "Combating Gang Activity in Prison," *Corrections.com*, 2008, www.corrections.com/news/article/18097 (accessed February 27, 2012).
37. Chad R. Trulson, James W. Marquart, Craig Hemmens, and Leo Carroll, "Racial Desegregation in Prison," *Prison Journal* 88 (2008): 270–299; Chad Trulson and James W. Marquart, *Judicial Intervention, Desegregation, and Inter-Racial Violence: A Case Study of Inmate Desegregation in a Southern Prison System*, unpublished manuscript (Huntsville, TX: Sam Houston State University, 2002).
38. Chad R. Trulson and James W. Marquart, "Inmate Racial Integration: Achieving Racial Integration in the Texas Prison System," *Prison Journal* 82 (2002): 498–525.
39. James W. Marquart and Chad R. Trulson, "First Available House: Desegregation in American Prisons and the Road to *Johnson v. California*," *Corrections Compendium* 31 (September–October, 2006): 1–5.
40. Hancock, "Combating Gang Activity in Prison."
41. For the influence that correctional officers can have on contributing to or defusing a rape-prone culture, see Helen M. Eigenberg, "Correctional Officers and Their Perceptions of Homosexuality, Rape, and Prostitution in Male Prisons," *Prison Journal* 80 (December 2000): 415–433.
42. 108th Congress, 2003, 117 Stat 972. See also Brenda V. Smith, "Analyzing Prison Sex: Reconciling Self-Expression with Safety," *Columbia Journal Gender and Law* 185 (2006).
43. Bureau of Justice Statistics, *Data Collection for the Prison Rape Elimination Act of 2003* (Washington, DC: U.S. Printing Office, 2004).
44. S. 1435[108]: *Prison Rape Elimination Act of 2003*; Public Law No: 108-79.
45. Allen J. Beck and Paige M. Harrison, *Sexual Victimization in State and Federal Prisons Reported by Inmates, 2007* (Washington, DC: Bureau of Justice Statistics, 2007), http://bjs.ojp.usdoj.gov/content/pub/pdf/svsfpri07.pdf (accessed February 27, 2012).
46. Jesse Walker, "Rape Behind Bars," *Reason* 35 (2003): 10–12.
47. Hensley, Koscheski, and Tewksbury, "Examining the Characteristics of Male Sexual Assault Targets in a Southern Maximum-Security Prison," pp. 667–679.
48. Christopher Hensley, Richard Tewksbury, and Tammy Castle, "Characteristics of Prison Sexual Assault Targets in Male Oklahoma Correctional Facilities," *Journal of Interpersonal Violence* 18 (June 2003): 595–606.
49. Mark S. Fleisher and Jessie L. Krienert, *The Myth of Prison Rape: Sexual Culture in American Prisons* (New York: Rowman & Littlefield, 2008).
50. Jennifer Stump, "Unit Riots at Beeville Prison," *Caller*, December 21, 1999.
51. *The Sun*, Yuma, Arizona, April 25, 2007.
52. *San Antonio Express News*, March 28, 2008.
53. "At Least Two Dead in Oklahoma Prison Riot," *USA Today*, May 19, 2008.
54. Mark Colvin, *From Accommodation to Riot: The Penitentiary of New Mexico in Crisis* (Albany: State University of New York Press, 1990).

55. Camille Graham Camp, *The Corrections Yearbook: Adult Correction 2002* (Middletown, CT: Criminal Justice Institute, 2003), p. 50.
56. S. C. Light, "Assaults on Prison Officers: Interactional Themes," *Justice Quarterly* 78 (1991): 243–251.
57. Ibid.
58. Donna L. Mailloux and Ralph C. Serin, "Sexual Assaults During Hostage Takings and Forcible Confinements: Implications for Practice," *Sexual Abuse: A Journal of Research and Treatment* 13 (July 2003): 161–170.
59. See "New York: Attica Survivors File $30M Suit for Damages," *Corrections Digest* 33 (2002): 7.
60. For the difficulties of negotiating with inmates during hostage taking, see Steven J. Romano, "Achieving Successful Negotiations in a Correctional Setting," *Corrections Today* 65 (April 2005): 114–118.
61. Colvin, *From Accommodation to Riot*. For an account of an attempt by inmates to defuse violence among inmates, see Christine Walrath, "Evaluation of an Inmate-Run Alternative to Violence Project: The Impact of Inmate-Inmate Intervention," *Journal of Interpersonal Violence* 16 (July 2001): 697–711.
62. For a history of violent behavior by staff members, see Mark Fleisher, *Warehousing Violence* (Newbury Park, CA: Sage Publications, 1989).
63. Crouch and Marquart, *An Appeal to Justice: Litigated Reform of Texas Prisons*.
64. Fay Dowker and Glenn Good, "The Proliferation of Control Unit Prisons in the United States," *Journal of Prisoners on Prisons* 4 (1993): 95–110; Holly J. Buckhalter, "Torture in U.S. Prisons," *Nation*, July 3, 1995, pp. 17–18.
65. Christopher J. Mumola, "Suicide and Homicide in State Prisons and Local Jails" (Washington, DC: Bureau of Justice Statistics, 2005), p. 1.
66. Ibid., p. 6.
67. Observations of Bartollas, who worked with self-destructive inmates for a number of years.
68. M. P. Huey and T. L. McNulty, "Institutional Conditions and Prison Suicide: Conditional Effects of Deprivation and Overcrowding," *Prison Journal* 85 (2005): 490–514.
69. Christine Tartaro, "An Application of Durkheim's Theory of Suicide to Prison Suicide Rates in the United States," *Death Studies* 29 (2005): 413–422.
70. Bruce B. Way, Richard Miraglia, Donald A. Sawyer, Richard Beer, and John Eddy, "Factors Related to Suicide in New York State Prisons," *International Journal of Law and Psychiatry* 28 (2005): 207.
71. Joseph Micielli, *The Stress and the Effects of Working in a High Security Prison* (Rockville, MD: National Institute of Justice, 2008).
72. Stephen Owen, "Occupational Stress Among Correctional Supervisors," *Prison Journal* 86 (2006): 164–181; Eugene Paoline, Eric Lambert, and Nancy Hogan, "A Calm and Happy Keeper of the Keys: The Impact of ACA Views, Relations with Coworkers, and Public Views on the Job Stress and Job Satisfaction of Correctional Staff," *Prison Journal* 86 (2006): 182–205; and Mike Vuolo and Candace Kruttschnitt, "Prisoners' Adjustment, Correctional Officers, and Context: The Foreground and Background of Punishment in Late Modernity," *Law and Society Review* 42 (2008): 307–314.
73. *Dothard v. Rawlinson*, 433 U.S. 321 (1977); *Gunther v. Iowa State Men's Reformatory*, 612 F.2d 1079 (6th Cir. 1979); *Ford v. Ward*, 471 F. Supp. 1095 (S.D.N.Y. 1978).
74. Incident reported to Bartollas.
75. From a survey of corrections officers done in Kentucky, this study found that rehabilitation received the strongest support of the various correctional ideologies, with female officers being more supportive of rehabilitation than males. See Richard Tewksbury and Elizabeth Ehrhardt Mustaine, "Correctional Orientations of Prison Staff," *Prison Journal* 88 (June 2008): 207–233.

On the morning of Wednesday, September 17, 2003, Kathy Boudin was released on parole from the Bedford Hills Correctional Facility. Boudin's departure ended a 22-year stay at the prison that left its mark on fellow prisoners and the programs that are available for their rehabilitation and health.[1]

On October 20, 1981, Kathy Boudin served as a decoy in the passenger seat of a U-Haul van in Nanuet, New York, from which armed men emerged and shot Nyack police officer Waverly Brown and police sergeant Edward O'Grady following the robbery of a Brinks armored truck. Boudin was one of 19 people convicted of participation in this Brinks robbery crime. She was incarcerated after her arrest and pleaded guilty in 1984 to first-degree robbery and second-degree murder. Her sentence was 20 years to life.

In the years that followed her incarceration, she reshaped her life as an inmate. Boudin started to work at the prison's Children's Center in 1984. She was the inmate coordinator of the parenting classes and the teen program. In 1994, the college-in-prison programs were discontinued throughout the nation. Kathy approached Michelle Fine, professor of psychology at the Graduate Center of City University of New York and they worked together to reestablish

college at the prison in Bedford. Eventually, they were able to get 12 colleges and universities to give faculty pro bono. Two staff people coordinated the program within the prison, and it worked

On October 21, 1981, police escort Kathy Boudin (top photo) into police headquarters after she was arrested for taking part in a deadly armored car heist. In the bottom photo, Boudin waves as she is released after serving more than 20 years at the Bedford Hills Correctional Facility, on September 17, 2003.

very well. In her 22 years in the Bedford Hills Correctional Facility, Boudin either initiated or was involved in more than a dozen programs for inmates.[2]

Kathy Boudin was paroled in 2003, the third time she went up for parole. She accepted a job as an AIDS counselor at St. Luke's-Roosevelt Hospital Center in New York City. Since her release, she has received her Ed.D. from Columbia University, Teachers College and is presently an adjunct assistant professor at Columbia Teachers College. Boudin has focused her work on the HIV/AIDS epidemic and criminal justice issues, including: women in prison; the mother–child relationship and parenting from a distance; adolescent relationships with incarcerated parents; restorative justice; and basic literacy inside correctional institutions.[3]

What we know is that women who commit violent crimes, some of whom are sentenced to many years in prison or even to death row, are not representative of those female offenders confined in long-term correctional institutions. Nor do many women prisoners have the impact on prison life (or in the community subsequent to their release) that Kathy Boudin has had. The average woman in prison, as the following sections will convey, is more likely to be a drug offender or a woman who has committed property offenses.

chapter

eight

THE PRISON EXPERIENCE: FEMALES

LEARNING OBJECTIVES

LO1 ▸ Identify the main reason for the rise in the imprisonment of women

LO2 ▸ Identify the findings of the classic studies of social structure in women's prisons

LO3 ▸ Discuss the contemporary studies of women doing time in prison

LO4 ▸ Understand that providing sufficient programs for incarcerated women with children is critical

LO5 ▸ Identify the serious issues of health care in women's prisons

LO6 ▸ Identify why professionalism is important in women's prisons

Photo of little boy hugging his inmate mother.

AP Photo/Stephen Morton

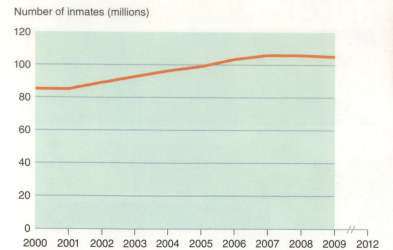

Number of inmates (millions)

FIGURE 8.1 Number of Sentenced Female Prisoners Under the Jurisdiction of State or Federal Correctional Authorities

Source: Heather C. West and William J. Sabol, *Prisoners in 2009* (Washington, DC: Bureau of Justice Statistics, 2010), Table 7, p. 22.

The treatment of women behind bars has come to the forefront of corrections. One reason is that there are now more females involved in the justice system, and their unique problems and issues have been identified. Before 1960, few women were in prison and independent women's prisons were relatively rare; most were attached to male institutions. Only four institutions for women were built between 1930 and 1950. In comparison, 34 women's prisons were constructed during the 1980s as crime rates soared.[4]

While relative to their number in the U.S. population, men are almost 14 times more likely than women to be incarcerated in a federal or state prison. Nonetheless, while the female inmate population is still relatively small, it is now more than 100,000, and increasing at a faster pace than the male population. Women prisoners now make up nearly 7 percent of the inmate population, compared to about 6 percent 10 years ago; the actual number of sentenced female prisoners under state or federal jurisdiction increased more than 20,000 during the past decade. See Figure 8.1 for the increase of women's imprisonment in recent years.

In Voices Across the Profession, Judy Anderson, warden of the Camille Griffin Graham women's prison in South Carolina, suggests that women prisoners have gender-specific needs, and this is an important factor in providing them adequate programming.

PRISONS FOR WOMEN: HISTORY AND CHARACTERISTICS

In the early days of prison history, women were confined in separate quarters in men's prisons and, like men, suffered from filth, overcrowding, and hard conditions. Women lodged in the Auburn penitentiary in New York were subject to beatings and sexual abuse by the male guards. African American and poor women were disproportionately incarcerated in all parts of the United States.

Even before the end of slavery, Quaker abolitionists and suffragists were at the forefront of the prison reform movement. **Elizabeth Fry** of England helped organize the women confined at London's Newgate Gaol in the early 1800s. Her brave and innovative work at Newgate with incarcerated women and their children was testimony to the fact that, with decent treatment, women convicts were redeemable. Fry challenged the rampant sexual abuse of institutionalized women and advocated that they be under the authority of other women and confined to their own institution. She also sought to substitute for the Quaker system of absolute silence a system that permitted inmates to communicate with each other and help each other reform. Fry was able to instill hope and dignity where there had been only despair. Today Elizabeth Fry Societies in Canada play an active role in exposing abuses in women's prisons.[5]

The Indiana Women's Prison, the first separate prison for women, was founded by a Quaker couple in 1873. Four years later, Massachusetts built an all-females state reformatory. Another American Quaker helped found the progressive women's reformatory at Bedford Hills. Other states gradually followed, and separate institutions for men and women became the norm, although there were exceptions. Fry's program, which emphasized women helping women, rehabilitation, religious education, and obedience, was instituted throughout North America.[6]

ELIZABETH FRY Quaker who brought reform to women confined in prison.

© Judy Anderson

"When I think about job satisfaction, it means a lot to me when I see staff members grow, accept new responsibilities, and move on with their careers. It is also meaningful when you see an inmate grow and believe that she can be successful when she returns to the community."

JUDY ANDERSON,
WARDEN

I have been warden of the Camille Griffin Graham Correctional Institution since 2003. I basically see myself as the mayor of a large urban city, which has a high crime rate and a large population of indigent people. The warden is responsible for providing all the services for inmates, which involves food, housing, education, medical, work, clothing, and anything in between.

Women come to prison through different pathways than men. They do time differently; they reenter and transition to the community differently. Consequently, we tailor our service delivery to meet their needs, not duplicate what is done with men. What we are trying to do is to be gender responsive, which recognizes the behavioral and social differences between female and male offenders, but we still have a long way to go. In the corrections system, most of our policies and procedures are designed for the majority, the men.

Women do their time more as process, while men are more interested in the bottom line. For example, women are able to forgive more easily than do men. They are usually not as violent. Men fight and move on. Women involved in a fight are upset; they need to do a lot of talking with verbal responses. For women, the bottom line is that everything is rational.

A typical woman who comes to prison is usually abused. She has self-medicated herself with drugs and alcohol. A male is typically part of her relationship piece of how she becomes involved in crime. There are gangs in some women's prisons, but if a woman has joined a gang on the outside, it is usually because of a man or a relationship issue. There is drug usage in a women's prison, but typically a woman gets/buys the drugs from another woman's prescribed medication.

The major challenge is that the warden needs to be everything to everybody. We need to focus on public safety, the welfare and jobs of employees, and, at the same time, we need to respond to the needs/concerns of the inmates. The task and challenge is to always balance the three. Another challenge, given the economy, is to find resources. It is necessary to find ways to provide services for funding we have lost. We have found that volunteers help to fill that void as we try to provide gender responsiveness and services for special needs offenders.

When I think about job satisfaction, it means a lot to me when I see staff members grow, accept new responsibilities, and move on with their careers. It is also meaningful when you see an inmate grow and believe that she can be successful when she returns to the community. It also means a great deal when you can make some system changes and have an impact on the field of corrections. I also like the fact that no two days are exactly alike and that I am also growing on the job.

Source: Interviewed in 2012.

Many significant aspects of contemporary corrections were pioneered by female administrators in charge of institutions for female offenders—for example, educational instruction, work release, and vocational activities. Prison reformers regarded women as good candidates for rehabilitation, partly because they were considered less dangerous than their male counterparts.

During the Progressive Era, cottage style reformatories were developed as an alternative to the harsh custodial institutions. Inmates of the custodial prisons, mostly African American women, suffered from the filthy conditions and violence inflicted by male guards. The new reformatories were usually staffed by women and aimed to correct women's moral behavior. Women were sentenced to the reformatories for various sexual offenses, including pregnancy outside marriage and unlawful sexual intercourse. By 1935, the progressive era was over, and reformatories and custodial prisons were merged. The legacy of the "cottage system" is evident at the woman's federal prison in Alderson, West Virginia, and in many state prisons, such as Bedford Hills in New York.[7]

The 1960s and 1970s, a period of civil rights awareness and protest by various oppressed groups, was also a time of reformist zeal concerning women in prison. Compassion was expressed for women who killed their husbands in self-defense and were charged with murder. There was also a huge outcry over prisoners such as Angela Davis and Joan Little. Davis was charged with abetting the escape of a violent prisoner, and Little was tried for killing her jailer during the act of rape.

The period of retrenchment of social services and the War on Drugs, which got underway in the 1980s and is continuing well into the twenty-first century, parallel a mass media campaign dramatizing crimes of violence. Women of color have been the most adversely affected by mandatory drug sentencing laws, mainly the harsh sentencing for crack cocaine. Another factor affecting both male and female prisoners is the vested interests of major corporations—the prison-industrial complex—and many local communities in the building and maintaining of prisons for their economic well-being.

LO1   RISE OF WOMEN'S IMPRISONMENT

Why is the female inmate population increasing? In addition to their committing more serious crimes, sentencing changes have helped put more women behind bars. Mandatory minimum sentences provide the same punishment for conspiracy to commit crimes, such as driving the getaway car, as for the instigator of the crime itself. According to the American Civil Liberties Union, women are increasingly caught up in the ever-widening net cast by current drug laws such as conspiracy laws and accomplice liability laws that extend criminal liability to the arrested offender's partners and relatives.[8] Accordingly, almost half of the women in prison today under these mandatory sentencing laws have been convicted of conspiracy. Sentencing laws fail to consider the reasons—including domestic violence, economic dependence, or dependent immigration status—that compel many women to remain silent. Mandatory minimum laws often subject women to the same—or in some cases harsher—sentences than the principals in the drug trade who are ostensibly the target of those policies.[9] This is an example of what we might call "equality with a vengeance," an equality of punishment meted out to women who violate the law.

Female offenders are more likely than males to be convicted of a nonviolent crime and be incarcerated for a low-level involvement in drug offenses, such as driving a boyfriend to make a drug deal. The female offender may end up serving a longer sentence than the boyfriend simply because she is less likely to work out a plea arrangement.[10]

The get-tough policies that produced mandatory and determinate sentencing statutes reduced the judicial discretion that has traditionally benefited women. As Meda Chesney-Lind points out, women were swept up in the get-tough movement and no longer receive the benefits of male chivalry. The use of sentencing guidelines means that such factors as family ties and employment record, two elements that usually benefit women during sentencing, are no longer being considered by some judges.[11] See Table 8.1 for estimated number of sentenced prisoners under state jurisdiction by offense and gender.

While the equality movement is under way, the prison is still a gendered organization, and some correctional administrators recognize that women often bring with them a set of needs that are different from the burdens faced by male inmates.

MYTH
Sentencing reform movements help keep people in the community and reduce incarceration.

FACT
While males may benefit from sentencing reforms, females suffer. Judicial discretion traditionally benefited women. Now gender-neutral sentences have placed more women behind bars.

TABLE 8.1 Sentenced Prisoners Under State Jurisdiction by Offense and Gender

Offense	All Inmates	Male	Female
Total	1,362,300	1,268,900	93,400
Violent	724,300	690,800	33,600
Property	261,200	235,500	27,700
Drug	242,200	218,200	24,000
Public Order	120,700	114,000	6,700

Source: Paul Guerino, Paige M. Harrison, and William J. Sabol, *Prisoners in 2010* (Washington, DC: Bureau of Justice Statistics, 2011), Table 16b, p. 28.

Characteristics of Women in Prison

Incarcerated women have typically had a troubled family life. Significant numbers were at-risk children, products of broken homes and the welfare system. Over half have received welfare at some time during their adult lives. As juveniles, they experienced a pattern of harsh discipline and abuse. Many claim to have been physically or sexually abused. This pattern continued in adult life; many female inmates were victims of domestic violence.[12]

Not surprisingly, many female offenders display psychological problems, including serious psychopathology.[13] One survey of incarcerated women in 12 nations, including the United States, found that 4 percent had psychotic illnesses; 12 percent, depression; and 42 percent, a personality disorder, including 21 percent with antisocial personality disorder.[14]

A significant number of female inmates report having substance abuse problems; more than three-fourths are serving time for nonviolent drug offenses.[15] Surveys show that about three-fourths have used drugs at some time in their lives, and almost half were involved with addictive drugs, such as cocaine, heroin, or PCP. Little difference exists in major drug use between male and female offenders when measured over their life span or at the time of their current arrest.

The cultural baggage that inmates bring into the prison setting is the end product of the drug wars on the streets and the War on Drugs in society. Caught up in the drug wars are minority women (Hispanic and African American) involved with gang members, foreigners arrested at airports as couriers for international drug syndicates, and violent and nonviolent offenders arrested for crime indirectly related to drug use. Race and class intersect in predictable ways to ensure that the persons most feared and resented by society are those who are shut away. Today, as Meda Chesney-Lind suggests, "street crime" has become a code word for "race." And racial tensions in the free community lay the groundwork for ethnic differences and resentments behind prison bars.[16]

The incarceration of so many women who are low-criminal risks yet face a high risk of exposure to HIV and other health issues because of their prior history of drug abuse presents a significant problem. One study of incarcerated women found that one-third of the sample reported that before their arrest they had traded sex for money or drugs; about one-quarter of these women reported trading sex for money or drugs "weekly or more often."[17] Such risky behavior significantly increases the likelihood of their carrying the AIDS virus or other sexually transmitted diseases.

The picture that emerges of the female inmate is troubling (see Exhibit 8.1). After a lifetime of emotional turmoil, physical and sexual abuse, and drug use, it seems improbable that overcrowded, underfunded correctional institutions can forge a dramatic turnaround in the behavior of at-risk female inmates. Many have

EXHIBIT 8.1 Characteristics of Women in Prison

- One in 703 African American females are imprisoned; compared to about 1 in 1,987 white females and 1 in 1,356 Hispanic females.

- Women in prison lack a solid employment history.

- They often have a history of poor physical health.

- They have a history of financial problems.

- They exhibit a distinct lack of education.

- They have received experiences of physical and sexual abuse.

- They have a history of substance misuse.

- They often have mental health and other problems.

- They are likely to be primary caregivers for their children.

Source: Amanda Noblet, "Women in Prison: A Review of the Current Female Prison System: Future Directions and Alternatives," Ph.D. dissertation and found in the *Internet Journal of Criminology 2008*, www.internetjournalofcriminology.com (accessed March 2, 2012).

WARD AND KASSEBAUM Classic study that claimed women adapted to imprisonment by forming homosexual alliances.

BUTCH The dominant, or male, role in a homosexual relationship in the prison society.

FEMME The docile, or female, role in a homosexual relationship in the prison society.

GIALLOMBARDO Classic study that identified that women were involved in fictive families in adapting to imprisonment.

FICTIVE FAMILIES A grouping of unrelated individuals who have assumed the traditional family roles of mother, father, grandparents, and so on.

EXHIBIT 8.2 Comparison of Classic Studies

Study	Prison Studied	Basic Finding
Ward and Kassebaum	Frontera Correctional Institution in California	Women cope with prison by establishing homosexual alliances.
Giallombardo	Federal reformatory for women in Alderson, West Virginia	Some women form fictive families in prison.
Hefferman	District of Columbia's women's reformatory in Occoquan, Virginia	Fictive kinship structure was present.

Sources: David A. Ward and Gene Kassebaum, *Women's Prisons and Social Structure* (Chicago: Anderson, 1965; Rose Giallombardo, *Society of Women: A Study of a Women's Prison* (New York: Wiley, 1966); Esther Hefferman, *Making It in Prison: The Square, the Cool, and the Life* (New York: Wiley, 1972).

lost custody of their children, a trauma that is more likely to afflict those who are already substance abusers and suffer from depression.[18] It should come as no surprise then that many female inmates feel strain and conflict, psychological conditions related to violent episodes.[19]

DOING TIME

The classic studies of women in prison found that prison culture for women was much different from that of men and revolved around sexual alliances with other female inmates. However, more recent studies have found that severe overcrowding, scarcity of resources, and emphasis on security now creates a much more austere and severe environment. As a result, women prisoners have a different response in some ways to imprisonment than was typically found in the past.

 # Classic Studies

There are three classic studies of women in prison: Ward and Kassebaum, Giallombardo, and Hefferman (see Exhibit 8.2).[20]

- **Ward and Kassebaum**: In their 1965 study of the Frontera Correctional institution in California, David A. Ward and Gene Kassebaum found that women attempted to deal with the painful conditions of confinement by establishing homosexual alliances. The researchers describe these prison love affairs as appearing to be unstable, short lived, explosive, and involving strict differentiation between the roles of "butch" and "femme." **Butch** is a dominant, or male, role. **Femme** is the docile, or female, role. The person in the butch role is expected to be strong, in control, and independent, and to pursue the femme.

- **Giallombardo**: Rose Giallombardo's 1966 study of the federal reformatory for women in Alderson, West Virginia, indicated a major difference between male and female prisoners. Among female inmates, membership in **fictive families** was more common than participation in homosexual activities and occurred earlier than sexual involvement. Giallombardo reported that the women at Alderson established familiar relationships similar to the relationships of the free world. A sort of family life—with "mothers" and "fathers," "grandparents," and "aunts' and "uncles"—was at the very center of inmate life at Alderson and provided a sense of belonging and identification that enabled inmates involved in "family affairs" to do easy time. Unlike male prisoners, the women at Alderson did not design the social system to combat the social and psychological deprivations of prison.

■ **Hefferman**: The 1972 research of Esther Hefferman at the District of Columbia's women's reformatory in Occoquan, Virginia, also supported the hypothesis that fictive kinship structure is present in women's prisons. Hefferman, along with Giallombardo, emphasized the concept of latent cultural identity as a factor leading to the formation of the fictive family. By this she meant the pre-institutional identity the female offender brings with her into the prison setting. Hefferman argued that women construct the kinship structure because they are socialized to conceive of themselves, their needs, and their peer relations primarily in terms of family roles and situations.

Prisons can be overcrowded, but many inmates are alone and isolated. Though women tend to form substitute family-like groupings, not all do—and for those who don't, the prison experience can be devastating.

© Hal Yeager/*Birmingham News*/Landov

Contemporary Prison Experience for Women

Several contemporary studies continue to document the existence of same-sex relations in women's prisons, but the widespread opinion today is that **kinship networks** are nowhere near as defined as one might believe reading the early studies.[21] In contrast, contemporary studies emphasize that social structure and relationships are only a small part of how women do prison time. Similarities do exist in how women do time today compared to the past, but the increased size of women's prisons, the emphasis on security, and the de-emphasis on programming have affected how women cope with prison life.

LO3 ▶ Barbara Owen's *In the Mix: Struggle and Survival in a Women's Prison* is a study that took place at the Central California Women's Facility, the world's largest female correctional facility. The basic question that framed her study was: how do women prisoners do time?[22] The following are her findings:

■ The culture that develops in a women's prison is "markedly different from the degradation, violence, and predatory structure of male prison life" because "the culture of the female prison seeks to accommodate these struggles rather than to exploit them."

■ The phase of a woman's criminal record and the number of previous prison terms contribute greatly to the prison experience.

■ Women prisoners, in comparing their imprisonment experiences to those of men prisoners, generally agreed that men show more solidarity than women.

■ Women are confined to administrative segregation for three major reasons: fighting, drug-related offenses, and assaults on staff.

■ Three general categories of exploitative relationships took place: (1) begins with a nonpayment of a friendly loan of food or cigarettes; (2) pursues a relationship with a naïve woman prisoner for exploitative purposes; and (3) involves outright extortion where an inmate who is thought to be weak is pressured to surrender her goods to another prisoner, either one time or as ongoing extortion.

■ Race tends to be de-emphasized much more than would be found in male prison culture and is not critical to prison culture.

HEFFERMAN Classic study that found the presence of fictive families in women's adaptation to prison life.

KINSHIP NETWORKS A type of prison socialization in which women deal with incarceration by becoming part of make-believe families.

THE MIX Owen's term for women's involvement in problematic prison behaviors and activities.

- No formal gang culture exists.

- Commitment to a criminal identity and stage in one's criminal and prison career are the most important contributions to one's style of doing time.

- The convict code has the following tenets: "Mind your own business," "The police are not your friend: stay out of their face," "If asked by staff, you do not tell," "Do not allow rat-packing; fight one on one only," "Take care of each other."

- In doing time, it is wise to stay out of "**the mix**," which is any behavior that can bring trouble or conflict with staff and other prisoners (e.g., involvement in drugs or fights).

Mark Pogrebin and Mary Dodge's interviewing of former female inmates who had done time in a western state also discovered that an important element of prison life for many women was dealing with fear and violence. Some reported that violence in women's prisons is common and that many female inmates undergo a process of socialization fraught with danger and volatile situations.[23] Confinement for women may produce severe anxiety and anger because of separation from families and loved ones and the inability to function in normal female roles. Unlike men, who direct their anger outward, female prisoners may turn to more self-destructive acts to cope with their problems. Female inmates are more likely than males to maim themselves and attempt suicide. One common practice among female inmates is self-mutilation, or carving. This ranges from simple scratches to carving the name of their boyfriend on their body or even complex statements or sentences ("To mother, with hate").[24]

Candace Kruttschnitt and Rosemary Gartner observed women's interactions in two California women's prisons, the Central Institution for Women (CIW) and the Valley State Prison for Women (VSPW), a high-security facility.[25] They found that imprisonment for women has changed over the past 40 years because today administrators place greater emphasis on custody and security, practice greater austerity, and give less attention to individuals. As a result, less is expected of prisoners, and in turn, inmates expect less from the prison administration and more from each other. Because administrators are preoccupied with the security and management of prisoners rather than rehabilitation, female inmates have become disaffected, suspicious, and isolated.[26]

While the structure of female social relations may be changing, Kruttschnitt and Gartner's study found that sexual relationships were still "very much a part of life" in prison. The researchers reason that because of the public's greater acceptance of same-sex relationships, there is now less regulation of prisoners' lives.[27]

Kruttschnitt and Gartner found that the prisoners in the two prisons they studied had three major ways of negotiating, or coping with, prison life:

- *Adopted style.* In this model, women associate with other prisoners and enjoy their associations. Few of these women report having problems with correctional officers.

- *Convict style.* This model involves spending time with only one or two others, or alone, and, as with the adopted style, these women enjoy their associations with other inmates. However, unlike the adopted class, they are highly likely to have difficulty dealing with correctional officers.[28]

- *Isolate style.* This model is characterized by preferring to be alone when not locked up in cells. Alienated from other prisoners, this negative and singular style gives female inmates the feeling that they have no control over their prison environment.

MYTH
Women form quasifamily structures in prison, with "mothers and fathers," "grandparents," and "aunts and uncles."

FACT
In contemporary prisons, female inmates may be more prone to mistrust their friendships with other women prisoners and refrain from forming close relationships.

The influence of the prison environment is seen in that in more punitive environments, women prisoners are least likely to approach their confinement in an adopted, as opposed to an isolate, manner. Women prisoners are also far more outspoken about what they see as inhumane treatment, abuse from staff, and arbitrary restrictions.

So, though women prisons are usually less violent, involve less gang activity, and do not reflect the racial tensions found in men's prisons, interpersonal relationships might be less stable and less familial than in the past. Inmates may be more prone to mistrust their friendships with other women prisoners and believe the primary motivation for interpersonal relationships involves economic manipulation.[29] In an era of high security in prison, female inmates may be forming a society that is more like males'.

Candace Kruttschnitt and Rosemary Gartner also interviewed 38 prisoners at the Valley State Prison for Women. Every one reported that the overriding concern was with control and security and that there was limited interest in helping inmates. Inmates felt that there was nothing for them to do except follow the rules. Prisoners felt that the institutional orientation was fundamentally aimed at maintenance and security. Some women even interpreted treatment by staff as intentional punitiveness. The women further felt that the administration had de-emphasized the potential for rehabilitation. The end result of this austere environment was poor relations among inmates.[30]

It may be this emphasis on control and security will increasingly take place in women's prisons, and this, in turn, will affect how women do time in the future. As it has in the Valley State Prison for Women, it will affect women prisoners' relationships with staff and other inmates, the quality of the prison environment, and the programming that is offered inmates.

See Exhibit 8.3 for a comparison of contemporary studies of women in prison.

SPECIAL ISSUES IN THE INCARCERATION OF WOMEN

The problems posed by motherhood in prison, the quality and adequacy of prison health care, and the sexual victimization of women prisoners are three pressing issues in women prisons.

Often located in rural areas miles away from inmates' families, women's prisons tend to develop a social structure that is quite different from that found in men's prisons. Some women form fictive families that replicate the family relationships they knew on the outside. "Married" couples may head such families, which occasionally also include a father figure. Women in these relationships give and receive a lot of love and nurturing.

EXHIBIT 8.3 A Comparison of Contemporary Studies of Women in Prison

Researchers	Location	Main Findings
K. Faith; Forsyth, et al.; Tewksbury and Koscheski; Severance	Studies located primarily in southern prisons	Documented the same-sex relations in women's prisons that were found in the classic studies
Barbara Owen	Central California Women's Facility	Found that women's imprisonment is similar to that of men in terms of inmate solidarity, exploitative relationships, gang culture, and inmate code
Pogrebin and Dodge	Western prisons	Revealed that fear and violence, including self-destructive coping mechanisms, are characteristic of inmates' lives
Kruttschnitt and Gartner	Central Institution for Women (California)	Found that female inmates have become more dissatisfied, suspicious, and isolated
Kruttschnitt and Gartner	Valley State Prison for Women (California)	Found that the overriding concern is with control and security, with limited interest in helping inmates

Motherhood in Prison

An estimated 80,000 incarcerated women, or about two-thirds of the women incarcerated in U.S. state prisons and nearly 60 percent of women confined in federal prisons, are parents to nearly 320,000 children under age 18.[31] Furthermore, most of these women were the heads of single-parent households prior to their confinement.[32] The separation of women prisoners from their children can be traumatic for all.[33] Prisons, and especially women's prisons, generally are located in remote, rural areas. Over time, family ties are broken. Yet prisoners' family relationships are very important not only for mental health reasons but for postrelease success. See Figure 8.2 for predictors of children's adjustment following parental incarceration and reunion.

While their mothers are incarcerated, children most frequently stay with maternal grandmothers, but other caretakers include the child's father or other relatives.[34] Imprisoned women express the most satisfaction when their children are placed with their maternal grandmothers, and when they have participated in the decision about where the children will live. In placing children with their maternal grandmothers, inmates feel relatively confident that they will encounter minimal difficulties when taking the children back upon release. If no suitable family alternatives are available, children may be placed in foster homes or put up for adoption. Those placements make it very difficult for mothers to regain custody after release.[35]

Imprisoned women are burdened with the knowledge that their own behavior has caused the separation from their children. This separation generates feelings of emptiness, helplessness, guilt, anger, and bitterness, and fear of loss or rejection by the children. With prolonged separation, mothers fear their children might establish stronger bonds of affection with caretakers than with them. Furthermore, mothers fear that teenage children staying with maternal grandparents may be arrested because of inadequate supervision.[36]

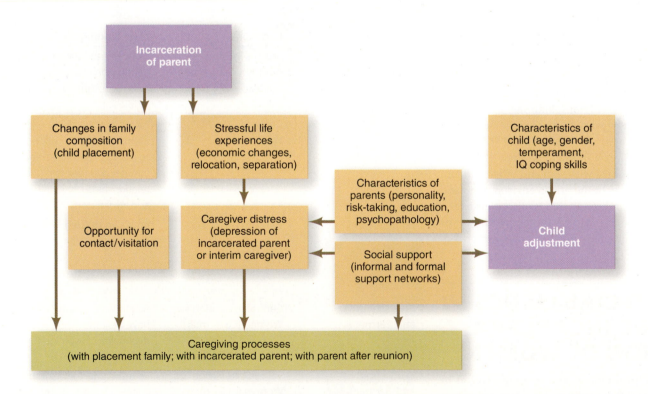

FIGURE 8.2 Predictors of Children's Adjustment Following Parental Incarceration and Reunion

Sources: Family Strengthening Policy Center, "Supporting Families with Incarcerated Parents" (Washington, DC: National Human Services Assembly, 2005), p. 9. Adapted from R. Parke and K. A. Clarke-Stewart, *Effects of Parental Incarceration on Young Children* (Washington, DC: U.S. Department of Health and Human Services, 2002).

Even more problems await inmates who are pregnant. The likelihood of pregnancy is high during imprisonment, with some prisoners sentenced to prison when they are already pregnant, and others becoming pregnant during home furloughs, work release, conjugal visits, or even through sexual intercourse or rape by prison staff. Studies of pregnancy outcome among women prisoners have revealed high rates of perinatal mortality and morbidity. The termination of prison pregnancy may not be possible even if the inmate desires it; under other circumstances the inmate may be forced by prison officials to have an abortion.[37]

LO4 Programs for Incarcerated Mothers

Several states have innovative programs for mothers of young children. California has a statute mandating the creation of a Mother-Infant-Care program, an alternative-sentencing project that allows 100 women with infants who are 6 months old or younger to live in one of the seven community-based facilities with their children and take parenting classes. Several hundred women have graduated from the program. The program at Bedford Hills in New York State is the one most written about. The Bedford Hills program provides a nursery where babies up to 18 months old can live with their mothers. A playroom is available for older children, who are encouraged to come and visit with their moms. The mother–child bonding has been excellent in this program, and the women learn child care skills. The Nebraska Correctional Center for Women, similarly, has a prison nursery and overnight visits for older children to maintain the bonds between mother and child. Children can stay up to five days a month. According to the male warden, the presence of children has a harmonizing effect on the whole population.[38] The Evidence-Based Corrections feature discusses an evaluation of these programs.

Inmate mothers are also treated well in some other countries. For example, the European Committee for Children of Imprisoned Parents (EUROCHIPS) advocates that attention be paid to the needs of children in maintaining ties with their incarcerated parents. The Swedish Prison and Probation Service ordered the following for all prisons in Sweden:

- Special leave will be granted for important events concerning children.

- Children should be allowed to telephone and speak directly to the parent. (In the past, children could only leave a message and ask the parent to call back, which frequently occurred several hours later.)

- Each new prisoner should be asked about his/her children.

- Flexible visiting hours for children need to be provided.[39]

One of the most crucial needs of women in prison is the ability to care for their young children. Here, incarcerated women hold their babies in a child development class given at the Indiana Women's Prison in Indianapolis. The prison is host to the Family Preservation Program, including the Wee Ones Nursery, which allows eligible offenders who deliver while incarcerated at IWP to reside with their infant at the facility for up to 18 months or the mother's earliest possible release date, whichever is sooner.

© Shaul Schwartz/Getty Images

MYTH Women in prison are young and unattached without families or kids.

FACT Two-thirds of the women incarcerated in U.S. state prisons and nearly 60 percent of women confined in federal prisons are mothers, and they have, collectively, 320,000 children under 18.

EVIDENCE-BASED CORRECTIONS

Prison Nursery Programs

It is now estimated that 4 percent of women in state prisons and 3 percent of women in federal prisons were pregnant at the time of admittance; about 6 percent of women in local jails were pregnant at the time of admittance. Despite this trend, there is no national policy that dictates what happens to children born to mothers who are under correctional supervision. The overwhelming majority of children born to incarcerated mothers are separated from their mothers immediately after birth and placed with relatives or into foster care. In a handful of states, women have other options: prison nurseries and community-based residential parenting programs.

Prison nursery programs allow a mother to parent her infant for a finite period of time within a special housing unit at the prison. Community-based residential parenting programs allow mothers to keep their infants with them while they fulfill their sentences in residential programs in the community. In either case, most mothers have committed low-level nonviolent offenses, face relatively short sentences, and will continue as their children's primary caregiver upon release.

A national study sponsored by the Women's Prison Association found that the number of prison-based nursery programs is growing, but such programs are still rare. Though every state has seen a dramatic rise in its women's prison population over the past three decades, only nine states have prison nursery programs in operation or under development.

Despite the fact that they are still few in number, research shows that these programs benefit mothers and children. When adequate resources are available for prison nursery programs, women who participate show lower rates of recidivism, and their children show no adverse affects as a result of their participation. By keeping mothers and infants together, these programs prevent foster care placement and allow for the formation of mother–child bonds during a critical period of infant development.

While such programs are an improvement, many women parenting their infants in prison nurseries could be doing so in the community instead. Most women in prison nursery programs present little risk to public safety. Community corrections programs have been shown to protect public safety and reduce recidivism at a fraction of the human and economic costs of prison. In the community, programs could operate according to prevailing community child health and development standards. Mothers would be able to access educational and vocational services while participating in a mother–child program, as they will be expected to serve as both mothers and employees after their release.

Source: Chandra Kring Villanueva, Sara From, and Georgia Lerner, *Mothers, Infants and Imprisonment, A National Look at Prison Nurseries and Community-Based Alternatives* (New York: Women's Prison Association, 2009), http://66.29.139.159/pdf/Mothers%20Infants%20and%20Imprisonment%202009.pdf (accessed March 2, 2012).

L05 ▶ Prison Health Care

The quality of health care in women's prisons varies from very good to grossly inadequate. Women in prison have unique health care needs that sometimes are not being met. As the prison population ages, these needs become critical.[40] Compared to men, women in prison have higher rates of illness. On the bright side, prison administrators now provide ready access to female-specific health care services, and initial physical and pelvic examinations, mammograms, and routine pregnancy screenings are performed. However, despite progress, there is much more to be done:[41]

- *Failure to refer seriously ill inmates for treatment and delays in treatment.* Women inmates suffering from treatable diseases such as asthma, diabetes, sickle cell anemia, cancer, late-term miscarriages, and seizures have little or no access to medical attention, sometimes resulting in death or permanent injury. Instances of failure to deliver life-saving drugs for inmates with HIV/AIDS have also been noted.

- *Lack of qualified personnel and resources and use of nonmedical staff.* There are too few staff to meet physical and mental health needs. This often results in long delays in obtaining medical attention; disrupted and poor quality treatment causing physical deterioration of prisoners with chronic and degenerative diseases, such as cancer; overmedication of prisoners with psychotropic drugs; and lack of mental health treatment. The use of nonmedical staff to screen requests for treatment is also common.

- *Charges for medical attention.* In violation of international standards, many prisons/jails charge inmates for medical attention, on the grounds that charging for health care services deters prisoners from seeking medical attention for minor matters or because they want to avoid work. In some supermax prisons, where prisoners cannot work at all, the U.S. Justice Department has expressed concern that charging prisoners impedes their access to health care.

- *Inadequate reproductive health care.* The National Institute of Corrections has stated that provision of gynecological services for women in prison is inadequate. Only half of the state prison systems surveyed offer female-specific services such as mammograms and Pap smears, and often entail a long wait to be seen.

- *Shackling during pregnancy.* Shackling of all prisoners, including pregnant prisoners, is policy in federal prisons and the U.S. Marshals Service and exists in almost all state prisons. Only two states have legislation regulating the use of restraints (belly chains, leg irons, and handcuffs). Shackling during labor may cause complications during delivery such as hemorrhage or decreased fetal heart rate. If a caesarian section is needed, a delay of even five minutes may result in permanent brain damage to the baby.

- *Lack of treatment for substance abuse.* The gap between services available and treatment needs continues to grow. The number of prisoners with histories of drug abuse is growing, but the proportion of prisoners receiving treatment has declined during the past decade.

- *Lack of adequate or appropriate mental health services.* A large percentage of women inmates experience sexual or physical abuse before coming to prison, and suffer posttraumatic stress disorder. Very few prison systems provide counseling. Women attempting to access mental health services are routinely given medication without opportunity to undergo psychotherapeutic treatment.[42]

In some cases, impetus for change has come through civil litigation. In *Plata v. Davis* (2002), the largest-ever prison class-action lawsuit, inmates alleged that California officials inflicted cruel and unusual punishment by their deliberate indifference to serious medical needs. The settlement agreement required that the California Department of Corrections improve its medical care procedures and policies and devote significant resources to ensure timely access to proper medical care.[43] In another California case, *Budd v. Cambra* (2002), the court ruled that the California Department of Corrections violated the law when it failed to license health care facilities that provide in-patient treatment to inmates throughout the state.

Sexual Abuse

All rape is an exercise of power, but some rapists have an edge that is more than physical; they operate within an institutionalized setting. According to Louis Rothenstein, a psychologist who worked for six years in the federal prison in Dublin, California, it was not uncommon for correctional officers to go into women's cells and have sex.[44] Complaints by women inmates and their advocates were ignored. "You would be blackballed if you were thought of as an advocate for the inmates," Rothenstein said.[45] "An internal code of silence shields the prison industry from public scrutiny," he added. The events at the notorious Middle Georgia Correctional Complex are even more scandalous. Women there sued the prison for sexual abuse in 1984 but had to wait eight years to win their case, in November 1992. In the end, 14 former employees—10 men, including the deputy warden, and 4 women—were indicted on sexual abuse charges, including rape, sexual assault, and sodomy, in "one of the worst episodes of its kind in the history of the

CAREERS in Corrections

CORRECTIONAL COUNSELOR

Preparation for the Job

A college education with an emphasis in criminology, social work, or counseling would be adequate preparation for the job. An M.A. in counseling or social work would even be greater preparation, and it would help secure employment in the Federal Bureau of Prisons.

Nature of the Job

The correctional counselor serves several functions in women's prisons. They are treatment agents who are responsible for providing casework to inmates, including interviewing inmates and providing the necessary paperwork that will process them through the institution, as well as providing for their particular concerns, such as phone calls and the welfare of family and children. They have the responsibility to be advocates who make certain that inmates receive proper medical care and are assigned to desired programs upon availability. They are resource developers who provide the link between the prisoner and the outside world, as they help inmates plan for their return to the community. Furthermore, they are advocates who ensure to the greatest possible extent that inmates are not deprived of their constitutional rights.

In performing these functions in state systems, counselors interview prisoners, their families, and other interested individuals or agencies to obtain personal history data; confer with administrative and medical personnel in formulating plans for work assignments, training, and other aids in institution adjustment; participate in disciplinary hearings; provide assistance in structuring the total institutional program for the individual prisoner; prepare reports and progress information for submission to the parole board; and develop case histories for use by psychiatrists and administrators for evaluation use in parole planning.

In the federal system, the correctional counselor is part of a unit team in a cell house. There are actually three individuals who have job responsibilities in the functional unit, or unit management, of the federal system that are similar to the role expectations of correctional counselors in state correctional systems.

nation's women's prisons."[46] The incidents took place in the warden's house, in a prison restroom, and in other areas.

Until recently, relatively little attention has been paid to the sexual assaults on female prisoners by their male guards. The International Women's Day organization documented more than 1,000 cases of sexual abuse of U.S. prisoners by correctional staff.[47] Extensive documentation was also provided by the Women's Rights Project of **Human Rights Watch**, an international nongovernmental organization. *All Too Familiar: Sexual Abuse of Women in U.S. State Prisons*, a 347-page report drawn from firsthand interviews, court records, and records of guards' disciplinary hearings, is astonishing in the graphic detail provided of everyday experiences of women in state prisons. It revealed that the extent of correctional officer-on-inmate abuse behind the closed doors of prisons is staggering.[48]

There continues to be extensive litigation concerning the sexual mistreatment of female inmates. Scandals have erupted in California, Georgia, Hawaii, Ohio, Louisiana, Michigan, Tennessee, New York, and New Mexico.[49] Most of them came to light only because of publicity surrounding legal suits. For example, in 2002, a jury awarded $15.4 million to 10 current and former prisoners at

HUMAN RIGHTS WATCH An international nongovernmental organization that is concerned with the rights of individuals, such as prisoners.

- The unit supervisor provides overall direction of the treatment that takes place in the unit; the unit supervisor is also responsible for maintaining open communication with staff outside the unit.

- The assistant unit supervisor has his or her caseload and also supervises other correctional counselors assigned to the unit.

- The correctional counselor is expected to use personal relationships, planned experiences, and peer-group interactions to meet the program objectives developed for each inmate.

Qualifications and Required Education

This position generally requires a college education, and supervisory counseling positions sometimes require an M.A. degree. Counselors are expected to have the following: knowledge of individual and group counseling techniques; knowledge of the goals and objectives of correctional treatment services; knowledge of the operations of a correctional facility; the ability to deal with persons with antisocial attitudes and to win their confidence; the ability to communicate effectively with others; and the ability to maintain records, prepare reports, and compose correspondence related to their jobs.

Job Outlook

With the continued construction of new prisons, as well as the promotions, retirements, and resignations of present correctional counselors, there will be a continuous need for people to fill correctional counselor positions in both men's and women's prisons.

Earnings and Benefits

The median salary for counselors with one to four years experience is $33,000; for those with five to nine years experience, $41,430; for those with 10 to 19 years experience, $45,130; and for those with 20 years or more experience, $78,000.

Sources: PayScale, www.payscale.com/research/US/Job=Correctional_counselor/Salary; Federal Bureau of Prisons, www.bop.gov; and Michigan Civil Service Commission, job specification for prison counselor, www.michigan.gov/mdcs (all sites accessed March 2, 2012).

Michigan's Robert Scott Correctional Facility for sexual abuse by male guards.[50] This sad story of sexual abuse was repeated a number of times in court filings related to a 2003 suit against individual New York Department of Corrections correctional officers, officials, and supervisors.[51]

Corrections Staff in Women's Prisons

Correctional administrators, correctional counselors and case workers, and women and men correctional officers are three categories of staff who have contact with inmates. Women have been superintendents of women's prisons since late in the nineteenth century, but today increasing numbers of women are seeking for and being appointed wardens of men's prisons.

The **correctional counselor** is the basic treatment officer in many adult correctional institutions. Female correctional counselors serve several functions in women's and men's prisons, as the Careers in Corrections box identifies.

CORRECTIONAL COUNSELOR The chief treatment officer in many correctional institutions, both male and female.

Female institutions are less violent than male correctional facilities. And while educational and vocational programs are sometimes lacking, some institutions have adopted innovative treatment methodologies. Here, female prison inmates at the Travis County Jail in Texas participate in a weekly meditation and yoga class as part of a drug-and-alcohol rehab program.

© Joshua Lutz/Redux

LO6 PROFESSIONAL-ISM IN WOMEN'S PRISONS

There is a growing movement to make the staff in women's prisons more competent and professional. What defines professionalism in a women's prison?

- A commitment to develop programming for inmates that deals with their present and helps them plan for the future

- A desire to treat inmates with dignity and respect

- A wide commitment to engage staff in prison management and operations

- A refusal to accept abusive treatment from staff toward inmates

- A determination to provide a safe environment for both inmates and staff

- A realization that staff training is a necessary aspect of a humane prison

- A desire to model positive behavior, both within and outside of the prison

- A willingness to pursue accreditation of their facility

Exhibit 8.4 examines the career of Elaine A. Lord, former superintendent of the Bedford Hills Correctional Facility in Bedford, New York, and articulates how she made a difference at this facility.

EXHIBIT 8.4 The Career of Elaine A. Lord

Elaine A. Lord began her career with the New York State Department of Correctional Services in 1975. In 1982, she was appointed deputy superintendent of program services at the Bedford Hills Correctional Facility, New York's only maximum-security facility for women. In July 1984, she was named superintendent of Bedford Hills and held this position until her retirement in March 2004. Bedford Hills housed approximately 820 inmates; sentences ranged from eight years to life. For this population, she and her staff had to think creatively and be willing to try new things in order to develop programs that were meaningful for women serving long sentences, often for committing violent crimes—women who had left families, especially children, behind.

In an interview, Lord said, "Our facility is known for its programs, and that is something we are very proud of. We get the inmates involved in the development of these programs, with some outside help. In this way, the inmates feel empowered and responsible for the success of the program, but even more important, I believe that it is the inmates who are in the best position to recognize and articulate the need for a particular program. The model for this philosophy came from Sister Elaine Roulette, a Sister of St. Joseph who began working at the prison 30 years ago and who has earned international recognition for her compassion and insight into the needs of incarcerated women and their children."

(Continued)

EXHIBIT 8.4 *(Continued)*

Lord continued: "The inmates conceive of a program and then connect with a civilian professional in that area: sometimes a college professor, a retired social worker, a professional in a particular field—people find us or we find them. As word of our program spreads, it becomes easier to find the support we need. Some of the women are now able to develop programs on their own, without outside help, and they serve as well as mentors to other women who are trying to develop programs. From a 'correctional' point of view, if we want the women to make proper choices, they really have to have the opportunity to do so in a meaningful way. The women have developed programs to deal with issues such as helping teens cope with prison life, parenting from a distance, AIDS counseling and education, an AIDS walk-a-thon, bringing college back into the facility, family violence, spiritual and religious enrichment, peer-tutoring for ABE and GED, and pre- and postnatal workshops."

She concludes: "I think the women at Bedford Hills have taught me and the other members of the staff that prison is not just about punishment; it can be about transformation as well. I have learned that if I do the best I can, if I continue to see the women as complex human beings who have much to offer themselves, each other, and society, if we can talk and commiserate and laugh, then we have formed a community. We have formed a place where the women can choose to change and grow—a safe place—away from the drugs and the abuse and the family violence and the poverty that often influenced their choices. Most of the women in Bedford Hills will leave some day. When they leave, my hope for them, and the thing that I work so hard to accomplish, is that they have gained something valuable as a result of having been here—a sense of self, a sense of worth, a sense of dignity, a sense that they can do something on the outside as a result of what they learned in prison. And most important of all, I want them to never, ever return to this place."

Source: Interviewed in 2002; and Commission on Safety and Abuse in America's Prisons, www.prisoncommission.org/public_hearing_3_witness_lord.asp (accessed March 2, 2012).

SUMMARY

LO1 ▶ Identify the main reason for the rise of the imprisonment of women

The female prison population is now more than 100,000 and is increasing at a faster pace than the male population. The rise in female imprisonment is traced largely to the mandatory harsh minimum sentences for drug possession and dealing.

LO2 ▶ Identify the findings of the classic studies of social structure in women's prisons

Classic studies indicated that the social structure in women's prisons included both make-believe families and same-sex relationship models. In recent decades, it appears that there is less evidence of make-believe families in women's prisons.

LO3 ▶ Discuss the contemporary studies of women doing time in prison

These studies examine daily experiences of women in prison:

- Some studies continue to find the existence of same-sex relations in women's prisons.

- Barbara Owen focuses on how women deal with the culture of prison life, especially those who are committed to a criminal identity.

- Pogrebin and Dodge discovered that an important aspect of prison life was dealing with fear and violence.

- Kruttschnitt and Gartner looked at how women negotiate or cope with prison life in one prison, and in another more secure women's prison, they examined how women deal with a facility which has as its dominant concern maintaining order and security, rather than helping inmates. They also considered how the increased control and security has affected how women cope with prison life.

LO4 ▶ Understand that providing sufficient programs for incarcerated women with children is critical

Motherhood in prison represents a serious issue for inmate mothers and a daunting challenge for correctional administrators. There are several

L05 Identify the serious issues of health care in women's prisons

These issues include inadequate reproductive care, shackling during pregnancy, lack of substance abuse treatment, lack of mental health services, failure to refer seriously ill inmates for treatment, delays in treatment, lack of qualified personnel and resources, and use of nonmedical staff. Adequate prison health care poses a difficult challenge because of rising costs, but nonetheless,

 L06 Identify why professionalism is important in women's prisons

Professionalism in a women's prison includes a desire to treat inmates with dignity and respect, a goal of maintaining a safe and humane environment for inmates, a refusal to be involved with abusive treatment toward inmates or corruption in any form, and a commitment to develop programming for inmates that will help them deal with the present and plan for the future.

Key Terms

Elizabeth Fry, 188
Ward and Kassebaum, 192
butch, 192
femme, 192

Giallombardo, 192
fictive families, 192
Hefferman, 193
kinship networks, 193

the mix, 194
Human Rights Watch, 200
correctional counselor, 201

 ## Critical Thinking Questions

1. Women are committing more crimes, but the real increase shows up in drug-related crimes. Why do you think that women are involved in more drug-related crimes now than in the past?

2. The typical female offender has children. How does motherhood affect her doing time?

3. "Women's inmate society establishes a substitute group in which women can identify or construct family patterns similar to those in the free world." Describe the family structure in a women's prison.

4. Sexual abuse of inmates is a problem in some women's prisons. What can be done about it?

5. How do the subcultures of men's and women's prisons differ?

6. Do you support a separate but equal women's criminal justice system? Why or why not?

 ## Thinking Like a Corrections Professional

You are a superintendent of a women's prison, and you have become familiar with the work of Elaine A. Lord while she was superintendent of the Bedford Hills Correctional Facility. You would like to develop in your facility the type of programming that is present at Bedford Hills. What steps would you take to accomplish this? What would you do first, second, and so forth? In thinking this out, be certain to include involvement of staff, inmates, and funding.

 ## Career Destinations

Interested in a career as a substance abuse counselor in a women's prison? This site describes substance abuse treatment of women in prison:
www.flahec.org/hlthcareers/subst.htm

Want to work with female inmates, helping them to get a second chance? The Women's Prison Association is a service and advocacy organization committed to helping women with criminal

justice histories realize new possibilities for themselves and their families:
www.wpaonline.org

While working in a women's institution you might be called upon to design a program to improve safety in order to create a more positive correctional climate. Check out:
www.ncjrs.gov/pdffiles1/nij/grants/225342.pdf

Notes

1. Abby Luby, Record Review, 2003, http://abbylu.com/pdfs/PROFILES/Kathy%20 Boudin%27s%20Impact.pdf (accessed March 1, 2012). See also articles on Kathy Boudin in the *New York Times*, May 18, 2003.
2. Ibid.
3. Faculty web page for the Columbia University School of Social Work, where Boudin is an adjunct assistant professor; last updated July 1, 2009.
4. Nicole Hahn Rafter, *Partial Justice* (New Brunswick, NJ: Transaction Books, 1990), pp. 181–182.
5. American Friends Service Committee, *Struggle for Justice: Report on Crime and Justice in America* (New York: Hill & Wang, 1971), p. 16.
6. Ibid.
7. For a history of women's prisons, see Samuel Walker, *Popular Justice: A History of American Criminal Justice* (New York: Oxford University Press, 1980).
8. American Civil Liberties Union, *Caught in the Net: The Impact of Drug Policies on Women and Families*, March 15, 2005, www.aclu.org/drug-law-reform/caught-net-impact-drug-policies-women-and-families (accessed March 1, 2012).
9. Ibid.
10. Polly Radosh, "Reflections on Women's Crime and Mothers in Prison: A Peacemaking Approach," *Crime and Delinquency* 48 (2002): 300–316.
11. Meda Chesney-Lind, "Patriarchy, Prisons, and Jails: A Critical Look at Trends in Women's Incarceration," paper presented at the International Feminist Conference on Women, Law, and Social Control, Mont Gabriel, Quebec, Canada, July 1991.
12. Seena Fazel and John Danesh, "Serious Mental Disorder in 23,000 Prisoners: A Systematic Review of 62 Surveys," *Lancet* 359 (2002): 545–561.
13. Rebecca Jackson, Richard Rogers, Craig Neuman, and Paul Lambert, "Psychopathy in Female Offenders: An Investigation of Its Underlying Dimensions," *Criminal Justice and Behavior* 29 (2002): 692–705.
14. Fazel and Danesh, "Serious Mental Disorder in 23,000 Prisoners."
15. Bureau of Justice Statistics, *Women Offenders* (Washington, DC: U.S. Department of Justice, 2000).
16. Meda Chesney-Lind and Lisa Pasko, *The Female Offender: Girls, Women, and Crime*, 2nd ed. (Newbury Park, CA: Sage Publications, 2004).
17. Gary Michael McClelland, Linda Teplin, Karen Abram, and Naomi Jacobs, "HIV and AIDS Risk Behaviors Among Female Jail Detainees: Implications for Public Health Policy," *American Journal of Public Health* 92 (2002): 818–826.
18. Christine Grella and Lisa Greenwell, "Correlates of Parental Status and Attitudes Toward Parenting Among Substance-Abusing Women Offenders," *Prison Journal* 86 (2006): 89–113.
19. Lee Ann Slocum, Sally Simpson, and Douglas Smith, "Strained Lives and Crime: Examining Intra-Individual Variation in Strain and Offending in a Sample of Incarcerated Women," *Criminology* 43 (2005): 1067–1110.
20. David A. Ward and Gene Kassebaum, *Women's Prisons and Social Structure* (Chicago: Anderson, 1965); Rose Giallombardo, *Society of Women: A Study of a Women's Prison* (New York: Wiley, 1966); Esther Hefferman, *Making It in Prison: The Square, the Cool, and the Life* (New York: Wiley, 1972).
21. K. Faith, *Unruly Women: The Politics of Confinement and Resistance* (Vancouver, BC, Canada: Press Gang Publishing, 2003); Craig J. Forsyth, Rhonda D. Evans, and D. Buck Foster, "An Analysis of Inmate Explanations for Lesbian Relationships in Prison," *International Journal of Sociology of the Family* 30 (2002): 66–77; C. Hensley, R. Tewksbury, and M. Koscheski, "Inmate-to-Inmate Sexual Coercion in a Prison for Women," *Journal of Offender Rehabilitation* 37 (2002): 77–87; and Theresa A. Severance, "The Prison Lesbian Revisited," *Journal of Gay and Lesbian Social Services* 17 (2004): 39–57.
22. Barbara Owen, "In the Mix: Struggle and Survival in a Women's Prison (Albany: State University of New York Press, 1998), pp. 1–2.
23. Mark Pogrebin and Mary Dodge, "Women's Accounts of Their Prison Experiences: A Retrospective View of Their Subjective Realities," *Journal of Criminal Justice* 29 (2001): 531–541.
24. Robert Ross and Hugh McKay, *Self-Mutilation* (Lexington, MA: Lexington Books, 1979).
25. Candace Kruttschnitt and Rosemary Gartner, *Marking Time in the Golden State: Women's Imprisonment in California* (Cambridge, UK: Cambridge University Press, 2005).
26. Ibid., p. 118.
27. Ibid., p. 92.
28. Ibid., pp. 133–134.
29. Kimberly R. Greer, "The Changing Nature of Interpersonal Relationships in a Women's Prison," *Prison Journal* 80 (December 2000): 442–468.
30. Kruttschnitt and Gartner, *Marking Time in the Golden State*, pp. 101, 105, and 107.
31. Family Strengthening Policy Center, "Supporting Families with Incarcerated Parents," (Washington, DC: National Human Services Assembly, 2005), p. 2. See also Jacquelyn L. Sandifer, "Evaluating the Efficacy of a Parenting Program for Incarcerated Mothers," *Prison Journal* 88 (2008): 423–445.
32. Craig J. Forsyth, "Pondering the Discourse of Prison Mamas: A Research Note," *Deviant Behavior: An Interdisciplinary Journal* 24 (2003): 269–280.
33. Phyllis E. Berry and Helen M. Eigenberg, "Role Strain and Incarcerated Mothers: Understanding the Process of Mothering," *Women and Criminal Justice* 15 (2003): 101.
34. Dorothy S. Rutz, "The Increase in Incarcerations Among Women and Its Impact on the Grandmother Caregiver: Some Racial Considerations," *Journal of Sociology and Social Welfare* 29 (September 2002): 179–197.
35. Joycelyn M. Baunach, "Parenting Programs in Women's Prisons," *Women and Criminal Justice* 14 (2002): 131–140.
36. Ibid.
37. Kristine Siefert and Sheryl Pimlott, "Improving Pregnancy Outcome During Imprisonment: A Model Residential Care Program," *Social Work* 46 (April 2001): 125–134.
38. For a description of these programs, see Katherine Stuart van Wormer and Clemens Bartollas, *Women and the Criminal Justice System* (Boston: Allyn & Bacon, 2007), pp. 164–165.
39. British Broadcasting Company (BBC), "Mothers in Prison," *Woman's Hour*, November 20, 2001.
40. General Accounting Office, *Women in Prison: Issues and Challenges Confronting U.S. Correctional Systems* (Washington, DC: U.S. Department of Justice, 1999).
41. Ibid.
42. Amnesty International, www.amnestyusa.org/our-work/issues/women-s-rights/violence-against-women?id=1108288 (accessed March 1, 2012).
43. Frank D. Russo, "California Senate Vote Today on $7 Billion Prison Health Care Construction Bill," *California Progress Report*, www.californiaprogressreport.com/site/california-senate-vote-today-7-billion-prison-health-care-construction-bill (accessed March 1, 2012).
44. See B. Stein, "Life in Prison: Sexual Abuse," *Progressive* (July 1996): 23–24. See also Nina Siegal, "Stopping Abuse in Prison," *Progressive* (April 2000): 31–33.
45. Stein, "Life in Prison: Sexual Abuse," p. 24.
46. *New York Times*, November 14, 1992, pp. 1, 7. For more sexual abuse cases, see United States District Court for the Eastern District of Wisconsin, 2008 U.S. Dist. Lexis 8488 (January 24, 2008, Decided).
47. International Women's Day, 2001. For examinations of the seriousness of this issue, see Cathy McCaniels-Wilson and Joanne Belknap, "The Extensive Sexual Violation and Sexual Abuse Histories of Incarcerated Women," *Violence Against Women* 14 (2008): 1090–1127; and Ashley G. Blackburn, Janet L. Mullings, and James W. Marquart, "Sexual Assault in Prison and Beyond: Toward an Understanding of Lifetime Sexual Assault Among Incarcerated Women," *Prison Journal* 88 (2008): 351–377.
48. Human Rights Watch, Women's Rights Project, All Too Familiar: Sexual Abuse of Women in U.S. State Prisons (New York: Human Rights Watch, 1996).
49. Chesney-Lind, *The Female Offender*. Iowa is another state in which prison officials have been sued. For information on these six suits, see William Petroski, "Sex in Prisons Costs Tax Payers," *Des Moines Sunday Register*, May 21, 2000, pp. 1A, 5A.
50. Tina Lam, "Jury Awards Women $15.4 Million for Sexual Abuse in Prison," *Detroit Free Press*, www.usatoday.com/news/nation/2008-02-02-prison-abuse_N.htm (accessed March 1, 2012).
51. Kari Lyderson, "Red Tape Lets Guards Rape Women Prisoners, Suit Argues," *New Standard*, www.november.org/stayinfo/breaking06/RapeSuit.html (accessed March 1, 2012).

In 1987, Michael Morton was convicted of murder, accused of killing his wife Christine. On October 4, 2011, Michael Morton walked out of a Williamson County (Texas) courtroom a free man after his murder conviction was overturned because of DNA evidence that another man had actually killed his wife. A bandana found at the scene of another murder contained the blood of Christine Morton and Mark A. Norwood, a known felon who lived in the area and who is now under investigation for both crimes. Michael Morton served nearly 25 years in prison before being released.

"Mr. Morton was the victim of serious prosecutorial misconduct that caused him to lose 25 years of his life and completely ripped apart his family. Perhaps even more tragically, we now know that another murder might have been prevented if law enforcement had continued its investigation rather than building a false case against Mr. Morton," said Barry Scheck, co-director of the Innocence Project, a nonprofit organization that takes on cases such as Morton's. "This tragic miscarriage of justice must be formally investigated and steps must be taken to hold police and prosecutors accountable."[1]

Morton would have never been convicted if the prosecution had turned over as required evidence pointing to his innocence. Among the evidence that was kept from the defense:

■ A statement by the victim's mother, who told police that the couple's 3-year-old child witnessed the murder and provided a chilling account of watching a man who was not his father beat Christine to death.

■ A report that a neighbor had on several occasions observed a man park a green van on the street behind the Morton's house, then get out and walk into the wooded area off the road.

■ A report that a check made out to Christine Morton by a man named John B. Cross was cashed with Christine's forged signature nine days after her murder.[2]

The Morton case is one of many that show that courts can make a mistake and innocent individuals are routinely sentenced to long terms in prison or even given the death penalty. It follows then that many prison inmates are not actually guilty of the crimes that put them behind bars. They would be at a significant legal disadvantage if their civil rights were denied. If prison inmates were unable to obtain legal representation or denied the right to bring their case to court, people like Michael Morton would never be able to earn their freedom.

AP Photo/*The Daily Texan*, Rebeca Rodriguez

Michael Morton waves to his parents, Bill and Patricia Morton, before his hearing on October 4, 2011, in Georgetown, Texas. Morton, who spent nearly 25 years in prison for his wife's murder, walked free after DNA tests showed another man was responsible. His attorneys say prosecutors and investigators kept evidence from the defense that would have helped acquit him at his trial.

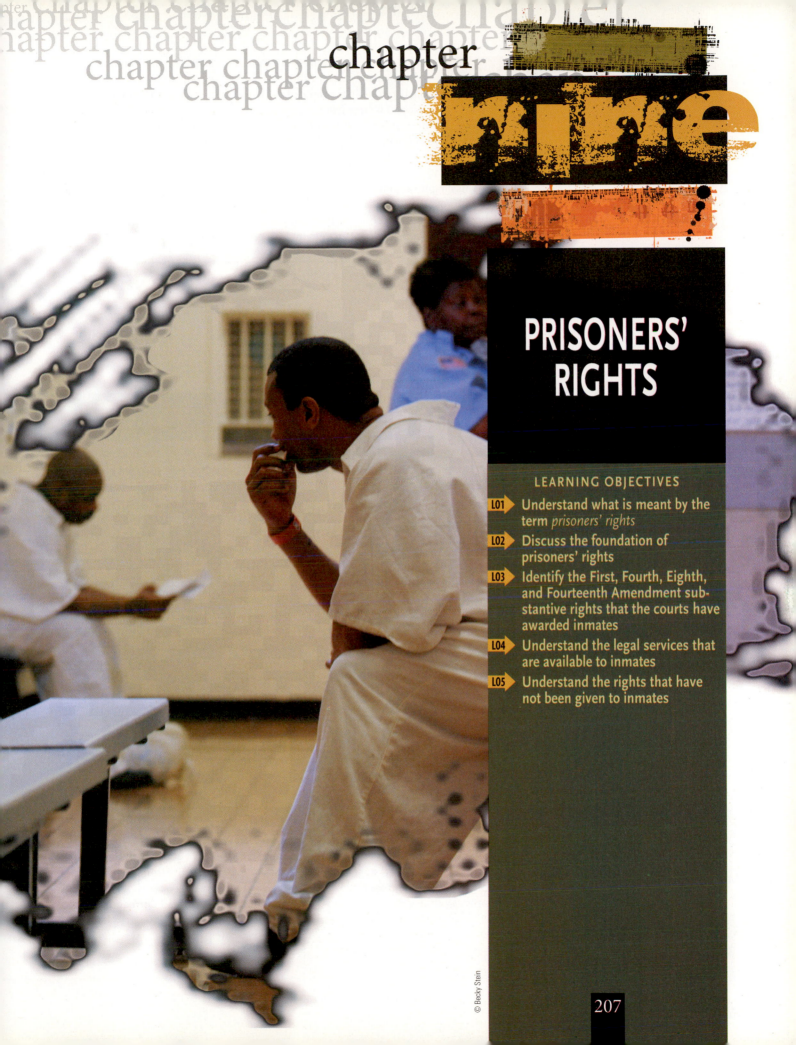

nine

PRISONERS' RIGHTS

LEARNING OBJECTIVES

L01 ▸ Understand what is meant by the term *prisoners' rights*

L02 ▸ Discuss the foundation of prisoners' rights

L03 ▸ Identify the First, Fourth, Eighth, and Fourteenth Amendment substantive rights that the courts have awarded inmates

L04 ▸ Understand the legal services that are available to inmates

L05 ▸ Understand the rights that have not been given to inmates

© Becky Stein

Proving innocence is only one aspect of the need for maintaining civil rights behind prison walls. Inmates also want to hold on to their constitutionally guaranteed rights, such as the right to practice religion and be free from cruel and unusual punishment while confined in a correctional facility. Over the past 50 years, the nation's court system has dealt with these issues and others. Case law has defined the rights of prisoners, in some instances expanding their ability to seek redress in the courts while in others restricting their rights and privileges.

This chapter examines the rights of convicted prisoners in some detail. In the Voices Across the Profession feature, Alvin J. Bronstein, the former director of the National Prison Project of the American Civil Liberties Union, puts the gains and losses of the prisoners' rights movement into perspective.

 ## WHAT DO WE MEAN BY PRISONERS' RIGHTS?

A *right* is a claim by an individual or group of individuals that another individual, a corporation, or the state has a duty to fulfill. Philosophers and jurists have written volumes about the source of rights. Legal positivists claim that the only rights

 # ACROSS the PROFESSION

"There is hope with a new generation of correctional administrators who are a cut above a lot of correctional administrators from the past in terms of inmates' concerns."

ALVIN J. BRONSTEIN,
DIRECTOR EMERITUS OF THE
NATIONAL PRISON PROJECT OF THE
AMERICAN CIVIL LIBERTIES UNION

Unfortunately, the gains of the 1960s, 1970s, and 1980s in terms of prisoners' rights were largely replaced by the Prison Litigation Reform Act of 1996. I stepped down from the Prison Project in January of 1996, and the Congress celebrated my departure by passing the Prison Litigation Reform Act in May of 1996. It was the result of a whole bunch of distortions by the National Association of Attorneys General, who published a top 10 list of all those cases that they claimed were causing problems. For example, in one of these cases they claimed that the prisoner was suing because he ordered creamy peanut butter from the commissary and got regular peanut butter. In fact, the peanut butter was not the real issue, but was mentioned as a minor example of the prison's inefficiency in a complaint that also described massive overcrowding and terrible medical care, which they ignored. Without any hearings, Congress passed it as a last minute amendment to the commerce department's budget.

It has made it very difficult for prisoners' litigation projects because of the onerous terms and exhaustion requirements of the act, including difficulties in filing and getting attorneys. Attorneys would no longer be getting fees at market rate, and it has been harder to get them involved. In contrast, I can remember in 1987 we had pending lawsuits in 27 states—major cases involving entire state systems, such as Tennessee, Alabama, Colorado, New Mexico, Maine, and Rhode Island. We had seven lawyers in our office, and we could not run around the country and take care of these cases without competent local lawyers being willing to help us.

The result of this is that, because of the Prison Litigation Reform Act, many things have gone back, perhaps not where they were, but there has been regression. Instead of having nineteenth-century prisons, we now have some nasty twentieth-century prisons. There continues to be a strong movement within the National Association of Attorneys General to keep the Prison Litigation Reform Act the way it is.

We also feel that there is hope with a new generation of correctional administrators who are a cut above a lot of correctional administrators from the past in terms of inmates' concerns. It is also helpful that the American Correctional Association is more sensitive than it has been to inmates' concerns and rights.

Source: Interviewed in 2008.

anyone possesses are those that are conferred by law[3]; others disagree, asserting that all human beings possess "natural" rights—from which legal rights are derived—necessary for survival in human society.[4] According to this view, laws that are inconsistent with natural rights cannot and should not survive. Examples would be the race laws of Nazi Germany and the apartheid laws of South Africa.

One reason that it is difficult to define inmate rights is because there is actually more than one view on the topic.

- *Legalistic/due process view.* Convicted felons do not have rights other than those conferred on them by law. In the United States, those rights are derived by the courts from the Constitution of the United States, from the state constitutions, and from the laws that Congress and the state legislatures enact. Inmates are entitled to due process of the law even in confinement.

- *Crime control view.* Inmates are criminals who have harmed others and must be made to pay for their misdeeds. Convicted criminals have, by definition, forfeited their right to freedom and liberty. The suffering they endure in confinement serves to deter future criminal behaviors. The fewer rights inmates have, the greater the deterrent effect of punishment.

- *Humanistic view.* Inmates are humans who have made mistakes and are being punished. Prisons are places of punishment, but they should not be punishing. If inmates are given the same rights and privileges as any citizen, their anger and resentment toward society will diminish, thereby aiding the rehabilitation process.

Considering these opposing viewpoints, in this chapter we use the following definition, which is a combination of humanistic and legalistic/due process, when we refer to inmate rights: Inmates must be given all the rights conferred on them by law, including due process rights, but their status as convicted felons has caused them to lose certain rights that free citizens have, including freedom and the ability to come and go as they wish.

 L02

FOUNDATIONS OF PRISONERS' RIGHTS LAW

The U.S. Constitution is the principal source of prisoners' rights, but federal and state statutes, legal precedents, federal civil rights lawsuits, and writs of *habeas corpus* are also important sources of prisoners' rights.

U.S. Constitution

Substantive criminal law primarily defines crimes, but the law of criminal procedure consists of the rules and procedures that govern the pretrial processing of criminal suspects and the conduct of criminal trials. The body of the Constitution and the first 10 amendments (added to the Constitution on December 15, 1791, and known as the **Bill of Rights**) are the main sources of the procedural law. The purpose of these amendments was to prevent the government from usurping citizens' personal freedoms. The U.S. Supreme Court's interpretation of these amendments has served as the basis for the creation of legal rights of the accused.

Statutes

States may award rights to prisoners beyond those granted by the U.S. Constitution or state constitution. **Statutes** tend to be written in more specific terms than are the U.S. Constitution or state constitutions. For example, the U.S. Supreme Court was asked in 1998 whether the Americans with Disability Act applied to state prisoners.

BILL OF RIGHTS The name given to the first 10 amendments to the U.S. Constitution, which are looked upon as fundamentally important in the processing of criminal defendants. Exhibit 9.1 sets out the most important amendments affecting inmates' rights.

STATUTES States may award rights to prisoners beyond those granted by the U.S. Constitution or state constitution.

EXHIBIT 9.1 Amendments to the Constitution that Affect Inmates' Rights

- The *First Amendment* grants freedom of religion, speech, the press, and assembly.

- The *Fourth Amendment* bars illegal "searches and seizures," a right especially important for the criminal justice system because it means that police officers cannot indiscriminately use their authority to investigate possible crime or arrest a suspect.

- The *Fifth Amendment* limits the admissibility of confessions that have been obtained unfairly. In the landmark case of *Miranda v. Arizona*, the Supreme Court held that a person accused of a crime has the right to refuse to answer questions when placed in police custody.[5]

- The *Sixth Amendment* guarantees a defendant the right to a speedy and public trial by an impartial jury, the right to be informed of the nature of the charges, and the right to confront any prosecution witnesses. It also contains the right of a defendant to be represented by an attorney, a privilege that has been extended to numerous stages of the criminal justice process, including pretrial custody, identification and lineup procedures, preliminary hearings, submission of a guilty plea, trial, sentencing, and postconviction appeal.

- The *Eighth Amendment* bars excessive bail or excessive fines imposed, as well as cruel and unusual punishment inflicted. This prohibition protects both the accused and convicted offenders from actions regarded as unacceptable by a civilized society, including corporal punishment and torture.

- The *Fourteenth Amendment* is the vehicle used by the courts to apply the protection of the Bill of Rights to the states. It affirms that no state may "deprive any person of life, liberty, or property, without due process of law."

In a unanimous decision the Court ruled that the statute's language included state prisoners.[6] The U.S. Congress is responsible for statutes dealing with problems concerning the entire nation. Congress passes laws defining federal crimes and punishments, authorizes programs in terms of criminal justice policies, and allocates funds for federal criminal justice agencies. Each state legislature enacts laws that govern the acts of that state and the individuals within that jurisdiction. In addition, state legislatures appropriate funds for state agencies, including corrections.

Legal Precedents

Previous court decisions, called **case law**, also affect court decisions. Judges create law or modify existing law when they make a decision in a particular case. They are guided by the Constitution and its Bill of Rights, state and federal statutes, and decisions in other cases. The precedent on an issue represents the collective body of judicial principles that a court considers when interpreting the law. Judges consider the principles involved in former decisions and apply them to the cases being decided. When a precedent establishes an important principle, or represents a change or new law, that precedent is known as a **landmark decision**. For example, in the important case *Holt v. Sarver*, federal courts intervened in the state prison system of Arkansas and addressed complaints of physical abuse by guards and inmate trustees on members of the general inmate population.[7] Trustees had been put in charge of fellow inmates and ruled with an iron hand. The Court found their abuse a violation of the Eighth Amendment's prohibition against cruel and unusual punishment. Following this decision, similar litigation was introduced in many other states, all but ending the trustee system in U.S. prisons.

Federal Civil Rights Lawsuits

Civil rights are rights that have been guaranteed and protected by the government. These laws are a protection against the denial of an individual's civil rights based on race, sex, age, religion, national origin, physical limitation, or previous condition of servitude. Civil rights lawsuits have covered issues such as public education, public housing, employment, voting, access to public facilities, and corrections. The U.S. Supreme Court has played a significant role in increasing government protections of civil rights to prisoners, including the right to sue people whom they feel violated their rights during trial. For example, in one recent case, two Mississippi men wrongfully sent to prison filed federal lawsuits against the medical experts who testified the men left bite marks on two slain children.[8]

Writ of *Habeas Corpus*

Habeas corpus represents the principal means by which state inmates attack the constitutionality of their convictions in federal courts. *Habeas corpus* has been called "the great writ of liberty." It is the means to show that individuals have the

CASE LAW The body of judicial precedent that is built on legal reasoning and previous interpretations of statutory laws.

LANDMARK DECISION When a precedent establishes an important principle, or represents a change or new law.

HABEAS CORPUS A Latin expression meaning "you have the body." A writ of *habeas corpus* brings a person before a court or judge to determine the legality of his or her restraint in custody.

right to be free from arbitrary arrests. *Habeas corpus* permits a federal judge to find a due process violation sufficient enough to overturn the judgment of numerous state judges and 12 jurors. Today, critics charge that *habeas corpus* often releases the convicted on technical principles of law, rather than on grounds of innocence or even for reasons of clemency. The Antiterrorism and Effective Death Penalty Act of 1996 greatly restricts the power of federal judges to award relief to state prisoners who file two or more *habeas corpus* applications. If an inmate asserts a claim that has been previously presented in a federal *habeas corpus* petition, the claim must be dismissed in all cases. See Figure 9.1 for the trends in habeas corpus petitions filed in U.S. District Court.

Petitions filed

FIGURE 9.1 Trends in *Habeas Corpus* Petitions Filed in U.S. District Court

Sources: John Scalla, *Prisoners Petitions Filed in U.S. District Courts, 2000, with Trends, 1980–2000* (Government Printing Office: Bureau of Justice Statistics, 2002); *Sourcebook of Criminal Justice Statistics* online, www.albany.edu/sourcebook/ (accessed March 28, 2012).

DEVELOPING PRISONERS' RIGHTS

While the above sources of law are the basis of prisoners' rights, they were not automatically applied or adopted. Quite the opposite. Prior to 1960, it was generally accepted that a convicted individual forfeited all rights not expressly granted by statutory law or correctional policy. Inmates were considered to be *civilly dead*. Convicted offenders, reasoned the U.S. Supreme Court, should expect to be penalized for their misdeeds and part of their punishment was the loss of freedoms ordinary citizens take for granted.

An examination of judges' actions over the years makes it possible to distinguish three phases of the prisoners' rights movement: (1) the convicted felon as-slave-of-the-state phase, (2) the high-water mark of the prisoners' rights movement, and (3) the crime control response of the federal and state courts

Convicted Felons as Slaves of the State

For most of the history of the United States, the prisoner has been a slave of state corrections—that is, prisoners lost all their rights when sentenced to prison. An 1871 case, *Ruffin v. the Commonwealth of Virginia*, expressed it this way: "[The prisoner] has, as a consequence of his crime, not only forfeited his liberty, but all his personal rights except those which the law in its humanity accords to him. He is for the time being the slave of the state."[9] One reason why prisoners lacked rights was that federal and state courts were reluctant to intervene in the administration of prisons unless the circumstances of a case clearly indicated a serious breach of the Eighth Amendment protection against cruel and unusual punishment. This judicial policy is referred to as the **hands-off doctrine**. The courts used three basic justifications for their neglect of prison conditions:

- Correctional administration was a technical matter best left to experts rather than to courts ill-equipped to make appropriate evaluations.

- Society as a whole was apathetic to what went on in prisons, and most individuals preferred not to associate with or know about offenders.

- Prisoners' complaints involved privileges rather than rights. Prisoners were considered to have fewer constitutional rights than other members of society.[10]

HANDS-OFF DOCTRINE The idea that persons sentenced to prison are not entitled to the same constitutional protections they enjoyed before conviction.

High-Water Mark of the Prisoners' Rights Movement

From 1966 to 1980, judges did a 180-degree reversal and became extensively involved in rulings on prisoners' rights. This about-face happened at the same time as the civil rights movement and the rise of the women's movement. It was a time of reform in American society, when social wrongs identified by African Americans, women, prisoners, and other groups were addressed.

In the 1960s, a number of cases held that the Black Muslim faith was an established religion and that members of the Nation of Islam were entitled to the same rights as members of other established religious groups. The federal courts have generally held that the religious rights granted to one religious group must be accorded to all such groups within a correctional facility.

Prisoners also sued to gain rights concerning personal correspondence, disciplinary procedures, and quality medical care. No area of correctional law has attracted as much attention as prisoner correspondence, largely because personal correspondence usually also involves an individual in the free community who was protected by the First Amendment. In an important case, *Procurier v. Martinez*, the U.S. Supreme Court ruled that "Censorship of prison mail works as a consequential restriction on the First and Fourteenth Amendment rights of those who are not prisoners."[11] What this meant is that citizens in the outside community have the right to correspond with prisoners without censorship of their mail. More recent court rulings have extended the rights of prisoner officials to censor inmate mail; see this section of First Amendment rights later in this chapter.

The high-water mark of the prisoners' rights movement was the *Wolff v. McDonnell* decision.[12] McDonnell, a prisoner, had filed a class-action suit against the state of Nebraska, claiming that its disciplinary procedures, especially those pertaining to the loss of "good time" (time subtracted from a sentence for good behavior), were unconstitutional.

The state court ruled that the defendant had not received the minimum requirements for disciplinary procedures. He petitioned the U.S. Supreme Court to restore the good time he had lost and to assess damages against corrections officials. The Supreme Court ruled that the state of Nebraska had properly enacted laws pertaining to the granting and revoking of good time. Nevertheless, the procedure used to revoke good time was found to be in violation of the due process rights granted in the Fourteenth Amendment.

A final major victory for inmates was in the area of medical rights. In *Estelle v. Gamble*, the court ruled that deliberate interference with serious medical needs constitutes cruel and unusual punishment.[13] Significantly, the suit also demonstrated that a complaint of system-wide deprivation of medical care receives a more sympathetic hearing than do complaints alleging inadequate medical care for an individual.

Crime Control Response by the Court

In the 1970s, court opinions shifted toward a more balanced position between prisoners' rights and legitimate institutional interest. This so-called **restraining hands doctrine** of the U.S. Supreme Court was obvious in four cases: *Baxter v. Palmigiano*,[14] *Enomato v. Clutchette*,[15] *Mecham v. Fano*,[16] and *Montanye v. Haymes*.[17]

Of these, the *Mecham v. Fano* decision most clearly expressed the restraining-hands doctrine because of its ruling that the prisoner is subject to the rules of the prison system: "Given a valid conviction, the criminal defendant has been constitutionally deprived of his liberty to the extent that the state may confine him and subject him to the rules of its prison system so long as conditions of confinement do not otherwise violate the Constitution."[18]

The 1981 *Rhodes v. Chapman* case, which held that the Southern Ohio Correctional Facility was not in violation of the Eighth Amendment for

RESTRAINING HANDS DOCTRINE
Supreme Court doctrine that gave correctional administrators freedom from excessive lower court interference.

double-celling inmates, was an even greater victory for prison officials.[19] In *Rhodes*, the Court ruled that double-bunking of prisoners was not cruel and unusual punishment. The Court ruled that conditions of confinement must not involve the wanton and unnecessary infliction of pain, nor may they be grossly disproportionate to the severity of the crime warranting imprisonment. But conditions that are not cruel and unusual under contemporary standards are not unconstitutional. To the extent such conditions are restrictive and even harsh, such as double-bunking, they are part of the penalty that criminals pay for their offenses against society.

Turner v. Safley remains the leading standard for evaluating prisoner free-expression claims.[20] Leonard Safley, a Missouri inmate, became involved with a female inmate at the Renz Correctional Institution in Cedar City, Missouri, which housed both male and female inmates at the time. After he was transferred to another prison, he planned to marry and wanted to correspond with his fiancée. Prison officials did not approve of the correspondence or the intended marriage, which in fact took place under court order. The case eventually landed in the U.S. Supreme Court, and while the Court struck down the restriction on inmate marriages, it ruled that inmate-to-inmate correspondence could be restricted. This case is significant because it changed the standard of review and made it possible for prison officials to make decisions on how to preserve the safety of the prison and inmates.[21]

In 1991, the Supreme Court ruled in the *Wilson v. Seiter* decision that uncomfortable conditions are not unconstitutional but are part of the penalty that inmates pay for committing crimes. The inmates claimed that the prison was too cold in the winter and too hot in the summer. The Court emphasized that to be in violation of constitutional rights, prison officials have to show deliberate indifference to inmates' basic needs. This became the standard for suits brought under Section 1983.[22]

LIMITING RIGHTS The inmate rights revolution soon clogged the appellate courts, prompting calls for limitations on inmate-sponsored litigation. The **Prison Litigation Reform Act (PLRA)**, which was passed by Congress and signed by President Clinton in 1996, limits the ability of prisoners to complain about conditions of confinement and to allege violation of their constitutional rights. The PLRA requires prisoners to either pay the full fee when filing a complaint ($150 in 1998) or to make an initial down payment followed by periodic installment payments. A three-strikes provision of this act prohibits an indigent prisoner from filing new lawsuits when the prisoner has previously filed frivolous or meritless claims. The PLRA appears to have had the greatest impact on civil rights prisoners, from whom the number of petitions filed dropped 20 percent from 1996 to 1997 and another 11 percent from 1997 to 1998.[23]

Inmates are also required to exhaust administrative remedies before they can take their complaints to the court system. The U.S. Supreme Court has decided two cases that define the scope of the exhaustion requirement—one dealing with a request for monetary relief and the other with allegations of excessive use of force. In *Booth v. Churner* (2001), a unanimous Court ruled that an inmate must go through the administrative processes before monetary relief could be granted.[24] In *Porter v. Nussle* (2002), a unanimous Court also made it clear that prisoners must use their grievance systems before going to court; there are no exceptions to this rule, even in situations where a grievance system cannot respond to an inmate's request for relief.[25]

SUBSTANTIVE RIGHTS OF INMATES

Through a slow process of legal review, the courts have granted inmates a number of **substantive rights** that have significantly influenced the entire correctional system. The most important of these rights are discussed in the following

PRISON LITIGATION REFORM ACT (PLRA) Passed by Congress in 1996, this act limits the ability of inmates to complain about conditions of confinement and to allege violations of their constitutional rights.

SUBSTANTIVE RIGHTS A right, such as life, liberty, or property, that is held to exist for its own sake and to constitute part of the legal order of society.

TIMELINE

Bell v. Wolfish
(1979)
Unannounced cell searches are necessary for security and order.

Theriault v. Carlson
(1977)
The First Amendment does not protect religions that are shams and are devoid of religious sincerity.

Thornburgh v. Abbott
(1989)
Restrictions on mailed publications to inmates are not allowed unless they meet a number of specified criteria.

Wolff v. McDonnell
(1974)
Disciplinary measures are necessary to lose "good time."

Whitley v. Albers
(1986)
A prisoner shot during a riot does not suffer cruel and unusual punishment if the action was taken to maintain discipline rather than to cause harm.

Wilson v. Seiter
(1991)
Prisoners must prove that cruel and unusual prison conditions exist because of the indifference of officials.

Procunier v. Martinez
(1974)
Censorship of inmate mail is subject to some restrictions.

Rhodes v. Chapman
(1981)
Double-celling is not unconstitutional.

1970	1975	1980	1985	1990	1995

Estelle v. Gamble
(1976)
Lack of proper medical care by the state is cruel and unusual punishment.

Bruscino v. Carlson
(1987)
Long-term lockdown is constitutional.

Lewis v. Casey
(1996)
Prisoners have a right of access to the courts, but this is different from the right of access to and use of a law library.

Meachum v. Fano
(1976)
Inmate is subject to the rules of the prison system.

Turner v. Safley
(1987)
Prison regulations that infringe on prisoners' rights are valid as long as they are reasonably related to the security and safety of the institution.

Ruiz v. Estelle
(1975)
Texas's correctional system is unconstitutional.

Hudson v. Palmer
(1984)
The Fourth Amendment does not apply to cell searches.

sections. Prisoners have sued to establish rights in four areas: (1) the right to physical security and the minimum conditions necessary to sustain life, (2) the right to receive their constitutionally guaranteed safeguards, (3) the right to challenge the legality of their convictions through the courts, and (4) the right to receive the benefit of reasonable standards and procedural protections. See the Timeline for the most significant U.S. Supreme Court decisions on prisoners' rights.

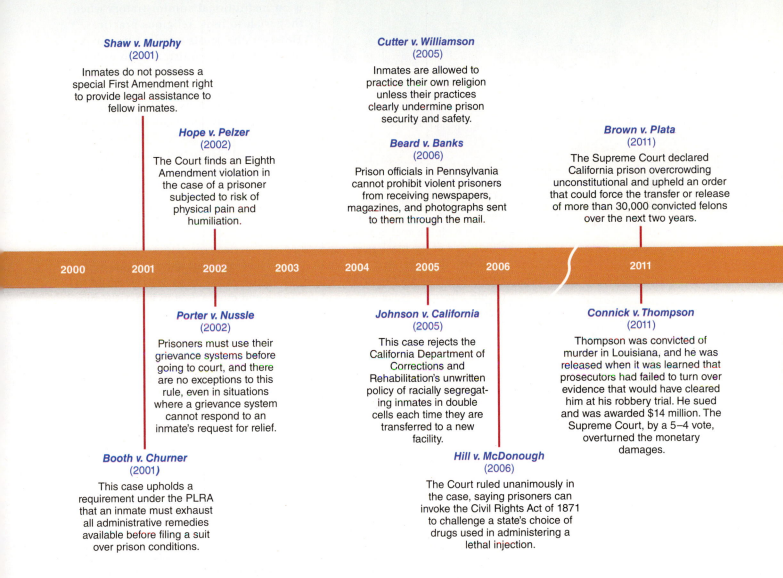

Shaw v. Murphy
(2001)
Inmates do not possess a special First Amendment right to provide legal assistance to fellow inmates.

Hope v. Pelzer
(2002)
The Court finds an Eighth Amendment violation in the case of a prisoner subjected to risk of physical pain and humiliation.

Cutter v. Williamson
(2005)
Inmates are allowed to practice their own religion unless their practices clearly undermine prison security and safety.

Beard v. Banks
(2006)
Prison officials in Pennsylvania cannot prohibit violent prisoners from receiving newspapers, magazines, and photographs sent to them through the mail.

Brown v. Plata
(2011)
The Supreme Court declared California prison overcrowding unconstitutional and upheld an order that could force the transfer or release of more than 30,000 convicted felons over the next two years.

2000 | 2001 | 2002 | 2003 | 2004 | 2005 | 2006 | 2011

Porter v. Nussle
(2002)
Prisoners must use their grievance systems before going to court, and there are no exceptions to this rule, even in situations where a grievance system cannot respond to an inmate's request for relief.

Johnson v. California
(2005)
This case rejects the California Department of Corrections and Rehabilitation's unwritten policy of racially segregating inmates in double cells each time they are transferred to a new facility.

Connick v. Thompson
(2011)
Thompson was convicted of murder in Louisiana, and he was released when it was learned that prosecutors had failed to turn over evidence that would have cleared him at his robbery trial. He sued and was awarded $14 million. The Supreme Court, by a 5–4 vote, overturned the monetary damages.

Booth v. Churner
(2001)
This case upholds a requirement under the PLRA that an inmate must exhaust all administrative remedies available before filing a suit over prison conditions.

Hill v. McDonough
(2006)
The Court ruled unanimously in the case, saying prisoners can invoke the Civil Rights Act of 1871 to challenge a state's choice of drugs used in administering a lethal injection.

First Amendment Rights

The rights of prisoners under the **First Amendment**—freedom of religion, speech, the press, and assembly—have been subject to significant legal challenges.

RELIGION Freedom of religion is a fundamental right guaranteed by the First Amendment. In general, the courts have ruled that inmates have the right to assemble and pray in the religion of their choice, but that religious symbols and practices that interfere with institutional security can be restricted.

FIRST AMENDMENT Congress shall make no law respecting an establishment of religion, or prohibiting the free exercise thereof; or abridging the freedom of speech, or of the press; or the right of the people peaceably to assemble, and to petition the government for a redress of grievances.

The courts have generally upheld freedom of religion behind bars, as long as religious practices do not interfere with institutional security. Here, a Jummah Congregational Prayer and Sermon session for Bilalian and African American Muslim inmates is led by the imam, Chaplain F. Rashid, in the Orange County (Florida) Jail.

Administrators can draw the line if religious needs become cumbersome or impossible to carry out for reason of cost or security. Granting special privileges can also be denied on the grounds that they will cause other groups to make similar demands. The federal courts have consistently held that the religious rights granted to one religious group must be accorded to all such groups within a correctional institution. Religious freedom has been looked upon as a preferred freedom; thus, the burden of proof is on institutional administrators when they wish to limit religious practices.[26] However, the courts usually have not required prison administrators to provide special diets, nor are they willing to allow the free exercise of religion to jeopardize the security and safety of the institution.

Religious rights resulted from lawsuits filed by smaller religious groups demanding that prison administrators give their parishioners the same religious rights granted members of established churches. Many of these legal actions were filed by the Nation of Islam, also known as the Black Muslims, an organization founded in Detroit by Wallace Fard Muhammad in 1930 with the goal of resurrecting the spiritual, mental, social, and economic conditions of the black men and women of America. The Nation of Islam also promoted the belief that worship of Allah will bring about universal peace. The courts eventually allowed Black Muslim ministers to conduct services and to permit Muslim prisoners access to the Koran and other religious materials. Subsequent rights were granted to other religious groups, such as Buddhists.[27]

While the Supreme Court recognized the right of inmates to practice their religion, the most important case on this issue limited absolute religious freedom and placed the security of an institution above the right to attend religious services. In *O'Lone v. Estate of Shabazz*, Muslim inmates in a minimum-security classification requested permission to attend services held in another section of the prison.[28] They argued that these services were essential to the practice of their religion. The request was denied on the basis of security. The Court upheld the denial, holding that "[w]hen a prison regulation impinges on inmates' constitutional rights, the regulation is valid if it is reasonably related to legitimate penological interests."[29]

In an important 2005 case, *Cutter v. Williamson*, the Court ruled that the Religious Land Use and Institutionalized Persons Act of 2000, which was intended to protect the rights of prisoners, is not an unconstitutional government promotion of religion.[30] Writing for the majority, Justice Ruth Bader Ginsburg stated, "It confers no privileged status on any particular religious sect, and singles out no bona fide faith for disadvantageous treatment." *Cutter* allows inmates to practice their own religion unless their practices clearly undermine prison security and safety.

RELIGIOUS FREEDOM RESTORATION ACT (RFRA)
In 1993, Congress passed the Religious Freedom Restoration Act (RFRA) as a reaction to concerns about restraining free exercise of religion. Congress rejected corrections officials' request to exclude jail and prison inmates from aspects of the act. Prior to this act, the inmate's exercise of religion could be restricted by prison officials if the restrictions were reasonably related to the maintenance of institutional security and discipline. The RFRA shifted the burden of proof from the prisoner to prison officials, who had to show that the restriction was necessary because of a compelling government interest.[31] In a 1997 case, the Supreme Court ruled that

the RFRA was unconstitutional except for the Federal Bureau of Prisons, which must still abide by the RFRA provisions.[32]

CENSORSHIP OF PERSONAL CORRESPONDENCE
Corrections officials have always felt that there is strong reason to place stringent limitations on inmate correspondence. Censorship of incoming mail is necessary, prison officials say, to detect contraband—including instruments of escape, pornographic materials, and narcotics or drugs. Censorship of outgoing correspondence is also necessary, they say, to protect the public from insulting, obscene, and threatening letters; to avoid defaming the prison; and to detect escape or riot plans.

In *Procunier v. Martinez* (1974), which was previously discussed, the U.S. Supreme Court defined the criteria for determining when the regulation of inmate correspondence constitutes a violation of First Amendment liberties. The Court ruled that the limitation of First Amendment freedoms must be no greater than is necessary or essential to the protection of the particular governmental interest involved.[33] This decision disappointed prison managers who wanted greater procedural restrictions on inmate correspondence, for the Supreme Court placed a relatively heavy burden of proof on prison censors. In *Thornburgh v. Abbott* (1989), the U.S. Supreme Court attempted to clear up lower court rulings concerning mailed publications with this ruling that publications must meet one of a number of criteria.[34] The Court went on to rule that unless one of these standards is met, the restrictions on the receipt of published material are not allowed.[35] In a 2001 case, *Shaw v. Murphy*, the Supreme Court ruled that inmates do not have a right to correspond with other inmates even if it concerns legal advice if prison administrators believe such correspondence undermines prison security.[36] In *Beard v. Banks* (2006), the Third Circuit Court of Appeals held that prison officials in Pennsylvania could not prohibit even the most violent prisoners from receiving photographs, newspapers, and magazines sent to them through the mail.[37]

ACCESS TO COURTS, LEGAL SERVICES, AND MATERIALS
Without the ability to seek judicial review of conditions causing discomfort or violating constitutional rights, the inmate must depend solely on the slow and often insensitive administrative mechanism of relief within the prison system. Therefore, the right of easy access to the courts gives inmates hope that their rights will be protected during incarceration. Courts have held that inmates are entitled to have legal materials available and be provided with assistance in drawing up and filing complaints. Inmates who help others, so-called jailhouse lawyers, cannot be interfered with or harassed by prison administrators.

FREEDOM OF THE PRESS AND OF EXPRESSION
With the lifting of the hands-off doctrine, courts have consistently ruled that only when a compelling state interest exists can prisoners' First Amendment rights be modified; correctional authorities must justify the limiting of free speech by showing that granting it would threaten institutional security. In one case, the court upheld the

JAILHOUSE LAWYERS Name given to inmates who develop an expertise in criminal law and help other inmates in preparing their cases.

Inmate Calvin Crawford is shown during a videotaped interview conducted by the *Naples Daily News* at a Florida state prison. Crawford, 35, has been in prison since 1992 when he was convicted in the shooting death of Judah Hamad, 22, a Fort Pierce grocery store owner. Inmates are permitted to speak to the press, but it is not a federal requirement that there be no administrative restrictions on the interview process. See the actual video interview at www.naplesnews.com/videos/detail/letter-inmate/.

While prisons are places of punishment, the courts have ruled that they cannot be punishing places. Certain privileges must be allowed. Here, in Washington State Penitentiary, inmate Torrey Baker whips up a tamale in a sandwich bag within the confines of his cell. Inmates at the Walla Walla prison have produced "The Convict Cookbook," which includes recipes that can be made inside a cell without a stove.

AP Photo/*Walla Walla Union–Bulletin*, Jeff Horner

EXHIBIT 9.2 First Amendment Cases

- *O'Lone v. Estate of Shabazz.* The Supreme Court limited absolute religious freedom and placed the security of the prison above the right to attend religious services.

- *Cutter v. Williamson.* The Supreme Court ruled that inmates are allowed to practice their own religion unless their practices clearly undermine prison security and safety.

- *Procurier v. Martinez.* The Supreme Court defined the criteria for determining whether regulation of inmate correspondence constitutes a violation of First Amendment liberties.

- *Thornburgh v. Abbott.* The Supreme Court ruled that publications must meet one of a number of current criteria to determine whether receipt would not be allowed.

- *Shaw v. Murphy.* The Supreme Court ruled that inmates do not have a right to correspond with other inmates even if it concerns legal action if prison administrators believe such correspondence undermines prison security.

- *Beard v. Banks.* The Third Court of Appeals held that prison officials in Pennsylvania could not prohibit even the most violent prisoners from receiving photographs, newspapers, and magazines sent to them through the mail.

- *Pell v. Procunier.* The Supreme Court ruled that prisoners do not have an automatic right to meet the press because legitimate state interest in security, order, and rehabilitation has to be considered.

- *Goodwin v. Oswald.* The Supreme Court stated that nowhere in state or federal law is the formation of prisoner unions outlawed or prohibited.

- *Jones v. North Carolina Prisoners' Union.* The Supreme Court held that a state regulation prohibiting prisoners from soliciting others to join a union and barring union meetings did not violate the First Amendment.

punishment of a prisoner who circulated materials calling for a collective protest against the administration.[38]

What about talking to the media? In *Pell v. Procunier* (1974), California inmates challenged prison rules that prohibited them from conducting interviews with the press. The Supreme Court ruled that prisoners do not have an automatic right to meet the press, because the legitimate state interest in security, order, and rehabilitation has to be considered.[39] The *Pell* decision solidified the balance test established in *Martinez*, but it also gave corrections officials the major role in determining when the interests of security, order, and rehabilitation were involved.

CENSORSHIP OF PUBLICATIONS AND MANUSCRIPTS The extent to which prison officials can censor the publications prisoners receive and can restrict the freedom of prisoners to publish articles and books while in prison has been the subject of much litigation. Although the courts have cautiously advised a broadening of these rights, they have reserved discretionary responsibility to prison administrators.

RIGHT TO ASSEMBLE Prisoners' right to assemble is also restricted. The emergence of prisoner unions in 10 states in the early 1970s brought about litigation on this subject.[40] *Goodwin v. Oswald* (1972) brought a decision upholding the right of prisoners to form unions. The Supreme Court stated that nowhere in state or federal law is the formation of prisoner unions outlawed or prohibited.[41] However, in *Jones v. North Carolina Prisoners' Union* (1977), the Supreme Court held that a state regulation prohibiting prisoners from soliciting others to join a union and barring union meetings did not violate the First Amendment.[42]

The *Jones* decision represented another setback for prisoners' rights. On the one hand, the Supreme Court extended the position in *Pell*, in which prison officials were looked to as the party that would decide when institutional security and order were threatened. On the other hand, the *Jones* decision extended the power of prison officials to limit First Amendment rights if they believed the potential existed for disruption of order.[43] See Exhibit 9.2 for these First Amendment cases.

Fourth Amendment Rights

The basic issue in the **Fourth Amendment** is proper search and seizure. The courts have consistently held that the protection the Fourth Amendment provides against unreasonable searches and seizures does not extend to prison. For example, *Moore v. People* (1970) concluded that searches conducted by prison officials "are not unreasonable as long as they are not for the purpose of harassing or humiliating the inmate in a cruel or unusual manner."[44]

Cell searches have raised the privacy issue. In *Bell v. Wolfish* (1979), the Supreme Court made it clear that unannounced cell searches, or "shakedowns," were necessary for security and order.[45] *Hudson v. Palmer* (1984) further shattered any hope that the Fourth Amendment would limit cell searches. The Court ruled that "the Fourth Amendment has no applicability to a prison cell."[46] Strip searches also have been allowed by the courts, which generally have permitted prison officials to conduct pat searches and body-cavity examinations in the name of institutional order and security.[47] See Exhibit 9.3 for cases concerned with Fourth Amendment rights.

EXHIBIT 9.3 Fourth Amendment Cases

- *Moore v. People*. The Supreme Court ruled that searches conducted by prison officials are not unreasonable unless they are designed to harass or humiliate the inmate in a cruel or unusual manner.

- *Bell v. Wolfish*. The Supreme Court made it clear that unannounced cell searches and shakedowns were necessary for security and order.

- *Hudson v. Palmer*. The Supreme Court ruled that the Fourth Amendment has no applicability to a prison cell, and cell searches, including strip searches, are necessary in the name of institutional order and security.

Eighth Amendment Rights

In the prison setting, the **Eighth Amendment** has been applied to living conditions, especially with painful executions, excessive corporal punishment, medical experimentation, and abuse of labor. The three principal tests of conformance with the Eighth Amendment deal with these questions: Does the punishment shock the conscience of a civilized society? Is the punishment unnecessarily cruel? Does the punishment go beyond legitimate penal aims? Considerable case law concerns violation of the Eighth Amendment by means of solitary confinement, physical abuse, deadly force, the death penalty, denial of access to medical treatment and services, and segregation.

SOLITARY CONFINEMENT The courts have generally supported the separation of troublesome prisoners from the general prison population. They have ruled that separation is necessary to protect the inmate, other prisoners, and the staff, and to prevent escapes. Although several courts have ordered the release of inmates from harsh solitary confinement, most courts have been unwilling to interfere unless the conditions were clearly "shocking," "barbarous," "disgusting," or "debasing." Court decisions often disagree whether cruel and unusual punishment existed when prisoners were denuded, exposed to the winter cold, and deprived of such basic necessities of hygiene as soap and toilet paper. For example, a federal district court in *Knop v. Johnson* (1987) ruled that cruel and unusual punishment existed when the state of Michigan failed to provide inmates with winter coats, hats, and gloves.[48] In *Harris v. Fleming* (1988), the federal court found that cruel and unusual punishment did not exist when an Illinois inmate was deprived of toilet paper for five days and soap, toothpaste, or a toothbrush for ten days.[49]

PHYSICAL ABUSE Not until the mid-1960s did a court decide that the disciplinary measure of whipping a prisoner with a leather strap constituted cruel and unusual punishment.[50] More recently, as discussed in Chapter 6, the court ruled in the *Madrid v. Gomez* decision (1995) that excessive and unnecessary

FOURTH AMENDMENT The right of the people to be secure in their persons, houses, papers, and effects, against unreasonable searches and seizures, shall not be violated, and no warrants shall issue but upon probable cause, supported by oath and affirmation, and particularly describing the place to be searched, and the persons or things to be seized.

EIGHTH AMENDMENT Excessive bail shall not be required, nor excessive fines imposed, nor cruel and unusual punishments inflicted.

force was used at the Pelican Bay State Prison in California in a variety of ways and circumstances.[51] There are two critical issues involving physical abuse:

- *Inmate on inmate.* The courts have generally been unwilling to impose liability on prison officials for failing to protect prisoners from physical abuse and sexual assault from other inmates. However, the courts have ruled that prison officials are liable for damages if they display indifference to attacks on inmates occurring inside the prison. The test of liability is "deliberate indifference" that requires something more than mere negligence and less than maliciousness.[52]

- *Correctional officer on inmate.* In one of the most influential cases in terms of force, *Hudson v. McMillian* (1992), Hudson, a Louisiana prison inmate, testified he had suffered minor bruises, facial swelling, loosened teeth, and a cracked dental plate after receiving a beating by two prison guards. The magistrate hearing the case ruled that respondents (staff) had violated the Eighth Amendment's prohibition on cruel and unusual punishments, and awarded Hudson damages. The court of appeals reversed the decision, holding that prisoners' charges of excessive force must prove "significant injury" and that Hudson could not prevail because his injuries were minor and required no medical attention. The case was appealed to the Supreme Court, which ruled that as long as force is used in a good faith effort to maintain control, there is no liability. It is only in instances when prisoners can prove that correctional officers acted maliciously that liability is held.[53]

MYTH Inmates can be abused by correctional officers and there is nothing they can do to get help.

FACT Inmates can sue for damages if they are injured by correctional staff members. However, they must show that the correctional officers acted maliciously and were not using force merely to maintain control of an unruly inmate.

DEADLY FORCE The use of deadly force in prison is not uncommon. Take for instance Corcoran Prison in California—during the past two decades, there have been more than 2,000 shooting incidents during which hundreds of inmates have been wounded and five killed (see Chapter 6).[54]

The courts have ruled that the use of deadly force is permissible to prevent the commission of a felony or the infliction of severe bodily harm.[55] These rulings permit the use of deadly force to prevent an inmate from escaping if a state has classified escape as a felony. Nevertheless, the courts have ruled that to avoid civil and criminal liability, deadly force must be used only as a last resort—after all other reasonable means have failed.

In *Whitley v. Albers* (1986), the Court set the standard for the use of deadly force. During the course of a riot at the Oregon State Penitentiary, a prison officer was taken hostage and placed on the upper tier of a two-tier cellblock. In an attempt to free the hostage, one of the officers shot an inmate in the knee. The Supreme Court ruled that prison officials are not liable for the use of deadly force unless it can be shown that they acted in a "wanton" manner, which is a difficult standard for attorneys to meet.[56]

MEDICAL TREATMENT AND SERVICES In early prisons, inmates' right to medical treatment was restricted through the "exceptional circumstances doctrine." Using this policy, the courts would hear only those cases in which the circumstances totally disregarded human dignity, while denying hearings to less serious cases. The cases that were allowed access to the courts usually represented a situation of total denial of medical care.

To gain their medical rights, prisoners have resorted to class-action suits (suits brought on behalf of all individuals affected by similar circumstances—in this case, poor medical attention). In the most significant case, *Newman v. Alabama* (1972), the entire Alabama prison system's medical facilities were declared inadequate.[57] The Supreme Court cited the following factors as contributing to inadequate care: insufficient physician and nurse resources, reliance on untrained inmates for paramedical work, intentional failure in treating the sick and injured, and failure to conform to proper medical standards. The *Newman* case forced corrections departments to upgrade prison medical facilities.

It was not until 1976, in *Estelle v. Gamble*, that the Supreme Court clearly mandated an inmate's right to have medical care.[58] Gamble had hurt his back in a Texas prison and filed suit because he contested the type of treatment he had received and questioned the lack of interest that prison guards had shown in his case. The Supreme Court said, "Deliberate indifference to serious medical needs of prisoners constitutes the 'unnecessary and wanton infliction of pain,' proscribed by the Eighth Amendment."[59] Gamble was allowed to collect monetary damages for his injuries.

In the *Pennsylvania Department of Corrections v. Yeskey* (1998) decision, Yeskey was sentenced to 18 to 30 months in a Pennsylvania prison. It was recommended by the sentencing court that he be placed in a motivational boot camp for first-time offenders. Successful completion of the boot camp would have made him eligible for parole in six months. However, prison officials refused his admission to the program because of his medical history of hypertension. Yeskey then filed suit alleging that his exclusion violated the Americans with Disabilities Act of 1990 (ADA). In a unanimous opinion written by Justice Antonin Scalia, the Supreme Court affirmed the lower court ruling, as it held that no "public entity" may discriminate against qualified disabled individuals due to their disability. The significance of this case is that the ADA also applies to state prisons.[60]

MYTH Prisons are hellholes lacking in basic human services such as proper medical care.

FACT The Supreme Court has mandated that inmates get proper medical care, and failure to provide adequate health services leaves them vulnerable for litigation. The provisions of the Americans with Disabilities Act of 1990 (ADA) must also be respected within prison walls.

CRUEL AND UNUSUAL PUNISHMENT

CRUEL AND UNUSUAL PUNISHMENT The concept of **cruel and unusual punishment** is founded in the Eighth Amendment of the U.S. Constitution. The term itself has not been specifically defined by the Supreme Court, but the Court has held that treatment constitutes cruel and unusual punishment when it does the following:

- Degrades the dignity of human beings[61]

- Is more severe (disproportional) than the offense for which it has been given[62]

- Shocks the general conscience and is fundamentally unfair[63]

- Is deliberately indifferent to a person's safety and well-being[64]

- Punishes people because of their status, such as race, religion, and mental state[65]

- Is in flagrant disregard of due process of law, such as punishment that is capriciously applied[66]

State and federal courts have placed strict limits on disciplinary methods that may be considered inhumane. Corporal punishment all but ended after the practice was condemned in *Jackson v. Bishop* (1968).[67] Although the solitary confinement of disruptive inmates continues,

A California Department of Corrections and Rehabilitation photo from May 22, 2011, shows prison overcrowding at the Solano State Prison in Vacaville, California. In *Brown v. Plata*, the U.S. Supreme Court ruled that conditions in California's overcrowded prisons were so bad that they violated the Eighth Amendment's ban on cruel and unusual punishment. The Court's decision called on the state to cut its prison population to no more than 110,000 inmates, meaning California will have to shed some 33,000 inmates to comply over the next two years. State officials can accomplish that by transferring inmates to local jails or releasing them.

its prolonged use under barbaric conditions has been held to be in violation of the Eighth Amendment. Courts have found that inmates placed in solitary have the right to adequate personal hygiene, exercise, mattresses, ventilation, and rules specifying how they can earn their release.

In *Hope v. Pelzer* (2002), the Supreme Court ruled that correctional officials who knowingly violate the Eighth Amendment rights of inmates can be held liable for damages.[68] Larry Hope, an Alabama prison inmate, was twice handcuffed to a hitching post for disruptive conduct. He was handcuffed above shoulder height, and when he tried moving his arms to improve circulation, the handcuffs cut into his wrists, causing pain and discomfort. He spent seven hours on the hitching post, during which he was given one or two water breaks but no bathroom breaks, and a guard taunted him about his thirst. Hope filed a suit against three guards charging them with violating his civil rights. The U.S. Supreme Court ruled that Hope's allegations established an Eighth Amendment violation. It ruled that among the "'unnecessary and wanton' inflictions of pain [constituting cruel and unusual punishment forbidden by the amendment] are those that are 'totally without penological justification.'" This determination is made in the context of prison conditions by ascertaining whether an official acted with "deliberate indifference" to the inmate's health or safety, a state of mind that can be inferred from the fact that the risk of harm is obvious. The Court reasoned that any safety concerns had long since ended by the time Hope was handcuffed to the hitching post, because he had already been subdued, handcuffed, placed in leg irons, and transported back to prison. The *Hope* case shows that correctional officials can be sued if their behavior violates an inmate's constitutional rights and that they or any reasonable person should have surmised that the behavior was in violation of accepted practices.

OVERALL PRISON CONDITIONS Prisoners have long had the right to the minimal conditions necessary for human survival, such as the necessary food, clothing, shelter, and medical care to sustain human life. A number of attempts have been made to articulate reasonable standards of prison care and to make sure they are carried out. Courts have held that, although people are sent to prison for punishment, it does not mean that prison should be a punishing experience.[69] In the 1994 case of *Farmer v. Brennan*, the Court ruled that prison officials are legally liable if, knowing that an inmate faces a serious risk of harm, they disregard that risk by failing to take measures to avoid or reduce it. Furthermore, prison officials should be able to infer the risk from the evidence at hand; they need not be warned or told.[70]

Although inmates retain the right to reasonable care, if there is a legitimate purpose for the use of governmental restrictions, they may be considered constitutional. For example, it might be possible to restrict reading material, allow strip searches, and prohibit inmates from receiving packages from the outside if the restrictions are legitimate security measures. If overcrowded conditions require it, inmates may be double-bunked in cells designed for a single inmate.[71]

RACIAL SEGREGATION On August 8, 2009, a riot in the California prison at Chino left hundreds injured, buildings burned, and property destroyed.[72] The disturbance was sparked by racial tensions between Latino and black inmates, and later sparked a great deal of controversy over the issue of racial segregation in prison: Should prisons be segregated to prevent violence among gangs like the Aryan Brotherhood, the Mexican Mafia, and the Black Guerrilla Family? Or should prisons be integrated like other institutions because any form of segregation is inherently unconstitutional?

The Alabama case of *Washington v. Lee* (1966) was the first judicial intervention on the desegregation of prisons.[73] Federal Judge Frank Johnson held that "this court can conceive of no consideration of prison security or discipline which will sustain the constitutionality of state statutes that on their face require complete and permanent segregation of the races in all Alabama penal facilities." The state was therefore ordered to provide for the total desegregation of all prisons within one year. This was done.[74] In the 2005 case *Johnson v. California*, Supreme Court reaffirmed the *Lee* decision when it ruled that racial segregation of prison inmates, in their cells or anywhere on prison grounds, is an inappropriate form of racial classification.[75] It left it open for lower courts to decide, using a standard of strict scrutiny, when segregation is inappropriate and unconstitutional. *Johnson* focused on the policy of segregating inmates upon their arrival at a prison. The Court ruled that if racial segregation was allowed for incoming inmates it would also be justified "in the dining halls, yards, and general housing areas." Segregation would only be allowed if a prison administrator could prove that there was a compelling interest in prison safety. The Court recognized that "prisons are dangerous places, and the special circumstances they present may justify racial classifications in some contexts." But these are only in the most extreme circumstances. It remains to be seen in light of the Chino riots whether the resolve to racially integrate prisons will be dampened and that courts—even when using a "strict scrutiny" standard—will find that integration, in many instances, is just too dangerous. Exhibit 9.4 sets out some critical Eighth Amendment cases that help define cruel and unusual punishment.

Fourteenth Amendment Rights

Due process is the major issue in the **Fourteenth Amendment**, especially related to disciplinary hearings and inmates helping each other to prepare their cases for appeal.

DUE PROCESS RIGHTS IN DISCIPLINARY HEARINGS

The 1974 *Wolff v. McDonnell* decision has been heralded as a landmark because of its impact on correctional administration and prisoners' rights.[76] In reviewing disciplinary procedures, the Supreme Court held that they were not equivalent to criminal prosecution and that during disciplinary hearings prisoners do not have the full due process rights of a defendant on trial. Nevertheless, the Court specified certain minimum requirements for disciplinary proceedings:

- The inmate must receive advanced written notice of the alleged rules infraction.
- The prisoner must be allowed sufficient time to prepare a defense against the charges.
- The prisoner must be allowed to present documentary evidence on his or her own behalf and therefore may call witnesses, as long as the security of the institution is not jeopardized.

EXHIBIT 9.4 Critical Eighth Amendment Cases

- *Knop v. Johnson.* A federal district court ruled that cruel and unusual punishment existed when the state of Michigan failed to provide inmates with winter coats, hats, and gloves.

- *Harris v. Fleming.* The federal court found that cruel and unusual punishment did not exist when an Illinois inmate was deprived of toilet paper for five days and soap, toothpaste, or a toothbrush for ten days.

- *Hudson v. McMillan.* The Supreme Court ruled that as long as force is used in a good faith effort to maintain control, there is no liability. It is only in instances when prisoners could prove the correctional officers acted maliciously that liability is held.

- *Whitley v. Albers.* The Supreme Court ruled that prison officials are not liable for the use of deadly force unless it can be shown that they acted in a "wanton" manner, which is a difficult standard for attorneys to meet.

- *Newman v. Alabama.* The Supreme Court ruled that the entire Alabama prison system medical facilities were inadequate and ordered that they be improved.

- *Estelle v. Gamble.* The Supreme Court ruled that "deliberate indifference" to "serious medical needs" of prisoners constitutes the "unnecessary and wanton infliction of pain," a violation against the prohibition of cruel and unusual punishment.

- *Pennsylvania Department of Corrections v. Yeskey.* The Supreme Court held that no public entity may discriminate against qualified disabled individuals due to their disability. The significance of this case is that the American Disability Act also applies to state prisons.

- *Jackson v. Bishop.* Corporal punishment all but ended after the practice was condemned in this case decided by the U.S. 8th Circuit Court.

- *Hope v. Pelzer.* The Supreme Court ruled the correctional officials who knowingly violate the Eighth Amendment rights of inmates can be held liable for damages.

- *Farmer v. Brennan.* The Supreme Court ruled that prison officials are legally liable if, knowing that an inmate faces a serious risk of harm, they disregard that risk by failing to take measures to avoid or reduce it.

- *Washington v. Lee.* The federal court in this Alabama case ordered the total desegregation of all prisons within one year.

- *Johnson v. California.* The Supreme Court ruled that racial segregation of prison inmates, in their cells or anywhere on prison grounds, is inappropriate use of racial classification.

FOURTEENTH AMENDMENT [*Section 1*]
All persons born or naturalized in the United States, and subject to the jurisdiction thereof, are citizens of the United States and of the State wherein they reside. No State shall make or enforce any law which shall abridge the privileges or immunities of citizens of the United States; nor shall any State deprive any person of life, liberty, or property, without due process of law; nor deny to any person within its jurisdiction the equal protection of the laws.

Racial conflict is a significant correctional issue. Inmates Tim Heffernan and Daniel Mabson talk while sitting on their adjacent bunks at the Sierra Conservation Center in Jamestown, California. Despite efforts by California prison officials to end one of the nation's last vestiges of institutionalized, government-mandated racial segregation, powerful race-based gangs violently oppose attempts to desegregate prison housing units. Blacks, whites, and Hispanics are willing to sleep side by side in bunk beds spaced an arm's length apart, but some would brawl or risk longer sentences rather than accept an inmate of another race in a bed above or below them in the same bunk bed stack.

AP Photo/Rich Pedroncelli

■ The prisoner is permitted to seek counsel from another inmate or a staff member when the circumstances of the disciplinary infraction are complex or the prisoner is illiterate.

■ The prisoner is to be provided with a written statement of the findings of the committee, the evidence relied upon, and the rationale for the action. A written record of the proceedings must also be maintained.[77]

Wolff v. McDonnell was significant because it standardized certain rights and freedoms within correctional facilities. Although inmates received some procedural safeguards to protect them against the notorious abuses of disciplinary meetings, they did not receive all the due process rights of a criminal trial. Nor did the Court question the right of corrections officials to revoke the "good time" of inmates.

LEGAL ASSISTANCE TO INMATES Until well past the time when the hands-off doctrine passed into obsolescence, correctional authorities were obsessed by their belief that prisoners should not trouble the courts with their complaints. Particularly discouraged were "writ writers," who prepared complaints for themselves and other prisoners. In many states, the preparation of writs was a disciplinary offense, calling for a session of punitive isolation.[78] Access to the courts was vigorously prevented. In 1941, the Supreme Court took notice of the obstacles to writs of *habeas corpus* in *Ex parte Hull*.[79]

Hull had filed for a writ of *habeas corpus*, only to have the papers he filed returned to him by prison officials without submission to the court. When ordered by the Supreme Court to show cause why Hull's petition for a writ should not be granted, the warden replied that he had issued a regulation that all such petitions had to be referred to the legal investigator for the parole board. The regulation went on to say that "documents submitted to [the investigator], if in his opinion are properly drawn, will be directed to the court designated or will be referred back to the inmate." Justice Frank Murphy's opinion pronounced this regulation invalid: "The state and its officers may not abridge or impair petitioner's right to … apply for a writ of *habeas corpus*."

In *Bounds v. Smith* (1977), in a 5–4 decision, the Court ruled that the state of North Carolina had a duty to provide adequate law libraries in each of its correctional facilities.[80] Although the state's proposal for a standard library is rather generous in its content, including the standard legal referral and state statutes, other states have gone far beyond North Carolina in the provision of law libraries, some of them so extensive as to be the envy of practicing attorneys.

In *Johnson v. Avery* (1969), the Supreme Court ruled that institutional officials may not prohibit inmates from assisting one another with legal work unless the institution provides reasonable legal assistance to inmates.[81] This decision denied the constitutionality of a Tennessee prison regulation that provided: "No inmate will advise, assist or otherwise contract to aid another, either with or without a fee, to prepare writs or other legal matters . . . Inmates are forbidden to set themselves up as practitioners for the purpose of promoting a business of writing writs." The Court ruled that inmates have the right to receive assistance from jailhouse lawyers. The Court also stated that the activities of the jailhouse lawyer could be restricted as to time and place, and that jailhouse lawyers could be prohibited from receiving fees for their services.[82] See Exhibit 9.5 for a selection of Fourteenth Amendment cases.

PROVIDING LEGAL SERVICES TO INMATES

While inmates have gained rights, it is critical to provide them with legal counsel so that they can avail themselves of their legal benefits and privileges. The **Innocence Projects** provide representation and investigative assistance to prison inmates who claim to be innocent of the crimes for which they were convicted. (See the Evidence-Based Corrections feature.)

The **grievance process** is another means available for inmates who feel that they have been unjustly treated or have been denied their rights. Nearly all of the grievance processes are set up by either the institution or the department of corrections. Grievances usually are submitted to someone in the institution and then go through a number of steps until they may end up in the director's office. If they cannot be resolved to the inmate's satisfaction on one level, they proceed to the next. Institutions vary on whether there is a time limit on processing the various steps.

A **corrections ombudsman** is a further means sometimes available for inmates who feel that they have been unjustly treated. A number of states have statewide corrections ombudsmen, including Iowa, Michigan, Minnesota, Montana, New Jersey, Texas, and Wisconsin. These programs have been successful at improving conditions in adult prisons by monitoring the relationship between prisoners and prison officials. The success of these programs depends upon the ombudsman's authority to pursue remedies and his or her ability to manage the competing interests of inmates and officials. If prisoners feel that the ombudsman lacks the ability to address their complaints adequately, they will be reluctant to be cooperative. However, if prison officials feel that the ombudsman is unreasonable, they will be reluctant to implement recommendations and may create additional obstacles to safeguarding prisoners' rights.[83] The Careers in Corrections job that receives attention in this chapter is the corrections ombudsman.

EXHIBIT 9.5 Fourteenth Amendment Cases

- *Wolff v. McDonnell.* The Supreme Court held that disciplinary procedures were not equivalent to criminal prosecution and that during disciplinary hearings prisoners do not have formal due process rights of the defendant on trial.

- *Ex parte Hull.* The Supreme Court held that the state or prison officials may not impair a petitioner's rights to apply for a writ of habeas corpus.

- *Bounds v. Smith.* The Supreme Court ruled that the state of North Carolina had a duty to provide adequate law libraries in each of its correctional facilities.

- *Johnson v. Avery.* The Supreme Court ruled that institutional officials may not prohibit inmates from assisting one another with legal work unless the institution provides reasonable legal assistance to inmates.

Originally given a life term for a series of rapes, teenager Jose Walle, 16, was resentenced to 65 years in prison in the courtroom of Judge Chet Tharpe after the U.S. Supreme Court ruled it was cruel and unusual punishment to sentence a juvenile to life in prison unless he committed a capital crime. After finishing his term, Walle must begin serving a 27-year sentence he received in Pinellas County, Florida, for a total of 92 years. At this time the Court is considering whether a life term for murder would be cruel and unusual for a teenager. Do you agree?

© ZUMA Wire Service/Alamy

THE IMPACT OF THE PRISONERS' RIGHTS MOVEMENT

Today, there is both good news and bad news about prisoners' rights. The good news is that over the past 40 years some of the bad conditions of the worst prisons have been corrected and prisoners have made gains in several areas. The improvements are undeniable and would not have been achieved without judicial intervention. Prisoners have made the greatest gains in the right to send and receive letters, but they also have made strides in their right to communicate with lawyers and the courts. Furthermore, the courts have permitted the right of religious freedom as long as it does not jeopardize institutional security. Courts also have been willing to rule on the totality of conditions in a prison setting when prisoners appeared to be undergoing severe dehumanization and deterioration in their

INNOCENCE PROJECTS These projects, found in a number of states, provide free legal assistance for those cases in which question remains regarding the legality of their convictions.

GRIEVANCE PROCESS A formalized arrangement in which inmates can register their complaints about the conditions of their confinement.

CORRECTIONS OMBUDSMAN An ombudsman (a Swedish word that means "representative") is a person or body that protects citizens against governmental abuses.

EVIDENCE-BASED CORRECTIONS

Wrongful Convictions

A wrongful conviction occurs when a person is convicted who is actually innocent of the crime and was no way involved in the incident that brought them to trial. While this turn of events can be devastating to those involved, such as Michael Morton, the subject of our opening vignette, no one actually knows how many prison inmates were innocent and wrongfully convicted. There are a number of reasons why the number of wrongful convictions remains unknown:

- No official or even unofficial statistics are kept.
- An acquittal is not a good measure of actual innocence.
- It is very difficult to unravel a case of actual innocence.
- Many prisoners falsely claim innocence.
- Criminal justice system personnel (police and prosecutors) deny that wrongful convictions occur and do not cooperate in uncovering miscarriages of justice.

There are now about 1 million felony convictions per year in state and federal courts. So even at a rate of .005 innocent people being falsely convicted each year, it is possible to estimate that 5,000 factually innocent persons are convicted of felonies in any given year.

To shed light on this important issue, legal scholar Samuel Gross examined hundreds of criminal cases over a 15-year period in which the convicted person was exonerated. Gross puts the number of exonerations at 340 between 1989 and 2003, the period he studied. Most known exonerations were for murder and rape cases. Yet a far larger number of serious felonies, including robbery, have not generated known cases of actual innocence. There is typically no biological evidence in robberies (and therefore no chance for DNA analysis) and the opportunities for mistaken eyewitness identification are greater. It stands to reason that many people imprisoned for robbery in the United States are actually innocent.

Gross also found that in 88 percent of the rape cases in the study, DNA evidence helped free the inmate. But biological evidence is far less likely to be available or provide definitive proof in other kinds of cases. Only 20 percent of the murder exonerations involved DNA evidence, and almost all of those were rape-murders. About 90 percent of false convictions in the rape cases involve misidentification by witnesses, and these errors very often occur across races: black men accused of raping white women made up a disproportionate number of exonerated rape defendants. Interracial rapes are uncommon, accounting for less than 10 percent of all rapes. But in half of the rape exonerations, black men were falsely convicted of raping white women. And while 29 percent of those in prison for rape are black, 65 percent of those exonerated of the crime are African American. Gross concludes that white Americans are much more likely to mistake one black person for another than to do the same for members of their own race.

Gross found that the leading causes of wrongful convictions for murder were quite different. These include false confessions and perjury by co-defendants, informants, police officers, or forensic scientists. In sum, the evidence found by Gross suggests that wrongful convictions are quite common and that giving inmates access to the courts to address these wrongs is essential.

Source: Samuel Gross, Kristen Jacoby, Daniel J. Matheson, Nicholas Montgomery, and Sujata Patil, "Exonerations in the United States, 1989 Through 2003," *Journal of Criminal Law and Criminology* 95 (2005): 523–560.

mental and physical well-being. It can be argued that many of these improvements are probably irreversible and that the states can be trusted to maintain constitutionally acceptable prisons.

The bad news is that overcrowding and its associated evils are reappearing and will be difficult to correct. Further bad news is that in too many states prisoners are expected to do "hard time" and not to enjoy the amenities that they were given in the past. With this social and political context, it has been more difficult for prisoners to win "cruel and unusual punishment" lawsuits. Another source of bad news is that federal courts, which were actively involved in prisoners' rights from the 1960s on, withdrew their receptivity to inmate suits in the 1990s. A final source of bad news is that the Prison Litigation Reform Act (PLRA), passed by Congress and signed by President Clinton in 1996, has limited the ability of prisoners to allege violations of their constitutional rights.

Prisoners may retain basic human rights, but they are not entitled to the same degree of constitutional protections that they enjoyed before conviction. The conditions of confinement can never satisfy prisoners. Convicts and their plight attract little public sympathy, so action to correct intolerable conditions is usually delayed until a crisis occurs. At that point, remedies must be drastic and thus costly, far more so than would be the case if farsighted planning, development, and fiscal support were available to implement changes as soon as they are needed.

CORRECTIONS OMBUDSMAN

Preparation for the Job

Preparation for such a career needs the proper academic credential for that state (states vary) and familiarity with the world of corrections. This ordinarily means that this person has worked in corrections, especially in institutional contexts.

Nature of the Job

The corrections ombudsman in those states that have a position or office investigates complaints that are: alleged to be contrary or inconsistent with the law or department of corrections practice; based on mistaken facts or irrelevant considerations; inadequately explained when reasons should have been revealed; inefficiently performed; unreasonable unfair or otherwise objectionable, even though in accordance with law. The corrections ombudsman does not investigate when: the complainant could reasonably be expected to use a different remedy or action; the complaint is trivial, frivolous, vexatious, or not in good faith; the complaint has been too long delayed to justify present examination. If an investigation discovers that a complainant has been treated improperly by a state agency, the office works with the agency involved to resolve the complaint through appropriate corrective action. Ombudsman programs can serve such functions as investigating allegations, monitoring facilities, conducting research, educating the community, providing recommendations for improvement, and, if needed, bringing litigation.

Qualifications and Required Education

States who have such offices vary in their qualifications and education. A college degree is typically required. Some ombudsmen are attorneys, while in other states a law degree is not required, but the ombudsman must be particularly skillful and experienced in handling complaints.

Job Outlook

Increased numbers of states are developing an office of corrections ombudsmen, and, accordingly, the outlook is good for employment in this area.

Earnings and Benefits

The salaries vary greatly from one state to another. Some ombudsmen are paid in the high $60,000s, while others receive compensation in the low $30,000s.

Sources: Nebraskalegislature.gov (accessed March 9, 2012); Prison Law Office: Protecting the Constitutional Rights of California Prisoners, www.prisonlaw.com (accessed March 9, 2012).

SUMMARY

L01 **Understand what is meant by the term *prisoners' rights***

Inmates must be given all the rights conferred on them by law, including due process rights, but their status as convicted felons has caused them to lose certain rights that free citizens have, including freedom and the ability to come and go as they wish.

L02 **Discuss the foundation of prisoners' rights**

The U.S. Constitution is the principal source of prisoners' rights, but federal and state statutes, legal precedents, federal civil rights lawsuits, and writs of *habeas corpus* are also important sources of prisoners' rights.

L03 **Identify the First, Fourth, Eighth, and Fourteenth Amendment substantive rights that the courts have awarded inmates**

Prisoners have made the greatest gains in the First, Fourth, Eighth, and Fourteenth Amendments, which include the right to send and receive letters, the right to communicate with lawyers and the courts, and the right of religious freedom as long as it does not jeopardize institutional security. Courts have also given relief on the totality of conditions in a prison setting when prisoners appeared to be undergoing severe dehumanization and deterioration in their mental and physical well-being.

 L04 ▶ **Understand the legal services that are available to inmates**

Inmates are free to find attorneys who will provide legal services for them (usually *pro bono*). In addition, there are a number of Innocence Projects throughout the nation; inmates might be successful in persuading one of these projects to take their case on. A few states have corrections ombudsmen, a nonsystem representative who is charged to protect citizens against legal abuse, and if inmates are doing time in a state that has a corrections ombudsman,

this may be an available legal service. The grievance process is another available service, where inmates can complain through this formalized arrangement if they feel they have been unjustly treated.

 L05 ▶ **Understand the rights that have not been given to inmates**

The good news about prisoners' rights is that some of the worst conditions of prisons have been corrected and inmates have made gains in several areas. The bad news is that overcrowding continues to be a problem in many prisons, inmates have lost some of the amenities they were given in the past, federal courts are not as actively involved in prisoners' rights as they were in the past, and the Prison Litigation Reform Act has limited the ability to allege violations of their constitutional rights.

Key Terms

Bill of Rights, 209
statutes, 209
case law, 210
landmark decision, 210
habeas corpus, 210
hands-off doctrine, 211

restraining hands doctrine, 212
Prison Litigation Reform Act (PLRA), 213
substantive rights, 213
First Amendment, 215
jailhouse lawyers, 217
Fourth Amendment, 219

Eighth Amendment, 219
cruel and unusual punishment, 221
Fourteenth Amendment, 223
Innocence Projects, 225
grievance process, 225
corrections ombudsman, 225

 ## Critical Thinking Questions

1. What did it mean to say that a convicted felon was "civilly dead"?
2. Summarize the most important cases establishing the hands-off doctrine.
3. Why is the right to due process so difficult to disentangle from institutional priorities?

4. What led to the hands-off doctrine of the courts?
5. Why has the implementation of prisoners' rights been so difficult for the courts?

 ## Thinking Like a Corrections Professional

You are a corrections ombudsman and discover that a warden of a maximum-security prison has been resistant to inmates' concerns. He has problems with a particular attorney who has become quite an advocate with inmates, whom he sees as continually challenging his authority in putting forward what she defines as rights of prisoners. He does not even want to permit this attorney to enter the prison.

How will you intercede in this situation? If the warden persists in disallowing the attorney's admittance to the prison, what will you do?

Another situation is that you have received complaints from several inmates that a particular major in the prison is involved directly or indirectly in the abuse of prisoners. He has the reputation of carrying a club and using it on inmates. Prison staff are afraid of him and will not testify against him; in addition, the warden supports him, claiming that he is one of the best staff members the prison has ever had.

How will you handle this situation? Will you attempt to involve external law enforcement officials? Why or why not?

Career Destinations

If you want to become involved in prisoners' rights, you can work with an inmate advocacy group. Learn more by going to some of their websites:

www.allofusornone.org

www.fcnetwork.org

If you are interested in becoming an ombudsman, check out:

www.ombudsassociation.org

To find out more about inmates' rights, go to:

http://public.findlaw.com/civil-rights/more-civil-rights-topics/prisoner-civil-rights-top/le5_6rights.html

Notes

1. Christina Caron, "Michael Morton Set Free After Spending Nearly 25 Years in Prison, Exonerated by DNA Evidence for His Wife's Murder," *ABC News*, October 4, 2011, http://abcnews.go.com/US/michael-morton-free-25-years-prison-exonerated-wifes/story?id=14663445 (accessed March 9, 2012).
2. Ibid.
3. Andrei Marmor, "The Nature of Law," *Stanford Encyclopedia of Philosophy* (Stanford, CA: Center for the Study of Language and Information, revised 2007).
4. John Locke was a great proponent of natural rights. See John C. Attig, *The Words of John Locke from the Seventeenth Century to the Present* (Westport, CT: Greenwood Press, 1985).
5. *Miranda v. Arizona*, 384 U.S. 436, 86 S.Ct. 1602, 16 L.Ed.2d 694 (1966).
6. *Pennsylvania Department of Corrections v. Yeskey*, 524 U.S. 206 (1998).
7. *Holt v. Sarver*, 309 F.Supp. 362 (E.D. Ark. 1970), affirmed, 442 F.2d 304 (8th Circuit, 1971).
8. "Exonerated Mississippi Men Sue over Bite Mark Testimony," *Picayune Item*, April 4, 2009, http://picayuneitem.com/statenews/x2079286911/Exonerated-Miss-men-sue-over-bite-mark-testimony (accessed April 19, 2012).
9. *Ruffin v. Commonwealth*, 62.790, at 796 (1871).
10. National Advisory Commission on Criminal Justice Standards and Goals, *Corrections* (Washington, DC: Government Printing Office, 1973), p. 18.
11. *Procunier v. Martinez*, 416 U.S. 396 (1974).
12. *Wolff v. McDonnell*, 418 U.S. 539 (1974).
13. *Estelle v. Gamble*, 429 U.S. 97 (1976).
14. *Baxter v. Palmigiano*, 425 U.S. 308 (1976).
15. *Enomato v. Clutchette*, 428 U.S. 308 (1976).
16. *Meacham v. Fano*, 427 U.S. (1976).
17. *Montanye v. Haymes*, 96 S.Ct. 2543 (1976).
18. *Meacham v. Fano*.
19. *Rhodes v. Chapman*, 29 Cr. L. rptr. 3061 (1961).
20. *Turner v. Safley*, 428 78, 1987.
21. For a review of this case, see David L. Hudson, Jr., *Turner v. Safley, High Drama, Enduring Precedent*, First Amendment Center. Accessed at www.firstamendmentcenter.org/turner-v-safley-high-drama-enduring-precedent (accessed March 9, 2012).
22. *Wilson v. Seiter*, 501 U.S. 294 (1991).
23. "Legislation Has Mixed Effect on Petitions," *Third Branch* 31 (April 1999). For a review of the courts and the PLRA, see Barbara Belbot, "Report on the Prison Litigation Act: What Have the Courts Decided So Far?" *Prison Journal* 84 (September 2004): 290–316.
24. *Booth v. Churner*, U.S. 731 (2001).
25. *Porter v. Nussle*, 534 U.S. 516 (2002).
26. See Christopher E. Smith, *Law and Contemporary Corrections* (Belmont, CA: Wadsworth, 1999).
27. *Cruz v. Beto*, 405, U.S. 319 (1972).
28. *O'Lone v. Estate of Shabazz*, 482 U.S. 342, 107 S.Ct. 1400, 96 L.Ed.2d 282 (1987).
29. Ibid., at 349.
30. *Cutter v. Wilkinson*, 544 U.S. 709 (2005).
31. Philip L. Reichel, *Corrections: Philosophies, Practices, and Procedures* (Boston: Allyn & Bacon, 2001), p. 528.
32. *Boerne v. Flores*, 521 U.S. 507 (1997).
33. *Procunier v. Martinez*, 416 U.S. 396 (1974).
34. *Thornburgh v. Abbott*, 490 U.S. 401 (1989).
35. Ibid.
36. *Shaw v. Murphy*, 532 U.S. 223 (2001).
37. *Beard v. Banks*, 548 U.S. 521 (2006).
38. *Roberts v. Papersack*, 256 F.Supp. 415 (M.D. 1966).
39. *Pell v. Procunier*, 417 U.S. 817 (1974).
40. C. Ronald Huff, "Unionization Behind the Walls," *Criminology* 12 (August 1974): 184–185.
41. *Goodwin v. Oswald*, 462 F.2d 1245-46 (3d Cir. 1972).
42. *Jones v. North Carolina Prisoners' Union*, 433 U.S. (1977).
43. C. Ronald Huff, "The Discovery of Prisoners' Rights: A Sociological Analysis," in *Legal Rights of Prisoners*, ed. G. P. Alpert (Beverly Hills, CA: Sage Publications, 1980), pp. 60–61.
44. *Moore v. People*, 171 Colorado 338, 467 P.2d (1970) .
45. *Bell v. Wolfish*, 441 U.S. 520 (1979).
46. *Hudson v. Palmer*, 82 L.Ed.2d 393 (1984).
47. See *Bell v. Wolfish*.
48. *Knop v. Johnson*, 667 F.Supp. 467 (1987).
49. *Harris v. Fleming*, 839 F.2d 1223 (1988).
50. *Jackson v. Bishop*, 404 F.2d 571 (8th Cir. 1968).
51. *Madrid v. Gomez*, 889 F.Supp. 1146 (N.D. Cal. 1995).
52. Ibid., at 843 n.8.
53. *Hudson v. McMillian*, U.S. 1 (1992).
54. Corey Weinstein, "Even Dogs Confined to Cages for Long Periods of Time Go Berserk," in *Building Violence: How America's Rush to Incarcerate Creates More Violence*, ed. John P. May and Khalid R. Pitts (Thousand Oaks, CA: Sage Publications, 2000), p. 116.
55. *Beard v. Stephens*, 372 F.2d 685 (5th Cir. 1967).
56. *Whitley v. Albers*, 475 U.S. 312 (1986).
57. *Newman v. Alabama*, 92 S.Ct. 1079, 405 U.S. 319 (1972).
58. *Estelle v. Gamble*, 429 U.S. 97 (1976).
59. Ibid.
60. *Pennsylvania Department of Corrections v. Yeskey*, 524 U.S. 206 (1998).
61. *Trop v. Dulles*, 356 U.S. 86, 78 S.Ct. 590 (1958); see also *Furman v. Georgia*, 408 U.S. 238, 92 S.Ct. 2726, 33 L.Ed.2d 346 (1972).
62. *Weems v. United States*, 217 U.S. 349, 30 S.Ct. 544, 54 L.Ed. 793 (1910).
63. *Lee v. Tahash*, 352 F.2d 970 (8th Cir., 1965).
64. *Estelle v. Gamble*, 429 U.S. 97 (1976).
65. *Robinson v. California*, 370 U.S. 660 (1962).
66. *Gregg v. Georgia*, 428 U.S. 153 (1976).
67. *Jackson v. Bishop*, 404 F.2d 571 (8th Cir. 1968).
68. *Hope v. Pelzer et al.*, 536 U.S. 730 (2002).
69. *Bell v. Wolfish*, 99 S.Ct. 1873–1974 (1979); also see "*Bell v. Wolfish*: The Rights of Pretrial Detainees," *New England Journal of Prison Law* 6 (1979): 134.
70. *Farmer v. Brennan*, 144 S.Ct. 1970 (1994).
71. *Rhodes v. Chapman*, 452 U.S. 337 (1981); for further analysis of *Rhodes*, see Randall Pooler, "Prison Overcrowding and the Eighth Amendment: The Rhodes Not Taken," *New England Journal on Criminal and Civil Confinement* 8 (1983): 1–28.
72. "Report Predicted Violence at Chino Prison Dorm Hit by Race Riots," *Los Angeles Times*, August 10, 2009, http://latimesblogs.latimes.com/lanow/2009/08/report-warned-of-violence-at-chino-prison-baracks-hit-by-race-riots.html (accessed March 9, 2012).
73. *Washington v. Lee*, 263 F.Supp. 27 (M.D. Alabama 1966). Affirmed, *Lee v. Washington*, 390 U.S. 333 (1968).
74. Ibid.
75. *Johnson v. California*, 543 U.S. 499 (2005).
76. *Wolff v. McDonnell*. 418 U.S. 539 (1974).
77. *Prisoner Law Reporter*, "Prison Discipline Must Include Notice," hearing of the Commission on Correctional Facilities and Services of the American Bar Association, Vol. 3 (July 1975): 51–53.
78. For examples of the measures taken to stamp out such activities, see Steve J. Martin and Sheldon Ekland-Olson, *Texas Prisons: The Walls Came Tumbling Down* (Austin: Texas Monthly Press, 1987), pp. 32–45, 50–58.
79. *Ex parte Hull*, 312 U.S. 546. Rehearing denied, 312 U.S. 716 (1941).
80. *Bounds v. Smith*, 430 U.S. 817 (1977).
81. *Johnson v. Avery*, 393 U.S. 483 (1969).
82. Smith, *Law and Contemporary Corrections*.
83. "Use of Ombudsman Programs in Juvenile Corrections," U.S. Department of Justice, Office of Juvenile Justice and Delinquency Prevention, www.ojjdp.gov/pubs/walls/sect-02.html (accessed March 8, 2012).

A commercial diving program conducted at the California Institution for Men at Chino has had quite an effect on inmates. Initiated and created in 1970 by the Marine Technology Training Center, this 11-month training includes a mix of academic and physical work totaling 2,000 hours of instruction, which is more than twice as much as required at some civilian diving schools. The diverse curriculum includes diving physics, navigation, report writing, air systems, welding, seamanship, blueprint reading, diesel engines, and marine construction. The intent of the program is to not only focus on technological skills, but also instill a professional attitude of determination, courage, and perseverance.[1]

This diving program was established at Chino under the guidance of Leonard Greenstone, a former U.S. Navy salvage diver and successful commercial diving contractor. The successful program has trained hundreds of men in commercial diving. In tracking 349 of the former graduates

of this vocational program, only 6 percent had returned to prison.[2]

The diving program at Chino Prison in California has trained hundreds of men in commercial diving, most of whom have made a successful adjustment in the community. The program was first established in 1970 and lasted for 33 years before it was eliminated during budget cuts in 2003. On December 1, 2006, the commercial diving center in Chino was reestablished as part of the renewed rehabilitation efforts of the California Department of Corrections and Rehabilitation.

The Chino divers are given jobs because of the school's strong reputation and a steady need for highly skilled labor in shipping, heavy construction, and the oil industry. Phil Newsum, executive director of the Association of Diving Contractors International, says that Chino graduates are among the best in the industry. "It all comes down to one question, 'Can you do the job?' They have shown over and over that they can."[3]

This is an exciting program and helps fulfill the responsibility of the Federal Bureau of Prisons and the states' departments of corrections, constitutionally mandated by federal and state courts, to provide programs and services to prisoners placed in their care. The federal government's Second Chance Act of 2007 authorized various grants to government agencies and nonprofit groups to provide a variety of services, including employment assistance, housing, substance abuse treatment, and family programming, that can help to reduce reoffending and parole violations.

CORRECTIONAL PROGRAMS AND SERVICES

© Becky Stein

LEARNING OBJECTIVES

LO1 Identify the role of treatment and services in prisons today

LO2 Discuss classification for treatment

LO3 Understand the individual-level treatment programs

LO4 Identify the group programs held in prisons

LO5 Discuss inmate self-help programs

LO6 Evaluate the quality of prison programs for inmates

LO7 Evaluate the quality of prison services for inmates

LO8 Understand how treatment in prison can become more effective

231

Many states have made efforts to inform soon-to-be-released inmates of specific programs to help them to better prepare for reentry. For example, in Maryland, the corrections department Education Libraries service is equipped with computers and other educational tools, which serve all the prerelease institutions in Maryland and help inmates prepare for life on the outside.[4]

It is true that prison programming has declined over time, and it is also true that inmates are more in need of substance abuse and alcohol abuse programs than mental health treatment programs. Inmates now have a greater interest in dealing with their substance abuse addictions and correctional authorities have the responsibility for providing meaningful treatment programs for those inmates receptive to them.[5]

In addition to treatment programs, state correctional authorities are responsible for providing adequate basic care of inmates, including academic education, vocational training, and religious services. The state or federal government is also required to provide medical and dental services to inmates, which are sometimes extremely expensive with the number of elderly inmates increasing. Recreation has long been important, even though recreational services have been cut with the current "eliminating the frills" emphasis of many correctional systems. The courts have further required that prisons have libraries, particularly libraries that provide the necessary law books for inmates.

What does it mean for the state to provide quality care to inmates? Should inmates have the same quality of medical care as individuals in the free community? How good does the food that the state serves inmates need to be? Does the state have any responsibilities for inmates' education beyond a GED? Does the state need to pay inmates for the work they do? These are the questions and issues that are addressed in this chapter.

Prison services can bring hope to some inmates. Here, Melinda Wilson, of Jacksonville, Florida (right), receives her GED diploma from Warden Norman Jenkins at the Homestead Correctional Institution in Homestead, Florida, on October 7, 2010. Wilson had a fourth-grade education when she was sentenced to 22 years for second-degree murder and robbery in 2007. But she dreamed of getting a high school diploma, something tangible to encourage her when "that worthless feeling" darkened her prison cell. She marched the prison hallway to "Pomp and Circumstance" wearing a blue cap and gown to receive her GED along with a handful of fellow inmates.

AP Photo/Alan Diaz

L01 ROLE OF TREATMENT AND SERVICES IN PRISON TODAY

Correctional treatment can be defined as any means to correct an offender's character, habits, attitudes, or behaviors so as to overcome his or her propensity toward crime. At its core, the contemporary correctional system rests on the belief in an individual's ability to change. While this view expresses optimism about the human spirit, most correctional administrators also are well aware that the prison is an extremely unfavorable setting for correctional treatment.[6]

As you may recall, treatment has been part of the correctional experience since the nineteenth century. However, correctional treatment came under pressure more than 30 years ago when sociologist Robert Martinson startled both correctional personnel and the public with the pronouncement that "with few and isolated exceptions, the rehabilitative efforts that have been reported so far have no appreciable effect on recidivism."[7] Douglas Lipton, Judith Wilks, and Martinson had surveyed 231 studies on offender rehabilitation which are found in their book, *The Effectiveness of Correctional Treatment: A Survey of Treatment Evaluation Studies.*[8] Their research review found that there was little benefit from treating inmates in prison.

Despite Martinson's dreary conclusion, a spirited debate over the "nothing works" thesis has continued to rage. Treatment proponents have dismissed Martinson's claim as overreaching. When Paul Gendreau and Robert R. Ross reviewed the published works on correctional rehabilitation programs, they found that many intervention programs reported success.[9] According to Gendreau and Ross, this success rate was "convincing evidence that some treatment programs, when they are applied with integrity by competent practitioners in appropriate target populations, can be effective in preventing crime or reducing recidivism.[10] Even Martinson eventually conceded that "contrary to [his] previous position, some treatment programs *do* have an appreciable effect on recidivism. Some programs are indeed beneficial."[11] Mark W. Lipsey and Francis T. Cullen's comprehensive review of the studies of correctional rehabilitation has found consistently positive effects on reducing recidivism, but they add that considerable variability exists in those effects depending on the type of treatment, its implementation, and the nature of the offenders to which it is applied.[12] In Voices Across the Profession, Diana Bailey,

VOICES ACROSS the PROFESSION

© Diana Bailey

"**Many offenders, especially when they are locked up for a while, see life as all about them. They have not necessarily thought of themselves in an employment career pathway context, and when you are doing a career assessment about them, they are totally enthralled.**"

DIANA BAILEY,
WORKFORCE DEVELOPMENT/
TRANSITION COORDINATOR

We have a variety of formal and informal career assessments of inmates inside the fence. Many offenders, especially when they are locked up for a while, see life as all about them. They have not necessarily thought of themselves in an employment career pathway context, and when you are doing a career assessment about them, they are totally enthralled. We are looking at their learning styles, interests and preferences, and work values. We are trying to work with their interests and skills, which many of them never knew they had. Teachers get to be creative in ferreting out their core competencies, trying to package their potential and to utilize their potential as much as possible.

The persons we are working with inside in the prisons frequently do not see themselves in terms of self-esteem or self-concept or as being part of any normal mainstream group. When they see a copy of their résumé, which looks cool and has legitimate skills on it, they feel really good about it. That is part of the skill development to get them ready for the horribly competitive workforce process they are going to be involved with when they get out. Even though we have low unemployment in Maryland, we are still suffering like nearly every other state. It is challenging for them to find employment in their area of career pathway and skill development.

Students also develop career portfolios, and they take those to either the one-stop career center or whatever service provider they may be linked up with. So, hopefully, they can hit the ground running when they get back to the community. When they leave the institution, for the most part, we have no further contact with them. We are hopeful that the providers can do their magic that we started inside the fence.

We also have at our maintaining institutions career centers that are very much like you would see in a public library. They have all the offender-specific and customized career development resources that would be useful for inmates doing career exploration or getting their résumé development taken care of. They usually will have sample applications and cover letters to help inmates, because most of them will be on their own when they leave us. Our goal is that they will have the skills to know what the career process is and to take it to the next step.

As a professional educator and a career development professional, the creativity of making a program and service delivery system for this population has been a real challenge. When it works, it is fabulous. When it does not work, it provides a high level of frustration. We think, what else could we have done? In many cases, [the problem is the] lack of support systems when they leave us. Increased skills give them improved self-esteem and more legal income necessary for economic self-sufficiency. Money means a lot to people; it gives them choices they might not have otherwise. The success stories may be few and far between, but when we have one, it is great.

Source: Interviewed in 2011.

workforce development/transition coordinator for the Maryland State Department of Education's Correctional Education Transition Mobile Unit, discusses a program for inmates that is used in the state of Maryland.

In sum, while Martinson's widely read review cast doubt on the effectiveness of correctional treatment, more recent reviews have found that programs can be highly effective under particular circumstances and with specific inmate populations, especially for those inmates who complete the programs. In the midst of these hopeful possibilities for treatment, there are at least two deterrents today that discourage the wider use of institutional programs:

- Overcrowded institutions, filled with inmate gangs, violence, and racial conflicts, require that the focus be on security and institutional survival.

- The "no frill" institutional emphasis found in many states cuts back on programming and treatment, as much as constitutionally is permitted.

CLASSIFICATION FOR TREATMENT

L02

In order to provide the most effective treatment, inmate needs are assessed at a classification center. Treatment effectiveness is thought to be maximized by matching inmate needs with the proper treatment modality. Proper classification is crucial to the efficient application of treatment because offenders are a diverse group, possessing a variety of behavioral issues and styles, as well as varying states of psychological health.

There are a number of classification systems used in American corrections. The earliest and the one that is most commonly used is **risk assessment**, used to assign inmates to high-, medium-, and low-risk caseloads. Another classification system is the **needs assessment**, used to record staff assessment of prisoners' problems, as well as the magnitude of these problems. Needs assessments are particularly essential for inmate reentry programs. See Figure 10.1, which includes needs related to prison adjustment. A third possible classification is the risk/needs assessment. The most widely used system of risk/needs assessment is the Level of Service Inventory-Revised (LSI-R). It includes such factors as criminal history, education/employment, leisure/recreation activities, companions, alcohol/drug use, and emotional/personal state. Even when inmates have been classified according to risk and needs assessment, there is an important consideration of their treatment amenability or likelihood of achieving success in the program, which is defined as the **responsivity principle**.[13]

In the 1980s, **SENTRY**, another classification method that has contributed to both treatment and the safety of inmates as well as staff, became the primary automated inmate management system for the Federal Bureau of Prisons. It provides immediate access to the current institutional population or community facility population. SENTRY further calculates all aspects of inmates' sentences and is the means by which inmates are assigned to specific facilities. SENTRY identifies inmates the court has determined need special evaluation, such as the need to separate inmates who have threatened each other, and records inmates' participation in disruptive groups and street gangs.[14]

Similar to the classification discussion in Chapter 5, which was focused more on institutional security rather than treatment, prison crowding makes it difficult to be able to provide an adequate assessment program concerning the treatment needs of inmates.

RISK ASSESSMENT Designed to predict new offenses or prison misconduct.

NEEDS ASSESSMENT Attempts to offer treatment-relevant information, such as social adjustment, hygiene, and level of family support.

RESPONSIVITY PRINCIPLE Maintains that programs should consider offenders' situations as well as characteristics that may become barriers to success in a correctional program.

SENTRY This system tracks and provides appropriate staff with access to critical inmate information, such as assignments, program completions, and inmate movement in every Federal Bureau of Prisons facility or while an inmate is in transit.

INITIAL INMATE CLASSIFICATION
ASSESSMENT OF NEEDS

NAME _____   NUMBER _____
       Last   First   MI

CLASSIFICATION CHAIRMAN _____   DATE _____ / _____ / _____

TEST SCORES:

                                                         _____
                                                          I.Q.

                                                          _____
                                                         Reading

                                                          _____
                                                          Math

NEEDS ASSESSMENT: Select the answer that best describes the inmate.

HEALTH:

| 1 Sound physical health, seldom ill | 2 Handicap or illness that interferes with functioning on a recurring basis | 3 Serious handicap or chronic illness, needs frequent medical care | _____ **code** |

INTELLECTUAL ABILITY:

| 1 Normal intellectual ability; able to function independently | 2 Mild retardation, some need for assistance | 3 Moderate retardation, independent functioning severely limited | _____ **code** |

BEHAVIORAL/EMOTIONAL PROBLEMS:

| 1 Exhibits appropriate emotional responses | 2 Symptoms limit adequate functioning, requires counseling, may require medication | 3 Symptoms prohibit adequate functioning, requires significant intervention, may require medication or separate housing | _____ **code** |

ALCOHOL ABUSE:

| 1 No alcohol problem | 2 Occasional abuse, some disruption of functioning | 3 Frequent abuse, serious disruption, needs treatment | _____ **code** |

DRUG ABUSE:

| 1 No drug problem | 2 Occasional abuse, some disruption of functioning | 3 Frequent abuse, serious disruption, needs treatment | _____ **code** |

EDUCATIONAL STATUS:

| 1 Has high school diploma or GED | 2 Some deficits, but potential for high school diploma or GED | 3 Major deficits in math and/or reading, needs remedial programs | _____ **code** |

VOCATIONAL STATUS:

| 1 Has sufficient skills to obtain and hold satisfactory employment | 2 Minimal skill level, needs enhancement | 3 Virtually unemployable, needs training | _____ **code** |

FIGURE 10.1 Assessment of Client Needs

Source: Patricia van Voorhis, Michael Braswell, and David Lester, *Correctional Counseling and Rehabilitation*, 6th ed. (Cincinnati: Anderson, 2007), p. 143.

Mentally ill inmates present a unique problem for correctional administrators. Here, public defender Jennifer Johnson (right) applauds client Carmen Morales for making improvements during a hearing at the Behavioral Health Court in San Francisco. Behavioral Health Court (BHC), a collaborative court with the San Francisco Superior Court, addresses the complex needs of mentally ill defendants with co-occurring substance use disorders by diverting them from jail and into appropriate community treatment. In this program, judges can offer a chance for users to go to rehab, get jobs, move into houses, find primary care physicians, and even remove their tattoos. There is enough data now to show that these alternative courts reduce recidivism and save money.

AP Photo/Eric Risberg

CORRECTIONAL TREATMENT METHODS

More than half of all prison inmates have experienced symptoms of a mental health problem or have had a recent history of mental disturbance. Consequently, all federal prisons and most state prisons and jail jurisdictions provide mental health services to inmates, including screening inmates at intake for mental health, problems, providing therapy or counseling by trained mental health professionals, and distributing psychotropic medications.[15]

Rehabilitation efforts begin early in the inmates' correctional experience and continue on until its end. While in the classification center, inmates are typed and presented with a series of conditions designed essentially to change and/or control their lifestyle, including getting help for a variety of problems (such as alcoholism, drug abuse, mental illness, etc.), mandatory meetings with treatment personnel, and a series of restrictions if they fail to partake in a treatment regime. Failure to abide by these conditions may result in loss of privileges, reduced good time, ineligibility for early release programs, and other penalties. This section presents a selection of therapeutic methods—individual, group, and self-directed programs that have been used nationally in correctional settings—and identifies some of their more salient features.

Individual-Level Treatment Programs

A number of different individual techniques are used within the prison, including insight-based therapy, behavior therapy, and cognitive-behavior therapy. These are reviewed below.

INSIGHT-BASED THERAPY It is common for prisons to employ insight-based therapy techniques for the treatment of mental and emotional disorders. There are many different types of insight-based therapy techniques, but in general they utilize insight, persuasion, suggestion, reassurance, and instruction so that inmates may see themselves and their problems more realistically and develop the desire to cope effectively with their fears and problems. (See Exhibit 10.1.)

Psychiatrists, clinical psychologists, and psychiatric social workers have used various versions of insight-based therapies in American prisons since the early twentieth century. Prisoners are encouraged to talk about past conflicts that cause them to express emotional problems through aggressive or antisocial behavior. The insight that inmates gain from this individual therapy supposedly helps them resolve the conflicts and unconscious needs that drove them to crime. As a final step, the inmate becomes responsible for his or her own behavior.

Insight-based therapies have some fundamental limitations in a prison context. Inmates usually do not see themselves as having emotional problems and are reluctant to share their inner thoughts with therapists. There are also staffing problems. Professional mental health staff make up only about 3 percent of agency staff, and they must provide a range of mental health services in U.S. prisons.[16] These

INSIGHT-BASED THERAPY Typically involves treatment designed to encourage communication of conflicts and insight into problems, with the goal being relief of symptoms, changes in behavior, and personality growth.

EXHIBIT 10.1 Insight-Based Therapies

Type	Treatment Goal	Qualifications of Therapist	Length of Treatment Period	Response from Offenders
Psychotherapy	Lead inmates to insight	Psychiatrist, psychologist, social worker	Long-term	Will examine individual problems with therapist
Transactional analysis	Lead inmates to insight	Psychiatrist, psychologist, trained nonprofessional, staff	Usually several months	Will examine individual problems in a group context and will learn a new approach to interpersonal relationships
Reality therapy	Help inmates to obtain basic needs	Psychiatrist, psychologist, trained nonprofessional, staff	Short period of time	Will learn to cope with reality, model responsible behavior, and determine right from wrong

staff are overworked because more than half of all prison and jail inmates have some form of mental health problem.[17] As a result, correctional treatment staff often have little time to conduct ongoing therapy. Instead, the few trained therapists in U.S. prisons are swamped with classification work and emergency cases.

BEHAVIOR THERAPY A second form of individual treatment, behavior therapy, rests on the assumption that desirable behaviors that are rewarded immediately and systematically will increase, and undesirable behaviors that are not rewarded or are punished will diminish or be extinguished. Behavior therapy uses positive and negative reinforcement to encourage desirable and extinguish undesirable behaviors. **Behavior modification** is the principal behavior therapy technique and is still practiced informally in a great many correctional institutions. It works like this: inmates receive additional privileges as they become more accepting of the institutional rules and procedures and as they give evidence of more positive attitudes.

The Evidence-Based Corrections feature looks at one successful attempt at modifying inmate behavior.

COGNITIVE-BEHAVIOR THERAPY Cognitive-behavior therapy (CBT) for offenders is based on the assumption that the foundations for criminal behavior are dysfunctional patterns of thinking. The intent is that by altering routine misinterpretations of life events, offenders can modify antisocial aspects of their personality and consequence behaviors. The goal of these interventions is to identify cognitive deficits linked to criminality, such as impulsivity, a concrete thinking style that

BEHAVIOR MODIFICATION A technique in which rewards or punishments are used to alter or change a person's behavior.

COGNITIVE-BEHAVIOR THERAPY (CBT) Therapy based on the assumption that the foundations for criminal behavior are dysfunctional patterns of thinking.

A counselor doing a mental health evaluation in the intake area at Georgia Diagnostic and Classification Prison in Jackson, Georgia. It is both a reception center (where inmates are evaluated and classified according to security level, mental health status, etc.) and a maximum-security prison where death row inmates are housed.

© Becky Stein

EVIDENCE-BASED CORRECTIONS

Getting Ready Program

The Getting Ready program is Arizona's common-sense approach to prerelease preparation designed to reduce postrelease recidivism. It is aimed at giving inmates better coping skills that can help them ease the shock of reentry.

The program begins on day one of incarceration and continues to the conclusion of every inmate's sentence. Getting Ready redefines the officer–offender relationship, shifting many responsibilities from the staff to the inmates and empowering both groups to function at substantively high levels. For example, officers do not tell inmates when to get up and when to go to sleep. Getting Ready does not just preach about what you ought to be doing when you get back to the real world. It brings the real world—what they call a "parallel universe"—into prison so that inmates in every custody level acquire and practice basic life skills from the first to the last day of their incarceration. In a sense, it involves adapting the prison life to resemble life in the community. One example is health care. Because health care costs are rising, Getting Ready helps prepare inmates to lower their medical costs upon release. It teaches them healthy habits—not smoking, eating healthy foods, exercising, and complying with medical directions—activities that will result in a lower co-pay on the outside. The Parallel Universe model has also been applied to inmates' work assignments. The program uses the U.S. Department of Labor's *Dictionary of Occupational Titles* to determine job categories and salaries and revises inmate pay to reflect what someone could expect to receive proportionately for performing this work in the community.

The same principle is applied to education. An inmate is not required to complete or further his education, but until he earns a GED—assuming he is academically able, which encompasses the vast majority of the population—he can be employed only in entry-level jobs, earning entry-level wages. Like in the real world, once they earn a GED, many other employment opportunities open up. In Getting Ready, a GED becomes a prerequisite to job training, better work assignments, and higher wages.

Getting Ready uses a three-tiered earned incentive system that changes the traditional paradigm. This system recognizes good behavior—greater acceptance of responsibility and better decision making—with rewards or incentives that can be earned over time, are appropriate to each custody level, and are prized by the population. For example, in Getting Ready, an inmate has to work very hard to earn a visit in which family members are allowed to bring food, and not all inmates in every custody level are eligible. Similarly, inmates who do well have the possibility of eating their meals in a less regimented setting, followed by a show or televised sports event, and the opportunity to buy snacks not ordinarily sold in the commissary.

Evaluations of the program indicate that since it was implemented, violence has been reduced, with inmate-on-inmate assaults decreasing 46 percent, inmate-on-staff assaults down 33 percent, suicides down 67 percent, and sexual assaults down 61 percent. The average one-year return rate for all releases in the two years before and after Getting Ready started improved 2.75 percent. Within this group of releases were 1,500 inmates who completed Getting Ready in its entirety. This group has done considerably better, as much as two years after release, than inmates of comparable risk who were not in the program.

Source: Dora Schriro, "Getting Ready: How Arizona Has Created a 'Parallel Universe' for Inmates," *National Institute of Justice Journal* 263 (2009), www.nij.gov/journals/263/getting-ready.htm (accessed March 5, 2012).

---

impinges on the ability to appreciate the feelings and thoughts of others, impairments in self-defeating behavior, egocentricity, inability to reason critically, peer interpersonal problem-solving skills, and a preoccupation with self.[18]

CBT in offender treatment targets the choices, thoughts, attitudes, and meaning systems that are associated with antisocial behavior as well as deviant lifestyle. It usually uses a training approach to teach new skills in areas where offenders showed deficits, such as generating alternative solutions, rather than reacting on first impulse; interpersonal problem awareness, evaluating consequences, opening up and listening to other perspectives; resisting peer pressure, soliciting feedback, taking on the person's well-being into account, and deciding on what is the most beneficial course of action.[19]

The CBT therapists act as teachers, and lessons are generally taught to groups in classroom settings. The lessons may include group exercises involving role-play, homework assignments, rehearsal, and intensive feedback and generally follow detailed lesson plans and structured curriculum.[20] People taking part in CBT learn specific skills that can be used to solve the problems they confront all the time as well as skills they can use to achieve legitimate goals and objectives. CBT first concentrates on developing skills to recognize distorted or unrealistic thinking when it happens, and then works toward changing that thinking or belief to mollify or eliminate problematic behavior.[21]

The most widely adopted of the cognitive-behavioral interventions is the **Cognitive Thinking Skills Program (CTSP)** developed by Robert Ross and Elizabeth Fabiano, which is now a core program in the Canadian Correctional System and has been implemented in the United States, Australia, New Zealand, and some European countries.[22]

CTSP was developed through a systematic review of all published correctional programs that were associated with reduced criminal recidivism. The researchers identified 100 evaluations of effective programs and discovered that all were designed to target offenders' thinking. Rigid thinking could be minimized by teaching participants creative thinking skills and providing them with prosocial alternatives to use when responding to interpersonal problems. Teaching offenders techniques of self-control could improve social adjustment. These interventions are core components of CTSP.[23]

A review of the literature leads to the conclusion that the combining element of cognition and behavioral approaches is found in the principle of self-reinforcement. This concept says that behavioral and cognitive changes reinforce each other. When cognitive change leads to changes in behavior, what takes place is a sense of well-being that strengthens the change in thought and, as a result, further strengthens the behavioral changes. This self-reinforcing feedback process is a key element of that cognitive-behavioral approach and is the basis for helping offenders understand the cognitive-behavioral process (see the "Cognitive-Behavioral Roadmap" in Figure 10.2).[24]

COGNITIVE THINKING SKILLS PROGRAM (CTSP) A cognitive-behavioral intervention, developed by Ross and Fabiana, designed to improve offenders' thinking processes.

COGNITIVE-BEHAVIOR THERAPY EFFECTIVENESS There is considerable research support that shows positive effects of cognitive-behavioral approaches with offenders:[25]

- A meta-analysis of 69 studies covering both behavior and cognitive-behavioral programs determined that the cognitive-behavioral programs are more effective in reducing rates of recidivism than the behavior programs. The mean reduction was about 30 percent for treated offenders.[26]

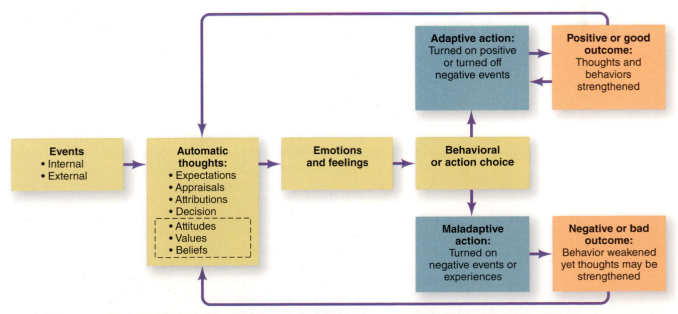

FIGURE 10.2 The Cognitive-Behavioral Roadmap: The Process of Learning and Change

Source: From Wanberg and Milkman, *Criminal Conduct and Substance Abuse Treatment: Strategies for Self-Improvement and Change: Pathways to Responsible Living: The Participant's Workbook.* Copyright © 2006 by Sage Publications, Inc. Reprinted by permission.

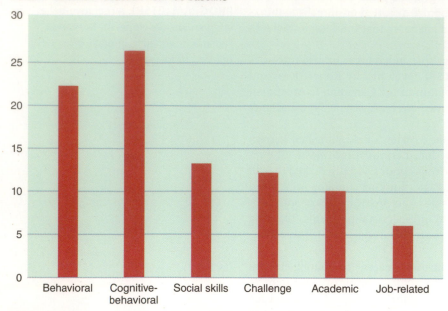

Percent recidivism reduction from .50 baseline

FIGURE 10.3 Mean Recidivism Effects for Skill-Building Programs

Source: From Mark Lipsey et al., *Improving the Effectiveness of Juvenile Justice Programs: A New Perspective on Evidence-Based Practice* (p. 26) as found at the following URL: http://cjjr.georgetown.edu/pdfs/ebp/ebppaper.pdf. Copyright © 2010 Center for Juvenile Justice Reform, Georgetown Public Policy Institute. Reprinted by permission.

- Other meta-analysis of correctional treatment concluded that cognitive-behavioral methods constituted critical aspects of effective correctional treatment.[27]

- Another study determined that the most effective interventions are those that employ cognitive-behavioral techniques to improve cognitive function.[28]

- There is strong evidence that positive results are more likely to take place among certain subgroups. For example, CTSP seems to be more effective with offenders over age 25 and with property offenders.[29] See Figure 10.3 for the recidivism effects for skill-building programs.

L04 ▶ Group Programs

In addition to individual-level therapies, most correctional institutions maintain group counseling programs. These programs help inmates to:

- Better control their emotions (understanding why they feel the way they do, learning how not to get too nervous or anxious, solving their problems creatively)

- Communicate effectively with others (understanding what people tell them and communicating clearly when they write)

- Deal with pressing legal concerns (keeping out of legal trouble and avoiding breaking laws)

- Efficiently manage general life issues (finding a job, dealing with difficult coworkers, being a good parent)

- Develop and maintain supportive social relationships (getting along with others, making others happy, making others proud)[30]

Some of the more common programs are discussed below.

DRUG AND ALCOHOL TREATMENT PROGRAMS The Federal Bureau of Prisons instituted its current drug treatment program 20 years ago and has adapted it in the years that followed to incorporate advances in correctional understanding of the problem. It uses cognitive-behavioral treatment and is implemented in a well-designed, evidence-based, modified therapeutic community. This extensive program includes drug abuse education, nonresidential drug abuse treatment for short-term offenders, and the Residential Drug Abuse Program (RDAP). This is the most intensive treatment program following the CBT model of treatment and is wrapped in a modified therapeutic model in which inmates learn what it is like in a prosocial community. Inmates live in a unit separate from the general population.

Translation Drug Abuse Treatment (TDAT) requires a continuation of drug abuse treatment in the community upon transfer to a residential reentry center (RRC). The primary responsibility of the regional TDAT staff is the monitoring of inmates' treatment progress during their stay in the RRC. Regional TDAT staff have developed a complex network of community-based contact to deliver treatment to inmates residing in an RRC or on home confinement. The regional TDAT key personnel work closely with probation to establish continual treatment as inmates leave Bureau custody and move to supervised release.[31]

Few states have developed this history or such a well-developed model for dealing with drug or alcohol offenders in prison, but there is an attempt in nearly every correctional system to provide some programming for these offenders. Treatment studies that have been done in prison populations have found that when drug programs are well integrated, using effective program elements and implemented carefully, these programs:

- Reduce relapse

- Reduce criminality

- Reduce recidivism

- Reduce inmate misconduct

- Reduced mental illness

- Reduce behavioral disorders

- Increase the level of the inmates' stake in societal norms

- Increase levels of education and employment upon returning to the community

- Improve health and mental health symptoms and conditions

- Improve relationships[32]

THERAPEUTIC COMMUNITIES

The **therapeutic community (TC)** treatment approach focuses on the total environment and uses all the experiences of that environment as the basic tools for therapeutic intervention. Evolving from the work of famed psychiatrist Maxwell Jones, this approach attempts to give persons within the therapeutic unit greater authority in the operation of their living units.[33]

An evaluation of the California Substance Abuse Treatment Facility (CSATF) found that it was associated with significant advantages for management of the prison—including lower rates of infractions, reduced absenteeism among correctional staff, and virtually no illicit drug use among prisoners.[34] While at one time more than 1,400 inmates received treatment, budget cuts have reduced that number to around 300 today.[35]

The Amity Prison TC in the J. Donovan Correctional Facility, a medium-security prison near San Diego, is one of the best-known therapeutic community programs. It provides intensive treatment to 200 male inmates who reside in a housing unit the last 9 to 12 months of their prison term. All participants are volunteers, and formal programming occurs four hours a day on weekdays. Amity also has a post-release program. Evaluations found the Amity treatment group had significantly lower rates of reincarceration, longer time to reincarcerate, and higher levels of employment than the control group.[36]

Self-contained therapeutic communities are difficult to establish in an institutional setting. Prison authorities are reluctant to delegate responsibility and authority to therapeutic communities and change rules to accommodate an atypical prison social system. However, therapeutic communities' recent success with treating drug abuse in prison has resulted in the increased development and use of these programs.[37] TCs have reduced recidivism when there is postprison support and follow-up treatment.[38] To ease acceptance of these programs, Therapeutic Communities of America has developed minimum standards and translated these standards into a formal accreditation process. The intent is to standardize the screening and selection process and to translate the broad standards into finding the ideal curriculum for various offenders. For example, how would a curriculum for mothers be different than for single men?[39]

ANGER MANAGEMENT

There is common agreement that anger is linked to violent criminal behavior in the community; to violent behavior, self-harm, and institutional conflict in the prison environment; and to failure to adjust on parole and postinstitutional release. As a result, **anger management programs**

THERAPEUTIC COMMUNITY (TC) A community treatment group designed to divert drug users from the criminal justice system; therapeutic communities vary in how much control they are given in prison settings.

ANGER MANAGEMENT PROGRAMS Programs designed to help inmates manage their anger, especially in interpersonal relations.

SELF-HELP PROGRAMS Programs from which inmates seek self-improvement, such as anger management, or express ethnic or cultural goals.

SERVICE PROJECT A worthy cause, such as disaster relief or peer counseling, in which inmates willingly participate.

are desired because of inmates' need for violence reduction techniques.[40] One survey of group psychotherapy services in correctional facilities indicated that anger therapy may be the most frequent form of group therapy offered within prison settings.[41] Anger management is frequently a part of drug treatment and sex offender treatment programs. Cognitive-behavioral approaches are often used as a means of helping inmates find ways to control their anger. Anger management or violence programs have also been implemented in other countries. For example, violence management programs are widely used in Australia.[42]

Yet, unlike other forms of prison treatment, such as drug abuse, little or no data are kept on anger management groups. One study that took place in a Midwestern low-security prison did find that those participants assigned to a treatment group had significant reduction in anger compared to those placed in the control group.[43]

Inmate Self-Help Programs

Departments of corrections frequently encourage inmates to establish **self-help programs**. These are run primarily by the inmates themselves and often express ethnic and cultural goals. Self-help groups meet in the evening or on the weekends. They usually are required to have staff sponsorship and establish governing bylaws and procedures.

Self-help programs offered in prison include Alcoholics Anonymous, Gamblers Anonymous, Toastmasters, Jaycees, Lifers, Dale Carnegie, Check Anonymous, Native American Spiritual and Cultural Awareness Group, yoga, transcendental meditation, tai chi, Insight Incorporated, Positive Mental Attitude (PMA), assertiveness training, anger management, stress management, life skills, moral development, and emotional maturity instruction.

HELPING OTHERS As part of the self-help initiative, some inmates are eager to become involved in **service projects**. These projects may have both self-help and service aspects or may focus on a needed institutional or community service. Some service projects are ongoing; others arise because of a disaster or emergency in the community. Service projects have included providing child care for prison visits, fighting forest fires and floods, adopting war orphans, doing peer counseling, recording books for the blind, training service dogs, donating blood, caring for rescued horses, participating as paramedics or in other lifesaving roles, and umpiring Little League games in the community.[44]

Sharon Richardson, an inmate at Bedford Hills Correctional Facility, in Bedford Hills, New York, and her yellow Labrador, Mitzie, show what Mitzie has learned. The dog has been trained to stare at Richardson every time she says, "Watch me." Richardson is one of about 30 women at the prison who take part in a program run by an organization called Puppies Behind Bars, which has inmates at several prisons in New York, New Jersey, and Connecticut help train service dogs to assist disabled people, including veterans returning from Iraq and Afghanistan.

© Joyce Dopkeen/*New York Times*/Redux

PRISON EDUCATION, VOCATIONAL, AND RELIGIOUS PROGRAMS

In addition to counseling and treatment, a correctional institution is responsible for providing all the necessary services to care for the physical, educational, recreational, and spiritual needs of inmates.

Academic Education

In adult institutions, academic education is usually available through adult basic education (ABE) programs, secondary and general education studies, postsecondary education programs, and social education programs. In a great many correctional systems, mandatory education is required of those inmates who manifest clearly defined educational deficiencies. College courses have been provided through live instruction, correspondence courses, television hookups, and release time, which allows inmates to attend educational institutions in the community. Community colleges have offered inmates courses leading to a two-year degree.

Improving inmates' educational skills may reduce recidivism through several mechanisms:

- Inmates who attain sufficient reading and writing skills for functional literacy may increase the possibility of lawful employment after release from prison. The importance of postrelease employment is an important consideration in staying crime-free. Therefore, educational programming in prison may reduce recidivism by improving job opportunities.

- The educational process may be helpful in reducing recidivism by facilitating the conscientiousness, maturation, and dedication that educational achievement requires. This view proposes that education may equip inmates to evaluate their environments and their decisions more thoughtfully and, as a result, make decisions that will assist them in remaining out of prison when released.

- The educational setting within the prison gives inmates an opportunity to interact with civilian employees in the context of a goal-oriented and nonauthoritarian relationship.[45]

Research studies have found that educational program participation was related to reduced rates of recidivism.[46] For example, one effort compared the impact of correctional education on re-arrest, reconviction, and reincarceration in Maryland, Minnesota, and Ohio, and found that participation in education resulted in lower rates of recidivism.[47] However, in spite of evidence that postsecondary correctional education (PSCE) reduces recidivism and improves institutional adjustment, prisoners have been denied access to higher education and Pell Grants, which provide college loans with beneficial repayment rules.[48] College prison programs have also been reduced, primarily because increasingly prison systems believe that prisoners do not need the frills of postsecondary schooling.[49]

Vocational Training

The need for vocational training has always been evident, because most inmates are educable and trainable but lack any regular work experience or any demonstrable skills in a trade. The basic purpose of vocational training, then, is to prepare inmates for jobs in the community.

The variety of vocational programs offered in men's prisons is impressive. Indeed, the Federal Bureau of Prisons UNICOR program lists 86 areas for which federal inmates are provided with vocational training opportunities; about 9,000 federal inmates complete training in at least one area each year.[50] In prisons across the nation, there are programs in printing, barbering, welding, meat cutting, machine shop work, electronics,

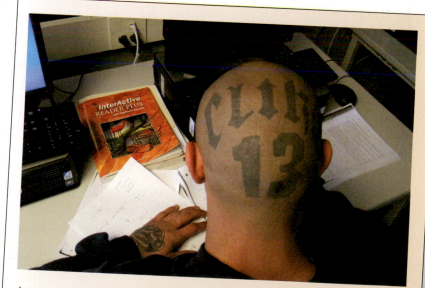

Inmates routinely take courses in an effort to earn a GED, receive specialized training, and even acquire college credit. Here, an inmate works on a reading assignment during a class at the High Desert State Prison, about 40 miles northwest of Las Vegas. More than 300 inmates at the prison receive adult education and vocational training from the Clark County School District through a partnership with the Nevada Department of Corrections

AP Photo/*Las Vegas Sun*, Paul Takahashi

baking, plumbing, computer programming, television and radio repair, bus repair, air conditioning maintenance, automotive body and fender repair, sheet metal work and repair, painting, blueprint reading, and furniture repair and upholstering.

Fewer vocational programs exist for women in correctional institutions. Vocational programs for women typically include cosmetology, secretarial training, business machine operation, data processing, baking and food preparation, and child care. But recently this pattern has been changing in some women's prisons. For example, Bedford Hills in New York offers women training in auto mechanics, electronics, and video technology, and the women's prison in Nebraska provides a course in truck driving. The Montana Women's Prison offers the "Prison Paws for Humanity" dog training program; there are several offenders currently involved with training dogs in this program.

Prison job fairs are offered in some prisons. The Federal Bureau of Prisons, Texas prisons, and Wisconsin prisons are among those correctional systems holding job fairs. At a 2008 fair at Wisconsin's Kettle Moraine Correctional Institution, 160 inmates participated in the job fair, which drew 33 employers and other exhibitors.[51]

Participation in vocational programs is seen as a means of reducing recidivism, based on the premise that the acquisition of vocational skills such as goal-setting, motivation, commitment, and learning of technical and nontechnical knowledge increases ex-offenders' legitimate employment opportunities following release.[52] David B. Wilson and colleagues found from an examination of 33 evaluations of vocational and work programs that "participants are employed at a higher rate and recidivate at a lower rate than nonparticipants."[53] Nonetheless, a sobering reality is that the crowded conditions in today's prisons only permit a small percentage of inmates to participate in vocational programs.

Religion

Religious instruction and services are always provided in federal, state, and private prisons. Full-time Protestant and Roman Catholic chaplains are available in most prisons. In some prisons, rabbis and imams come in from the outside community to conduct services for Jewish and Muslim inmates. Religious services include Sunday Mass and morning worship, confession, baptism, instruction for church membership, choir, and religious counseling.

The emphasis on religion in prison has recently grown, due in part to President George W. Bush's creation of a White House Office of Faith-Based and Community Initiatives. In 2003, Florida Governor Jeb Bush dedicated the first faith-based prison in the United States, a 750-bed medium-security facility for men in Lawtey, Florida. In 2004, Florida converted what was then the all-male Hillsborough Correctional Institution to the nation's first faith-based correctional facility for women. At least five states—Texas, Kansas, Minnesota, Florida, and Iowa—have opened new prison facilities in which the central philosophy involves religious teaching. In March 2004, the Corrections Corporation of America (CCA) announced its interest in developing faith-based correctional facilities. This private corporation is partnering with the Institute in Basic Life Principles, a Chicago-based prison ministry group, to develop faith-based programming that will be eventually extended to all 64 CCA jails, detention centers, and prisons throughout the United States. Missouri and Florida also opened facilities for youthful offenders based on faith-based principles.[54] See Exhibit 10.2 for what takes place in a Florida faith- and character-based prison. The Urban Institute conducted an evaluation of both Lawtey and Hillsborough, the two Florida faith- and character-based correctional institutions. Overall, "staff, inmates, and volunteers overwhelmingly find value in the FCBI [faith- and character-based institution] model and believe that it is achieving its goals of changing inmate behaviors, preparing inmates for successful reentry, and ultimately reducing recidivism."[55]

PROVIDING SERVICES TO INMATES

In addition to treatment, prison authorities provide basic human services to inmates. In some cases, these services are the result of legal cases brought by inmates demanding better treatment. The courts have mandated that medical services, visitation with family, and the use of a sufficient law library are constitutional rights of prisoners.

Medical Services

Medical services have become one of the most important issues of corrections, particularly because of infectious disease (HIV, AIDS, hepatitis B, hepatitis C, tuberculosis), female health issues, and elderly prisoners' medical concerns.

Key questions are: What kind of services should the state and the federal government provide for inmates? And what can the state and federal government afford? Most states spend about $2,500 a year for each inmate's health care, but some states spend more and others less. The quality of medical care varies from state to state and even from one prison to another within that state. Thirty-five out of 43 state correctional systems have initiated a **fee-for-medical-services policy** to reduce the major expense of health services. These fees range from $2 to $8 for each requested and nonemergency appointment; some states even charge for each prescription.

Visitation

Many inmates are married or have close families and friends, and a stay in prison strains relationships. To help inmates deal with the disruption caused by a prison sentence, most correctional institutes allow visitation privileges.

The quality of the visitation process has improved in recent years. Visiting arrangements tend to fall into the following categories: (a) closed visits, (b) limited-contact visits, (c) informal-contact visits, (d) freedom of grounds, and (e) conjugal or family visits. For a while, the general trend was to permit prisoners much more physical contact than they had been allowed in the past, but this trend began to change in the final years of the twentieth century.

Conjugal visits, or family visits, are permitted in a few states for inmates who have earned privileges. Conjugal visits usually mean that prisoners enjoy 24 or 48 hours of privacy with their families. A trailer is frequently provided for

EXHIBIT 10.2 Wakulla Correctional Institution, Crawfordville, Florida: A Faith- and Character-Based Prison

- Admittance to Wakulla is voluntary, as is program participation by the inmates. Entry into the program does not depend upon the inmate's faith preference or lack thereof, but rather on his or her behavior and desire to participate in the available special programs.

- Wakulla has a capacity of 1,622 inmates. Faith- and character-based activities take place each day of the week during daylight hours. During normal work hours, inmates are assigned to regular work assignments or education classes.

- Two other faith- and character-based institutions in Florida—Lawtey and Hillsborough Correctional Institutions—house 780 male inmates and 292 female inmates, respectively.

- The enthusiasm for faith- and character-based programs has been overwhelming, evidenced by the more than 300 inmates on a waiting list to enter such a program.

- Of the more than 15,000 volunteers statewide, more than 600 support the Wakulla program with services and other resources.

- Programs available to inmates include Victim Impact Panels, life skills, personal growth, family life, parenting, AA, NA, mentoring, anger management, and MAD DADS (Men Against Destruction/Defending Against Drugs and Social-Disorder).

- Many different faiths are represented at Wakulla, including inmates with no faith preference. Some of the faiths include Christianity, Islam, Jehovah's Witnesses, Seventh-Day Adventist, Judaism, Mormonism, Nation of Islam, and Buddhism.

- State funds may be expended for programs that further secular goals, but not for programs that further religious indoctrination. All related religious materials are donated.

- While it is too soon to calculate recidivism rates, inmates in faith- and character-based programs have proven to have fewer fights, get fewer disciplinary reports, and may even have fewer crisis mental health events (seasonal depression, anxiety attacks, explosive anger, etc.).

- Twenty-one states are operating or developing faith-based residential programs, but among these:
  - Florida is the only state with an entirely faith- and character-based institution.
  - Florida is the only state where the duration of the program can last until release. The duration for other states is 12 to 18 months.

Source: Florida Department of Corrections, Wakulla Correctional Institution, www.dc.state.fl.us/secretary/press/2005/FaithBasedWakulla.html (accessed March 6, 2012).

FEE-FOR-MEDICAL-SERVICES POLICY A correctional system policy in which inmates are charged for health care.

CONJUGAL VISITS A visit lasting one or two days during which prisoners can enjoy private visitation with their families.

Candace McCann, an inmate at the Rockville Correctional Facility in Rockville, Indiana, talks to her aunt, Margaret Earlywine, from her prison unit. McCann can also watch by video as her 7-year-old daughter, live from Earlywine's home three hours from the prison, draws a picture, models an outfit, or shows off lost teeth. Using ATM-like kiosks developed by a Florida company, the Rockville facility was among the first to allow inmates to link up with families at home.

AP Photo/Michael Conroy

MYTH	FACT
Prisoners are kept away from their families, resulting in divorce and family break-up.	Many states, including California, New York, and Connecticut, allow conjugal visits that give inmates private time with their families that can last up to two days.

the visit. The wife or other family member brings food to prepare, and a correctional officer checks on the inmate once a day or so. These programs have been expanded in most participating states to include female prisoners. Mississippi instituted a program of conjugal visitation in the 1950s; in 1968, the California Correctional Institution at Tehachapi instituted family visitation. More recently, California, Connecticut, Mississippi, New Mexico, New York, and Washington began programs of family visitation.

The Library

In recent years, prison libraries have been expanded and made available to all inmates. Inmates in most prisons are now permitted to obtain books from the state library if they are not available at the prison. In contrast to the days when the books were kept in the warden's office or in other inaccessible places, well-equipped law libraries generally are available for inmate use.

Prison Industries

Several prison industries programs developed in the late nineteenth century: contract system, piece-price system, lease system, and public account system, The first three of these systems involved partnerships between the state and private business that resulted in marketing the goods produced by inmate labor to the public. The major difference in these systems was found in who supervised the inmate labor: the state supervised prisoners under the piece-price system; private business supervised inmates under the contract and lease systems. The public account system involved direct sales by state-run industries to the public.

Resistance from labor unions and local businesses resulted in the passage of state and federal law in the twentieth century that prohibited inmate-made goods from competition in the free market. The Hawes-Cooper Act of 1929 permitted states to bar out-of-state prison-made goods from sale in the receiving state. In 1940, the Sumners-Ashurst Act was enacted, making transportation of prison-made goods in interstate commerce a federal crime. The passage of this final piece of federal legislation resulted in most of those few states that had not yet adopted the state-use system soon doing so.

There are several approaches to prison industry:

- *The prison provides space and a labor pool of inmates to hire.* Within this model, a company supervises the inmates and makes all decisions related to personnel, wages, and products. An example of this is the Free Venture Model, a federal program that began in Connecticut and now extends to 16 states, which attempts to achieve productive labor with private-sector efficiency, wages, and relevance. The goal of the Free Venture Model is a realistic work environment with a full workday. Inmate wages are based on output, and training for job skills can be transferred to work in the community.[56] Another well-known example takes place at the Eastern Oregon Correctional Institution in Pendleton, Oregon. Inside Oregon Enterprises is the employer, and inmates make a line of T-shirts, jeans, and jackets, known as Prison Blues.

■ *The prison becomes a temporary personnel service.* One example of this is telemarketing from prison. About a dozen states, including Arizona, California, Iowa, and Oregon, have call centers in state and federal institutions in which inmates are employed in telemarketing jobs.[57]

■ *The institution employs inmates for prison industry and pays them a wage.* Federal Prison Industries is the most noteworthy example of a correctional system developing a highly successful industrial program for inmates. FPI has continually made a profit through the sale of goods to federal agencies; it is entirely self-sustaining and operates without appropriating any funds. FPI pays prisoners reasonably well, at least in comparison with the pay they would receive in most state systems.

Typically, inmates choose to become involved in prison industry because it enables them to earn much-needed money, even though the hourly wages for most states are pitifully low. Inmates can make 20 to 30 cents an hour in state prisons, over $1.00 an hour in Federal Prisons Industries (UNICOR), or, if working for private industry in some prisons, $10 to $15 dollars an hour.

LO8 Making Correctional Treatment More Effective

Evaluation of education, vocation, and work programs indicates that they may be able to lower recidivism rates and increase postrelease employment.[58] Research shows that inmates who have completed higher levels of education find it easier to gain employment upon

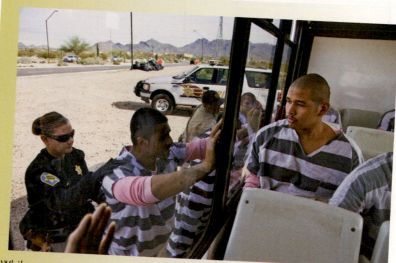

While most correctional institutions struggle to include the most contemporary treatment methods in their daily routines, including psychological counseling efforts, others rely on more old-fashioned methods to convince inmates to "go straight." Here, inmates of a chain gang get searched for contraband after weeding duty before they get on the bus that will take them back to Estrella Jail in Phoenix, Arizona. Estrella Jail is also home to America's only female chain gang. Inmates stay in their cells 23 hours a day during "lock down" unless they are out on chain gang duty, for which they can volunteer. There is no television or organized recreation provided.

© Scott Houston/Corbis

Correctional administrators are creating programs to ease reentry and cut down on recidivism. Here, inmate Mayda Hernandez enjoys time with her children, Ruben, 8, Gerardo, 4, and Eduardo, 11, after they opened gifts during a Christmas event for 15 female inmates in the Harris County Sheriff's Office Reentry Services Program in Houston, Texas. The inmates had presents donated by Navidad en el Barrio to give their children. The women are minimum-risk inmates who have had good relationships with their children. The inmates are also working with Reentry Services in setting goals for a successful transition back into the community in efforts to reduce recidivism. Children accompanied by adults can visit inmates during routine visitation days but without physical contact.

AP Photo/*Houston Chronicle*, Melissa Phillip

Community correctional centers enable residents to keep jobs in the community, helping to maintain their bond to family and friends. Here, William Palmer, employment services representative with Alvis House Community Corrections Center, passes out copies of the employment guide to Alvis House residents during an education consulting session at a facility in Columbus, Ohio.

AP Photo/Paul Vernon

EXHIBIT 10.3 Principles and Components of Effective Programs

- Teach interpersonal skills.

- Teach academic skills training, which includes adult basic education and general equivalency diplomas. This teaches the offender how to participate in education activities and how to read, write, and utilize basic arithmetic.

- Provide vocational skills training, which teaches how to acquire and maintain employment in order to fulfill financial obligations and how to engage in purposeful activity and postrelease employment.

- Make use of behavioral modification techniques.

- Use cognitive-behavioral therapy. This focuses on engaging in accurate self-appraisal and goal setting, solving problems effectively, maintaining self-control, and displaying prosocial values.

- Stress improving moral reasoning.

- Offer sex-offender interventions, particularly cognitive restructuring, which teaches the inmate to control self-destructive or other destructive behavior.

- Provide drug abuse treatment. Combine in-prison therapeutic communities with follow-up community treatment.

Sources: David Wilson, Leana Bouffard, and Doris Mackenzie, "A Quantitative Review of Structured, Group-Oriented, Cognitive-Behavioral Programs for Offenders," *Criminal Justice and Behavior* 32 (2005): 172–204; Mark Lipsey and David Wilson, "Effective Intervention for Serious Juvenile Offenders: A Synthesis of Research," in *Serious and Violent Juvenile Offenders: Risk Factors and Successful Interventions*, ed. Rolf Loeber and David Farrington (Thousand Oaks, CA: Sage Publications, 1998); and Joan Petersilia, *When Prisoners Come Home* (New York: Oxford University Press, 2003), pp. 176–177.

release and consequently are less likely to recidivate over long periods.[59]

It is also possible that a combination of efforts rather than a single approach can have beneficial results—such as combining institutional treatment with postrelease aftercare.[60] So although not all programs are successful for all inmates, many treatment programs are effective, and some participants, especially younger clients, have a better chance of success on the outside than those who forgo treatment.[61]

Effective programs are set up by an inspired individual or group of individuals, have unified teamwork on the part of the staff, have a transmittable philosophy of life, trust offenders with decision-making responsibilities, help offenders develop needed skills, are regarded as unique and different by offenders, avoid conflict with formal decision makers, avoid isolation from social institutions (such as the family and the school), and provide a support network following release or graduation (see Exhibit 10.3).[62]

The strategy for improving the effectiveness of correctional treatment has argued for some time that it is necessary to discover what works for which offenders in what contexts. In other words, correctional treatment could work if *amenable* offenders were offered *appropriate* treatment by *matched* workers in environments *conducive* to producing maximal effects.

Accordingly, if offenders are placed in the right programs at the optimal time for them to benefit from treatment, then program integrity becomes a matter of major importance.[63] Program integrity requires that effective intervention delivers the services to the offenders that they claim to deliver; that treatment has sufficient strength to accomplish goals; that program personnel are equipped to deliver the specified services; and that treatment is not only matched to the interest and needs of offenders, but has the flexibility to be modified according to the changing interests and needs of offenders.[64] Effective implementation of treatment ultimately depends on research to provide the information on who should get what treatment, when treatment is best given, and what frequency and intensity of treatment is necessary. It would certainly appear that the increasingly wide use of evidence-based practices will improve the effectiveness of correctional treatment.

SUMMARY

LO1 ▶ **Identify the role of treatment and services in prisons today**

The role of treatment and services in prisons today is to provide opportunities for inmates to profit from confinement and to provide adequate, basic care of inmates.

LO2 ▶ **Discuss classification for treatment**

The role of classification is to define the needs of inmates as well as the available programs that can meet those needs.

LO3 ▶ **Understand the individual-level treatment programs**

The three main individual techniques used within the prison include insight-based therapy, behavior therapy, and cognitive-behavior therapy. The treatment programs that are offered within prisons today tend to be more drug- and behavior-oriented than in the past and much less based on psychological models and insight.

LO4 ▶ **Identify the group programs held in prisons**

The therapeutic community (TC) and anger management programs are two of the most widely used group treatments in prison. The therapeutic community approach focuses on the total environment and uses all the experiences of that environment as the basic tools for therapeutic intervention. Anger management programs are designed to help inmates manage their inappropriate anger outbursts.

LO5 ▶ **Discuss inmate self-help programs**

Inmate self-help programs are run primarily by the inmates themselves and are designed to help inmates improve themselves, such as anger management, or express ethnic or cultural goals.

LO6 ▶ **Evaluate the quality of prison programs for inmates**

Prison programs include academic education, vocational training, and religious instruction and services. The quality of these programs varies from one prison to another, but they do face the problem that prison overcrowding makes it difficult for inmates to have available popular vocational training programs.

LO7 ▶ **Evaluate the quality of prison services for inmates**

The constitutionally mandated services provided to inmates include medical services, visitation, the library, and recreation. Inmates have long complained about some of these services, especially medical care, but overall they have recently been provided quality medical care.

LO8 ▶ **Understand how treatment in prison can become more effective**

If offenders are placed in the right programs at the optimal time for them to benefit from treatment, the likelihood increases that they will benefit from treatment. It is also possible that a combination of efforts rather than a single approach can have beneficial results.

Key Terms

risk assessment, 234
needs assessment, 234
responsivity principle, 234
SENTRY, 234
insight-based therapy, 236

behavior modification, 237
cognitive-behavior therapy (CBT), 237
Cognitive Thinking Skills Program (CTSP), 239
therapeutic community (TC), 241

anger management programs, 241
self-help programs, 242
service project, 242
fee-for-medical-services policy, 245
conjugal visits, 245

❓ Critical Thinking Questions

1. Although it is generally agreed that treatment does not work well in prison, treatment programs exist in nearly every American prison. Why?

2. In some prisons, inmates receive excellent care. Is it fair for them to receive better medical care than many citizens in the community?

3. Do you think that prisoners should have to pay for their food, board, medical care, and other services? Why or why not?

4. You are inside. The parole board tells you to get some therapy. Every choice mentioned in this chapter is available to you. Which will you choose? Why?

5. Is it exploitation of inmates for prison industries to make large profits but pay inmates so little?

Thinking Like a Corrections Professional

You are the chairperson of a congressional committee that has been asked to evaluate faith- and character-based prisons. How will you do this? Do you think that your committee and you will visit existing faith- and character-based prisons? Will your committee and you consider the following questions?

■ How is it possible for a faith- and character-based prison to exist and still honor the separation of church and state?

■ Could this type of program be placed in another prison (a unit or cellblock) if it were not state financed?

What other questions do you think you will consider? What will your final recommendations be?

Career Destinations

If you want to become a drug counselor, you may first want to read up on the most effective drug treatment programs in prisons today:

www.malibuhorizon.com/best-drug-rehab-treatment-centers.aspx

Another career possibility is correctional educator. To learn more, go to the site of the Correctional Education Association:

www.ceanational.org/

State correctional authorities routinely post jobs for correctional counselors. You can search for one in your state at this site:

http://federalgovernmentjobs.us/

Notes

1. California Department of Corrections and Rehabilitation, *Staff News: Communicating with Professionals in Corrections and Parole* (December 15, 2006): 1, 7.
2. Ibid.
3. Kevin Johnson, "Prison Diving Program Anchors Former Inmates," *USA Today*, July 14, 2008.
4. Maryland State Department of Education, http://marylandpublicschools.org/msde/ (accessed March 5, 2012).
5. Statements recently expressed to one of the authors by inmates he interviewed in various prisons across the nation.
6. Rudiger Ortmann, "The Effectiveness of Social Therapy in Prison: A Randomized Experiment," *Crime and Delinquency* 46 (April 2000): 214–232.
7. Robert Martinson, "What Works? Questions and Answers About Prison Reform," *Public Interest* (Spring 1974): 21–54.
8. Douglas Lipton, Robert Martinson, and Judith Wilks, *The Effectiveness of Correctional Treatment: A Survey of Treatment Valuation Studies* (New York: Praeger Press, 1974).
9. Paul Gendreau and Robert Ross, " Effective Correctional Treatment: Bibliotherapy for Cynics," *Crime and Delinquency* 27 (October 1979): 463–489.
10. Robert R. Ross and Paul Gendreau, eds., *Effective Correctional Treatment* (Toronto: Butterworth, 1980), p. viii; Paul Gendreau and Robert R. Ross, "Revivification or Rehabilitative Evidence," *Justice Quarterly* 4 (September 1987): 349–407.
11. Robert Martinson, "New Findings, New Views: A Note of Caution Regarding Sentencing Reform," *Hofstra Law Review* 7 (Winter 1979): 244.

12. Mark W. Lipsey and Francis T. Cullen, "The Effectiveness of Correctional Rehabilitation: A Review of Systematic Reviews," *Annual Review of Law and Social Science* 3 (2007): 297–320. See also Francis T. Cullen, "The Twelve People Who Saved Rehabilitation: How the Science of Criminology Made a Difference," *Criminology* 43 (2005): 1–42; Doris Layton MacKenzie, *What Works in Corrections: Reducing the Criminal Activities of Offenders and Delinquents* (New York: Cambridge University Press, 2006); Edward E. Rhine, Tina L. Mawhorr, and Evalyn C. Parks, "Implementation: The Bane of Effective Correctional Programs," *Criminology and Public Policy* 5 (2006): 347–358.
13. Patricia Van Voorhis, Michael Braswell, and David Lester, *Correctional Counseling and Rehabilitation*, 6th ed. (Cincinnati: Anderson, 2007), pp. 137, 146.
14. Office of the Inspector General, "Select Application Controls Review of the Federal Bureau of Prisons Sentry Database System," July 2003, www.usdoj.gov/oig/reports/BOP/a0325/app8.htm (accessed March 5, 2012).
15. Doris James and Lauren Glaze, *Mental Health Problems of Prison and Jail Inmates* (Washington, DC: Bureau of Justice Statistics, 2006), http://bjs.ojp.usdoj.gov/content/pub/pdf/mhppji.pdf (accessed March 29, 2012).
16. Eve Kupersauin, "Inmates Getting MH Care, but Quality Unknown," *Psychiatric News* 36 (2001): 6.
17. James and Glaze, *Mental Health Problems of Prison and Jail Inmates*.
18. Gerald G. Gaes, Timothy J. Flanagan, Lawrence L. Motiuk, and Lynn Stewart,

"Adult Correctional Treatment," *in Crime and Justice, 26th Edition: Prisons*, ed. Michael Tonry and Joan Petersilia (Chicago: University of Chicago Press, 1999), pp. 374–375.
19. Harvey Milkman and Kenneth Wanberg, *Cognitive-Behavioral Treatment: A Review and Discussion for Correctional Professionals* (Washington, DC: National Institute of Corrections, 2007), p. 5.
20. Ibid.
21. Sesha Kethineni, and Jeremy Braithwaite, "The Effects of a Cognitive-Behavioral Program for At-Risk Youth: Changes in Attitudes, Social Skills, Family, and Community and Peer Relationships," *Victims and Offenders* 6 (2011): 93–116.
22. Patricia van Voorhis, Lisa M. Spruance, P. Neal Ritchey, Shelley Johnson Listwan, and Renita Seabrook, "The Georgia Cognitive Skills Experiment: A Replication of Reasoning and Rehabilitation," *Criminal Justice and Behavior* 31 (2004): 282–305.
23. Ibid.
24. Ibid.
25. Ibid.
26. Frank S. Pearson, Douglas S. Lipton, Charles M. Cleland, and Dorline S. Yee, "The Effects of Behavioral/Cognitive-Behavioral Programs on Recidivism," *Crime and Delinquency* 48 (2002): 476–496.
27. Milkman and Wanberg, *Cognitive-Behavioral Treatment*, p. xix.
28. Ibid.
29. Pearson, Lipton, Cleland, and Yee, "The Effects of Behavioral/Cognitive-Behavioral Programs on Recidivism."
30. Dianna Newbern, Donald Dansereau, and Urvashi Pitre, "Positive Effects on Life Skills Motivation and Self-Efficacy: Node-Link

Maps in a Modified Therapeutic Community," *American Journal of Drug and Alcohol Abuse* 25 (1999): 407–410.

31. Federal Bureau of Prisons, *Substance Abuse Treatment*, www.bop.gov/inmate_programs/substance.jsp (accessed March 5, 2012).
32. Ibid.
33. Maxwell Jones, *Social Psychiatry in Prison* (Baltimore: Penguin Books, 1968).
34. Michael Prendergast, David Farabee, and Jerome Cartier, "The Impact of In-Prison Therapeutic Community Programs on Prison Management," *Journal of Offender Rehabilitation* 32 (2001): 3–78.
35. Personal conversation with facility staff, March 28, 2012.
36. Ibid.
37. Gerald Melnick, Josephine Hawke, and Harry K. Wexler, "Client Perceptions of Prison-Based Therapeutic Community Drug-Treatment Programs," *Prison Journal* 84 (2004): 121–127.
38. George De Leon, Gerald Melnick, George Thomas, David Kressel, and Harry K. Wexler, "Motivation for Treatment in a Prison-Based Therapeutic Community," *American Journal of Drug and Alcohol Abuse* 26 (2000): 33–46.
39. W. N. Welsh and G. Zajac, "A Census of Prison-Based Drug Treatment Programs: Implications for Programming, Policy, and Evaluation," *Crime and Delinquency* 50 (2004): 108–133.
40. Ibid.
41. Steven D. Vannoy and William T. Hoyt, "Evaluation of an Anger Therapy Intervention for Incarcerated Adult Males," *Journal of Offender Rehabilitation* 39 (2004): 40.
42. University of South Australia, Forensic and Applied Psychology Research Group, www.unisa.edu.au/faprg/ (accessed March 5, 2012).
43. Vannoy and Hoyt, "Evaluation of an Anger Therapy Intervention for Incarcerated Adult Males," p. 40.
44. For animal programs in prison, see Gennifer Furst, *Animal Programs in Prison: A Comprehensive Assessment* (Boulder, CO: Lynne Rienner Publishers, 2011).
45. Gaes, Flanagan, Motiuk, and Stewart, "Adult Correctional Treatment," pp. 374–375.

46. Lauren O'Neill, Doris Layton MacKenzie, and David M. Bierie, "Educational Opportunities Within Correctional Institutions: Does Facility Type Matter?" *Prison Journal* (2007): 311–327; J. Bouffard, D. L. MacKenzie, and L. Hickman, "Effectiveness of Vocational Education and Employment Programs for Adult Offenders: A Methodology-Based Analysis of the Literature," *Journal of Offender Rehabilitation* 31 (2000): 1–41; and David B. Wilson, Catherine A. Gallagher, and Doris L. MacKenzie, "A Meta-Analysis of Corrections-Based Education, Vocation, and Work Programs for Adult Offenders," *Journal of Research in Crime and Delinquency* 47 (November 2000): 347–368.
47. Stephen J. Steurer, Linda Smith, and Alice Tracy, *OCE/CEA: Three-State Recidivism Study*, report submitted to the Office of Correctional Education (Washington, DC: Correctional Education Association; Department of Education, 2001).
48. Joshua Page, "Eliminating the Enemy: The Import of Denying Prisoners Access to Higher Education in Clinton's America," *Punishment and Society* 6 (2004): 357–378.
49. United States General Accounting Office, *Prisoner Releases: Reintegration of Offenders into Communities* (Washington, DC: U.S. General Accounting Office: 2001).
50. Federal Bureau of Prisons, www.bop.gov (accessed March 5, 2012).
51. Dan Benson, "Prison Job Fair Gives Inmates a Rehearsal for Life Outside," *Journal Sentinel*, September 29, 2008.
52. Wilson, Gallagher, and MacKenzie, "A Meta-Analysis of Corrections-Based Education, Vocation, and Work Programs for Adult Offenders," p. 361.
53. Ibid.
54. Nancy G. LaVigne, Diana Brazzell, and Kevonne Small, *Evaluation of Florida's Faith- and Character-Based Institutions: Final Report* (Washington, DC: Urban Institute, 2007). For a discussion of those who volunteer for faith-based programs, see Scott D. Camp, Jody Klein-Saffran, Okyun (Karl) Kwon, Dawn M. Daggett, and Victoria Joseph,

"An Exploration into Participation in a Faith-Based Prison Program," *Criminology and Public Policy* 5 (2006): 529–550.
55. LaVigne, Brazzell, and Small, *Evaluation of Florida's Faith- and Character-Based Institutions: Final Report*.
56. Connecticut Department of Corrections, *Free Venture Model in Correction* (Hartford, CT: Department of Corrections, n.d.).
57. Jon Swartz, "Inmates vs. Outsourcing, *USA Today*, July 6, 2004.
58. Wilson, Gallagher, and MacKenzie, "A Meta-Analysis of Corrections-Based Education, Vocation, and Work Programs for Adult Offenders," pp. 347–368.
59. Mary Ellen Batiuk, Paul Moke, and Pamela Wilcox Rountree, "Crime and Rehabilitation: Correctional Education as an Agent of Change—A Research Note," *Justice Quarterly* 14 (1997): 167–80.
60. Megan Kurlychek and Cynthia Kempinen, "Beyond Boot Camp: The Impact of Aftercare on Offender Reentry," *Criminology and Public Policy* 5 (2006): 363–388.
61. David Farrington and Brandon Welsh, "Randomized Experiments in Criminology: What Have We Learned in the Last Two Decades?" *Journal of Experimental Criminology* 1 (2005): 9–38.
62. Dr. Martin Groder, the late psychiatrist and pioneer of therapeutic communities, advocated these common elements of effective programs throughout his career. We discussed these principles during interviews one of the authors had with Dr. Groder; the last was in 2002.
63. Evidence-based practices are one of the common requirements of correctional programs today; this has to do with referring and using other programs that have been found to be effective. See Edward J. Latessa, "The Challenge of Change: Correctional Programs and Evidence-Based Practices," *Criminology and Public Policy* 4 (2004): 547–560.
64. See Lipsey and Cullen, "The Effect of Correctional Rehabilitation: A Review of Systematic Reviews," pp. 297–320.

In 1997, Steven Cunningham, a convicted killer, told authorities that he had also killed a 15-year-old girl named Angela Correa 10 years earlier. His confession (along with DNA evidence) eventually helped clear Jeffrey Mark Deskovic, one of Angela's high school classmates, who was wrongfully imprisoned for 16 years for the crime. Retesting of DNA recovered from Correa's body had matched it to Cunningham, who was already serving a 20-to-life sentence for another murder committed several years later. Cunningham at first denied his role in the killing, but eventually confessed to raping and strangling Correa, a sophomore at Peekskill High School in New York.[1]

Deskovic, like many freed inmates, has struggled to rebuild his life. For six months, he got by on $137 a month in disability checks and $150 in food stamps from the federal government. Earning money through speech and newspaper articles about wrongful convictions, he paid rent for the first time in his life, for an apartment the county subsidized because of his depression and post-traumatic stress disorder. He enrolled at Mercy College in Dodds Ferry, New York, on a $22,000 scholarship, but found relationships with females as well as his male peers difficult.[2]

While some correctional experts believe that anyone can be successfully treated and rehabilitated in prison, others point to repeat killers such as Steven Cunningham and say that they are untreatable, unrepentant, and should never be released or paroled. There is little if any evidence that incarceration reduces an offender's risk of reoffending upon return to the community.[3] Cunningham knew another innocent man had been convicted for a crime he himself had committed, but chose to say and do nothing for 16 years, even though he was already in prison! Perhaps he thought that he might one day be paroled and a second murder conviction would ruin his chances for early release. Should violent criminals ever be given the chance of early release? Is it fair to the victim of the crime and/or future victims?

Jeffrey Mark Deskovic with one of his lawyers, Barry Scheck, at a news conference, September 20, 2006, upon his release from prison. Deskovic was wrongly imprisoned for 16 years for killing a young girl; another man, Steven Cunningham, was the actual killer.

eleven

PAROLE AND RELEASE TO THE COMMUNITY

LEARNING OBJECTIVES

LO1 Understand parole practices today

LO2 Know how the parole board functions

LO3 Identify the rules of those parolees released to the community

LO4 Understand the procedures involved in the revocation of parole

LO5 Be able to identify why people fail on parole

LO6 Identify some of the rights that ex-offenders have lost

AP Photo/Mark Humphrey

Parole is one of the most controversial aspects of the criminal justice process. What makes parole so controversial is that there are offenders such as Steven Cunningham who, in the public's mind, should never be paroled. Some people find it offensive to have them come up for parole at certain intervals. Then there are other ex-offenders who commit violent crimes and the question is raised why they were paroled in the first place. This chapter considers the problems and possibilities of parole, including other means of returning inmates to the community. We will first discuss parole practices and then examine the importance of reentry for ex-offenders leaving prison.

PAROLE PRACTICES

As you may recall (Chapter 1), the origins of parole can be traced to the work of Alexander Maconochie, superintendent of a penal colony on Norfolk Island, Australia. Maconochie issued "marks" encouraging positive behavior and let inmates serve their sentences in stages, each increasing in responsibility. The final stage was a **ticket of leave**.

Later, influenced by Maconochie, Sir Walter Crofton established the "Irish mark system" in which inmates could earn early release by positive behavior. He created the four stages of graduated release: solitary confinement, special prison, open institution, and ticket of leave.

The Irish system was well received, appeared to have low rates of recidivism, and penologists from the United States began to urge bringing these ideas of graduated release to the United States.[4]

Zebulon R. Brockway presented a paper on the Irish mark system at the First Correctional Congress in 1870, and when he was appointed superintendent of Elmira Reformatory (opened in 1876), he adopted the mark system. Brockway would release inmates conditionally to the community once they demonstrated reformation, and there they would be supervised by state agents. Parole, as it was called, rapidly spread across the United States. But it was not until 1944 that all states had adopted the indeterminate sentence and the use of parole.

Extent of Parole Today

Today, most inmates return to society and try to resume their lives. For the majority of these inmates, their reintegration into society comes by way of **parole**—the planned community release and supervision of incarcerated offenders before the expiration of their full prison sentences. There are about 820,000 people on parole, a number that has increased over the past decade. Each year about 550,000 inmates are released on parole, and up until 2009, the number of parole entries increased each year (see Figure 11.1).[5]

L01 Principles of Parole

Regardless of its format, parole is based on the following principles:

- The state extends to offenders a privilege by releasing them from prison before their full sentence is served.

- The state also enters a release contract with offenders in exchange for their promise to abide by certain conditions.

After many years behind bars, nothing seems familiar to parolees. The pace of life sometimes startles them, causing them to feel like outsiders in their own communities. The Fortune Society is dedicated to helping inmates make a successful adjustment back into society and believes in a world where all who are at-risk, incarcerated, or formerly incarcerated can become positive, contributing members of society. Their work supports successful reentry of formerly incarcerated men and women and promotes alternatives to incarceration. In this photo, Betty Wilson teaches Nolen Ruiz how to make vegetarian lasagna at the Fortune Society, where former prisoners can learn to cook for their families.

© Chester Higgins Jr./*New York Times*/Redux

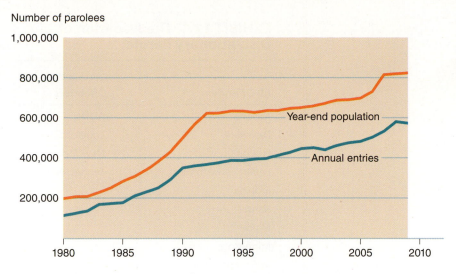

Number of parolees

FIGURE 11.1 Annual Parole Populations and Entries to State Parole

Source: Lauren E. Glaze and Thomas P. Bonczar, *Probation and Parole in the United States, 2009* (Washington, DC: Bureau of Justice Statistics, 2010), Tables 5 and 12, pp. 5 and 33.

■ Offenders who violate the law or the conditions of parole can be returned to prison to complete their sentences.

■ The state retains control of parolees until they are dismissed from parole.

DISCRETIONARY PAROLE The decision to release inmates is made by a parole board.

MANDATORY PAROLE RELEASE Inmate is released on parole when the unserved portion of the maximum prison term equals good time.

Types of Parole

The format of parole is determined by statutory requirement. In indeterminate sentencing states, after an inmate has served the minimum sentence his or her case is reviewed by a parole board, a duly constituted body of men and women who review inmate cases and determine whether offenders have reached a rehabilitative level sufficient to deal with the outside world. The board also dictates what specific parole rules parolees must obey. After reviewing the case, they have the discretion to release the inmate to serve the remainder of his or her sentence in the community.

This use of **discretionary parole** has been abolished in 13 states and the federal government, and four states have abolished discretionary parole for certain offenses (see Exhibit 11.1 for the states that have abolished it). See Figure 11.2 for the percentage of parolees by type of release. In the remaining jurisdictions that use determinate sentencing models, the amount of time a person must remain in prison is a predetermined percentage of the sentence, assuming there are no infractions or escape attempts. Referred to as **mandatory parole release**, under this model the inmate is released when the unserved portion of the maximum prison term equals his or her earned good time (less time served in jail awaiting trial).[6]

In some states, sentences can be reduced by more than half with a combination of statutory and earned good time. If the conditions of their release are violated, mandatory releasees can have their

Most inmates leave prison before the completion of their sentence and are placed on parole. Here, Michael Franzese (left), a former captain in the Colombo crime family, leaves the ball park after coaching an all-star Little League team. Franzese spent three years in federal prison in the late 1980s for racketeering and tax conspiracy. Then, he says, he decided to leave the Mafia. Much to his surprise and that of many law enforcement officials, the decision has not proven fatal. After another stint in prison for parole violation from 1991 to 1994, Franzese says he left his life of crime and has planted new roots in Los Angeles—promoting hip-hop concerts, developing real estate, and pursuing his true passion, coaching Little League baseball.

© Lee Celano/*New York Times*/Redux

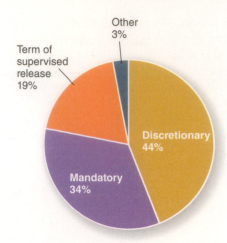

FIGURE 11.2 Adults on Parole by Type of Release from Prison

Source: Lauren E. Glaze and Thomas P. Bonczar, *Probation and Parole in the United States, 2009* (Washington, DC: Bureau of Justice Statistics, 2010), Table 21, p. 42.

EXHIBIT 11.1 The Abolition of Discretionary Parole

All Offenders	Certain Violent Offenders
Arizona	Alaska
Delaware	Louisiana
Florida	New York
Federal government	Tennessee
Indiana	
Kansas	
Maine	
Minnesota	
Mississippi	
North Carolina	
Oregon	
Virginia	
Washington	
Wisconsin	

MYTH

Every inmate, save those serving life for murder, has a right to get parole if they behave well in prison.

FACT

The Supreme Court has ruled that there is no legal right to parole. All inmates are entitled to is an opportunity to be heard by a parole-granting authority and a statement of reasons if their parole is denied.

good time revoked and be returned to the institution to serve the remainder of their unexpired term.

The remaining inmates are released for a variety of reasons, including expiration of their term, commutation of their sentence, and court orders to relieve overcrowded prisons.[7] In a few instances, inmates are released after their sentence has been commuted by a board of pardons or directly by a governor or even the president of the United States. About 15 percent of prison inmates are released after serving their entire maximum sentence without any time excused or forgiven. And despite the efforts of correctional authorities, about 7,000 inmates escape every year from state and federal prisons (the number of escapes is actually declining, due in part to better officer training and more sophisticated security measures).[8]

The Parole Board

The **parole board** is administered by an independent agency (autonomous model) or is part of a single large department that runs all state correctional programs (consolidated model). The parole board is an independent agency in all but five states (Maryland, Michigan, Minnesota, Ohio, and Texas), but parole field services are administered by the department of corrections in two-thirds of the states.

The duties of the parole board are as follows:

- To select and place prisoners on parole
- To aid, supervise, and provide continuing control of parolees in the community
- To determine when the parole function is completed and to discharge from parole
- To determine whether parole should be revoked, if violations of conditions occur

PAROLE BOARD An official panel that determines whether an inmate serving an indeterminate sentence is ready for parole.

The majority of states have a full-time parole board. The membership of state parole boards varies from three to nineteen. New York has the largest parole board with nineteen members. Twenty-two jurisdictions have five members; ten jurisdictions have three. In nineteen states, the governor appoints the parole board; Wisconsin and Ohio are the only states that appoint members from a civil service list. Very few states require specific professional qualifications for board members.

The board's authority to grant or deny parole is based on its assessment of the risk of the inmate to the community as well as his or her readiness to return to community life. Parole decisions are made in a number of ways. Some jurisdictions have the entire board interview eligible inmates; in other jurisdictions, only part of the board interviews. A few jurisdictions use hearing examiners to interview inmates. Some states do not interview inmates at all; they make their decisions based solely upon written reports.

PAROLE GUIDELINES   In nearly all states that still authorize parole, authorities have further restricted parole by setting specific standards that inmates must meet to be eligible for release. Many of these states use formal risk prediction instruments or **parole guidelines** to structure the parole decision-making process. Parole guidelines are actuarial devices that predict inmates' risk of recidivism based on crime and offender background information. The guidelines produce a "seriousness" score for each offender by summing the points assigned for various background characteristics (higher scores mean greater risk). Prisoners with the least serious crimes and the lowest statistical probability of reoffending are the first to be released.[9]

Many guidelines are based on the U.S. Parole Commission's salient factor score (SFS). In use since 1981, the salient factor score is based on:

- Number of previous convictions/adjudications
- Number of previous commitments that were more than 30 days
- Age at current offense
- Recent three-year prison commitment-free period
- Heroin/opiate or other drug dependency
- Whether inmate is older

The SFS places the inmate in one of four risk categories: very good, good, fair, or poor. Accordingly, parole officials consider this score in deciding whether parole is to be granted and, if so, what level of supervision will be needed.[10]

Despite these advantages, few states currently rely primarily on parole guidelines or risk prediction instruments for making release decisions. Maryland, Ohio, Pennsylvania, Virginia, and Washington do still use risk assessment instruments, but in each of these instances, risk assessment scores are strictly advisory.[11]

PAROLE GRANT HEARINGS   Discretionary parole decisions are made at a parole grant hearing. At this hearing, the full board or a selected subcommittee reviews information, may meet with the offender, and then decides whether the parole applicant has a reasonable probability of succeeding outside of prison. Each parole board has its own way of reviewing cases.

In a few states, such as Ohio, parole board members meet face to face with the applicant before a decision is made. A face-to-face meeting can be beneficial because the hearing panel can get feedback from inmates to more thoroughly evaluate parole readiness. Parole board officials, many of whom have varied professional training and experience, can use these meetings to assess an inmate's sincerity and readiness for release.[12] In addition, parole boards will look at the inmate's crime, institutional record, and willingness to accept responsibility before making the release decision. Some jurisdictions rely on standardized tests that predict whether a potential parolee may recidivate upon release.[13] Inmates who

PAROLE GUIDELINES   Actuarial devices predicting the risk of recidivism based on information about the offender and the crime.

maintain their innocence may find that denying responsibility for their crimes places their release date in jeopardy. The requirement that they admit guilt or culpability is especially vexing for those inmates who are actually innocent and who actively refuse to accept their institutional label of "convicted criminal."[14]

One of the major issues concerning parole board decision making is whether it has racial disparity effects. Kathryn D. Morgan and Brent Smith's study of parole in Alabama found that race did not have a significant impact on decisions at the preliminary screening stage or the parole release stage. They found that 42 percent of the African American inmates up for parole were released, compared to 43 percent of the white inmates, a finding that supports equal treatment in the parole grant decision.[15]

Most states have recently taken measures to ensure due process at parole grant hearings. For example, about half of the states now permit counsel to be present and witnesses to be called. Verbatim transcripts are frequently kept of the hearings. Furthermore, inmates are typically provided with both a written and an oral explanation of the parole decision. However, inmates continue to be denied access to their files, which means they are unable to determine why their case was decided the way it was.

Characteristics of Those on Parole

Regardless of the method of their release, former inmates face the formidable task of having to readjust to society. This means regaining legal rights they may have lost on their conviction, reestablishing community and family ties, and finding employment. After being in prison, these goals are often difficult to achieve. The typical characteristics of adults on parole are that they are predominantly male; are divided between white and African American as well as a strong Hispanic or Latino representation; are being supervised by a parole officer and have a sentence length of one year or more; and were sentenced for drug, violent, or property offenses, in that order (see Figure 11.3).

L03 ## The Parolee in the Community

Once released into the community, the typical parolee is given a set of rules and conditions that must be obeyed—standard conditions applicable to all parolees and special conditions tailored to particular parolees. These may include:

- Reporting to the parole agent within 24 hours of prison release

- Not carrying weapons

- Reporting changes of address and employment

FIGURE 11.3 Characteristics of Adults on Parole

Source: Lauren E. Glaze and Thomas P. Bonczar, *Probation and Parole in the United States, 2009* (Washington, DC: Bureau of Justice Statistics, 2010), Tables 17–19.

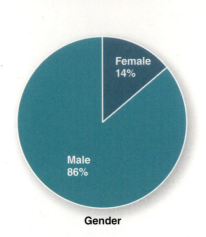

Gender

- Female 14%
- Male 86%

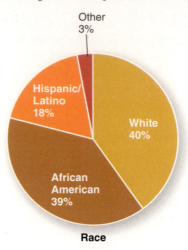

Race

- Other 3%
- Hispanic/Latino 18%
- White 40%
- African American 39%

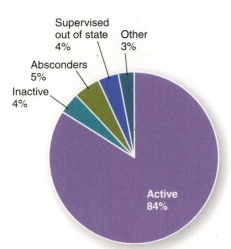

Status of supervision

- Supervised out of state 4%
- Other 3%
- Absconders 5%
- Inactive 4%
- Active 84%

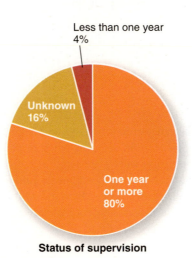

Status of supervision

- Less than one year 4%
- Unknown 16%
- One year or more 80%

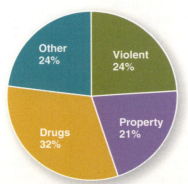

Type of offender

- Other 24%
- Violent 24%
- Property 21%
- Drugs 32%

- Not traveling more than 50 miles from home or not leaving the county for more than 48 hours without prior approval from the parole officer
- Obeying all parole agent instructions
- Seeking and maintaining employment or participating in education/work training
- Not committing crimes
- Submitting to search by police and parole officers[16]

Parolees who violate these rules may have parole revoked and be sent back to the institution to serve the remainder of their sentence. Once in the community, the parolee is supervised by a trained staff of parole officers who help him or her search for employment and monitor the parolee's behavior and activities to ensure that the conditions of parole are met. In Voices across the Profession, probation/parole officer supervisor Jennifer Reynoldson offers her perspective on some of the challenges faced by these officers.

Voices ACROSS the PROFESSION

© Jennifer Reynoldson

" Mentoring and changing lives is meaningful work that has a significant impact on the offender as well as the community. "

JENNIFER REYNOLDSON,
PROBATION/PAROLE OFFICER
SUPERVISOR

As a probation/parole officer supervisor in the largest judicial district in Iowa, there are multiple facets to effectively supervising community-based offenders on probation and parole. Research clearly shows that the implementation and utilization of evidence-based practices into daily case work with offenders has an impact on reducing recidivism and promoting positive change with offenders. It is the mission of the district as well as each officer to protect the public, employee, and offender during the course of their daily case management work with offenders. As a supervisor, it is my responsibility to work with probation and parole officers to ensure that they are utilizing the most successful techniques to assist in this process.

The fundamentals of evidence-based practices include assessing offender risk, identifying criminogenic need areas, and targeting those areas with cognitive-based interventions to reduce risk. It is the philosophy of the department that offenders will be supervised according to their risk and need level rather than by charge type. This means that a high-risk offender who is only on supervision for simple misdemeanor will receive the same intensive supervision as a felony offender with the same amount of risk. Why would we do that? If you are the victim of domestic violence and your partner has tried to stab you with a knife, beaten you in front of your children or held you hostage, and then is charged with a simple assault charge, it becomes clear why our department has chosen to focus on risk rather than charge type. As a side note, domestic violence calls are the most dangerous made by law enforcement and corrections.

We focus our limited resources on medium- to high-risk offenders and are able to reduce their risk significantly if evidence-based practices are incorporated into all aspects of their case management.

Evidence-based practices also clearly demonstrate that the most effective parole officers are those who can effectively build a working alliance and develop good rapport with the offenders they supervise. Effective officers will utilize a strength-based approach during office appointments that incorporates motivational interviewing techniques to help promote change. Think about your own experience in college, high school, or even grade school. Who was your favorite teacher and why? Most answer that their favorite teacher was funny, cared about them, and taught them things they didn't know before. The same can be said for our most successful parole officers. Those who have those traits get the best results.

Working in corrections is always challenging; you are required to think on your feet, make sound decisions, be a people person as well as have good organizational skills. However, it is also very rewarding. Mentoring and changing lives is meaningful work that has a significant impact on the offender as well as the community.

Source: Interviewed in 2011.

Parole officers' work takes them to many different locales where they must help people with a variety of serious social and personal problems. Here, parolees Tony DeWeese, Blaine Clayton, and Jason Marshal talk with parole officer Roland Asuncion in the yard during a break in classes at the drug treatment program for parolees in Folsom, California.

© Brian Baer/MCT/Landov

Parole is generally viewed as a privilege granted to deserving inmates on the basis of their good behavior while in prison. Parole has two conflicting sides, however. On the one hand, the paroled offender is allowed to serve part of the sentence in the community, an obvious benefit for the deserving offender. On the other hand, since parole is a privilege and not a right, the parolee is viewed as a dangerous criminal who must be carefully watched and supervised. The conflict between the treatment and enforcement aspects of parole has not been reconciled by the criminal justice system, and the parole process still contains elements of both.

To overcome these roadblocks to success, the parole officer may have to play a much greater role in directing and supervising clients' lives than the probation officer. In some instances, parole programs have become active in creating new postrelease treatment-oriented programs designed to increase the chances of parole success. In other instances, parole agencies have implemented law enforcement–oriented services that work with local police agencies to identify and apprehend parolees who may have been involved in criminal activity.[17]

THE PAROLE OFFICER

State parole agencies now employ nearly 65,000 full-time and 2,900 part-time workers, almost equally split between male and female full-time parole officers. Their average caseload is 38 active parolees for each full-time position devoted to parole supervision.[18] There are some communities in which parole officers continue to see service as an important part of the job. But for the most part, parole officers are seen and view themselves as control agents.[19]

Parole officers have much in common with probation officers. Both perform duties that are investigatory and regulatory. They face similar role conflicts and frustrations. Both cope with excessive caseloads, both lack community resources, and both may be inadequately trained. In fact, in many states the same officer provides both probation and parole services. In separated departments, state-administered parole services usually pay officers somewhat better than do county-funded probation services. Parole officers also tend to be older and more experienced in the criminal justice system than probation officers. See Voices Across the Profession and Careers in Corrections for the parole officer's job.

Surveillance and Constraint

Parole agents are powerful legal actors. Some states equip them with legal authority to carry and use firearms. Parole agents have legal authority to search persons, places, and property without fulfilling the requirement imposed by the Fourth Amendment. They are able to order arrests without probable cause and to confine without bail. Parole agents also are able to recommend revocation of parole for new crimes or for technical violations of the conditions of parole.

Agents' authority extends into the wider community. Their power to search applies to households where a parolee is living and to businesses where a parolee is working.[20] The search does need to be done within a constitutional framework.

© James Young

> "I see offenders coming out of prison all the time depressed, saying, "I am a felon, no one will hire me." You have to say to them, "Some won't—let's find the ones who will.""

JAMES YOUNG
PROBATION/PAROLE OFFICER

I currently supervise high-risk parolees. I carry a lower caseload than most agents to be able to supervise the offenders I have more effectively. The offenders I supervise all have curfews, they are required to report in the office more frequently, and they are placed on a color code to submit to drug and alcohol tests. Once I sign them up to parole they are given a color. They are then required to call a phone number twice a week. If their color comes up, they must come into the office the next morning and provide a urine sample. Since this is not one of the best parts of the job, the duties are shared by all probation and parole officers on a rotating basis. The positive results are then reported to the supervising officer for referring the offender to treatment or report to the court.

My street partner and I also conduct home checks and pre-parole checks; we will enter the offender's house and visit with the offender and their family members. We take note of the offender or family member's demeanor, cleanliness of the home, who is in the home, whether anyone is drinking or looking suspicious. We may check rooms, refrigerators, or areas outside the house for contraband. We do not carry weapons. We have pepper spray and a handheld radio to keep in contact with Polk County Sheriff's dispatch. They record all calls and check on us if we have been in a home for an extended period of time.

The area of parole that I am most excited about is what we call the reentry program. Years ago our only concern was to the public, and we would watch the offender until they made a mistake or broke a parole condition and sent them right back to the institution. Now we are working with the offender, placing them in programming that will help them get a job, take care of their mental health needs, connect them with the programs that will help them with basic daily needs, and most of all involve the family and their prosocial friends to help them get though this difficult period of transition in their life. I see offenders coming out of prison all the time depressed, saying, "I am a felon, no one will hire me." You have to say to them, "Some won't—let's find the ones who will." If you can move an offender from the institution to the home, provide them with solid information, point them in the right direction for meaningful work, and have regular contacts with spouses, parents, and adult children to help, you can have an offender who feels good about himself. He is productive, he is being a father again and supportive of his spouse, with a very good chance of staying out of the institution.

Source: Interviewed in 2011.

Because of the power and privilege, the relationship that develops between parole officer and parolee is much more adversarial than supportive. Parolees see officers' weapons (in those states that approve carrying of weapons) and handcuffs and know the officers can have them returned to prison. In turn, parole officers know that some parolees are dangerous and capable of assaulting them.

Supervision of Parolees

Five states' agencies account for nearly half of the adults under parole supervision: California, Texas, Illinois, New York, and Pennsylvania.[21] A number of technologies are being used to aid supervision by parole agencies nationwide. These include handheld computers, electronic kiosks, concealed weapons detection to increase officer safety, and face and voice recognition technologies. Parole officers also use drug and alcohol testing, remote alcohol and drug monitoring, new technologies for monitoring sex offenders, such as penile plethysmographs, and computer surveillance software.[22] These technologies are changing the nature of parole supervision, the manner in which drug and alcohol tests are conducted, and locating and tracking parolees within geographical boundaries.[23] The TechnoCorrections feature discusses the use of GPS to monitor sex offenders.

CAREERS in Corrections

PAROLE OFFICER

Job Preparation

In addition to a college education, a volunteer experience in a probation/parole agency or a residential work release program would be looked upon in a favorable way during the job interview process.

Nature of the Job

Parole officers identify and supervise offenders who are eligible for conditional release from prison before they have completed their sentences. To merit parole, inmates must obey rules, perform prison jobs well, and show progress in rehabilitation and therapy programs. Some parole officers work inside correctional facilities, preparing reports for parole boards. They assess inmates' lives before and during incarceration, how prisoners' families will affect their community adjustment, and what job prospects inmates might have if released. Based on officers' reports and interviews with inmates and their families, the boards choose certain prisoners for release. Field officers work with parolees once they have returned to their communities. They help parolees find jobs, schools, or treatment programs. For example, former drug addicts may have to enroll in programs that help them stay off drugs. If parolees have financial problems, officers direct them to community agencies that can provide welfare benefits and other financial support. Some officers supervise halfway houses in which small groups of parolees live together to share experiences and lend each other support. Drug therapists, psychiatrists, and social workers often help with this supervision.

Qualifications and Required Education

A bachelor's degree in sociology, psychology, criminology, or correctional science is usually preferred. In addition, many agencies require one or two years of work experience in correctional institutions or other social agencies or a master's degree in sociology or psychology. Applicants must generally take written, oral, psychological, and physical examinations. In most states, parole officers must pass training programs and certification tests.

Job Outlook

Employment of parole officers is expected to grow through 2014. Mandatory sentencing guidelines, which call for longer prisoner terms and few opportunities for parole, are being reconsidered in many states because of budgetary constraints and court decisions. If additional prisoners gain early release, more parole officers may be needed to supervise them. Jobs for parole officers should also open up as experienced workers retire or leave the field.

Earnings and Benefits

Earnings vary depending on location and experience. The median salary for all parole officers is around $40,000 a year. The lowest 10 percent earn less than $26,000 per year, and the highest 10 percent more than $46,000 per year. Supervisors and directors often earn much more.

Sources: "Parole Officer Job Description, Career as a Parole Officer," http://careers.stateuniversity.com/ (accessed March 8, 2012). See also the American Correctional Association; American Federation of State, County, and Municipal Employees; and National Council on Crime and Delinquency.

INTENSIVE SUPERVISION PAROLE (ISP) The most at-risk parolees are placed on **intensive supervision parole (ISP)**. These programs use limited caseload sizes, treatment facilities, the matching of parolee and supervisor by personality, and shock parole (which involves immediate short-term incarceration for parole violators to impress them with the seriousness of a violation). ISP clients

INTENSIVE SUPERVISION PAROLE (ISP) More extensive supervision than is given for most parolees.

Electronic monitoring has been used to keep probationers under surveillance and is now being adopted for use with parolees. One prominent example is New Jersey's Sex Offender Monitoring Pilot Project Act, which became law in August 2005, authorizing the New Jersey State Parole Board to subject up to 250 of the state's most dangerous registered sex offenders to round-the-clock global positioning system (GPS) monitoring. The program was required because the state parole board's caseload of more than 4,300 sex offenders is one of the largest in America, mainly due to the passage of Supervision for Life sentencing guidelines for sex offenders. Today, sex offenders make up nearly a third of the parole caseload, with a net increase of about 45 new sex offenders each month.

An analysis of 225 sex offenders that have been subject to GPS monitoring in New Jersey found that only one of these high-risk sex offenders had been charged with a new sex crime while under GPS supervision. The lone offender was arrested at the crime scene, but even if he had left the scene, the GPS data was available to pinpoint his presence at the time and place of the crime, and was ready to serve as a vital aid to the investigation.

The following case examples demonstrate ways in which the state parole board's GPS monitoring has intercepted violations by sex offenders and has helped law enforcement agencies work together to protect the public.

■ In Sussex County, GPS tracking data revealed that a sex offender was repeatedly staying at an address other than his registered address. The unauthorized address turned out to be the residence of his girlfriend, who had an infant in the home. This data was turned over to the prosecutor's office. The sex offender was investigated and charged with violations of Megan's Law for failing to stay at his approved address.

■ In Burlington County, a sex offender's past victim reported the sex offender was stalking her. A review of GPS tracking data revealed that the sex offender had been at the former victim's place of employment and near her home. This information was turned over to the prosecutor's office.

■ In Union County, the GPS monitoring program tracked a Tier III sex offender to a residential mental health treatment facility where it turned out he was employed. Parole officers investigated and determined the sex offender did not register his employment with the prosecutor's office as required under Megan's Law. The prosecutor was notified, and the subject was suspended from his employment as it was determined that his commitment offense involved elderly victims.

The New Jersey project's success may herald increased use of GPS monitoring for parolees in the community.

Source: New Jersey Parole Board, "Report on New Jersey's GPS Monitoring of Sex Offenders," www.state.nj.us/parole/docs/reports/gps.pdf (accessed March 8, 2012).

---

are required to attend more office and home visits than routine parolees. ISP may also require frequent drug testing, a term in a community correctional center, and electronic monitoring in the home. More than 17,000 parolees are under intensive supervision; 1,400 of these are monitored electronically by computer.

Evaluations of ISP programs have produced mixed results. Some show that they may actually produce a higher violation rate than traditional parole supervision because limiting caseload size allows parole officers to supervise their clients more closely and spot infractions more easily.[24] However, some evaluations do show that under some conditions a properly run ISP program can significantly reduce recidivism upon release. The key factors may be parole officer orientation (a balance between social service and law enforcement seems to work best) and a supportive organizational environment in which the program is being run.[25]

In some jurisdictions, a unified department of probation and parole carries out field investigations. Here, Chelsea Klostreich (left) and Lucinda Carroll (center), parole and probation officers with Washington County, Oregon, check on the household of a man on parole for a domestic violence charge. The officers travel in pairs for safety.

© Torsten Kjellstrand/*Oregonian*/Landov

The fact that so many parolees have had their parole revoked, resulting in their return to prison, has attracted the interest of policy makers. An examination of the high rates of revocation reveals that a large percentage of parolees have been returned to prison for **technical violations**.[26] What this means is that they have been returned to prison for violating the conditions of parole, rather than for a new crime. For example, in California, two-thirds of parolees returned to prison are parole violators.[27]

Is There a Legal Right to Parole?

What happens if the parole authority denies early release, but the inmate believes he is deserving of parole? Perhaps he has witnessed other inmates receiving parole who have similar institutional records. Can he question the parole board's decision via the courts? The Supreme Court answered this question in 2011 when it ruled in the consolidated cases of *Swarthout v. Cooke* and *Cate v. Clay* that due process requirements are satisfied when a prisoner has an opportunity to be heard and is provided a statement of the reasons why parole is denied; there is in essence no absolute or legal right to receiving parole. The first case, *Swarthout v. Cooke*, involved Damon Cooke, who was incarcerated in California for attempted first-degree murder. In 2002, the California Board of Prison Terms rejected his parole request. California law provides that if the board denies parole, the prisoner can seek judicial review. Subsequently the California superior court, the California court of appeal, and the California supreme court all denied Cooke's petitions, prompting him to seek federal assistance. Similarly, *Cate v. Clay* began with the 1978 conviction of Elijah Clay for first-degree murder. In 2003, the board found Clay suitable for parole, but the governor reviewed the case and found Clay unsuitable for parole. After going through the state process, Clay filed a claim in federal court. The district court concluded that the governor's reliance on the nature of Clay's original offense rather than his prison behavior violated his right to due process. The Ninth Circuit affirmed, concluding that the governor's decision was unreasonable.

The Supreme Court reversed both decisions, holding that the Due Process Clause requires fair procedures in parole hearing. However, it held that both Cooke and Clay received adequate process because they were allowed an opportunity to be heard and were provided a statement of the reasons why parole was denied. The courts do not have the right to step in and conclude the parole board (and governor's) decisions were faulty. If the process is fair, then the inmate must live with the outcome.[28]

Parole Revocation

There are also legal issues involved when a parolee violates the rules of his release. This process begins when the parole officer decides if and when to file a complaint against a parolee. In some states, regulations guide or even mandate specific responses to violations, which restricts parole officers' discretion. However, parole officers have significant discretionary power.[29] Opsal and colleagues found that in Colorado, parole officers used race, ethnicity, gender, pivotal categories, and therapeutic needs to construct and made the decision when and whether to file a complaint.[30]

In **Morrissey v. Brewer** (1972), the U.S. Supreme Court first ruled on procedures for **revocation of parole**. Morrissey was a bad-check writer who had been paroled from the Iowa State Penitentiary. Seven months after his release, his parole was revoked for a technical violation, and he was returned to prison. At about the same time, a second petitioner, Booher, was returned to prison without opportunities on a technical parole violation. Both men petitioned for *habeas corpus* on the grounds that they had been denied due process of the law and returned to prison without opportunities to defend themselves at an open hearing. The two cases were consolidated for appeal and eventually reached the U.S. Supreme Court.

TECHNICAL VIOLATIONS Parole violations that pertain to behavior that is not crime, such as the failure to refrain from alcohol use.

MORRISSEY V. BREWER Supreme Court ruled on procedures for revocation of parole.

REVOCATION OF PAROLE A formal procedure that takes place when a parole board, after listening to the parolee and his or her parole officer and their witnesses, decides that parole must end because the offender committed a new crime or violated the conditions of parole.

In his opinion, Chief Justice Warren Burger laid down the essential elements of due process for parole revocation. The first requirement was a hearing before an "uninvolved" hearing officer, who might be another parole officer or perhaps an "independent decision maker," who would determine whether there was reasonable cause to believe that a parole violation had taken place. If so, the parolee might be returned to prison, subject to a full revocation hearing before the parole board.

The actual revocation procedures begin when the parole officer requests a warrant based on an alleged violation of parole. A parole officer, a warrant officer, or a police officer can issue a warrant. Once parolees are in custody, they are given a list of the charges against them. The next step in this process, which tends to vary from state to state, gives prisoners an opportunity to challenge at a preliminary hearing the allegation of violation and to confront adverse witnesses, including parole officers. The hearing officer is usually a senior officer, whose chief task is to determine whether there are reasonable grounds for believing that parolees have violated one or more of the conditions of parole—that is, whether there is "probable cause." If probable cause exists, parolees are held in custody for a revocation hearing. If probable cause is not found, parolees are returned to supervision.

A more comprehensive revocation hearing is held to determine whether the violation of parole is serious enough to justify returning parolees to prison. If parole is not revoked, parolees are returned to supervision. Jurisdictions vary greatly in determining how much time revoked parolees should spend in prison. They also vary in their decisions on whether parolees should receive credit for the time they spend under parole supervision. In complying with the requirements of due process imposed in *Morrissey v. Brewer*, parole officers and parole boards have focused their attention on the processing of violating cases. However, instead of receiving praise from the political system for its get-tough approach, the parole system has received criticism for its high return rates, because of the ongoing problem of prison overcrowding and its fiscal implications.

HOW SUCCESSFUL IS PAROLE?

Despite all efforts to treat, correct, and rehabilitate incarcerated offenders, a majority still return to prison shortly after their release.[31] An important federally sponsored study of more than 270,000 prisoners released in 15 states found that two-thirds of parolees were re-arrested, half were reconvicted, and about 25 percent resentenced to prison within three years of leaving prison. Within three years, about 52 percent were back in prison, serving time for a new prison sentence or for a technical violation of their release, such as failing a drug test, missing an appointment with their parole officer, or being arrested for a new crime.[32] A similar study of about 300,000 parole discharges found that more than half either absconded or were returned to jail or prison.[33] These data show that most offenders fail upon re-entry into the community and failure is most likely to take place soon after release (see Table 11.1). Why failure rates are so great and what is being done to alleviate the problem are topics discussed in the following sections.

 ## Why Do People Fail on Parole?

The specter of recidivism is especially frustrating to the American public: it is so difficult to apprehend and successfully prosecute criminal offenders that it seems foolish to grant them early release so they can prey on more victims. This problem is exacerbated when the parolee is a chronic, frequent

MYTH Most former inmates succeed on parole.

FACT Sadly, most inmates recidivate soon after they are released from prison. The longer they are out, the better their chances of success.

While many parolees fail, others can make a successful adjustment to society. Here, parolee Lorlei Sontag, 37, talks to the accountability panel at the Wichita Parole Office. Kansas is a leader in a spreading national effort to make parole more effective in reducing violations and reincarcerations as it protects the public and seeks to help more offenders go straight.

offender. Parole failure is still a significant problem, and a growing portion of the correctional population consists of parolees who failed on the outside. Why has the phenomenon of parole failure remained so stubborn and hard to control?

The very nature of the prison experience itself may be a factor: the psychological and economic problems that lead offenders to recidivism are rarely addressed by a stay in prison. Once released from prison, offenders face a multitude of difficulties. They remain largely undereducated, unskilled, and usually without solid family support systems. When they return to society, it may be to the same destructive neighborhood and social groups that prompted the original law-violating behavior.[34] It is also possible that parole failure is tied to the releasee's own lifelong deficits. Most research efforts indicate that a long history of criminal behavior, an antisocial personality, and childhood experiences with family dysfunction are all correlated with postrelease recidivism.[35]

PERSONAL MARRIAGE AND FAMILY ISSUES Recidivism may be a by-product of the disruptive effect a prison experience has on personal relationships. Ex-inmates may find their home life torn and disrupted when they are finally released.[36] Wives of inmates report that they have to face the shame and

TABLE 11.1 Success on Parole

Study	Populations	Outcome
Hughes and James	270,000 released prisoners in 15 states	Two-thirds arrested within three years for felony or serious misdemeanor; about 25 percent were back in prison.
Lowenkamp and Latessa	7,306 offenders placed in community-based programs	Programs were more effective with higher-risk offenders than with lower-risk ones. Moderate and high-risk offenders had a 70 percent success rate.
U.S. Department of Justice 2002 Trends Study	297,851 parole discharges	45.3 percent were successful completions and 51.7 percent were returned to jail or prison.
U.S. Department of Justice 2005	503,800 parole discharges	45 percent were successful completions and 38 percent were returned to jail or prison.

Sources: Timothy Hughes and Doris James, "Inmates Returning to the Community After Serving Time in Prison," www.bjs.gov/content/pub/pdf/reentry.pdf (accessed March 8, 2012); Christopher T. Lowenkamp and Edward J. Latessa, "Increasing the Effectiveness of Correctional Programming Through the Risk Principle: Identifying Offenders for Residential Placement," *Criminology and Public Policy* 4 (2005): 263–290; Bureau of Justice Statistics, *New Release*, April 2004; Bureau of Justice Statistics, *Bulletin*, November 2006.

stigmatization of having an incarcerated spouse while withstanding a barrage of calls from their jealous husbands on the "inside," who try to monitor their behavior and control their lives. Family visits to the inmate become traumatic and strain relationships because they often involve strip searches and other invasions of privacy.[37] Sensitive to these problems, some states have instituted support groups designed to help inmates' families adjust to their loneliness and despair.[38]

State correctional authorities have developed programs that help inmates adjust to reentry, by providing prerelease treatment or postrelease care. Christopher Lowenkamp and Edward Latessa studied more than 7,000 offenders placed in 53 community-based residential programs as part of their parole. Offenders who successfully completed residential programming were compared with offenders under parole/postrelease control who were not placed in residential programs. Lowenkamp and Latessa found that residential programs were particularly effective with higher-risk offenders and that residential treatment helped the most troubled inmates make a successful reentry into society.[39]

The Evidence-Based Corrections feature discusses another initiative designed to help inmates successfully return to society.

EVIDENCE-BASED CORRECTIONS

Serious and Violent Offender Reentry Initiative (SVORI)

The Serious and Violent Offender Reentry Initiative (SVORI) program is designed to improve reentry outcomes along five dimensions: criminal justice, employment, education, health, and housing. SVORI programs are encouraged to implement a multiphased approach. Although the structure varies, programs usually plan at least one prerelease phase and at least one postrelease phase. The prerelease, institutionally based phase generally entails the selection of eligible participants and the initiation of SVORI programming and services. During the prerelease phase, most programs begin the development of a reentry plan for each participant. This plan usually assesses basic needs (e.g., medical services, food, shelter, and clothing). Most programs plan to provide a wide array of services to SVORI participants, including case management, treatment plan development, and release plan development. A transition team develops a schedule involving case management, employment services, supervision and monitoring, transitional housing, treatment, and aftercare. As in the prerelease phase, the

program offers a wide range of services to SVORI participants in the postrelease phase including:

- Substance abuse treatment
- Mental health counseling
- Medical and/or dental services
- Employment and/or education training
- Housing assistance
- Faith-based services
- Other services such as parenting skills, domestic violence awareness, life skills, and/or anger management

Many SVORI programs offer participants support from the community following the completion of their parole term. During this sustaining phase, program administrators encourage participants to maintain contact with personal social support networks and to be involved in community reintegration activities.

A number of detailed evaluations of the programs have been undertaken, and the findings have been mixed. The evaluators have determined that participants in SVORI programs are more likely to receive services than comparable nonparticipants. From release through 15 months postrelease, SVORI participants appear to be doing

well—moderately better than non-SVORI participants—across a wide range of outcomes. About one-third report living in their own residences. In contrast to pre-incarceration findings, few reported that they currently lived with people who abused alcohol or drugs. Nearly three-fourths had worked since release. However, results indicate that, compared to non-SVORI participants, SVORI participants show no discernible differences on outcomes with respect to recidivism, housing, substance abuse, and physical and mental health. What seemed to be the problem? Simply put, offenders face important challenges upon returning to their communities. These challenges include finding suitable housing and employment and obtaining affordable health care (including substance abuse treatment and mental health counseling). Results from the SVORI evaluation support the notion that successful reentry of returning offenders cannot be tied to one process (such as, in this example, the provision of services).

Sources: Christy Visher and Pamela Lattimore, "Study Examines Prisoners' Reentry Needs," NIJ Update, April 2008, www.ncjrs.gov/pdffiles1/nij/222475.pdf (accessed March 8, 2012); National Institute of Justice, "Evaluation of the Serious and Violent Offender Reentry Initiative," July 26, 2011, http://nij.gov/topics/corrections/reentry/evaluation-svori.htm (accessed March 8, 2012).

Losing Rights

Ex-inmates may find that going straight is an economic impossibility. It is particularly difficult in the present job market, with so many out of work. Many employers are reluctant to hire people who have served time. Even if a criminal record does not automatically prohibit all chance of employment, why would an employer hire an ex-con when other applicants are available? If they lie about their prison experience and are later found out, ex-offenders will be dismissed for misrepresentation. Research shows that former inmates who gain and keep meaningful employment are more likely to succeed on parole than those who are unemployed or underemployed.[40] One reason that ex-inmates find it so difficult to make it on the outside is the legal restrictions they are forced to endure. These may include bans on certain kinds of employment, limits on obtaining licenses, and restrictions on their freedom of movement. One survey found that a significant number of states still restrict the activities of former felons.[41] In general, states have placed greater restrictions on former felons as part of the get-tough movement. These have been described as "invisible punishments" that reduce the rights and privileges of those convicted of crimes.[42]

However, courts have considered individual requests by convicted felons to have their rights restored. It is common for courts to look at such issues as how recently the criminal offense took place and its relationship to the particular right before deciding whether to restore it. An additional frustration results from the civil disabilities imposed on convicted felons. The get-tough movement of the 1980s increased the statutory restrictions placed on parolees. Ex-offenders confront legal and social barriers that stand between them and job opportunities. Examinations of statutory barriers indicate that as many as 300 occupations require licenses that are unobtainable by persons with felony convictions. Felons are not likely to find work as nurses, barbers or beauticians, real estate salespersons, or cashiers, or to work in places where alcoholic beverages are sold. Limited work experience, lack of training, difficulty in accepting supervision, and unrealistic expectations about income and promotion also put ex-offenders seeking jobs at a disadvantage. Dealing with the public and with coworkers is not a skill learned in prison, so ex-offenders are unlikely candidates for any job calling for interaction with strangers.

The **disenfranchisement laws** or civil disabilities extend into many other areas of the convicted felon's life. Fourteen states permanently deny convicted felons the right to vote (most other states restrict this right until felons fulfill their sentences). Their criminal records may preclude them from retaining parental rights, may be grounds for divorce, and may bar them from serving on a jury, holding public office, and owning firearms.

Recidivism may be a by-product of the disruptive effect a prison experience has on personal relationships. Ex-inmates may find their home life torn and disrupted when they are finally released. Some try to do something about their problems. Adam Gaines, 40, of Owings Mills, Maryland, has firsthand experience of watching his children flounder. He was freed last year after 13-and-a-half years in prison for robbery. Now, he is trying to be the father he never was to a son who dropped out of school in the 10th grade, another son who is just starting high school, and a teenage daughter who had a baby and dropped out of school. Working out with his son Shane, 14, is part of his career objectives: Gaines is studying to be a fitness teacher.

© Fred R. Conrad/*New York Times*/Redux

CORRECTIONAL LIFE
Jeff: An Ex-offender Outside

"I think the hardest thing about coming out of prison to the free world is finding a job. I was born with two strikes, being black and male. Then, once a man gets a criminal record, that is the third strike. They say they want you to make it, but everywhere you go—state agency, job interview with private employer—you are met with the same look. It is the look that says you're unwanted, and no matter how many help-wanted signs are in the windows, it always seems they want everyone's help but mine. What makes it even more difficult is that while we were in prison we gained very few viable skills, nothing that can really help you out in society. So that when you get out, most of us are unequipped to make it."

DISENFRANCHISEMENT LAWS Civil disabilities facing parolees when they return to the community.

Eight jurisdictions require ex-offenders to register with a police department on release from prison.

A number of experts and national commissions have condemned the loss of rights of convicted offenders as a significant cause of recidivism. Consequently, courts have generally moved to eliminate the most restrictive elements of post-conviction restrictions.[43]

What Can Be Done to Improve Parole Effectiveness?

One way of improving parole effectiveness is to analyze the factors that predict parole success or failure and then build programs around the results. A number of attempts have been made to isolate these factors. In one such attempt, Joe Graffam and colleagues conducted a large-scale study to examine the employability of ex-offenders and prisoners. They found that aside from those with an intellectual or psychiatric disability, those with a criminal background were deemed as less likely than other disadvantaged groups to obtain and maintain employment. They found that six broad domains influence the reintegration of ex-offenders:

- Personal conditions

- Rehabilitation and counseling support

- Employment and training support

- Social network/environment

- Accommodation

- The criminal justice system[44]

Similarly, Christy Visher and Jeremy Travis found that recidivism is affected by several factors: (a) personal and situational characteristics, including peers, family, community, and state-level policies, (b) incarceration experiences, and (c) the period after release.[45]

It may be possible to create effective parole programs built around these criteria. For example, California created a statewide, community-based correctional program that was intended to reduce parole recidivism. The Preventing Parolee Crime Program (PPCP) provided employment services, housing assistance, substance abuse treatment, and literacy training to thousands of parolees. The study found that the PPCP produced modest reductions in recidivism and parole absconding, and created the potential for substantial long-term cost savings. The fact that its positive effects were strongest for parolees who completed their services taught the lesson that future program designers and administrators should consider including mechanisms to improve service utilization and parolee retention.[46]

Criminologist Joan Petersilia has a number of recommendations to improve parole effectiveness. They include the following:

- *Parole offices should incorporate neighborhood parole supervision.* The key components of what some consider the new parole model are to strengthen parolees' linkages with law enforcement and the community, to offer a full-service model of parole, and to attempt to change the ex-offenders' lives through personal, family, and neighborhood interventions.

- *Parole administrators should establish and test reentry courts and community partnerships.* The motive is to engage the broader community and the justice system in monitoring and assisting ex-offender reintegration. This has been called the Reentry Partnership Initiative (RPI).

- *Policy makers should establish procedures for ex-prisoners to regain full citizenship.* This issue is one of establishing some procedure by which some parolees can move beyond their criminal records.[47]

TARGETING TIME, PLACE, AND OFFENDERS Corrections expert James Byrne suggests that another effective approach may be front-loading the intensity of parole supervision—that is, closely supervising parolees as soon as they are released from prison and cutting back on supervision as they adjust to the community. We know that most people fail on parole soon after they are released from prison; about 10 percent of all offenders are arrested during their first month back in the community. Therefore, concentrating community supervision resources at the start of an offender's parole term might be effective, since that is when they are more likely to reoffend.[48]

Byrne also suggests that resources may be directed at parolees who pose the greatest threat to the community. To date, 31 states have passed legislation allowing the use of lifetime community supervision for targeted groups of offenders, most notably sex offenders and offenders convicted of homicide. While these offenders actually have a low reoffending rate, their close supervision may be reassuring to the community, their victims, and the community corrections agencies responsible for supervising the offender.

Finally, Byrne suggests that effective parole supervision must be community oriented. Community supervision strategies should consider community-level risks posed by parolees and then assign community corrections officers to specific geographic areas rather than to specific caseloads. Those areas that need the most help are already at risk to crime and lack resources to prevent its occurrence. Parole officers assigned to these areas can make the most difference.[49]

Second Chance Act

On April 9, 2008, President George Bush signed the Second Chance Act into law. Receiving bipartisan support in both chambers of Congress, the bill was supported by a broad spectrum of leaders representing law enforcement, corrections, the courts, and local government. This first-of-its-kind legislation authorizes various grants to government agencies and nonprofit groups to provide employment assistance, substance abuse treatment, housing, family programming, mentoring, victim support, and other services that can help reduce reoffending and violations of probation and parole. If properly financed and carried out, the act could cut recidivism and ruinous prison costs for states by helping them develop programs that former inmates need to build viable, crime-free lives. The Second Chance Act was funded for $100 million for fiscal year 2010, $83 million for fiscal year 2011, and President Obama requested $100 million for fiscal year 2012. In late 2011, the House Appropriations Committee provided $70 million in their House bill, but the Senate bill for fiscal year 2012 eliminated funding for the Second Chance Act.[50]

SUMMARY

L01 ▸ **Understand parole practices today**

Discretionary parole has now been abolished in 13 states, but for those states that have parole it is based on the following principles:

■ The state extends to offenders a privilege by releasing them from prison before their full sentence is served.

■ The state also enters a release contract with offenders in exchange for their promise to abide by certain conditions.

■ Offenders who violate the law or conditions of parole can be returned to prison to complete their sentences.

■ The state retains control of parolees until they are dismissed from parole.

L02 ▸ **Know how the parole board functions**

Parole decisions can be made with an entire board interviewing eligible inmates; in other jurisdictions, only part of the board interviews eligible inmates. Hearing examiners are used in some jurisdictions to interview inmates. Some states, rather than interviewing inmates, make their decisions based solely upon written reports. Nearly all states still authorizing parole have further restricted parole by setting specific standards that inmates must meet to be eligible for release. Some states use formal risk prediction instruments or parole guidelines to structure the parole decision-making process.

L03 ▶ Identify the rules of those parolees released to the community

The parolee released to the community is typically given a set of rules and conditions that must be obeyed. These include reporting to the parole officer within 24 hours; not carrying weapons; obeying all parole agent instructions; not traveling more than 50 miles from home or leaving the county without permission; not committing crimes; seeking and maintaining employment.

L04 ▶ Understand the procedures involved in the revocation of parole

Revocation of parole takes place when a parole board decides, while granting the parolee due process rights, that parole must end because the offender committed a new crime or violated the conditions of parole. The actual revocation procedures begin when the parole officer requests a warrant based on an alleged violation of parole. The next step involves parolees being given an opportunity to challenge at a preliminary hearing the allegation of violation and to confront adverse witnesses. If probable cause is found to exist by the hearing officer, the parolee is held in custody for a revocation hearing.

L05 ▶ Be able to identify why people fail on parole

People fail on parole for a number of reasons: the very nature of the prison experience itself; a multitude of difficulties faced upon release, include remaining largely undereducated, unskilled, and usually without solid family support systems; and personal marriage and family issues. In addition, they frequently must return to the same neighborhoods and social groups that prompted their law-violating behavior in the first place.

L06 ▶ Identify some of the rights that ex-offenders have lost

Legal restrictions that parolees face include bans on certain kinds of employment, limits on obtaining licenses, loss of voting privileges, and restrictions on the freedom of movement.

Key Terms

ticket of leave, 254
parole, 254
discretionary parole, 255
mandatory parole release, 255

parole board, 256
parole guidelines, 257
intensive supervision parole (ISP), 262
technical violations, 264

Morrissey v. Brewer, 264
revocation of parole, 264
disenfranchisement laws, 268

 # Critical Thinking Questions

1. "Parole boards are arbitrary and discriminatory and they ought to be abolished," says John Q. Liberal. "Yes, but so is the whole criminal justice system," says Sally Moderate. "At least the boards are trying to remedy inequities." What are likely to be the reasons behind each opinion?

2. Technical violators of parole are filling our prisons and aggravating problems related to prison crowding. What is your evaluation of technical violations of parole? For example, if a parolee moves in with his girlfriend and does not tell his parole officer, is this justification for returning him to prison?

3. Some states claim that an ex-offender's record should be made public. Does an ex-offender have any rights of privacy?

4. Suppose you have been convicted of a felony and have served 30 months in your state's penitentiary. You will be released on parole next week. How will your parents, husband or wife, children, and friends receive you? What will you do about getting a job? Will the university readmit you without any special processing? How are you going to discuss the last 30 months with your friends, some of whom do not know that you were in prison?

Thinking Like a Corrections Professional

The new governor of your state believes that ex-offenders should be given more rights. She has appointed you as chair of a special task force to prepare a report for her. What rights will you recommend that a released inmate ought to have? Which privileges should inmates be allowed to become full citizens? In other words, what degree of rights, privileges, and freedom will your task force recommend for ex-offenders?

Career Destinations

Learn more about becoming a parole officer at: www.legal-criminal-justice-schools.com/Criminal-Justice-Degrees/Parole-Officer.html

A number of states post listings for parole officers. Here is one in Texas:
www.tdcj.state.tx.us/vacancy/hr-home/parole.htm

Notes

1. Fernanda Santos, "Inmate Enters Guilty Plea in '89 Killing," *New York Times*, March 15, 2007.
2. Fernanda Santos, "Vindicated by DNA, but a Lost Man on the Outside," *New York Times*, November 25, 2007, www.nytimes.com/2007/11/25/us/25jeffrey.html (accessed March 7, 2012).
3. David Farabee, *Rethinking Rehabilitation: Why Can't We Reform Our Criminals?* (Washington, DC: AEI Press, American Enterprise Institute, 2005).
4. A. A. Bruce, *Parole and Indeterminate Sentences* (Springfield, Illinois, Parole Board, 1928).
5. Lauren E. Glaze and Thomas P. Bonczar, "Probation and Parole in the United States, 2009," *Bureau of Justice Statistics Bulletin* (Washington, DC: U.S. Department of Justice, 2010).
6. Ibid.
7. Kathryn D. Morgan and Brent Smith, "The Impact of Race on Parole Decision-Making," *Justice Quarterly* 25 (June 2008): 413.
8. Ibid.
9. Joan Petersilia, *When Prisoners Come Home: Parole and Prisoner Reentry* (New York: Oxford University Press, 2003), p. 71. See also "What Works in Community Corrections: An Interview with Dr. Joan Petersilia," the Pew Center on the States, Public Safety Performance Project, November 2007, www.pewcenteronthestates.org/initiatives_detail.aspx?initiativeID=31336 (accessed March 8, 2012).
10. Petersilia, *When Prisoners Come Home.*
11. Ibid., p. 72.
12. Sandra Crockett Mack and Khalil Osiris, "Successful Reentry, One Case at a Time," *Corrections Today* 69 (2007): 50–55.
13. Caroline Kröner, Cornelis Stadtland, Matthias Eidt, and Norbert Nedopil, "The Validity of the Violence Risk Appraisal Guide (VRAG) in Predicting Criminal Recidivism," *Criminal Behavior and Mental Health* 17 (2007): 89–100.
14. Kathryn Campbell and Myriam Denov, "The Burden of Innocence: Coping with a Wrongful Imprisonment," *Canadian Journal of Criminology and Criminal Justice* 46 (2004): 139–164.
15. Morgan and Smith, "The Impact of Race on Parole Decision-Making."
16. Petersilia, *When Prisoners Come Home*, p. 82.
17. Brian Parry, "Special Service Unit: Dedicated to Investigating and Apprehending Violent Offenders," *Corrections Today* 63 (2001): 120.
18. Thomas P. Bonczar, *Characteristics of State Parole Supervising Agencies, 2006* (Washington, DC: Bureau of Justice Statistics Special Report, 2008), p. 1.
19. James M. Byrne, "The Social Ecology of Community Corrections: Understanding the Link Between Individual and Community Change," *Criminology and Public Policy* (May 2008).
20. Patrick A. Langan and David J. Levin, *Recidivism of Prisoners Released in 1994* (Washington, DC: Bureau of Justice Statistics, 2002).
21. Bonczar, *Characteristics of State Parole Supervising Agencies, 2006.*
22. Byrne, "The Social Ecology of Community Corrections."
23. Petersilia, *When Prisoners Come Home*, p. 90.
24. David Z. Zanis, Frank Mulvaney, Donna Covello, Arthur I. Alterman, Barry Savity, and William Thompson, "The Effectiveness of Early Parole to Substance Abuse Treatment Facilities on 24-Month Criminal Recidivism," *Journal of Drug Issues* (2003): 223–236.
25. Mario Paparozzi and Paul Gendreau, "An Intensive Supervision Program that Worked: Service Delivery, Professional Orientation, and Organizational Supportiveness," *Prison Journal* 85 (2005): 445–466.
26. James A. Wilson, "Bad Behavior or Bad Policy? An Examination of Tennessee Release Cohorts, 1993–2001," *Criminology and Public Policy* 3 (2005): 485–526.
27. Joan Petersilia and Robert Weisberg, "Parole in California: It's a Crime," *Los Angeles Times*, April 23, 2006, http://articles.latimes.com/2006/apr/23/opinion/op-petersilia23 (accessed March 8, 2012).
28. *Swarthout v. Cooke* and *Cate v. Clay*, 562 U.S. ___ (2011).
29. Tara Opsal, Sara Steen, and Peter Lovegrove, "Understanding Parole Officers' Assessment of Risk and Need: The Role of Race, Ethnicity, and Gender in Filing Revocation Complaints," unpublished paper, 2011. See also Jeff Lin, Ryan Grattet, and Joan Petersilia, "'Back-End Sentencing' and Reimprisonment: Individual, Organizational and Community Predictors of Parole Sentencing Decisions," *Criminology* 4 (2010): 759–795.
30. Ibid.
31. Wilson, "Bad Behavior or Bad Policy?"
32. Timothy Hughes and Doris James, "Inmates Returning to the Community After Serving Time in Prison," www.bjs.gov/content/pub/pdf/reentry.pdf (accessed March 8, 2012).
33. Bureau of Justice Statistics, *New Release*, April 2004; and Bureau of Justice Statistics, *Bulletin*, November 2006.
34. Jeremy Travis and Joan Petersilia, "Reentry Reconsidered: A New Look at an Old Question," *Crime and Delinquency* 47 (2001): 291–313.
35. James Bonta, Moira Law, and Karl Hanson, "The Prediction of Criminal and Violent Recidivism Among Mentally Disordered Offenders: A Meta-Analysis," *Psychological Bulletin* 123 (1998): 123–142; Arthur J. Lurigio, "Effective Services for Parolees with Mental Illnesses," *Crime and Delinquency* 47 (2001): 446–461; Larry Brimeyer, "Iowa Implements Mental Health Re-entry Program," *Corrections Today* 65 (2003): 38–41; Jeffrey Draine, Nancy Wolff, Joseph E. Jacoby, Stephanie Hartwell, and Christine Deucios, "Understanding Community Re-entry of Former Prisoners with Mental Illness: A Conceptual Model to Guide New Research," *Behavioral Sciences and the Law* 23 (2005): 689–707.
36. Beth Huebner, "Racial and Ethnic Differences in the Likelihood of Marriage," *Justice Quarterly* 24 (2007): 156–183.
37. Laura Fishman, *Women at the Wall: A Study of Prisoners' Wives Doing Time on the Outside* (New York: State University of New York Press, 1990).
38. Leslee Goodman Hornick, "Volunteer Program Helps Make Inmates' Families Feel Welcome," *Corrections Today* 53 (1991): 184–186.
39. Christopher T. Lowenkamp and Edward J. Latessa, "Increasing the Effectiveness of

Correctional Programming Through the Risk Principle: Identifying Offenders for Residential Placement," *Criminology and Public Policy* 4 (2005): 263–290. For an article that challenges the findings of Lowenkamp and Latessa, see James M. Byrne and Faye S. Taxman, "Crime (Control) Is a Choice: Divergent Perspectives on the Role of Treatment in the Adult Corrections System," *Criminology and Public Policy* 4 (2005): 291–310.

40. T. E. Hanlon, D. N. Nurco, R. W. Bateman, and K. E. O'Grady, "The Response of Drug Abuser Parolees to a Combination of Treatment and Intensive Supervision," *Prison Journal* 78 (1999).

41. Kathleen Olivares, Velmer Burton, and Francis Cullen, "The Collateral Consequences of a Felony Conviction: A National Study of State Legal Codes Ten Years Later," *Federal Probation* 60 (1996): 10–17.

42. Jeremy Travis, "Invisible Punishment: An Instrument of Social Exclusion," in *Invisible Punishment: The Collateral Consequences of Mass Imprisonment*, ed. Marc Mauer and Meda Chesney-Lind (Washington, DC: New Press, 2002), p. 16.

43. See, for example, *Bush v. Reid*, 516 P.2d 1215 (Alaska, 1973); *Thompson v. Bond*, 421 F.Supp. 878 (W.D. Mo., 1976); *Delorne v. Pierce Freightlines Co.*, 353 F.Supp. 258 (D. Or., 1973); *Beyer v. Werner*, 299 F.Supp. 967 (E.D. N.Y., 1969).

44. Joe Graffam, Alison Shinkfield, Barbara Lavelle, and Wenda McPherson, "Variables Affecting Successful Reintegration as Perceived by Offenders and Professionals," *Journal of Offender Rehabilitation* 40 (2004): 147–171.

45. Christy A. Visher and Jeremy Travis, "Transitions from Prison to Community," *Annual Review of Sociology* 29 (2003): 89–113.

46. Sheldon X. Zhang, Robert E. L. Roberts, and Valerie J. Callanan, "Preventing Parolees from Returning to Prison Through Community-Based Reintegration," *Crime and Delinquency* 52 (October 2006): 551–571. In a 2012 issue of *Criminology and Public Policy* devoted to employment-based reentry for parolees, there is strong emphasis placed on how to improve the effectiveness of reentry programs for parolees that target employment. *Criminology and Public Policy* 11 (February 2012).

47. Petersilia, *When Prisoners Come Home*, pp. 172–211.

48. James Byrne, *The New Generation of Concentrated Community Supervision Strategies: Focusing Resources on High Risk Offenders, Times, and Places*, report prepared for the Public Safety Performance Project, the Pew Charitable Trusts, Washington, DC, 2009.

49. Ibid.

50. Reentry Policy Council, reentrypolicy.org/government_affairs/second_chance_act (accessed March 8, 2012).

There are a number of tragic stories of aging prisoners in the California correctional system who are ineligible for parole. One of the most touching is that of Helen Leheac, who at 88 years old was nearly blind and deaf, her mind enfeebled by Alzheimer's, and in the terminal stages of kidney failure. Helen had hoped to be released from prison and spend her last days in a transitional home for formerly incarcerated women.[1] But after she had served 19 years behind bars on a conspiracy-to-murder conviction, the parole board told her that she remained a risk to public safety if she were freed and denied her request for release.

On January 5, 2009, Helen died of pneumonia in a hospital near the Central California Women's Facility (CCWF) in Chowchilla, where she was confined. She was shackled at her waist and

© Gloria Killian

Gloria Killian, a former inmate of the California Institution for Women (CIW) in Corona, is now a strong prisoners' rights advocate. As a former law student, Killian was assigned to the prison law library, where she worked for 14 years providing legal assistance to other inmates. She worked extensively with battered women and developed specialized legal services for many different areas of the prison. After being incarcerated for 16 years, Killian's conviction was overturned on appeal. Once released, she started her own nonprofit organization called Action Committee for Women in Prison, whose mission is to advocate for the humane and compassionate treatment of incarcerated women and to work for the release of all women who are unjustly imprisoned.

ankles, with two guards at her bedside.

Gloria Killian, a former inmate of the California Institution for Women (CIW) in Corona and now a strong prisoners' rights advocate, comments, "It's a terrible injustice, what's going on in those prisons. There's nothing worse than being sick and being in prison. These people are not a threat to society. They couldn't hurt a fly if they wanted to. And besides, it's too expensive to keep them incarcerated."

"The board gives us a release date, and the governor takes it away," said Jane Benson, 60, a prisoner of 22 years at CIW. She succeeded in persuading the parole board to free her the fourth time she came up for parole. But she said her luck ran out when her papers reached the governor's desk.

chapter
TWELVE

SPECIAL PRISON POPULATIONS

LEARNING OBJECTIVES

LO1 Understand the problems of inmates with a substance-involved history

LO2 Be aware what challenges and problems sex offenders bring to the prison

LO3 Know some of the issues terrorists present to the correctional system

LO4 Understand the prison experience of HIV inmates

LO5 Identify the world faced by chronic mentally ill inmates while they are in prison

LO6 Understand the plight of elderly inmates while incarcerated and what is involved in their care

LO7 Understand the problems faced by illegal immigrants in U.S. prisons

AP Photo/Rich Pedroncelli

With tougher sentencing laws, it is projected that by 2030 there will be 33,000 geriatric inmates in California prisons alone, costing the state at least a $1 billion a year. There are presently 525 women aged 55 and over in the state's three prisons housing women—CIW, CCWF, and Valley State Prison for Women (VSPW).[2]

Elderly inmates provide unique management problems for staff. How is it possible to treat this special needs group in a manner that is compassionate and humane? It also illustrates how the prison population today is not a homogenous community but as diverse and varied as the nation itself. Inmates bring with them a myriad of social problems, and this chapter will consider eight types of inmates, grouped in the following three categories: (1) **special offense inmates**—inmates with substance abuse histories, sex offenders, and terrorists; (2) **special needs inmates**—HIV inmates and inmates with chronic mental health issues; and (3) **special population inmates**—elderly inmates and inmates who are illegal immigrants. Problems posed by each type to the correctional environment and to community settings when they are released are discussed in some detail, followed by a discussion of the programs that are now being employed to help members of these subgroups adjust to the institution and to the community upon their release.

Mary Leftridge Byrd, a corrections professional for 30 years, served as superintendent of three correctional institutions housing women and men and led two state prerelease systems. Over the years, she has worked as parole agent and as assistant warden in four state correctional systems. More recently, she served as deputy secretary, division of Offender Treatment and Reentry Programs, for the Washington State Department of Corrections, where her responsibilities included inmate programs, victim's services, corrections education, religious services, chemical dependency treatment, and reentry initiatives. In Voices Across the Profession, she tells what she liked about being a warden, including working with difficult or special populations, and what she feels she accomplished in her work in corrections.

SPECIAL OFFENSE INMATES

Special offense inmates are linked together because of their prior criminal/deviant behavior issues. Some are violent offenders, others are substance abusers, and some present problems to correctional administrators because they engage in multiple-offense patterns, such as violent drug-gang members, and others are domestic or international terrorists. Three special offense inmates are considered in this section: inmates with substance abuse histories, which includes such offenders as street-level drug dealers, drug traffickers, "mules" who carry drugs for others, and alcoholics whose crimes are directly related to drinking problems; the **sex offenders** group, which includes rapists and pedophiles; and terrorists.

 LO1

Corrections and Substance-Involved Inmates

The problems of substance-involved inmates are certainly not a small matter: many offenders report that they were under the influence of drugs and alcohol when they committed crime.[3] Over 50 percent of inmates in federal prisons are drug offenders.[4] Over 30 percent of inmates in state prisons are serving time for drug offenses.[5] (See Exhibit 12.1.)

PROBLEMS OF WORKING WITH SUBSTANCE-INVOLVED INMATES
Narcotics or alcohol can become a special challenge when an inmate comes into the prison addicted and may crash from a sudden withdrawal. A sudden withdrawal from alcohol, for example, can throw the inmate's system into shock and may cause cardiac arrest, kidney failure, or hallucinations.

SPECIAL OFFENSE INMATES Inmates who are involved in substance abuse, are sex offenders, or are terrorists.

SPECIAL NEEDS INMATES These include HIV inmates and inmates with chronic mental health issues

SPECIAL POPULATION INMATES These include the elderly prisoner, and the illegal immigrant inmate.

SEX OFFENDERS A variety of offenders including the child molester, the pedophile, and the rapist.

© Mary Leftridge Byrd

> " When I got into this two decades ago, you never heard anybody talk about planning, seeking, or focusing on a career in corrections. So it's great to think about leaving a legacy of influencing young people and trying to bring some enthusiasm about this profession with them and for them. "

MARY LEFTRIDGE BYRD,
CORRECTIONAL EXECUTIVE

I absolutely loved this work [as a warden]. What an opportunity to intercede in someone's life—I'm talking about both staff and inmates now. With my staff being so young, here was an opportunity to actually raise a young professional, and we've gotten to the point in this country where somebody may actually say they want to be a warden when they grow up. When I got into this two decades ago, you never heard anybody talk about planning, seeking, or focusing on a career in corrections. So it's great to think about leaving a legacy of influencing young people and trying to bring some enthusiasm about this profession with them and for them.

Inmate populations were brown, black, white, and sometimes blue. They were old, young, terminally ill, articulate, dependent, informed, strong, fragile women and men who often presented many challenges. They were men and women from the mountains, the city, the seaside, and the country. As one inmate once said to me, "Warden, you know how to deal with men from the woods and men from the hood." I took that as a compliment.

I have served as superintendent or warden of institutions that house mentally ill women and men who live in the same housing areas as those who have had long histories of drug abuse and addiction. I have also been involved with those who had histories of domestic violence, both as survivors and as perpetrators. Inmates could be elderly or very young and extraordinarily violent or extremely vulnerable. We had inmates who were living with HIV/AIDS. We always needed to remember that beyond the problems inmates bring to us, they were still daughters and sons, fathers and mothers, and relatives to people in the community, and we needed to treat them in a respectful way.

What did I like about being a warden? Where else could I have the opportunity to be involved in ensuring the provision of medical care along with the emotional and spiritual support often needed when someone is seriously or terminally ill? Where else could I have the opportunity to learn a lot about facilities, management, and physical plant maintenance? Where else could I have the opportunity to become active in a dynamic education system without certification? Where else would I have the ability to insist on hanging artwork in a public facility? Where else could I have the opportunity to be directly involved and accountable for the financial administration of a large organization? Where else could I have the opportunity to be involved with the culinary arts on such a large scale? Where else could I get involved in law enforcement as we were there? Think about our K-9 units, contraband interdiction efforts, investigations, sweeps and searches. Where else could I be involved in ministry? There is no question that my work is based on my own spirituality. For years I have believed I am called to do this. The longer I remain in the field, the more readily I acknowledge this calling, but my ministry is based more on behavior than through spoken words.

When asked about my management philosophy—no matter what office I am leading—I need only six words: 'Do justly, walk humbly, love mercy.' I am ever grateful to be on a journey that gives so much, especially the ever-present privilege to teach and the opportunity to learn.

Source: Interviewed in 2011.

Some inmates, desperate to continue their substance-abusing lifestyle, will actually produce homemade alcohol within the institution. An alcohol-based contraband that is found in nearly every prison is called "prison hooch" or sometimes "rook," which is a concentrated form of alcohol and can be made in a variety of ways. Much of the inmate world in some prisons focuses around the drug/alcohol economy—buying, using, selling, and bartering. Not surprisingly, violence invariably erupts from this economy. In the Correctional Life feature, a long-term Pennsylvania inmate tells how he has learned to do time. He also gives some information on how he sells drugs in prison.

EXHIBIT 12.1 Substance-Abusing Inmates and Criminal Activity in Prisons

A report by the National Center on Addiction and Substance Abuse (CASA) at Columbia University revealed that substance abuse inmates were involved in these inmate offenses:

- 78 percent of violent crimes

- 83 percent of property crimes

- 77 percent of public order, immigration or weapon offenses, and probation/parole violations

The CASA report also found that substance abuse inmates were:

- Four times likelier to receive income through illegal activity

- Twice as likely to have had at least one parent who abused alcohol or other drugs when they were children

- 41 percent likelier to have some family criminal history

- 20 percent less likely to have completed at least high school

- 20 percent likelier to be unemployed a month before incarceration

Source: Lauren Duran and Sulaiman Berg, *Behind Bars: Substance Abuse and America's Prison Population*, the National Center on Addiction and Substance Abuse at Columbia University, press release, 2010, www.casacolumbia.org/templates/PressReleases.aspx?articleid=592&zoneid=79 (accessed March 12, 2012).

CORRECTIONAL LIFE

Charles: Making the Best of Prison Time

"I'm here listening to soft music and thinking. I've been thinking about deals [drugs] on the yard. I spend a lot of time in the corner where the card game is. I keep the book—who owes who. The only time I leave the area is when I am making a drug deal. While out, I scan the yard. We call it "prowling." I need to know who is doing what. If you sell a certain drug, you try and beat your competitor to the punch. Also, it's good to know who has been buying what, so you know how much the user owes out. If you let the drug user go too far, he will take the lockup. He might give you up to get out of lockup and then you are in lockup."

PROGRAMS FOR SUBSTANCE-INVOLVED INMATES

About 90 percent of all state and federal prisons in the United States offer some form of substance abuse counseling, and about one in eight inmates have participated in a substance abuse treatment program while incarcerated.[6] Alcoholics Anonymous (AA), Narcotics Anonymous (NA), and other drug programs are also conducted in prisons. Some programs are brought into the prisons by AA or NA members from the community. Others are conducted by staff members.[7]

Evaluations of drug treatment programs have determined that treatment services should be based on the following:

- A clear and consistent treatment philosophy

- An atmosphere of empathy and safety

- The recruitment and maintenance of committed, qualified treatment staff

- Clear and unambiguous rules of conduct

- The use of ex-offenders and ex-addicts as role models, staff, and volunteers

- The use of peer role models and peer pressure

- The provision of relapse prevention programs

- The establishment of continuity of care throughout custody and community aftercare

- The integration of treatment evaluations into the design of the program

- The maintenance of treatment program integrity, autonomy, flexibility, and openness[8]

There is evidence that prisoners assigned to prison-based drug treatment programs have better prison adjustment than those in the general population.[9] There is also evidence that drug-involved offenders are less likely to recidivate if they receive treatment behind prison walls.[10] Offenders who enter and complete in-prison residential treatment are less likely to experience new arrests and substance use during the first six months following release.[11] Nonetheless, despite this success, relatively few at-risk inmates receive treatment while incarcerated.[12] In the Evidence-Based Corrections feature, one of the more widely used and successful programs to treat substance-abusing inmates is discussed.

Sex Offenders

About 10 percent of prisoners in state prisons and 1 percent in federal facilities have been convicted of a sex offense. This number does vary from one state to another.[13] In 2008, a Texas man named James Kevin Pope was sentenced to

EVIDENCE-BASED CORRECTIONS

Therapeutic Communities

Because substance abuse is super-prevailing among correctional clients, some correctional facilities have been reformulated into therapeutic communities that apply a psychological, experimental learning process and rely on positive peer pressure within a highly structural environment. The therapeutic community (TC) for the treatment of drug abuse and addiction has existed for about 40 years. In general, TCs are drug-free residential settings that use treatment stages that reflect increased levels of personal and social responsibility. Peer influence, applied through a variety of group processes, is used to help individuals learn and assimilate social norms and develop more effective social skills.

TCs differ from other treatment approaches principally in their use of the community, comprising treatment staff with those in recovery, as key agents of change. This approach is often referred to as "community as method." TC members interact in structural and nonstructural ways to influence attitudes, perceptions, and behavior associated with drug use.

The community itself, including staff and program participants, becomes the primary method of change. They work together as members of a "family" in order to create a culture where community members confront each other's negative behavior and attitudes and establish an open, trusting, and safe environment. The TC approach then relies on mutual self-help. It also encourages personal disclosure rather than the isolation of the general prison culture.

In addition to the importance of the community as a primary agent of change, a second fundamental TC principle is "self-help," a process that ensures that the individual and treatment are the main contributors to the change process. Mutual self-help means that individuals also assume partial responsibility for the recovery of their peers, an important aspect of an individual's own treatment.

Is It Effective?

Treating substance-abuse inmates has proved difficult even with such highly touted programs as the therapeutic community. For three decades, the National Institute on Drug Abuse has conducted several large studies to advance scientific knowledge of the outcome of drug abuse treatment. These studies collected data from over 65,000 individuals submitted to publicly funded treatment agencies, including TCs and other types of program (i.e., methadone maintenance, outpatient drug abuse, short-term inpatient, and drug detoxification programs. Data were collected during the treatment stage and in a series of follow-ups that focused on outcomes that occurred 12 months and longer after treatment.

These studies found that participation in a TC was associated with several positive outcomes. For example, the Drug Abuse Treatment Outcome Study I (DATOS), the most recent long-term study of drug treatment outcomes, shows that those who successfully completed treatment in a TC had lower levels of cocaine, heroin, and alcohol use, criminal behavior, unemployment, and indicators of depression than they had before treatment.

Success rates for TC programs may be shaped by the way individual programs are administered and the effectiveness of treatment delivery. For example, there is evidence that those inmates who recently completed TC programs have significantly lower recidivism rates than non-attendees and are more likely to seek treatment once they return to the community. In addition when run successfully, TC programs seem effective in reducing re-arrest and reincarceration rates.

Sources: National Institute of Drug Abuse Research Series, *Therapeutic Community*, www.drugabuse. gov/publications/research-reports/therapeutic-community (accessed March 12, 2012); Sheldon X. Zhang, Robert E. L. Roberts, and Kathryn E. McCollier, "Therapeutic Community in a California Prison, Treatment Outcomes After 5 Years," *Crime and Delinquency* 37 (2011): 82; Mitchell Miller and Helen Miller, "Considering the Effectiveness of Drug Treatment Behind Bars, Findings from the South Carolina RSAT," *Justice Quarterly* 28 (2011): 70–86.

40 life prison terms for sexually assaulting young girls over a two-year period. He received a life sentence for each sex assault conviction. At the request of prosecutors, Pope was sentenced to serve the sentences consecutively, adding up to 4,060 years behind bars; parole eligibility would begin in the year 3209.[14]

While Pope's sentence was extreme, increased prosecution and conviction, as well as longer and harsher sentences, have contributed significantly to increased numbers of sex offenders in prisons. Other signs of the get-tough attitude toward sex offenders are laws permitting the indefinite confinement of rapists and child molesters who are viewed as too dangerous for release at the end of their court-imposed sentences. The state of Washington had the first such law, and Kansas, New Jersey, and Wisconsin have

Convicted pedophiles Bill Price (in the cap) and Paul George are shown taking part in a group therapy session at Atascadero State Hospital. Coalinga State and Atascadero State mental hospitals in central California host a "civil commitment" program for sexual criminals who have served their time in a state penitentiary but are not deemed safe for release by the court system. Inmates at the mental hospitals can choose to participate in a phased program of therapy designed to rehabilitate the sexual offender, most of whom are pedophiles. The treatment has not been proven medically viable on a large scale as of yet, and only a handful of inmates have been released back into society after serving time at hospitals such as Coalinga and Atascadero.

© Eros Hoagland/Redux

adopted similar laws.[15] With their release, these offenders, especially those convicted of offenses against children, are faced with Megan's Law and the National Sex Offender Registry.

PROBLEMS OF WORKING WITH SEX OFFENDERS
The child molester, or pedophile, has long had difficulty with prison adjustment. Other inmates, many of whom have families and children on the outside, want to set an example and convince child molesters that they will pay dearly for their crimes. In many prisons, unless pedophiles are placed in protective custody, they are likely to be sexually assaulted or even killed. Yet, in other prisons, prison classification has been successful in placing sex offenders in relatively safe environments; in these institutions, pedophiles are not harmed as they do their time.

Many studies have shown the recidivism rate of sex offenders to be extremely low, especially when compared to the recidivism rates of other types of offenders. Sex offenders are much more likely to commit another sex crime than an offender previously convicted of a different category of crime; still, the recidivism rate of sex offenders is about 5 to 10 percent.[16] In Exhibit 12.2, Washington State's program for sex offenders is discussed in some detail.

CIVIL COMMITMENT FACILITIES
Legislatures in some states have recently taken another step in controlling sexual offenders by passing laws that permit a diagnosis of sex offenders as sexually violent predators. When a person is convicted of a sex offense, he receives a penal sanction, usually a prison sentence. Once the inmate is nearing release, the state can file a petition to have the offender involuntarily and indefinitely committed to a mental institution or correctional facility that blends both a correctional facility and a mental institution. An evaluation by a mental health professional is required as well as a probable cause hearing to determine whether to label the offender a sexually violent predator. If he is so labeled, and following the completion of his prison sentence, the offender is confined to a mental health facility until judged by mental health professionals to no longer constitute a danger to the community. Sixteen states have now passed laws to involuntarily commit sexually violent predators.[17]

Under these civil commitment programs, almost 3,000 pedophiles, rapists, and other sex offenders are being held indefinitely in civil commitment facilities, secure institutions that provide mental health treatment. They cost taxpayers from four to eight times more than keeping offenders in prison. The U.S. Supreme Court has upheld the constitutionality of the laws, primarily because their aim is to furnish treatment if possible, not punish offenders twice for the same crime. The Supreme Court weighed in on this issue in 1997, in the case of *Kansas v. Hendricks.*[18] Leroy Hendricks was a repeat child molester. As the end of his prison sentence neared, state prosecutors became concerned that upon his release he would continue victimizing children. In accordance with Kansas's Sexually Violent Predator Act, they filed to have Hendricks civilly committed as soon as he was released from prison. Hendricks appealed, claiming that it violated the law against double jeopardy. The case eventually made it to the Supreme Court, which ruled that the Kansas act did not violate double jeopardy because it was a civil action and was designed to protect the safety of innocent people rather than punish an offender. The Court ruled that indefinite commitment was not equal to a life sentence because the prisoner-cum-patient is "permitted immediate release upon a showing that the individual is no longer dangerous or mentally impaired." After the decision Leroy Hendricks remained locked up at a cost of $185,000 a year—more than eight times the cost of a prison sentence in that state. When it was announced that he was moving to a group home in 2006, his transfer was protested by community residents. On April 28, 2006, the Kansas Supreme Court prevented the state from moving Hendricks out of a special treatment program for violent sexual predators to a group home in rural Leavenworth County. Now in his 70s, Hendricks spends most days in a wheelchair or leaning on a cane, because of circulation ailments, diabetes, and the effects of a stroke. There is a good chance that he may not live long enough to "graduate" from treatment.[19]

Terrorists in Prison

L03

While the Guantánamo Bay Naval Base detention camp is still in operation, many convicted **terrorists** are now being housed in federal maximum-security prisons and are part of the general prison population. On October 1, 2011, while 171 prisoners remained at Guantánamo, the Federal Bureau of Prisons reported that it was holding 269 inmates with charges that they are connected with international terrorism and 93 reported to have a connection to domestic terrorism.[20] In addition, 600 prisoners are packed into the makeshift prison on the American air base at Bagram in Afghanistan.[21] The United States Penitentiary Administrative Maximum Facility (ADX) is the supermax prison of the Federal Bureau of Prisons and holds many of the convicted terrorists, including Zacarias Moussaoui, who wanted to be one of the 9/11 hijackers; Wadih El Hage, Osama bin Laden's former private secretary; and Ramzi Yousef, the leader of the first World Trade Center attack in 1993.[22]

EXHIBIT 12.2 Sex Offender Treatment in Prison

An estimated 95 percent of sex offenders sentenced to prison eventually return to the community. That makes the Twin Rivers Sex Offender Treatment Program for men at the Monroe Correctional Complex and a similar program at the Washington Correction Center for Women in Gig Harbor valuable tools in the struggle to help them become law-abiding citizens.

The Department of Corrections knows treatment is not a cure for sexual deviancy. Therefore, the Monroe program's three main goals are:

- Helping offenders learn to reduce and manage risk

- Providing information to help the department and its community partners monitor and manage offenders more effectively

- Evaluating and improving treatment

Treatment begins with comprehensive assessments that include psychological tests, clinical interviews, and other techniques designed to define treatment goals and strategies for each offender. Counselors study what has sparked past offenses and then help to define the attitudes, thinking, and behavior skills that are needed to reduce the likelihood of reoffending. Program participants receive individual and group therapy. Group sessions generally have 12 to 14 members and meet from 6 to 10 hours per day. Additional classes and sessions address sexual deviancy, life skills, and other topics.

Offenders vary widely in their motivation and commitment to change. Treatment is likely to be successful to the extent that offenders are able to:

- Recognize and understand the factors that contributed to their offense(s)

- Monitor themselves and their environment to detect changes indicating that their risk to reoffend is increasing

- Develop the skills necessary to intervene, manage, and reduce risky behavior

- Remain willing and able to apply monitoring and intervention skills in a timely and effective manner, including seeking outside assistance when necessary

Treatment priority is given to the highest-risk offenders. But lower-risk offenders may be admitted for such factors as the offender:

- Used a high level of violence when committing his or her crime

- Likely committed more offenses than his or her official record shows

- Expresses an intention to commit future sex offenses

- Engages in sexually aggressive behavior in prison

- Experiences thoughts and fantasies related to sexually abusive behavior and is bothered by them

Offenders can be terminated from treatment for assaults and fighting, sexual behavior, violating the confidentiality of others in the program, failing to make progress in treatment, or being placed in a high security category (such as maximum). Offenders are expected to continue receiving treatment for up to three years after leaving prison through aftercare programs available throughout the state.

The Washington Corrections Center for Women in Gig Harbor offers similar treatment for approximately 10 of the 25 female sex offenders incarcerated there.

Source: "Sex Offender Treatment in Prison," www.doc.wa.gov/community/sexoffenders/prisontreatment.asp (accessed March 12, 2012).

TERRORIST One who acts with premeditated and politically directed violence directed against noncombatants.

When Guantánamo is closed down, its terrorist inmates will be transferred to traditional prisons in the United States or elsewhere. Correctional administrators will then have to decide how to control this special population: should they be given the same rights and privileges of other inmates or kept under much tighter control?

One major issue has been accusations that convicted terrorists held in maximum security prisons are able to freely communicate with the outside world, encouraging future terrorist attacks from their jail cells. Media news reports indicate that individuals convicted of committing terrorist acts against the United States have been allowed to recruit terrorists because the Federal Bureau of Prisons allows them very generous pen pal privileges. In one notorious incident, convicted terrorists were able to contact, from their prison in the United States, individuals in a Spanish terror cell, including Mohamed Achraf, who later allegedly led a plot to bomb Spain's National Court building in Madrid.[23] See Exhibit 12.3 for the various types of terrorist groups.

Using Torture

One of the most controversial issues surrounding the treatment of suspected terrorists is the use of torture to gain information. While most people loathe the thought of torturing anyone, some experts argue that torture can sometimes be justified in what they call the **ticking bomb scenario**. Suppose the government found out that a captured terrorist knew the whereabouts of a dangerous explosive device that was set to go off and kill thousands of innocent people. Would it be permissible to engage in the use of torture on this single suspect if it would save the population of a city? Legal scholar Alan Dershowitz argues that torturing terrorists in custody can be

TICKING BOMB SCENARIO This scenario proposes that a dangerous explosive device is set to go off and kill thousands of people and, therefore, it might be necessary to take extreme measures, such as torture, on a subject to extract information from him or her.

EXHIBIT 12.3 Types of Terrorist Groups

Revolutionary Terrorism

Revolutionary terrorists use violence to frighten those in power and their supporters in order to replace the existing government with a regime that holds acceptable political or religious views. Terrorist actions such as kidnapping, assassination, and bombing are designed to draw repressive responses from governments trying to defend themselves. These responses help revolutionaries to expose, through the skilled use of media coverage, the government's inhumane nature. The original reason for the government's harsh response may be lost as the effect of counterterrorist activities is felt by uninvolved people.

Political Terrorism

Political terrorism is directed at people or groups who live in close connection but who (a) oppose the terrorists' political ideology or (b) the terrorists define as "outsiders" who must either be exiled or destroyed. Political terrorists want the government to be more sensitive to their views and see things their way. In the United States, right-wing terrorist groups are organized around such themes as white supremacy, pro-life, militant tax resistance, and religious revisionism. On the left, domestic political terror groups are involved in violent actions to protect the environment and support animal rights (known as eco-terrorism).

Nationalist Terrorism

Nationalist terrorism promotes the interests of a minority ethnic or religious group that believes it has been persecuted under majority rule and wishes to carve out its own independent homeland. In Spain, the Basque Fatherland and Liberty (Euskadi Ta Askatasuna, or ETA) is devoted to establishing a Basque homeland; in the Middle East, Hamas and Hezbollah fight for the destruction of Israel and the establishment of a Palestinian state.

Retributive Terrorism

Rather than fighting for a homeland, retributive terrorists fight for a cause. Their enemies are not local groups whom they oppose or have conflict with, but rather people anywhere whose ideology and/or religion they find objectionable. Rather than a unified central command, they are organized in far-flung nets. Not located in any particular nation or area, they have no identifiable address. They are capable of attacking anyone at any time with great destructive force. They may use technology to attack their targets' economic infrastructure—such as through computers and the Internet—and actually profit from the resulting economic chaos by buying or selling securities in advance of their own justified under some circumstances, especially to prevent damaging terror attacks. To ensure that torture is not used capriciously, Dershowitz proposes the creation of a "torture warrant" that can only be issued by a judge in cases where (a) there is an absolute need to obtain immediate information in order to save lives and (b) there is probable cause that the suspect has such information and is unwilling to reveal it to law enforcement agents. The suspect would be given immunity from prosecution based on information elicited by the torture; it would only be to save lives. The warrant would limit the torture to nonlethal means, such as sterile needles being inserted beneath the nails to cause excruciating pain without endangering life.[24]

RARE RECIDIVISM In contrast with the record at Guantánamo, where the Defense Department says that about 25 percent of those released are suspected or known of subsequently joining militant groups, it appears extremely rare for federal inmates with past terrorist ties to plot violence following release. About 300 have been quietly released, and the government keeps a close eye on them. Before prisoners are released, FBI agents generally interview them, and probation officers track them for a number of years.[25] Exhibit 12.4 sets out a comparison of these special offense categories.

attack. Because they do not hope to regain a homeland or a political voice, they are willing to engage in suicide missions to achieve their goals.

State-Sponsored Terrorism

State-sponsored terrorism occurs when a repressive government regime forces its citizens into obedience, oppresses minorities, and stifles political dissent. Death squads and the use of government troops to destroy political opposition parties are often associated with political terrorism. Countries known for encouraging violent control of dissidents include Brazil, Colombia, Guatemala, Honduras, Peru, Iraq, and the Sudan.

Cult Terrorism

Some cults may be classified as terror groups because their leaders demand that followers prove their loyalty through violence or intimidation. These destructive cults are willing to have members commit violence, including murder. Members typically follow a charismatic leader who may be viewed as having godlike powers or even the reincarnation of an important religious figure. The leader and his or her lieutenants commonly enforce loyalty by severe discipline and by physically preventing members from leaving the group. They may go through doomsday drills, and maintain a siege mentality, fearing attacks from the government. It is not uncommon for such destructive groups to begin stockpiling weapons and building defensive barricades.

Criminal Terrorism

Sometimes terrorist groups become involved in common-law crimes such as drug dealing and kidnapping, even selling nuclear materials. Their illegal activities may on occasion become so profitable that they replace the group's original focus. In some cases there has been close cooperation between organized criminal groups and guerillas. In other instances the relationship is more superficial. For example, the Revolutionary Armed Forces of Colombia imposes a tax on Colombian drug producers, but evidence indicates that the group cooperates with Colombia's top drug barons in running the trade. In some instances, the line between being a terrorist organization with political support and vast resources and being an organized criminal group engaging in illicit activities for profit becomes blurred. What appears to be a politically motivated action—such as the kidnapping of a government official for ransom—may turn out to be merely a crime for profit.

Sources: Sanjeev Gupta, Benedict Clements, Rina Bhattacharya, and Shamit Chakravarti, "Fiscal Consequences of Armed Conflict and Terrorism in Low- and Middle-Income Countries," *European Journal of Political Economy* 20 (2004): 403–421; Andrew Chen and Thomas Siems, "Effects of Terrorism on Global Capital Markets," *European Journal of Political Economy* 20 (2004): 349–356; Lawrence Miller, "The Terrorist Mind: A Psychological and Political Analysis, Part II," *International Journal of Offender Therapy and Comparative Criminology* 50 (2006): 255–268; Chris Dishman, "Terrorism, Crime, and Transformation," *Studies in Conflict and Terrorism* 24 (2001): 43–56.

EXHIBIT 12.4 Comparison of Special Offense Inmates

Inmate	Number in Prison	Treatment Access	Recidivism Rates
Substance-involved inmates	High percentage	About 1 in every 8 substance-abusing inmates receive adequate treatment	High rates of recidivism upon release
Sex offenders	About 10 percent in state prisons and 1 percent in federal prisons	Relatively few receive adequate treatment	Very low, 5 to 10 percent repeat their criminal offenses
Terrorists	1,100 or so spread over several prisons	N/A	Low for those who have been released from federal prisons

SPECIAL NEEDS INMATES

Special needs inmates include a variety of people with particular mental or physical conditions that require that they either be separated from the general prison population and/or receive unique treatment tailored to their particular circumstance. Inmates bring many physical health issues to the prison, including high rates of tuberculosis, hepatitis, and HIV, and these health issues have an effect on budgets, staff, and other inmates. In addition, as a group, inmates have high rates of chronic mental health issues, including depression, anxiety, and some psychosis. Included in this group are HIV inmates and inmates with chronic mental health issues.

L04 ▶ ## Corrections and the HIV-Infected Inmate

Inmate populations include a high percentage of individuals in AIDS risk groups, particularly intravenous drug users.[26] At last count, 21 states reported testing all inmates for HIV at admission or sometime while in custody, and the Federal Bureau of Prisons (BOP) and 47 states reported testing prisoners if they have HIV-related symptoms or if they requested an HIV test. The BOP and 40 states test inmates after they are involved in an incident in which a prisoner is exposed to a possible HIV transmission, and the BOP and 10 states test inmates who belong to specific high-risk groups. In addition, Missouri, Alabama, Florida, Texas, and Nevada test all inmates for HIV upon their release.[27]

PROBLEMS OF WORKING WITH HIV INMATES HIV inmates are integrated with the general population in all but three states. Alabama, Mississippi, and South Carolina house the HIV-infected separately but integrate them into vocational and educational programs.[28] California moves all patients with AIDS to a medical facility in Vacaville to prevent the spread of the disease.

Working with this population raises a number of questions: Should patients with AIDS be hospitalized, segregated, or paroled? Should officers be notified when an inmate tests positive? How about notifying past or prospective sexual partners? Does educating inmates about safe sex and needle hygiene imply that the state condones sexual behavior and drug use in prison? Does this education obligate prison officials to provide the means for prisoners to practice safe sex and good needle hygiene while imprisoned?

PROGRAMS FOR HIV/AIDS INMATES Prison programs increasingly are informing inmates about the risk of unsafe sex and drug abuse. Prison personnel tend to be extremely cautious about contact with and treating inmates with HIV/AIDS. Nonetheless, a number of programs and initiatives have been created. Several states (including Vermont and Mississippi) and local jurisdictions (such as New York City, San Francisco, Philadelphia, and Washington, D.C.) are providing condoms to inmates, while others make bleach available to inmates to disinfect needles. The Corrections Demonstration Project of the Centers for Disease Control and Prevention (CDC) and the Health Resources Services Administration are attempting to fund and promote programs for HIV- and AIDS-infected inmates.[29] Under the Corrections Demonstration Project, four state grantees (California, Florida, New Jersey, and New York) have created HIV prevention/peer education programs within correctional institutions. These services include weekly new inmate orientation to describe the available HIV prevention services (New Jersey) and prerelease health education sessions for inmates who are returning to the community (California). Three of the state jurisdictions, California, New Jersey, and New York, are offering peer educator training to both HIV-positive and HIV-negative inmates. These programs hope to build associations with correctional officials and medical staff and to implement the needed services in prisons without placing a burden on correctional budgets.

Some prison systems have worked with outside agencies to help HIV/AIDS inmates adjust to prison life and prepare for reentry. In San Quentin prison in California, Centerforce, a private nonprofit institution, has been training inmates as peer HIV educators. Twice a year, volunteers are solicited to receive the comprehensive peer education training and then to work as peer educators within the prison. About 40 peer educators are trained each year. Centerforce personnel conduct focus groups to assess the service needs of inmates living with HIV, and to get feedback from them about primary prevention programs at the prison. Peer educators provide individual support for inmates newly diagnosed in prison and for HIV-positive inmates who have not been previously incarcerated. Centerforce has developed a two-week, eight-session health promotion intervention for HIV-positive inmates preparing to be released from prison. The sessions include such topics as self-esteem, health maintenance, community resources, stress management, substance use, legal issues, and barriers to care after release as well as a resource fair to introduce community service providers. In addition, peer educators conduct one-to-one sessions to help inmates learn techniques to prevent them from acquiring or transmitting HIV after release from prison. During these sessions, an individual's HIV risk is assessed, an individualized risk-reduction plan is created, and referrals are given. Sessions are conducted within two weeks of release from prison.[30]

Corrections and Chronic Mentally Ill Inmates

According to a recent national survey, more than half of all prison and jail inmates (56 percent of state prisoners, 45 percent of federal prisoners, and 64 percent of local jail inmates) have a mental health problem. See Exhibit 12.5 for data on inmates who reported symptoms of a mental disorder.

PROBLEMS OF WORKING WITH CHRONIC MENTAL HEALTH INMATES Prisoners with chronic mental health problems typically have had behavioral problems before incarceration and many get involved in substance abuse. An estimated 61 percent of state prisoners and 44 percent of jail inmates who

---

EXHIBIT 12.5 Inmates Who Reported Symptoms of a Mental Disorder

- 54 percent of local jail inmates had symptoms of mania, 30 percent major depression, and 24 percent psychotic disorder, such as delusions or hallucinations.

- 43 percent of state prisoners had symptoms of mania, 23 percent major depression, and 15 percent psychotic disorder.

- 35 percent of federal prisoners had symptoms of mania, 16 percent major depression, and 10 percent psychotic disorder.

Female inmates have higher rates of mental health problems than male inmates—in state prisons, 73 percent of females and 55 percent of males; in federal prisons, 61 percent of females and 44 percent of males; and in local jails, 75 percent of females and 63 percent of males.

Source: Doris J. James and Lauren E. Glaze, *Mental Health Problems of Prison and Jail Inmates* (Washington, DC: Bureau of Justice Statistics Special Report, 2006), p. 1.

A mentally ill inmate (right) talks to members of the mental health treatment team, (from left) psych technician Anthony Ramos, social worker Lee Penchansky, and psychologist Dr. Charlene Green inside the Idaho Maximum Security Institution near Boise, Idaho. The inmate is one of many of Idaho's mentally ill sent to the prison for treatment because there are no other adequate facilities. He is too sick to be treated as an outpatient and too dangerous for lower-level security hospitals.

AP Photo/Troy Maben

have a mental health problem had a current or past violent offense. About a quarter of both state prisoners (25 percent) and jail inmates (26 percent) had served three or more prior sentences before incarceration. Inmates with a mental health problem also had high rates of substance dependence or abuse in the year before their admission:

- 74 percent of state prisoners and 76 percent of local jail inmates were dependent on or abusing drugs or alcohol.

- 37 percent of state prisoners and 34 percent of jail inmates said they had used drugs at the time of their offense.

- 13 percent of state prisoners and 12 percent of jail inmates had used methamphetamines in the month before their offense.

In addition, these inmates bring other problems to the prison setting. About a quarter of both state prisoners and jail inmates with mental problems also report past physical or sexual abuse. About one in three state prisoners with mental health problems, one in four federal prisoners, and one in six jail inmates had received mental health treatment since admission. Taking a prescribed medication was the most common type of treatment—27 percent in state prisons, 19 percent in federal prisons, and 15 percent in local jails.[31]

Because inmates with chronic mental health problems present such a challenge for correctional administrators, efforts have been made to develop screening instruments to identify and classify them in an efficient manner. These instruments are discussed in Exhibit 12.6.

PROGRAMS FOR PRISONERS WITH CHRONIC MENTAL HEALTH ISSUES How did the population of mentally ill inmates get so large? In the 1960s, the government began closing state-run hospitals due to budget cuts and court orders forbidding the institutionalization of mentally ill people unless they received proper treatment. As a result, the number of people hospitalized for mental illness has significantly declined. Fifty years ago, the United States had nearly 600,000 state hospital beds for people suffering from mental illness; today, that number has dwindled to 40,000. Many wound up on the street and in the courts. Many Americans receive mental health treatment in prisons and jails rather than hospitals or treatment centers. New York City's Rikers Island jail alone holds an estimated 3,000 mentally ill inmates at any given time.[32]

While the number of inmates with mental health problems is significant, treatment

MYTH
One reason why male inmates are more violent and dangerous than female inmates is because males have a higher rate of mental illness.

FACT
The rate of mental illness among females in prison is actually higher than males. Almost three-quarters of women in prison suffer from mental illness.

Considering the significant problems posed by mentally ill inmates, it is important for correctional administrators to develop tools to quickly identify inmates who are in need of special services. Most clinical evaluations are time consuming and expensive, so a brief but effective screening is available. Researchers funded by the National Institute of Justice have created and tested two brief mental health screening tools and found that they are likely to work well in correctional settings. These tools are the Correctional Mental Health Screen (CMHS) and the brief Jail Mental Health Screen (BMHS).

The CMHS uses separate questionnaires for men and women. The version for women (CMHS-W) consists of eight yes/no questions and the version for men (CMHS-M) contains twelve yes/no questions about content and lifetime indications of serious mental disorders. Six questions regarding symptoms in the inmate's history of mental illness are the same on both questionnaires: the remaining questions are unique to each gender. Some of the questions are:

- Have you ever had worries you just can't get rid of?

- Some people feel that their mood changes frequently—as if they spend every day on an emotional roller coaster. Does this sound like you?

- Do you get annoyed when friends or family complain about their problems? Or do people complain that you are not sympathetic to their problems?

- Have you ever felt like you didn't have any feelings, or felt distant or cut off from other people or from your surroundings?

- Has there ever been a time when you felt so irritable that you found yourself shouting at people or starting fights or arguments?
  Do you often get in trouble at work or with friends because you act excited at first but then lose interest in projects and don't follow through?

- Do you tend to hold grudges or give people the silent treatment for days at a time?

Each screen takes about three to five minutes to administer. It is recommended that male inmates who answer yes to six or more questions and female inmates who answer yes to five or more questions be referred for further evaluation.

BHMS

The BHMS has eight yes/no questions, takes about two to three minutes and requires minimum training to administer. It asks six questions about current mental disorders plus two questions about history of hospitalization and medication for mental or emotional problems. Inmates who answer yes to two or more questions about current symptoms or answer yes to either of the other two questions are referred for further evaluation. Corrections classification officers, intake staff, or nursing staff can administer the screen.

Validation test results show that these tests are effective instruments that can be used to identify depression, anxiety, PTSD, some personality disorders, and the presence of any undetected mental health problems.

Sources: Andrew L. Goldberg and Brian R. Higgins, *Brief Mental Health Screening for Corrections Intake*, www.ncjrs.gov/pdffiles1/nij/215592.pdf (accessed March 12, 2012); National Institute of Justice, *Mental Health Screens for Corrections*, May 7, 2007, www.ncjrs.gov/pdffiles1/nij/216152.pdf (accessed March 12, 2012).

has been less than adequate and services for mentally ill inmates have been highly criticized. This has prompted advocacy groups to file lawsuits and lobby legislatures to promote relief for the mentally ill inmate. For example, in 2006, the Advocacy Center for Persons with Disabilities filed a federal lawsuit against the state of Florida, alleging that it was violating the civil rights of hundreds of mentally ill convicts and inmates awaiting trial by leaving them jailed and without treatment. In 2007, New York legislators passed a bill outlawing solitary confinement for mentally ill inmates after a study found that such isolation—to which mentally ill prisoners are often subjected—worsened psychiatric symptoms and often led to self-mutilation or suicide attempts.[33] Exhibit 12.7 sets out the treatment access and postrelease success of special needs inmates.

SPECIAL POPULATION INMATES

The third type of unique inmate is those in special populations, whose status creates problems for prison administrators. The elderly prisoner and the illegal immigrant inmate are two forms of special population inmates.

EXHIBIT 12.7 Comparison of Special Needs Inmates

Inmate	Number in Prison	Treatment Access	Recidivism Rates
HIV-infected	No national data	Providing medical care and some psychological counseling	Postrelease success is typical of the average inmate
Chronic mental health issues	About half of inmates have mental health problems	Usually medication and some direct intervention when crisis situations take place	High recidivism rates when returned to the community

Corrections and the Elderly Inmate

LO6

Today there are more than 120,000 inmates aged 50 and over in state or federal prisons, more than twice as many as a decade earlier.[34] The aging of the prison population has come about from longer sentences resulting from the get-tough-on-crime measures that impose truth-in-sentencing, mandatory sentences, and three-strikes laws, and an increasing number of older people convicted of sex crimes and murder.[35] This number is sure to rise: the U.S. population aged 65 and older is estimated to grow from 35 million in 2000 to 78 million in 2050, and the number of those aged 85 and older will increase from 4 million to 31 million.[36] It is projected by Brie Williams, a geriatrician at the San Francisco Veterans Administration (VA) Medical Center that "by 2030, one-third of the U.S. prison population will be geriatric."[37]

There are different adjustment rates for elderly prisoners. The longer the amount of time remaining to be served, the harder it usually is for the elderly person to deal with confinement. Background factors, such as level of education and marital status, can also affect the adjustment of the elderly. Some inmates, especially those imprisoned early in life, are more institutionally dependent than others. Some have higher morale and are more involved in programs and prison life than others. There is the problem that in many prisons there is little programming or specialized treatment geared for elderly inmates.[38]

PROBLEMS OF WORKING WITH THE ELDERLY INMATE The elderly prisoner is vulnerable to victimization and requires special attention when it comes to medical treatment, housing, nutrition, and institutional activities. The care of the elderly is extremely expensive. For example, the average cost of housing an inmate over 60 is $70,000 a year, which is about three times the average cost for other prisoners.[39]

Inmates over 50 are also more likely to have health and mental health problems than noninstitutionalized Americans

Martha Staggs, 68, listens to a question during an interview at the Julia Tutwiler Prison for Women in Wetumpka, Alabama. Staggs, who was convicted of murdering her husband in 2003, was diagnosed with colon cancer and after surgery the cancer spread to her liver. Her chemotherapy and medical bills total more than $67,000 a year. The cost of elderly or infirm inmates to Alabama's underfunded, overcrowded prison system has prompted several lawmakers to support a bill that would expedite parole dates for those prisoners. Is there any point in keeping someone like Staggs behind bars or would an elderly inmate such as her be better off being treated in the community?

AP Photo/Rob Carr

because they often come from poor backgrounds, have a greater likelihood of drug and alcohol abuse, and have more restricted access to health care.[40]

Some elderly prisoners find prison physically difficult to manage. One study of 120 female prisoners aged 55 or older in a California prison found that 69 percent of the women reported that at least one prison activity of daily living was very difficult to perform. These women also had higher rates of hypertension, asthma or other lung disease, and arthritis.[41] Another study found that nearly 40 percent of state inmates 55 and older have a recent history of mental health problems or disorders.[42]

Ronald H. Aday and others have reported that older prisoners need more orderly conditions, safety precautions, emotional feedback, and familial support than younger prisoners. They are particularly uncomfortable in crowded conditions, tend to prefer small groups, and want time alone.[43]

One of the problems of working with elderly prisoners is that increasing numbers of these prisoners have violent records or are sex offenders. One study conducted in the Deerfield Correctional Center in Virginia, which includes a large population of geriatric inmates, found that 75 percent had violent records and nearly 30 percent were sex offenders.[44] This record means that while the elderly demand special care, high security measures still must be maintained.[45]

MYTH Most people are released from prison and there are relatively few elderly inmates.

FACT Today, there are more 120,000 inmates aged 50 and over in state or federal prisons, more than twice as many as a decade earlier.

LO7 Corrections and the Illegal Immigrant

Few issues create as much controversy as immigration and crime. Concerns over the effects of immigration have existed for a long time, and bans against criminal aliens represented some of the earliest restrictions on immigration in the United States.[46] More recently, policies adopted in the mid-1990s have greatly expanded the scope of acts for which noncitizens may be expelled from the United States. Even so, calls to curtail immigration, especially illegal immigration, appeal to public fears about immigrants' involvement in criminal activities.[47]

Ironically, concern about the criminal activity of immigrants is rampant despite growing evidence that they actually have very low crime rates. According to "Crime, Corrections, and California: What Does Immigration Have to Do with It?"—a report released by the Public Policy Institute of California—immigrants are far less likely than the average U.S. native to commit crime in California.[48] Significantly lower rates of incarceration and institutionalization among foreign-born adults suggest that long-standing fears of immigration as a threat to public safety are unjustified. See Exhibit 12.8 for the key findings.

Illegal immigrants are an emerging correctional population. The Willacy Detention Center in Raymondville, Texas, is used by the U.S. Immigration and Customs Enforcement (ICE) agency to keep illegal immigrants in detention before they are deported. On December 18, 2008, 116 Salvadoran nationals—83 men and 33 women—were woken up at 4 A.M. and transported in buses under strict surveillance to be flown back to El Salvador. Here, prison guards at the Willacy facility frisk female detainees before embarking for the airport.

EXHIBIT 12.8 Key Findings About Immigrants

- People born outside the United States make up about 35 percent of California's adult population but represent only about 17 percent of the state prison population.

- U.S.-born adult men are incarcerated in state prisons at rates up to 3.3 times higher than foreign-born men.

- Among men aged 18 to 40—the age group most likely to commit crime—those born in the United States are 10 times more likely than immigrants to be in county jail or state prison.

- Noncitizen men from Mexico aged 18 to 40—a group disproportionately likely to have entered the United States illegally—are more than 8 times less likely than U.S.-born men in the same age group to be in a correctional setting (0.48 percent versus 4.2 percent).

Source: Kristin F. Butcher and Anne Morrison Piehl, "Immigration Has Little To Do With California Crime" Press Release, Public Policy Institute of California, February 25, 2008. Reprinted by permission of Public Policy Institute of California. www.ppic.org/main/publication.asp?i=776.

The findings are striking because immigrants in California are more likely to be young and male and to have low levels of education—all characteristics associated with higher rates of crime and incarceration. Yet the report shows that institutionalization rates of young male immigrants with less than a high school diploma are extremely low, particularly when compared with U.S.-born men with low levels of education. The low rates of criminal involvement by immigrants may be due in part to current U.S. immigration policy, which screens immigrants for criminal history and assigns extra penalties to noncitizens who commit crime.[49]

Despite the evidence indicating that both legal and illegal immigrants are less crime prone than native-born Americans, John Hagan and Alberto Palloni have found that the public's fear of illegal immigrants leads to higher levels of detention among Hispanic immigrants who actually break the law. Their findings suggest that Hispanics may suffer an increased burden at the pretrial release stage, because of both racism and anti-immigrant attitudes.[50] Stephen Demuth and Darrell Steffensmeier's analysis of this issue found conclusive evidence that anti-immigrant attitudes may contribute to the overdetention of immigrants who do break the law.[51]

Today, state and federal prisons hold more than 90,000 noncitizens, a number that has been steadily growing. More than two-thirds of the noncitizens in state or federal prisons are held by three jurisdictions: the Federal Bureau of Prisons and the California and Texas Departments of Corrections.[52]

PROBLEMS ILLEGAL IMMIGRANTS BRING TO THE PRISON

Illegal immigrants have a number of unique problems that must be addressed by correctional administrators. They may be recruited into ethnically compatible gangs. They frequently have difficulty in communicating with staff because their ability to use English is limited. Consequently, the growing number of non-English-speaking inmates requires that correctional staff become bilingual. If needs are not met, prison unrest may result.

PROGRAMS FOR ILLEGAL IMMIGRANTS
The Bureau of Immigration and Customs Enforcement (ICE)—the federal agency that has jurisdiction over immigrant detention—is now in the process of creating **family detention centers**, minimum-security residential facilities that would house entire families and provide schooling for children, recreational activities, and access to religious services.

FAMILY DETENTION CENTERS
Minimum-security residential facilities that provide schooling for children, recreational activities, and access to religious services.

CAREERS in Corrections
FORENSIC PSYCHOLOGIST

Preparation for the Job

Forensic psychology is the interaction of psychology and the law. Psychologists interested in this line of applied work should have experience working in prisons, jails, rehabilitation centers, police departments, law firms, schools, or government agencies. To prepare for the job, they should gain experience working directly with attorneys, defendants, offenders, victims, pupils, families, or with patients within the state's corrections or rehabilitation centers.

Nature of the Job

Forensic psychologists apply the knowledge and scientific methods from the field of psychology in legal settings. They evaluate the mental health of parolees, run inmate mental health programs, and provide counseling to victims. Moreover, in the court system, forensic psychologists consult with attorneys to assess individuals' mental health to determine how their mental state relates to the trial. They may help in crafting sentences based on the criminal defendant's clinical needs. Finally, they consult with law enforcement in order to apprehend criminals; for example, they might create a psychological profile of a suspect to predict their behavior.

Qualifications and Required Education

A forensic psychologist will need either a master's or doctorate degree. A master's degree will qualify forensic psychologists for entry level work in places such as police departments, prisons and jails, and mental health centers. The two more advanced programs are a doctorate of philosophy (Ph.D.) in psychology and a doctorate of psychology (Ps.D.) in forensic psychology. The differences are actually clear; the two programs have two different foci depending on the career goals of a future forensic psychologist. A Ph.D. in psychology will prepare students for administrative or management positions in law enforcement and health organizations. Ps.D. training prepares students for providing mental health treatment and being a court witness.

Job Outlook

The number of educational institutions that offer graduate programs in forensic science is relatively small, so entry into a program is competitive. But with the recognition of the importance of psychological factors in behavior and functioning, the employment outlook is good.

Earnings and Benefits

A forensic psychologist's mean annual salary is $74,250. The majority of these psychologists make between $51,520 and $93,870 a year.

Sources: Bureau of Labor Statistics, United States Department of Labor Psychologists, *Occupational Outlook Handbook*, 2008–2009 edition, www.bls.gov/oco/ocos056.htm (accessed March 13, 2012); British Psychological Society, www.bps.org.uk (accessed March 13, 2012); Marisa Mauro, "What Is Forensic Psychology?" June 7, 2010, "Take All Prisoners" blog, *Psychology Today*, www.psychologytoday.com/blog/take-all-prisoners/201006/what-is-forensic-psychology (accessed March 30, 2012).

This concept has been condemned by human rights groups and immigrant rights organizations as punitive and unnecessary, but immigration authorities embrace it as a deterrent against families crossing the border as a group and to ensure that immigrants show up for their court hearings and leave the country when ordered deported.

EXHIBIT 12.9 Comparison of Special Population Inmates

Inmate	Number	Treatment Access	Recidivism Rates
Elderly inmates	More than 120,000 inmates and growing all the time	Provide expensive medical care, some in separate facilities	Low, many never leave prison
Illegal immigrants	About 90,000 noncitizens	Placing them in family detention centers	N/A but probably high

Illegal immigrants who commit criminal offenses typically are required to be punished for these offenses, such as being sent to prison and doing their time, before they are subjected to being deported.

When family detention centers began operations, correctional administrators immediately faced protests and lawsuits charging that the children were living in substandard conditions. Children were given hospital scrubs to wear, forbidden to have toys, and allowed only one hour of recreation per day. After a legal settlement, children are now allowed to wear pajamas, move freely around the center, and bring toys into their rooms. There also have been changes made to the facility, including adding individual bathrooms, adding murals, and replacing metal doors.[53]

Exhibit 12.9 compares the treatment and recidivism of special population inmates. Because these populations are large and growing, specialized correctional personnel are now required to give them proper treatment. One of these, the forensic psychologist, is discussed in the Careers in Corrections feature.

SUMMARY

L01 Understand the problems of inmates with a substance-involved history

Inmates with a substance-involved history, especially drug-addicted inmates, need treatment while incarcerated and, at the same time, they pose particular challenges to maintaining a lawful environment if they are involved in drug use and trafficking to other inmates.

L02 Be aware what challenges and problems sex offenders bring to the prison

Sex offenders are more numerous in prison than in the past. The major categories of sex offenders are the rapist and the child molester. It is the child molester who traditionally has had a difficult time in the prison environment, but improved classification in some states has resulted in sex offenders being safer than they have been in the past. Some sex offenders face civil commitment when they are released from prison.

L03 Know some of the issues terrorists present to the correctional system

Terrorists are presently largely housed in Guantánamo Bay facility, as well as federal facilities on the mainland. The projected closing of Guantánamo Bay will mean that nearly 200 detainees will be transferred to traditional prisons. Correctional administrators will then have to decide how to control the special population.

L04 Understand the prison experience of HIV inmates

HIV inmates are highly represented in inmate populations, particularly intravenous drug users. In all but three states, Alabama, Mississippi, and South Carolina, they are integrated with the general population.

L05 Identify the world faced by chronic mentally ill inmates while they are in prison

Chronic mentally ill inmates are also highly represented in prison populations. It has been found that half or more of inmates in today's prisons have some form of mental health problem, and with some inmates their behavior is so extreme that they need psychiatric intervention and medication. They face ridicule, harassment, and the possibility of various forms of victimization from other inmates and very little in terms of programs and other means, other than medication, to help them cope with prison life.

 Understand the plight of elderly inmates while incarcerated and what is involved in their care

Elderly inmates are extremely costly to care for, both in maintaining their physical well-being and in providing for them during the final days of their lives. One of the tasks of prison staff is to protect them

from exploitative inmates. The management and care of these inmates require proper programming, a safe environment, and a sensitive and concerned staff.

L07 ▶ Understand the problems faced by illegal immigrants in U.S. prisons

Illegal immigrants are another special population in prison settings. More than two-thirds of noncitizen inmates are held in the Federal Bureau of Prisons and the California and Texas Departments of Corrections. Even though illegal immigrants do pose problems, such as when they become involved in a violent prison gang, they ordinarily present little difficulty during the time they are detained.

Key Terms

special offense inmates, 276
special needs inmates, 276
special population inmates, 276

sex offenders, 276
terrorist, 281

ticking bomb scenario, 282
family detention centers, 290

 ## Critical Thinking Questions

1. Is there a better way to handle vulnerable inmates than to put them in the prison population or to isolate them in protective custody?

2. What should the role of correctional staff be with inmates who are dying?

3. Which group of inmates discussed in this chapter do you think poses the greatest problem for staff?

4. Which group of inmates discussed in this chapter do you think has the greatest problem with prison life?

5. Why is the role of the correctional supervisor so important in handling the special population inmates discussed in this chapter?

Thinking Like a Corrections Professional

The warden calls you and other lieutenants together and tells you that prison suicides have become a major problem. There have been three so far this month, and the current year has the highest number of suicides in the history of the prison.

As the senior correctional supervisor, he wants you to chair a team to study this problem and make recommendations that will reduce the incidents of suicides. What will you do—first, second, and third? Are prison suicides something that can be reduced through management procedures?

Career Destinations

If you want to work with geriatric inmates, you might refer to the American Geriatrics Society:
www.americangeriatrics.org

If you are interested in counseling sex offenders, you may want to go to the Washington State Sex Offender Treatment Provider Program website, which has information regarding health care providers, regulations for professional practice, and contact information:

www.doh.wa.gov/hsqa/professions/Sex_Offender_Treatment_Provider/

You might also want to check out the National Association of Forensic Counselors:
www.nationalafc.com

Notes

1. Viji Sundaram, "Golden Girls Behind Bars: Aging Population Yearn for Freedom," *New America Media*, February 9, 2009, http://new americamedia.org/ (accessed March 12, 2012).
2. Ibid.
3. James P. Wojtowicz, Tongyin Liu, and G. Wayne Hedgpeth, "Factors of Addiction: New Jersey Correctional Population," *Crime and Delinquency* 53 (2007): 471–500.
4. William J. Sabol, Heather Couture, and Paige M. Harrison, *Prisoners in 2006* (Washington, DC: Bureau of Justice Statistics, 2007), p. 10.
5. Ibid., p. 24.
6. Sarah Goodrum, Michelle Station, Carl Leukefeld, J. Matthew Webster, and Richard T. Purvis, "Perceptions of a Prison-Based Substance Abuse Treatment Program Among Some Staff and Participants," *Journal of Offender Rehabilitation* 37 (2006): 27–46.
7. See Stephen K. Valle and Dennis Humphrey, "American Prisons as Alcohol and Drug Treatment Centers: A Twenty-Year Reflection, 1988–2000," *Alcoholism Treatment Quarterly* 20 (2002): 83–106.
8. Michael L. Prendergast and Henry K. Wexler, "Correctional Substance Abuse Treatment Programs in California: A History Perspective," *Prison Journal* 84 (2004): 12–13.
9. Michael L. Prendergast, Elizabeth A. Hall, and Harry K. Wexler, "Multiple Measures of Outcome in Assessing a Prison-Based Drug Treatment Program," *Journal of Offender Rehabilitation* 37 (2003): 65–94.
10. Sheryl Pimlott Pubiak, Carol J. Boyd, Janie Slayden, and Amy Young, "The Substance Abuse Treatment Needs of Prisoners: Implementation of an Integrated Statewide Approach," *Journal of Offender Rehabilitation* 41 (2005): 1–19. See also Bernadette Pelissier, "Gender Differences in Substance Use Treatment Entry and Retention Among Prisoners with Substance Use Histories," *American Journal of Public Health* 94 (2004): 1418–1424. See also Steven Belenko, "Assessing Released Inmates for Substance-Abuse-Related Service Needs," *Crime and Delinquency* 52 (2006): 94–113.
11. Bernadette Pelissier, Susan Wallace, Joyce Ann O'Neil, Gerald G. Gaes, Scott Camp, William Rhodes, and William Saylor, "Federal Prison Residential Drug Treatment Reduces Substance Use and Arrests After Release," *American Journal of Drug and Alcohol Abuse* 27 (2001): 315–337. See also Neal P. Langan and Bernadette M. Pelissier, "The Effect of Drug Treatment on Inmate Misconduct in Federal Prisons," *Journal of Offender Rehabilitation* 34 (2002): 21–30.
12. Steven Belenko and Jordan Peugh, "Estimating Drug Treatment Needs Among State Prison Inmates," *Drug and Alcohol Dependence* 77 (2005): 269–281.
13. *Sex Offending and Sex Offenders: Theories, Factors, and Treatment,* InsidePrison.com, April 2006, www.insideprison.com/Sex-Offending-and-Offenders.asp (accessed March 14, 2012).
14. Associated Press, "Texas Man Gets 4,060 Years in Prison," *New York Daily News*, July 2, 2008.
15. William M. DiMascio, *Seeking Justice: Crime and Punishment in America* (New York: Edna McConnell Clark Foundation, 1995), p. 22.
16. Tim Bynum, *Recidivism of Sex Offenders*, CSOM Publication, 2001, www.csom.org/pubs/recidsexof.html (accessed March 14, 2012). See also *Sex Offending and Sex Offenders*.
17. These 16 states are Arizona, California, Florida, Illinois, Iowa, Kansas, Massachusetts, Minnesota, Missouri, New Jersey, North Dakota, South Carolina, Texas, Virginia, Washington, and Wisconsin.
18. *Kansas v. Hendricks*, 521 U.S. 346 (1997).
19. Monica Davey and Abby Goodnough, "Doubts Rise as States Hold Sex Offenders After Prison," *New York Times*, March 4, 2007.
20. Scott Shane, "Beyond Guantánamo, a Web of Prisons, *New York Times*, December 11, 2011, p. 1.
21. Eric Schmitt, "Two Prisons, Similar Issues for President," *New York Times*, January 27, 2009, pp. A1, A16.
22. Scott Pelley, "Supermax: A Clean Version of Hell," *60 Minutes*, October 14, 2007.
23. United States Senate, "Schumer: Bureau of Prisons Process Must Be Examined and Fixed Immediately, Pen Pal Privileges for Terrorists Must Stop," March 1, 2005.
24. Alan M. Dershowitz, *Shouting Fire: Civil Liberties in a Turbulent Age* (New York: Little, Brown, 2002); and Dershowitz, "Want to Torture? Get a Warrant," *San Francisco Chronicle*, January 22, 2002.
25. Shane, "Beyond Guantánamo," p. 26.
26. Camille Graham Camp and George M. Camp, *The Corrections Yearbook 2002: Adult Corrections* (Middletown, CT: Criminal Justice Institute, 2002), p. 52.
27. Bureau of Justice Statistics, *HIV in Prisons, 2006* (Washington, DC: U.S. Department of Justice, 2008). For an argument that contracting HIV in prison is no small issue, see Kimberly R. Jacob Arriola, "Debunking the Myth of the Safe Haven: Toward a Better Understanding of Intraprison HIV Transmission," *Criminology and Public Policy* 5 (2006): 137–148.
28. T. M. Hammett, P. Harmon, and L. M. Maruschak, *1996–1997 Update: HIV/AIDS, STDs, and TB in Correctional Facilities* (Washington, DC: National Institute of Justice, 1999).
29. Ronald Braithwaite and Kimberly Arriola, "Male Prisoners and HIV Prevention: A Call for Action Ignored," *American Journal of Public Health* 93 (2003): 759–763.
30. Centerforce, "Collaborative Programs in HIV, STD and Hepatitis Prevention," www.caps.ucsf.edu/projects/Centerforce/ (accessed March 14, 2012).
31. Ibid.
32. M. J. Stephey, "De-Criminalizing Mental Illness," *Time* magazine, August 8, 2007, www.time.com/time/health/article/0,8599,1651002,00.html (accessed March 14, 2012).
33. Ibid.
34. "Elderly Inmates Swell Prisons, Driving Up Health Care Costs," *Nation*, www.usatoday.com/news/nation/2004-02-28-elderly-inmates_x.htm (accessed March 14, 2012).
35. Ibid.
36. The American Geriatrics Society, www.americangeriatrics.org/specialists/ (accessed March 14, 2012).
37. Quoted in Steve Tokar, "Prisons Not Adapting to Needs of Aging Inmate Population," University of California Newsroom, 2006.
38. "Elderly Inmates Swell Prisons, Driving Up Health Care Costs."
39. Ibid.

40. Anthony A. Sterns and Greta Lax, "The Growing Wave of Older Prisoners: A National Survey of Older Prisoner Health, Mental Health and Programming," *Corrections Today* 70 (August 2008): 70–76.

41. Tokar, "Prisons Not Adapting to Needs of Aging Inmate Population."

42. D. J. James and L. E. Glaze, *Mental Health Problems of Prison and Jail Inmates* (Washington, DC: Bureau of Justice Statistics, 2006). See also Rebecca S. Allen, Laura Lee Phillips, Lucinda Lee Roff, Ronald Cavanaugh, and Laura Day, "Religiousness/ Spirituality and Mental Health Among Older Male Inmates," *Gerontologist* 46 (2008): 692–697; and Steven J. Caverley, "Older Mentally Ill Inmates: A Descriptive Study," *Journal of Correctional Health Care* 12 (2006): 1–7.

43. Sterns and Lax, "The Growing Wave of Older Prisoners."

44. Eva Russo, "Growing Old Behind Bars," *Richmond Times-Dispatch*, March 4, 2009.

45. Viji Sundaram, "Golden Girls Behind Bars."

46. Daniel Kanstroom, *Deportation Nation: Outsiders in American History* (Cambridge, MA: Harvard University Press, 2007).

47. Kristin F. Butcher and Anne Morrison Piehl, "Crime, Corrections, and California: What Does Immigration Have to Do with It?" Public Policy Institute of California, *California Counts: Population Trends and Profiles* 9 (February 2008): 1, www.ppic.org/main/publication. asp?i=776 (accessed March 14, 2012).

48. Ibid.

49. Ibid., pp. 1–2.

50. John Hagan and Alberto Palloni, "Sociological Criminology and the Mythology of Hispanic Immigration and Crime," *Social Problems* 46 (1999): 615–632.

51. Stephen Demuth and Darrell Steffensmeier, "The Impact of Gender and Race-Ethnicity in the Pretrial Release Process," *Social Problems* 51 (May 2004): 222–242.

52. U.S. Department of Justice, Bureau of Justice Statistics, "Jail Inmates at Midyear 2007," www.bjs.gov/content/pub/pdf/jim07.pdf (accessed March 14, 2012).

53. Anna Gorman, "Immigration Agency Plans New Family Detention Centers," *Los Angeles Times*, May 18, 2008.

On March 30, 2007, Ronell Wilson was sentenced to die for the murder of two police detectives.[1] Wilson looked away as a judge made official what a jury of seven men and five women had found in January. Uniformed detectives filled the wooden seats of the vast courtroom. The widows of his victims sat with their children. Wilson's mother watched from the front row of the gallery.[2]

"It is the judgment of the court," said Judge Nicholas G. Garaufis of the Federal District of Brooklyn, "that the defendant Ronell Wilson is sentenced to death." Quietness filled the courtroom. The trial had lasted more than two months. The jurors found Wilson guilty of executing undercover detectives James V. Nemorin and Rodney J. Andrews on Staten Island in March 2003.

Everyone in the courtroom had heard of the details of Wilson's deprived upbringing at the Stapleton House project on Staten Island, of his bedwetting, of his juvenile crime, of his street gang involvement,

© Aaron Lee Fineman

Ronell Wilson, convicted of shooting and killing two undercover detectives, James V. Nemorin and Rodney J. Andrews, is shown being escorted from court. In the course of a sting operation, Wilson and a teenaged accomplice ordered the detectives to drive to a remote area, then Wilson shot both officers in the head, execution style. Should the killing of a police officer in the line of duty be punished by death?

and of his plan to rob the two detectives. They also heard a surveillance recording of Wilson shooting one detective in the back of the head and then pause to make the other beg for his life.

This sentence of death was the first in a federal court in New York since the Rosenbergs were executed in the 1950s for espionage. Judge Garaufis said, "This is a very sobering day for everyone. It's the end of one process, and the beginning of another process."

On July 2, 2010, a prosecutor's procedural mistake led to Wilson's death penalty being lifted, at least temporarily. On October 20, 2010, an appeals court refused to revisit the death penalty that was voided by the mistake. So, unless a federal appeals court overturns the voided decision, Ronell Wilson will serve a sentence of natural life, without the possibility of parole.[3]

chapter

Thirteen

CAPITAL PUNISHMENT AND THE DEATH ROW INMATE

LEARNING OBJECTIVES

LO1 Describe what public opinion is concerning the death penalty

LO2 Be able to compare the importance of aggravation versus mitigation concerning the death penalty

LO3 Discuss the position of the U.S. Supreme Court concerning the death penalty

LO4 Identify the position of the Supreme Court concerning the importance of race and the death penalty

LO5 Discuss the Supreme Court's rulings on the execution of mentally impaired inmates and juveniles

LO6 Describe how correctional officers working on death row regard their jobs

LO7 Identify how inmates on death row adjust to their situation

LO8 Evaluate whether the death penalty deters murder

AP Photo/Rick Bowmer, File

297

Capital punishment, as the Wilson case reveals, is a topic that stirs deep emotional reactions in both supporters and opponents. With this trial, as with every murder trial, the outcome is viewed from various perspectives. The victims' surviving families and children, as well as the police community, strongly supported giving Ronell Wilson the death sentence. The state's representative, the prosecutor, played his role in persuading the jury to bring back the recommendation for a death sentence. In contrast, the defendant and his attorneys viewed the proceeding through a much different lens. With this case, as with nearly all death penalty cases, they saw flaws in the process. The defendant's prior background and personal problems were ignored by the judge, who seemed to want vengeance rather than justice. We know errors can be and have been made in capital trials. Should the chance that an innocent person may be executed outweigh the need for retribution? Should Wilson get off with a life sentence in view of the murders he committed?

In Voices Across the Profession, Kelly Culshaw Schneider, a group supervisor in the Ohio Public Defender's Death Penalty Division, tells what troubles her about the death penalty.

 ACROSS the PROFESSION

KELLY CULSHAW SCHNEIDER
ATTORNEY

© Kelly Culshaw Schneider

"What I do and what my office does are extremely important. Regardless of what your personal opinion is concerning the death penalty, most of us would agree that if your state is going to be in the business of killing people, you want to make sure that the Constitution is followed and that the rules are applied as carefully as possible to make sure that the people who get the ultimate penalty are the most deserving.

Kelly Culshaw Schneider has been with the office of the Ohio Public Defender since becoming an attorney in 1997. She began as an assistant public defender in the Death Penalty Division and is now a group supervisor. Being certified by the Ohio Supreme Court has allowed Schneider to practice before the Ohio Supreme Court, the United States Court of Appeals from the Sixth Circuit for the Northern and Southern District of Ohio, and the United States Supreme Court.

"I like coming to work because I went to law school to become a public defender. That is what I've always wanted to do. I believe in the criminal justice system and the right to a defense. This is a job, especially with death penalty cases, where you can really make a difference.

"After being here 10 years, my general impression of the death penalty is that it has some real fairness issues. From the trial through to the end, there isn't a lot of rhyme or reason to who gets death and

who gets life. Secondly, it doesn't seem like the death penalty is applied equally. My clients are predominantly from a poor socioeconomic class. They are generally black and most of them have killed a white person. That is how the statistics play out in Ohio. Third, when you look at how relief is granted, you can see the unfairness issues. You can put two cases next to each other that are virtually identical and one gets relief and the other doesn't.

"What I do and what my office does are extremely important. Regardless of what your personal opinion is concerning the death penalty, most of us would agree that if your state is going to be in the business of killing people, you want to make sure that the Constitution is followed and that the rules are applied as carefully as possible to make sure that the people who get the ultimate penalty are the most deserving."

Kelly Culshaw Schneider is cognizant that many of her defendants had really poor representation at the trial level and are in desperate need of somebody who will put some time and energy on their case. "It is especially important to be a public defender in the death penalty arena," she adds, "because of the finality of the penalty." That is why she feels that her office and other offices like the Ohio Public Defender's office "must be vigilant about the defendant's constitutional rights."

Source: Interviewed in 2011.

CAPITAL PUNISHMENT AS A SENTENCE

The ultimate disposition in sentencing is the decision by the court to take the life of a convicted defendant. There have been more than 14,500 executions carried out in the United States, beginning with the execution of Captain George Kendall in 1608. Until the year 2000, the general trend in the second half of the twentieth century was an increase in the number of persons under sentence of death; the number of persons under sentence of death has declined since 2000 (see Figure 13.1). As of 2011, 36 states and the Federal Bureau of Prisons held 3,158 inmates under sentence of death, 15 fewer inmates than at year-end 2009. There has also been a decline in the number of yearly executions, today less than 50 people are executed yearly (see Figure 13.2). Between January 1 and December 19, 2011, 13 states executed 43 inmates, which was 3 fewer than the number executed as of the same date in 2010.[4] Three states accounted for more than half of the executions carried out during this period: Texas executed 13 inmates, Alabama executed 6, and Ohio executed 5. Of the 43 executions carried out during this period, all were by lethal injection. No women were executed during this period.[5] Although most of the executions through U.S. history have

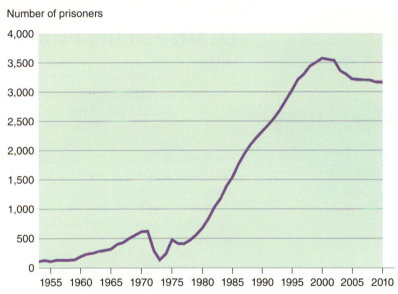

Number of prisoners

FIGURE 13.1 Number of Persons Under Sentence of Death

Tracy L. Snell, *Capital Punishment, 2010 Statistical Tables* (Washington, DC: Bureau of Justice Statistics, U.S. Department of Justice, 2011).

Executions

FIGURE 13.2 Number of Persons Executed in the United States

Tracy L. Snell, *Capital Punishment, 2010 Statistical Tables* (Washington, DC: Bureau of Justice Statistics, U.S. Department of Justice, 2011).

Source: Tracy L. Snell, *Capital Punishment, 2010 Statistical Tables* (Washington, DC: Bureau of Justice Statistics, U.S. Department of Justice, 2011).

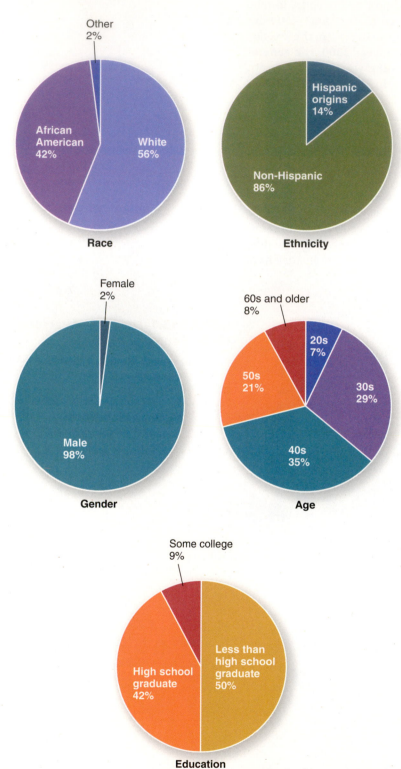

THE DEATH PENALTY IN CONTEMPORARY SOCIETY

On December 2, 2005, with his final words, "God bless everybody in here," Kenneth Boys became the 1,000th prisoner to be put to death in the United States since capital punishment was reinstated in 1976.[7] The death penalty has become an institution. Two driving forces in this institution are public opinion about capital punishment and political support for the death penalty. Although the death penalty still receives high approval in the United States, it is not as well received internationally.

Death Penalty Profile

Of those under sentence of death at year-end 2011, 55 percent were white and 42 percent were black. The 388 Hispanic inmates under sentence of death accounted for 14 percent of inmates with a known ethnicity. Ninety-eight percent of inmates under sentence of death were male, and 2 percent were female. The race and gender of those under sentence of death has remained relatively unchanged since 2000 (see Figure 13.3).[8]

Researchers Mark Cunningham and Mark Vigen found that an overwhelmingly large number of death row inmates are Southern males, frequently intellectually limited and academically deficient, with developmental histories of trauma, family disruption, and substance abuse. The rates of psychological disorders among death row inmates are high, with the conditions of confinement seeming to aggravate or precipitate these disorders. In contrast to what is traditionally thought, research findings reveal that the majority of death row inmates do not exhibit violence in prison, even when they are in more open institutional settings.[9]

Lethal injection is now the predominant method of execution and is used in 36 states and the federal government. In addition to lethal injection, 16 states authorized an alternative method of execution (see Figure 13.4). Nine states authorized electrocution; three states, lethal gas; three states, hanging; and two states, firing squad. For states that authorize multiple methods of execution, the method is generally selected by

LETHAL INJECTION The predominant method of execution, used in 35 states and by the federal government.

been for murder and rape, federal, military, and state laws have given the death penalty for other crimes, such as robbery, kidnapping, killing that takes place during drug trafficking, treason, espionage, and desertion from military service.[6]

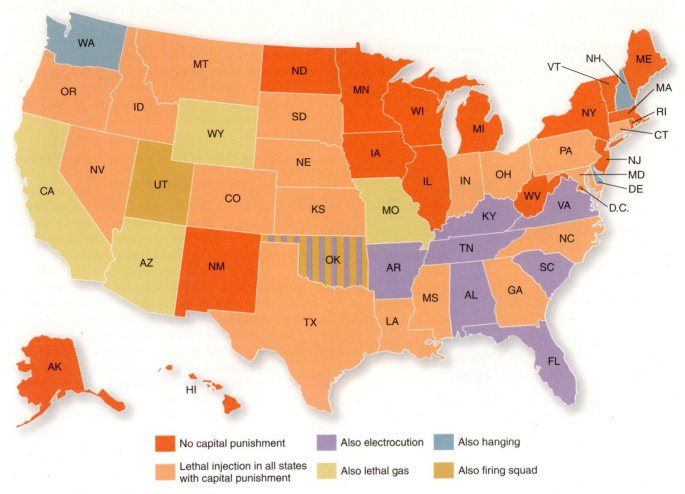

Source: Tracy L. Snell, *Capital Punishment, 2010 Statistical Tables* (Washington, DC: Bureau of Justice Statistics, U.S. Department of Justice, 2011).

FIGURE 13.4 Modes of Execution

the condemned prisoner. Exhibit 13.1 sets out each state's current death penalty policy.[10]

Public Opinion

American public opinion on the death penalty shifted dramatically during the twentieth century. Ever since 1939, the Gallup Poll has asked the public, "Do you favor or oppose the death penalty for persons convicted of murder?" For several decades in the twentieth century, support for the death penalty gradually declined. As recently as 1978, a Roper poll found that 66 percent of the population opposed the death penalty. However, in the last two decades of the twentieth century as the violent crime rate skyrocketed public opinion changed and a great majority of Americans, more than 80 percent, favored executions.[11] Some evidence indicates, however, that when the public is presented with the alternative of life imprisonment without the possibility of parole (LWOP), there is less support (about 50 percent) for the death penalty.[12]

MYTH The general public wholeheartedly supports the death penalty.

FACT While it is true that when surveyed about 80 percent of the public supports capital punishment, support erodes when they are given a choice such as life without parole for convicted killers. Wrongful convictions may convince many people that the use of the death penalty is just too risky.

EXHIBIT 13.1 Death Penalty Policy by State

States with the Death Penalty	States without the Death Penalty
Alabama	Alaska
Arizona	Hawaii
Arkansas	Illinois
California	Iowa
Colorado	Maine
Connecticut	Massachusetts
Delaware	Michigan
Florida	Minnesota
Georgia	New Jersey
Idaho	New Mexico
Indiana	North Dakota
Kansas*	Rhode Island
Kentucky	Vermont
Maryland	West Virginia
Mississippi	Wisconsin
Missouri	**ALSO**
Montana	District of Columbia
Nebraska	
Nevada	
New Hampshire*	
New York	
North Carolina	
Ohio	
Oklahoma	
Oregon**	
Pennsylvania	
South Carolina	
South Dakota	
Tennessee	
Texas	
Utah	
Virginia	
Washington	
Wyoming	
ALSO	
U.S. Government	
U.S. Military*	

* Indicates jurisdictions with no executions since 1976.

** Under moratorium from executions until the end of the current governor's term in 2015.

Source: Reprinted with permission of the Death Penalty Information Center, www.deathpenaltyinfo.org/states-and-without-death-penalty (accessed April 8, 2012).

What factors influence public opinion about the death penalty? Reports of erroneous executions in newspapers and news magazines as well as popular books about people released from death row because they were found to be innocent can influence public perceptions. Former death row inmates who have become public figures and win the sympathy of the general public by their work behind bars can also have an effect.[13]

International Opposition to the Death Penalty

The trend worldwide is to abolish the death penalty. According to human rights watchdog agency Amnesty International, over half the countries in the world have abolished the death penalty, either in law or practice. In Europe, the death penalty has been transformed from a national issue to an international human rights issue.[14] A total of 31 countries abolished the death penalty in law or in practice during the last 10 years, but China, Iran, Saudi Arabia, the United States, and Yemen remain among the most frequent executioners, some in direct contradiction of international human rights law. The total number of executions officially recorded by Amnesty International in 2010 went down from at least 714 people in 2009 to at least 527 in 2010, excluding China. China is believed to have executed thousands in 2010 but continues to maintain its secrecy over its use of the death penalty. Amnesty officials claim that while executions may be on the decline, a number of countries continue to pass death sentences for drug-related offences, economic crimes, sexual relations between consenting adults, and blasphemy, violating international human rights law forbidding the use of the death penalty except for the most serious crimes. A significant proportion of the executions or death sentences recorded in 2010 in China, Egypt, Indonesia, Iran, Laos, Libya, Malaysia, Thailand, the United Arab Emirates, Saudi Arabia, and Yemen were for drug-related offences. Iran, Pakistan, Saudi Arabia, Sudan, and the United Arab Emirates ignored international prohibitions in 2010 and imposed death sentences on individuals who were below 18 years of age when the crimes were committed.[15]

Death Penalty Appeals

A criminal defendant is convicted in a capital trial where he or she is charged with murder. In this first phase of the trial, the **guilt/innocence phase**, the jury determines whether the accused is guilty or not guilty of the capital offense for which he or she is charged. In the second, the **punishment phase**, the jury determines whether the person will be sentenced to death or life in prison.

The convicted defendant in a capital case will begin a process of lengthy appeals in both state and federal appeals court. The average time spent on California's death row is 17.5 years; the last five executions in California took place after the condemned prisoners had spent more than 20 years on death row.[16] In recent years, states that often utilize the death penalty have made an attempt to shorten the process of appeals. It is not unusual for large law firms to become involved in a case and provide counsel far superior to what the defendant received at his or her trial. A convicted defendant can decide not to pursue appeals, and his or her execution will take place in a few years.

Most cases are first heard in the state court of appeals. This is usually an automatic direct appeal, and the case will be examined for trial error and to determine if the case is consistent with similar death penalty cases. State review courts seldom overturn a conviction. The U.S. Supreme Court is then petitioned for a writ of *certiorari*, which is a written order to the lower court to send the records forward for a review. If the Supreme Court denies review, as it usually does, the stage of postconviction review begins. At this second stage, with the challenge from death row inmates that they have received ineffective or incompetent trial counsel, new counsel is appointed by the court. The new counsel typically raises questions about the fairness of the trial, such as tainted evidence, incompetent legal representation, or prosecutorial or police misconduct. If the trial court denies the appeal, it may be filed again with the state court of appeals. Typically, the state court of appeals denies the petition, and the defense counsel petitions the U.S. Supreme Court.

Demonstrators protest the death penalty in Paris, France. According to Amnesty International, 139 countries have abolished the death penalty. Nonetheless, about 20 countries have carried out executions in recent years and at least 676 executions were known to have been carried out worldwide in 2011, an increase of more than 100 since 2010. The increase is largely due to executions in Iran, Iraq, and Saudi Arabia. However, the total does not include the thousands of people who were believed to have been executed in China.

© Fanny/REA/Redux

This ends the second stage, and the third stage, the federal *habeas corpus* stage, is filed in the U.S. district court in the state that convicted the defendant. If this petition is denied by the U.S. district court, it is submitted to the U.S. court of appeals. A denial of the petition by the U.S. appeals court will send it forth again to the U.S. Supreme Court to intercede. When all appeals have been exhausted, including efforts to get the U.S. Supreme Court to intercede, the attorneys for the convicted prisoner usually approach the governor of the state and ask for a stay of the execution or clemency (see Figure 13.5).[17]

A number of reasons exist why the review process takes 10 or more years from conviction to execution:

- *Possibility of error.* Because of the terrible consequences of a false conviction in a death penalty case, it is critical to determine if any error influenced the outcome of the trial process. James S. Liebman and colleagues, in studying 4,578 appeals between 1973 and 1995, found that the overall rate of error in capital punishment cases in the United States is a staggering 68 percent. Two out of every three cases reviewed by the courts during this time period were deeply flawed.[18]

- *Complex process.* Death penalty appeals are very complex and take time to weave from one stage to the other.

- *Appellate delay.* Due to case pressure and overload, appeals courts, especially on the federal level, take a lengthy period of time to respond to a case before them. Federal judges tend to submit findings that are more extensive and better researched than is ordinarily true in those filed by state appeals courts.

GUILT/INNOCENCE PHASE In a capital trial, the phase in which the jury determines whether the accused is guilty or not guilty of the capital offense for which he or she is charged.

PUNISHMENT PHASE In a capital trial, the phase in which the jury determines whether the person will be sentenced to death or life in prison.

Source: James S. Liebman, Jeffrey Fagan, and Valerie West, *A Broken System: Error Rates in Capital Cases 1973–1995* (New York: Columbia University School of Law, 2000), p. 22.

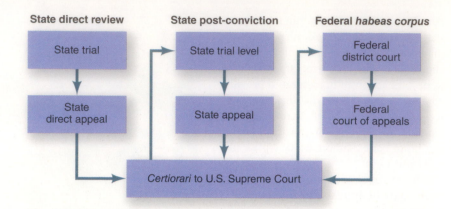

State direct review
- State trial
- State direct appeal

State post-conviction
- State trial level
- State appeal

Federal *habeas corpus*
- Federal district court
- Federal court of appeals

Certiorari to U.S. Supreme Court

To reduce the number of appeals, federal court rulings have placed limits on their use in death penalty cases. The Supreme Court dealt with this issue when Warren McCleskey returned to the Supreme Court for another attempt to overturn his sentence.[19] In a decision announced on April 15, 1991, Justice Anthony Kennedy wrote for a 6–3 majority rejecting McCleskey's claim of racial bias and went on to pronounce a new rule on such appeals. Henceforth, "a failure to press at the outset a claim of constitutional defect will be excused only *if* the inmate can show that something actually prevented raising that issue and can prove that the claimed defect made a difference in the outcome of the verdict or sentence."[20] McCleskey was executed on September 25, 1991.

Another method to limit appeals is to restrict the use of *habeas corpus* (see Chapter 9). Prisoners on death row argue in such a writ that their detention as condemned persons is based on some error in the administration of the law.

Despite the fact that it is difficult to appeal a capital sentence, many cases have been brought before the court system. In the following sections, some of the more important legal rulings are discussed in some detail.

Representative Hank Johnson, D-Georgia, reveals a shirt that reads "I am Troy Davis" as Davis's sister Martina Correia speaks with the media across the street from the Georgia Diagnostic and Classification Prison. Troy Anthony Davis was convicted for the 1989 murder of Savannah police officer Mark Allen MacPhail. On August 17, 2009, the U.S. Supreme Court ordered a federal district court in Georgia to consider and rule on whether new evidence "that could not have been obtained at the time of trial clearly establishes Davis's innocence." It instructed the trial court to "receive testimony and make findings of fact" about whether new evidence clearly established Davis's innocence. However, after considering the new evidence the Georgia court let Davis's conviction stand. In all, Davis had his execution stayed four times over the course of his 22 years on death row, but multiple legal appeals during that time failed to prove his innocence and he was executed on September 21, 2011.

AP Photo/Paul Abell

LEGALITY OF THE DEATH PENALTY

The constitutionality of the death penalty has been a major concern to both the nation's courts and its concerned social scientists. Lawyers have debated in the federal courts whether capital punishment is cruel and unusual, as stated in the Eighth Amendment to the Constitution. Whether it is *cruel* depends on one's perspective, but because it is favored by so many and has been in use for so long, the death penalty is not *unusual* and therefore not constitutionally banned per se. It is difficult to argue that the Constitution bans the death penalty, because the creators made reference to capital crimes, and executions were carried out at the time the Constitution was written. But times have changed, and the Constitution is a flexible document.

Consequently, there have been numerous legal challenges to the use of the death penalty. Some of the most critical ones are discussed in the following section.

L02

Use of Discretion: Aggravation versus Mitigation

In 1972, in one grand gesture, the U.S. Supreme Court in *Furman v. Georgia* swept away the death penalty in every state and spared the lives of men and women on death row.[21] The *Furman* case was the climax of a long battle against the death penalty. One of the campaigners was the NAACP, acutely sensitive to the fact that African Americans have been disproportionately given the death penalty. *Furman* involved an African American man accused and convicted of murder and rape. Georgia law allowed the judge to impose capital punishment at his or her personal discretion. In a 5–4 decision, the Supreme Court relied on the "equal protection" provision of the Fourteenth Amendment to overturn the sentence, as well as the "cruel and unusual punishment" provision of the Eighth Amendment. In his option, Justice William O. Douglas wrote:

Public opinion on the death penalty is often shaped by high profile cases. Damien Echols was held on death row in Arkansas for 16 years, after he was convicted in 1994 of the triple murder of three 8-year-old West Memphis boys. Echols claimed he never met the youngsters, Christopher Byers, Stevie Branch, and Michael Moore, and he never went into the Robin Hood Hills woods where they were killed. He said he was at home in Marion, a small community bordering West Memphis, talking on the phone for hours with a couple of other teens when the murders were committed. After DNA evidence proved their innocence, Echols and his co-defendants Jason Baldwin and Jessie Misskelley were released in 2011, having served 18 years and 78 days in prison.

© Stan Carroll/*Commercial Appeal*/Landov

> The high service rendered by the "cruel and unusual" clause is to require legislatures to write penal laws that are even-handed, non-selective, and non-arbitrary, and to require judges to see to it that general laws are not applied sparsely, selectively, and spottily to unpopular groups.[22]

Douglas went on to hold that the Georgia law violated the Fourteenth Amendment because, like the laws of the other states authorizing the death penalty, it provided the courts with so much discretionary freedom that judges could impose capital punishment on only a select group of people—the poor, the unpopular, and racial minorities. The Supreme Court did not completely rule out the use of capital punishment as a penalty. Rather, it objected to the arbitrary and capricious manner in which it was imposed. After *Furman*, many states changed statutes that had allowed jury discretion in imposing the death penalty. In some states, this was accomplished by enacting statutory guidelines for jury decisions; in others, the death penalty was made mandatory for certain crimes only. Despite these changes in statutory law, no further executions were carried out while the Court pondered additional cases concerning the death penalty.

In July 1976, the Supreme Court ruled on the constitutionality of five state death penalty statutes. In the first case, *Gregg v. Georgia*, the Court found valid the Georgia statute holding that a finding by the jury of at least one "aggravating circumstance" out of ten is required in pronouncing the death penalty in murder cases.[23] In the *Gregg* case, for example, the jury imposed the death penalty after finding beyond a reasonable doubt two aggravating circumstances: (1) the offender was engaged in the commission of two other capital felonies, and (2) the offender committed the offense of murder for the purpose of receiving money and other financial gains (for example, an automobile).[24]

FURMAN V. GEORGIA U.S. Supreme Court decision that declared the death penalty unconstitutional.

GREGG V. GEORGIA U.S. Supreme Court decision that superseded *Furman v. Georgia* and declared the death penalty constitutional if certain conditions are met.

AGGRAVATION When a jury finds a first-degree murder conviction on a defendant at the end of the trial phase, the defendant is then tried in a second phase, referred to as the penalty phase. The task of the prosecution is to establish that the sentence should be death because the aggravating causes in the case exceed mitigating causes.

MITIGATION During the penalty phase of the jury proceedings, the defense attempts to establish that there are greater mitigating causes than aggravating causes and the jury should bring in a recommendation for less than death (usually for life imprisonment without the possibility of parole).

McCLESKEY V. KEMP The Supreme Court ruled that race did not enter into the decision of the Georgia court and that there was no evidence of racial bias.

The issue of **aggravation** versus **mitigation** was further defined in the California case *Pulley v. Harris* (1984). Here the question was whether California law was unconstitutional because it did not require that the sentencing court compare the facts of the case with the disposition of other similar cases in order to ensure that the sentence was proportional to the seriousness of the crime.[25] The Supreme Court decided that California's death penalty law could be imposed if the California court could find that one or more of seven "special circumstances" were present: (1) murder for profit, (2) murder perpetrated by an explosion, (3) murder of a police officer on active duty, (4) murder of a victim who was a witness to a crime, (5) murder committed in a robbery, (6) murder with torture, or (7) murder by a person with one or more previous convictions of murder. In *Pulley v. Harris*, the murder was committed in the course of a robbery, a fact that satisfied the constitutional requirement of proportionality, and the Court ruled that Harris was eligible for execution.[26] In a more recent case, *Kansas v. March* (2006), the Supreme Court ruled that the Kansas death penalty scheme, which directs imposition of the death penalty when mitigating factors stand equal with aggravating factors, is constitutional.[27]

LO3 In sum, capital punishment is constitutional if state statutes clearly provide that, during the sentencing process, these conditions are met:

1. The court is informed about the defendant's background and criminal history.
2. Mitigating factors affecting culpability are brought to the attention of the court.
3. There are standards to guide trial courts in making the sentencing decision.
4. Every death sentence is reviewed by a state appellate court.[28]

Since resumption of the death penalty, the Court has dealt with a number of critical issues defining when, how, and with whom the penalty can be employed.

Administering Death

Most states have discontinued use of traditional methods of execution such as hanging and the electric chair and now rely on lethal injection. In 2008, the U.S. Supreme Court ruled in *Baze v. Rees* that Kentucky's lethal injection protocol satisfies the Eighth Amendment. Lethal injection is used for capital punishment by the federal government and 35 states, at least 30 of which (including Kentucky) use the same combination of three drugs. Kentucky's lethal injection protocol reserves to qualified personnel, with at least one year's professional experience, the responsibility for inserting the intravenous (IV) catheters into the prisoner.[29] The Court ruled that such procedures are constitutionally acceptable and do not amount to cruel and unusual punishment.

LO4 ## Race and the Death Penalty

A significant argument of abolitionists is that the death penalty is used in a racist fashion and therefore violates constitutional guarantees of due process and equal protection. The critical case on this issue concerns the murder trial of **McCleskey v. Kemp** (1987).[30] McCleskey was an African American man who was convicted in 1978 of the murder of a white police officer during an armed robbery. He contended that the imposition of the death penalty was cruel and unusual because African American men killing white victims are sentenced to death with greater frequency than white men killing white victims.

In this infamous 1928 photo, Ruth Snyder, sentenced to death for the murder of her husband, is shown being executed in the electric chair in Sing Sing Prison. The final moments of her execution were caught on film by a miniature plate camera strapped to the ankle of Tom Howard, a photographer working for the *New York Daily News*.

© Tom Howard/*NY Daily News* Archive/Getty Images

In support of this contention, McCleskey presented to the Supreme Court a study by Professor David Baldus showing the following: In Georgia, 22 percent of African American defendants with white victims received the death penalty, but only 8 percent of white defendants with white victims received the death penalty. Only 3 percent of white defendants charged with killing African American victims were sentenced to death. Prosecutors sought the death penalty in the cases of 70 percent of African American defendants killing white victims, but capital punishment was sought for only 32 percent of white defendants killing African American victims. It was argued that the figures showed that Georgia courts and prosecutors were discriminatory in their application of the laws.[31]

Justice Lewis Powell, writing for a 5–4 Supreme Court majority, rejected this argument. He held in this particular case that race did not enter into the decision of the Georgia court, and regardless of national data trends, there was no evidence of bias in the present case.[32] Although the Supreme Court was not swayed by charges of racial bias in the *McCleskey* decision, it has ruled that jury selection cannot be tainted by racial bias. In the 2003 case of *Miller-El v. Cockrell*, the African American defendant was convicted of capital murder in 1986 and sentenced to death. Miller-El's attorneys argued that prosecutors excluded African Americans from jury duty in Dallas County, Texas. The lower courts refused to consider his claim, but the Supreme Court disagreed, saying that the prosecutors had used their peremptory challenges to eliminate 91 percent of the eligible African Americans. The stated reasons for eliminating African Americans from the jury pool also applied to some white jurors who were not challenged and did serve on the jury. The Court further noted that the prosecution used underhanded techniques in order to eliminate African Americans. Moreover, a memo existed that instructed prosecutors to eliminate jurors based on race, ethnic background, and religion.[33]

John Donohue examined capital punishment in Connecticut from 1973 to 2007, a 34-year period, and did a comprehensive evaluation of 4,686 murders. He found that arbitrariness and discrimination were defining features of capital punishment sentences in this state. He especially found the racial effect evident (minority defendants with white victims were far more likely to be sentenced to death than others).[34]

L05 # Execution of Mentally Impaired Prisoners

Amnesty International contends that humanitarian standards require that people with mental impairment not be subjected to the death penalty. Amnesty International cites a 1988 recommendation by the United States Committee on Crime Prevention and Control that "persons suffering from mental retardation or extremely limited mental competence should not be executed for their acts." In 1989, the United States Economic and Social Council adapted a similar resolution. Despite such pronouncements, the mentally impaired continued to be executed in the United States. On August 16, 2000, John Satterwhite, a 53-year-old man who had been diagnosed as having both mental impairment and paranoid schizophrenia, died by lethal injection by the state of Texas. Satterwhite had been sentenced to death for the 1979 murder of Mary Francis Davis during the robbery of a shop in San Antonio.[35]

In 2002, the Supreme Court ruled in *Atkins v. Virginia* that execution of the mentally retarded was unconstitutional.[36] Daryl Atkins, who had an IQ of 49, was sentenced to death for killing Eric Nesbitt in a 7-Eleven store's parking lot. Justice John Paul Stevens, writing for the majority, noted that since the *Penry v. Lynaugh* case, in which the Supreme Court had upheld the execution of the retarded, a national consensus had emerged rejecting such execution. He added that the number of states prohibiting such executions had increased from two to eighteen.[37] The Court found his arguments persuasive and ended the practice of executing the mentally challenged.

Execution of Mentally Ill Persons

According to Amnesty International, since 1983 more than 60 inmates diagnosed with mental illness have been executed in U.S. prisons. Amnesty International argues that executing these inmates who cannot understand the nature of or reason for their punishment serves no deterrent or retributive purpose. In addition, common law has traditionally maintained that persons with mental illness may be incapable of pursuing available appeals or preparing themselves for death, in keeping with humanitarian or religious principles.[38]

In 1986, in *Ford v. Wainwright*, the Supreme Court heard the case of a person who became mentally deficient after receiving a death sentence.[39] In prison, Ford began to exhibit extremely delusional behavior. He claimed that the Ku Klux Klan was part of a conspiracy forcing him to commit suicide and that his female relatives were being tortured and sexually abused elsewhere in the prison. Writing for the majority, Justice Thurgood Marshall ruled that the Eighth Amendment prohibits the state from executing persons with mental illness because the accused person must understand that he or she has been sentenced to death and the reasoning behind this decision. Marshall found the alternative offensive to humanity.[40]

A 1991 Arkansas case thrust the execution of the mentally ill into the national limelight. Ricky Ray Rector had killed a police officer and another citizen and then shot himself in the temple, lifting three inches off his brain and leaving himself with the competence of a small child. Rector was convicted at trial and given the death penalty. In prison, he howled day and night, jumping around and giving no indication that he realized he was on death row and would be executed. The Supreme Court rejected his appeal. The issue of how competence should be determined is an important consideration complicating whether a mentally ill person should be executed or not. Typically, states' expert witnesses will find that the defendant is competent, while defenses' expert witnesses will find that the defendant is unable to understand the legal procedures that are taking place. Another issue concerns the morality of treating a person's mental illness so that they can be executed. Although the Court has not directly addressed this issue, the 1990 *Washington v. Harper* ruling found that a state could require an inmate to take a drug to control his schizophrenia.[41]

Execution of Juveniles

International human right treaties prohibit executing anyone under 18 years of age. The International Covenant on Civil and Political Rights, the U.N. Convention on the Rights of the Child, and the American Convention on Human Rights all have provisions to this effect. Indeed, more than 100 countries have laws specifically excluding the execution of juveniles or may be presumed to exclude such executions as they are parties of one of the above treaties. Seven countries since 1990 are known to have executed inmates who were under 18 years of age at the time of the crime—Congo, Iran, Nigeria, Pakistan, Saudi Arabia, the United States, and Yemen. Since 1994, 20 executions of those who were juveniles when they committed the crime have taken place, including 13 in the United States.[42]

The United States is one of the few nations that has executed juvenile offenders. In a 1988 case, **Thompson v. Oklahoma**, Wayne Thompson was 15 when he was arrested along with his half brother—then age 27—for the shooting and stabbing to death of Charles Keene. The Court ruled by a 5–3 vote that "the Eighth and Fourteenth Amendments prohibit the execution of a person who was under 16 years of age at the time of his or her offense."[43] In the 1989 case **Stanford v. Kentucky**, the question had to do with the eligibility of a murderer for execution when the crime was committed while he was a minor.[44] Stanford was 17 years and 4 months old when he was sentenced to death. Writing for a divided court, Justice Antonin Scalia ruled that inasmuch as common law prescribed 14 as the minimum age for execution, the sentence of a 17-year-old did not violate the

THOMPSON V. OKLAHOMA U.S. Supreme Court decision that prohibits execution of juveniles under age 16 at the time of the offense.

STANFORD V. KENTUCKY U.S. Supreme Court decision allowing the execution of juveniles who were age 17 at the time of the crime.

Eighth Amendment proscription against cruel and unusual punishment.[45] All debate over the possible use of capital punishment as a sanction for juveniles ended with the 2005 case of *Roper v. Simmons* when the Court held that executing those who commit their crimes as juveniles is neither consistent with the Constitution nor in keeping with the standards of a civilized society.[46]

Administrative Issues and the Death Penalty

A **death-qualified jury** means that any person opposed in concept to capital punishment is removed during *voir dire*. Defense attorneys are opposed to death-qualified juries because they bar those citizens who oppose the death penalty from serving as jurors. Defense attorneys believe that these citizens may be more liberal and less likely to convict defendants. Consequently, death qualification creates juries that are not representative of the public opposing the death penalty.

In *Witherspoon v. Illinois*, the Supreme Court upheld the practice of removing jurors who are opposed to the death penalty.[47] The Court further made it easier to convict people in death penalty cases when it was ruled that jurors could be excused if their views on capital punishment were deemed by a trial judge to "prevent or substantially impair the performance of their duties."[48] The Court further ruled that jurors can be excused because of their opposition to the death penalty at the guilt phase of a trial, in spite of the fact that the issue of capital punishment would not need to be considered until a separate sentencing hearing.[49] In addition, the Court ruled in *Lockhart v. McCree* (1986) that removing those who oppose capital punishment does not violate the Sixth Amendment provision that juries represent a fair cross-section of the community and, as a result, unfairly tips the scale toward juries that are prone to convict defendants in capital cases.[50] Thus, it would appear that, at least for the present, prosecutors are able to excuse jurors who believe that the death penalty is immoral or wrong.

See the Timeline for the significant U.S. Supreme Court decisions on the death penalty.

WORKING ON DEATH ROW

The conditions on death row vary among the states that house condemned prisoners. All states except Missouri and Tennessee segregate death row prisoners from the general prison population. Meals are usually served in condemned prisoners' cells. If inmates are permitted to purchase a television, they may do so but generally can receive only local channels. They can read until they fall asleep, no matter how late it might be, because each cell typically has individually controlled light switches. Inmates generally live in windowless cells. They cannot see or hear what is going on outside the prison. Attorneys can almost always visit five or more times each week, and condemned prisoners can have one or two family visits a week. A few days before their scheduled execution, prisoners are frequently taken from their cells to another prison in which the execution will take place.[51]

A number of staff members are involved with death row inmates: classification officers who process newly arriving inmates, the correctional officers and supervisors who are directly responsible for the inmates, mental health personnel, the chaplain, and the emergency medical technicians who insert the IVs that will send three fatal drugs through the condemned inmate's veins.

ROPER V. SIMMONS U.S. Supreme Court decision that disallows the execution of juveniles who committed a capital crime under the age of 18.

DEATH-QUALIFIED JURY During *voir dire*, any person opposed to capital punishment may be dropped from the jury pool.

TIMELINE

Legal Challenges to the Death Penalty

Stanford v. Kentucky
(1989)

Eighth Amendment does not probibit the death penalty for crimes committed at age 16 or 17.

Pulley v. Harris
(1984)

No constitutional requirement for a proportionality review of sentences in comparable cases in a state.

Penry v. Lynaugh
(1989)

Mental retardation is no bar to capital punishment.

Payne v. Tennessee
(1991)

Eighth Amendment does not prohibit admission of "victim impact" evidence.

McCleskey v. Kemp
(1987)

Rejects racial injustice of the death penalty.

Furman v. Georgia
(1972)

Overturns death penalty in Georgia.

1970	1975	1980	1985	1990	1995

Gregg v. Georgia
(1976)

Declares death penalty in Georgia is constitutional.

Thompson v. Oklahoma
(1988)

Prohibits execution of juveniles under age 16.

Ford v. Wainwright
(1986)

Prohibits the state from executing the insane.

L06 ▶ # Working with Death Row Inmates

A group of correctional officers and supervisors are responsible for inmates on death row. They seem to be positive about their jobs, and inmates, in turn, generally feel that they are being treated with respect.[52] When asked how he liked his job, one death row correctional officer replied, "It is a job. These guys are going to die, and we try to treat them decently. We do everything we can for them."[53]

Because of the length of time between conviction and execution, officers working on death row may develop relationships with the inmates and even develop a form of rapport. Officers do experience a sense of loss when inmates are moved to where they will be executed, but they do not usually feel that they are putting them to death. They are merely doing their job. It is easier for officers when inmates are transferred to another facility to be executed than when the executions take place in the same institution.

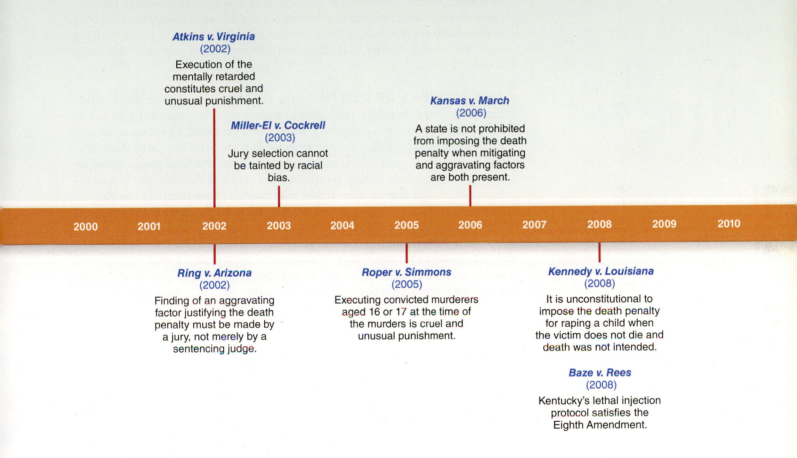

Atkins v. Virginia
(2002)

Execution of the mentally retarded constitutes cruel and unusual punishment.

Miller-El v. Cockrell
(2003)

Jury selection cannot be tainted by racial bias.

Kansas v. March
(2006)

A state is not prohibited from imposing the death penalty when mitigating and aggravating factors are both present.

| 2000 | 2001 | 2002 | 2003 | 2004 | 2005 | 2006 | 2007 | 2008 | 2009 | 2010 |

Ring v. Arizona
(2002)

Finding of an aggravating factor justifying the death penalty must be made by a jury, not merely by a sentencing judge.

Roper v. Simmons
(2005)

Executing convicted murderers aged 16 or 17 at the time of the murders is cruel and unusual punishment.

Kennedy v. Louisiana
(2008)

It is unconstitutional to impose the death penalty for raping a child when the victim does not die and death was not intended.

Baze v. Rees
(2008)

Kentucky's lethal injection protocol satisfies the Eighth Amendment.

Execution Teams

Death work culminates in the **deathwatch**, which is generally 24 to 48 hours. It is usually supervised by a team of correctional officers who report to the prison warden; the warden or his or her representative is legally mandated to preside over the execution.

Teams are likely to view the execution as a shared responsibility. The deathwatch team officers feed inmates on the "row," observe them, escort them to the shower and exercise areas, prepare them for execution, escort them to the death chamber, and secure them for execution. Members of this team have the responsibility of explaining to condemned inmates what is going to happen to their personal property, when and how long they can talk with family in the final hours before execution, and how the warden has a phone line available to hear any stay of execution that might be forthcoming from the courts or the governor's office.[54]

Those who carry out the execution are part of what is known as an **execution team**. The officers who make up the execution team usually say that they cope

DEATHWATCH The period, generally 24 to 48 hours, before the execution; usually supervised by a team of correctional officers.

EXECUTION TEAM Those who carry out the execution.

with their jobs by focusing on the routine. One supervisor, who has the rank of major, described his duties succinctly: "We make sure everything is done correctly."[55] Each person on the team has a particular job to do, and they attempt to do it in a professional but detached way. They see themselves as doing a job that society requires someone to do, and they take pride in the way they conduct themselves as they carry out the law.

Donald A. Cabana wrote a gripping account of the time he was warden of the Mississippi State Penitentiary at Parchman, and supervised two executions. In this book, which is recommended reading, he says, "Capital punishment exacts a toll on those who must carry it out."[56] Nor is working on death row an easy job for a correctional officer. Inmates have different ways of coping with their sentence of death, but it is difficult for a correctional officer not to be affected by this environment. Officers must deal with emotions of guilt because they administered death. When asked, one officer echoed what a number of fellow officers think about these events: "After it is over, you get to thinking about the inmate. You try to block out what happened but you can't—his death is there."[57]

THE PROCESS OF DEATH In the final few hours before death, while procedures vary somewhat from state to state, a prisoner receives his or her final visits from family and attorney. He or she is provided a final meal, usually whatever is requested. The warden and chaplain visit and stay until the execution is over. Witnesses arrive, and the inmate makes the final preparations. In some states, the male inmate receives a fresh set of clothes and the female inmate a dress. The inmate is permitted to shower and is connected to an electro-cardiogram (EKG) machine, which will remain until the heart stops and death has taken place.

Executions are quite ritualized and involve a series of precise steps. It is the responsibility of the strap-down team, usually a six-person group, to escort the condemned from their cells to the execution room and secure them to the execution table. Each is assigned responsibility for one body part, such as the left arm or the left leg. This process keeps them from focusing on what they are preparing the condemned for and diffuses responsibility. One officer who performed this duty for 15 years notes, "We each have a duty to do it as efficiently as we can. The day is important enough that we want it to go without a hitch."[58]

When the straps are securely fastened, then it is up to the warden to give the signal to begin the execution. The warden usually stands at the head of the person strapped on the gurney, and the prison chaplain stands at his or her feet. When the medical technician or the trained officer injects the two lethal chemicals, death usually comes in a few minutes.

The first drug, sodium thiopental, ensures that the prisoner does not experience any pain associated with the paralysis and cardiac arrest caused by the second and third drugs, pancuronium bromide and potassium chloride. According to the U.S. Supreme Court, the actual insertion of the intravenous (IV) catheter must be made by a person who has at least one year's professional experience. The execution team has the responsibility to mix the drugs and load them into syringes, and the warden and deputy warden must remain in the execution chamber to observe the prisoner and watch for any IV problems while the execution team administers the drugs from another room. If the prisoner is not unconscious within 60 seconds after the sodium thiopental's delivery, a new dose must be given at a secondary injection site before the second and third drugs are administered.[59] A physician examines the body and pronounces death.

The execution process is concluded when the strap-down team reenters the death chamber, unfastens the straps around the body, and transfers it to another gurney. The body is loaded into a waiting hearse and taken to a local funeral home, where it is either claimed by the family or interred by the state. The death certificate usually says "state-ordered homicide."[60]

LIVING ON DEATH ROW

Inmates living on death row share experiences like no others. There appear to be at least four types of inmate responses to death row:

- Some continue to reiterate their innocence, and they may even go to their execution claiming innocence.

- Some focus on legal appeals and court work.

- Some have a religious experience and adopt a new religious identity.

- Some become quite depressed, ruminating over struggles and difficulties of adjusting to death row.

In the midst of these responses, inmates deal with a variety of anxieties on death row—arranging meetings with their attorneys, waiting for rulings from appeal courts, desiring correspondence from their families, and looking forward to upcoming family visits. Another source of anxiety is when the date of execution is approaching for their incarcerated friends or themselves.

One inmate on death row in Ohio talks about the trauma when a condemned prisoner is taken from death row to the prison where he will be executed:

> Last week they came and got a guy down the cellblock. We had been friends for a number of years, and we had served time together in a number of "joints" in this state. He knew his time was up, but we didn't believe it was going to happen until they came and got him. This place hasn't been the same since that [about a week ago]. I don't think I've slept since that. I know my time is coming and, as I told you before, I'm innocent. The state is going to kill an innocent man. I just feel nervous; I can't relax. I can't get it off my mind that my time is coming too.[61]

For a more extensive statement from a death row inmate in Georgia, see the Correctional Life feature.

For some, living on death row means preparing for the end. Here, on February 15, 2012, George Rivas speaks from death row in the Allan Polunsky Unit prison in Livingston, Texas, about his part in the crime rampage of the Texas Seven. On December 13, 2000, Rivas's gang overpowered workers at the Texas Department of Criminal Justice Connally Unit prison in Kenedy and stole the workers' clothes, broke into the prison's armory to get guns, and drove away in a prison truck. They committed several robberies, including two in Houston, and then 11 days later, gunned down Irving, Texas, police officer Aubrey Hawkins. In the end, Rivas was executed by lethal injection on February 29, 2012 at 6:22 P.M.

AP Photo/Fort Worth Star-Telegram, Ron T. Ennis

ARGUMENTS FOR AND AGAINST THE DEATH PENALTY

Defenders of the death penalty make several arguments supporting their position and, at the same time, those who oppose the death penalty base their arguments on several positions. The following sections outline both the **retentionist arguments** and the **abolitionist arguments**.

Retentionist Arguments

- *Deterrence.* Punishment has a deterrent value. Crime is a rational process, and therefore it only stands to reason that the possibility of a death sentence will deter some of those who are contemplating murder.[62]

- *Fairness.* It is only fair that "cold-blooded" killers pay for their crimes with their own lives. In Walter Berns's eloquent essay, he draws on humanity's anger against Nazi war criminals to justify capital punishment for retribution.[63]

- *Threat of recidivism.* Defenders of the death penalty charge that life imprisonment does not protect society, because prisoners who have

RETENTIONIST ARGUMENTS Defenders of the death penalty make several arguments supporting their positions, including its deterrent value, fairness, and life imprisonment does not sufficiently protect society.

ABOLITIONIST ARGUMENTS Those who oppose the death penalty base their arguments on several positions, including the moral issue, the constitutional issue, and the pragmatic issues.

CORRECTIONAL LIFE

"James: Inmate Voice from Death Row

James A. Lee reflects what it is like being on death row in the Georgia Department of Corrections.

"When someone gets a death sentence, his or her whole world caves in. Nothing, nor anyone, can prepare one for the mental torture that follows! Being separated from friends, family, and loved ones, and knowing that life will be soon going on without you is not easy to handle.

"The best way to deal with and cope with these things is to constantly stay busy! Reading, writing, exercise, or whatever; just don't sit still. An idle mind will collapse on you and then the torture really begins. Others deal with it by medication to help strengthen their minds. But this is a form of detachment, an escape from reality if you will.

"As for the 'biggie,' the death sentence and execution, it's hard in the beginning. It's daily torture, but as time progresses it becomes less and less powerful over you. In a day-to-day atmosphere, I never think of it. When I see family or friends on visits, I'm reminded of it. But over time, it loses its power to torture you."

James A. Lee closed this 2008 letter he wrote for this book with these words: "Thank you for this opportunity to voice myself! May all your frowns be found upside down."

Source: James A. Lee, letter to the author, 2008. "

Those opposed to the death penalty include people whom you might think would be supporters. Ronnie Sandoval (left) and Lorrain Taylor comfort each other as they hold photos of their slain children at a news conference where they joined others in supporting a November 2012 ballot initiative to end the death penalty, held in Sacramento, California, August 29, 2011. Sandoval's son, Arthur Carmona, was murdered in Santa Ana in 2008 and Taylor's twin sons were gunned down together in Oakland in 2000. Both mothers spoke against the death penalty and support the initiative that would replace capital punishment with life prison terms.

AP Photo/Rich Pedroncelli

committed murder are usually eligible for parole after a period of time, or if they are given a life sentence, they commit another murder while they are incarcerated.[64]

Abolitionist Arguments

- *The moral issue.* Moralists who reject the death penalty as a response to crime, even the crime of murder, hold that it is state-administered homicide. The moralist's argument goes on to a consideration of the inevitable caprice in the administration of the death penalty. In addition, this argument makes the point that the majority of men and women executed have been African American or Hispanic, in spite of all the precautions against prejudice that have been built into the judicial process. Does race influence the death penalty? Consider the Evidence-Based Corrections feature.

- *The constitutional issue.* Challenges to the legitimacy of capital punishment have built their case against the death penalty by the ambiguous language of the Eighth and Fourteenth Amendments. What this challenge is all about is that the death penalty is unconstitutional.

- *The pragmatic issues.* The possibilities of errors, incompetent and inexperienced defense counsels, police officers who are not truthful, and prosecutors who repress evidence are some of the reasons why wrongful individuals are convicted and given the sentence of death. The recent releases from death row because of wrongful convictions are a reminder of the accuracy of this concern. The other pragmatic issue is the costliness of the death penalty; it is several times more expensive than confining an inmate for the duration of his or her life. A few state studies are as follows:

- Maryland: The state has incurred costs of $37.2 million for each of the state's five executions since they reenacted the death penalty.

- New Jersey: The state's death penalty cost taxpayers $253 million since 1983, a figure that is over and above the costs incurred by the state under a sentence of life without parole instead of death.

- Kansas: The state concluded that capital cases are 70 percent more expensive than comparable non-death-penalty cases.

- Florida: The state would save $51 million each year by punishing all first-degree murders with life in prison without parole.

- California: The state spends $90 million dollars annually above and beyond the ordinary costs of the justice system on capital cases.

- Texas: Each death penalty case in Texas costs taxpayers about $2.3 million, about three times the costs of imprisoning someone in a single cell at the highest security level for 40 years.[65]

EVIDENCE-BASED CORRECTIONS

Racial Intolerance and Support for the Death Penalty

Why do people support the death penalty? Is it based on an actual belief that capital punishment deters murder or do other forces influence public attitudes? According to James Unnever and Francis Cullen's research, support for capital punishment, here and abroad, may reflect cross-group conflict and animosity. Public opinion is fueled by perceived or actual threats by outside groups—the dominant group's fear that its privileges are being eroded by the demands of a minority and the minority group's belief that it can enhance its position by challenging the existing racial/ethnic order. Members of the privileged group can claim that their prejudices toward the outsiders are justified because these minorities are disrupting society by being overly criminal. Unnever and Cullen argue that associating criminality with "others" helps justify the belief in harsh criminal justice policies such as the death penalty.

Unnever and Cullen found that data collected in the United States confirmed their views that racial intolerance predicts not only pro-death-penalty attitudes but also support for punitive crime-control measures. Using survey data from a number of other nations, they found that public support for capital punishment is related to beliefs about racial and ethnic minorities. The data show that individuals in France, Belgium, the Netherlands, West and East Germany, Italy, Luxembourg, Denmark, Great Britain, Greece, Spain, Finland, Sweden, and Austria who expressed racial and ethnic prejudice were more likely to support harshly punishing criminals. Racial intolerance was one of the most substantive predictors of punitiveness. People with more years of education were less likely and those who were conservatives were more likely to embrace punitive sentiments. However, punitiveness was not related to racial/ethnic intolerance in Portugal and Ireland, possibly because these two countries have more benign race relations than most others.

In conclusion, Unnever and Cullen found that support for capital punishment may rely less on the need for safety and is more likely a response to racial and ethnic conflict and anger.

Source: James Unnever and Francis Cullen, "Racial-Ethnic Intolerance and Support for Capital Punishment: A Cross-National Comparison," *Criminology* 48 (2010): 831–879.

L08 DOES THE DEATH PENALTY DETER MURDER?

Defenders of the death penalty, as stated above, make several arguments supporting their positions. They claim that this punishment is justified because it provides incapacitation and is a deterrent to murder. They assert further that the death penalty provides justice for victims' families, that individuals who commit heinous crimes deserve the death penalty, and that it is proportional.

Contemporary opposition to capital punishment is generally based on beliefs about the possibility of error; the unfair use of discretion; no deterrence effect; racial, gender, and other biases; brutality unacceptable to a free society; and the expense of executions (up to $3 million per execution, which is considerably more than life imprisonment).

Yet the absolute key issue in the death penalty debate is whether this punishment can lower the murder rate. Even with its brutality and cruelty, the claim could be made that the death penalty could be justified if it proved to be an effective deterrent that would save innocent lives. As suggested by this chapter, those who favor the death penalty claim that it has real deterrent value and those who oppose it deny it has real deterrent value. Which position is correct?

The particular focus on the empirical research on the death penalty is whether the death penalty serves as a more effective deterrent than life imprisonment for capital crimes such as homicide. The methods that have been employed include the following:

- *Immediate impact studies.* This approach attempts to calculate the effects a well-publicized execution has on the short-term murder rate.

Years on death row take a toll on inmates. Here, a death row inmate stands in his cell at Lieber Correctional Institution near Ridgeville, South Carolina. Inmates at the facility spend about 23 hours a day in a cell so narrow they can touch both walls at the same time and just long enough to accommodate a set of bunk beds, a toilet, and a sink.

AP Photo/Lou Krasky

■ *Time-series analysis.* This approach compares long-term trends in capital punishment rates and murder.

■ *Contiguous-state analysis.* This approach compares murder rates in states with the death penalty to the murder rates of a similar state that has abolished the death penalty.

The majority of researchers have failed to find any deterrent effect of the death penalty. There is little evidence that murder rates rise when a state abolishes capital punishment any more so than murder rates decrease when the death penalty is adopted. The murder rate is further similar both in states that use capital punishment and neighboring states that have abolished the death penalty.

Despite this lack of empirical verification, some recent studies have concluded that executing criminals may, in fact, bring the murder rate down. Newer studies, using sophisticated data analysis, have been able to uncover a more significant association. James Yunker, using a national data set, has found evidence that there is a deterrent effect of capital punishment now that the pace of executions has accelerated.[66] Economists Hashem Dezhbakhsh, Paul H. Rubin, and Joanna M. Shepherd performed an advanced statistical analysis on county-level homicide data and found that each execution leads to an average of 18 fewer murders.[67]

These efforts contradict findings that capital punishment fails as a deterrent. So on the one hand, the most recent research indicates that if the death penalty was used more frequently, it is possible that the tipping point would be reached, and execution can become an effective deterrent measure. On the other hand, capital punishment still carries significant baggage: since 1976, more than 100 people have been wrongfully convicted and sentenced to death in the United States. And according to research sponsored by the Pew Foundation, a majority of death penalty convictions have been overturned, many due to "serious, reversible error," including egregiously incompetent defense counsel, suppression of exculpatory evidence, false confessions, racial manipulation of the jury, "snitch" and accomplice testimony, and faulty jury instructions.[68] So after years of study, the value of the death penalty remains a topic of considerable debate.

SUMMARY

LO1 ▶ **Describe what public opinion is concerning the death penalty**

American public opinion shifted dramatically in the twentieth century. As recently as 1978, one public opinion poll found that 66 percent of the population opposed the death penalty. However, in the last two decades of the twentieth and into the twenty-first century, with the rising violent crime rates, public opinion changed and a great majority of Americans, more than 80 percent, favored

the death penalty. Some evidence exists that when the public is presented with the alternative of life imprisonment without the possibility of parole, the support declines (about 50 percent) for the death penalty.

LO2 ▶ **Be able to compare the importance of aggravation versus mitigation concerning the death penalty**

The first phase of the death penalty trial determines guilt or innocence. If the jury finds that a person is guilty of first-degree murder, then the court process enters the penalty phase. For a person to be condemned to death in the penalty phase, the jury must find that the aggravation factors (why the defendant should be put to death) are greater than the mitigation factors (why the defendant should not be put to death).

L03 **Discuss the position of the U.S. Supreme Court concerning the death penalty**

The death penalty has received mixed support from the U.S. Supreme Court, but, with certain exceptions, the Court has consistently found the death penalty does not constitute cruel and unusual punishment.

L04 **Identify the position of the Supreme Court concerning the importance of race and the death penalty**

Jury selection cannot be tainted by racial bias, but unless the defense can prove that racial bias is involved, race is not a factor in the execution process.

L05 **Discuss the Supreme Court's rulings on the execution of mentally impaired inmates and juveniles**

The Supreme Court has opposed execution of juveniles under 18 and the execution of the mentally impaired.

L06 **Describe how correctional officers working on death row regard their jobs**

Correctional workers on death row believe that they have a duty to do and try to perform it as efficiently as they can. They want to treat the condemned with dignity and respect.

L07 **Identify how inmates on death row adjust to their situation**

Death row inmates attempt to adjust to their situation in a variety of ways. Some focus on their cases, others have a religious experience and see themselves through their new identity, while many ruminate about the struggles and difficulties they have in adjusting to death row.

L08 **Evaluate whether the death penalty deters murder**

There has been continuous debate and much research conducted to determine whether the death penalty deters murder, and at the end of the day, the evidence seems to conclude that the death penalty does not deter murder in our society.

Key Terms

 # Critical Thinking Questions

1. Do we need the death penalty to satisfy our need for revenge? Is it possible for society to give up the death penalty?

2. What is the purpose of taking the life of a murderer who is mentally ill?

3. What do you think is the most persuasive argument for the death penalty?

4. What do you think is the most persuasive argument against the death penalty?

5. What do the recent stances of the U.S. Supreme Court suggest will be the future of the death penalty in this nation?

Thinking Like a Corrections Professional

In your state, the governor has suspended all executions, citing troubled executions and wrongful convictions in other states, and plans to appoint a commission. You have been appointed to head this commission to consider the humanity and constitutionality of the death penalty. Your commission will include doctors, lawyers, scientists, and law enforcement officials.

As the chair of this commission, what would you do, in the order in which you would do it? (First action, second, third,

fourth, etc.) What information would your commission need to make its report? What do you think would be the outcome of your commission's report? For example, if the report should conclude that the problems related to the death penalty make it unconstitutional, what do you think the governor or his successor would do? In answering this question, remember that your state has executed a number of people in the modern era of the death penalty.

Career Destinations

If you oppose the death penalty, you might someday work for the American Civil Liberties Union. Check out their death row page, which includes summaries and analy-

sis of ethical, legal, and political issues relating to capital punishment:

www.aclu.org/capital/

Notes

1. The following account is taken from James Barton, "Geography and Emotion Helped Sway Jurors' Vote," *New York Times*, February 1, 2007, www.nytimes.com/2007/02/01/nyregion/01death.html (accessed March 14, 2012).
2. Ibid.
3. Ibid.
4. Tracy L. Snell, *Capital Punishment, 2010 Statistical Tables* (Washington, DC: Bureau of Justice Statistics, U.S. Department of Justice, 2011), http://bjs.ojp.usdoj.gov/content/pub/pdf/cp10st.pdf (accessed April 8, 2012).
5. Ibid.
6. Bureau of Justice Statistics, *Capital Punishment Statistics, 2008*, http://bjs.ojp.usdoj.gov/content/pub/pdf/cp08st.pdf (accessed April 8, 2012).
7. Andrew Buncombe, "U.S. Turns Against Death Penalty as 1,000th Prisoner Is Executed," *Common Dreams News Center*, November 29, 2006.
8. Snell, *Capital Punishment, 2010 Statistical Tables*.
9. Mark D. Cunningham and Mark P. Vigen, "Death Row Inmate Characteristics, Adjustment, and Confinement: A Critical Review of the Literature," *Behavioral Sciences and the Law* 20 (2002): 191–210.
10. Snell, *Capital Punishment, 2010 Statistical Tables*.
11. Joseph Carroll, *Gallup Poll: Who Supports the Death Penalty?* www.deathpenaltyinfo.org/gallup-poll-who-supports-death-penalty (accessed March 14, 2012).
12. Ibid.
13. Karen S. Miller, *Wrongful Capital Convictions and the Legitimacy of the Death Penalty* (New York: LFB Scholarly Publishing LLC, 2006); and Michael Mello, *The Wrong Man: A True Story of Innocence on Death Row* (Minneapolis: University of Minnesota Press, 2001).
14. Marie Gottschalk, *The Prison and the Gallows: The Politics of Mass Incarceration in America* (England: Cambridge University Press, 2006), p. 227.
15. Amnesty International, "Death Penalty in 2010: Executing Countries Left Isolated After Decade of Progress," www.amnesty.org/en/news-and-updates/report/death-penalty-2010-executing-countries-left-isolated-after-decade-progress (accessed April 8, 2012).
16. Terri Figueroa, "Appeals Process Drag On for Years in Death Penalty Cases," *North County Times*, February 5, 2006.
17. James S. Liebman, Jeffrey Fagan, and Valerie West, *A Broken System: Error Rates in Capital Cases, 1973–1995* (New York: Columbia University School of Law, 2000).
18. Ibid. See also, concerning the possibility of wrongful convictions, D. Michael Risinger, "Innocents Convicted: An Empirically Justified Factual Wrongful Conviction Rate," *Journal of Criminal Law and Criminology* 97 (2007): 761–806; and James D. Unnever and Francis T. Cullen, "Executing the Innocent and Support for Capital Punishment: Implications for Public Policy," *Criminology and Public Policy* 4 (2005): 3–38.
19. *McCleskey v. Kemp*, 438 U.S. 586 (1991).
20. Ibid.
21. *Furman v. Georgia*, 408 U.S. 238 (1972).
22. Ibid.
23. *Gregg v. Georgia*, 428 U.S. 153, 96 S.Ct. 2909, 49 L.Ed.2d 859 (1976).
24. Ibid., at 205–207, 96 S.Ct. at 2940–41.
25. *Pulley v. Harris*, 104 S.Ct. 881 (1984).
26. Ibid.
27. *Kansas v. March*, 548 U.S. 263 (2006).
28. *Pulley v. Harris*.
29. *Baze et al. v. Rees, Commissioner, Kentucky Department of Corrections, et al.*, 0–7-5439, 217 S.W. 3d 207 (2008).
30. *McCleskey v. Kemp*.
31. Ibid.
32. Ibid.
33. *Miller-El v. Cockrell*, 537 U.S. 322 (2003).
34. John Donohue, "Capital Punishment in Connecticut, 1973–2007: A Comprehensive Evaluation from 4,686 Murders to One Execution," http://works.bepress.com/john_donohue/87/ (accessed March 14, 2012). For a discussion of this study, see Lincoln Caplan, "The Random Horror of the Death Penalty," *New York Times*, January 7, 2012, www.nytimes.com/2012/01/08/opinion/sunday/the-random-horror-of-the-death-penalty.html (accessed March 14, 2012).
35. Amnesty International website, www.amnesty.org (accessed March 14, 2012).
36. *Atkins v. Virginia*, 122 S.Ct. 2242 (2002).
37. Ibid.
38. Amnesty International website.
39. *Ford v. Wainwright*, 477 U.S. 399 (1986).
40. Ibid.
41. *Washington v. Harper*, 494 U.S. 210 (1990).
42. Amnesty International website.
43. *Thompson v. Oklahoma*, 487 U.S. 815 (1988).
44. *Stanford v. Kentucky*, 109 S.Ct. 2969 (1989).
45. Ibid.
46. *Roper v. Simmons*, 543 U.S. 551 (2005).
47. *Witherspoon v. Illinois*, 391 U.S. 550 (1968).
48. *Wainwright v. Witt*, 499 U.S. 412, 105 S.Ct. 844, 83 L.Ed.2d 841 (1985).
49. Ibid.
50. *Lockhart v. McCree*, 476 U.S. 162, 106 S.Ct. 1758, 90 L.Ed.2d 137 (1986).
51. Michael Taylor, "Peterson to Begin Life on Death Row," *San Francisco Chronicle*, March 17, 2005.
52. As an expert witness in nearly 20 death row cases, Bartollas has interviewed inmates on death row and talked with officers responsible for these inmates. It is unusual for conflict to be present among officers and inmates.
53. Ibid.

54. Robert Johnson, *Death Work: A Study of the Modern Execution Process* (Pacific Grove, CA: Brooks/Cole, 1990), pp. 70–71.

55. Sara Rimer, "Working on Death Row: A Special Report: In the Busiest Death Chamber, Duty Carries Its Own Burdens," *New York Times*, December 17, 2000.

56. Donald A. Cabana, *Death at Midnight: The Confession of an Executioner* (Boston: Northeastern University Press, 1996), p. xi.

57. Ken Hausman, "Researcher Enters Minds of Death-Row Officers," *Psychiatry News* 36 (2001): 6.

58. Ibid.

59. *Baze et al. v. Rees*.

60. Rimer, "Working on Death Row: A Special Report."

61. Inmate told Bartollas this in October 2004.

62. This was the argument expressed by James Q. Wilson, Ernest van den Haag, and more recent economists and others.

63. Water Berns, *For Capital Punishment* (New York: Basic Books, 1979).

64. Bartollas has been an expert witness in a number of cases in which inmates who had committed a previous murder committed another murder while incarcerated.

65. Death Penalty Information Center, *Costs of the Death Penalty*, 2011, www.deathpenaltyinfo.org/costs-death-penalty (accessed March 14, 2012).

66. James Yunker, "A New Statistical Analysis of Capital Punishment Incorporating U.S. Postmoratorium Data," *Social Science Quarterly* 82 (2001): 297–312.

67. Hashem Dezhbakhsh, Paul H. Rubin, and Joanna M. Shepherd, "Does Capital Punishment Have a Deterrent Effect? New Evidence from Postmoratorium Panel Data," *American Law and Economics Review* 5 (2003): 344–376.

68. Pew Foundation, "Death Penalty," www.pewcenteronthestates.org (accessed March 14, 2012).

In March 2007, in response to reports of sexual abuse of youth at the Texas Youth Commission institutions, Governor Rick Perry placed the entire Texas Youth Commission under conservatorship in order to guide and reform the agency.[1] The charges of sexual abuse first broke in 2005 when a Texas Ranger investigation corroborated sexual contacts between residential males and two top supervisors at the West Texas State School in Pyote; the correctional employees were permitted to resign without charges being filed. Lawmakers found evidence that some youth residents had received lengthened sentences for refusing to have sex with correctional officers.

At the governor's request, Ed Owens, then interim executive director of the Texas Youth Commission, asked Dr. David W. Springer to form a Blue Ribbon Task Force charged with defining a new rehabilitation system and developing evidence-based practices that could effectively treat and manage delinquents. The findings would be reviewed by a panel consisting of a youth official, prosecutors, and civil rights advocates. In the wake of the scandal, the Youth Commission's board of directors resigned and many other top officials were ousted.[2]

In a 2010 report, *Sexual Victimization in Juvenile Facilities*, the Bureau of Justice Statistics conducted the first nationally representative survey of sexual abuse among adjudicated youth in residential juvenile facilities. This BJS study surveyed 26,550 adjudicated youth held in state operated and large local or privately operated juvenile facilities.

It was found that an estimated 12 percent of youth in state facilities and large nonstate facilities (representing 3,220 youth nationwide) reported experiencing one or more incidents of sexual victimization by another youth or faculty staff member in the previous months or since admission.

- About 2.6 percent of youth (700 nationwide) reported an incident involving a peer

Students line up near their bunks in a dormitory at the West Texas State School, site of a notorious sex scandal. In April 2007, former Texas Youth Commission administrators Ray Brookins and John Paul Hernandez were indicted by a grand jury for improper behavior with juvenile residents. Brookins, the juvenile prison's former assistant superintendent, was accused of having an improper relationship with a student and sexual activity with a person in custody. Hernandez, the school's principal, was charged with sexual assault and having an improper relationship with a student and sex with a prisoner. This problem is not confined to Texas; similar scandals have occurred in juvenile institutions in other jurisdictions. There have been reports of abusive treatment of youth in Arkansas, Arizona, Connecticut, Georgia, Florida, Hawaii, Indiana, Louisiana, Maryland, Mississippi, Nevada, New Jersey, Oklahoma, Puerto Rico, and South Dakota.

and, alarmingly, 10.3 percent (2,730) reported an incident involving facility staff.

- About 4.3 percent of youth (1,150) reported having sex or other sexual activity with facility staff as a result of some type of force; 6.4 percent of youth (1,710) reported contact with facility staff without force or threat.

Approximately 95 percent of all youth reporting staff sexual misconduct said they had been victimized by female staff. In 2008, 42 percent of staff in state juvenile facilities were female.[3] In the midst of this bad news about juvenile institutionalization, there is good news from California. In the last decade, California has closed eight of its eleven juvenile facilities and successfully turned the responsibility for its nonviolent offenders over to the counties. Governor Jerry Brown also wants to complete the transformation and phasing out of the three remaining state facilities that hold 1,000 more serious offenders. The state realizes that it will need to develop different facilities for managing violent young offenders. Spending on the system has dropped by almost half, from nearly $500 million to about $245 million and the state has cut its juvenile population from about 10,000 in the mid-1990s to about 1,000 today. Some critics are concerned that without a state juvenile system to hold violent offenders, prosecutors may try more young people as adults, but the state can prevent this by monitoring and penalizing counties that overprosecute juveniles and by allowing for extended custody in local facilities for those juveniles who have committed more serious crimes.[4]

chapter
Fourteen

THE JUVENILE OFFENDER

LEARNING OBJECTIVES

LO1 Identify the early development of juvenile justice

LO2 Understand the disposition of probation, including how it is administered and by whom and recent trends in its use

LO3 Distinguish between community treatment and institutional treatment for juvenile offenders

LO4 Know the nature of aftercare for juvenile offenders and comment on recent innovations in juvenile aftercare and reentry programs

LO5 Understand how the juvenile is transferred and tried in adult court

LO6 Be able to identify the plight faced by juveniles sent to adult prisons

Dormitory-style rooms at the Fred C. Nelles Youth Correctional Facility in Whittier, California, February 10, 2004.

© Monica Almeida/New York Times/Redux

321

JUVENILE JUSTICE SYSTEM A system established over 100 years ago to provide for the care of law-violating youth.

JUVENILE DELINQUENT An underage minor who engages in antisocial activities that are defined as criminal behavior by the state's legal code.

STATUS OFFENDER A juvenile who engages in an act that is considered illegal because of his or her age, such as running away, disobedience, or truancy.

The victimization of youths in the Texas juvenile training schools is a sad commentary on institutionalization in the **juvenile justice system**, and the widespread nature of juvenile sexual victimization is even more sobering from the National Bureau of Justice Statistics survey. California's closing of training schools is a hopeful sign that juvenile institutionalization is experiencing widespread reform. Independent of but interrelated with the adult criminal justice system, the juvenile justice system is primarily responsible for dealing with minors who violate the criminal law (**juvenile delinquents**) and also those youth who have not committed crimes but are incorrigible, truants, runaways, or unmanageable—behaviors forbidden for underage children (**status offenders**).

This chapter examines how youthful offenders are handled by the juvenile justice system. It also considers boot camps and adult prisons as placements for juvenile offenders, juveniles' transfer to adult courts, and the changing sentencing structures for juvenile offenders. These are critical issues because so many juveniles who have been processed through the justice system later end up in the adult correctional system.

Voices Across the Profession gives us a glimpse into the world of Jean Tomlinson, who started working in the juvenile justice field as a juvenile correctional officer. She worked her way up the career ladder and became the first female

Voices ACROSS the PROFESSION

© Jean Tomlinson

"Interventions with the family are an important area. These children come from broken homes, dysfunctional in so many ways."

JEAN TOMLINSON
SUPERINTENDENT

I have a real passion for the juvenile justice system and look upon it as my calling. I think [corrections] students today are much more aware of the adult system than they are of juvenile justice issues. When I talk in my classes about juveniles whose crimes

are very similar to adult crimes—such as drug dealers, sex offenders, murderers, attempted murderers, and car thieves—students are amazed. I may talk about an 11-year-old sex offender who might have had six or seven victims. [Students] are somewhat naïve about the crimes that kids can commit at an early age. In Texas, once you are involved in the juvenile justice system, you are with them until you are 21.

I feel that we need to focus on a couple of different areas. Interventions with the family are an important area. These children come from broken homes, dysfunctional in so many ways. For example, a child being used as a pornographic object, and the mother is making money off of her children. I believe that if a kid is locked up, the family should have counseling and therapy as long as the kid is locked up. The next focus is to separate minor and more serious offenders. In Texas we put our 11-years-olds in with our 19- and 20-year-olds. The younger kids are still pliable and amenable to rehabilitation, and they want the approval of adults and people around them. After they are 16, they are either really entrenched in gangs or expect to go to the pen and want to go to the pen. And that is when they begin to hurt the guards.

Private versus State Operations

In the private versus the state, I did not like working for the for-profit operation very much. I was used to working with budgets in state operations. I was superintendent of this private facility and had been there 45 days or so when I was told, "You need to cut your budget by 10 percent." I asked them, "How do you want me to do this? Where do you want me to start?" They said, "Start with clothing." I looked outside, and there was a foot of snow. And my kids had not been issued jackets. I thought that guy was out of his mind.

The private operation was paying staff $7 an hour. With the state we pay better, and we have better insurance. With the high turnover, the kids would know when guards were green, and they would start playing all the tricks. They set them up for failure immediately. They get the guards to bring cigarettes, pop, drugs, and all sorts of stuff. [Private operation staff] are much easier to exploit than staff in state institutions. This is their second income. They would have the kids' parents send money [directly] to the officers' homes.

Source: Interviewed in 2008.

director of security for the Texas Youth Commission. She was responsible for all the intakes into the system, making certain they were classified correctly and had their adjudication documents, and assigning them to the proper facility after they had been assessed. She eventually became superintendent of a for-profit 155-bed facility for males aged 10 to 15. Then she became the assistant superintendent of a 240-bed facility in south Texas, which was a regional facility.

LO1

HISTORY OF THE JUVENILE JUSTICE SYSTEM

Juvenile justice in the United States began in the colonial period and continued to use English practices. The family, the cornerstone of the community in colonial times, was the source and primary means of social control of children. The law was uncomplicated; the only law enforcement officials were town fathers, magistrates, sheriffs, and watchmen; and the only penal institutions were jails for prisoners awaiting trial or punishment. Juvenile lawbreakers did not face a battery of police or other authorities, nor did they have to worry that practitioners of the juvenile justice system would try to rehabilitate or correct them. They only had to concern themselves with being sent back to their families for punishment.

As children got older, however, the likelihood increased that they would be dealt with more harshly by colonial law. The state, even in those early days, clearly was committed to raising its children correctly and making them follow society's rules. Indeed, this early practice appears to have been incorporated into the early Massachusetts Puritan code, which was a model for the U.S. Constitution of 1787.

The state became even more concerned about the welfare of its children in the 1800s. Increased urbanization, industrialization, and bureaucratization were changing the face of America. In the cities particularly, increasing numbers of youths were seemingly out of control. Reformers searched for ways to teach them traditional values, and the asylum and the training school were developed to help the state maintain its control.

The Concept of *Parens Patriae*

The early courts took control of juveniles under the concept of **parens patriae**, a Latin term used to signify the role of the king as the father of his country. The concept was first used by English kings to establish their right to intervene in the lives of the children of their vassals—children whose position and property were of direct concern to the monarch.[5] As time passed, the monarchy used *parens patriae* more and more to justify its intervention in the lives of families and children in order to protect their general welfare.[6] *Parens patriae* was brought over and used in American courts, being formalized in the case of *Ex parte Crouse* in 1838, which gave the courts a legal basis for intervening in the lives of children. The Bill of Rights, the Pennsylvania Supreme Court ruled, did not apply to minors and the state could legitimately confine minors who needed "protection." This meant that juveniles did not have the right to counsel or trial by jury, and could be confined even in the absence of criminal behavior.

Child Savers and the Origin of the Juvenile Court

By the end of the 1800s, much of the U.S. population lived in urban areas and worked in factories. Cities were large and growing, and waves of immigrants were inundating the nation's shores with millions of people destined to remain poor. Conditions in the cities were shocking; there was much poverty, crime, disease, mental illness, and dilapidation. The cities' children were viewed as unfortunate

PARENS PATRIAE A medieval English doctrine that sanctioned the right of the Crown to intervene in natural family relations whenever a child's welfare was threatened.

TIMELINE

In re Winship (1970)
In delinquency matters, the state must prove its case beyond a reasonable doubt.

Kent v. United States (1966)
Courts must provide the "essentials of due process" in transferring juveniles to the adult system.

Breed v. Jones (1975)
Waiver of a juvenile to criminal court following adjudication in juvenile court constitutes double jeopardy.

Eddings v. Oklahoma (1982)
Defendant's youthful age should be considered a mitigating factor in deciding whether to apply the death penalty.

Stanford v. Kentucky (1989)

Thompson v. Oklahoma (1988)
Minimum age for death penalty is set at 16.

Graham v, Florida (2010)
Supreme Court ruled that juveniles may not be sentenced to a life in prison without parole for any crime short of homicide.

| 1965 | 1970 | 1975 | 1980 | 1985 | 1990 | 2005 | 2010 |

McKeiver v. Pennsylvania (1971)
Jury trials are not constitutionally required in juvenile court hearings.

Oklahoma Publishing Company v. District Court (1977)

Schall v. Martin (1984)
Preventive "pretrial" detention of juveniles is allowable under certain circumstances.

Roper v. Simmons (2005)
Minimum age for death penalty is set at 18.

Smith v. Daily Mail Publishing Company (1979)
The press may report juvenile court proceedings under certain circumstances.

In re Gault (1967)
In hearings that could result in commitment to an institution, juveniles have four basic constitutional rights.

Source: Howard N. Snyder and Melissa Sickmund, *Juvenile Offenders and Victims 2006 National Report* (Pittsburgh: National Center for Juvenile Justice, 2006), p. 101.

---

victims of the urban scene. The concept of *parens patriae* was used by so-called "child savers" to control the lives of poor and immigrant children. The child-saving philosophy can be seen in a statement by Judge Gustav L. Schramm, who was the first juvenile court judge of Allegheny County (Pittsburgh), Pennsylvania: "Neither umpire nor arbiter, [the juvenile court judge] is the one person who represents his community as *parens patriae*, who may act with the parents, or when necessary even in place of them, to bring about behavior more desirable."[7] The child-saving movement culminated in passage of the Illinois Juvenile Court Act of 1899, which established the nation's first independent juvenile court. For the first time the distinction was made between children who were neglected and those who were delinquent. Delinquent children were those under the age of 16 who violated the law. Most important, the act established a court and a probation program specifically for children. In addition, the legislation allowed children to be committed to institutions and reform programs under the control of the state. The key provisions of the act were these:

- A separate court was established for delinquent and neglected children.

- Special procedures were developed to govern the adjudication of juvenile matters.

- Children were to be separated from adults in courts and in institutional programs.

- Probation programs were to be developed to assist the court in making decisions in the best interests of the state and the child.[8]

The attractiveness of the juvenile court philosophy resulted in almost all states setting up juvenile courts. In fact, by 1928, only 2 of 31 states had not passed a juvenile court statute.

After 60 years of operation, the juvenile court was heavily criticized because it operated informally and defendants were given few constitutional rights. Children would be tried without lawyers and did not have the right to confront witnesses or have juries. Then, in the critical case of *In re Gault* (1967), the Supreme Court granted juveniles due process rights, including an attorney. See the Timeline for Supreme Court decisions of special relevance to juvenile justice.

CONTEMPORARY JUVENILE JUSTICE

Today, every state maintains an independent juvenile system that traditionally is based on a policy of treatment, rehabilitation, and care for needy children. This system is charged with the care and treatment of minor children who have been found to have violated the state's penal code but because they fall under a statutory age limit, which is most commonly 17 or 18 years of age, society has chosen to treat them differently and separately from more experienced and adult offenders.

Keeping within this framework of treatment and rehabilitation, there is a wide choice of correctional treatments available for juveniles. These can be divided into two major categories: community treatment and institutional treatment. **Community treatment** refers to efforts to provide care, protection, and treatment for juveniles in need. These efforts include probation, treatment services (such as individual and group counseling), restitution, and other programs. **Institutional treatment facilities** are correctional centers operated by state and county governments. These facilities restrict the movement of residents through staff monitoring, locked exits, and interior fence controls.

Similarities Between Juvenile and Adult Justice Systems

The fact is that considerable similarity exists between the juvenile and adult justice systems. Both consist of three basic subsystems and interrelated agencies. The flow of justice in both is supposed to be from law violation to police apprehension, judicial process, judicial disposition, and rehabilitation in correctional agencies. The basic vocabulary is the same in the juvenile and adult systems, and even when the vocabulary differs, the intent remains the same.

Note the following terms that refer to the juvenile and adult systems:

Adjudicatory hearing is a trial.

Aftercare is parole.

Commitment is a sentence to confinement.

Detention is holding in jail.

Dispositional hearing is a sentencing hearing.

Juvenile court officer is a probation officer.

Minor is a defendant.

Petition is an indictment.

Petitioner is a prosecutor.

COMMUNITY TREATMENT Treatment provided to juveniles in the community versus an institutional context.

INSTITUTIONAL TREATMENT FACILITY A correctional institution that provides long-term treatment for juveniles.

EXHIBIT 14.1 Similarities and Differences Between the Juvenile and Adult Justice Systems

Similarities	Differences
■ Police officers use discretion with both juvenile and adult offenders.	■ Juveniles can be arrested for acts that would not be criminal if they were adults (status offenders).
■ Juvenile and adult offenders receive *Miranda* and other constitutional rights at time of arrest.	■ Age determines the jurisdiction of the juvenile court; age does not affect the jurisdiction of the adult court.
■ Juveniles and adults can be placed in pretrial facilities	■ Parents are deeply involved in the juvenile process but not in the adult process.
■ The juvenile court and the adult court use proof beyond a reasonable doubt as the standard for evidence.	■ Juvenile court proceedings are more informal, while adult court proceedings are formal and open to the public.
■ Plea bargaining may be used with both juvenile and adult offenders.	■ Juvenile court proceedings, unlike adult proceedings, are not considered criminal; juvenile records are generally sealed when the age of majority is reached. Adult records are permanent.
■ Convicted juvenile and adult offenders may be sentenced to probation services, residential programs, or institutional facilities.	
■ Boot camps are used with juvenile and adult offenders.	■ Juvenile courts cannot sentence juveniles to jail or prison; only adult courts can issue such sentences.
■ Released institutional juvenile and adult offenders may be assigned to supervision in the community.	

Respondent is a defense attorney.

Taking into custody is arresting a suspect.

Both the juvenile and adult systems are under fire to get tough on crime, especially on offenders who commit violent crimes. Both must deal with excessive caseloads and institutional overcrowding, must operate on fiscal shoestrings, and face the ongoing problems of staff recruitment, training, and burnout. Exhibit 14.1 further describes the common ground and differences between the juvenile and adult justice systems.

The remainder of this chapter is divided into three parts: Juvenile corrections in the community, institutionalized juveniles, and juveniles in the adult system. The first two parts, juveniles in community-based treatments and juveniles in long-term juvenile institutions, will attempt to identify what is different about the juvenile and adult justice processes, rather than discuss what is similar about the juvenile and adult justice system processing of offenders.

JUVENILE CORRECTIONS IN THE COMMUNITY

Probation and other forms of community treatment for juvenile offenders generally refer to nonpunitive legal disposition for delinquent youths, emphasizing treatment without incarceration.

LO2 ► Probation

Probation is the primary form of community treatment used by the juvenile justice system. A juvenile who is on probation is maintained in the community under the supervision of an officer of the court. Probation also encompasses a set of rules and conditions that must be met for the offender to remain in the community. Juveniles on probation may be placed in a wide variety of community-based treatment programs that provide services ranging from group counseling to drug treatment.

Traditional probation is still the backbone of community-based corrections. About 400,000 juveniles are placed on formal probation each year, which amounts to more than 60 percent of all juvenile dispositions. The use of probation has increased significantly since 1993, when around 224,500 adjudicated youths were placed on probation.[9] These figures show that regardless of public sentiment, probation continues to be a popular dispositional alternative for judges. It can be seen that a major difference between juvenile and adult probation officers is that the juvenile probation officers' duties are focused more on treatment, contact with families, and providing specialized services to juveniles. In contrast, the adult probation officer—while retaining responsibilities for treatment intervention—emphasizes more public safety and surveillance of offenders.

In the juvenile court, probation is often ordered for an indefinite period. Depending on the statutes of the jurisdiction, the seriousness of the offense, and the juvenile's adjustment on probation, youths can remain under supervision until the court no longer has jurisdiction over them (that is, when they reach the age of majority). State statutes determine whether a judge can specify how long a juvenile may be placed under an order of probation. In most jurisdictions, the status of probation is reviewed regularly to ensure that a juvenile is not kept on probation needlessly. Generally, discretion lies with the probation officer to discharge youths who are adjusting to the treatment plan.

Although juvenile probation services continue to be predominantly organized under the judiciary, recent legislative activity has been in the direction of transferring those services from the local juvenile court judge to a state court administrative office. Whether local juvenile courts or state agencies should administer juvenile probation services is debatable. In years past, the organization of probation services depended primarily on the size of the program and the number of juveniles under its supervision. Because of this momentum to develop unified court systems, many juvenile court services are being consolidated into state court systems.

Like the adult system, the juvenile justice system has developed intermediate probation/alternative sanction programs such as intensive supervision probation, electronic monitoring (EM), and house arrest.[10] A number of states, including Georgia, New Jersey, Oregon, and Pennsylvania, are experimenting with statewide intensive programs for juveniles. In addition, more and more juvenile court judges, especially in metropolitan juvenile courts, are placing high-risk juveniles on small caseloads and assigning them more frequent contact with a probation officer than would be true of traditional probation.

The use of EM in juvenile justice has been gradually gaining acceptance. Twenty years ago, only 11 juvenile programs used EM.[11] Today, EM programs are widely used in juvenile justice programs throughout the United States.

Alternative Community Sanctions for Juveniles

Some juveniles need more intense confinement than can be provided by probation even if it is supplemented with intermediate sanctions such as house arrest and electronic monitoring. To meet the needs of these youth, the juvenile justice system has developed a set of community correctional programs. Some are residential, requiring that youth spend a period of time in a nonsecure facility while typically going to school and other activities during the day. Others are nonresidential programs that allow clients to live at home while receiving services in the community.

Residential programs are typically divided into four major categories: (1) group homes, (2) family group homes, (3) wilderness programs, and (4) boot camps. One residential program that would not be found in the adult system is **wilderness programs**, sometimes called "survival programs," which take place in settings such as the mountains, the woods, the beach, and the desert. The intent of these survival programs is to improve youths' self-confidence and sense of self-reliance.

RESIDENTIAL PROGRAMS Programs conducted for the rehabilitation of youthful offenders within community-based and institutional settings.

WILDERNESS PROGRAMS Programs that occur in a wooded area, the mountains, desert, or a lake where adolescents are taught survival skills and cooperation with others.

GROUP HOMES Nonsecure residences that provide counseling, education, job training, and family living.

FAMILY GROUP HOMES Group homes that are run by a family rather than by a professional staff.

NONRESIDENTIAL PROGRAMS Programs for youthful offenders that usually do not confine them overnight.

Group homes are staffed by a small number of qualified persons, and generally house 12 to 15 youngsters. The institutional quality of the environment is minimized, and youths are given the opportunity to build a close relationship with the staff. Youths reside in the home, attend public schools, and participate in community activities in the area.

Family group homes combine elements of foster care and group home placements. Troubled youths have an opportunity to learn to get along in a family-like situation, and at the same time the state avoids the startup costs and neighborhood opposition often associated with establishing a public institution.

Boot camps for youthful offenders, like those for adult offenders, developed in the mid-1980s and 1990s. Emphasizing military discipline, physical training, and regimented activity for periods typically ranging from 30 to 120 days, these programs endeavor to shock juvenile delinquents out of committing further crimes. A fair assessment may be that the quality of boot camps depends largely on how much they tailor their programs to participants' maturity levels and how effective they are in implementing and sustaining effective aftercare services.[12] However, the follow-ups on boot camps are mixed concerning their effectiveness.[13] The disappointing recidivism results, as well as charges of abuse, have prompted Georgia, Florida, Maryland, Arizona, and South Dakota to shut down or reevaluate this get-tough approach with juveniles.[14]

In **nonresidential programs**, youths remain in their homes and receive counseling, education, employment, diagnostic, and casework services at the community-based center. A counselor or probation officer gives innovative and intensive support to help the youth remain at home. Family therapy, educational tutoring, and job placement may all be part of the program.

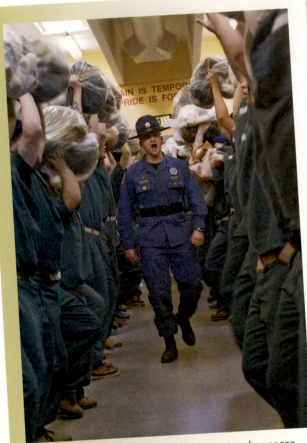

Boot camps were once viewed as a correctional panacea. For example, the Colorado Corrections Alternative Program offered reduced prison sentences for men and women convicted of nonviolent crimes. The program was open to prisoners age 30 or younger. During the 90-day program, offenders also took addiction-recovery classes and worked on GEDs, if needed. A 2004 review of the program that showed 36 percent of those who completed the program 12 years earlier had gotten in more trouble with the law, compared with 52 percent of those who were qualified for the program but did not volunteer for it. The last class graduated in 2010 when rising recidivism rates cancelled out program benefits. But the deciding factor leading to the closure of the program was that it became too costly. As fewer inmates qualified or volunteered for the program, the cost per inmate rose from $78 a day to $110 in a single year (2010).

Is Community Treatment Effective?

Community-based programs continue to present a promising alternative for juvenile corrections:

- Some states have found that residential and nonresidential settings produce comparable or lower recidivism rates. There is evidence that youths in nonsecure settings are less likely to become recidivists than those placed in more secure settings.

- Community-based programs have lower costs and are especially appropriate for large numbers of nonviolent juveniles and those guilty of lesser offenses.

- Public opinion on community corrections remains positive. Many citizens prefer community-based programs for all but the most serious juvenile offenders.[15]

As jurisdictions continue to face high rates of violent juvenile crime and ever-increasing costs for juvenile justice services, community-based programs will play an important role in providing rehabilitation of juvenile offenders and ensuring public safety. See Exhibit 14.2 for the comparison between community-based treatment in the juvenile and adult systems.

EXHIBIT 14.2 Comparison Between Juvenile and Adult Justice Systems

Justice System	Role of the Courts	Community Treatment	Institutional Treatment
Juvenile system	Judicial court referral to proper placement. Appeals are rarely used.	Probation and various forms of residential and nonresidential treatment.	Short-term and long-term treatment. Some of the long-term training schools have violent residents' cultures.
Adult system	More complex court system and appeals are commonplace.	Also has probation and various forms of intermediate sanctions.	Large, much larger than juvenile facilities and inmates stay longer, sometimes for the remainder of their sentence, or are even executed.

JUVENILE INSTITUTIONS TODAY: PUBLIC AND PRIVATE

Juveniles who are repeat offenders or commit very serious crimes may find themselves in secure facilities variously called training schools, reform schools, or locked facilities. These house the most dangerous, chronic juvenile offenders in institutions that can resemble adult facilities.

Most juveniles are housed in public institutions administered by state agencies: child and youth services, health and social services, corrections, or child welfare.[16] In some states these institutions fall under a centralized system that covers adults as well as juveniles. Recently, a number of states have removed juvenile corrections from an existing adult corrections department or mental health agency. However, the majority of states still place responsibility for the administration of juvenile corrections within social service departments.

Supplementing publicly funded institutions are private facilities that are maintained and operated by private agencies funded or chartered by state authorities. The majority of today's private institutions are relatively small facilities holding fewer than 30 youths. Many have a specific mission or focus (for example, treating females who display serious emotional problems). Although about 80 percent of public institutions can be characterized as secure, only 20 percent of private institutions are high-security facilities.

Population Trends in Juvenile Corrections

Whereas most delinquents are held in public facilities, most status offenders are held in private facilities. At last count, there were about 70,000 juvenile offenders being held in public (49,000) and private (21,000) facilities in the United States. While the number of juveniles held in custody increased rapidly (41 percent) in the 1990s, it has been in decline since the year 1999, when 120,000 juveniles were being kept in secure confinement.[17]

The juvenile custody rate varies widely among states. Some (such as New Hampshire and Vermont) have fewer than 100 kids in custody per 100,000 population, while others (such as Wyoming and North Dakota) have more than 400 per 100,000 in secure custody.

In an important study, criminologist Daniel Mears found that there are three main explanations for why some states incarcerate juveniles at a much higher rate than others: (1) they have high rates of juvenile property crime and adult violent crime; (2) they have higher adult custody rates; and (3) there is a "cultural acceptance of punitive policies" in some parts of the country. Interestingly, Mears found that Western and Midwestern states were more likely to have higher

Some juvenile institutions, including boot camps, feature a strict regime of physical training. Here, Jack Madden does push-ups during morning exercises in the Future Soldiers Program at the Pendleton Juvenile Correctional Facility. The Future Soldiers Program gives selected juvenile offenders the chance for an early release pending the completion of boot-camp-like military training and life-style experience. Officials in charge of the program at Pendleton are seeking to coordinate with area military recruiters to send graduates to active service upon their release.

© Andy Kropa/Redux

juvenile incarceration rates than Southern states, thus calling into question the widely held view that the South is disproportionately punitive.[18]

Institutionalized Juveniles

The typical resident of a juvenile facility is a 17-year-old male incarcerated for an average stay of 3.5 months in a public facility or 4 months in a private facility. Private facilities tend to house younger children, while public institutions provide custodial care for older children, including a small percentage of youths between 18 and 21 years of age. Most incarcerated youths are person, property, or drug offenders. See Figure 14.1 for a profile of institutionalized juveniles.

RACIAL INEQUALITY Racial disparity in juvenile disposition is a growing problem that demands immediate public scrutiny.[19] Minority youths accused of delinquent acts are less likely than white youths to be diverted from the court system into informal sanctions and are more likely to receive sentences involving incarceration. Today, a disproportionate number of minority youth are still being held in locked facilities.

In response, many jurisdictions have initiated studies of racial disproportion in their juvenile justice systems, along with federal requirements to reduce disproportionate minority confinement (DMC), as contained in the Juvenile Justice and Delinquency Prevention Act of 2002.[20] While some progress has been made, many challenges remain, including the basic need to identify factors that contribute to DMC. There are success stories, such as those listed below:

- New Jersey, by implementing the Juvenile Detention Alternatives Initiative (JDAI) of the Annie E. Casey Foundation, is one of several localities that has produced significant reductions in DMC. Across five counties in New Jersey, the disparities dropped significantly between youth of color held in detention rather than being placed in community alternatives versus white youth similarly charged being detained rather than placed in the community.

- Peoria County, Illinois, has reduced disproportionate referrals of youth of color to the juvenile justice system by working with schools to strengthen school-based conflict resolution protocols and student retention/inclusion.

- Travis County, Texas, has reduced disproportionate incarceration of youth of color for technical probation violations with a sanction supervision program that instead offers intensive case management and probation services to youth and families.

- Baltimore County has reduced by 50 percent secure detention of African American youth resulting from bench warrants for failing to appear in court by instituting a reminder call program.[21]

While the DMC initiative was begun with great promise, the Evidence-Based Corrections feature shows that achieving racial justice can often be a difficult path.

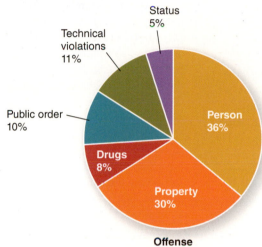

FIGURE 14.1 **Institutionalized Juveniles**

Source: Howard N. Snyder and Melissa Sickmund, *Juvenile Offenders and Victims 2006 National Report* (Pittsburgh: National Center for Juvenile Justice, 2006), Ch. 7.

GENDER DIFFERENCES: MALES Males make up the great bulk of institutionalized youth, and most treatment programs are directed toward their needs. In many ways their experiences mirror those of adult offenders. Research efforts confirm the notion that residents do in fact form cohesive groups and adhere to an informal inmate culture.[22] The more serious the youth's record and the more secure the institution, the greater the adherence to the inmate social code. Male delinquents are more likely to form allegiances with members of their own racial group and to attempt to exploit those outside the group. They also scheme to manipulate staff and take advantage of weaker peers. However, in institutions that are treatment oriented, and where staff–inmate relationships are more intimate, residents are less likely to adhere to a negativistic inmate code.

GENDER DIFFERENCES: FEMALES The number of females in juvenile institutions is far lower than males; nationally, females account for 13 percent of juvenile offenders in residential placement. Feminists believe that young women are still being forced to endure a double standard in the juvenile justice system because it is male-dominated and designed to "protect" young girls from their own sexuality.[23] Girls are more likely than boys to be incarcerated for status offenses.

The same double standard that brings a girl into an institution continues to exist once she is in custody. Females tend to be incarcerated for longer terms than males. In addition, institutional programs for girls tend to be oriented toward reinforcing traditional roles for females. Most of these programs also fail to take account of the different needs of African American and Caucasian females, as in the case of coping with past abuse.[24] Institutions for girls are generally more restrictive than

EVIDENCE-BASED CORRECTIONS

Disproportionate Minority Confinement/Contact (DMC)

The disproportionate minority confinement/contact (DMC) directive was designed to ensure that youthful offenders, regardless of their race or position in the social structure, receive equitable treatment within the juvenile justice system. Recently Michael Lieber and his associates examined the impact of the DMC on the processing of juvenile offenders within a state juvenile justice system. They chose Iowa for their study because it is one of the states that was selected to serve as a model for the implementation of strategies to reduce DMC. Their research focused on the extent that race influences decision makers, and whether the implementation of the DMC effort would result in the reduction or elimination of a race effect on decision-making outcomes. After controlling for a wide array of variables, they found that African Americans were more likely than whites to be referred at intake for further proceedings both before and after the implementation of the DMC initiative. The relative influence of race on intake decision making did not change following the implementation of the DMC initiative.

In some instances the researchers found that the DMC created an effect in opposition to what was intended. During the decade prior to the implementation of the DMC mandate, white adolescents who committed property offenses were less likely than African Americans to be referred to juvenile court for further proceedings. However, during the decade after the implementation of the DMC mandate, whites who committed property offenses were more likely than African Americans to be referred to juvenile court for further proceedings. While this change can be viewed as a movement toward equality, it actually was an overcorrection. Rather than helping African American youths, it penalized white offenders.

Decision making was influenced by gender and family household structure. African American males were more likely than white males to receive a court referral, and this racial disadvantage remained in the post-DMC period. After DMC was in place, African Americans who came from single-parent households were more likely to be referred to juvenile court than those who resided in two-parent households, although this was not the case for whites. Stated differently, after the DMC mandate, the effects of race became more covert and indirect, operating through family structure. One might conclude that this result reflects decision makers' reliance on stereotypes involving assessments of the African American single-parent family as dysfunctional and less able than either the white single-parent household or the African American two-parent household to supervise and socialize children effectively. In sum, there was little or no evidence that the DMC legislation impacted decision makers to rely less on race and more on legal and extralegal considerations at intake. The DMC initiative, to some extent, may have reduced the influence of being African American on the judicial decision-making process, but not quite in the manner anticipated.

Source: Michael Leiber, Donna Bishop, and Mitchell Chamlin, "Juvenile Justice Decision-Making Before and After the Implementation of the Disproportionate Minority Contact (DMC) Mandate," *Justice Quarterly* 28 (2011): 460–492.

those for boys, and they have fewer educational and vocational programs and fewer services. Institutions for girls also do a less-than-adequate job of rehabilitation.

EXHIBIT 14.3 Effectiveness of Juvenile Institutions

- The purpose of these programs is to rehabilitate youths to become well-adjusted individuals and send them back into the community to be productive citizens.
- Despite good intentions, however, the goal of rehabilitation is rarely attained, due in large part to poor implementation of the programs.[25]
- A significant number of juvenile offenders commit more crimes after release,[26] and some experts believe that correctional treatment has little effect on recidivism.[27]
- However, a large-scale empirical review of institutional treatment programs found that serious juvenile offenders who receive treatment have recidivism rates about 10 percent lower than similar untreated juveniles, and that the best programs reduced recidivism by as much as 40 percent.[28]
- The most successful of these institutional treatment programs provide training to improve interpersonal skills and family-style teaching to improve behavioral skills.

Institutional Treatment for Juveniles

Nearly all juvenile institutions implement some form of treatment programs that are similar to what have been previously described for adult settings: counseling, vocational and educational training, recreational programs, and religious counseling. In addition, most institutions provide medical programs as well as occasional legal service programs. Generally, the larger the institution, the greater the number of programs and services offered. See Exhibit 14.3 for effectiveness of juvenile correctional care.

The Careers in Corrections feature focuses on an important actor in the effort to care for juveniles in institutional settings: the social worker.

The Legal Right to Treatment

The primary goal of placing juveniles in institutions is to help them reenter the community successfully. Therefore, lawyers claim that children in state-run institutions have a legal right to treatment. A number of cases—*Inmates of the Boys' Training School v. Affleck* in 1972, *Nelson v. Heyne*, *Morales v. Turman*—found that juveniles do have a right to treatment.[29] In a more recent case, *Pena v. New York State Division for Youth*, the court held that the use of isolation, hand restraints, and tranquilizing drugs at Goshen Annex Center violated the Fourteenth Amendment right to due process and the Eighth Amendment right to protection against cruel and unusual punishment.[30]

The right to treatment has also been limited. For example, in *Ralston v. Robinson*, the Supreme Court rejected a youth's claim that he should continue to be given treatment after he was sentenced to a consecutive term in an adult prison for crimes committed while in a juvenile institution.[31] In the *Ralston* case, the offender's proven dangerousness outweighed the possible effects of rehabilitation. Similarly, in *Santana v. Callazo*, the U.S. First Circuit Court of Appeals rejected a suit brought by residents at the Maricao Juvenile Camp in Puerto Rico on the grounds that the administration had failed to provide them with an individualized rehabilitation plan or adequate treatment. The circuit court concluded that it was a legitimate exercise of state authority to incarcerate juveniles solely to protect society if they are dangerous.

MYTH All correctional clients have the right to treatment.

FACT Actually, while adults have no such right, juveniles do. The Supreme Court has ruled in a number of cases that juveniles cannot be held in secure treatment unless there is an effort to provide them with adequate care and rehabilitative services.

JUVENILE AFTERCARE AND REENTRY

Aftercare in the juvenile justice system is the equivalent of parole in the adult criminal justice system. When juveniles are released from an institution, they are placed in an aftercare program of some kind, so that youths who have been institutionalized are not simply returned to the community without some transitional assistance. Whether individuals who are in aftercare as part of an indeterminate sentence remain in the community or return to the institution for further rehabilitation depends on their actions during the aftercare period. Aftercare is an extremely important stage in the juvenile justice process because few juveniles age out of custody.[32]

There is an ongoing effort to improve conditions at juvenile institutions, but many seem like adult prisons. Cells at the Connecticut Juvenile Training School in Middletown house all but the state's most serious juvenile offenders, and the school is gearing up for a likely increase in its population and an infusion of about $40 million a year. This is due to a 2010 state law that raised the age at which juveniles are automatically charged as adults from 16 to 18, and resulted in more youthful offenders being treated in juvenile facilities.

© Joyce Dopkeen/*New York Times*/Redux

Preparation for the Job

Budding social workers should gain experience volunteering in group homes, after-school programs, and working in the community with at-risk kids.

Nature of the Job

Social casework, organizational processing of residents, services to residents, and maintenance of community contact are the duties of the social worker. Social workers are expected to make use of the principles of social casework in their therapeutic intervention with residents, the purpose of which is to determine the kind of help they need. Social workers guide residents throughout the institutional process, up to representing them at periodic reviews before an administrative board and ultimately recommending each client for release (unless they have been given a mandatory sentence). Social workers write frequent evaluation reports on each resident's progress, copies of which are usually sent to the social worker's supervisor, to the central office of the youth commission or department of corrections, and to the youth's aftercare officer. Furthermore, the social worker is expected to do all of the prerelease paperwork when the institutional release procedure has determined that a youth is ready to leave the institution. There is a wide range of community-contact responsibilities, which might include determining why parents have not written and encouraging them to visit, reporting on the medical condition

Postinstitutional Supervision of Juveniles

Juveniles in aftercare programs are supervised by parole caseworkers or counselors whose job is to maintain contact with the juvenile, make sure that a corrections plan is followed, and show interest and caring. The counselor also keeps the youth informed of services that may assist in reintegration and counsels the youth and his or her family. Unfortunately, aftercare caseworkers, like probation officers, often carry such large caseloads that their jobs are next to impossible to do adequately. New models of aftercare and reentry have been aimed at the chronic and/or violent offender. The Intensive Aftercare Program (IAP) model developed by David Altschuler and Troy Armstrong offers a continuum of intervention for serious juvenile offenders returning to the community following placement.[33]

Aftercare Revocation Procedures

Juvenile parolees are required to meet established standards of behavior, which are similar to those of adults on parole. If these rules are violated, the juvenile may have his parole revoked and be returned to the institution. Most states have extended the same legal rights enjoyed by adults at parole

August Collins (left), a caseworker with the Youth Empowerment Project (YEP), guides King Sanchez IV, 19, through paperwork at the GED offices in New Orleans. YEP, a re-entry program for teenagers coming home from the state's juvenile facilities, has a waiting list for its services. Post-release care is a significant element of a successful return to the community, and recent funding cutbacks have endangered these important programs.

© Jennifer Zdon/Times–Picayune

of any hospitalized family member, informing residents should a death occur in the family, contacting aftercare officers about a resident's special concerns, and counseling parents when conflict seems to be present in the home.

Qualifications and Required Education

An undergraduate degree in sociology, social work, or criminology is required in most juvenile institutional settings. Many correctional systems also require the applicant to pass an intelligence and aptitude test. To be promoted to social worker supervisor frequently requires a master's degree in social work, criminology, or sociology.

Job Outlook

The job outlook continues to be good for institutional social workers for both state and private institutions.

Earnings and Benefits

Social workers in state facilities receive a higher salary than do social workers in private institutions. Some social workers in county facilities make higher salaries than do those in state facilities and some do not. The average salary in state facilities ranges from $25,000 to $50,000.

Source: "Institutional Child Care Worker," http://careers.stateuniversity.com/pages/702/Institutional-Child-Care-Worker.html (accessed March 16, 2012).

---

revocation hearings to juveniles who are in danger of losing their aftercare privileges.

 L05

WAIVER TO THE ADULT COURT

Because of concern over violent juvenile offenders and the threat they pose to the community, state legislatures have passed laws permitting juveniles to be transferred or waived to adult court, where they can be tried and punished as adults. Waiver is a very serious issue because it means that a minor child can be sent to an adult prison institution where they will interact with and be influenced by experienced criminals. See Exhibit 14.4 for the relationship between juvenile behavior and a life of crime.

States vary widely in the criteria they use in making this waiver decision. Some states focus on the age of the offender, and others consider both age and offense. Vermont (age 10), Georgia, Illinois, and Mississippi (age 13) transfer children at very young ages. More states transfer juveniles at 14 than at any other age; seven states transfer juveniles at either 15 or 16 years of age.

The offenses juveniles commit are also important in the waiver decision.

EXHIBIT 14.4 The Youthful Offender and a Future Life of Crime

One of the areas that has received vast examination is the relationship between juvenile behavior and adult crime. The following findings receive support:

- Adolescent gang involvement contributes to a likelihood of involvement in street crime and arrests in adulthood.

- Some evidence exists that delinquents who become adult offenders are somewhat more likely than other delinquents to have had more seriously offensive delinquent careers.

- Cumulate disadvantage of some delinquents (individual and parental deficits) make drug use and gang involvement more attractive, lead to dropping out of school and unemployment into their adult years, and, in turn, these antisocial behaviors continue from childhood delinquency into adult crime.

- Childhood victimization with females, especially sexual victimization, can contribute to adult involvement with drugs and prostitution.

- Being institutionalized as a juvenile seriously compromises adult adjustment.

- Some studies have found a relationship between such factors as poor parental supervision, parental rejection, parental criminality, or delinquent siblings and late adult criminality.

Sources: Marvin D. Krohn, Jeffrey T. Ward, Terence P. Thornberry, Alan J. Lizotte, and Rebekah Chu, "The Cascading Effects of Adolescent Gang Involvement Across the Life Course," *Criminology* 49 (November 2011): 991–1025; Nadine Lanctot, Stephen A. Cernkovich, and Peggy C. Giordano, "Delinquent Behavior, Official Delinquency, and Gender: Consequences for Adult Functioning and Well-Being," *Criminology* 45 (2007): 191–222; and Brian Francis, Keith Soohill, and Alex R. Piquero, "Estimation Issues and Generational Changes in Modeling Criminal Career Length," *Crime and Delinquency* 53 (January 2007): 3–37.

EXHIBIT 14.5 Types of Waiver to Adult Court

- *Judicial waiver.* The juvenile court makes the decision to waive a juvenile to the adult court.

- *Prosecutorial waiver.* Some states give prosecutors the authority to decide whether to try juveniles in either juvenile or adult court.

- *Statutorial exclusion.* Certain offenses are excluded from juvenile court, thereby automatically transferring juveniles to adult court.

Some states permit waiver for any criminal offense, whereas others waive only those offenses specifically mentioned in the state's statutes. Many states permit waiver to the adult court if the juvenile previously has been adjudicated delinquent or has a prior criminal conviction. Depending on the state, three major mechanisms are used to waive juveniles: judicial waiver, prosecutorial waiver, and statutorial exclusion (see Exhibit 14.5).

Methods of Waiver

Except where state laws mandate that a youth be tried in adult court, someone has to make the decision to waive a youth. **Judicial waiver**, the most widely used transfer mechanism, involves the actual decision-making process that begins when the juvenile is brought to intake. Predictably, the mechanisms used vary by state. In some states, intake personnel, juvenile prosecutors, or judges make the decision, based in part on the age or offense criteria.

In other states, the prosecutor or judge in the adult court may decide where a juvenile is to be tried. The decision is determined by the requirements of the state and the way the intake officer, prosecutor, or judge interprets the youth's background. Typically, the criteria used include the age and maturity of the child; the child's relationship with parents, school, and community; whether the child is considered dangerous; and whether court officials believe that the child may be helped by juvenile court services.

Other state jurisdictions give prosecutors the authority to decide whether to try juveniles in either juvenile or adult courts. Nevada, Vermont, and Wyoming permit charges to be filed in either juvenile or adult court for any criminal offense, but most states specifically mention in their juvenile codes precisely which offenses may be tried in either court.

Some states have a **statutorial exclusion** of certain offenses from juvenile court, thereby automatically transferring perpetrators of those offenses to adult court. The statutes also, however, spell out the minimum age that youths must reach before they may be transferred to adult court.

Treating Juveniles as Adults

Although waivers are still relatively infrequent and have recently decreased in number, they are an important issue in juvenile justice. Significantly, juveniles waived to adult court are not always the most serious and violent offenders. With adult courts' massive caseload and their limited judicial experience with sentencing youths, little evidence exists that adult court judges know what to do with juveniles appearing before them.

Juveniles sentenced in adult courts are subject to the same range of dispositions as are adults. Cases may be dismissed or offenders may be found guilty. If found guilty, youths may be released to the care of their parents, placed on probation, fined, ordered to pay restitution, or referred to a social agency qualified to deal with their problem. But a very controversial disposition is the placement of youths in adult correctional facilities.

The crowding, violence, and exploitative relationships found in adult prisons make this disposition extremely questionable. Furthermore, although some states have attempted to develop special institutions for juveniles, even these appear to have the same characteristics as adult prisons. Youths who are placed in them can no better protect themselves than they can in adult facilities. Given the young age of even the most violent of these offenders, society has the task of deciding whether any type of adult institutional placement is appropriate for these youths.

The California Youth Authority has long extended its jurisdiction over youthful offenders to those up to 23 years of age. North Carolina was one of the first states to develop Youthful Offender Camps for 16- to 18-year-old males. In the 1990s,

JUDICIAL WAIVER The procedure of relinquishing the processing of a particular juvenile case in adult criminal court, also known as certifying or binding over to the adult court.

STATUTORIAL EXCLUSION Certain juvenile offenses in some states are automatically transferred to adult court.

Colorado, New Mexico, and Minnesota also developed transitional, or intermediate, systems between the juvenile and adult systems. Intermediate sentencing for youthful offenders that bridges the juvenile and adult systems certainly appears to be a positive means to keep some juveniles out of adult correctional facilities.

Youths in Adult Prisons

LO6

Adult prisons are a world apart from most training schools. Prisons are much larger, sometimes containing several thousand inmates and covering many acres of ground. Life on the inside is usually austere, crowded, and dangerous, and institutionalized youths are particularly subject to sexual victimization and sexual assault. Richard E. Redding concluded from his review of the programming that juveniles receive in adult correctional facilities: "Once incarcerated in adult facilities, juveniles typically receive fewer age-appropriate rehabilitative, medical, mental health and educational services, and are at greater risk of physical and sexual abuse and suicide."[34]

Each year, an estimated 4,000 new court commitments are admitted to state adult prison systems.[35] Providing for the care and special needs of juvenile offenders in adult facilities is proving to be a real problem. The youthful offenders may be as young as 13 and feel overwhelmed by older and more aggressive offenders. With their need to be part of something, youthful offenders tend to be highly impressionable and easily used or manipulated.[36] Some may be pressured into joining prison gangs and violent groups.

In the Correctional Life feature, a 17-year-old sentenced to life without parole tells what prison initially was like for him.

Punishing Juveniles: The Death Penalty and Life in Prison

The execution of minor children has not been uncommon in our nation's history; at least 366 juvenile offenders have been executed since 1642.[37] However, on March 1, 2005, the U.S. Supreme Court, in the case of *Roper v. Simmons*, put an end to the practice of the death penalty for juveniles in the United States. At issue was the minimum age that juveniles who were under the age of 18 when they committed their crimes could be eligible for the death penalty.[38] At the time, 16- and 17-year-olds were eligible for the death penalty; 21 states permitted the death penalty for juveniles.[39] A total of 72 juvenile offenders were on death row at the time.[40] In a 5–4 decision, the Court ruled that the juvenile death penalty was in violation of the Eighth Amendment's ban on cruel and unusual punishment. In its decision, the Court found that juveniles lack the maturity and sense of responsibility found in adults.[41]

What about a life sentence? Barry Feld, an opponent of life sentences for kids, argues that the Supreme Court's reasoning in *Roper v. Simmons* should also be applicable to cases in which juvenile offenders receive life sentences without the possibility of parole.[42] Feld proposes that "states formally recognize youthfulness as a mitigating factor by applying a 'youth discount' to adult sentence lengths."[43] On May 17, 2010, the Court agreed with Feld. It ruled on two Florida cases involving youths sentenced to life in prison for non-homicide crimes. One (*Sullivan v. Florida*) was convicted of raping a 72-year-old woman when he was 13; the other (*Graham v. Florida*) involved a home invasion robbery by a 17-year-old.[44] In its decision, the Court stated:

> The Constitution prohibits the imposition of a life without parole sentence on a juvenile offender who did not commit homicide. . . . A state need not guarantee the offender eventual release, but if it imposes a sentence of

CORRECTIONAL LIFE
Joshua: Can I Survive?

"At 17, for me at least, prison was many things. There is the fear. We've all seen the movies where the young kid (it's always the young kid) comes into prison and is quickly fed upon by the predators. He's raped or beaten, made a punk or killed, sometimes all of the above. I have a very active imagination, so I could foresee every possible bad outcome, played out in vivid detail inside my head. You tell yourself, "I'll be strong! I'll do whatever it takes to survive," but the fear is still there. Everything is so uncertain. You have no idea what to expect. It's a feeling of flux, and for a time your life simply doesn't belong to you. It's like you were a caterpillar sealed away inside your cocoon. You're constantly changing. You have to learn to adapt to your new environment. You're not sure what you'll have to become to come out okay.

It's a proving ground also. You're constantly tested, by yourself and others. Will he, won't he, is he, can he? The other inmates, as well as staff, feel you out to see if you're a snitch, a bitch, a gossip, or a "stand up" or "solid" guy. They want to know if they can use you, or if you're strong and take care of yourself.

Do I deserve to be here? Probably! Regardless of my age, what I did was wrong. Regardless of my mental status at the time of the crime, what I did resulted in a spouse who lost his wife, four young kids growing up without a mother, and an innocent person losing her life. Do I feel guilty? Not as much as I used to. As the years pass and the more I go through, it's harder to feel sorry or guilty."

Source: Interviewed by Clemens Bartollas.

life it must provide him or her with some realistic opportunity to obtain release before the end of that term.[45]

But juveniles who commit murder can still die in prison for crimes they committed when they were minors. They can be sentenced in adult court to remain in prison for the duration of their natural lives without the possibility of parole (LWOP). Locking up the juvenile for the rest of his or her life may be cruel punishment, but it is not unusual. There are currently 2,390 people in this nation who are serving life sentences for crimes they committed as juveniles. There are 73 juveniles who committed crimes when they were 13 and 14. Nationally, 59 percent of the juveniles serving life sentences without the possibility of parole had no prior criminal convictions before being placed in prison for life.

Forty-two states presently allow life without parole for minors. California has 225 inmates serving life sentences for crimes committed as minors. In Pennsylvania, estimates range from 360 to 443 inmates serving life without parole for offenses committed as juveniles (see Figure 14.2).[46]

HELPING CHILDREN IN CUSTODY
The state of Washington has attempted to manage imprisoned youthful offenders more effectively. In 1997, the state enacted Senate Bill 3900 defining the jurisdiction, custody, and management requirement for juvenile offenders. This legislation requires juvenile offenders to be placed in adult prisons for serious offenses such as aggravated murder. In addition, it dictates the housing and educational requirements for youthful offenders within the department of corrections (DOC) as follows:

- An offender under the age of 18 who is convicted in adult criminal court and sentenced to the DOC must be placed in a housing unit, or a portion of a housing unit, separated from adult inmates.

- The offenders may be housed in an intensive management unit or administrative segregation unit, if necessary, for the safety or security of the offender or the staff.

FIGURE 14.2 State-by-State Map of Juveniles Serving Life Without Parole

Source: Frontline, "When Kids Get Life," May 21, 2009.

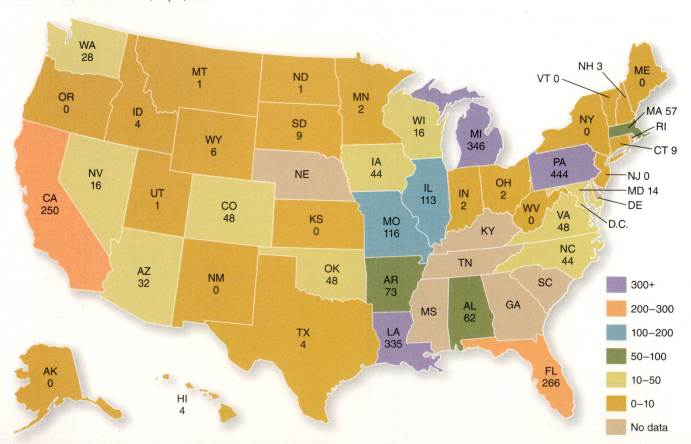

- The DOC must provide an educational program to an offender under the age of 18 who is incarcerated at a DOC facility. The program must enable the offender to obtain a high school diploma or general equivalency diploma (GED).[47]

Female youthful offenders are placed at the Washington Corrections Center for Women (WCCW), and males are confined at the Clallam Bay Corrections Center. A multidisciplinary team was formed in September 1997 in order to meet the challenge of accommodating juveniles in adult prisons. This team has been concerned with providing a safe and secure environment; an environment distant from adult offenders' contact and influences; programs and services similar to those available to the general population; and an educational program offering credit for a high school diploma or GED.[48]

Some variations on the practice of confining a juvenile in an adult institution do exist among the states. In some jurisdictions, states have no alternative but to place juveniles in adult institutions if the courts require incarceration. Some states can, under special circumstances, place youths in either juvenile or adult institutions, yet other states can refer juveniles back to juvenile court for their disposition. In some instances, very young offenders are sent to juvenile facilities but then are transferred to adult institutions when they come of age. Recognizing the dangers and inadequacies of placing juveniles with adults, some jurisdictions have developed special institutions for these younger adult offenders.

SUMMARY

L01 **Identify the early development of juvenile justice**

Juvenile justice in the United States began in the colonial period. It changed in the twentieth century with a number of significant U.S. Supreme Court cases, in which juveniles were given more due process rights.

L02 **Understand the disposition of probation, including how it is administered and by whom and recent trends in its use**

Probation is the most widely used method of community treatment. Youths on probation must obey rules given to them by the court and participate in some form of treatment program. If rules are violated, youths may have their probation revoked. Behavior is monitored by probation officers. Formal probation accounts for more than 60 percent of all juvenile dispositions, and its use has increased significantly in the last decade.

L03 **Distinguish between community treatment and institutional treatment for juvenile offenders**

Community treatment for juveniles consists of probation, residential programs, house arrest, and electronic monitoring. The secure juvenile institution was developed in the mid-nineteenth century as an alternative to placing youths in adult prisons. Youth institutions evolved from large, closed institutions to cottage-based education- and rehabilitation-oriented institutions.

L04 **Know the nature of aftercare for juvenile offenders and comment on recent innovations in juvenile aftercare and reentry programs**

Aftercare in the juvenile justice system is the equivalent of parole in the adult criminal justice system. Juveniles released from institutions are placed in an aftercare program, so that they are not simply returned to the community without some transitional assistance. New types of programs include the Intensive Aftercare Program (IAP), which offers a continuum of intervention for serious juvenile offenders returning to the community following placement.

L05 **Understand how the juvenile is transferred and tried in adult court**

Juveniles can be transferred to adult court through a judicial waiver by a juvenile court judge; by prosecutorial discretion in jurisdictions that give prosecutors the authority to try juveniles in either juvenile or adult courts; or by statutorial exclusion in those states that automatically transfer juveniles who commit certain offenses to adult court.

L06 **Be able to identify the plight faced by juveniles sent to adult prisons**

About 4,000 juveniles are sent to adult prison each year. Providing for the special needs of juveniles in adult prisons poses a serious problem. Youthful offenders often feel overwhelmed by older and more aggressive offenders.

Key Terms

juvenile justice system, 322
juvenile delinquent, 322
status offender, 322
parens patriae, 323
community treatment, 325

institutional treatment facility, 325
residential programs, 327
wilderness programs, 327
group homes, 328
family group homes, 328

nonresidential programs, 328
aftercare, 333
judicial waiver, 336
statutorial exclusion, 336

 ## Critical Thinking Questions

1. Would you want a community treatment program for juvenile offenders in your neighborhood? Why or why not?

2. If youths violate the rules of probation, should they be placed in a secure institution?

3. What are the most important advantages of community treatment for juvenile offenders?

4. What is the purpose of juvenile probation? Identify some conditions of probation and discuss the responsibilities of the juvenile probation officer.

5. Has community treatment generally proven successful?

6. Why have juvenile boot camps not been effective in reducing recidivism?

7. Is there such a thing as a good juvenile correctional institution?

 ## Thinking Like a Corrections Professional

As a local juvenile court judge, you have been assigned the case of Jim Butler, a 13-year-old juvenile so short he can barely see over the bench. On trial for armed robbery, the boy has been accused of threatening a woman with a knife and stealing her purse. Barely a teenager, he already has a long history of involvement with the law. At age 11 he was arrested for drug possession and placed on probation; soon after, he stole a car. At age 12 he was arrested for shoplifting. Jim is accompanied by his legal guardian, his maternal grandmother. His parents are unavailable because his father abandoned the family years ago and his mother is currently undergoing inpatient treatment at a local drug clinic. After talking with his attorney, Jim decides to admit to the armed robbery. At a dispositional hearing, his court-appointed attorney tells you of the tough life Jim has been forced to endure. His grandmother states that, although she loves the boy, her advanced age makes it impossible for her to provide the care he needs to stay out of trouble. She says that Jim is a good boy who has developed a set of bad companions; his current scrape was precipitated by his friends.

A representative of the school system testifies that Jim has above-average intelligence and is actually respectful of teachers. He has potential, but his life circumstances have short-circuited his academic success. Jim himself shows remorse and appears to be a sensitive youngster who is easily led astray by older youths.

You must now make a decision. You can place Jim on probation and allow him to live with his grandmother while being monitored by county probation staff. You can place him in a secure incarceration facility for up to three years. You can also put him into an intermediate program such as a community-based facility, which would allow him to attend school during the day while residing in a halfway house and receiving group treatment in the evenings. Although Jim appears salvageable, his crime was serious and involved the use of a weapon. If he remains in the community, he may offend again; if he is sent to a correctional facility, he will interact with older, tougher kids. What mode of correctional treatment would you choose?

 ## Career Destinations

If you are interested in working with juveniles, you can learn about innovative programs sponsored by Homeboy Industries. Its mission is to assist at-risk and former gang-involved youths to become contributing members of the community through a variety of services:
www.homeboy-industries.org

This site can help you see what is required to become a juvenile institutions officer:

www.co.monterey.ca.us/personnel/documents/ specifications/60F88.pdf

Or a juvenile probation officer:
www.co.lancaster.pa.us/courts/cwp/view. asp?a=472&Q=389322

Notes

1. Ralph Blumenthal, "Texas, Addressing Sexual Abuse Scandal, May Free Thousands of Its Jailed Youths," *New York Times*, March 24, 2007.
2. David W. Springer, *Transforming Juvenile Justice in Texas: A Framework for Action* (Austin, TX: Blue Ribbon Task Force Report, 2007).
3. Allen J. Beck, Paige M. Harrison, and Paul Guerino, *Sexual Victimization in Juvenile Facilities Reported by Youth, 2008–09* (Washington, DC: U.S. Government Printing Office; Bureau of Justice Statistics, 2010), p. 1.
4. "Some Good News from California's Justice System," *New York Times*, January 16, 2012, p. A2.
5. Douglas Besharov, *Juvenile Justice Advocacy—Practice in a Unique Court* (New York: Practicing Law Institute, 1974), p. 2.
6. D. R. Rendleman, *"Parens Patriae*: From Chancery to the Juvenile Court," *South Carolina Law Review* (1971), p. 209.
7. Gustav L. Schramm, "The Judge Meets the Boy and His Family," *National Probation Association 1945 Yearbook*, pp. 182–194.
8. Anthony M. Platt, *The Child Savers: The Invention of Delinquency* (Chicago: University of Chicago Press, 1969).
9. Howard N. Snyder and Melissa Sickmund, *Juvenile Offenders and Victims: 2006 National Report* (Pittsburgh: National Center for Juvenile Justice, 2006), pp. 174–175.
10. TDCJ-Community Justice Assistance Division, *Electronic Monitoring: Agency Brief* (n.d.), p. 1.
11. Joseph B. Vaughn, "A Survey of Juvenile Electronic Monitoring and Home Confinement Programs," *Juvenile and Family Court Journal* 40 (1989): 4, 22.
12. Snyder and Sickmund, *Juvenile Offenders and Victims*, p. 187.
13. Doris Layton MacKenzie, David B. Wilson, Gaylene Styve Armstrong, and Angela R. Gover, "The Impact of Boot Camps and Traditional Institutions on Juvenile Residents: Perceptions, Adjustment, and Change," *Journal of Research in Crime and Delinquency* 38 (August 2000): 279–313; Jean Bottcher and Michaele Ezell, "Examining the Effectiveness of Boot Camps: A Randomized Experiment with a Long-Term Follow-Up," *Journal of Research in Crime and Delinquency* 42 (2005): 309–320; and Jerry Tyler, Ray Darville, and Kathi Stalnaker, "Juvenile Boot Camps: A Descriptive Analysis of Program Diversity and Effectiveness," *Social Sciences Journal* 38 (2001): 445–460.
14. Alexandra Marks, "States Fall Out of (Tough) Love with Boot Camps," *Christian Science Monitor*, December 27, 1999, p. 1.
15. Ira Schwartz, *Juvenile Justice and Public Policy* (New York: Lexington Books, 1992), p. 217.
16. Data used in this section come from the Office of Juvenile Justice and Delinquency Prevention, "Juveniles in Corrections," www.ojjdp.gov/ojstatbb/corrections/qa08201.asp (accessed April 8, 2012).
17. Ibid.
18. Daniel P. Mears, "Exploring State-Level Variation in Juvenile Incarceration Rates: Symbolic Threats and Competing Explanations," *Prison Journal* 86 (2006): 470–490.
19. John F. Chapman, Rani A. Desai, Paul R. Falzer, and Randy Borum, "Violence Risk and Race in a Sample of Youth in Juvenile Detention: The Potential to Reduce Disproportionate Minority Confinement," *Youth Violence and Juvenile Justice* 4 (2006): 170–184.
20. Heidi M. Hsia, George S. Bridges, and Rosalie McHale, *Disproportionate Minority Confinement: 2002 Update: Summary* (Washington, DC: Office of Juvenile Justice and Delinquency Prevention, 2004).
21. Coalition for Juvenile Justice, *Disproportionate Minority Contact (DMC), Facts and Resources*, www.juvjustice.org/media/factsheets/factsheet_12.pdf (accessed April 8, 2012).
22. Christopher Sieverdes and Clemens Bartollas, "Security Level and Adjustment Patterns in Juvenile Institutions," *Journal of Criminal Justice* 14 (1986): 135–145.
23. Several authors have written of this sexual double standard. See E. A. Anderson, "The Chivalrous Treatment of the Female Offender in the Arms of the Criminal Justice System: A Review of the Literature," *Social Problems* 23 (1976): 350–357; G. Armstrong, "Females Under the Law: Protected but Unequal," *Crime and Delinquency* 23 (1977): 109–120; Meda Chesney-Lind, "Judicial Enforcement of the Female Sex Role: The Family Court and the Female Delinquent," *Issues in Criminology* 8 (1973): 51–59; Meda Chesney-Lind, "Juvenile Delinquency: The Sexualization of Female Crime," *Psychology Today* 19 (1974): 43–46; Allan Conway and Carol Bogdan, "Sexual Delinquency: The Persistence of a Double Standard," *Crime and Delinquency* 23 (1977): 13–35; Meda Chesney-Lind and Randall G. Shelden, *Girls, Delinquency, and the Juvenile Justice System*, 3rd ed. (Belmont, CA: Wadsworth, 2004).
24. Kristi Holsinger and Alexander M. Holsinger, "Differential Pathways to Violence and Self-Injurious Behavior: African American and White Girls in the Juvenile Justice System," *Journal of Research in Crime and Delinquency* 42 (2005): 211–242.
25. Doris Layton MacKenzie, "Reducing the Criminal Activities of Known Offenders and Delinquents: Crime Prevention in the Courts and Corrections," in *Evidence-Based Crime Prevention*, ed. Lawrence W. Sherman, David P. Farrington, Brandon C. Welsh, and Doris Layton MacKenzie (New York: Routledge, 2006, rev. ed.), p. 352.
26. Patrick A. Langan and David J. Levin, *Recidivism of Prisoners Released in 1994* (Washington, DC: Bureau of Justice Statistics, 2002).
27. David Farabee, *Rethinking Rehabilitation: Why Can't We Reform Our Criminals?* (Washington, DC: American Enterprise Institute, 2005); for a rebuttal of this view, see James M. Byrne and Faye S. Taxman, "Crime (Control) Is a Choice: Divergent Perspectives on the Role of Treatment in the Adult Corrections System," *Criminology and Public Policy* 4 (2005): 291–310.
28. Mark W. Lipsey and David B. Wilson, "Effective Intervention for Serious Juvenile Offenders: A Synthesis of Research," in *Serious and Violent Juvenile Offenders: Risk Factors and Successful Interventions*, ed. Rolf Loeber and David P. Farrington (Thousand Oaks, CA: Sage Publications, 1998).
29. *Inmates of the Boys' Training School v. Affeck*, 346 F. Supp. 1354 (D.R.I. 1972); *Nelson v. Heyne*, 491 F.2d 353 (1974); *Morales v. Turman*, 383 F.Supp. 53 (E.D. Texas 1974).
30. *Pena v. New York State Division for Youth*, 419 F. Supp. 203 (S.D.N.Y. 1976).
31. *Ralston v. Robinson*, 102 S.Ct. 233 (1981).
32. Joan McCord, Cathy Spatz Widom, and Nancy A. Crowell, *Juvenile Crime, Juvenile Justice*, Panel on Juvenile Crime: Prevention, Treatment, and Control (Washington, DC: National Academy Press, 2001), p. 194.
33. David M. Altschuler and Troy L. Armstrong, "Juvenile Corrections and Continuity of Care in a Community Context—The Evidence and Promising Directions," *Federal Probation* 66 (2002): 72–77.
34. Richard E. Redding, "Juvenile Offenders in Criminal Court and Adult Prison: Legal, Psychological, and Behavioral Outcomes," *Juvenile and Family Court Journal* 50 (1999): 1–20.
35. Snyder and Sickmund, *Juvenile Offenders and Victims*, p. 186.
36. Salvador A. Godinez, "Managing Juveniles in Prison," *Corrections Today* 61 (April 1999): 132–133.
37. Victor L. Streib, *The Juvenile Death Penalty Today: Death Sentences and Executions for Juvenile Crimes, January 1, 1973–September 30, 2003* (Ada, OH: Claude W. Pettit College of Law, Ohio Northern University, October 6, 2003), p. 3.
38. *Roper v. Simmons*, 125 S.Ct. 1183 (2005).
39. Erica Goode, "Young Killer: Bad Seed or Work in Progress?" *New York Times*, November 25, 2003.
40. Adam Liptak, "Court Takes Another Step in Reshaping Capital Punishment," *New York Times*, March 2, 2005.
41. *Roper v. Simmons*.
42. Barry C. Feld, "A Slower Form of Death: Implications of *Roper v. Simmons* for Juveniles Sentenced to Life Without Parole," *Notre Dame Journal of Law, Ethics and Public Policy* 22 (2008): 9–65.
43. Ibid., p. 10.
44. *Graham v. Florida*, 560 U.S. _____ (2010) (decided May 17, 2010).
45. Ibid.
46. Robert Barnes, "Supreme Court Restricts Life Without Parole for Juveniles," *Washington Post*, May 2010, www.washingtonpost.com/wp-dyn/content/article/2010/05/17/AR2010051701355.html (accessed March 16, 2012).
47. Gary Fleming and Gerald Winkler, "Sending Them to Prison: Washington State Learns to Accommodate Female Youthful Offenders in Prison," *Corrections Today* 61 (April 1999): 132–133.
48. Ibid., p. 133.

In 2008, 78 New Jersey corrections officers and civilian employees were fired for infractions that included possessing drugs, improper relationships with inmates, and not showing up for work. That year, the state awarded 622 commendations but also issued 937 final disciplinary actions. Some employees saved lives and confiscated weapons, while others placed colleagues and inmates in harm's way.[1] The corrections department issued a statement, saying in part, "It proves that we are meticulous about policing ourselves. . . . The commissioner is absolutely determined to punish those who endanger themselves and coworkers."[2]

The most common reason for disciplinary action was lateness or excessive absences. Several employees were fired, along with dozens more suspended or reprimanded, for not showing up. Five employees were terminated for being "unduly familiar"

Office of Attorney General for the State of New Jersey

Eugene Braswell, shown here, was caught up in the corruption scandal involving New Jersey correctional officers. He had been a senior state correction officer working at Northern State Prison, but in 2011, Braswell pleaded guilty to first-degree cocaine trafficking and second-degree official misconduct. Braswell admitted that he and his co-conspirators transported 22 kilograms of cocaine, wrapped in heat-sealed plastic bags and hidden in the roof panels of the vehicle they were driving from a buy in Texas. His co-conspirators pleaded guilty to second-degree conspiracy charges and received 7 years in prison; Braswell faces 15 years.

with or having "inappropriate relationships" with inmates. Besides absenteeism, most firings were drug related. Two employees refused to take a drug test, and three others failed them. A typist was found with two baggies of suspected marijuana, and an officer was caught at home with a half-ounce of cocaine. One officer was fired for accepting bribes, and a lieutenant lost his job after pleading guilty to aggravated assault.[3]

Yet, at the same time, hundreds of officers and employees were praised for good work. On several occasions, officers prevented inmates from committing suicide. Others received commendations for seizing contraband: some stopped visitors with drugs and others found cell phones and shanks. Officers were also applauded for their actions outside the state's prisons, such as stopping to assist at the scene of a motor vehicle accident.[4]

Fifteen

TODAY'S CORRECTIONS PROFESSIONAL: CHARACTERISTICS, CHALLENGES, AND OPPORTUNITIES

LEARNING OBJECTIVES

LO1 Know how far professionalism has brought corrections

LO2 Be able to define professionalism and the need of it

LO3 Identify how correctional administrators can foster professionalism

LO4 Know the present challenges for advancement in professionalism

LO5 Define the major challenges facing corrections in the present

LO6 Identify whether punishment or reform will dominate the future landscape of corrections

The New Jersey experience illustrates the challenges facing correctional administrators in contemporary society. The report of the commendations, suspensions, and termination of correctional officers in New Jersey reveals that some officers are committed to their careers and perform at a high level, while others' job performance is such that they place fellow officers and the security of the institution in jeopardy. It is sometimes necessary to fire them.

One of the underlying themes of this book is that the committed corrections professional can have an exciting and fulfilling career and, at the same time, can make a difference in inmates' lives. The Voices Across the Profession features in the book have echoed this theme over and over. As Jim Bruton says in Chapter 1, "we resolve to go to work each day believing that offenders can change and that we can have an impact on their lives."

Yet there are challenges to the job. Overcrowded and sometimes violent prisons, lengthy sentences given to offenders, and high rates of recidivism, to name a few. While correctional administrators have little or no control over these issues, what takes place in community-based corrections and in prisons and jails is very much their responsibility. What adds to the challenge of corrections today is the changing landscape of corrections and what it will look like in decades to come. The hope is that with this changing landscape corrections will become more humane in the treatment of offenders, more respectful of human rights, and more effective in preparing those who have violated society's laws for responsible community living.

We begin with a discussion of professionalism and a career in corrections. In Voices Across the Profession, Ray Stanelle, a senior investigator for

VOICES ACROSS the PROFESSION

© Ray Stanelle

> "Corrections is in my blood, and I am quite passionate about it. It is a great career."

RAY STANELLE,
SENIOR INVESTIGATOR FOR DRUG
INTERDICTION AND INTELLIGENCE

I joined the Georgia Department of Corrections as a correction officer in June of 1994 when I was 45 years old. I attended Georgia College and State University and earned my B.S., with a major in criminal justice. During this time, I also completed a course in comparative law and corrections in England and Spain, next earning my M.P.A. with criminal justice as my discipline of concentration.

I must say I learned more about inmates and prisons and policy and procedures as a correction officer than I could have ever learned in a classroom. As a correction officer, I supervised inmates in the dormitory and also on inside details. The atmosphere of a dormitory changes with each shift, and each shift is a world unto itself. I was later assigned the position of disciplinary investigator where I remained until leaving to become a probation officer in 1997. I loved my probation officer job, which was very demanding and challenging. I ran a tight ship and expected all probationers to adhere to the terms and conditions of their probation. For all the tough talk, I discovered that by being consistent and fair, and by setting high standards, I had probationers completing probation who had never completed anything in their lives. I learned that if you expected excellence, their chance of success improved greatly.

I left probation when I was chosen to become an internal affairs investigator for the Georgia Department of Corrections. I left this position after four years to become a chief counselor, then became an acting deputy warden. I missed working in the field and jumped at an opportunity to return to internal affairs, where I investigated everything from excessive force to assaults, rapes, suicides, and inmate deaths. I have found this to be meaningful work. For example, I worked with one of my investigators for eight months and finally solved how a death row inmate was getting Internet pagers smuggled to him. The investigation took us from Georgia to Italy and then on to Singapore. The reward was the day we arrested the culprit who had been smuggling the pagers into the prison. I became a senior investigator for drug interdiction and intelligence, a job I still hold today.

Corrections is in my blood, and I am quite passionate about it. It is a great career. I would recommend it to students reading this book.

Source: Interviewed in 2011.

drug interdiction and intelligence with the Georgia Department of Corrections, discusses his work in the current correctional system.

PROFESSIONALISM IN CORRECTIONS

In its original form, discipline in American prisons was rough and physical, and public flogging was not unusual. One famous warden allowed himself to be photographed in the act of flogging a misbehaving prisoner, explaining to the watching press that "these men aren't here for playing hooky from Sunday School."[5]

Until 1966, when the federal courts outlawed the practice, punishment was harsh and physical. The strap was used to punish prisoners in Mississippi and Arkansas. The strap was made of leather, 3 to 5 feet in length and about 4 inches wide, with a wooden handle 8 to 12 inches long. Arkansas had an informal requirement that strapping be limited to 10 blows on the buttocks at a time for any single offense. Sometimes, though not always, the prisoner posterior might be bare. Southern prisons employed convict guards for perimeter security and to maintain order in the fields and cellblocks. Their methods were straightforward and rough. While convicts working as guards were not supposed to administer the strap, this rule was frequently breached.[6]

The correctional system has come a very long way from what is now referred to as the Dark Ages of Corrections. Today the system focuses on *professionalism*, a loosely defined term that refers to a set of character strengths and personal values directed at providing the highest quality service to others in the workplace, both colleagues and clients.

Professionalism brought corrections into the modern age and will guide it into the future. However, reaching this standard did not occur overnight. In this section, we discuss a few of the steps taken in the past to reach the current standard of corrections professionalism.

Emerging Professionalism

Those who view corrections through the lens of reform conclude that the government must strike a balance between individual rights and collective needs. This balance, reflecting a long history of constitutional government, is weighed on the side of individual rights.

Meeting these goals has been another matter. Reformers have advanced corrections and moved it toward professionalism. One early reformer, Richard A. McGee, changed the nature of corrections in California by upgrading the physical plants and staffing patterns, by institutional research, and by developing alternatives to imprisonment. Another, Kenneth Stoneman, closed Vermont's only maximum-security prison in the 1970s. Lloyd McCorkle, instead of building more prisons, developed a network of satellites in New Jersey at other human services institutions. Kenneth F. Schoen was instrumental in laying out the principles of Minnesota's groundbreaking community correction act. James V. Bennett closed Alcatraz, opened Marion, planned Morgantown, and created a professional bureaucracy at the Federal Bureau of Prisons. Elayn Hunt, before her death, was leading the Louisiana corrections system out of its dark ages.

STAFF TRAINING AND DEVELOPMENT The Federal Bureau of Prisons and a number of states began to emphasize staff training in the early 1970s. It was not long before state corrections training academies were established across the nation. In the late 1970s, the American Correctional Association (ACA) Commission on Accreditation established its training standards, which had wide influence on the field of corrections. One of its standards was to require 120 hours for preservice and 40 hours for annual in-service training. The National Institute of Corrections (NIC) and the Association of State Correctional Administrators (ASCA) were other agencies that began to offer training for correctional staff. Correctional officers, similar to law enforcement officers, began their service in training academies, and various levels of management staff soon had programs established for them. One of the advantages of staff training is that it ensures a uniform way to do the job. Staff training was one of the most important impetuses toward professionalism of American corrections.

IMPLEMENTING GENDER AND RACIAL INTEGRATION The acceptance of women in corrections took a long time, and it was not until midway through the twentieth century that women were widely accepted in positions of leadership. Since that time, women have been directors or commissioners of corrections, many have been superintendents of women's prisons, and an increasing number have been wardens of men's prisons, even maximum-security ones. In addition to Elayn Hunt, who was Louisiana corrections commissioner between 1972 and 1976, women such as Ward Murphy in Maine, Ali Klein in New Jersey, and Ruth L. Rushen in California in the 1980s became the heads of adult corrections. In 1992, Kathleen M. Hawk was appointed director of the Federal Bureau of Prisons, and in 2009, Collette S. Peters became the first female director of the Oregon Department of Corrections. By the end of the twentieth century, women represented about 10 percent of wardens and superintendents of the 900 statewide correctional facilities for men.

In the twentieth century, pioneered by the Federal Bureau of Prisons, most state systems began to actively recruit minority staff for positions at all levels. Bob Matthews, a Bureau of Prisons warden, noted that "as an African American, the thing that impressed me about Norm Carlson was he did a lot to advance equal opportunity in the Bureau. Norm selected the first African-American assistant director and regional director."[7] Matthews thought Attica's violent uprising had made a big impression on Carlson. He was aware that most federal prisons, like state prisons, were in rural areas and staffed by whites, but with a large minority-inmate population. Not surprisingly, according to Matthews, there would often be a lack of understanding and communication. He explained, "Norm recognized he had to have some staff that looked like the people who were locked up. Norm moved ahead of the problem on this one, and in my mind, he gets a lot of kudos for advancing equal opportunity hiring."[8]

EMPHASIS ON ETHICS AND INTEGRITY Both corrections and law enforcement agencies realized in the late twentieth century that an emphasis on integrity was critically important in being recognized as professional entities. Persons of integrity demonstrate over a period of time that they are honest. They also show that there are no contradictions between what they say and what they do. Thus, "standing tall" is not something that can be earned in a day or a week. It occurs over a substantial period of time during which this integrity is tested on a regular basis. The credibility and honesty of these people are reflected in everything they say and do.

Corrections staff with integrity seem to have the ability to maintain their composure, regardless of the circumstances taking place around them. No matter how volatile an incident may be or how much they are upset by the behavior of other staff members or inmates, they are able to keep their cool. This calmness is reassuring to others because they know that even in the worst conditions, you can count on these people to keep their wits about them and stay focused on what has to be done to resolve the situation.

The American Correctional Association's Code of Ethics has contributed to this emphasis on ethics and integrity (see Exhibit 15.1). The code has statements regarding respecting the civil rights of others; treating every situation with concern for the

A male prisoner is searched by a female corrections officer in the Santa Ana, California, city jail. It is common today to have male officers in female prisons and female officers in male prisons. Are there benefits to this arrangement? Are there also drawbacks?

welfare of those involved; refraining from using one's position to secure personal privileges or advantages; and respecting, promoting, and contributing to a workplace that is healthy, safe, and free of harassment in any form.[9]

Implementation of standards and accreditation, spearheaded by the American Correctional Association, has developed across the nation. In 2012, there were 1,289 correctional services across the United States that have received accreditation from the ACA accreditation program.[10]

Professionalism Today

The present status of professionalism in corrections includes the following:

- The definition of professionalism
- The need for professionalism
- The difference between a professional and a nonprofessional
- The ways a correctional leader can foster professionalism
- What remains to be done to attain greater professionalism

DEFINITION OF PROFESSION-ALISM Corrections professionals, rather than following a script or providing minimum service, undertake a specialized set of tasks and complete them, believing passionately in what they do, never compromising their standards or values, and caring about clients even if they happen to be criminal offenders. Corrections professionals, as is true of other types of professionals, are experts at their work. They see their commitment to the organization as having the objective of obtaining the highest standards of excellence. As we briefly touched on at the beginning of this book, becoming a corrections professional means:

- Seeing oneself as a person of integrity
- Treating offenders with dignity and respect
- Modeling positive behaviors to both inmates and staff
- Refusing to accept unethical behavior from fellow staff members
- Doing what is possible to create a positive workplace

EXHIBIT 15.1 American Correctional Association's Code of Ethics

Preamble

The American Correctional Association expects of its members unfailing honesty, respect for the dignity and individuality of human beings and a commitment to professional and compassionate service. To that this end we subscribe to the following principles.

1. Member shall respect and protect the civil and legal rights of all individuals.
2. Member shall treat every professional situation with concern for the welfare of the individuals involved and with no intent to personal gain.
3. Member shall maintain relationships with colleagues to promote mutual respect within the profession and improve the quality of service.
4. Members shall make public criticism of their colleagues or their agencies only when warranted, verifiable, and constructive.
5. Members shall respect the importance of all disciplines within the criminal justice system and work to improve cooperation with each segment.
6. Members shall honor the public's right to information and share information with the public to the extent permitted by law but subject to individuals' right to privacy.
7. Members shall respect and protect the right of the public to be safeguarded from criminal activity.
8. Members shall refrain from using their position to secure personal privileges or advantages.
9. Members shall refrain from allowing personal interest to impair objectivity in the performance of duty while acting in an official capacity.
10. Members shall refrain from entering into any formal or informal activity over agreement which presents a conflict of interest or is inconsistent with the conscientious performance of duties.
11. Members shall refrain from accepting any gifts, services, or favors that is or appears to be improper or implies an obligation inconsistent with the free and objective exercise of professional duties.
12. Members shall clearly differentiate between personal views/statements and views/statements/positions made on behalf of the agency or Association.
13. Members shall report to appropriate authorities any corrupt or unethical behavior in which there is sufficient evidence to justify review.
14. Members shall refrain from discriminating against any individual because of race, gender, creed, national origin, religious affiliation, age, disability, or any other type of prohibited discrimination.
15. Members shall preserve the integrity of private information; they shall refrain from seeking information on individuals beyond that which is necessary to implement responsibilities and perform their duties; members shall refrain from revealing nonpublic information less expressively authorized to do so.
16. Members shall make all appointments, promotions, and dismissals in accordance with established civil service rules, applicable contract agreements, and individual merit, rather than furtherance of personal interest.
17. Members shall respect, promote, and contribute to a workplace that is safe, healthy, and free of harassment in any form.

Source: Adopted by the Board of Governors and Delegate Assembly in August 1994 and updated in 2009. Reprinted by permission of the ACA. Available online at www.aca.org/pastpresentfuture/ethics.asp (accessed April 5, 2012).

- Being committed to making a difference

- Being a proactive leader, anticipating and preventing problems before they occur

- Remembering that institutional security must always come first

- Maintaining a clean institution; cleanliness and orderliness of the institution are absolute necessities in correctional leadership

- Remembering the importance of accountability, attention to detail, and following the schedule

- Being a person who listens

- Keeping your personal stuff from getting in the way and refusing to permit your personal problems or issues keep you from doing an effective job

- Going the second mile for offenders, especially in community supervision, if it is the right thing to do

NEED FOR PROFESSIONALISM IN CORRECTIONS The encouraging changes that have taken place in recent decades are an indication of the influence of professionalism. Professionalism is affected by how staff dress, how they speak, and how they behave. Workplace attitudes also tell a lot about the level of professionalism in an organization. Professional employees maintain positive, can-do attitudes, even when faced with stressful situations. Professionalism and commitment to the organization are demonstrated by limiting absences, possessing high productivity, and effectively communicating with others.[11] There is still progress to be made, but the commitment of the professionals within the ranks of corrections has brought it a long way, and it is this same commitment that will ensure an even more positive day for corrections in the future.

PROFESSIONAL AND NONPROFESSIONAL To the professional, the job represents a career, a career in which he or she can grow and contribute. To the nonprofessional, the job represents merely a job, a paycheck. There is no commitment to the organization. He or she puts in the time and sees no reason to give any more of self than is absolutely necessary. Unprofessional workplace conduct includes frequent tardiness, poor contact with inmates, and low employee morale. Nonprofessional behavior is also involved in participating in workplace gossip, turning on mobile devices, and using the institution for personal issues. For example, a nonprofessional staff member who has the reputation of sharing all the rumors and "lowdowns" on staff and inmates throughout the institution—much of which information may be unverified, offensive, and of a personal nature—can be very destructive to the quality of institutional life. A nonprofessional staff member who is reported as falling asleep or nodding off while on duty assignment can threaten the security of the institution and the safety of other staff. Finally, it can be argued that almost every major correctional crisis is preceded by systematic failure to perform the job.[12]

See Voices Across the Profession, which addresses some of the key questions about professionalism. In this statement, Norman Carlson defines a professional as a person who has a long-term commitment to a field of endeavor, which generally includes some preparation for his or her job. The nature of professionalism, according to Carlson, is such that a professional is one who is committed to the agency and is constantly learning and growing, and who seeks to learn from others. This person does whatever is necessary to stay current and up to date. The professional, emphasizes Carlson, has a high standard of personal ethics, both on and off the job. This person treats others with respect, including subordinates and inmates. Part of the commitment of the professional is to make the organization better. You foster professionalism, according to Carlson, by articulating the need for and justification of professionalism in a correctional context. The professional

NORMAN C. CARLSON,
FORMER DIRECTOR OF THE FEDERAL
BUREAU OF PRISONS

There are several definitions associated with the term "professionalism." The classical definition generally refers to an advanced degree in a specialty area of study, licensure, and required involvement in continuing education. Vocations such as medicine, dentistry, and law are traditional examples of this type of professionalism.

Another common use of the term describes individuals who, through combinations of academic study and employment experience, have prepared themselves and made a long-term commitment to a particular occupational field. The emphasis is on the long-term commitment or career in an occupational field as compared with a shorter-term job which requires little or no advanced preparation. Administrators of criminal justice agencies, such as law enforcement and corrections, fall into this category of professionalism.

In my opinion, correctional administrators must be committed to managing the agency for which they are responsible in a manner that will maximize the overall contribution to community safety. Their long-term goal should be to improve programs and operations in a manner that will enhance effectiveness and serve to benefit the public. To accomplish this, a professional administrator needs to keep abreast of the academic literature and integrate what research and evaluation have demonstrated to be effective. The principal focus is on making changes which will improve the agency's performance.

As role models, correctional administrators must set high standards for themselves in terms of integrity and ethical conduct, both on and off the job. They need to insure through example that everyone in the organization, staff as well as clients, are treated with respect and dignity. Relationships with subordinates should reinforce the notion that all staff are important and that their thoughts and opinions are welcomed.

Source: Interviewed in 2012. Norman Carlson, director of the Federal Bureau of Prisons from 1970 to 1987, is acknowledged as one of the corrections pioneers who contributed as much as anyone to the development of professionalism.

is aware that it is absolutely necessary for an organization to pursue professional behavior if it wants to move forward.

 FOSTERING PROFESSIONALISM Unquestionably, professionalism in corrections depends on the leadership of top administrators, including directors or commissioners of state or federal systems as well as wardens and superintendents of correctional institutions. What is encouraging is the number of outstanding correctional leaders who are advocating professional leadership today. Some of these leaders include the following:

- Frank Wood was warden of two maximum-security prisons in Minnesota and later commissioner of corrections in Minnesota. One of his contributions was the importance of proactive leadership.

- Patrick McManus, former commissioner of corrections in Kansas and corrections official in Minnesota, warns that too many corrections professionals have permitted the political realities to set the tone and agency for corrections.

- Chase Riveland, former commissioner of corrections in Washington State, is pleased with the improvements that have taken place in the corrections field, but is concerned how fiscal constraints are restricting the programs and policies of corrections.

- Kathleen Hawk Sawyer, former director of the Bureau of Prisons, emphasizes the importance of values, principles, and convictions; articulating your goals and expectations clearly; leading by example; and maintaining perspective and balance.

- William Sondervan, former director of the Maryland Division of Corrections, suggests that "if you are a good warden, you can almost smell, taste, and touch when things are going well or when things are going wrong."

- David Crist, warden of Minnesota's Correctional Center at Stillwater, adds that "The warden can develop and motivate staff by listening, by allowing them to experiment with new approaches while you are mentoring them, by training them, and then occasionally by allowing them to make their own mistakes as long as the consequences are not going to be too dramatic."

- Dr. Reginald Wilkinson, former director of corrections for Ohio's Department of Rehabilitation and Corrections, adds that a "well-managed facility is clean and orderly, the grounds are well kept, the officers are well groomed, the facility is well painted, and it is not cluttered. A well-managed facility also has a lower level of incidence of violence, few positive drug tests, and prisoners are engaged in meaningful work experiences, vocational programs, and educational programs."

- Jim Bruton, a former Minnesota warden, gave more advice to aspiring proactive wardens: "Correctional institutions don't run safely by accident, they run well by design. It takes a proactive approach, leaving no area of the institution without explicit detail and accountability."

These top-notch administrators, as well as many others, fostered professionalism by their pursuit of proactive leadership, by developing a culture of excellence, by promoting evidence-based practices, by overcoming as much as possible the dichotomy between custody and treatment, by their pursuit of integrity, and by encouraging staff to be involved in learning and growing.

WHAT REMAINS TO BE DONE Professional ideals are sometimes hard to achieve, but the following are important processes in terms of attaining greater professionalism:

- Corrections staff cannot control overcrowded prisons, but they must do everything possible to reduce the violence and drug trafficking of prison life.

- It is necessary to suspend or terminate staff who abuse inmates and violate their rights.

- It is difficult to talk about professionalism when the no-frills and get-tough approaches with inmates result in taking needed programs and services away from them.

- Professionalism is further challenged by the fiscal constraints that currently exist in corrections; correctional administrators are expected to do more with less.

- It is important that correctional organizations develop greater clarity on their purpose—why the organization exists, what their mission is, what resources are needed to support the purpose and mission, and what the future direction of the organization should be.

- There needs to be a national set of principles and philosophy on what is acceptable behavior toward residents in community-based programs and inmates in prisons. Accreditation provides the broad map of what is expected in correctional care, but the subtle things expected from staff need further clarity and explanation.

- The quality of prisons has improved from the past, but there continue to be too many inhumane new prisons. New construction does not always result in a prison conducive to humane incarceration.

- The level of professionalism is very much affected by the ability to recruit the right staff and, once they are recruited, to explain the principles and behaviors that are expected from them.

- The continuation of correctional officers' commitment to a culture that sanctions abuse and mistreatment of prisoners must be eradicated. One way this can be done is to videotape any disciplinary interaction between correctional officers and inmates and to remind officers that charges will be brought in court if they violate the rights of inmates.

- The salaries of correctional personnel in the community and institutional contexts need to be continually increased. The salaries of these staff in some jurisdictions are still far too low. One advantage of increased salaries is that college-educated applicants are more frequently attracted to these positions.

- Administrative correctional staff must be willing to step forth when colleagues are out of line. This may come to the point of termination if that should be necessary.

- Private correctional facilities too frequently pay inadequate salaries to staff, have inferior construction, and fail to provide needed services for inmates. Private companies, if they intend to be in the corrections business, must maintain the standards of federal and state corrections.

"Corrections is not for the faint of heart," was an expression that the late John P. Conrad, noted corrections practitioner, author, and consultant, used to make.[13] And it is true! Corrections is not an easy job, either in the community or in correctional institutional settings. However, as you read the many Voices Across the Profession features found in this text, a common theme emerges time after time, and it is that individuals find corrections to be a very rewarding career.

The internal affairs investigator has one of the most important jobs in corrections, as it is his or her responsibility to regulate the quality of institutional life as well as what takes place in the community. That role is set out in the Careers in Corrections feature.

CORRECTIONS TODAY

The present landscape of corrections can be divided into community-based corrections and prisons. Under community-based corrections, the most important considerations are the continued movement toward a risk-management system, the continued popularity of restorative justice, the wide use of technology, fiscal constraints, the evidence of best practice, and the increased emphasis on reentry. Under prisons, the most pressing concerns include prison overcrowding, tightening budgets and scarcity, the changing nature of prison populations, the wide use of technology, and the increased use of evidence-based programs.

Matthew Conner speaks to an auditorium of students at Camden Catholic High School in Cherry Hill, New Jersey, about his incarceration. Conner, 29, spoke as a participant in Project PRIDE, a New Jersey Department of Corrections program that brings minimum-security inmates to schools to talk about their experiences with drugs and alcohol. Conner was a college student heading home after a night of living it up when he ran through a red light at Pennsylvania and Baltic Avenues in Atlantic City early one morning in July 2001. The result: His best friend was killed and he was sentenced to 10 years in prison. Conner has delivered this talk about 15 times now, each time reliving the night that became a nightmare and changed his life forever.

AP Photo/*Press of Atlantic City*, Danny Drake

CAREERS in Corrections
INTERNAL AFFAIRS INVESTIGATOR

Preparation for the Job

This is one of the more valued careers in corrections, but it requires becoming familiar with correctional facilities, and it takes considerable experience to accomplish this.

Nature of the Job

One of the most desirable jobs within a correctional agency is that of the internal affairs investigator. Few jobs offer the variety of daily challenges that confront the investigator. The investigator's job consists of identifying individual involvement, whether by internal personnel or public citizens, that is suspected of criminal infractions of an administrative, civil, or criminal nature.

One case may involve allegations of personal dealings between staff and inmates, while another case may involve allegations of physical abuse of inmates by staff, or perhaps even an inmate-on-inmate assault, sometimes ending in a homicide. Yet another case may involve staff or public involvement in smuggling contraband such as drugs over the guard line and into the facility. Anything of a criminal nature that occurs outside prison can and does occur inside the prison—things like theft, prostitution, assaults, blackmail, robbery, suicide, rape, and homicide. When a crime occurs, it is incumbent upon the internal affairs investigator to use every tool at his or her disposal to take sworn statements and conduct interviews, gather evidence, and, if applicable, utilize a polygraph examiner ("lie detector"). The internal investigator must have the ability to fully conduct and document criminal investigations. In order to effectively function in this capacity, he or she must have a reputation of faultless character that goes hand in hand with being above reproach. In addition, he or she must have the knowledge and ability needed to prepare legal arrest warrants, search warrants, and court orders. Lastly, he or she

Community-Based Corrections Has Evolved into a Risk-Management System

In probation and parole, as well as intermediate sanctions, the movement will continue to be a **risk-management system**. Agencies' strategies will move toward actuarial calculation and control, drug-testing technologies, such as urinalysis, and classification systems. This emerging bureaucratic-managerial state will emphasize strategies that will better ensure public protection. The most widely used of these strategies will be a combination of probation and incarceration, intensive probation, and electronic monitoring and house arrests. More conditions will continue to be placed on offenders under community supervision, which may result in increased detention and violations.

Restorative Justice Continues to Be Popular in Community-Based Corrections

The expansion of restorative justice, as discussed in Chapter 4, is one of the most exciting movements in corrections today. Restorative justice has recently been coupled with intermediate sanctions. From the grassroots level to state and local

RISK-MANAGEMENT SYSTEM A correctional system that is focused more on regulating and controlling offenders than on providing treatment or services for them.

must have the training and experience to safely facilitate legal arrests based on impeccable documentation needed for prosecution and for ensuring effective and factual testimony in court.

The successful investigator maintains a professional contact network with county, state, and federal law enforcement officials. Also, the investigator must have a working knowledge of the growth, presence, and dangers of security threat groups, more popularly known as gangs. Such contacts often include a network of confidential informants.

Qualifications and Required Education

A career path for someone interested in becoming an investigator begins with a college degree. Strong oral and written communication skills are required. The qualifications further consist of practical experience in the field. For instance, the fundamental experience learned during a short tour of duty as a correctional officer would give one the opportunity to learn through experience practical knowledge that just cannot be learned in a classroom or text. If one is going to be investigating crime in a prison setting, it makes sense to have worked in that environment.

Job Outlook

There is comparatively little turnover of internal investigators. The challenging nature of the job, along with its prestige, makes this position highly sought after.

Earnings and Benefits

This job pays an annual salary in the range of $32,000 to over $62,000, with approximately $47,000 considered the midpoint salary.

Source: The basis of this 2011 statement was provided by Ray Stanelle, who is an internal investigator for the Georgia Department of Corrections.

headquarters, restorative justice is rapidly gaining momentum both in the United States and internationally.

Community-Based Corrections Has an Increased Emphasis on Reentry

Reentry is likely to be one of the areas of corrections that will receive greater emphasis in the years to come. There are more than 500,000 inmates being released back into the community each year.[14] The combined high rates of recidivism, resurgence of a belief in rehabilitation, and overcrowded prisons make it mandatory for correctional officials to improve the prospects for success when parolees return to the community. For too long, parolees have returned to the community without receiving adequate treatment and are unprepared for life in conventional society. It is anticipated that some of the barriers for employment may be reduced and that more successful drug and/or alcohol abuse programs will reduce the rates of addictive behavior. Still, with the current state of the economy in U.S. society, it will be difficult for ex-offenders to find employment when so many citizens have lost their jobs and are unemployed.

Community-Based Corrections and Fiscal Constraints, Technocorrections, and Evidence of Best Practices

A constant theme of those who work in corrections today, from federal, state, county, and private corrections, is that you must do more with less. Corrections is facing, perhaps even more so, the economic downsizing that is found throughout American life. The text has emphasized evidence-based practices, and many of the Voices talk about how they must demonstrate these practices. (See the Evidence-Based Corrections feature for another example.) Unquestionably, even at a time when funding is

EVIDENCE-BASED CORRECTIONS

Hawaii's HOPE

The HOPE (Hawaii's Opportunity Probation with Enforcement) program is designed to keep people on probation by threatening them at a formal "warning" hearing with "swift and certain" punishment, rather than severe sanctions, for violating terms of probation. The program is geared to drug-involved offenders. Before HOPE, probationers in Hawaii typically received notice of drug tests as much as a month ahead of time. Under HOPE, probationers are given a color code at the warning hearing. Every morning, they must call a hotline to hear which color has been selected for that day. If it is their color, they must appear at the probation office before 2 P.M. for a drug test. If a HOPE probationer fails to appear for the drug test, a bench warrant is issued and served immediately. A probationer who fails the random drug test is immediately arrested and within 72 hours is brought before a judge. If the probationer is found to have violated the terms of probation, he or she is immediately sentenced to a short jail stay. Typically, the term is several days, servable on the weekend if the probationer is employed; sentences increase for successive violations.

HOPE differs from other programs by:

- Focusing on reducing drug use and missed appointments rather than on drug treatment and imposing drug treatment on every participant.
- Mandating drug treatment for probationers only if they continue to test positive for drug use or if they request a treatment referral. A HOPE probationer who has a third or fourth missed or "dirty" drug test may be mandated into residential treatment as an alternative to probation revocation.
- Requiring probationers to appear before a judge only when a violation is detected—in this respect, HOPE requires less treatment and court resources than drug courts.
- Having probationers who are employed serve any jail time, at least initially, on a weekend so they do not jeopardize their employment.

Because only a small fraction of HOPE probationers receive mandated treatment, the program can afford to use intensive long-term residential treatment, rather than relying primarily on outpatient drug-free counseling as do most diversion programs and drug courts.

Careful evidence-based evaluations of the HOPE program found:

- It is more cost-efficient because it covers a large number of clients while delivering intensive treatment to those who prove to need it.
- It puts a smaller strain on treatment capacity by avoiding the situation in which clients for whom treatment is mandated crowd out clients who voluntarily seek treatment.
- Because the treatment mandate follows repeated failures, it helps break through denial; an offender who has spent three brief spells in jail for dirty drug tests may find it hard to keep telling himself that he is in control of his drug use.

One study of the program, in which randomly selected samples of general-population probationers were compared to a similar group of HOPE probationers, found that after one year the HOPE probationers were:

- Fifty-five percent less likely to be arrested for a new crime
- Seventy-two percent less likely to use drugs
- Sixty-one percent less likely to skip appointments with their supervisory officer
- Fifty-three percent less likely to have their probation revoked

As a result, HOPE probationers served or were sentenced to 48 percent fewer days, on average, than the control group of traditional probationers. Probationers assigned to HOPE had large reductions in positive drug tests and missed appointments, and were significantly less likely to be arrested during follow-up at 3 months, 6 months, and 12 months. They averaged approximately the same number of days in jail for probation violations, serving more but shorter terms. They spent about one-third as many days in prison on revocations or new convictions.

Source: National Institute of Justice, "'Swift and Certain' Sanctions in Probation Are Highly Effective: Evaluation of the HOPE Program," www.nij.gov/topics/corrections/community/drug-offenders/hawaii-hope.htm (accessed April 9, 2012).

limited and hard-line tactics continue, especially in institutional contexts, using best practices is a reality of the present and increasingly the wave of the future. Finally, technocorrections has become a firm fixture of community-based corrections.

TECHNOLOGY-DRIVEN SECURITY
Technology that has been developed to increase internal and external security in correctional institutions.

Prisons Are Overcrowded

There is reason to think that prison populations are leveling out and perhaps, at least with state prisons, declining.[15] There is some reason to celebrate the decrease in 2010 of the prison population numbers. Still, most correctional systems, including jails and prisons, exceed designed or ideal populations. And it remains to be seen whether meaningful reductions will proceed at a pace to have a significant impact on prison crowding. The problem is that broad-based and deep changes in sentencing and corrections practices have yet to emerge.[16]

The Changing Nature of Prison Populations

Prison inmates are getting older, with skyrocketing health costs. Greater numbers of sex offenders are being incarcerated. Chronic mental health inmates are finding themselves in jails and prisons in increased numbers. Terrorists are being referred to correctional systems, and illegal immigrants are finding themselves in correctional contexts.

Violence Within the Prison

The high levels of violence in many prisons continues to remain high. A culture of violence, the presence of gangs, and the trafficking of drugs in prisons make it difficult to provide a safe environment for staff and inmates.

Technocorrections

As the prison population remains crowded, and the number of high-risk problem groups such as convicted terrorists grows, correctional administrators must seek new and efficient means of maintaining order and security within prison walls. Rather than relying on traditional methods of security and control, the correctional system is entering a new phase of technocorrections, which involves using technology rather than personnel to monitor prison populations. Today, **technology-driven security** is designed to maintain not only perimeter security but internal security and inmate control as well. For example, perimeters now have motion detectors that transmit movement to a centralized command center for immediate response, infrared image detectors that use handheld devices no bigger than a flashlight, and better and stronger physical barriers that make escape nearly impossible.

Community corrections has relied for quite some time on technology to monitor offenders. As you may recall, electronic monitoring (EM) has been widely used in probation and parole services. New methods of technology are being explored to provide probation and parole officers with tools to better manage their caseloads by doing their jobs more effectively and efficiently. See the TechnoCorrections feature on what is being planned for the future.

Here, a 3D facial recognition program demonstrates how biometrics can be used to identify suspected terrorists at airports or other ports of entry. Biotmetrics, including facial recognition and retinal scans, are ushering in a new era of homeland security.

© Ian Waldie/Getty Images

What does the future hold for techno-corrections? There is little question that in the future technology will play an increasing role in correctional security and management. One area of growing importance is the control of illegal contraband that is smuggled into the prison, such as cell phones and the electric chargers that power them. Inmates use these devices to communicate with confederates on the outside, ordering them to intimidate witnesses, smuggle drugs and weapons into the facility, or plan future crimes. Today, correctional administrators are testing a variety of scanning and detection devices that can help them detect illegal contraband, from a cell phone to a knife. Devices using radio waves can track prisoner and staff movements within an institution. New computer programs may help predict where problems are most likely to occur. One recent pilot project at the Graterford State Correctional Institution in Pennsylvania tested a millimeter wave imaging system to scan visitors. The imaging system can look through clothing to detect weapons, cell phones, and nonmetallic objects. Currently used by the Transportation Security Administration (TSA) to scan passengers, the system requires people entering the institution to step into a "portal," which looks like a booth. The system beams radio energy in the millimeter wave spectrum from antennas that rotate around the person. The energy is reflected, and scanners produce an image of the body and any objects hidden beneath the clothing. The system was used for more than a year, and officials believe it was successful.

To address privacy concerns, prison officials used a privacy screen that cut out the most explicit views but still allowed the system to signal if something was hidden beneath a person's clothing. Graterford officials also set up laptop computers when they introduced the system so visitors could see for themselves how the images looked. The Graterford system completed between 400 and 600 scans in a typical week, and each scan was completed in seconds. Overall, the millimeter wave system improved the contraband situation at Graterford; on several occasions, the system detected cell phones. Yet the system's greatest success may be its deterrent effect: people who knew about the system did not even try to smuggle.

Portable Systems

Another innovation now being tested is devices to detect nonmetallic objects, such as improvised weapons made of wood or hard plastics. The Weapons and Non-permitted Devices Detector, or WANDD, is a handheld system similar to handheld metal detectors. The WANDD scans fully clothed people for contraband hidden under their clothing. Although designed specifically to spot nonmetallic contraband, it detects metal as well.

Unlike millimeter wave systems that use radio energy, the WANDD uses sound waves—akin to sonar—to detect objects. The device "listens" to the sound waves that bounce back to it, detecting hidden objects under clothing. A prototype is now being tested at the Virginia Peninsula Regional Jail in Williamsburg. The device has been found to work well with various clothing fabrics, including standard jumpsuits. The WANDD prototype successfully detected objects such as cell phones, plastic knives, guns, and credit cards.

Tracking Prisoners and Pinpointing Prison Hotspots

Corrections officials are also beginning to test radio frequency identification (RFID) technology, which uses small transponders called "tags" to track movements. RFID tags can be attached to or incorporated into a variety of objects, such as wristbands.

Each tag has an integrated circuit and a tiny antenna to handle radio signals and can be used with a network of sensors—called RFID readers—to track movements. For example, a few correctional institutions have used the systems to provide information on prisoners' movements and to alert staff if there is an unusual concentration of people in a certain area. Movement information can be stored in computers and could prove useful in investigations to determine who was present in a certain part of a building at a particular time. Similarly, the Florida Department of Corrections (DOC) is testing a computerized system that predicts potential trouble spots within prisons, allowing managers to assign extra staff or take other actions to prevent violence and other problems. The effort involves using data warehousing and data mining techniques to pinpoint where trouble is most likely to occur. Dubbed CO-TAS (Correctional Operational Trend Analysis System), the system uses historical information and computerized number crunching to give supervisors a reading of the "climate" of a facility or parts of a facility, right down to individual cells. COTAS uses information about prisoners—such as age, gang membership, escape attempts, violent incidents, and medical and psychological conditions—to predict potential trouble spots. CO-TAS is now available to administrators in Florida's 137 correctional facilities. These include 60 prisons and a variety of other operations such as work camps. If COTAS is found to be effective, the Florida DOC will make copies of the software available to correctional institutions around the nation.

Source: Philip Bulman, "Using Technology to Make Prisons and Jails Safer," *NIJ Journal*, March 2009, www.ncjrs.gov/pdffiles1/nij/225764.pdf (accessed April 7, 2012).

The Dangers of Technocorrections

While technocorrections holds the promise of providing greater security and control, it also brings with it a unique set of problems. The danger is that increasingly technology-driven corrections will result in a sterile and isolated environment for inmates, in which contact with staff is greatly reduced or even nonexistent. Prisons, it is true, will be more secure, in both external and internal security, but they may also be less humane, and it is hard to imagine that this environment will not have an adverse effect on prisoners as they return to the community. Technology can also provide a false sense of security in both community-based and institutional settings. For example, knowing where someone is does not mean that it is possible to know what he or she is doing.

Another main threat of technocorrections, especially if it is used in the community to keep track of offenders, may be that it offers a low-cost method of expanding state control over people in the name of public safety.[17] Right now the correctional population remains at a high level and critics are searching for ways to reduce the inmate population. If security and control become less costly and more effective, less attention may be paid to the development of policies that reduce correctional populations, and the current policy of requiring those convicted of crime to remain behind bars longer can be maintained at no additional costs. Lowering the costs of imprisonment may become especially attractive to the public at a time when the crime rate has dropped as the prison population has soared.

Development of technocorrections could also mean that more people could be labeled criminals and monitored in the community at low cost, a scenario that will provide legislators with greater incentive to expand the net of justice. Deviant, unpopular, or just unconventional behaviors, ranging from body piercing to political activism, may be labeled "criminal," simply because there are inexpensive methods to monitor the behavior. This is the **net widening** issue which many critics of corrections are quick to voice.

The issues of privacy and civil rights are also a concern. Laws requiring the registration of sex offenders are now commonplace. Should we also implant chips in their bodies so they can be monitored by GPS systems? Another example is that since the 9/11 terrorist attacks, facial recognition biometrics has been developed. It is threatening because it can be deployed secretly and can be invisible to those surveyed. Yet, in an effort to apprehend criminals and suspected terrorists, should it be used more extensively? Other biometric identifiers that are available include handprints, vein dimensions, iris patterns, retina blood vessels, body odor, voice recognition, and the way we walk. Should this technology be expanded to apprehend criminals even though all of us would be caught in this genetic profiling?[18]

NET WIDENING Increasing the number of people contacted by or under the jurisdiction of the justice system.

L06 ▶ CORRECTIONS AND THE FUTURE

Gazing into a crystal ball in an attempt to predict the future of corrections is extremely problematic. It is likely that overpopulation of prisons will continue to be a problem. Fiscal constraints, evidence of best practices, technocorrections, and restorative justice will also continue. However, the most important consideration in the future is whether continued repression or reform will dominate the corrections landscape.

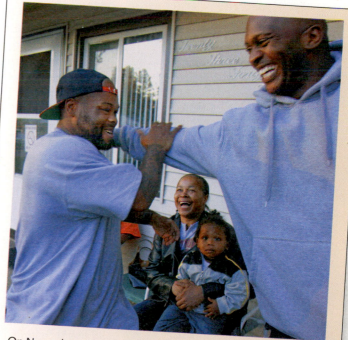

On November 1, 2011, in Springfield, Illinois, Antwain Black, 36 (left), celebrates his freedom with friends and family after being released early from Leavenworth Prison. Black was among the first of potentially thousands of inmates who are being released early from federal prison because of an easing of the harsh penalties for crack that were enacted in the 1980s, when the drug was a terrifying new phenomenon in America's cities. Changes in the law may finally help reduce overcrowding in the prison system.

AP Photo/Seth Perlman

Glimpses of Reform

A number of well-respected corrections experts believe that the get-tough movement has peaked and that a reversal in public policy may be on the horizon. Economic concerns may have reopened conversations about the desirability of retributive policies. Recent economic downturns have created a context in which old ideas about punishment may have become unconvincing and new ideas such as restorative justice and community initiatives may have newfound validity. A number of states—Arkansas, Iowa, Nevada, New York, Washington, and Wisconsin—have produced reform changes that focus on reforming the drug laws and reducing the length of incarceration, especially for nonviolent offenders.[19] Some states, such as Colorado and Kansas, are closing prisons. In March 2009, Kentucky lawmakers passed a bill that enhances the credits some prisoners can earn toward release. Michigan has been freeing some inmates who have yet to serve their maximum sentence. New Jersey has replaced jail time with community programs or other sanctions for offenders who violate parole. In March 2009, Governor Bill Richardson of New Mexico signed legislation to repeal the state's death penalty.[20] (See Exhibit 15.2 for reforms in 2010.)

In Voices Across the Profession, corrections expert Mark Kleiman discusses his ideas on an alternative to mass punishment.

While these reform efforts are encouraging, on balance the overwhelming evidence still supports a continuation of the get-tough mood and its consequences to the management of prisons in the decades to come. It is unlikely that the various interest groups involved will give up without considerable resistance about what a retributive

VOICES ACROSS the PROFESSION

© Mark Kleiman

"The first step in getting away from brute force is to want to get away from brute force: to care more about reducing crime than about punishing criminals, and to be willing to choose safety over vengeance when the two are in tension."

MARK KLEIMAN,
PROFESSOR OF PUBLIC POLICY, UCLA
SCHOOL OF PUBLIC AFFAIRS

We have been trying to solve our crime problem with brute force: building more and more prisons and jails. Is there an alternative to brute force? There is reason to think so, and pieces of that alternative approach can be seen working in scattered places throughout the world of crime control. But the first step in getting away from brute force is to want to get away from brute force: to care more about reducing crime than about punishing criminals, and to be willing to choose safety over vengeance when the two are in tension.

Justice both requires and limits punishment. Laws, customs, and institutional arrangements—including the Constitution and ideas such as "innocent until proven guilty"—limit, and ought to limit, the range of options. Still, thinking about the advantages and disadvantages—what economists quaintly call "benefits" and "costs"—of different approaches to crime control is one place to start the inquiry.

One way to frame the general problem of crime-control policy is

"What set of actions would result in the least total harm and cost, from crime and crime-control efforts combined?" Neither across-the-board lenity nor maximum severity offers the right answer to that question. In order to squeeze the maximum crime prevention benefit from every prisoner-day of incarceration, we need to learn to deliver the minimum effective dose of punishment and to make as much use as possible of convincing and clearly communicated threats rather than actual punishments.

Since punishment is always a cost and not a benefit, we should also be alive to the many possibilities to reduce offending without punishment: everything from a later school day (to shorten the burglary-friendly time period when adolescents are out of school but grown-ups have not returned from work) to removing highly criminogenic environmental lead to sending nurses to visit first-time mothers in need of coaching.

Source: Mark Kleiman, Professor of Public Policy in the UCLA School of Public Affairs, 2012.

EXHIBIT 15.2 Key Criminal Justice Police Reforms and Legislation Passed in 2010

State	Reform	State	Reform
Arizona	Enacted the Arizona Medical Marijuana Act, which protects seriously ill patients from state prosecution for using limited amounts of medical marijuana.	Michigan	Revised conditions for parole eligibility by establishing legislative intent to improve access to rehabilitative programs.
California	Authorized medical parole for prisoners who are permanently incapacitated. Reduced the penalty for marijuana possession to a non-arrestable infraction.	New Hampshire	Enacted presumptive parole for prisoners whose length of stay exceeds the minimum sentence.
Colorado	Modified penalties for certain drug possession offenses. Established revocation policy for technical parole violations. Directed the cost savings from reducing parole revocations towards reentry services. Raised the age of presumptive prosecution for certain juvenile defendants from 14 to 16.	New Jersey	Relaxed mandatory minimums by authorizing court to waive or reduce parole ineligibility or grant probation for certain drug offenses. Strengthened reentry policy, including opting out of the federal lifetime ban on food stamps for persons with felony drug offenses. Allowed possession of medical marijuana for chronically ill patients.
Connecticut	Enacted statewide "Ban the Box" measure, which delays inquiry from public employers regarding the criminal history of job applicants until job candidates are interviewed for the position.	New Mexico	Established statewide "Ban the Box" policy, which removes questions regarding criminal history from public employment applications.
Delaware	Amended state code to count prisoners at their last place of residence prior to incarceration for the decennial census.	New York	Modified policy regarding how incarcerated persons are counted for the decennial census. Adopted policy requiring the notification of voting rights.
District of Columbia	Authorized possession of medical marijuana for persons with certain chronic illnesses, including glaucoma and cancer.	Pennsylvania	Authorized the parole board to divert certain technical parole violators from prison to parole violation centers for treatment.
Illinois	Modified felony property threshold amounts to account for inflation.	Rhode Island	Reformed probation revocation policy by authorizing release for probationers acquitted of new criminal charges.
Indiana	Established rehabilitation-based discharge for certain long-term prisoners.	South Carolina	Modified sentencing structure for certain criminal offenses. Eliminated crack powder sentencing disparity.
Kansas	Allowed medical parole for certain terminally ill prisoners.	Tennessee	Authorized sentencing alternatives for nonviolent property offenses.
Louisiana	Exempts expungement fees in certain cases.	Vermont	Codified policy to reduce the rate of incarceration. Authorized early discharge from unlimited supervision for certain probationers.
Maryland	Modified census policy regarding the inclusion of incarcerated persons. Enacted medication protocol for mentally ill persons released from local facilities.	Virginia	Established alternatives to detention policy for juveniles tried as adults.
Massachusetts	Authorized parole eligibility for certain prisoners incarcerated at the county level. Adopted "Ban the Box" measure, which eliminates criminal history questions on an initial public employment application.	Wyoming	Directed law enforcement officers to use risk assessment when detaining juvenile defendants.

TABLE 15.1 Comparing Past, Present, and the Future of Corrections

	Punishment	Amenities	Inmate Culture	Staff Control
Past	The "dark ages of corrections," brutality toward inmates	Few	Inmate code and inmate solidarity	Absolute control
Present	No brutality, but extended lockups	Extensive	Culture split into gangs, racial groups	Staff sometimes feel out of control
Future	Extended use of supermax prisons	Less than in the past	Lack of inmate solidarity	More control than in the past

philosophy has meant to corrections philosophy and practices. Correctional reform measures still have a long way to go—or to express this another way, the philosophy of punishment in the United States is not likely to change in the near future.

Correctional Careers and the Future

There is every reason to believe that a correctional career in the future will be even more promising than in the present. Salaries will continue to go up, as well as health care and retirement benefits. The morale of correctional staff will likely continue to increase, with the influx of college-educated staff, the increased safety that technocorrections brings, and the growth of professionalism in corrections.

SUMMARY

L01 **Know how far professionalism has brought corrections**

It was not that long ago that corrections was considered to still be in the "Dark Ages," but corrections has come a long way in terms of professionalism in the past ten years or so. Staff development and training, an emphasis on ethics and integrity, and the implementation of standards and accreditation have contributed to the professionalization of corrections.

L02 **Be able to define professionalism and the need of it**

Corrections professionals undertake a specialized set of tasks and complete them, believe passionately in what they do, never compromise their standards or values, and care about clients, even if they happen to be criminal clients. Professionals are committed to the organization and have the objective of obtaining the highest standards of excellence.

L03 **Identify how correctional administrators can foster professionalism**

Correctional administrators can foster professionalism by their pursuit of proactive leadership, by developing a culture of excellence, by promoting evidence-based practices, by overcoming as much as possible the dichotomy between custody and

treatment, by their pursuit of integrity, and by encouraging staff to be involved in learning and growing.

L04 **Know the present challenges for advancement in professionalism**

For attaining greater professionalism in corrections, it is important to develop clarity on the institution's purpose and mission; generate developed principles and a philosophy on what is acceptable behavior toward residents in community-based programs and inmates in prisons; emphasize the necessity of recruiting the right staff and once they are recruited, provide top-notch training for them; and upgrade the salaries of correctional levels on all levels.

L05 **Define the major challenges facing corrections in the present**

These challenges include overcrowded prisons, tightening budgets and scarcity, continued movement toward risk-management systems in community-based corrections, continued popularity of restorative justice, increased emphasis on re-entry, using best practices, the changing nature of prison populations, violence within the prison, and wide use of technology in community-based and institutional corrections.

Identify whether punishment or reform will dominate the future landscape of corrections

There are signs that reform from retributive policies may be taking place in some states, but the overwhelming evidence probably supports a continuation of the get-tough mood and its consequences to sentencing and to the management of prisons in the twenty-first century.

Key Terms

risk-management system, 352

technology-driven security, 355

net widening, 357

 ## Critical Thinking Questions

1. How is professionalism ultimately involved in all of the issues in this chapter?

2. How difficult do you think it would be to be a corrections professional?

3. How can technology be both an advantage and a disadvantage to corrections?

4. What would you find attractive about a corrections career?

 ## Thinking Like a Corrections Professional

One of the tasks of being a corrections professional today is that you are expected to do more with less. How would you do this if you were a director of probation? What cuts could you make without affecting the quality of services? How would you relieve the anxiety of staff who are afraid of losing their jobs? What more can you do in this time of fiscal austerity?

 ## Career Destinations

Want to become a correctional investigator? This site may help:
www.indeed.com/q-Correctional-Investigator-jobs.html

Another approach is to look for work with a private correctional firm:
www.correctionscorp.com/careers/careers-security/

Notes

1. Katherine Santiago, "Seventy-Eight N.J. Corrections Workers Fired in 2008," *Star-Ledger*, Newark, New Jersey, August 30, 2009.
2. Ibid.
3. Ibid.
4. Ibid.
5. Elam Lynds, warden of the New York State Prison at Auburn, made this statement. Cited in W. David Lewis, *From Newgate to Dannermora: The Rise of the Penitentiary in New York, 1996–1848* (Ithaca, NY: Cornell University Press, 1965), p. 51.
6. See *Jackson v. Bishop*.
7. Clemens Bartollas, *A Model of Correctional Leadership: The Career of Norman A. Carlson* (Alexandria, VA: American Correctional Association, 2010), p. 132.
8. Ibid., pp. 132–133.
9. American Correctional Association, www.aca.org (accessed March 20, 2012).
10. Spokesperson for the American Correctional Association reported this information in 2012.
11. Rose Johnson, *Topics of Professionalism in the Workplace*, http://smallbusiness.chron.com/topics-professionalism-workplace-25820.html (accessed April 5, 2012).
12. Gene Atherton, "The Professionalism and Safety Connection," *Corrections.com*, www.corrections.com/news/article/18532 (accessed April 5, 2012).
13. Conrad said this to one of the authors on a number of occasions; it can also be found throughout his publications.
14. Lauren E. Glaze and Thomas P. Bonczar, *Probation and Parole in the United States, 2010* (Washington, DC: Bureau of Justice Statistics, 2011).
15. See Chapter 6.
16. Malcolm C. Young, "Getting Prison Numbers Down—for Good," *Inside Criminal Justice*, January 1, 2012.
17. The following relies heavily on Tony Fabelo, "Technocorrections: The Promises, the Uncertain Threats," www.ncjrs.gov/pdffiles1/nij/181411.pdf (accessed April 5, 2012).
18. Neal Katyal, "Review: Architecture as Crime Control," *Architecture of Control* (October 18, 2007); "Privacy Today; A Review of Current Issues," www.mindfully.org/Technology/Privacy-Rights-Clearinghouse1oct02.htm (accessed April 5, 2012).
19. Jennifer Steinhauer, "To Cut Costs, States Relax Prison Policies," *New York Times*, March 24, 2009.
20. Ibid., pp. 12–16.

abolitionist arguments Those who oppose the death penalty base their arguments on several positions, including the moral issue, the constitutional issue, and the pragmatic issues.

administrative-control model A model that contends that the management style of the prison has influence over what takes place in inmate culture.

aftercare The supervision of juveniles who are released from correctional institutions so that they can make an optimal adjustment to community living. Also, the status of a juvenile conditionally released from a treatment or confinement facility and placed under supervision in the community.

aggravation When a jury finds a first-degree murder conviction on a defendant at the end of the trial phase, the defendant is then tried in a second phase, referred to as the penalty phase. The task of the prosecution is to establish that the sentence should be death because the aggravating causes in the case exceed mitigating causes.

anger management programs Programs designed to help inmates manage their anger, especially in interpersonal relations.

argot A form of slang inmates use in prison settings to express how they feel.

Auburn cellblock An austere prison setting in Auburn, New York, in which inmates were made to endure great suffering.

Auburn silent system A system first used in the prison in Auburn, New York, that demanded silence from all prisoners at all times, even when they were eating or working together.

bail bond The means, financial or property, used to release a defendant from jail.

bail bondsman Bonding agents lend money for a fee to people who cannot make bail. They normally charge a percentage of the bail amount.

Bail Reform Act of 1966 Federal legislation that further spurred the bail reform

movement by urging pretrial release for all noncapital cases unless the defendant appeared unlikely to return to court.

Bail Reform Act of 1984 This federal act formalized preventive detention provisions for those considered dangerous or unlikely to return to court.

Beccaria, Cesare Bonesana One of the founders of the classical school of criminology, who advocated that punishment should be public, immediate, and necessary.

behavior modification A technique in which rewards or punishments are used to alter or change a person's behavior.

bench, or unsupervised, probation A type of probation in which probationers are not subject to supervision.

Bentham, Jeremy One of the founders of the classical school of criminology, who believed that the law should accomplish the utilitarian purpose of the protection of society.

Big House A type of large fortress-like prison that dominated corrections in the early part of the twentieth century.

Bill of Rights The name given to the first 10 amendments to the U.S. Constitution, which are looked upon as fundamentally important in the processing of criminal defendants.

blameworthy The law defines that a person is criminally liable for his or her behavior.

booking The process of admitting an arrestee or sentenced misdemeanant to jail.

bridewells Houses of corrections run by local authorities to teach habits of industry to vagrants and idlers.

Brockway, Zebulon Superintendent of the Elmira reformatory in New York.

butch The dominant, or male, role in a homosexual relationship in the prison society.

campus style design Open prison design that allows some freedom of movement; the units of the prison are housed in a complex of buildings surrounded by a fence.

case law The body of judicial precedent that is built on legal reasoning and previous interpretations of statutory laws.

Clemmer, Donald Known for his research at Menard Correctional Center; coined the term *prisonization*, which defines how inmates learn to adapt to prison while taking on the prison culture.

Code of Hammurabi Law code issued during the reign of Hammurabi of Babylon. The law of *lex talionis* makes its appearance in this code, one of the first comprehensive views of the law.

cognitive-behavior therapy Therapy based on the assumption that the foundations for criminal behavior are dysfunctional patterns of thinking.

Cognitive Thinking Skills Program (CTSP) A cognitive-behavior intervention, developed by Ross and Fabiana, designed to improve offenders' thinking processes.

community corrections act (CCA) State-based acts through which local governments that participate receive subsidies for diverting minor offenders from state prisons.

community service Requires an offender to perform a certain number of work hours at a private nonprofit or government agency.

community treatment Treatment provided to juveniles in the community versus an institutional context.

concurrent sentences One or more sentences imposed at the same time and served simultaneously.

conjugal visits A visit lasting one or two days during which prisoners can enjoy private visitation with their families.

consecutive sentences One or more sentences imposed at the same time and served one after the other.

contraband Unauthorized materials possessed by prisoners.

correctional counselor The chief treatment officer in many correctional institution, both male and female.

Correctional Services Corp. v. Malesko Defines the protections and rights of inmates in private corporations' facilities.

corrections The institutions and methods that society uses to correct, control, and change the behavior of convicted offenders.

corrections ombudsman An ombudsman (a Swedish word that means "representative") is a person or body that protects citizens against governmental abuses.

courtyard style design A prison design in which corridors surround a courtyard. Housing, educational, vocational, recreational, prison industry, and dining areas face the courtyard.

Crofton, Walter Prison reformer who developed the Irish mark system, which eventually spread to the United States and influenced the development of parole.

cruel and unusual punishment Punishment that involves torture or the infliction of unnecessary and wanton pain.

death-qualified jury During *voir dire*, any person opposed to capital punishment may be dropped from the jury pool.

deathwatch The period, generally 24 to 48 hours, before the execution; usually supervised by a team of correctional officers.

deferred prosecution programs Those referred to these programs benefit from having their charges dropped upon their successful completion.

deferred sentence A sentence that delays conviction on a guilty plea until the sentenced offender has successfully served his or her probation term.

deprivation model A model that views the losses experienced by an inmate during incarceration as one of the costs of imprisonment.

determinate sentence Sentencing that imposes a sentence for a definite term. Its main forms are flat-time sentences, mandatory sentences, and presumptive sentences.

discretionary parole The decision to release inmates is made by a parole board.

disenfranchisement laws Civil disabilities facing parolees when they return to the community.

dispute resolution programs Programs whose purpose is to keep minor conflicts between criminals out of the criminal courts. Most are based on mediation.

Eastern State Penitentiary A fortress-like prison in Philadelphia consisting of seven wings radiating from a control hub. Prisoners were kept in solitary confinement. It became a model for prisoners in several European countries.

Eighth Amendment Excessive bail shall not be required, nor excessive fines imposed, nor cruel and unusual punishments inflicted.

equity goal of punishment That offenders usually gain from criminal violations makes it seem just and right that they repay society and victims for losses, expenses, and damages that result from their crimes.

evidence-based programs This approach is an analysis of programs with scientifically approved methods to discover what works with which offenders.

execution team Those who carry out the execution.

external classification system Determines the level of security and control needed for the incoming prison population.

family detention centers Minimum-security residential facilities that provide schooling for children, recreational activities, and access to religious services.

family group homes Group homes that are run by a family rather than by a professional staff.

federal sentencing guidelines These guidelines were adopted by Congress and until the U.S. Supreme Court ruled otherwise were to be binding on federal judges.

fee-for-medical-services policy A correctional system policy in which inmates are charged for health care.

femme The docile, or female, role in a homosexual relationship in the prison society.

fictive families A grouping of unrelated individuals who have assumed the traditional family roles of mother, father, grandparents, and so on.

financial restitution Payment of a sum of money by an offender either to the victim or to a public fund for victims of crime.

First Amendment Congress shall make no law respecting an establishment of religion, or prohibiting the free exercise thereof; or abridging the freedom of speech, or of the press; or the right of the people peaceably to assemble, and to petition the government for a redress of grievances.

First Correctional Congress A congress held in Cincinnati in 1870 to present progressive ideas about corrections, which resulted in the formulation of the Declaration of Principles.

first-generation jail Focuses on staff providing linear/intermittent surveillance of inmates, which they do by patrolling the corridors and observing inmates in their cells.

Fourteenth Amendment [*Section 1*] All persons born or naturalized in the United States, and subject to the jurisdiction thereof, are citizens of the United States and of the State wherein they reside. No State shall make or enforce any law which shall abridge the privileges or immunities of citizens of the United States; nor shall any State deprive any person of life, liberty, or property, without due process of law; nor deny to any person within its jurisdiction the equal protection of the laws.

Fourth Amendment The right of the people to be secure in their persons, houses, papers, and effects, against unreasonable searches and seizures, shall not be violated, and no warrants shall issue but upon probable cause, supported by oath and affirmation, and particularly describing the place to be searched, and the persons or things to be seized.

Fry, Elizabeth Quaker who brought reform to women confined in prison.

Furman v. Georgia U.S. Supreme Court decision that declared the death penalty unconstitutional.

general deterrent effect The idea that punishing one person for his or her criminal acts will discourage others from committing similar acts.

Giallombardo Classic study that identified that women were involved in fictive families in adapting to imprisonment.

Gill, Howard B. Developed the "scamp" system at the Norfolk Prison colony in Virginia.

good time A deduction of time awarded to inmates for good behavior.

Gregg v. Georgia U.S. Supreme Court decision that superseded *Furman v. Georgia* and declared the death penalty constitutional if certain conditions are met.

grievance process A formalized arrangement in which inmates can register their complaints about the conditions of their confinement.

group homes Nonsecure residences that provide counseling, education, job training, and family living.

guilt/innocence phase In a capital trial, the phase in which the jury determines whether the accused is guilty or not guilty of the capital offense for which he or she is charged.

habeas corpus A Latin expression meaning "you have the body." A writ of *habeas corpus* brings a person before a court or judge to determine the legality of his or her restraint in custody.

hands-off doctrine The idea that persons sentenced to prison are not entitled to the same constitutional protections they enjoyed before conviction.

Hefferman Classic study that found the presence of fictive families in women's adaptation to prison life.

houses of corrections Workhouses where vagrants were forced to work to achieve the purposes of discipline and punishment.

Howard, John English sheriff who advocated jail reform.

Human Rights Watch An international nongovernmental organization that is concerned with the rights of individuals, such as prisoners.

importation model A model that suggests that the influences prisoners bring into the prison affect their process of imprisonment.

incapacitation Isolating offenders to protect society.

indeterminate sentence Sentence that permits early release from a correctional institution after the offender has served a required minimum portion of his or her sentence.

inmate code An unwritten but powerful code regulating inmates' behavior; inmates codes are functional to both inmates and prison administrators because they tend to promote order within the walls.

inmate disturbance A disturbance, either violent or nonviolent, that brings disruption or even closes down the prison.

Innocence Projects These projects, found in a number of states, provide free legal assistance for those cases in which question remains regarding the legality of their convictions.

insight-based therapy Typically involves treatment designed to encourage communication of conflicts and insight into problems, with the goal being relief of symptoms, changes in behavior, and personality growth.

institutional treatment facility A correctional institution that provides long-term treatment for juveniles.

intensive probation Supervision that is far stricter than standard probationary supervision.

intensive supervision parole (ISP) More extensive supervision than is given for most parolees.

internal classification system Determines the cell or housing unit where inmates will be housed as well as facility programs to which they are assigned.

jail A facility that is authorized to hold pretrial detainees and sentenced misdemeanants for periods longer than 48 hours.

jailhouse lawyers Name given to inmates who develop an expertise in criminal law and help other inmates in preparing their cases.

judicial reprieve Permitted judges to suspend judgment until offenders could seek a pardon or gather new evidence.

judicial waiver The procedure of relinquishing the processing of a particular juvenile case in adult criminal court, also known as certifying or binding over to the adult court.

just deserts Punishment that is commensurate with the seriousness of the offense or the harm done.

juvenile delinquent An underage minor who engages in antisocial activities that are defined as criminal behavior by the state's legal code.

juvenile justice system A system established over 100 years ago to provide for the care of law-violating youth.

kinship networks A type of prison socialization in which women deal with incarceration by becoming part of make-believe families.

landmark decision When a precedent establishes an important principle, or represents a change or new law.

lethal injection The predominant method of execution, used in 35 states and by the federal government.

Maconochie, Alexander Served as director of the prison colony in Australia and set up the "mark" system.

Madrid v. Gomez The judge in this case found that staff at the Pelican Bay Prison in California had used excessive and unnecessary force on inmates.

mandatory minimum sentence The imposition of sentences required by statute for those convicted of a particular crime with specific circumstances, such as selling drugs to a minor close to a school or robbery with a firearm.

mandatory parole release Inmate is released on parole when the unserved portion of the maximum prison term equals good time.

Manhattan Bail Project A Vera Institute of Justice program that provided ROR release for eligible defendants, which influenced later bail reform movements.

mass incarceration A term given to the high rates of incarceration in the United States.

maximum-security prison A prison in which complete control of any and all prisoners can be applied at any time.

McCleskey v. Kemp The Supreme Court ruled that race did not enter into the decision of the Georgia court and that there was no evidence of racial bias.

medical model The idea that criminality is a sickness that can be cured through psychological intervention.

medium-security prison A prison with single or double fencing, guarded towers or closed-circuit television monitoring, sally-port entrances, and zonal security systems to control inmate movement within the institution.

minimization of system penetration A diversion whose purpose is to minimize the offender's contact with the justice process as much as possible.

minimum-security prison A prison with relaxed perimeter security, sometimes without fences or any other means of external security.

mitigation During the penalty phase of the jury proceedings, the defense attempts to establish that there are greater mitigating causes than aggravating causes and the jury should bring in a recommendation for less than death (usually for life imprisonment without the possibility of parole).

the mix Owen's term for women's involvement in problematic prison behaviors and activities.

monastic confinement Prisons established by the Church in the Middle Ages for those laity involved in offensive acts, such as incest and magic.

Montesquieu, Charles-Louis de Secondat, Baron de One of the founders of the classical school of criminology, who advocated the moderation of punishment.

Morrissey v. Brewer Supreme Court ruled on procedures for revocation of parole.

needs assessment Attempts to offer treatment-relevant information, such as social adjustment, hygiene, and level of family support.

net widening Increasing the number of people contacted by or under the jurisdiction of the justice system.

new-generation jail A facility with a podular architectural design that emphasizes the interaction of inmates and staff.

new penology A new approach in probation and other community-based corrections that focuses more on administrative control and regulation than on treatment and offering services.

no-frills policy Inmates will receive the bare minimum of food, services and programs, and medical care required by law.

nolle prosequi A formal entry in the record of the court indicating that the prosecutor does not intend to proceed any further in this case.

nonlegal factors in sentencing These include contextual factors, social class, gender, age, and victim characteristics.

nonresidential programs Programs for youthful offenders that usually do not confine them overnight.

parens patriae A medieval English doctrine that sanctioned the right of the Crown to intervene in natural family relations whenever a child's welfare was threatened.

parole The conditional release from confinement of an offender serving an indeterminate sentence.

parole board An official panel that determines whether an inmate serving an indeterminate sentence is ready for parole.

parole guidelines Actuarial devices predicting the risk of recidivism based on information about the offender and the crime.

penal harm A current movement that believes the purpose of corrections is to punish offenders as severely as possible.

penitentiary A prison in which persons found guilty of a felony are isolated from normal society.

Pennsylvania model A penal system based on the belief that most prisoners would benefit from the experience of incarceration.

percentage bail Defendants deposit about 10 percent of the bail amount with the court clerk.

presentence investigation (PSI) An investigation whose main purposes are to help the court decide whether to grant probation, to determine the conditions of probation, to determine the length of the sentence, and to decide on community-based or institutional placement for the defendant.

presumptive sentencing Sentencing in which the legislature sets penalties for criminal acts.

pretrial release Release from jail or a pretrial detention center pending adjudication of the case.

preventive detention Retaining in jail defendants who are deemed dangerous or likely to commit crimes while awaiting trial.

prison classification A method of assessing inmate risks and needs that balances the security concerns of the institution with treatment needs of the individual.

prison culture The values, norms, and attitudes that inmates form in terms of institutional survival.

prison gang A group of inmates who are bound together by mutual interests, have identifiable leadership, and act in concert to achieve a specific purpose that generally includes the conduct of illegal activity.

prison-industrial complex A term given to describe the multimillion-dollar prison-building boom in which powerful corporate interest groups, large businesses, and politicians join together to profit from the burgeoning corrections industry.

prisonization The process by which inmates learn and internalize the customs and culture of prison.

Prison Litigation Reform Act (PLRA) Passed by Congress in 1996, this act limits the ability of inmates to complain about conditions of confinement and to allege violations of their constitution rights.

Prison Rape Elimination Act (PREA) This act established "zero tolerance" for rape in custodial settings, required data collection on the incidence of rape in each state, and established a National Prison Rape Elimination Commission.

prison riot Collective response of inmates that is violent, in which they strike out against what they consider unfair prison conditions.

prison violence Can vary from riots to staff assaults, inmate assaults, staff assaults of inmates, or self-inflicted violence.

proactive warden An approach to prison management that is focused on anticipating problems before they occur.

probation A form of punishment that permits a convicted offender to remain in the community, under the supervision of a probation officer and subject to certain conditions set by the court.

professionalism The conduct, aims, or qualities that characterize or make a profession or professional person.

protective custody A form of segregation, not for punishment but intended to isolate potential victims from predators.

punishment phase In a capital trial, the phase in which the jury determines whether the person will be sentenced to death or life in prison.

racial disparity in sentencing An actual pattern of racial discrimination in sentencing.

radial design In this wheel-shaped configuration, corridors radiate like spokes from a control center at the hub.

recognizance Permitted offenders to remain free if they promised to pay their debts to the state.

reformatory model A penal system for youthful offenders featuring indeterminate sentencing and parole, classification of prisoners, educational and vocational training, and increased privileges for positive behavior.

rehabilitation Changing an offender's character, attitudes, or behavior patterns so as to diminish his or her criminal propensities.

reintegrative philosophy A correctional approach aimed at returning offenders to the community as soon as possible.

release on own recognizance (ROR) The release without bail of defendants who appear to have stable ties in the community and are a good risk to appear for trial.

residential programs Programs conducted for the rehabilitation of youthful offenders within community-based and institutional settings.

responsivity principle Maintains that programs should consider offenders' situations as well as characteristics that may become barriers to success in a correctional program.

restorative justice Making amends to the victim or to society for the harm resulting from a criminal offense.

restraining hands doctrine Supreme Court doctrine that gave correctional administrators freedom from excessive lower court interference.

retentionist arguments Defenders of the death penalty make several arguments supporting their positions, including its deterrent value, fairness, and life imprisonment does not sufficiently protect society.

retribution Something given or demanded as repayment for wrongdoing; "getting even" for violating the social contract on which the law is based.

revocation of parole A formal procedure that takes place when a parole board, after listening to the parolee and his or her parole officer and their witnesses, decides that parole must end because the offender committed a new crime or violated the conditions of parole.

revocation of probation A violation of the rules or terms of probation or the commitment of a new crime, which may result in the offender being placed in an institution.

Richardson v. McKnight Supreme Court held that correctional officers employed by a private firm are not entitled to a qualified immunity from suit by prisoners, charging a section 1983 violation.

risk assessment Designed to predict new offenses or prison misconduct.

risk management system A correctional system that is focused more on regulating and controlling offenders than on providing treatment or services for them.

Roper v. Simmons U.S. Supreme Court decision that disallows the execution of juveniles who committed a capital crime under the age of 18.

second-generation jail Staff use remote supervision as they remain in a secure control booth surrounded by inmate pods or living areas.

security threat groups (STGs) The name that law enforcement and corrections officials give to groups that exhibit ganglike activity.

segregation A punishment unit in which inmates are separated from other inmates and are fed in their cells. Unlike the past, inmates must be adequately fed and permitted some time out of their cells to exercise.

selective incapacitation Identifying high-rate offenders and providing for their long-term incarceration.

self-help programs Programs from which inmates seek self-improvement, such as anger management, or express ethnic or cultural goals.

sentencing guidelines Federal and state guidelines intended to ensure fair sentencing by ending the reduction of terms in prison by grants of parole, ensuring that persons committing similar crimes serve similar terms, and ensuring that sentences reflect the severity of the criminal conduct.

sentencing sanctions The various types of sentences that can be awarded by the courts.

SENTRY This system tracks and provides appropriate staff with access to critical inmate information, such as assignments, program completions, and inmate movement in every Federal Bureau of Prisons facility or while an inmate is in transit.

service project A worthy cause, such as disaster relief or peer counseling, in which inmates willingly participate.

sex offenders A variety of offenders including the child molester, the pedophile, and the rapist.

sexual victimization Forcing an inmate to submit sexually to one or more inmates.

shock probation The offender, his or her attorney, or the sentencing judge can submit a motion to suspend the remainder of a sentence after a felon has served a period of time in prison.

signature bond Generally given for minor offenses and based on the defendant's written promise to appear in court.

situational model A model that suggests that prison culture is influenced by situations rather than remaining constant and can vary over time and place.

special needs inmates These include HIV inmates and inmates with chronic mental health issues

special offense inmates Inmates who are involved in substance abuse, are sex offenders, or are terrorists.

special population inmates These include the elderly prisoner, and the illegal immigrant inmate.

specific deterrence The idea that an individual offender will decide against repeating an offense after experiencing the painfulness of punishment for that offense.

split sentence A sentence requiring an offender to spend a period of time in jail before being placed on probation in the community.

Stanford v. Kentucky U.S. Supreme Court decision allowing the execution of juveniles who were age 17 at the time of the crime.

status offender A juvenile who engages in an act that is considered illegal because of his or her age, such as running away, disobedience, or truancy.

statutes States may award rights to prisoners beyond those granted by the U.S. Constitution or state constitution.

statutorial exclusion Certain juvenile offenses in some states are automatically transferred to adult court.

substantive rights A right, such as life, liberty, or property, that is held to exist for its own sake and to constitute part of the legal order of society.

suicide watch programs Inmates are placed in special cells and are supervised more frequently, usually every 30 minutes or less.

supermax prison Most secure of all prison systems, in which there is typically a 23-hour lockdown.

supervised release Requires more frequent contact with pretrial officers, phone calls, and officer interviews.

sureties Individuals who would agree to make themselves responsible for offenders who had been released from custody.

Sykes, Gresham Developed a typology of prison social roles and inmate culture.

technical violation (probation) A probationer violates one of the rules of probation, such as looking for a job.

technical violations (parole) Parole violations that pertain to behavior that is not crime, such as the failure to refrain from alcohol use.

technology-driven security Technology that has been developed to increase internal and external security in correctional institutions.

telephone-pole design This prison has a long central corridor serving as the means for prisoners to go from one part of the prison to another. Extending out from the corridor are cross-arms containing housing, school, shops, and recreation areas.

terrorist One who acts with premeditated and politically directed violence directed against noncombatants.

therapeutic community (TC) A community treatment group designed to divert drug users from the criminal justice system; therapeutic communities vary in how much control they are given in prison settings.

third-party custody Takes place when the court assigns custody of the defendant to an individual or agency that promises to ensure his or her appearance in court.

Thompson v. Oklahoma U.S. Supreme Court decision that prohibits execution of juveniles under age 16 at the time of the offense.

three-strikes laws Rules for repeat offenders that require long sentences without parole for conviction of a third or higher-order felony.

ticket of leave In Maconochie's system of graduated release, this was the final stage.

ticking bomb scenario This scenario proposes that a dangerous explosive device is set to go off and kill thousands of people and, therefore, it might be necessary to take extreme measures, such as torture, on a subject to extract information from him or her.

total institution Term coined by Irving Goffman to describe an institution that has total control over all aspects of those confined there.

Treatment Alternatives to Street Crime (TASC) A treatment program designed to divert minor drug abusers away from the criminal justice system.

true diversion A diversion program where the offender has his or her criminal prosecution dropped upon successful completion of this program.

truth-in-sentencing A close connection between the imposed sentence and the actual time served in prison. The time that offenders actually serve on their sentence.

unsecured bail Allows defendants' release without a deposit or bail arranged through a bondsman.

Ward and Kassebaum Classic study that claimed women adapted to imprisonment by forming homosexual alliances.

wilderness programs Programs that occur in a wooded area, the mountains, desert, or a lake where adolescents are taught survival skills and cooperation with others.

Be aware that "*n*" or "*nn*" following a page reference indicates one or more note numbers on a page.

SUBJECT INDEX

A

Abolitionist arguments against death penalty, 314
Abortion and women prisoners, 197
ACLU (American Civil Liberties Union)
    on tasers, 171
    and women prisoners, 190
Action Committee for Women in Prison, 274
Active phone line systems, 91–92
Adjustment to incarceration
    jail, adjustment to, 117
    men, difficulties of, 165
Administration. *See also* Wardens
    of jails, 110–111, 117–119
    of prisons, 152–156
Administrative control theory, 168, 178
Administrative detention (AD), 147
Administrative remedies, prisoners exhausting, 213
Adopted style of coping, 194–195
Adoption of children with incarcerated mothers, 196
Adult basic education (ABE) programs, 242–243
Adult Internal Classification System (AICS), 165
Adult Internal Management System (AIMS), 165
Advanced Vehicle Interrogation and Notification system (AVIAN), 151
Advocacy Center for Persons with Disabilities, 286–287
African Americans
    in corrections work, 346
    death penalty and, 306–307
    disproportionate minority confinement (DMC), 330–331, 332
    federal sentencing guidelines and, 43
    in jail populations, 116–117
    in juvenile institutions, 330–331
    parole board decisions and, 258
    in prison populations, 24, 139
    sentencing and, 49–50
    suicide by, 177
    women prisoners as, 192
    wrongful convictions and, 226
AFSCME (American Federation of State, County, and Municipal Employees), 179
Aftercare, 333–334
    revocation procedures, 334–335
Age. *See also* Elderly inmates; Juvenile offenders
    of jail inmates, 116
    of prison populations, 138
    sentencing and, 49
Aggravation *vs.* mitigation issue, 306
Alcohol abuse. *See* Substance abuse
Alcoholics Anonymous (AA), 242, 278
Alderson reformatory, West Virginia, 192–193
All Too Familiar: Sexual Abuse of Women in U.S. State Prisons (Human Rights Watch), 200
Almshouses, 13
Alvis House Community Corrections Center, 248
Amends, making, 103
American Convention on Human Rights, 308
American Correctional Association (ACA), 26
    Code of Ethics, 346–347
    Commission on Accreditation, 128, 142, 345
    prisoners' rights and, 208

American Indians. *See* Native Americans
Americans with Disabilities Act (ADA) of 1990
    boot camps, medical history of prisoner and, 221
    prisoners' rights and, 209–210
Amnesty International, 302, 303
    mentally ill persons and death penalty, 308
    mentally impaired persons and death penalty, 307
Anger management, 242
    probation and, 68
Anger management programs, 241–242
Anti-Drug Abuse Act of 1986, 47
Antiterrorism and Effective Death Penalty Act of 1996, 211
Appeals of death penalty, 302–304
Architectural designs of prisons, 148–159
Argot language of inmates, 168
Arizona
    Estrella Jail, 18
    Getting Ready program, 238
Aryan Brotherhood, 169, 222
Assaults. *See also* Physical/sexual abuse; Violence
    Getting Ready program and, 238
Assemble, right of prisoners to, 218
Assertiveness training, 242
Association of Diving Contractors International, 230
Association of State Correctional Administrators (ASCA), 346
Atascadero State mental hospital, 280
Atkins v. Virginia (2002), 307, 311, 318*nn*36, 37
Atlanta Federal Penitentiary, 141
Attica Prison riots, New York, 137, 174, 176, 346
Attorney–client privilege and prisoners' rights, 210
Attorneys. *See also* Defense attorneys; Legal services
    in Death Penalty Division, 298
    on death row, 309
    prosecutors, 35
    public defenders in Death Penalty Division, 298
Auburn Penitentiary, New York, 17–18, 188
    silent system, 18
Automobiles
    ignition interlock devices, 93
    under-vehicle surveillance systems, 151

B

Backroom deals, 21
Backscatter imaging system for concealed weapons, 151
Bail, 112
    percentage bail, 113
    reforms, 113–114
    signature bonds, 113
    unsecured bail, 112
Bail bonds, 112
Bail bondsmen, 112
Bail Reform Act of 1966, 113–114
Bail Reform Act of 1967, 114
Baldwin Inmate Boot Camp, Georgia, 139
Banishment, 13
Basic Life Principles, 244
Baxter v. Palmigiano (1976), 212, 229*n*14
Baze et al. v. Rees (2008), 306, 311, 318*n*29, 319*n*59
Bearden v. Georgia (1983), 74, 81*n*54

Beard v. Banks (2006), 215, 217, 218, 229*n*37
Beard v. Stephens (1967), 229*n*55
Bedford Hills Correctional Facility, New York, 188, 190
    Boudin, Kathy and, 186
    Lord, Elaine A. and, 202–203
    Mother-Infant Care program, 197
    Puppies Behind Bars program, 242
Behavioral Health Court, San Francisco, 236
Behavior modification, 237
Bell v. Wolfish (1979), 214, 219, 229*nn*45, 49, 69
Bench probation, 76
Beyer v. Werner (1969), 273*n*43
The Big House: Life Inside a Supermax Security Prison (Bruton), 5
Big House era, 165–166
Bill of Rights
    and juvenile offenders, 323
    and prisoners' rights, 209–210
Biometric Inmate Tracing System (BITS), 129
Biometrics, 129, 151, 355
    dangers of, 357
Black Americans. *See* African Americans
Black Gangster Disciple Nation, 169
Black Guerrilla Family, 169, 222
Black Muslims, 169, 212, 216
Black Panthers, 169
Blakely v. Washington (2004), 43, 47, 52*n*19
Blameworthiness, 6
Body orifice security scanner (BOSS) systems, 34
Body-scanning screening system, 151
Boerne v. Flores (1997), 229*n*32
Booking, 112
Boot camps, 86, 87, 100–102
    evaluation of, 100
    for juvenile offenders, 328, 330
    medical history of prisoner and, 221
Booth v. Chumer (2001), 213, 215, 229*n*24
Booth v. Maryland (1987), 73–74, 80*n*43
Boulder County Jail, Colorado, 122–123
Bounds v. Smith (1977), 224, 225, 229*n*80
Branding, 12, 15
Breed v. Jones (1976), 324
Bridewells, 13
Brown v. Plata (2011), 215, 221
Bruscino v. Carlson (1987), 214
Buddhist prisoners, rights of, 216
Budd v. Cambra (2002), 199
Bugs, 22
Bureau of Justice Statistics' *Sexual Victimization in Juvenile Facilities* report, 320
Bureau of Prisons. *See* Federal Bureau of Prisons
Burning, 15
Bush v. Reid (1973), 273*n*43
Butch females, 192

C

California. *See also* Pelican Bay State Prison, California; San Quentin Prison, California
    Behavioral Health Court, San Francisco, 236
    Board of Prison Terms, 264
    California Institution for Women (CIW), 274

Inmate-balance theory, 178
Inmates. *See* Prisons and prisoners
Inmates of the Boys' Training School v. Affleck (1972), 333, 341*n*29
Innocence Project, 206
    legal representation through, 225
In re Gault (1967), 324, 325
In rem proceeding, civil forfeiture as, 88
In re Winship (1970), 324
Inside Oregon Enterprises, 247
Insight-based therapy, 236–237
Insight Incorporated, 242
Institutional treatment facilities for juvenile offenders, 325
Integrating correctional services, 142
Integrity in corrections work, 346–347
Intensive Aftercare Program (IAP) for juvenile offenders, 334
Intensive supervision probation (ISP), 58, 76–77, 87, 262–263
    in juvenile justice system, 327
Intermediate sanctions, 82–107. *See also* Community-based corrections; Electronic monitoring (EM)
    continuum of, 85–86
    criticisms of, 104
    future of, 104
    problem-solving courts, 85
Internal affairs investigators, 352–353
Internal classification systems, 164
International Brotherhood of Teamsters, 179
International Covenant on Civil and Political Rights, 308
International Women's Day organization, 200
Internet, sex offenders registering on, 56
In the Mix: Struggle and Survival in a Women's Prison (Owen), 193–194
Intolerance and death penalty, 315
Investigations
    presentence investigation reports (PSIs), 73
    presentence investigations, 37
    by probation officers, 72–73
Iowa Consortium for Substance Abuse Research and Evaluation, University of Iowa, 130
Iran, death penalty in, 302, 308
Irish mark system, 254
Isolate style of coping, 194–195

J

J. Donovan Correctional Facility, California, 241
Jackson v. Bishop (1968), 221, 223, 229*nn*50, 67, 361*n*6
Jail-Based Assessment and Treatment Project (Iowa), 130
Jailhouse lawyers, 217
Jail Mental Health Screen (BMHS), 287
Jails, 21
    adjustment to jail, 117
    administration of, 110–111, 117–119
    biometrics in, 129
    booking in, 112
    classification of inmates, 112
    contemporary jails, 115
    corrections officers in, 124–125
    defined, 110
    direct-supervision (DS) jails, 120–121
    first-generation jails, 119
    fourth-generation jails, 121
    gangs in, 117, 118
    history of, 111–112
    idleness of inmates in, 126
    local administration of, 118
    mentally ill inmates, 126–127
    in Middle Ages, 13
    monitoring inmates in, 129
    new generation jails, 120–121
    OmniView Total Supervision (OVTS) jails/prisons, 121
    overcrowding in, 117, 126
    populations of, 115–117
    programs in, 122–123
    second-generation jails, 119–120
    state administration of, 118–119
    structure of, 117–119
    suicide by inmates, 127, 128
    trends shaping, 128–129
    violence in, 127
Jamaican Posse, 169
Jaycees, 242
Job fairs at prisons, 244
Johnson v. Avery (1969), 224, 225, 229*n*81
Johnson v. California (2005), 215, 223, 229*n*75
Jones v. North Carolina Prisoner's Unions (1977), 218, 229*n*42
Judges, 36–37. *See also* Probation
    corrections and, 20
    discretion in sentencing, 40
    judicial reprieve, 58
Judgments, deferred programs, 63
Judicial reprieve, 58
Judicial waiver of juveniles, 336
*Julia Tutwiler Prison for Women, Alabama, 288
Jurisdiction over prisons, 139–144
Jury trials. *See also* Death penalty
    death-qualified jury, 309
    judges and, 36
    prisoners' rights and, 210
Just deserts, 6
    intermediate sanctions and, 84
    probation and, 67
    theory of, 10
Juvenile courts
    history of, 323–325
    waiver of juvenile offenders to adult court, 335–336
Juvenile delinquents, defined, 322
Juvenile Justice and Delinquency Prevention Act (JJDPA) of 2002, 116, 330
Juvenile justice system, 322. *See also* Juvenile offenders
    adult system, comparison to, 325–326, 329
    alternative community sanctions for, 327–328
    contemporary system, 325–326
    effectiveness of, 332
    history of, 323–325
    parens patriae doctrine, 323, 324
    population trends in, 329–330
    private institutions in, 329
    probation in, 326–327
    public institutions in, 329
    terminology of, 325–326
    U.S. Supreme Court decisions on, 324, 333
Juvenile offenders, 320–341
    in adult prisons, 337
    adults, treatment as, 336–337
    aftercare for, 333–335
    boot camps for, 328, 330
    death penalty for, 308–309, 337–338
    effectiveness of community programs, 328–329
    future life of crime and, 335
    gender and, 331–332
    help for, 338–339
    in jails, 116
    life imprisonment for, 337–338
    postrelease programs for, 334
    racial disparity among, 330–331
    reentry programs, 334–335
    sexual victimization of, 172, 320
    treatment programs for, 332–333
    waiver to adult court, 335–336
Juvenile probation, 58

K

Kansas
    Leavenworth Prison, 23, 149–150
    prison closings in, 134
    Sexually Violent Predator Act, 280
Kansas v. Hendricks (1997), 280–281, 294*n*18
Kansas v. March (2006), 306, 311
Kennedy v. Louisiana (2008), 311
Kent v. United States (1966), 324
Kettle Moraine Correctional Institution, Wisconsin, 244
Kidnapping, death penalty for, 300
Kinship networks of women prisoners, 193
Knop v. Johnson (1987), 219, 223, 229*n*48

L

Language of inmates, 168
Laos, death penalty in, 302
Latin Kings, 169
Latino Americans. *See* Hispanic Americans
Law libraries, prisoner access to, 224
Lawtey prison, Florida, 244
LCS Correctional Services, 142
Leavenworth Prison, Kansas, 23, 149–150
Lee v. Tahash (1965), 229*n*63
Legal issues. *See also* Prisoners' rights
    of death penalty, 305–309
    juvenile offenders, treatment of, 333
    wardens and, 153
Legal services, 217
    Fourteenth Amendment and prisoners' rights to legal assistance, 224
    for inmates, 225
Legislature and corrections, 20
Lethal gas, execution by, 300–301
Lethal injection, 299, 300–301, 306
    administration of, 312
Level of Service Inventory-Revised (LSI-R), 234
Lewis v. Casey (1996), 214
Lex talionis, 12
Libraries in prisons, 246
    law libraries, prisoner access to, 224
Libya, death penalty in, 302
Lieber Correctional Institution, South Carolina, 316
Life imprisonment
    for juvenile offenders, 337–338
    without possibility of parole (LWOP), 301, 338
Lifers, 242
Life skills courses, 242
Lifetime community supervision, 270
Life without possibility of parole (LWOP), 301, 338
Literacy tutoring in jails, 123
The Little Book of Circle Processes: A New/Old Approach to Peacemaking (Pranis), 101
Locally administered probation departments, 68
Lockhart v. McCree (1986), 309, 318*n*50
Lockups, 111
Lockyer v. Andrade (2003), 45, 47
Los Angeles County Jail, 118, 126

M

Madrid v. Gomez (1995), 148, 159*n*50, 219–220, 229*nn*51, 52
Mail of prisoners. *See* Censorship
Malaysia, death penalty in, 302
Management and Training Corporation, 142
Mandatory minimum sentences, 44–45
Mandatory parole, 255
Manhattan Bail Project, 113–114
Manhattan Court Employment Project, 63
Maricao Juvenile Camp, Puerto Rico, 334
Marine Technology Training Center, 230
Marion Federal Penitentiary, Illinois, 141, 150
Marriage
    between inmates, 213
    parolees, issues of, 266–267
Maryland
    House of Corrections, 134
    State Department of Education's Correctional Education Transition Mobile Unit, 233–234
Massachusetts, juvenile offenders in, 323

Mass incarceration, 22
Maximum-security prisons, 146, 147
    Big House era, 165–166
    typical day at, 163
McCleskey v. Kemp (1991), 306–307, 310, 318*nn*19, 30–32
McKeiver v. Pennsylvania (1967), 324
Meacham v. Fano (1976), 212, 214, 229*nn*16, 18
Medical care. *See* Health care
Medical model of rehabilitation, 19
Medium-security prisons, 145
Megan's Laws, 56, 263
Mempa v. Rhay (1967), 74, 81*n*51
Menard Prison, Illinois, 166–167
Mental health. *See also* Mentally ill inmates
    probation and, 65–66
    women prisoners, care for, 199
Mental hospitals, sex offenders committed to, 280
Mentally ill inmates, 126–127, 285–287
    death penalty and, 308
    diversion programs and, 236
    elderly inmates, 288–289
    rape and, 175
    screening tools for, 287
    services and programs for, 286–287
    violence and, 178
    women prisoners, 191
Mentally impaired persons, execution of, 307–308
Methadone programs, 279
Metropolitan correction centers (MCCs), 120
Mexican Mafia, 169, 222
Mexikanemi, 169
Michigan
    Flint Citizens Probation Authority, 63
    prison closings in, 134
    Robert Scott Correctional Facility, 201
Middle Ages
    judicial reprieve in, 58
    punishment in, 12–13
Middle Georgia Correctional Complex scandal, 199–200
Military law, death penalty under, 300
Miller-El v. Cockrell (2003), 307, 311, 318*n*33
Millimeter wave systems, 356
Minimization of system penetration, 62
Minimum-security prisons, 145
Minimum sentences, 40
    mandatory minimum sentences, 44–45
Minnesota
    Faibault Correctional Facility, 136
    Oak Park Heights Correctional Facility, 150, 163
    Sentencing Grid, 42
Minnesota v. Murphy (1984), 74, 80*n*45
Minorities. *See* Race
Miranda v. Arizona (1966), 210, 229*n*5
Mission of prisons, 142
Mississippi State Penitentiary at Parchman, 312
Mitigation, aggravation *vs.,* 306
The mix, 194
Monastic confinement, 13
Monitoring. *See also* Electronic monitoring (EM);
  Global positioning systems (GPS) monitoring
    heartbeat monitoring, 151
    jail inmates, 129
Montana Women's Prison's Prison Paws for
  Humanity program, 244
Montanye v. Haymes (1976), 212, 229*n*17
Moore v. People (1970), 219, 229*n*44
Morales v. Turman (1974), 333, 341*n*29
Morality
    death penalty and, 314
    moral development courses, 242
Morrissey v. Brewer (1972), 81*n*50, 264–265
Mother-Infant Care program, 197
Mothers in prison, 196–198. *See also* Pregnant
  inmates
    international treatment of, 197

nursery programs in prisons, 197, 198
    programs for, 197–198
MRI (magnetic resonance imaging), 151
Mule Creek State Prison, California, 9
Multnomah Drug Court Program, Oregon, 95
Murder. *See also* Death penalty
    deterrence, death penalty and, 315–316
    lifetime community supervision for, 270
    wrongful convictions for, 226
Mutilations, 15

N

NAACP (National Association for the Advancement
  of Colored People) on death penalty, 305
Narcotic Control Act, 46
Narcotics Anonymous (NA), 278
National Advisory Commission on Criminal Justice
  Standards, 58
National Association of Attorneys General (NAAG),
  208
National Association of Drug Court Professionals
  (NADCP), 97
National Center on Addiction and Substance Abuse
  (CASA), Columbia University, 278
National Committee on Community Corrections, 61
National Guard, 179
National Institute of Corrections (NIC), 346
    on classification, 164–165
Nationalist terrorism, 282
National Sheriffs' Association, 128
Nation of Islam, 169, 212, 216
Native Americans
    circle sentencing and, 102–103
    in jail populations, 116–117
Native American Spiritual and Cultural Awareness
  Group, 242
Navidad en el Barrio, 247
Nebraska Correctional Center for Women, 197
Needs assessment for services and programs, 234–235
Neighborhood parole supervision, 269
Nelson v. Heyne (1974), 333, 341*n*29
Neo-Nazis, 169
Net widening, 357
Nevada's High Desert State Prison, 243
Newgate Gaol, London, 17, 188
New generation jails, 120–121
New Jersey
    corrections scandal, 342
    prison closings in, 134
    Project PRIDE, 351
    Rahway Penitentiary, 150
    Sex Offender Monitoring Pilot Project Act, 263
    Trenton Penitentiary, 150
Newman v. Alabama (1972), 223, 229*n*57
New Mexico State Prison riots, 174, 176
New penology, 67–68
New York. *See also* Auburn Penitentiary, New York;
  Bedford Hills Correctional Facility, New York
    Attica Prison riots, 137, 174, 176, 346
    Camp Gabriels, 134
    Elmira Reformatory, 13, 15, 18–19, 254
    Goshen Annex Center, 333
    NYPD (New York Police Department), 110
    Penal System, 17–18
    Rikers Island, 110
    Rockefeller laws, 46
    Sing Sing Correctional Facility, 146
    Tombs Prison, 110, 126
    Vera Institute of Justice, 87
Nigeria, execution of juveniles in, 308
9/11 attacks, 281
No-frills policy, 137, 162
Nolle prosequi, 21–22
Nonlegal factors in sentencing, 48–49
Nonlethal electrified fences, 151
Nonresidential programs for juvenile offenders, 328
Norfolk Prison Colony, Virginia, 13, 19

Norway massacre, 2011, 2
Nursery programs in prisons, 198
NYPD (New York Police Department), 110

O

Of Crimes and Punishment (Beccaria), 13–14
Ohio
    Death Penalty Division, Ohio, 298
    Public Defender, 298
*Oklahoma Publishing Company v. District of
  Columbia* (1977), 324
Oklahoma State Reformatory at Granite riots, 176
Older inmates. *See* Elderly inmates
O'Lone v. Estate of Shabazz (1987), 216, 218, 229*nn*28, 29
OmniView Total Supervision (OVTS) jails/prisons, 121
OMVI (operating motor vehicle while intoxicated), 115–116
"On the Chopping Block: State Prison Closings"
  (Sentencing Project), 134
Oregon
    Eastern Oregon Correctional Institution, 247
    Inside Oregon Enterprises, 247
    Multnomah Drug Court Program, 95
Outpatient drug abuse programs, 279
Overcrowding, 22, 355
    in federal penitentiaries, 141
    in jails, 117, 126
    violence and, 178

P

Pakistan, death penalty in, 302, 308
Parallel Universe model, 238
Paramilitary model for security, 178
Pardons, 256
Parens patriae doctrine, 323, 324
Parole, 21, 252–273. *See also* Intensive supervision
  probation (ISP); Recidivism
    characteristics of parolees, 258
    combined parole and probation departments,
      68–69
    defined, 254
    disenfranchisement laws, 268–269
    due process rights and, 264–265
    effectiveness of, 265–267
    evidence-based programs and success in, 11
    failure, reasons for, 265–266
    grant hearings, 257–258
    guidelines, 257
    improving effectiveness of, 269–270
    legal right to, 264
    lifetime community supervision, 270
    losing rights and, 268–269
    personal relationships and, 266–267
    principles of, 254–255
    revocation of, 264–265
    rules for parolees, 258–260
    salient factor score (SFS) for, 257
    Second Chance Act of 2008, 270
    Serious and Violent Offender Reentry Initiative
      (SVORI) program, 266
    targeting parole supervision, 270
    technical violations, 264
    truth-in-sentencing laws and, 46
    types of, 255–256
Parole boards, 256–257
Parole officers, 260–264
    careers as, 259, 261, 262
    neighborhood parole supervision, 269
    responsibilities of, 260–261
    supervision of parolees, 261–262
Passive phone line systems, 92
Payne v. Tennessee (1991), 52*n*40, 310
Pedophiles. *See* Sex offenders
Pelican Bay State Prison, California, 147–148
    prison gang members in, 170

RICO (Racketeer Influenced and Corrupt Organization Act), 88
Rights of prisoners. *See* Prisoners' rights
Rikers Island, New York, 110
Ring v. Arizona (2002), 311
Riots, 174–176
    Chino prison riots, California, 222–223
    in jails, 127
    types of, 176
Risk assessment
    probation and, 67–68, 75
    for services and programs, 234
Risk-management system, 352
Risk-need-responsivity (RNR) model, 68
Rita v. United States (2007), 47
Robbery, death penalty for, 300
Robert Scott Correctional Facility, Michigan, 201
Roberts v. Papersack (1996), 229*n*36
Robinson v. California (1962), 229*n*65
Rockefeller laws (New York), 46
Rockville Correctional Facility, Indiana, 246
Rook, 278
Roper v. Simmons (2005), 309, 311, 337, 341*nn*38, 41
Ruffin v. the Commonwealth of Virginia (1871), 211, 229*n*9
Ruiz v. Estelle (1976), 214
Rummel v. Estelle (1980), 46

S

Salient factor score (SFS), 257
Salvation Army Misdemeanant Program (SAMP), 69
Sanctions. *See also* Intermediate sanctions
    graduated sanctions systems and probation, 75
    sentencing sanctions, 39
San Francisco, California
    Behavioral Health Court, 236
    Veterans Administration (VA) Medical Center, 288
San Quentin Prison, California, 24, 148, 180
    Centerforce program, 285
Satellite Monitoring and Remote Tracking (SMART) program, 92
Saudi Arabia, death penalty in, 302, 308
Scamp system, 19
Scanning and detection devices, 356
Schall v. Martin (1984), 324
Search and seizure
    by parole officers, 261
    prisoners' rights and, 210, 219
    probationer's home, warrantless search of, 74
Second Chance Act of 2008, 230, 270
Second-generation jails, 119–120
Security housing units (SHUs), 147
    violence in, 147–148
Security threat groups (STGs), 168–169
Segregation of prisoners, 222–223
    disciplinary segregation (DS), 147
    in maximum-security prisons, 146
Selective incapacitation, 9
Self-help programs, 242
Self-inflicted violence, 177–178
Self-mutilation by women prisoners, 194
Sentences and sentencing. *See also* Death penalty; Minimum sentences; Probation; Sentencing guidelines
    age and, 49
    circle sentencing, 102–103
    concurrent sentencing, 37–38
    consecutive sentencing, 37–38, 39
    contextual factors and, 48
    deferred sentences and probation, 76
    determinate sentences, 41
    discretion in, 40
    excessively long sentences, 47–48
    gender and, 49
    good time, 38–39, 46
    indeterminate sentences, 40–41

    by judges, 36–37
    Minnesota Sentencing Grid, 42
    models, 39–40
    nonlegal factors in, 48–49
    presumptive sentencing, 41–42
    racial disparity and, 49–50
    sanctions, 39
    social class and, 49
    split sentencing, 86, 87, 97–98
    structured sentences, 41–42
    three-strikes laws, 45–46
    timeline for sentencing in U.S., 46
    truth-in-sentencing laws, 46
    victim characteristics and, 49
    violent felons, sentencing of, 47
Sentencing guidelines, 41
    evaluations of federal guidelines, 43
    federal sentencing guidelines, 43
    legality of, 43–44
Sentencing Project, 134
Sentencing Reform Act of 1984, 43, 46
SENTRY classification method, 234
Serious and Violent Offender Reentry Initiative (SVORI) program, 267
Service dog training programs, 242
Service Employees International Union (SEUI), 179
Service projects, 242
Services. *See* Programs and services
Sex Offender Monitoring Pilot Project Act, New Jersey, 263
Sex offenders, 56, 274. *See also* Rape
    civil commitment facilities, 280–281
    Good Lives Model (GLM), 78
    Internet, registering on, 56
    lifetime community supervision for, 270
    monitoring methods, 261, 263
    problems of working with, 280
    treatment in prison, 281
    working in prison with, 278–281
Sexual abuse. *See* Physical/sexual abuse
Sexual assault. *See* Physical/sexual abuse; Rape
Sexually Violent Predator Act (Kansas), 280
Sexual Victimization in Juvenile Facilities (Bureau of Justice Statistics), 320
Sexual Violence in the Texas Prison System (Austin), 175
Shackling of pregnant inmates, 199
Shakedowns of cells, 219
Shaw v. Murphy (2001), 215, 217, 218, 229*n*36
Sheridan Correctional Center, Illinois, 60
Sheriffs. *See* Jails
Shock probation, 76, 86, 87, 97–98
Shockwave area denial system, 171
Short-term inpatient drug-abuse programs, 279
Sick call disturbances, 174
Sierra Conservation Center, California, 224
Signature bonds, 113
Sing Sing Correctional Facility, New York, 146
Sit-down strikes, 174
Situational model, 168
Sixth Amendment
    and prisoners' rights, 210
    sentencing guidelines and, 43–44
Skill-building programs, 240
Slave of the state, prisoners as, 211
Smith v. Daily Mail Publishing Company (1979), 324
Social class
    of jail populations, 117
    sentencing and, 49
Social cost of corrections, 24
Social education programs, 242–243
Social learning techniques and probation, 68
Social workers, 334–335
    psychiatric social workers and insight-based therapy, 236–237
Solano State Prison, California, 221
Soldiers of Aztlan, 169

Solem v. Helm (1983), 46
Solitary confinement, prisoners' rights and, 219
Somers Prison, Connecticut, 150
South Oxnard Challenge Program, California, 103
Spanish terrorists, 282
Special needs inmates, 274, 284–287
    comparison of, 288
        HIV-infected inmates, 284–285
        mentally ill inmates, 285–287
Special offense inmates, 276–284. *See also* Sex offenders
    comparison of, 284
    terrorist inmates, 281–283
Special population inmates, 274, 287–292. *See also* Elderly inmates; Illegal immigrant inmates
    comparison of, 292
    illegal immigrant inmates, 289–292
Specific deterrence, 8
The Spirit of Laws (Montesquieu), 12
Split sentencing, 86, 87, 97–98
Stanford v. Kentucky (1989), 308–309, 310, 318*nn*44, 45, 324
State-administered probation departments, 68
State departments of corrections, 141–142
    improving services of, 141–142
The State of the Prisons in England and Wales (Howard), 13
State-sponsored terrorism, 282
State-subsidized jails, 118–119
Status offenders, 322
Statutes and prisoners' rights, 209–210
Statutorial exclusion, waiver of juveniles by, 336
Stay of execution in death penalty cases, 303
Stocks and pillory, 111
Strategic Anti-Violence Unit (SAV-U), 78
Street crime and women prisoners, 191
Stress management, 242
Strip searches, 219
Structured sentences, 41–42
Substance abuse
    anger management programs and, 242
    criminal activity in prisons, 278
    detoxification programs, 279
    electronic monitoring (EM) and, 93
    inmates, working with, 276–278
    in jails, 117
    mentally ill inmates and, 286
    probation and, 65–66, 76
    programs for inmates, 278
    Serious and Violent Offender Reentry Initiative (SVORI) program and, 267
    suicide and, 178
    therapeutic communities (TCs), 241, 279
    treatment programs in prisons, 240–241
    women prisoners and, 191
Substance Abuse and Mental Health Services Administration (SAMHSA), 127
Substance abuse counselors, 96
Substantive rights of inmates, 213–224
Successful parole, elements of, 11
Suicide
    Getting Ready program and, 238
    by inmates, 177–178
    by jail inmates, 127, 128
Suicide watch programs, 128
Sullivan v. Florida (2010), 337
Sumners-Ashurst Act of 1940, 246
Supermax prisons, 146–148
    evaluation of, 149
    prison gang members in, 170
    pros and cons of, 147
    terrorists in, 281
    violence in, 147–148
Supervised release, 113
Supervision by probation officers, 72–73
Supreme Court. *See* U.S. Supreme Court
Sureties, 58

Surveillance by probation officers, 72–73
Survival
    juvenile offenders, programs for, 327
    violence and, 178
Swarthout v. Cooke (2011), 264, 272n28
Sweden, treatment of incarcerated mothers in, 197
System overload, 22

T

Tai chi, 242
Talbert House, 99
Tapia v. United States (2011), 40, 47, 52n11
Targeted interventions, 10
Tasers, 171
Tate v. Short (1971), 106n9
Tattle Tale, 93
Tattoos of prison gangs, 169
Technical violations
    of parole, 264
    of probation, 64, 74–75
Technocorrections, 354–355
    dangers of, 357
    prison security and, 150–151
Technology-driven security, 355–356
Telephone-pole design for prisons, 148, 150
Telephones
    cell phones in prisons, 34
    passive phone line systems, 92
Terrorism. *See also* Terrorist inmates
    criminal forfeiture and, 88–89
Terrorist inmates, 281–283
    recidivism and, 283
    torture, use of, 283–284
    types of terrorist groups, 282–283
Texas
    Aryan Brotherhood of Texas, 169
    Harris County Sheriff's Office Reentry Services
        Program, 247
    prison gangs in, 169
    Three Rivers prison riots, 176
    Travis County Jail, 202
    West Texas State School in Pyote, 320
    Willacy Detention Center, 289
    William G. McConnel Unit riot, 174
    Youth Commission institutions, 320
Texas Syndicate, 169
Thailand, death penalty in, 302
Therapeutic communities (TCs), 241, 279
Therapeutic Communities of America, 241
Theriault v. Carlson (1977), 214
Third-party custody, 113
Thompson v. Bond (1976), 273n43
Thompson v. Oklahoma (1988), 308, 310, 318n43, 324
Thornburgh v. Abbott (1989), 214, 217, 218, 229nn34, 35
Three Rivers, Texas Federal Prison riots, 176
Three-strikes laws, 45–46, 47
    excessively long sentences and, 48
Tickets-of-leave, 14, 254
Ticking bomb scenario, 283
Timeline for corrections, 12–13
Time-series analysis of death penalty, 316
Toastmasters, 242
Tombs Prison, New York, 110, 126
Too Good to Be True (Mason), 143
Torture, 12, 283–284
Total institutions, 162, 164
Transactional analysis, 237
Transcendental meditation (TM), 242
Translation Drug Abuse Treatment (TDAT), 240–241
Transmitter wristbands, 151
Transportation of prisoners, 12–13
Transportation Security Administration (TSA), 356
Travis County Jail, Texas, 202
Treason, death penalty for, 300
Treatment. *See* Programs and services
Treatment Alternatives to Street Crime
    (TASC), 62, 64

Trenton Penitentiary, New Jersey, 150
Trop v. Dulles (1958), 229n61
Truancy, electronic monitoring (EM) and, 93
True diversion, 62
Truth-in-sentencing laws, 46
Turner v. Safley (1987), 213, 214 229n20
Twin Rivers Sex Offender Treatment Program,
    Washington, 281

U

U.N. Convention on the Rights of the Child, 308
Under-vehicle surveillance systems, 151
UNICOR program (Federal Bureau of Prisons),
    140–141, 243–244, 247
United Arab Emirates, death penalty in, 302
United States v. Booker (2005), 44, 47, 52n20
United States v. Granderson (1994), 74–75, 81n55
United States v. Knights (2001), 74, 80n47
Unsupervised probation, 76
Upgrading prison standards, 142
U.S. Appeals Courts, death penalty appeals to, 303
U.S. Committee on Crime and Prevention Control,
    307
U.S. Comptroller General's probation study, 58
U.S. Constitution. *See also* Bill of Rights; specific
    amendments
        death penalty and, 314
        juvenile offenders and, 323
        prisoners' rights and, 209–210
U.S. Department of Justice
    on parole effectiveness, 266
    probation studies, 58–59
U.S. Department of Labor's *Dictionary of Occupa-
    tional Titles,* 238
U.S. Immigration and Customs Enforcement (ICE),
    289, 290
U.S. Parole Commission's salient factor score (SFS),
    257
U.S. Probation and Pretrial Services, 69
U.S. Sentencing Commission, 43, 46
U.S. States Penitentiary Administrative Maximum
    Facility (ADX), 281
U.S. Supreme Court. *See also* Case law
    on censorship of prison mail, 212
    on prisoners' rights, 209–210, 212–215
    on probationers' rights, 74
    on Religious Freedom Restoration Act (RFRA) of
        1993, 216–217
    restraining hands doctrine, 212–213
    on revocation of probation, 74
    significant decisions on prisoners'
        rights, 214–215
    on three-strikes laws, 45
    writ of *certiorari,* 303

V

Valley State Prison for Women (VPW), California,
    194
Vera Institute of Justice, New York, 87
Vermont model, 103
Victim–offender conferencing, 103–104
Victims and victimization. *See also* Physical/sexual
    abuse; Rape
        notification systems, 93
        sentencing and, 49
        victim–offender conferencing, 103–104
Video cameras, sexual assault risk and, 174
Violence. *See also* Riots
    anger management programs and, 241–242
    explanations of, 178
    Getting Ready program and, 238
    inmate-on-inmate violence, 176–177
    in jails, 127
    male prisoners and, 174–176
    prison gangs and, 169–170
    in prisons, 355
    self-inflicted violence, 177–178

staff, inmate assaults on, 176
staff assaults on inmates, 177
    in supermax prisons, 147–148
    women prisoners and, 194
Violent Crime Control and Law Enforcement Act of
    1994, 46, 47, 97
Virginia
    Deerfield Correctional Center, 289
    Norfolk Prison Colony, 13, 19
    Peninsula Regional Jail, Williamsburg, 356
    Williamsburg, jails in, 111
Visitation programs, 245–246
    family visitation, 246
Vocational programs, 243–244
    Federal Prison Industries (FPI/UNICOR)
        programs, 140–141
Voir dire and death-qualified jury, 309
Voluntary lock-downs, 174

W

Wackenhut Corrections, 142, 143, 144
Wainwright v. Witt (1985), 318nn48, 49
Waiver of juvenile offenders to adult
    court, 335–336
Wakulla Correctional Institution, Florida, 245
Walnut Street Jail, Philadelphia, 13, 15
Ward and Kassebaum study, 192
Wardens, 152–156
    fiscal management by, 153
    institutional monitoring by, 153
    legal issues, involvement in, 153
    planning by, 153
    policy, determination of, 153
    proactive wardens, 154–155
    staff development by, 153
War on Drugs and women prisoners, 191
Warrantless searches of probationer's home, 74
Washington
    Clallam Bay Corrections Center, 339
    Corrections Center for Women
        (WCFCW), 150, 339
    juvenile offenders, help for, 338–339
    State Reformatory, 167
    Total Abstinence Society, 58
    Twin Rivers Sex Offender Treatment
        Program, 281
Washington, D.C. *See* District of Columbia
Washington v. Harper (1990), 308
Washington v. Lee (1966), 222–223, 229nn73, 74
Weapons and Non-permitted Devices Detector
    (WANDD), 356
Weekend programs in jails, 122
Weems v. United States (1910), 229n62
Wee Ones Nursery program, 197
West Texas State School in Pyote, 320
West Virginia's Alderson reformatory, 192–193
Whipping post, 111
Whipping prisoners, 111, 219
White House Office of Faith-Based and Community
    Initiatives, 244
Whitley v. Albers (1986), 214, 223, 229n56
WikiLeaks, 91
Wilderness programs for juvenile offenders, 327
Willacy Detention Center, Texas, 289
William G. McConnel Unit, Beeville, Texas,
    riot in, 174
Williamsburg, Virginia, jails in, 111
Williams v. New York State (1949), 73–74, 80nn41, 44
Wilson v. Seiter (1991), 213, 214, 229n22
Wisconsin's Kettle Moraine Correctional Institu-
    tion, 244
Witherspoon v. Illinois (1968), 309, 318n47
Wolff v. McDonnell (1974), 212, 214, 223–224, 225,
    229nn12, 76
Women prisoners, 186–204. *See also* Mothers in
    prison; Pregnant inmates
        adopted style of coping, 194–195